More praise

DIVAS, DAMES & L___

"Hoorah!
We've seen at least 100 reprints of the Golden Age Wonder Woman comics, 99 reprints of Supergirl and 98 reprints of Sheena, Queen of the Jungle, but what of the scores of more obscure, but equally wonderful Golden Age heroines—and there were scores of them! Their old comics are scarce as hen's teeth. And even if you can afford them, you dare not read them because each time you take the comic out of its plastic bag another little piece rots away and falls off, like the mummy in the horror movies. Now Mike Madrid has fixed that problem with *Divas, Dames & Daredevils:* in one beautifully designed collection he reprints the blood-and-thunder stories of twenty-eight Golden Age comic book heroines, from girl reporter Penny Wright, Feature Writer, to the exotic likes of Fantomah, Mystery Woman of the Jungle, and The Sorceress of Zoom. Some of them wear costumes, some just dress in snappy 1940s frocks, but whether fighting crooks or Nazis or outer-space aliens, these beautiful dames are in control, and they don't need anybody to rescue them. Lovers of Golden Age comics and strong women everywhere thank you, Mike Madrid!"

—Trina Robbins, *author of Pretty in Ink:*
Women Cartoonists 1896–2013

"Essential reading for anyone interested in the history of how women have been portrayed in comics."
—Johanna Draper Carlson,
Comics Worth Reading

"Provide[s] fantastic documentation of how many female characters were created during this era—some with surprisingly progressive personalities and stories to boot. The author's passion for heroines and fascination with those who have been left behind are palpable. . . . Wholly enjoyable as an impressive, detailed collection shining a light on heroines long ago neglected."—*Publishers Weekly*

"Madrid presents the cream of a very ripe crop of empowered comic book heroines and introduces them quite eloquently, accentuating readers' enjoyment of the stories themselves but also making readers aware of why the stories matter so much regardless of the era in which they are read. A valuable reference book of comics history, recommended for graphic novels collections."—Alger C. Newberry, *Library Journal*

"*Divas, Dames & Daredevils: Lost Heroines of Golden Age Comics* is an entertaining, insightful, fun salute to these courageous women from the past. You feel like a friend at the comics shop is sharing a whole new world to you. You'll want to share this pop history collection, too."—Will Harris, *ComicsBlend.com*

"*Divas, Dames & Daredevils* introduces us to the female scientists, flying aces, secret agents, and fearless reporters who fought for justice during the Second World War—as well as to their fantastic warrior goddess sisters who shared the pages of golden age comics. Femme and fatale, these gals projected a confident take-no-guff fierceness that upended cultural ideas about femininity and femaleness. Moxie saved the day—but if necessary these heroines could throw a punch as good as any man, if not better. Madrid's meticulous and passionate research provides a window into a seemingly lost *herstory* of patriotism, bravery, and progressive ways of thinking about female agency and adventure. This collection, and the engaging context provided throughout, ensure that these dames, divas, and daredevils will not be forgotten."—Jennifer K. Stuller, author of *Ink-Stained Amazons and Cinematic Warriors: Superwomen in Modern Mythology*

"A fascinating, in-depth exploration . . . it's the perfect time to look back at some of the daring dames from the dawn of the artform." —Jason Motes, *ScienceFiction.com*

"A nice tribute to a forgotten era of comics."
—KC Carlson, *Westfield Comics blog*

DIVAS

DAMES

LOST HEROINES OF

EXTERMINATING ANGEL PRESS

& DAREDEVILS

GOLDEN AGE COMICS

Compiled and annotated by MIKE MADRID
Foreword by Maria Elena Buszek, Ph.D.

EXTERMINATING ANGEL PRESS
"Creative Solutions for Practical Idealists"
Visit **www.exterminatingangel.com** to join the conversation
info@exterminatingangel.com

Exterminating Angel book design by Mike Madrid
Typesetting by John Sutherland
Cover illustration by Charles A. Winter
Back cover illustration by Barbara Hall

ISBN: 978-1-935259-23-7
eBook ISBN: 978-1-935259-24-4
Library of Congress Control Number:2013933702

Distributed by
CONSORTIUM BOOK SALES & DISTRIBUTION
(800) 283-3572
www.cbsd.com

PRINTED IN THE
UNITED STATES OF AMERICA

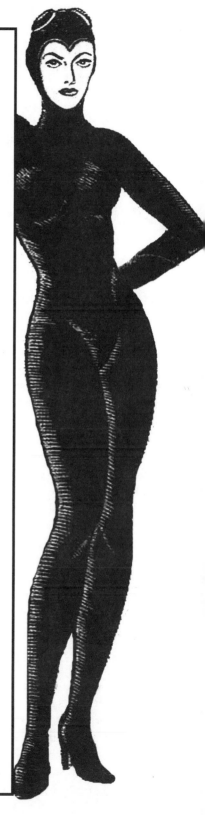

"SHEBAM! POW! BLOP! WIZZ!"

Foreword by Maria Elena Buszek, Ph.D.

In their 1968 duet "Comic Strip," legendary French singer/songwriter Serge Gainsbourg teamed up with another legend, film vixen Brigitte Bardot, to jump on the Pop Art bandwagon. The sonic equivalent of a Roy Lichtenstein painting come to life, Gainsbourg's lyrics invite the audience to join him in a comic-book world of word bubbles, adventure, and romance, punctuated by the English-language interjections of Bardot: "SHEBAM! POW! BLOP! WIZZ!" In a video the pair filmed for the song, Bardot is depicted as a comic-book heroine who springs forth from a life-sized painting—an Amazonian queen bursting onto his scene.

Bardot's superheroine was inspired not only by 'high' art's renewed interest in pop-culture genres like comic books, but by the simultaneous emergence of real-life heroines at what was probably the height of the era's activism. From the civil rights and anti-colonialist movements to the blossoming women's and gay liberation groups, women rose to prominence as the most visible—and, often, sexy—symbols of the massive societal changes taking place in the '60s.

But this upheaval—and these startling superheroines—were not so much a revolution so much as an evolution. Western perspectives on class, race, gender and sexuality have been changing for centuries, through the Enlightenment and the Industrial Revolution. And we of the 21st century are still in the midst of that evolution. In the United States, the cultural shifts brought on by the crises surrounding the Great Depression and World War II got the government involved. First, on a limited scale, there was the equal-rights hiring philosophy of New Deal projects, and then more broadly, as the massive depletion by the war of traditionally-privileged white men found the country in need of all its citizens, no matter how previously marginalized. As President Franklin D. Roosevelt bluntly put it in his 1942 Columbus Day speech: "In some communities employers dislike to hire women. In others they are reluctant to hire Negroes. We can no longer afford to indulge such prejudice." The country's military, government offices, and industry responded not only by hiring, but by recruiting women as well—encouraging and even glamorizing roles that for generations had been considered beyond women's physical and mental capabilities.

Pop culture followed suit. The period's cinema, music, and pin-ups cherry-picked scrappy models of femininity that had emerged during the Depression, updated in line with new demands being made upon women in the global urgency of WWII. And, as Mike Madrid demonstrates in this rediscovery of the era's "lost heroines," comic books also contributed to the cause. In his long-overdue valentine to these forgotten female characters, Madrid has provided us with a look at, and thoughtful contextualization, of the range of women one could expect to find—from Mother Hubbard to Lady Satan, plain Jane (Martin) to Mysta of the Moon—in this golden age of comics.

In keeping with the spirit of the era, most of these little-known heroines justified their extraordinary feats in connection with the war effort: alongside the famous exploits of Amazon-princess-turned-Axis-basher Wonder Woman, Madrid uncovers not just the more humble wartime warrior Pat Patriot, but also ordinary "superheroines" like nurses Jane Martin and Pat Parker, whose extraordinary contributions reflected the real-life heroics of women at war. Indeed, the war seemed to find glamorous women of mystery like Lady Satan and Madame Strange, the supernatural powers of Mother Hubbard and jungle queen Fantomah, and even the ancient

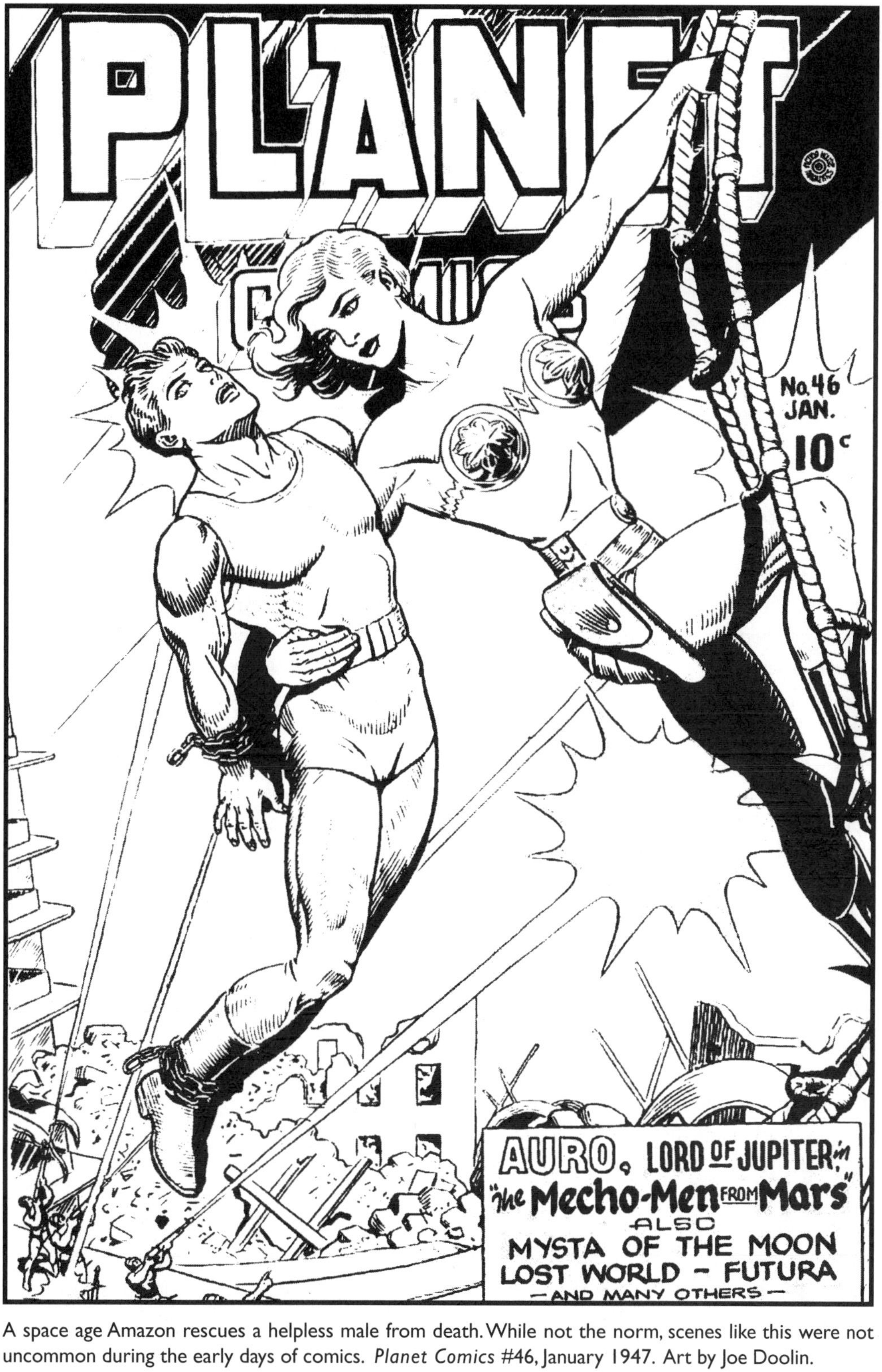
PLANET
No. 46
JAN.
10¢
AURO, LORD OF JUPITER in
"the Mecho-Men FROM Mars"
ALSO
MYSTA OF THE MOON
LOST WORLD - FUTURA
-AND MANY OTHERS-

A space age Amazon rescues a helpless male from death. While not the norm, scenes like this were not uncommon during the early days of comics. *Planet Comics* #46, January 1947. Art by Joe Doolin.

Greek goddess Diana all leaping to the Allies' defense. These fantastic stories were inspired by the real-life drama of the war.

In the same way that real women's contributions to WWII opened doors in other realms, many of the characters Madrid spotlights demonstrate these gains as well. While the war effort clearly needed nurses and pilots overseas, just as it needed factory workers on the home front, Madrid's book reminds us that the wartime lack of male workers at home also produced "lady" lawyers, journalists, and investigators—whose exploits fit neatly with the male-dominated conventions of adventure comics—as well as artists, who joined the ranks of male illustrators by producing some of the very work we see in this book. (Unsurprisingly, it was women artists like Barbara Hall, Fran Hopper, and Claire Moe who produced some of the more exciting and unconventional heroines in *Divas, Dames & Daredevils*.)

Alas, when the war ended the fate of comic-book heroines continued to reflect those of their real-life counterparts. The same country that demanded women question their traditional lot in life during the war soon demanded just as adamantly that it was now their duty to return from the home front to the home. Pop culture reflected this shift by idealizing images of women to fit the culture's demand for a return to more conventional gender roles. Comics themselves became segregated into "girls'" and "boys'" genres, and it's telling that almost none of the heroines featured in this book survived to the 1950s. The result of this shift, as Madrid laments, was the start of a decades-long "era where comic book heroines had to be little more than pretty."

But—as the "Comic Strip" with which I began attests—once unleashed, these heroines did not pass so easily into the historical ether. Like the women who inspired them, these strong female comic-book characters gave society a taste of what exciting new roles women might take on when given the opportunity. They also stubbornly remained in the cultural subconscious. While artists like Lichtenstein and Andy Warhol may have looked to the more vapid corners of comic-book romance and children's illustrations for inspiration, painter Mel Ramos opened the door wider to reintroduce characters discussed by Madrid, like Fantomah and Señorita Rio. For comic book fans like Ramos, these unruly models of femininity from the war years surely stuck in his childhood memory, just as they no doubt rematerialized as young women in his midst began to more closely resemble these golden-age heroines as the 1960s wore on. It's no accident that the first issue of *Ms. Magazine*, published in July 1972, featured Wonder Woman (in a cover illustration by DC Comics artist Murphy Anderson) as symbolic of both the history that the era's women's liberation movement sought to honor, and the power the movement felt in its rediscovery.

That Wonder Woman has reappeared on many occasions on the cover of *Ms.* (most recently, on its 40th anniversary issue in the Fall of 2012) is a testament to the fact—if I may flesh out Madrid's concluding analysis of these *Divas, Dames & Daredevils*—that these characters are worth revisiting to see how women lived in the golden age of comics. And more than that—to remind us how far women today still need to go.

Maria Elena Buszek, Ph.D., an Associate Professor of Art History at the University of Colorado Denver, is the author of *Pin-Up Grrrls: Feminism, Sexuality, Popular Culture*. Her writing has appeared in *Bust* magazine, *Art Journal*, *Archives of American Art Journal*, and *TDR: The Journal of Performance Studies*.

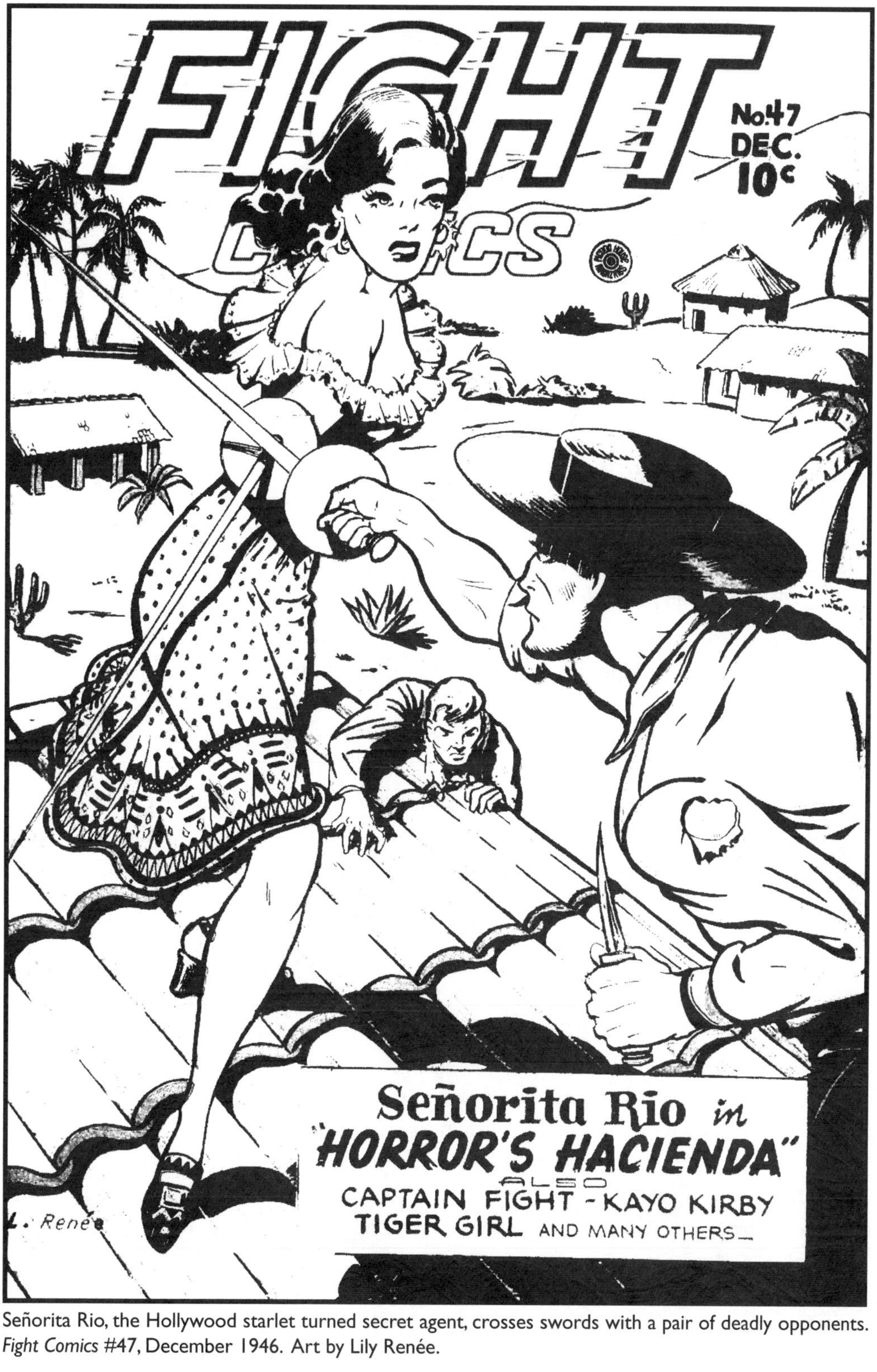
FIGHT COMICS
No. 47
DEC.
10¢
Señorita Rio in
"HORROR'S HACIENDA"
ALSO
CAPTAIN FIGHT - KAYO KIRBY
TIGER GIRL AND MANY OTHERS
L. Renée

Señorita Rio, the Hollywood starlet turned secret agent, crosses swords with a pair of deadly opponents. *Fight Comics* #47, December 1946. Art by Lily Renée.

GOLDEN YEARS

Everyone thinks of the 1970s as being a decade of bell-bottoms, mood rings and disco balls. There were certainly plenty of those. But growing up during that time, I also recall the '70s as being an era of great nostalgia. "Old is in, and we are happily awash in the sleek and gaudy period that stretched from the '20s through the '30s and into the '40s," wrote *Life Magazine*, in a 1971 cover story on the nostalgia craze. The poster shop at the local shopping mall started selling reproductions of old Hollywood movie posters. New films of that time like "Cabaret," "Paper Moon," and "The Great Gatsby" were bringing the '20s and '30s back to life. I didn't know anything about fashion, but I knew my older sister and her friends were painting their nails red and wearing '40s style dresses. So I was aware of all this, but it was too young to affect me. Or so I thought.

By the early '70s, I had been reading comic books for a few years. At that time it was a very casual hobby. I mainly bought a comic book if its cover looked good, or if there was an interesting female character inside. I was vaguely aware of how long some of the famous superheroes had been around, but I didn't necessarily give it much thought. I remember seeing a comic book that reprinted a Batman story from the 1940s. That was my first introduction to the concept that comic books actually had a history.

My favorite place to kill time at the shopping mall was the B. Dalton Bookseller. My life changed the day I found the section called "humor." In among the collections of *New Yorker* cartoons and *Peanuts* comic strips were histories of comic books. I felt like I had stumbled into Aladdin's cave. Here were stories about Superman and Batman from the 1940s. They looked and acted differently than the way they were being presented in contemporary comics. And there were all of these other fascinating characters that I'd never heard of, like Plastic Man, The Spirit, and Sheena. Week after week I'd go back to that bookstore and pore over *The Great Comic Book Heroes* by Jules Feiffer and *The Steranko History of Comics* to see what new bit of information I could glean. Especially intriguing was the collection of 1940s Wonder Woman stories that *Ms. Magazine* produced. All of these stories seemed wilder than what I was reading in comics at the time. The characters brimmed with fire and vibrancy. Soon I was haunting my local library and repeatedly checking out books like *Comix* by Les Daniels, and *All In Color For A Dime* by Dick Lupoff, to learn as much as I could about comic book history. The '70s nostalgia bug had bit me. I had discovered the Golden Age of Comics, and had started down the road to comic book geekdom.

Over the years I became a more serious comic collector. I started going to comic book conventions. I read every book I could find on comics. Eventually I even wrote a book of my own called "*The Supergirls*," which was a history of comic book superheroines. After "*Supergirls*" was published, I began hearing from readers. Many had no idea that the history of comic books stretched back to the late 1930s. They told me that reading "Supergirls" made them want to learn more about the early comics, and specifically about the female characters that appeared in them. It was great to hear this. I felt that in some small way I might have done for these readers what those authors in the '70s had done for me.

Recently I found myself going back to revisit comic books of the '30s and '40s. I knew quite a bit about the more famous comic book heroines of that era, characters like Phantom Lady, The Black Cat, and Miss Fury. But I wound up encountering dozens of characters I knew little about, or even had never heard of. As I read the amazing adventures of obscure heroines like Madame Strange, Calamity Jane, and The Magician From Mars, I felt like that ten-year old kid who was discovering old comics for the first time.

While there are a number of heroines I would like to have included in a collection like this, I focused on the ones that I have dubbed as 'lost'. These are characters you may have heard of, but whose stories you never had the chance to read. Or they may be women who only made a few appearances and then disappeared. They may have been lost, but you will find they are definitely unforgettable. I invite you to meet a group of daring heroines from the early days of comic books who will surprise and entertain you, I hope as much as they have me.

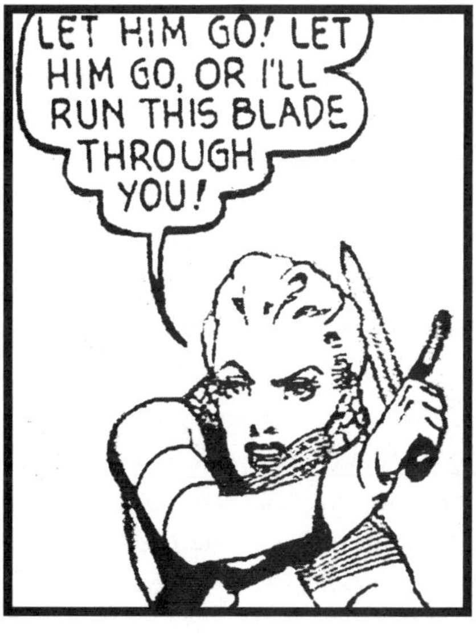
LET HIM GO! LET HIM GO, OR I'LL RUN THIS BLADE THROUGH YOU!

A CAST OF THOUSANDS

Imagine you are in a present-day comic book shop. Take a glance over the shelves of comic books and you're likely to see many familiar titles—*Superman, Batman, The Incredible Hulk, Wonder Woman, Spider-Man, Fantastic Four, Iron Man, Catwoman, and X-Men*. These are all the names and faces and colorful costumes that we've come to expect to see on comic book shelves for decades.

Now imagine you're looking at a similar rack of comic books from 70 years ago. First off, there were no specialty comic book shops then—those didn't appear in America in great numbers until the 1970s. So if these were the 1940s, you'd be looking at comics at a newsstand, a drug store or a candy shop. And the assortment of titles would look different from what we're used to seeing—*Champion Comics, Crackajack Funnies, Hit Comics, Heroic Comics, Wings Comics, Planet Comics, Military Comics, Jungle Comics, Wonderworld Comics, All-American Comics, Thrilling Comics, Air Fighters Comics*. These were anthology titles, and they were the mainstay of the comic book industry from the late 1930s to the mid '50s—the era that has come to be known as the Golden Age of comic books.

The comic book industry in great part grew out of pulp magazines. Pulps offered cheap, often titillating fiction. Whether it was detective stories, science fiction or horror tales, fantasies or westerns, each issue featured work by different writers. After Superman made his 1938 debut, comic books became the hot ticket on the newsstand. Pulp magazine publishers began switching formats from written stories to illustrated stories, still using the same formula of presenting several different stories per issue.

The anthology concept made sense in the early days of comics, when publishers were trying to figure out what would attract readers to the fledgling medium. Rather than bank on the appeal of a single character, publishers would offer readers an assortment of stories in each anthology title. Very few of these stories continued from issue to issue. Most were self-contained, and were told in few pages, sometimes six or less. This was a new medium, and writers knew their readers had no prior history with these characters. So the writing was tight and well–handled. The reader was taken on a journey filled with action, danger, plot twists, and some humor, all wrapped up in less than ten pages.

Since superheroes were such an exciting new concept, most of the anthology titles had a popular crime-fighting hero as their headliner. So, Superman starred in *Action Comics*, Batman in *Detective Comics*, and Captain Marvel in *Whiz Comics*. The characters featured in the rest of the issue could have been another superhero or two, a detective, perhaps a tuxedo-clad sorcerer, a dashing soldier of fortune or a science fiction hero. A humor or "funny animal" feature usually rounded out the issue. These comics were forty-two, fifty-two, sixty-four or more pages for a dime—a fantastic variety show in every issue. If any of these features proved to be unpopular with readers, the publisher could simply replace it with a new one. And if any heroes proved to be very popular, like Superman or Batman, they could be spun off into their own titles.

Since the 1960s, two publishers—DC Comics and Marvel—have dominated the comic book industry. During the Golden Age, there were over forty different publishers competing for a reader's dime. So over forty publishers, over a span of roughly fifteen years, produced multiple anthology titles every month, each one averaging about seven features per issue. This produced a literal flood of characters on the newsstands—a colorful cast of thousands for comic book readers to enjoy. Some of these anthology titles were popular and lasted for years, others lasted one year or even only one issue. Some characters like Superman, Batman, and Captain America have survived until today. But there are scores of obscure heroes like The Iron Skull, Doctor Frost, Minimidget, Human Meteor, Mr. Justice, Yank and Doodle, Steel Fist, The Phantom Sphinx, and Blackout that didn't hit the big time, and are forgotten now.

And then there were the women. Only a handful of women headlined their own anthology titles, most notably Sheena, the Queen of the Jungle in *Jumbo Comics*, Mary Marvel in *Wow Comics*, and of course Wonder Woman in *Sensation Comics*. But, the anthology titles provided a home for many other women. Many of the anthology titles had a woman as one of their features, presumably to attract female readers. Modern day comic book readers might be surprised at the broad spectrum of heroines in Golden Age comics—daring masked vigilantes, queens of lost civilizations and intergalactic warriors, crafty reporters and master spies, witches and jungle princesses, goddesses and regular gals. The common perception is that Wonder Woman was the only heroine to fight for justice in the 1940s. While she is the most well-known and enduring heroine, there were lots of others. Characters like Lady Fairplay, Miss Espionage, Margo the Magician, Senorita Rio, Iron Lady, and X of the Underground also paraded across the comic book page. Their time may have been brief, but they no doubt inspired some young reader with their combination of bravery and beauty.

In these very early days of comic books, there weren't as many established rules about how women characters *should* or *shouldn't* act. As a result, many of these Golden Age heroines feel bold and modern as we read them today. They are presented as fearless and unapologetic about their strength. They can fly a plane as easily as most people can drive a car. They're smart, competent, and funny. While many are drawn in a sexy manner, they are the heroic centerpieces of their stories. They don't wait for a man to make the decisions for them. When a crisis occurs, these heroines take action, no matter how dangerous the situation. Those around them have confidence in their abilities. "I knew I could count on you!" a grateful man tells Pat Patriot, after she has accepted an assignment that everyone else has refused. In truth, many of these female characters possess the same sort of authority and confidence as the males. "That's how you really want to measure an action heroine— can that role be replaced by a male?" notes sociologist Katy Gilpatric in the documentary *Wonder Women! The Untold Story of American Superheroines*. Many modern day readers feel that superheroines have always been the second-class citizens of the comic book world. But the portrayal of women as less powerful, less capable, and less heroic than men didn't become widespread until the 1950s, when heroines like Batwoman were told that fighting crime was too dangerous for a female. It took the Women's Liberation Movement of the 1970s to change the representation of women in comics, and return them more to the way they had been depicted thirty years earlier.

Another stereotype about women in comics is that they are obsessed with love and romance, and want nothing more than to settle down and get married. Again, this was a character trait that began to be written into stories more regularly starting in the 1950s. Heroines like the Invisible Girl and the Wasp were portrayed as marriage-minded women who let the men in their lives order them around. But the heroines you will meet here are different. Romance is often not even an element of their stories. These women lead the same kinds of adventurous lives that men do, and they don't express any need to change that in order to get married. Some of these heroines, like the space pilot Gale Allen, even push romantic liaisons aside when they interfere with her job. That's not to say that these women don't have emotions. It's just that they show that they can control them, in the same way a man can. Overall these stories don't express the idea that it's a hindrance to be a woman, which was the case in the '50s and much of the '60s.

The heroines in this collection are not among the most famous in comic book history. They are, as the book's title calls them, "lost" heroines. Some had long careers; some made only one appearance. What these women may lack in big names they make up with heroic swagger. They stride through these stories in larger-than-life style, modern day heirs of American tall tale heroes. But they are also a reflection of their times. Keep in mind that the majority of these stories were produced during World War Two. Everyone needed to take part in helping the war effort, including women. During WWII, women were stepping out of traditional roles to work in war plants, serve in the military, and fly planes. So it makes sense that women in comic books would be presented in a heroic fashion.

Still, not all comic book readers during the Golden Age were ready for strong female heroes. Beginning in 1940, the aviation-themed anthology *Wings Comics* featured the adventures of Jane Martin, a gallant nurse turned spy who could fly a plane and handle a gun. Perusing the pages where readers' letters were printed reveals some differences of opinions between male and female readers regarding a proper woman's role in comic books. The sentiments expressed in these letters sound strangely similar to those of today's female

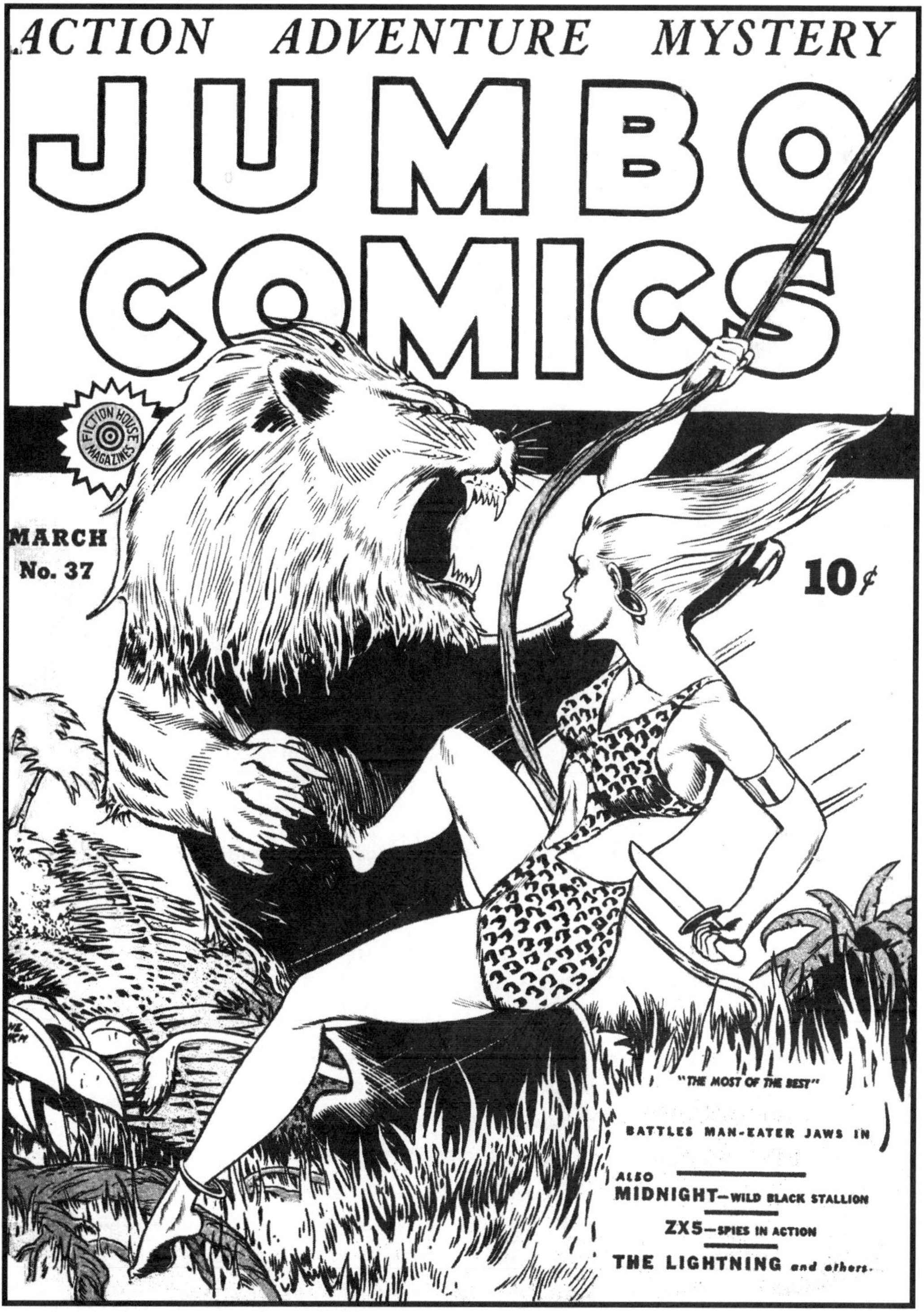
ACTION ADVENTURE MYSTERY
JUMBO COMICS
FICTION HOUSE MAGAZINES
MARCH
No. 37
10¢
"THE MOST OF THE BEST"
BATTLES MAN-EATER JAWS IN
ALSO
MIDNIGHT—WILD BLACK STALLION
ZX5—SPIES IN ACTION
THE LIGHTNING and others.

Sheena, Queen of the Jungle was the first heroine of comic books. Making her American debut in 1938, she established the image of the comic book heroine—powerful, brave, but also sexually attractive to men. *Jumbo Comics* #37, March 1942. Art by Dan Zolnerowich.

comic book readers:

In *Wings* #31 (1943) a reader named John writes:

"Someone is going to drop a high explosive bomb if you don't get rid of Jane Martin, Secret Agent (ha, ha!). A woman's place is in the home or maybe a nurse, and I mean a NURSE."

A few months later in *Wings* #35 (1943), a reader named Evelyn writes:

"We girls are sick and tired of boy heroes."

In that same issue, Charlotte adds her opinion, including a call for sisterhood among female readers:

"I believe that any and every comic book needs the feminine touch…To my way of thinking we girls should stick together!"

In *Wings* #43 (1944), Clyde expresses his desire for Jane Martin to curb her violent ways:

"I think Jane Martin could be tuned down or removed permanently…It's not that I don't like girls. The more the merrier, but I just don't go for a 'Pistol-packin' mamma'!"

And finally, in *Wings* #46 (1945), Barbara has a message for publishers who don't think females read comic books:

"I'd like to say that we girls don't sit home reading the wallpaper. You know we like comic books too. What do you say, girls?"

Publishers *did* know that girls read comics. When superheroes became less popular after the end of WWII, publishers began to create new comics that would attract female readers. But they produced romantic stories, not heroic ones. It was felt that girls would find stories about dating and marriage more appealing than tales of adventurous women. When the Comic Code was instituted in 1954 in an effort to clean up comic books, it further affected the way women were portrayed. The Comic Code not only made sure that women were no longer drawn in an overly sexualized manner, but also that they be written in more traditional roles. And so, for the next decade or more, pretty but demure women who took a backseat to men populated comic books.

The stories in this book come *before* that more conservative era. These stories give us a glimpse into comic books in their infancy. Like other media that developed in the 20th century—movies, television, and rock 'n' roll—the earliest works often feel crude by today's standards. The writing in these stories is often raw and the art is sometimes simplistic. But there is a real vibrant quality to these stories. This is before comics were intended just as reading for kids, when they were simply *entertainment*. This was era when women could still be bold and powerful, and even dangerous. These women could crack a joke one minute and a crook's jaw the next. This was a time before comic books became corporate, and marketing plans, toy lines, and big summer blockbuster movies determined what types of stories would be told. This was a time when comics were fun.

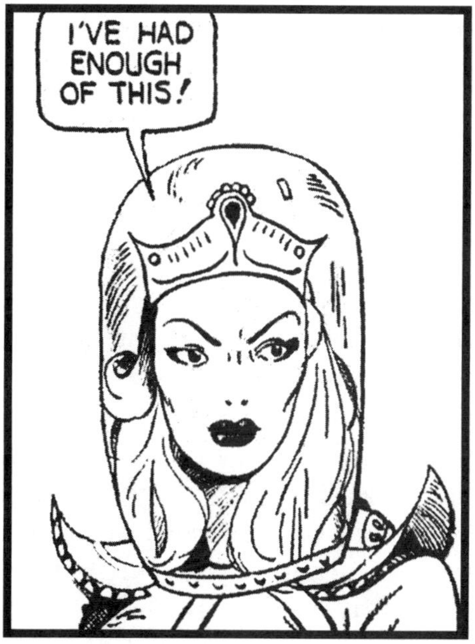
I'VE HAD ENOUGH OF THIS!

WOMEN AT WAR

A line of Americans marches across a broad, empty plain. There are men and women from all walks of life—farmers and bakers, doctors and nurses. Their ranks stretch out to disappear beyond the horizon behind them. Their hands are raised as they cheer on the young woman who leads them. She is dressed in a blue blouse, red and white striped skirt, a flowing red cape, and a broad belt emblazoned with a star. She holds aloft the torch of liberty to light the way. She has the determined look of a leader on her face. The text on a curling scroll describes the scene:

> *"The Spirit of 1941 – similar to that of '76 – is embodied in a young girl who rises above the ranks to lead her people in ridding our country of its enemies—"*

This is how comic book readers were introduced to Pat Patriot. Like another heroic young woman from 500 years earlier, Pat is rallying her people to defend democracy and freedom. It's no wonder she is called "America's Joan of Arc." It's August of 1941, and America will not enter WWII for another four months. But comic books began waging war on the Axis powers well before the Japanese attack on Pearl Harbor on December 7, 1941.

After Superman's 1938 debut, every manner of superhero began to fill the pages of comics. There were heroes with incredible strength, others that could run at amazing speed. Some controlled fire, some electricity, some magnetism. Some heroes could fly, and others could breathe underwater. Heroes dressed up as every conceivable animal that writers could think of—Batman, The Owl, Red Panther, Hawkman, Black Condor. There was even a hero called The Zebra. They were all ready and willing to battle great evil. But the heroes of the early comics needed an enemy that was worthy of their fantastic abilities—a cause noble enough to rally around. And then, as if made to order, World War II arrived.

WWII was a devastating tragedy that took much of the world decades to recover from.

But it was also the shot in the arm that the relatively new medium of comics needed to ensure it would be a success. Comics presented big sweeping ideas of good and evil, and here was a real battle of good and evil taking place before the eyes of the world. The United States was a nation built by immigrants, and its citizens had been seeing the lands of their origins suffering under the attacks of the Axis powers since the late 1930s. As the 1940s dawned, the world waited to see if the United States would come to the aid of its allies in Europe and Asia. But in October of 1940, President Franklin Roosevelt was still saying that the United States would not be sending American troops into the battles being waged overseas. Comic books, however, were not waiting for an official declaration of war to get involved.

The American people were being told that a specter was casting its shadow across the country. Comic books presented stories of evil foreign spies working within the nation's borders, and the heroic efforts of valiant Americans to crush this vermin. The Nazis and the Japanese were presented as cruel and insidious foes perfectly suited for the grand drama of comic books. A veritable battalion of patriotic, star-spangled, Axis-bashing superheroes would be created to deal with this secret menace. But some of the first characters to enter the war were not fighters, but angels of mercy.

As early as 1940, nurse Jane Martin had already marched across battlefields from Marseille to Alexandria, as she brought "her brave succor to men in battle…risking all for the dying and wounded." That same year, farmer's daughter Lee Preston joined the Red Cross and flew the danger-filled skies of China and Europe to bring medical supplies to the battlefronts. When an officer congratulated Lee on completing yet another hazardous mission, she replied with the cool reserve of a combat veteran, "Thank you sir, but serving the wounded is my job!" By May of 1941, another nurse, this one named Pat Parker, joined the fray. Readers were told, "Soldiers do not all fight in trenches. English women battle as valiantly as their men…Pat Parker ranks with the best of these gallant women-at-war." These women were in the thick of battle, and didn't hesitate to pull a gun if the situation called for it. But their number one job was helping the needy.

Back in America, comics were turning into a big propaganda machine. The Shield, comics' first red, white and blue hero debuted in 1940, followed by Captain America the following year. In anticipation of the impending United States entry into the war, comic books exploded with a battalion of patriotic heroes throughout 1941–U.S. Jones, the Spirit of '76, the American Crusader, the Bald Eagle, Super American, Unknown Soldier, Captain Battle, Captain Fearless, Captain Fight, Captain Victory, Captain Glory, Captain Flag, Captain Courageous, Captain Freedom. The war was practically won before it had even started, as these star-spangled heroes were literally drawn punching Hitler in the nose.

1941 produced its share of patriotic heroines as well. USA, Miss Victory, Pat Patriot, and Miss America all made their debuts, with Wonder Woman rounding out the list in December of that year, the same month as the Pearl Harbor attacks.

While all of these ladies trounced their share of Axis foes during WWII, Pat Patriot's debut as "America's Joan of Arc" leading her people to victory suggests a role that is uniquely female in wartime–the woman as symbol of inspiration and hope. Pat Patriot

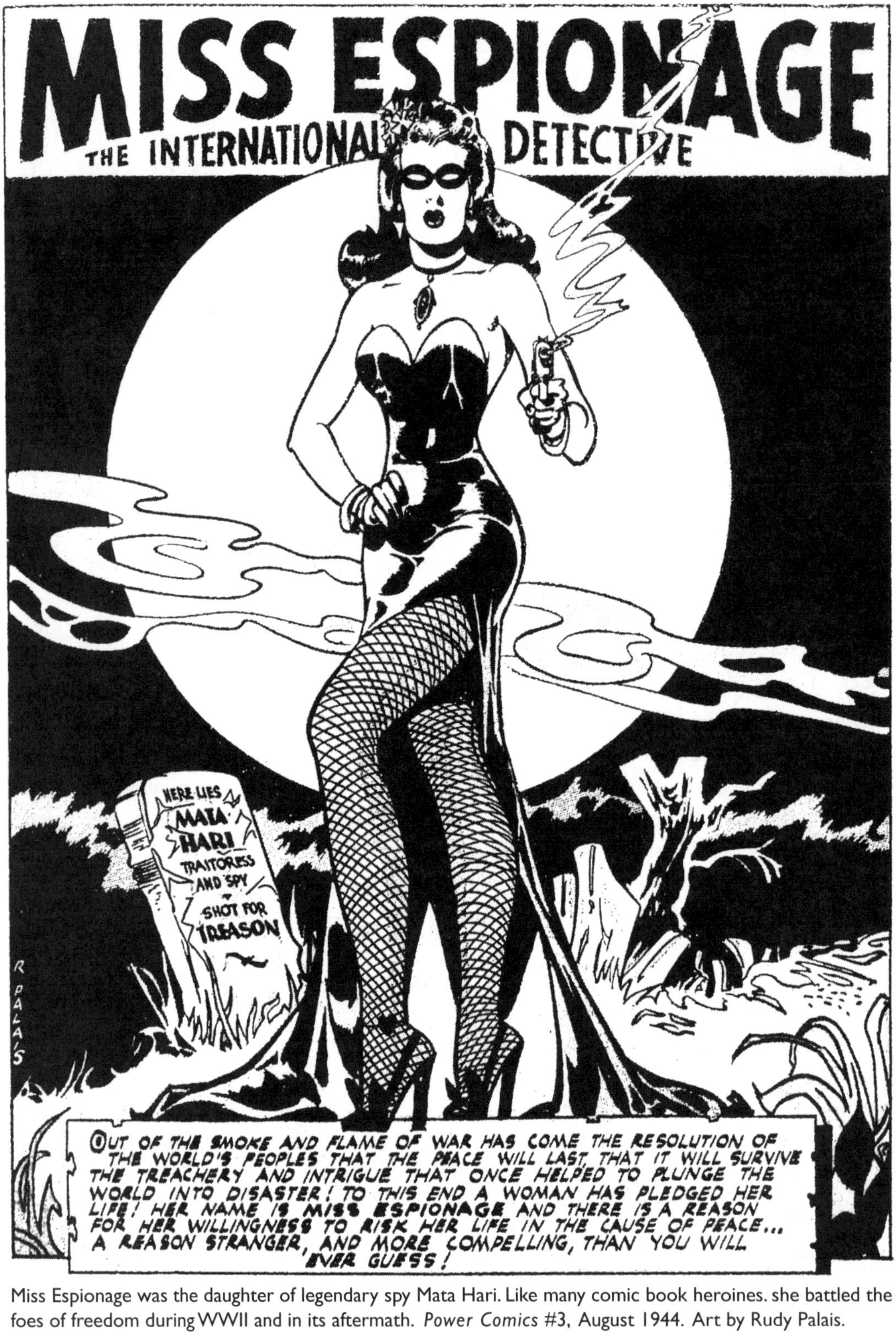
MISS ESPIONAGE
THE INTERNATIONAL DETECTIVE
HERE LIES MATA HARI TRAITORESS AND SPY SHOT FOR TREASON
R PALAIS
OUT OF THE SMOKE AND FLAME OF WAR HAS COME THE RESOLUTION OF THE WORLD'S PEOPLES THAT THE PEACE WILL LAST, THAT IT WILL SURVIVE THE TREACHERY AND INTRIGUE THAT ONCE HELPED TO PLUNGE THE WORLD INTO DISASTER! TO THIS END A WOMAN HAS PLEDGED HER LIFE! HER NAME IS MISS ESPIONAGE AND THERE IS A REASON FOR HER WILLINGNESS TO RISK HER LIFE IN THE CAUSE OF PEACE... A REASON STRANGER, AND MORE COMPELLING, THAN YOU WILL EVER GUESS!

Miss Espionage was the daughter of legendary spy Mata Hari. Like many comic book heroines. she battled the foes of freedom during WWII and in its aftermath. *Power Comics* #3, August 1944. Art by Rudy Palais.

started out as Patricia Patrios, a woman working in an airplane factory. The name "Patrios" sounds Greek, suggesting that Pat comes from an immigrant family, and as such would embrace American democratic ideals. When plucky Pat complains to her boss about the bad working conditions at the factory, he promptly fires her. That night, Pat performs in an amateur play, wearing a red, white and blue costume. After an attempt is made on her life, Pat suspects that something suspicious is going on back at the war plant. Still clad in her patriotic costume, she goes to investigate. After a series of misadventures, Pat captures a group of Axis spies operating in the airplane factory. When the workers see the victorious young woman resplendent in her patriotic garb, they dub her 'Pat Patriot'. "Young lady, it was only through your courage that those men were discovered and captured. You are the spirit of Americanism!"

Pat Patriot's career was not as long as Captain America's. Her adventures were over by the middle of 1942. But "America's Joan of Arc" also provided something to readers that some of the bellicose male super-patriots might have overlooked—a sense of comfort during bad times. One story closes with the heroine making a radio broadcast: "And so, the words of Pat Patriot ring out over the country, bringing assurance to thousands of worried persons as she fights for peace and democracy…"

Let's meet some of the brave women who defended democracy in WWII—

JANE MARTIN— Jane Martin, "the modern Florence Nightingale," began aiding the wounded on battlefields throughout the war zones in September 1940. In her early stories, Jane's aviator fiancé Tom arrives at the last minute to save the brave nurse. But he disappears after a few months, leaving Jane to handle the action as nurse, pilot, and occasional spy. The story presented here is from 1942, and shows Jane as both compassionate healer and valiant freedom fighter, delivering supplies and weapons to the needy. Later that same year, Jane became a full-time spy who traveled to exotic locales on dangerous assignments, much to the displeasure of some male readers. Jane Martin ended her long career in *Wings Comics* as a reporter in 1950.

PAT PARKER, WAR NURSE— Pat Parker debuted as a courageous English nurse who was also a skilled pilot in the May 1941 issue of *Speed Comics*. In her second adventure, Pat gains notoriety after she captures a German U-boat off the coast of Great Britain, prompting her to create the secret identity of War Nurse. As War Nurse, Pat travels across war-ravaged Europe in her battle against the Axis powers. In September 1942, Pat recruits a group of young women, consisting of British Ellen, Russian Tanya, American Penny, and Chinese Mei Ling. They become the Girl Commandos, one of the first all-female teams in comic books. Pat eventually dropped her War Nurse identity, but continued to lead the Girl Commandos until 1946. This story was drawn by artist Barbara Hall, one of the many female artists who worked during the Golden Age.

MADAME STRANGE— When Madame Strange was described as "mysterious, beautiful and cloaked with an unknown identity," they weren't joking. Who is she? What was the source of her great strength, speed and courage? We'll never know. All readers knew was that Madame Strange was an "American girl reporter" who travelled to exotic locations to relentlessly hunt down spies. But all you *really* needed to know about Madame Strange was not to mess with her. "Talk fast or I'll snap your arm!" she declares, as she grapples with an opponent in her first appearance in 1941's *Great Comics*. Madame Strange was one of the most physical female superheroes, and challenged the concept that comic book heroines were weak flowers. *Great Comics* only lasted three issues, and with its demise went one of the most fearless, two-fisted ladies of WWII.

PAT PATRIOT— Like War Nurse, Pat Patriot was a woman with no special powers who donned a red, white and blue costume to help the war effort. "America's Joan of Arc" traveled the country as a sort of morale booster, battling spies wherever she went. In this story, Pat braves the depths of the ocean and even ventures inside of a volcano (in her high heels) to track down enemy agents. Although most of Pat's time was spent protecting the homefront, in her final appearance, she traveled to Burma to lead a battalion of 100 female soldiers, all naturally wearing uniforms with skirts and high heels. Pat Patriot appeared in *Daredevil Comics* between 1941-42.

LADY SATAN— The love of freedom was incentive for many comic book heroines to fight the Axis powers. Lady Satan's motive was revenge. This story tells the origin of an unnamed woman who loses everything at the hands of the Nazis. Dubbing herself Lady Satan, she moves to Paris, where she becomes a spy and foe of the fascists. Wielding her deadly chlorine gas gun, Lady Satan only made a couple of appearances during the war. She returned in 1946, but was now a supernatural detective with black magic powers. The wartime Lady Satan appeared in *Dynamic Comics* in 1941-42.

BLACK VENUS— Like Lady Satan, vengeance was a motive for the slinky aviatrix called Black Venus to wage a one-woman war on the Axis. All of the servicemen were sweet on USO canteen hostess Mary LeRoche, but none knew of her tragic past. Before the war, she had been an exotic dancer in Paris. When Mary spurned the advances of a cruel Japanese officer, he had her fiancé killed. Using her stage name "Black Venus" as her *nom de guerre*, Mary took to the skies to fight for freedom and democracy.

Although Black Venus had plenty of admirers, she flew strictly solo. "…no matter how many people are around, I will always be alone!", Black Venus muses, as her plane flies into the sunset. Once the war was over, Black Venus' stories revolved around her efforts to rehabilitate veterans returning home from battle. Black Venus fought the good fight in *Contact Comics* from 1944-46.

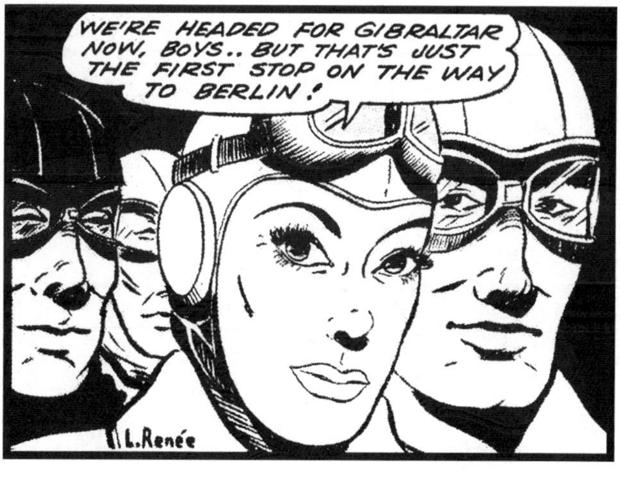
WE'RE HEADED FOR GIBRALTAR NOW, BOYS.. BUT THAT'S JUST THE FIRST STOP ON THE WAY TO BERLIN!
L. Renée

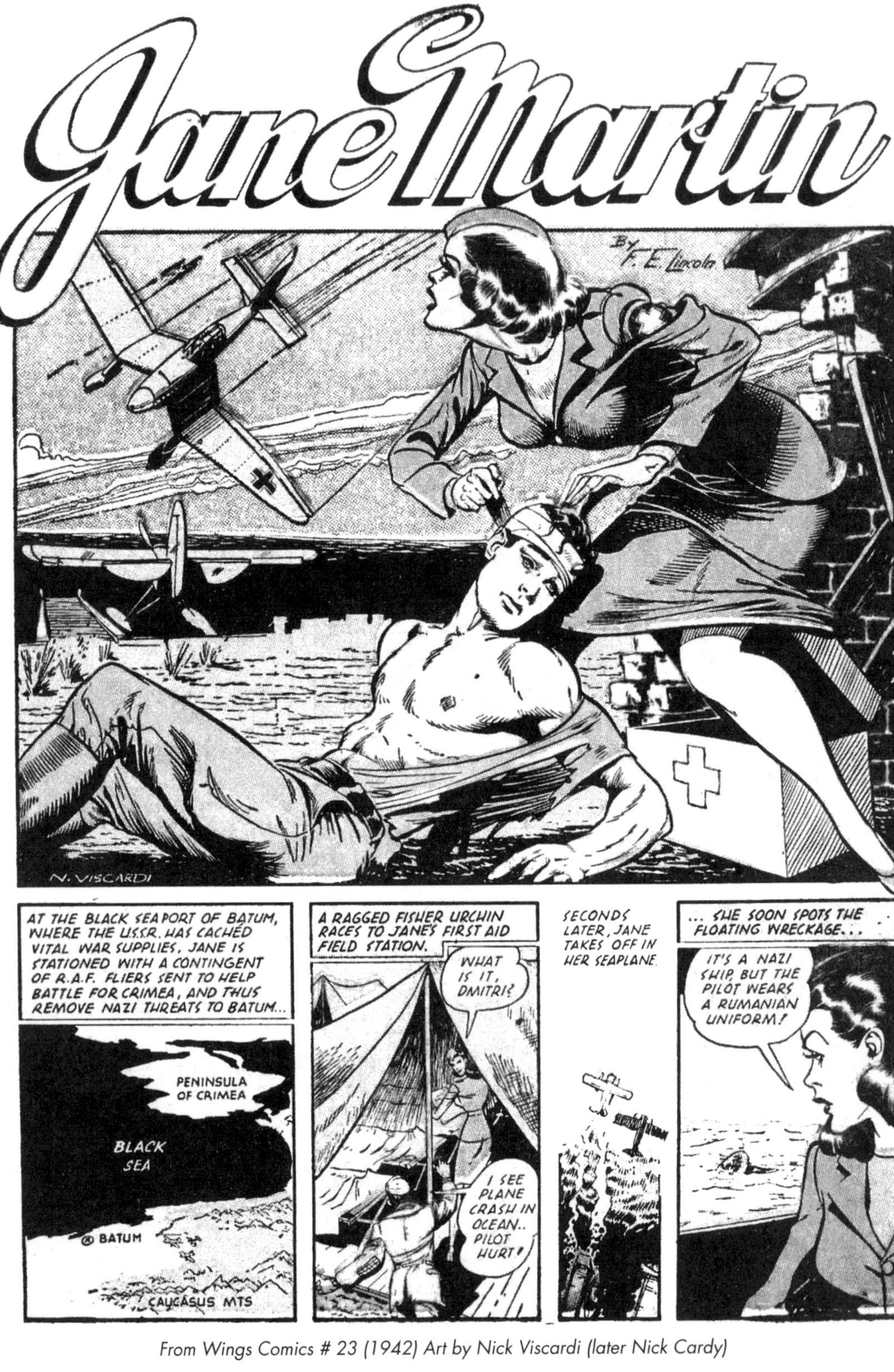
Jane Martin
By F. E. Lincoln
N. VISCARDI
AT THE BLACK SEAPORT OF BATUM, WHERE THE U.S.S.R. HAS CACHED VITAL WAR SUPPLIES, JANE IS STATIONED WITH A CONTINGENT OF R.A.F. FLIERS SENT TO HELP BATTLE FOR CRIMEA, AND THUS REMOVE NAZI THREATS TO BATUM...
PENINSULA OF CRIMEA
BLACK SEA
BATUM
CAUCASUS MTS
A RAGGED FISHER URCHIN RACES TO JANE'S FIRST AID FIELD STATION.
WHAT IS IT, DMITRI?
I SEE PLANE CRASH IN OCEAN.. PILOT HURT!
SECONDS LATER, JANE TAKES OFF IN HER SEAPLANE.
... SHE SOON SPOTS THE FLOATING WRECKAGE...
IT'S A NAZI SHIP, BUT THE PILOT WEARS A RUMANIAN UNIFORM!

From Wings Comics # 23 (1942) Art by Nick Viscardi (later Nick Cardy)

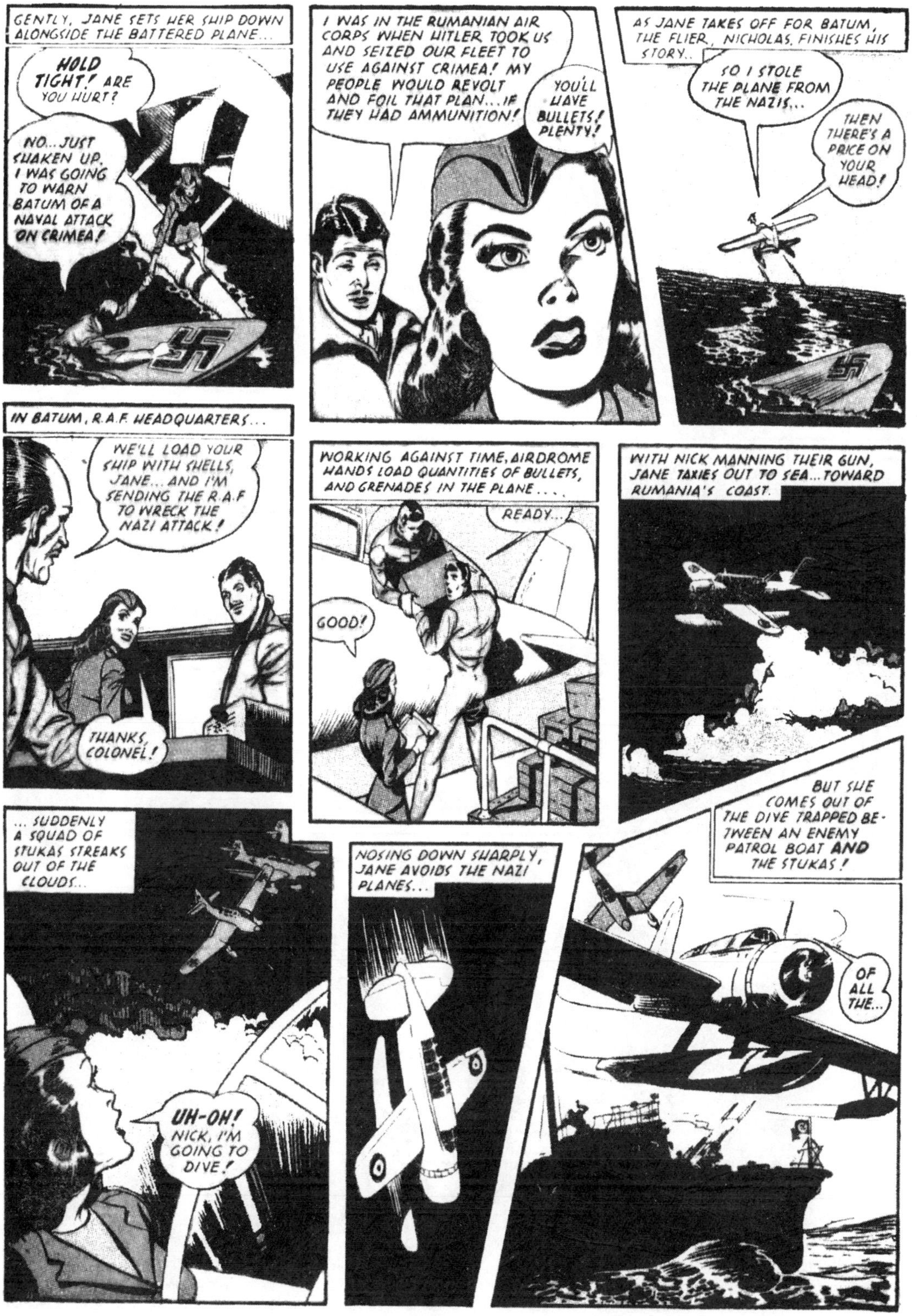
GENTLY, JANE SETS HER SHIP DOWN ALONGSIDE THE BATTERED PLANE...
HOLD TIGHT! ARE YOU HURT?
NO... JUST SHAKEN UP. I WAS GOING TO WARN BATUM OF A NAVAL ATTACK ON CRIMEA!
I WAS IN THE RUMANIAN AIR CORPS WHEN HITLER TOOK US AND SEIZED OUR FLEET TO USE AGAINST CRIMEA! MY PEOPLE WOULD REVOLT AND FOIL THAT PLAN... IF THEY HAD AMMUNITION!
YOU'LL HAVE BULLETS! PLENTY!
AS JANE TAKES OFF FOR BATUM, THE FLIER, NICHOLAS, FINISHES HIS STORY..
SO I STOLE THE PLANE FROM THE NAZIS...
THEN THERE'S A PRICE ON YOUR HEAD!
IN BATUM, R.A.F. HEADQUARTERS...
WE'LL LOAD YOUR SHIP WITH SHELLS, JANE... AND I'M SENDING THE R.A.F TO WRECK THE NAZI ATTACK!
THANKS, COLONEL!
WORKING AGAINST TIME, AIRDROME HANDS LOAD QUANTITIES OF BULLETS, AND GRENADES IN THE PLANE....
READY...
GOOD!
WITH NICK MANNING THEIR GUN, JANE TAXIES OUT TO SEA... TOWARD RUMANIA'S COAST.
... SUDDENLY A SQUAD OF STUKAS STREAKS OUT OF THE CLOUDS...
UH-OH! NICK, I'M GOING TO DIVE!
NOSING DOWN SHARPLY, JANE AVOIDS THE NAZI PLANES...
BUT SHE COMES OUT OF THE DIVE TRAPPED BE-TWEEN AN ENEMY PATROL BOAT AND THE STUKAS!
OF ALL THE...

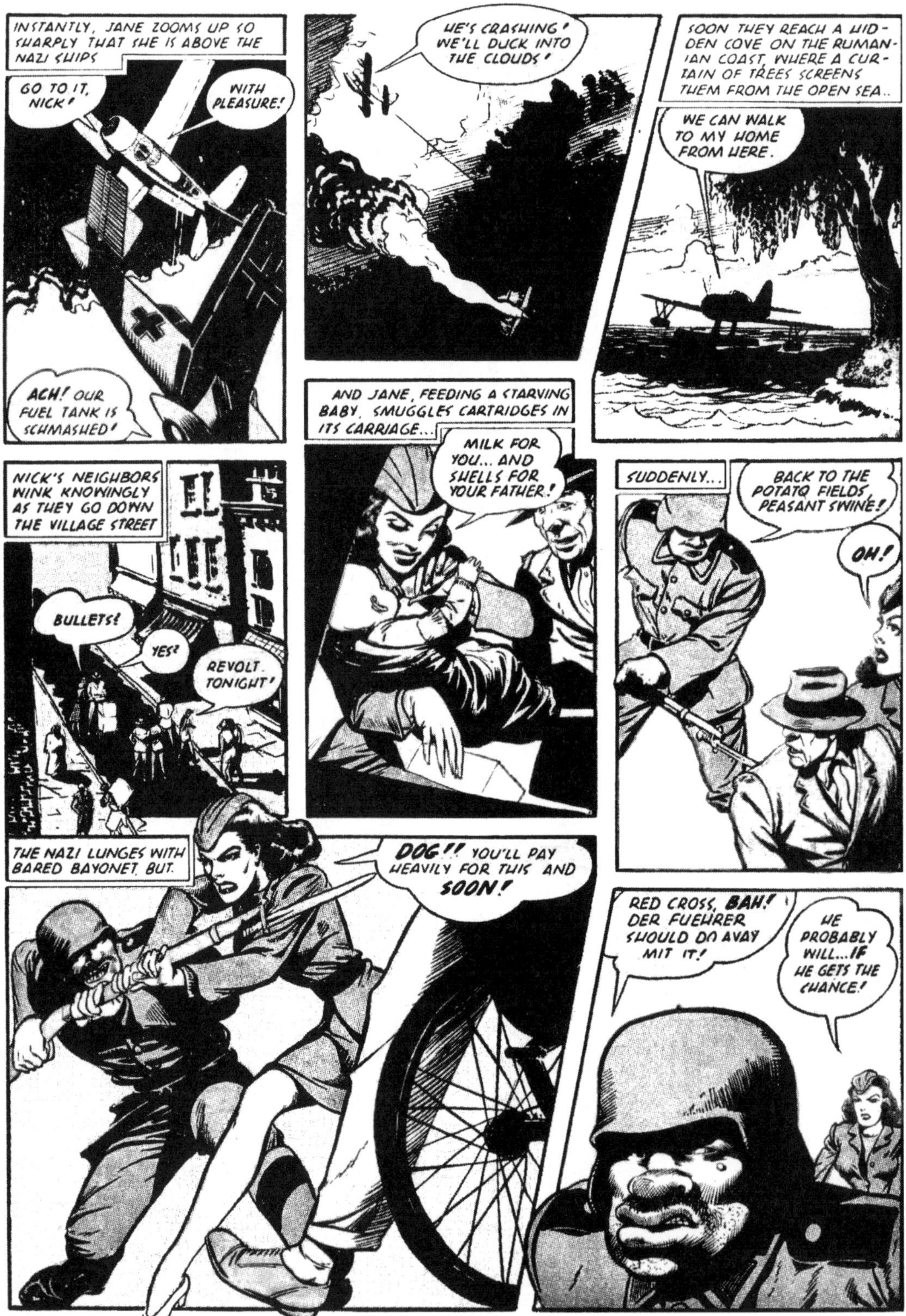
INSTANTLY, JANE ZOOMS UP SO SHARPLY THAT SHE IS ABOVE THE NAZI SHIPS
GO TO IT, NICK!
WITH PLEASURE!
ACH! OUR FUEL TANK IS SCHMASHED!
HE'S CRASHING! WE'LL DUCK INTO THE CLOUDS!
SOON THEY REACH A HIDDEN COVE ON THE RUMANIAN COAST, WHERE A CURTAIN OF TREES SCREENS THEM FROM THE OPEN SEA..
WE CAN WALK TO MY HOME FROM HERE.
NICK'S NEIGHBORS WINK KNOWINGLY AS THEY GO DOWN THE VILLAGE STREET
BULLETS!
YES?
REVOLT. TONIGHT!
AND JANE, FEEDING A STARVING BABY, SMUGGLES CARTRIDGES IN ITS CARRIAGE...
MILK FOR YOU... AND SHELLS FOR YOUR FATHER!
SUDDENLY...
BACK TO THE POTATO FIELDS, PEASANT SWINE!
OH!
THE NAZI LUNGES WITH BARED BAYONET, BUT.
DOG!! YOU'LL PAY HEAVILY FOR THIS AND SOON!
RED CROSS, BAH! DER FUEHRER SHOULD DO AVAY MIT IT!
HE PROBABLY WILL...IF HE GETS THE CHANCE!

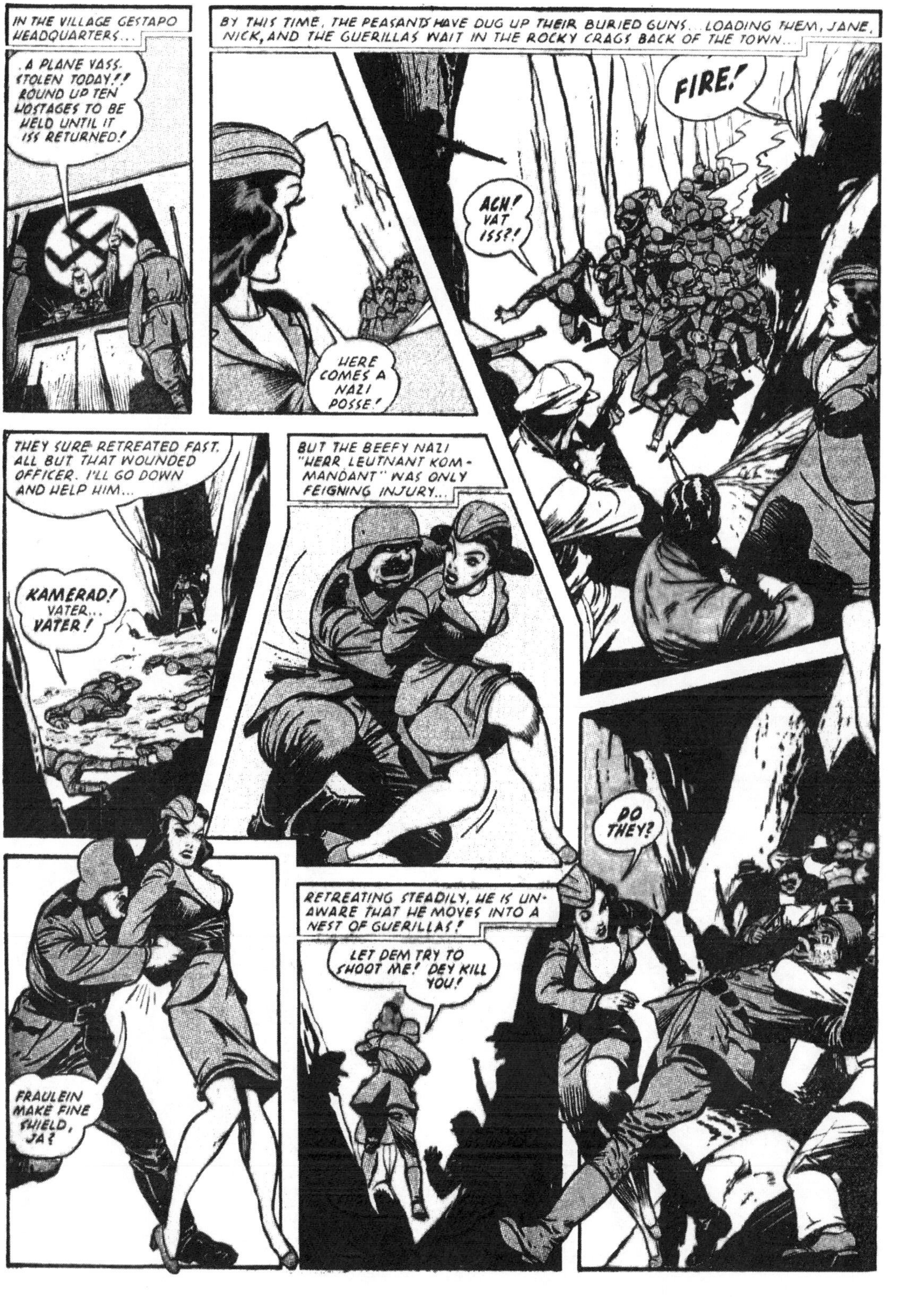
IN THE VILLAGE GESTAPO HEADQUARTERS...
..A PLANE VASS STOLEN TODAY!! ROUND UP TEN HOSTAGES TO BE HELD UNTIL IT ISS RETURNED!
BY THIS TIME, THE PEASANTS HAVE DUG UP THEIR BURIED GUNS... LOADING THEM, JANE, NICK, AND THE GUERILLAS WAIT IN THE ROCKY CRAGS BACK OF THE TOWN...
HERE COMES A NAZI POSSE!
FIRE!
ACH! VAT ISS?!
THEY SURE RETREATED FAST. ALL BUT THAT WOUNDED OFFICER. I'LL GO DOWN AND HELP HIM...
KAMERAD! VATER... VATER!
BUT THE BEEFY NAZI "HERR LEUTNANT KOMMANDANT" WAS ONLY FEIGNING INJURY...
DO THEY?
FRAULEIN MAKE FINE SHIELD, JA?
RETREATING STEADILY, HE IS UNAWARE THAT HE MOVES INTO A NEST OF GUERILLAS!
LET DEM TRY TO SHOOT ME! DEY KILL YOU!

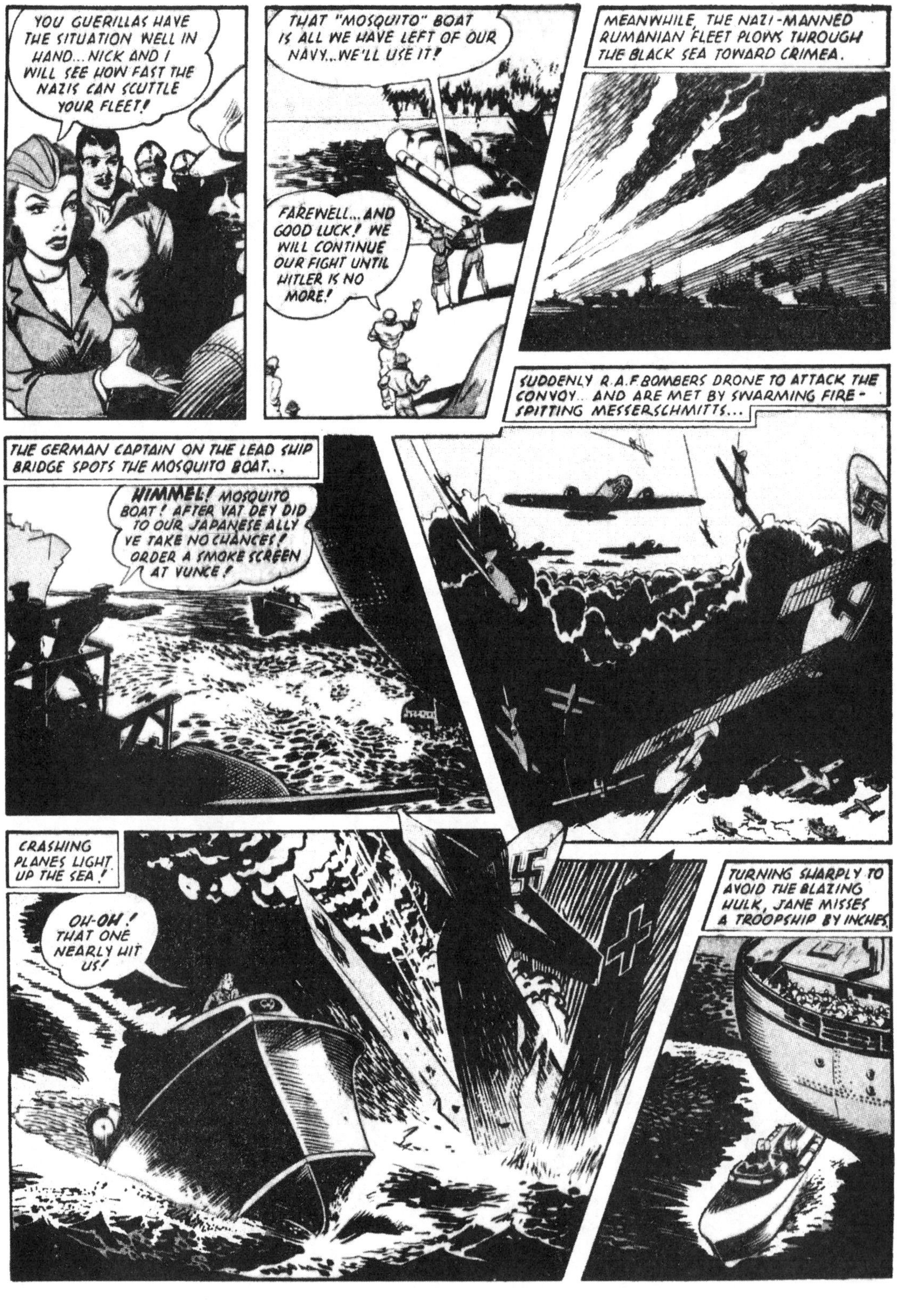
YOU GUERILLAS HAVE THE SITUATION WELL IN HAND... NICK AND I WILL SEE HOW FAST THE NAZIS CAN SCUTTLE YOUR FLEET!
THAT "MOSQUITO" BOAT IS ALL WE HAVE LEFT OF OUR NAVY... WE'LL USE IT!
FAREWELL... AND GOOD LUCK! WE WILL CONTINUE OUR FIGHT UNTIL HITLER IS NO MORE!
MEANWHILE, THE NAZI-MANNED RUMANIAN FLEET PLOWS THROUGH THE BLACK SEA TOWARD CRIMEA.
SUDDENLY R.A.F. BOMBERS DRONE TO ATTACK THE CONVOY... AND ARE MET BY SWARMING FIRE-SPITTING MESSERSCHMITTS...
THE GERMAN CAPTAIN ON THE LEAD SHIP BRIDGE SPOTS THE MOSQUITO BOAT...
HIMMEL! MOSQUITO BOAT! AFTER VAT DEY DID TO OUR JAPANESE ALLY VE TAKE NO CHANCES! ORDER A SMOKE SCREEN AT VUNCE!
CRASHING PLANES LIGHT UP THE SEA!
OH-OH! THAT ONE NEARLY HIT US!
TURNING SHARPLY TO AVOID THE BLAZING HULK, JANE MISSES A TROOPSHIP BY INCHES

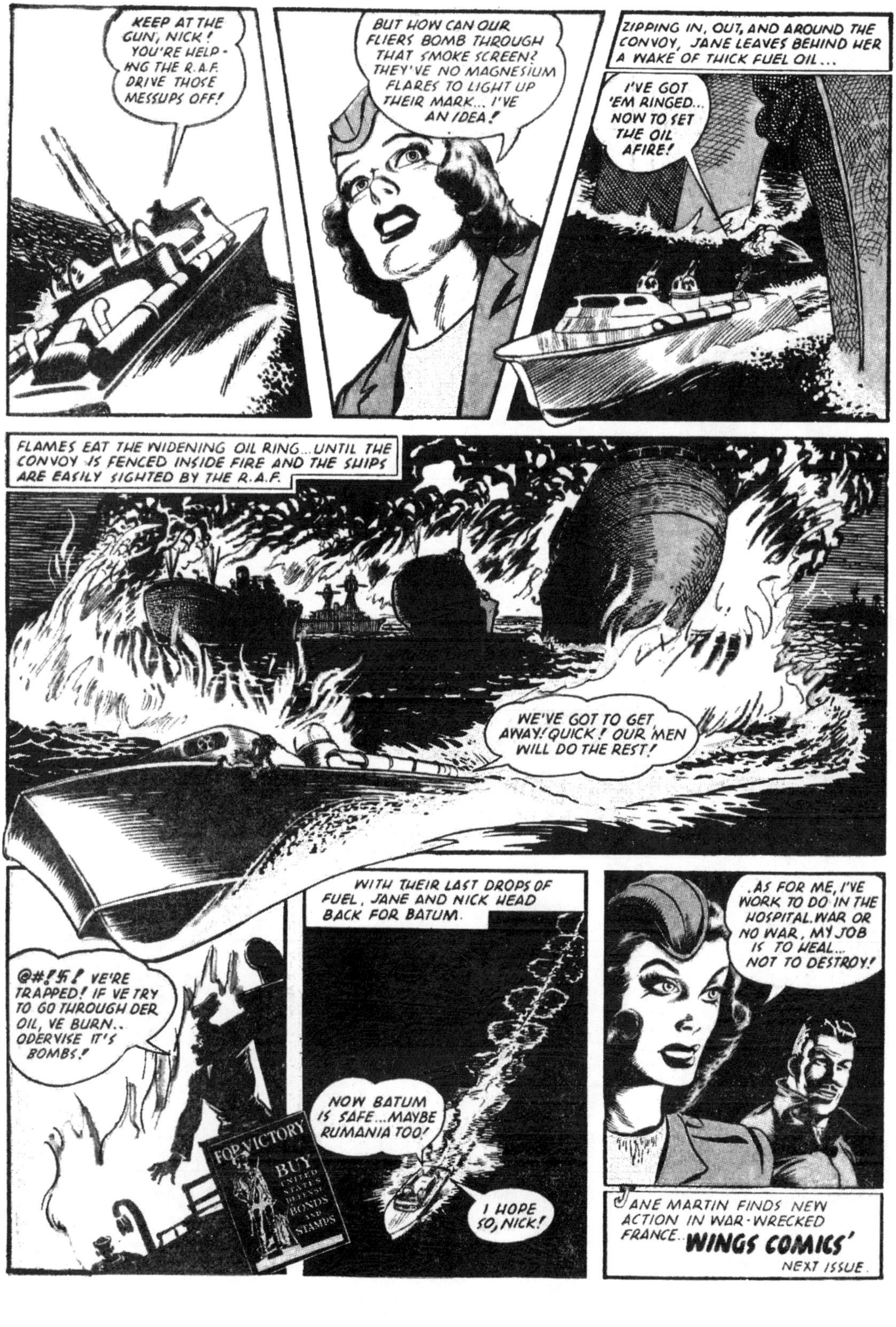
KEEP AT THE GUN, NICK! YOU'RE HELPING THE R.A.F. DRIVE THOSE MESSUPS OFF!
BUT HOW CAN OUR FLIERS BOMB THROUGH THAT SMOKE SCREEN? THEY'VE NO MAGNESIUM FLARES TO LIGHT UP THEIR MARK... I'VE AN IDEA!
ZIPPING IN, OUT, AND AROUND THE CONVOY, JANE LEAVES BEHIND HER A WAKE OF THICK FUEL OIL...
I'VE GOT 'EM RINGED... NOW TO SET THE OIL AFIRE!
FLAMES EAT THE WIDENING OIL RING... UNTIL THE CONVOY IS FENCED INSIDE FIRE AND THE SHIPS ARE EASILY SIGHTED BY THE R.A.F.
WE'VE GOT TO GET AWAY! QUICK! OUR MEN WILL DO THE REST!
@#!卐! VE'RE TRAPPED! IF VE TRY TO GO THROUGH DER OIL, VE BURN.. ODERVISE IT'S BOMBS!
FOR VICTORY BUY UNITED STATES DEFENSE BONDS AND STAMPS
WITH THEIR LAST DROPS OF FUEL, JANE AND NICK HEAD BACK FOR BATUM.
NOW BATUM IS SAFE... MAYBE RUMANIA TOO!
I HOPE SO, NICK!
AS FOR ME, I'VE WORK TO DO IN THE HOSPITAL. WAR OR NO WAR, MY JOB IS TO HEAL... NOT TO DESTROY!
JANE MARTIN FINDS NEW ACTION IN WAR-WRECKED FRANCE.. WINGS COMICS' NEXT ISSUE.

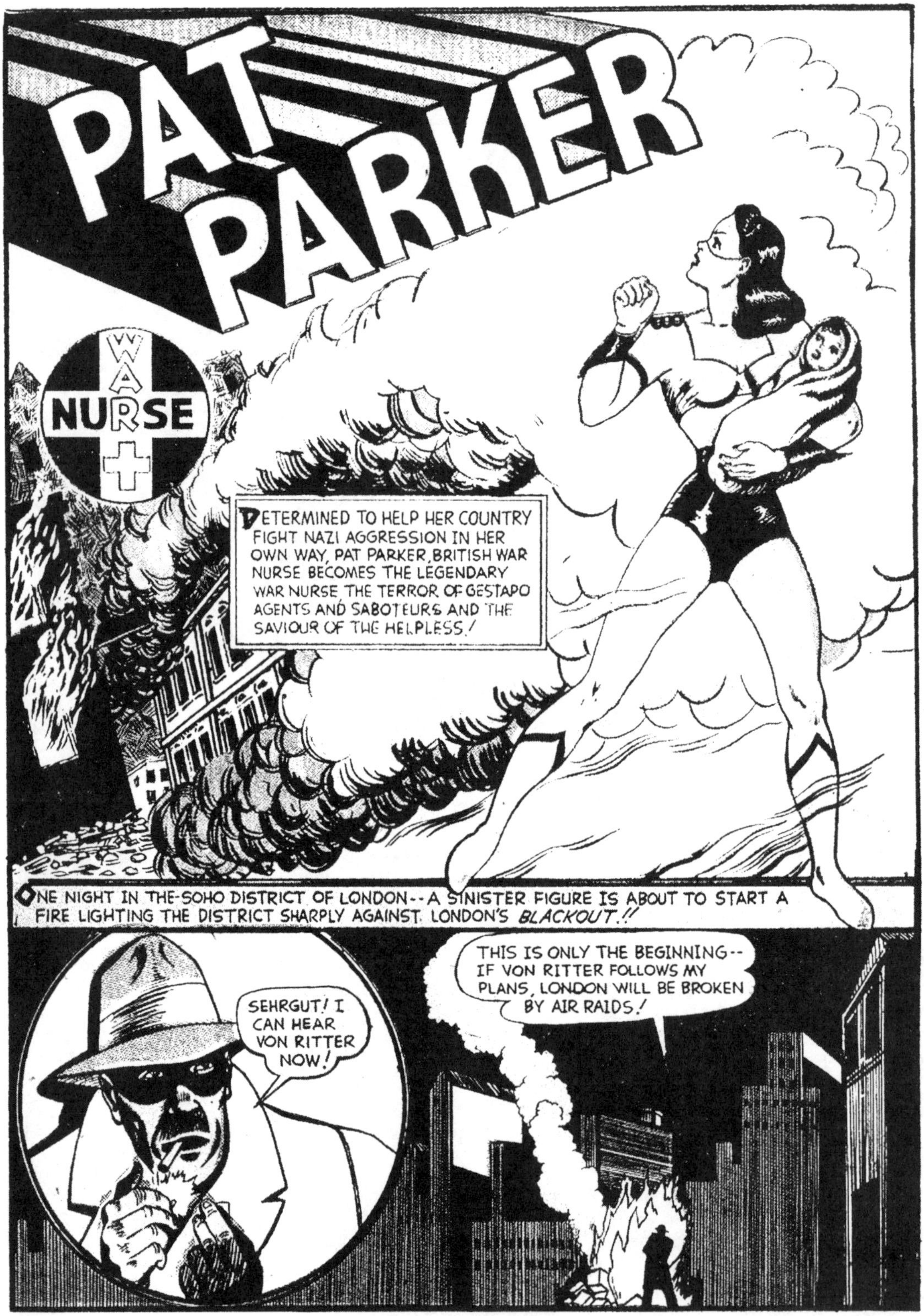
PAT PARKER
WAR NURSE
DETERMINED TO HELP HER COUNTRY FIGHT NAZI AGGRESSION IN HER OWN WAY, PAT PARKER, BRITISH WAR NURSE BECOMES THE LEGENDARY WAR NURSE, THE TERROR OF GESTAPO AGENTS AND SABOTEURS AND THE SAVIOUR OF THE HELPLESS!
ONE NIGHT IN THE SOHO DISTRICT OF LONDON-- A SINISTER FIGURE IS ABOUT TO START A FIRE LIGHTING THE DISTRICT SHARPLY AGAINST LONDON'S BLACKOUT!!
SEHRGUT! I CAN HEAR VON RITTER NOW!
THIS IS ONLY THE BEGINNING-- IF VON RITTER FOLLOWS MY PLANS, LONDON WILL BE BROKEN BY AIR RAIDS!

From Speed Comics #17 (1942) Art by Barbara Hall

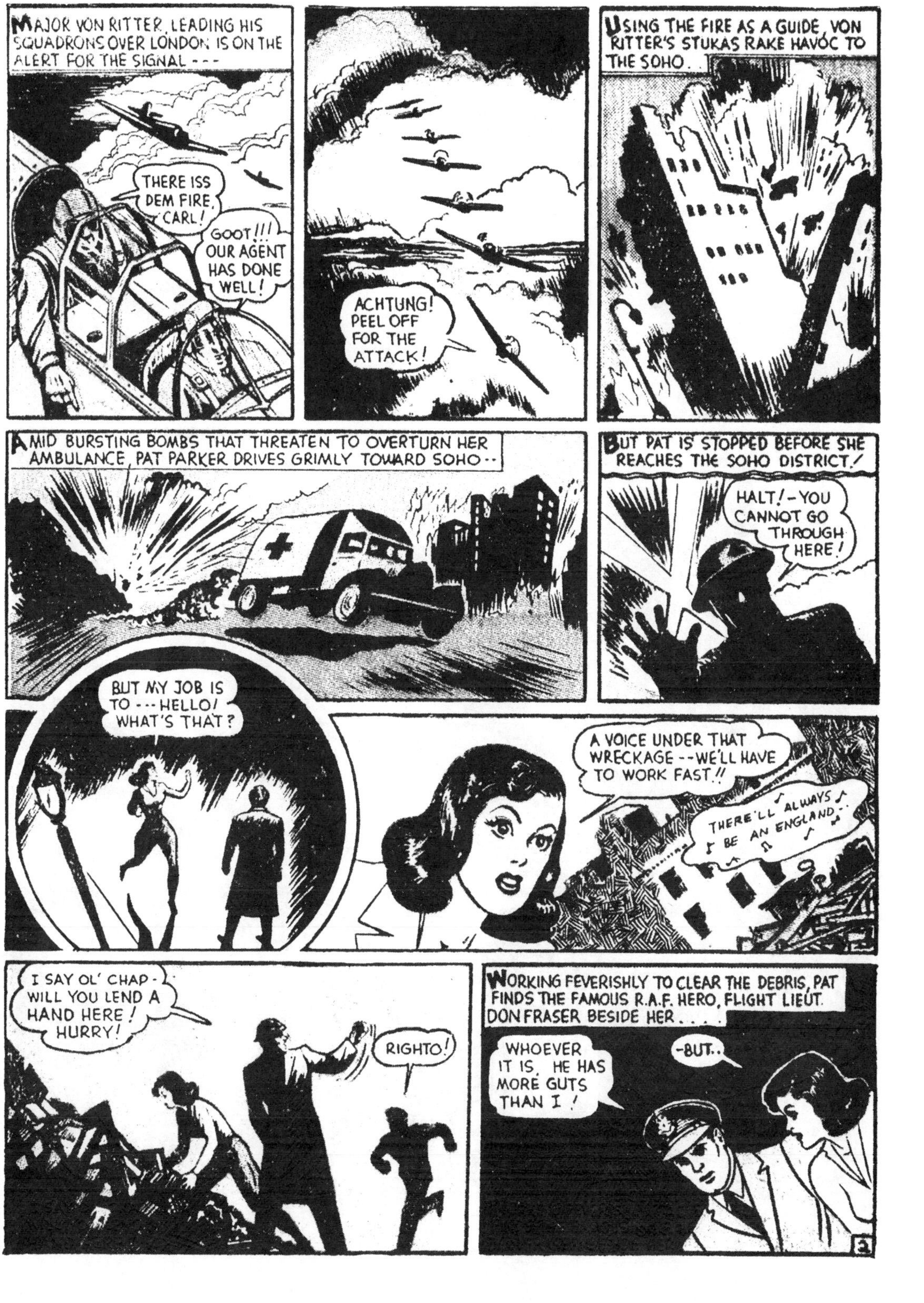
MAJOR VON RITTER, LEADING HIS SQUADRONS OVER LONDON IS ON THE ALERT FOR THE SIGNAL ---
THERE ISS DEM FIRE, CARL!
GOOT!!! OUR AGENT HAS DONE WELL!
ACHTUNG! PEEL OFF FOR THE ATTACK!
USING THE FIRE AS A GUIDE, VON RITTER'S STUKAS RAKE HAVOC TO THE SOHO.
AMID BURSTING BOMBS THAT THREATEN TO OVERTURN HER AMBULANCE, PAT PARKER DRIVES GRIMLY TOWARD SOHO --
BUT PAT IS STOPPED BEFORE SHE REACHES THE SOHO DISTRICT!
HALT! - YOU CANNOT GO THROUGH HERE!
BUT MY JOB IS TO --- HELLO! WHAT'S THAT?
A VOICE UNDER THAT WRECKAGE -- WE'LL HAVE TO WORK FAST!!
THERE'LL ALWAYS BE AN ENGLAND...
I SAY OL' CHAP - WILL YOU LEND A HAND HERE! HURRY!
RIGHTO!
WORKING FEVERISHLY TO CLEAR THE DEBRIS, PAT FINDS THE FAMOUS R.A.F. HERO, FLIGHT LIEUT. DON FRASER BESIDE HER . . . .
WHOEVER IT IS, HE HAS MORE GUTS THAN I!
-BUT..
3

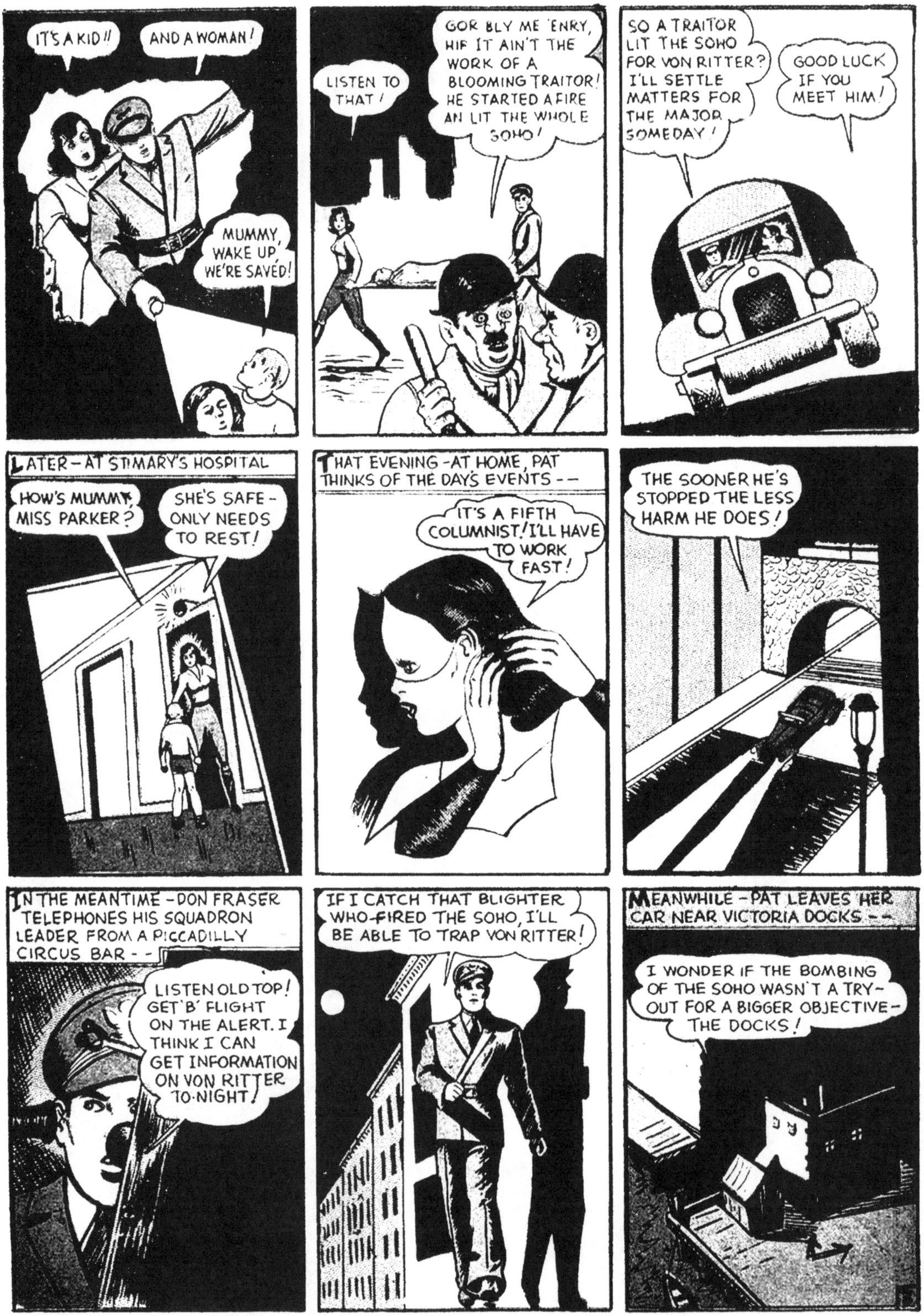
IT'S A KID!!
AND A WOMAN!
MUMMY, WAKE UP, WE'RE SAVED!
LISTEN TO THAT!
GOR BLY ME 'ENRY, HIF IT AIN'T THE WORK OF A BLOOMING TRAITOR! HE STARTED A FIRE AN LIT THE WHOLE SOHO!
SO A TRAITOR LIT THE SOHO FOR VON RITTER? I'LL SETTLE MATTERS FOR THE MAJOR SOMEDAY!
GOOD LUCK IF YOU MEET HIM!
LATER - AT ST. MARY'S HOSPITAL
HOW'S MUMMY, MISS PARKER?
SHE'S SAFE - ONLY NEEDS TO REST!
THAT EVENING - AT HOME, PAT THINKS OF THE DAY'S EVENTS --
IT'S A FIFTH COLUMNIST! I'LL HAVE TO WORK FAST!
THE SOONER HE'S STOPPED THE LESS HARM HE DOES!
IN THE MEANTIME - DON FRASER TELEPHONES HIS SQUADRON LEADER FROM A PICCADILLY CIRCUS BAR --
LISTEN OLD TOP! GET 'B' FLIGHT ON THE ALERT. I THINK I CAN GET INFORMATION ON VON RITTER TO-NIGHT!
IF I CATCH THAT BLIGHTER WHO FIRED THE SOHO, I'LL BE ABLE TO TRAP VON RITTER!
MEANWHILE - PAT LEAVES HER CAR NEAR VICTORIA DOCKS --
I WONDER IF THE BOMBING OF THE SOHO WASN'T A TRY-OUT FOR A BIGGER OBJECTIVE - THE DOCKS!

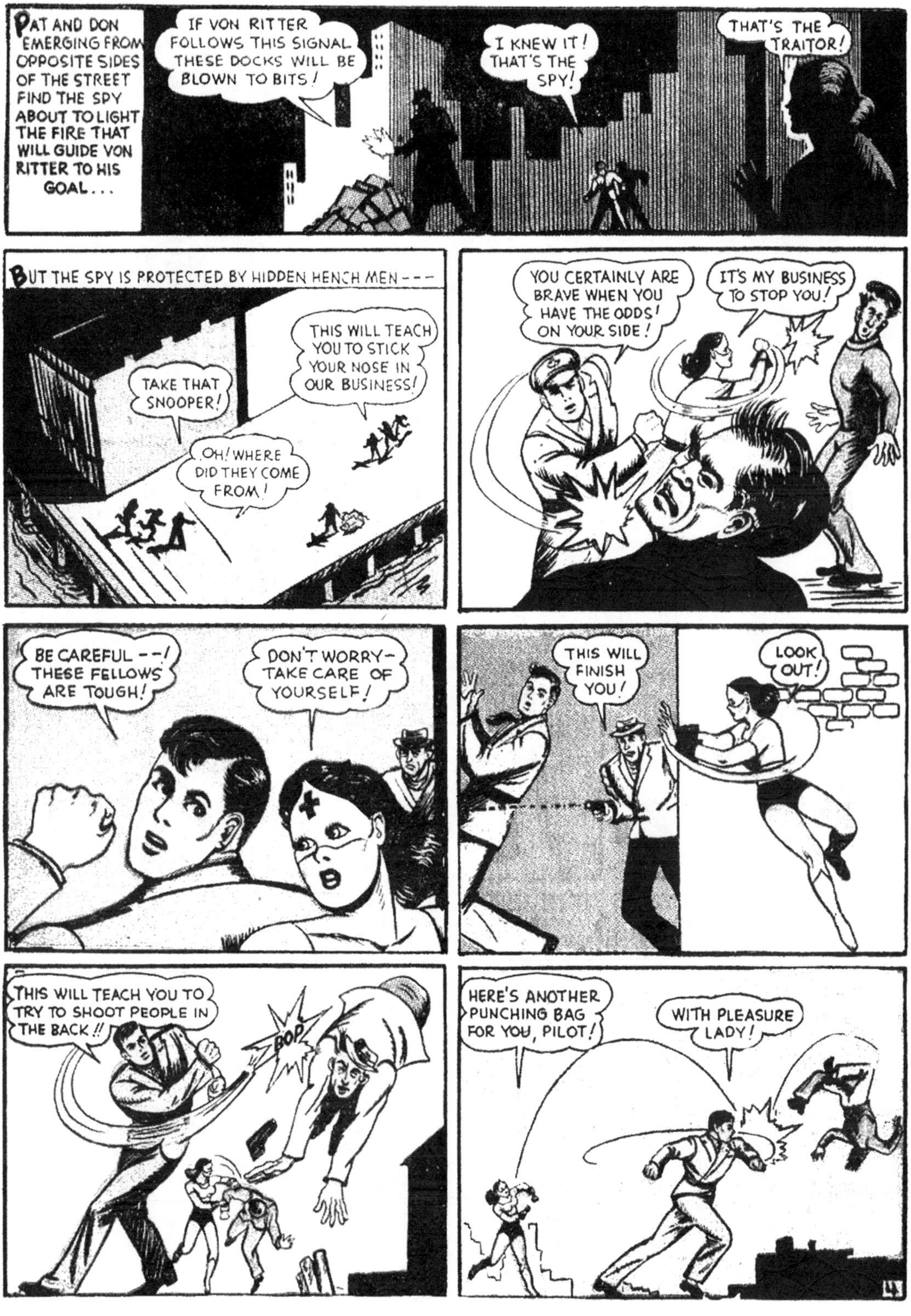
PAT AND DON EMERGING FROM OPPOSITE SIDES OF THE STREET FIND THE SPY ABOUT TO LIGHT THE FIRE THAT WILL GUIDE VON RITTER TO HIS GOAL...
IF VON RITTER FOLLOWS THIS SIGNAL THESE DOCKS WILL BE BLOWN TO BITS!
I KNEW IT! THAT'S THE SPY!
THAT'S THE TRAITOR!
BUT THE SPY IS PROTECTED BY HIDDEN HENCH MEN---
TAKE THAT SNOOPER!
THIS WILL TEACH YOU TO STICK YOUR NOSE IN OUR BUSINESS!
OH! WHERE DID THEY COME FROM!
YOU CERTAINLY ARE BRAVE WHEN YOU HAVE THE ODDS! ON YOUR SIDE!
IT'S MY BUSINESS TO STOP YOU!
BE CAREFUL --! THESE FELLOWS ARE TOUGH!
DON'T WORRY- TAKE CARE OF YOURSELF!
THIS WILL FINISH YOU!
LOOK OUT!
THIS WILL TEACH YOU TO TRY TO SHOOT PEOPLE IN THE BACK!!
BOP
HERE'S ANOTHER PUNCHING BAG FOR YOU, PILOT!
WITH PLEASURE LADY!

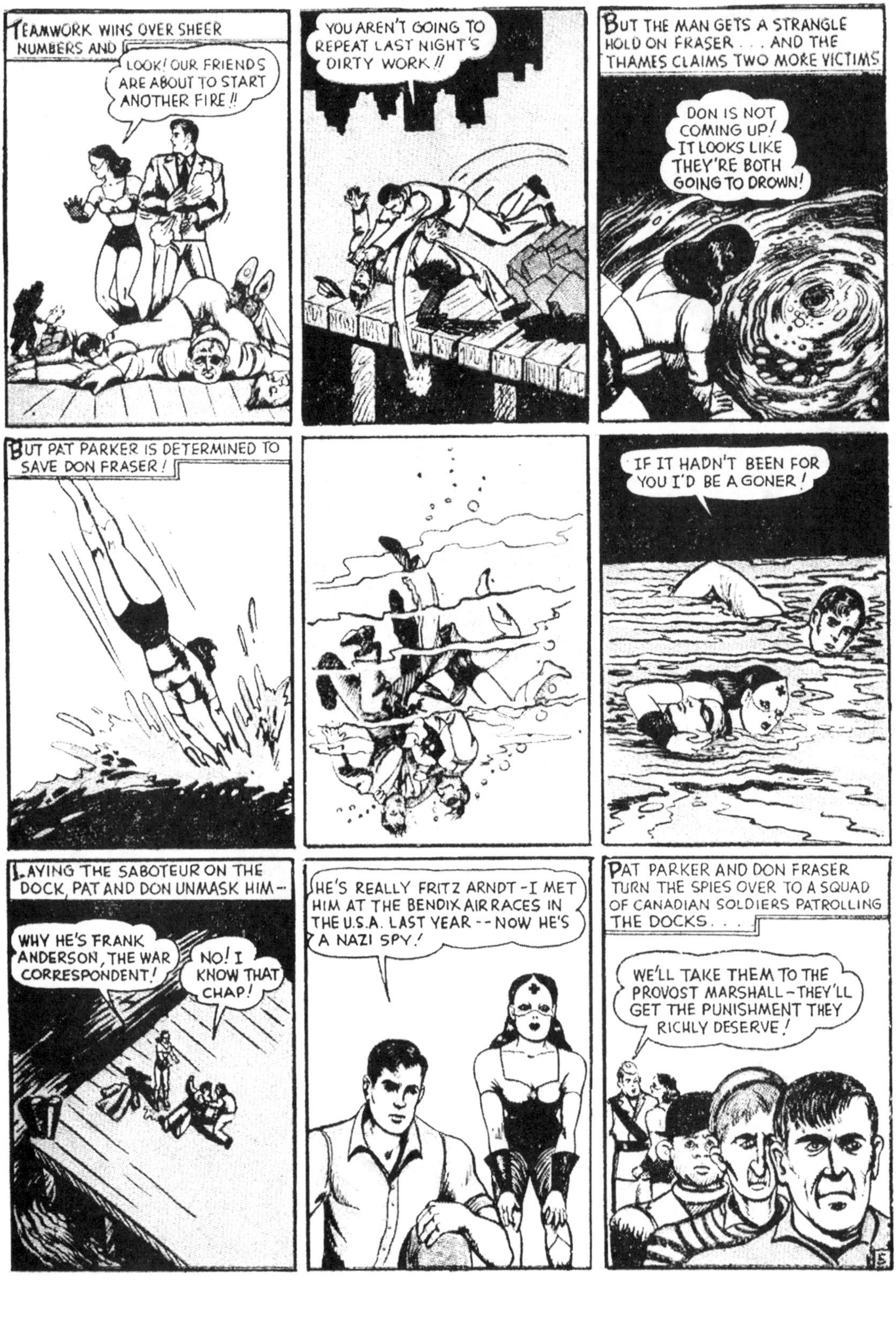
TEAMWORK WINS OVER SHEER NUMBERS AND
LOOK! OUR FRIENDS ARE ABOUT TO START ANOTHER FIRE !!
YOU AREN'T GOING TO REPEAT LAST NIGHT'S DIRTY WORK !!
BUT THE MAN GETS A STRANGLE HOLD ON FRASER . . . AND THE THAMES CLAIMS TWO MORE VICTIMS
DON IS NOT COMING UP! IT LOOKS LIKE THEY'RE BOTH GOING TO DROWN!
BUT PAT PARKER IS DETERMINED TO SAVE DON FRASER!
IF IT HADN'T BEEN FOR YOU I'D BE A GONER!
LAYING THE SABOTEUR ON THE DOCK, PAT AND DON UNMASK HIM--
WHY HE'S FRANK ANDERSON, THE WAR CORRESPONDENT!
NO! I KNOW THAT CHAP!
HE'S REALLY FRITZ ARNDT - I MET HIM AT THE BENDIX AIR RACES IN THE U.S.A. LAST YEAR -- NOW HE'S A NAZI SPY!
PAT PARKER AND DON FRASER TURN THE SPIES OVER TO A SQUAD OF CANADIAN SOLDIERS PATROLLING THE DOCKS . . .
WE'LL TAKE THEM TO THE PROVOST MARSHALL - THEY'LL GET THE PUNISHMENT THEY RICHLY DESERVE!

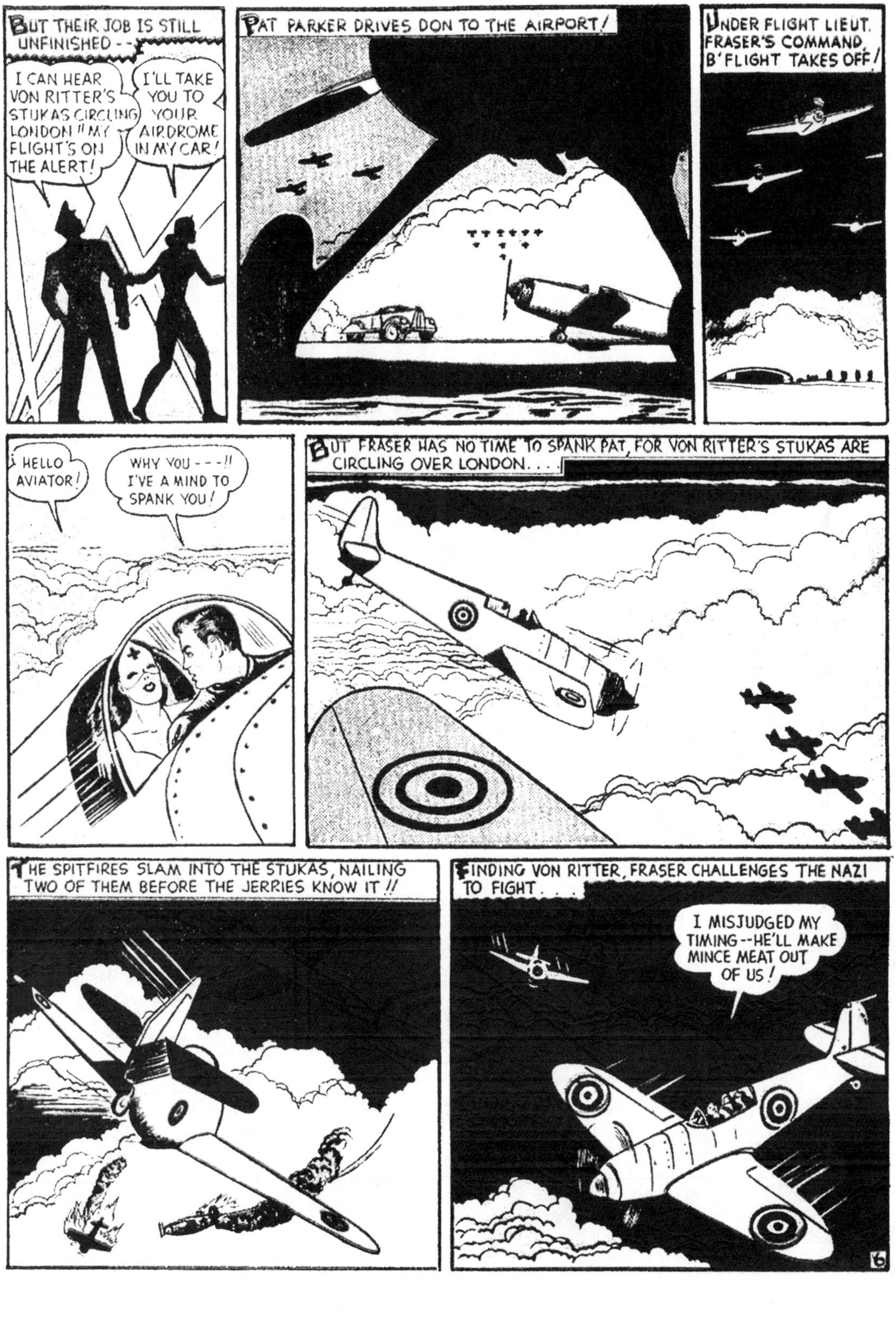
BUT THEIR JOB IS STILL UNFINISHED - -
I CAN HEAR VON RITTER'S STUKAS CIRCLING LONDON !! MY FLIGHT'S ON THE ALERT!
I'LL TAKE YOU TO YOUR AIRDROME IN MY CAR!
PAT PARKER DRIVES DON TO THE AIRPORT!
UNDER FLIGHT LIEUT. FRASER'S COMMAND, B' FLIGHT TAKES OFF!
HELLO AVIATOR!
WHY YOU - - -!! I'VE A MIND TO SPANK YOU!
BUT FRASER HAS NO TIME TO SPANK PAT, FOR VON RITTER'S STUKAS ARE CIRCLING OVER LONDON. . .
THE SPITFIRES SLAM INTO THE STUKAS, NAILING TWO OF THEM BEFORE THE JERRIES KNOW IT !!
FINDING VON RITTER, FRASER CHALLENGES THE NAZI TO FIGHT. . .
I MISJUDGED MY TIMING--HE'LL MAKE MINCE MEAT OUT OF US!
6

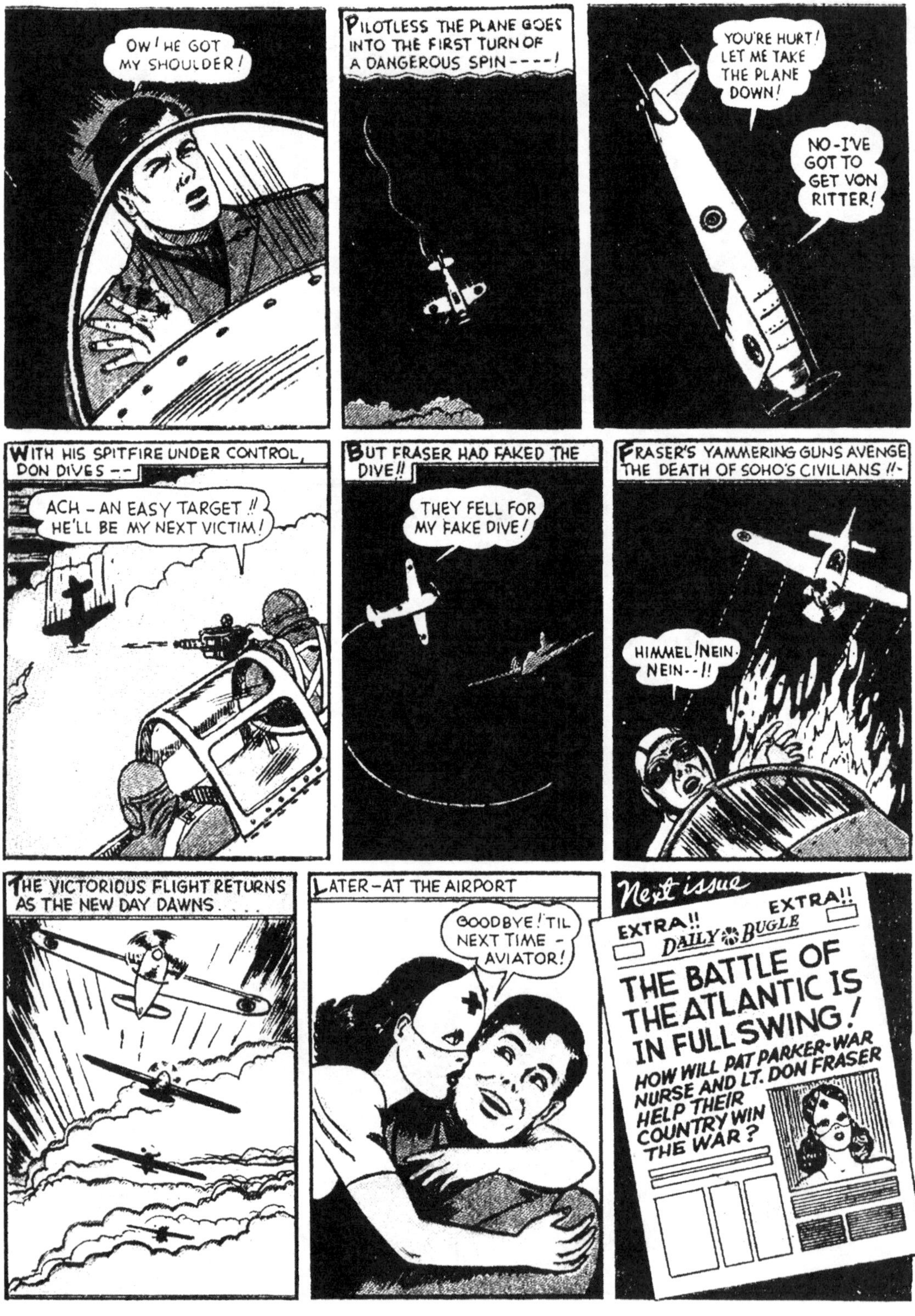
OW! HE GOT MY SHOULDER!
PILOTLESS THE PLANE GOES INTO THE FIRST TURN OF A DANGEROUS SPIN----!
YOU'RE HURT! LET ME TAKE THE PLANE DOWN!
NO-I'VE GOT TO GET VON RITTER!
WITH HIS SPITFIRE UNDER CONTROL, DON DIVES --
ACH - AN EASY TARGET !! HE'LL BE MY NEXT VICTIM!
BUT FRASER HAD FAKED THE DIVE!!
THEY FELL FOR MY FAKE DIVE!
FRASER'S YAMMERING GUNS AVENGE THE DEATH OF SOHO'S CIVILIANS !!-
HIMMEL! NEIN. NEIN--!!
THE VICTORIOUS FLIGHT RETURNS AS THE NEW DAY DAWNS. . .
LATER-AT THE AIRPORT
GOODBYE! 'TIL NEXT TIME - AVIATOR!
Next issue
EXTRA!!
EXTRA!!
DAILY BUGLE
THE BATTLE OF THE ATLANTIC IS IN FULL SWING!
HOW WILL PAT PARKER-WAR NURSE AND LT. DON FRASER HELP THEIR COUNTRY WIN THE WAR?

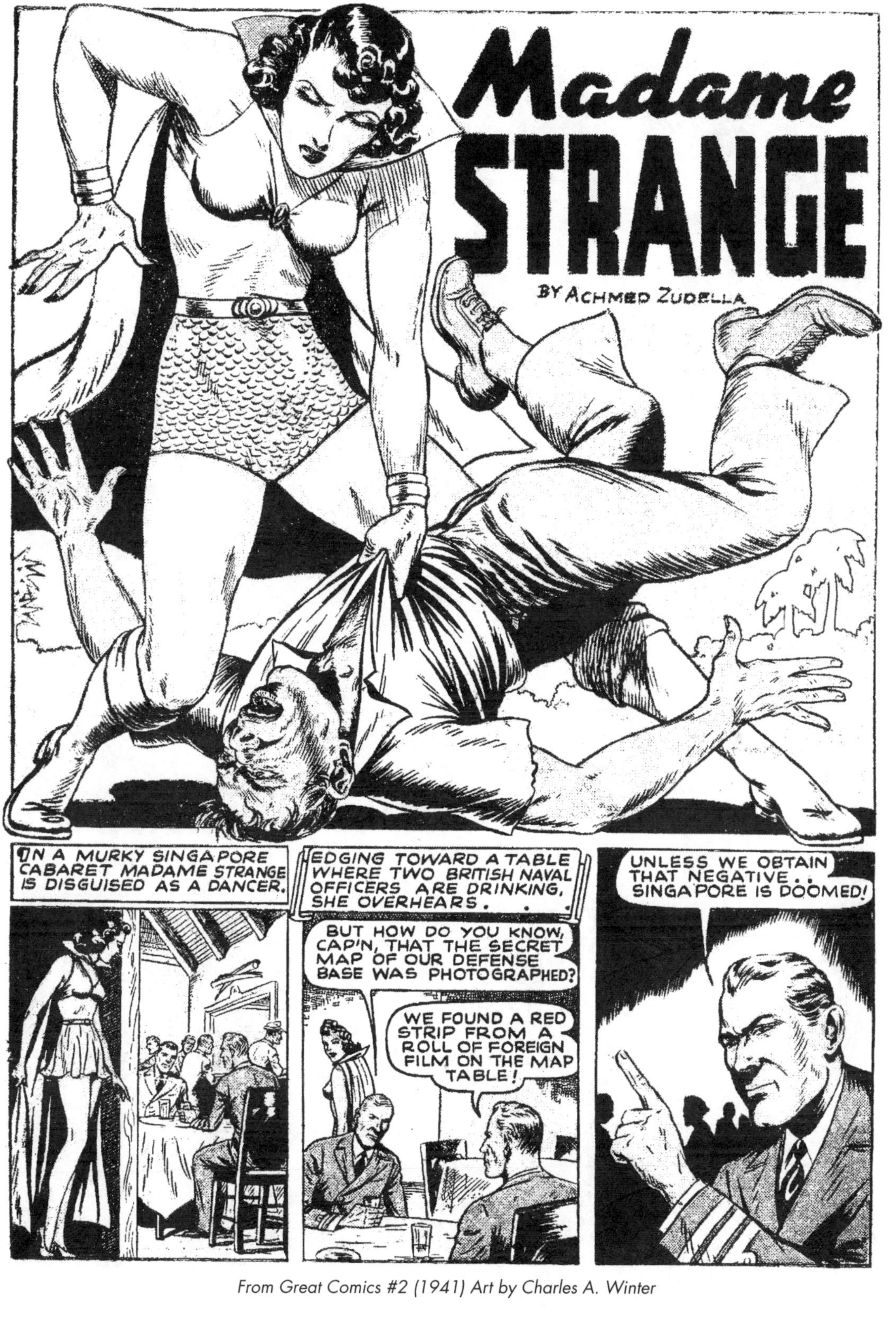
Madame
STRANGE
BY ACHMED ZUDELLA
IN A MURKY SINGAPORE CABARET MADAME STRANGE IS DISGUISED AS A DANCER.
EDGING TOWARD A TABLE WHERE TWO BRITISH NAVAL OFFICERS ARE DRINKING, SHE OVERHEARS . . .
BUT HOW DO YOU KNOW, CAP'N, THAT THE SECRET MAP OF OUR DEFENSE BASE WAS PHOTOGRAPHED?
WE FOUND A RED STRIP FROM A ROLL OF FOREIGN FILM ON THE MAP TABLE!
UNLESS WE OBTAIN THAT NEGATIVE . . SINGAPORE IS DOOMED!

From Great Comics #2 (1941) Art by Charles A. Winter

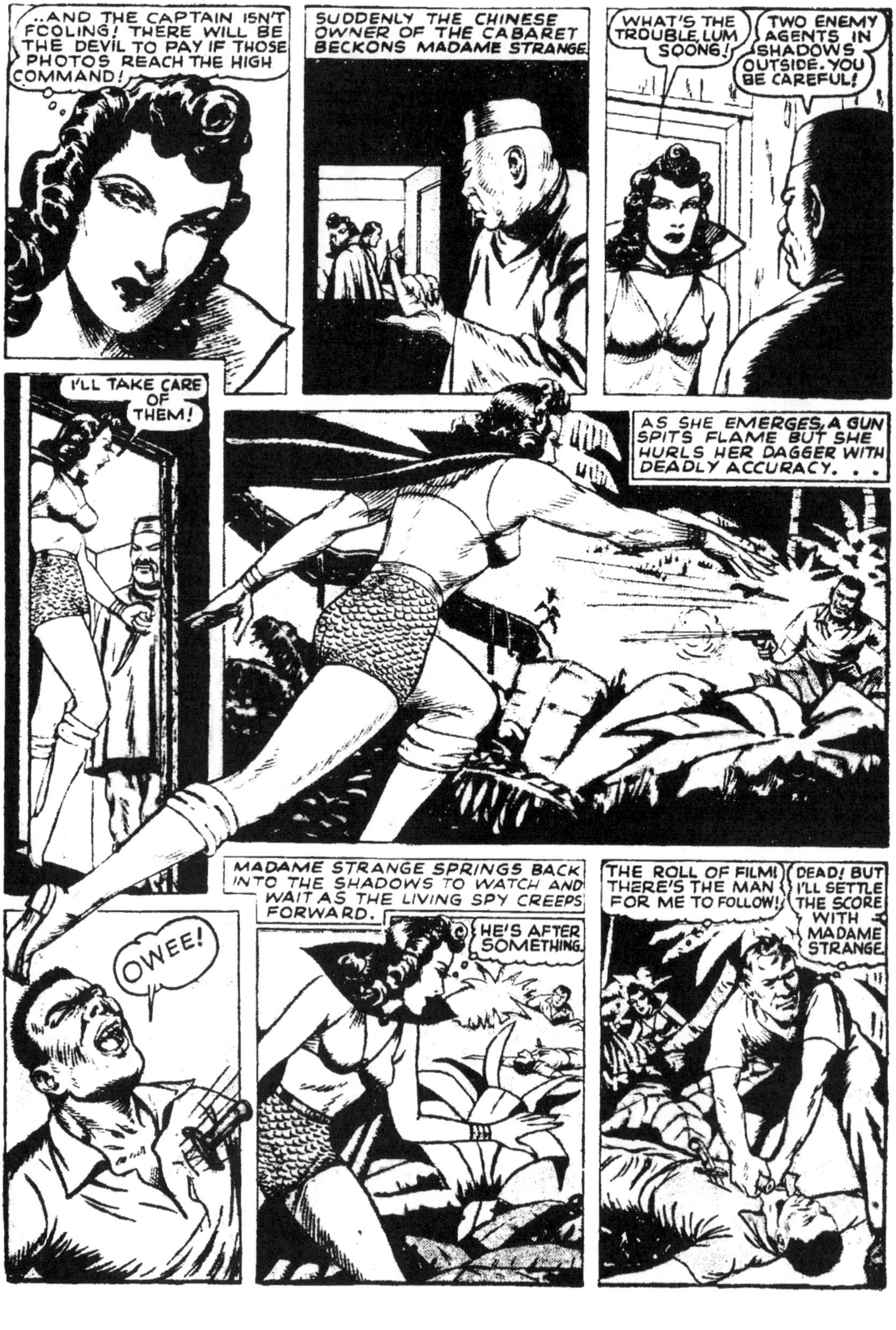
..AND THE CAPTAIN ISN'T FOOLING! THERE WILL BE THE DEVIL TO PAY IF THOSE PHOTOS REACH THE HIGH COMMAND!
SUDDENLY THE CHINESE OWNER OF THE CABARET BECKONS MADAME STRANGE.
WHAT'S THE TROUBLE, LUM SOONG!
TWO ENEMY AGENTS IN SHADOWS OUTSIDE. YOU BE CAREFUL!
I'LL TAKE CARE OF THEM!
AS SHE EMERGES, A GUN SPITS FLAME BUT SHE HURLS HER DAGGER WITH DEADLY ACCURACY. . .
OWEE!
MADAME STRANGE SPRINGS BACK INTO THE SHADOWS TO WATCH AND WAIT AS THE LIVING SPY CREEPS FORWARD.
HE'S AFTER SOMETHING.
THE ROLL OF FILM! THERE'S THE MAN FOR ME TO FOLLOW!
DEAD! BUT I'LL SETTLE THE SCORE WITH MADAME STRANGE.

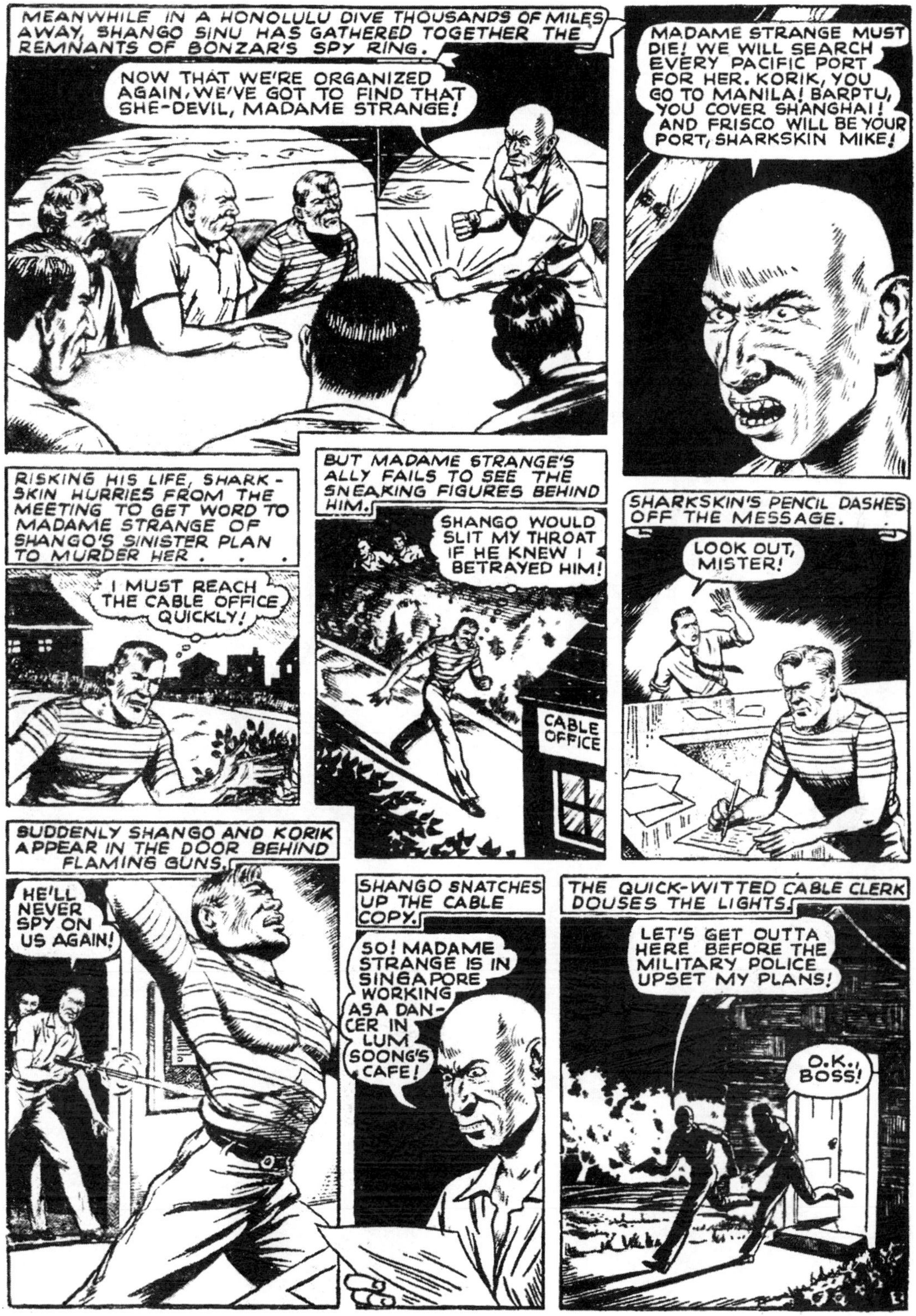
MEANWHILE IN A HONOLULU DIVE THOUSANDS OF MILES AWAY, SHANGO SINU HAS GATHERED TOGETHER THE REMNANTS OF BONZAR'S SPY RING.
NOW THAT WE'RE ORGANIZED AGAIN, WE'VE GOT TO FIND THAT SHE-DEVIL, MADAME STRANGE!
MADAME STRANGE MUST DIE! WE WILL SEARCH EVERY PACIFIC PORT FOR HER. KORIK, YOU GO TO MANILA! BARPTU, YOU COVER SHANGHAI! AND FRISCO WILL BE YOUR PORT, SHARKSKIN MIKE!
RISKING HIS LIFE, SHARK-SKIN HURRIES FROM THE MEETING TO GET WORD TO MADAME STRANGE OF SHANGO'S SINISTER PLAN TO MURDER HER . . .
I MUST REACH THE CABLE OFFICE QUICKLY!
BUT MADAME STRANGE'S ALLY FAILS TO SEE THE SNEAKING FIGURES BEHIND HIM.
SHANGO WOULD SLIT MY THROAT IF HE KNEW I BETRAYED HIM!
CABLE OFFICE
SHARKSKIN'S PENCIL DASHES OFF THE MESSAGE.
LOOK OUT, MISTER!
SUDDENLY SHANGO AND KORIK APPEAR IN THE DOOR BEHIND FLAMING GUNS.
HE'LL NEVER SPY ON US AGAIN!
SHANGO SNATCHES UP THE CABLE COPY.
SO! MADAME STRANGE IS IN SINGAPORE WORKING AS A DANCER IN LUM SOONG'S CAFE!
THE QUICK-WITTED CABLE CLERK DOUSES THE LIGHTS.
LET'S GET OUTTA HERE BEFORE THE MILITARY POLICE UPSET MY PLANS!
O.K., BOSS!

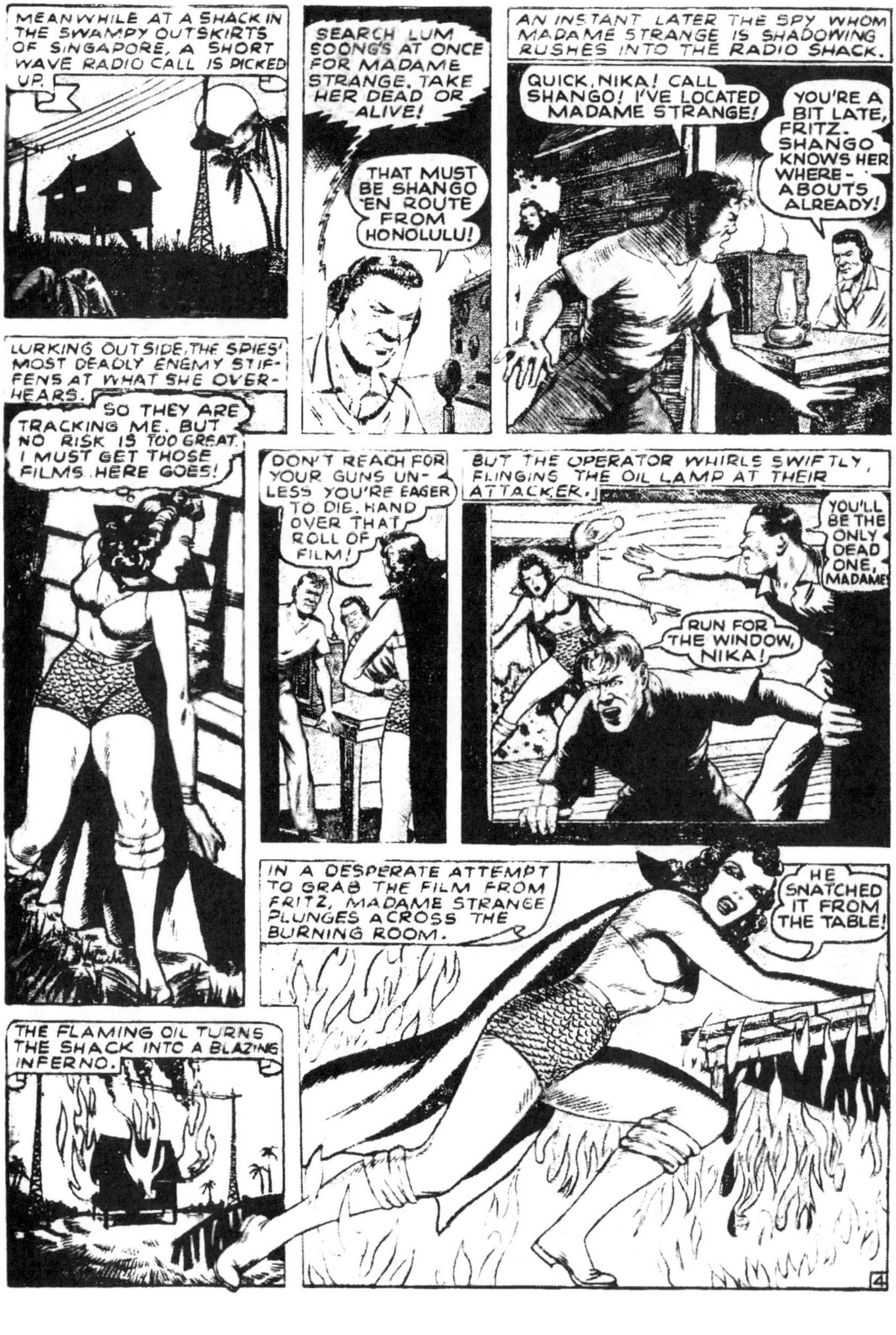

MEANWHILE AT A SHACK IN THE SWAMPY OUTSKIRTS OF SINGAPORE, A SHORT WAVE RADIO CALL IS PICKED UP.
SEARCH LUM SOONG'S AT ONCE FOR MADAME STRANGE. TAKE HER DEAD OR ALIVE!
THAT MUST BE SHANGO 'EN ROUTE FROM HONOLULU!
AN INSTANT LATER THE SPY WHOM MADAME STRANGE IS SHADOWING RUSHES INTO THE RADIO SHACK.
QUICK, NIKA! CALL SHANGO! I'VE LOCATED MADAME STRANGE!
YOU'RE A BIT LATE, FRITZ. SHANGO KNOWS HER WHERE-ABOUTS ALREADY!
LURKING OUTSIDE, THE SPIES' MOST DEADLY ENEMY STIFFENS AT WHAT SHE OVERHEARS.
SO THEY ARE TRACKING ME. BUT NO RISK IS TOO GREAT. I MUST GET THOSE FILMS. HERE GOES!
DON'T REACH FOR YOUR GUNS UNLESS YOU'RE EAGER TO DIE. HAND OVER THAT ROLL OF FILM!
BUT THE OPERATOR WHIRLS SWIFTLY, FLINGING THE OIL LAMP AT THEIR ATTACKER.
YOU'LL BE THE ONLY DEAD ONE, MADAME!
RUN FOR THE WINDOW, NIKA!
IN A DESPERATE ATTEMPT TO GRAB THE FILM FROM FRITZ, MADAME STRANGE PLUNGES ACROSS THE BURNING ROOM.
HE SNATCHED IT FROM THE TABLE!
THE FLAMING OIL TURNS THE SHACK INTO A BLAZING INFERNO.
4

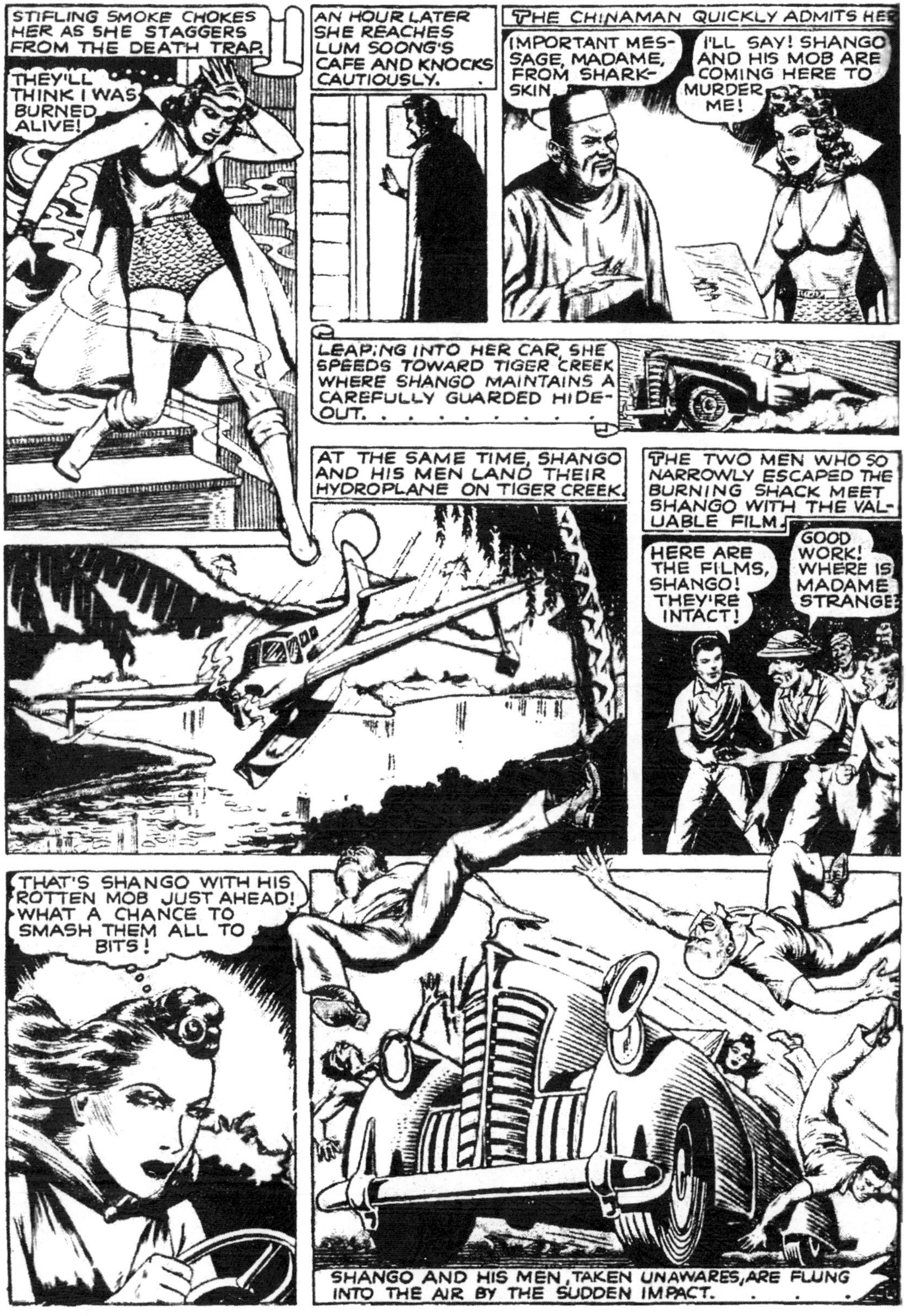
STIFLING SMOKE CHOKES HER AS SHE STAGGERS FROM THE DEATH TRAP.
THEY'LL THINK I WAS BURNED ALIVE!
AN HOUR LATER SHE REACHES LUM SOONG'S CAFE AND KNOCKS CAUTIOUSLY.
THE CHINAMAN QUICKLY ADMITS HER
IMPORTANT MESSAGE, MADAME, FROM SHARKSKIN.
I'LL SAY! SHANGO AND HIS MOB ARE COMING HERE TO MURDER ME!
LEAPING INTO HER CAR, SHE SPEEDS TOWARD TIGER CREEK WHERE SHANGO MAINTAINS A CAREFULLY GUARDED HIDE-OUT. . . . .
AT THE SAME TIME, SHANGO AND HIS MEN LAND THEIR HYDROPLANE ON TIGER CREEK.
THE TWO MEN WHO SO NARROWLY ESCAPED THE BURNING SHACK MEET SHANGO WITH THE VALUABLE FILM.
HERE ARE THE FILMS, SHANGO! THEY'RE INTACT!
GOOD WORK! WHERE IS MADAME STRANGE?
THAT'S SHANGO WITH HIS ROTTEN MOB JUST AHEAD! WHAT A CHANCE TO SMASH THEM ALL TO BITS!
SHANGO AND HIS MEN, TAKEN UNAWARES, ARE FLUNG INTO THE AIR BY THE SUDDEN IMPACT. . . .

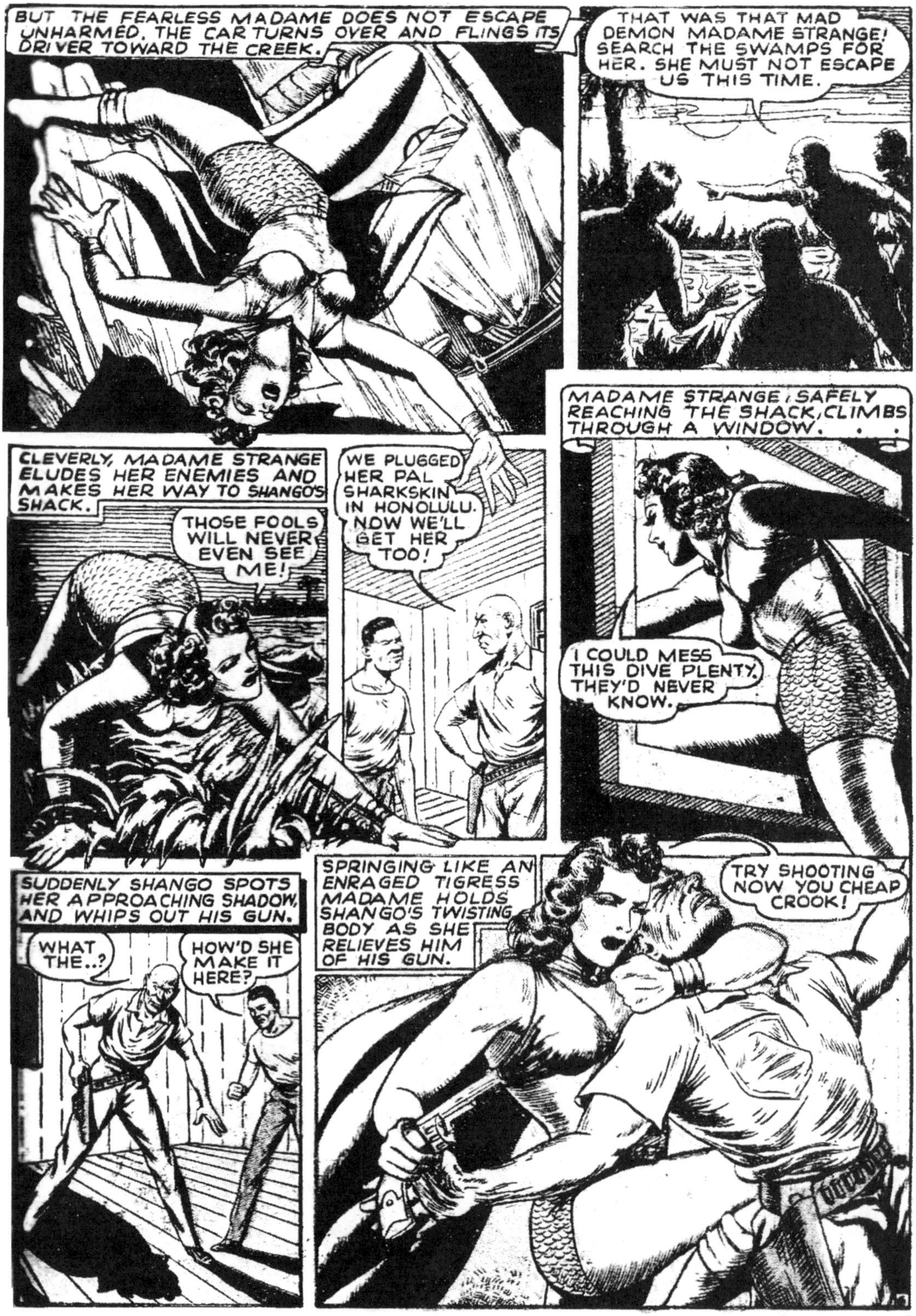
BUT THE FEARLESS MADAME DOES NOT ESCAPE UNHARMED. THE CAR TURNS OVER AND FLINGS ITS DRIVER TOWARD THE CREEK.
THAT WAS THAT MAD DEMON MADAME STRANGE! SEARCH THE SWAMPS FOR HER. SHE MUST NOT ESCAPE US THIS TIME.
CLEVERLY, MADAME STRANGE ELUDES HER ENEMIES AND MAKES HER WAY TO SHANGO'S SHACK.
THOSE FOOLS WILL NEVER EVEN SEE ME!
WE PLUGGED HER PAL SHARKSKIN IN HONOLULU. NOW WE'LL GET HER TOO!
MADAME STRANGE, SAFELY REACHING THE SHACK, CLIMBS THROUGH A WINDOW. . .
I COULD MESS THIS DIVE PLENTY. THEY'D NEVER KNOW.
SUDDENLY SHANGO SPOTS HER APPROACHING SHADOW, AND WHIPS OUT HIS GUN.
WHAT THE..?
HOW'D SHE MAKE IT HERE?
SPRINGING LIKE AN ENRAGED TIGRESS MADAME HOLDS SHANGO'S TWISTING BODY AS SHE RELIEVES HIM OF HIS GUN.
TRY SHOOTING NOW YOU CHEAP CROOK!

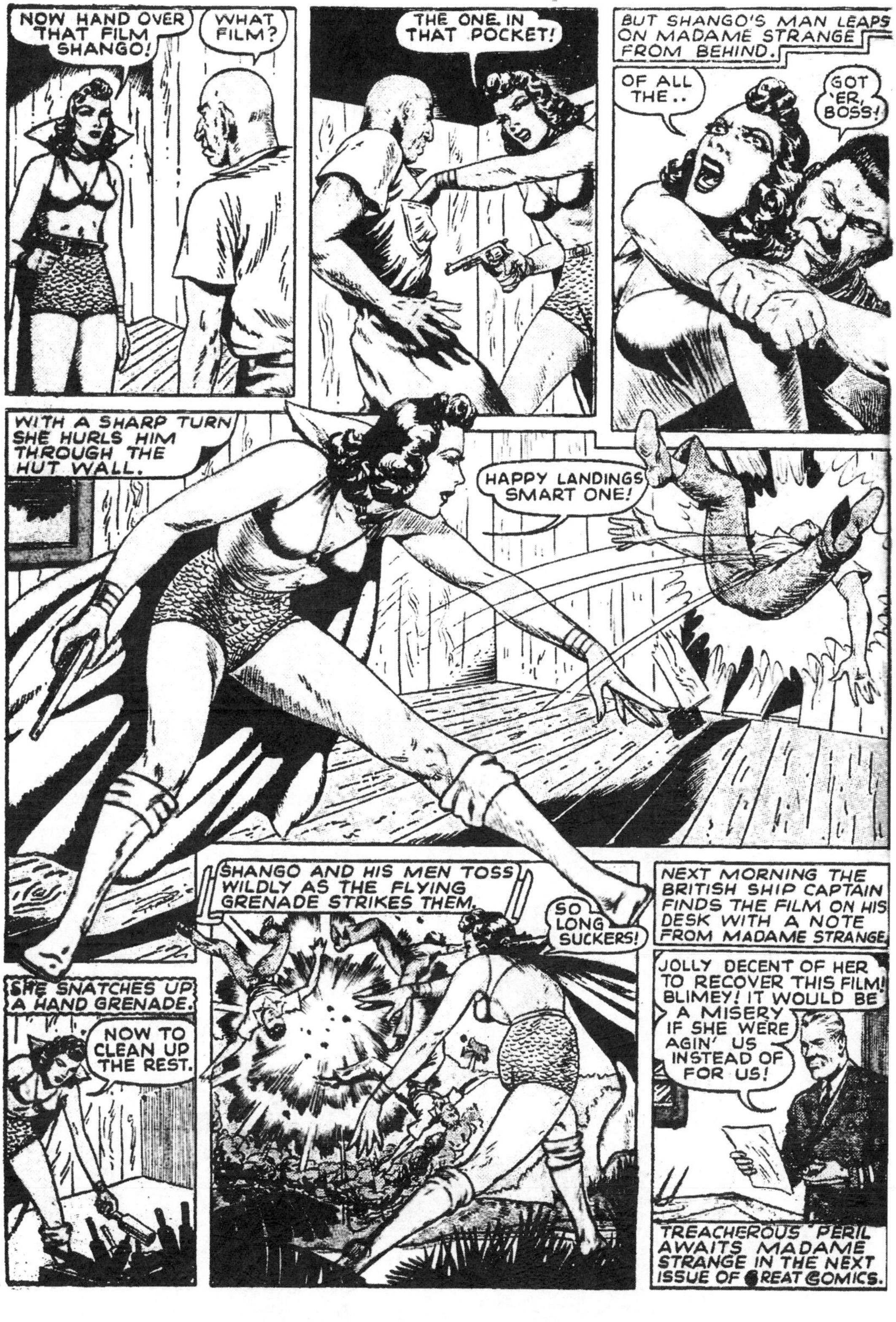

NOW HAND OVER THAT FILM SHANGO!
WHAT FILM?
THE ONE IN THAT POCKET!
BUT SHANGO'S MAN LEAPS ON MADAME STRANGE FROM BEHIND.
OF ALL THE..
GOT 'ER, BOSS!
WITH A SHARP TURN SHE HURLS HIM THROUGH THE HUT WALL.
HAPPY LANDINGS SMART ONE!
SHE SNATCHES UP A HAND GRENADE.
NOW TO CLEAN UP THE REST.
SHANGO AND HIS MEN TOSS WILDLY AS THE FLYING GRENADE STRIKES THEM.
SO LONG SUCKERS!
NEXT MORNING THE BRITISH SHIP CAPTAIN FINDS THE FILM ON HIS DESK WITH A NOTE FROM MADAME STRANGE.
JOLLY DECENT OF HER TO RECOVER THIS FILM! BLIMEY! IT WOULD BE A MISERY IF SHE WERE AGIN' US INSTEAD OF FOR US!
TREACHEROUS PERIL AWAITS MADAME STRANGE IN THE NEXT ISSUE OF GREAT COMICS.

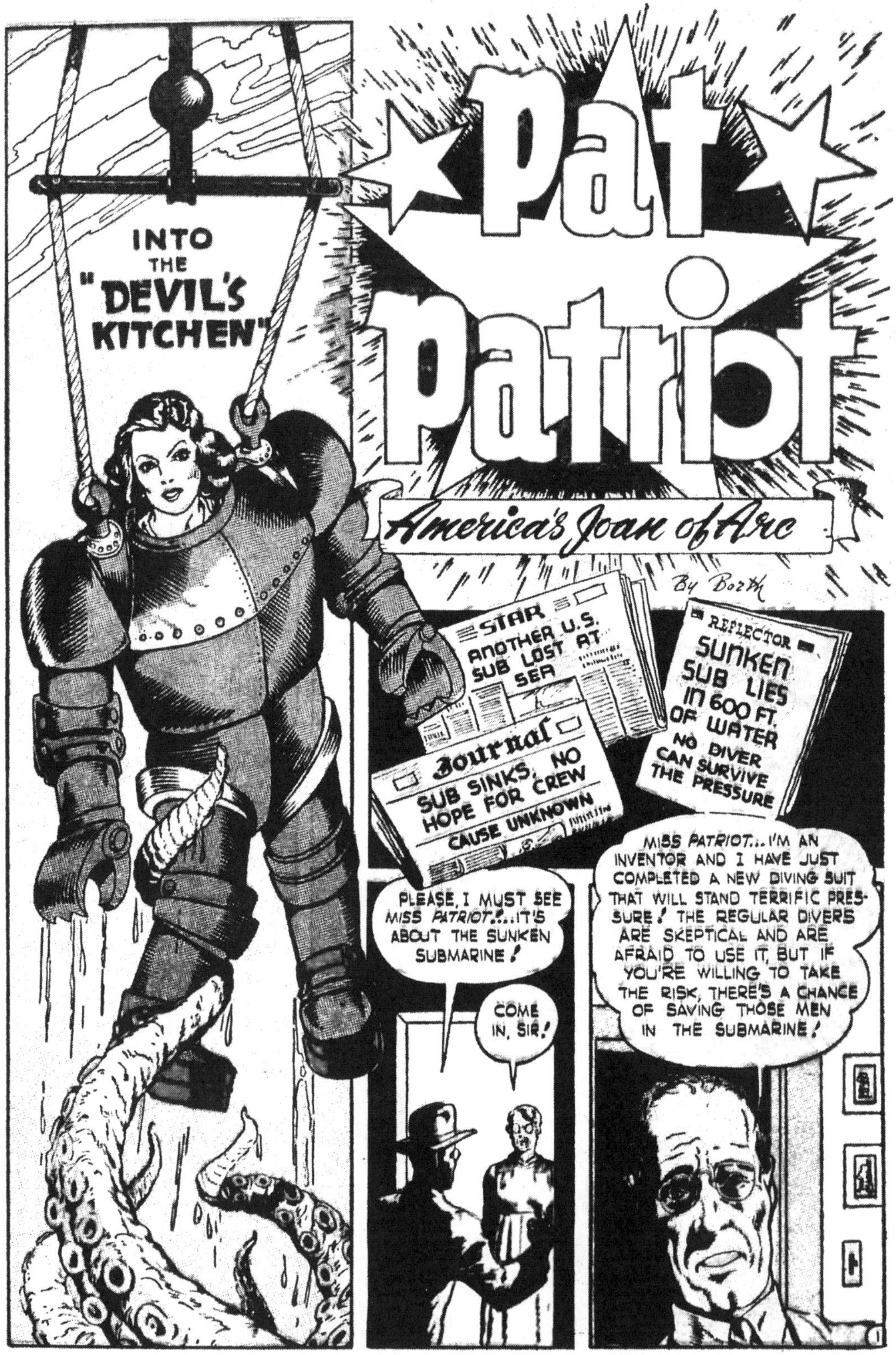
Pat Patriot
America's Joan of Arc
By Borth
INTO THE "DEVIL'S KITCHEN"
STAR ANOTHER U.S. SUB LOST AT SEA
REFLECTOR SUNKEN SUB LIES IN 600 FT. OF WATER NO DIVER CAN SURVIVE THE PRESSURE
Journal SUB SINKS, NO HOPE FOR CREW CAUSE UNKNOWN
PLEASE, I MUST SEE MISS PATRIOT!...IT'S ABOUT THE SUNKEN SUBMARINE!
COME IN, SIR!
MISS PATRIOT... I'M AN INVENTOR AND I HAVE JUST COMPLETED A NEW DIVING SUIT THAT WILL STAND TERRIFIC PRESSURE! THE REGULAR DIVERS ARE SKEPTICAL AND ARE AFRAID TO USE IT, BUT IF YOU'RE WILLING TO TAKE THE RISK, THERE'S A CHANCE OF SAVING THOSE MEN IN THE SUBMARINE!

From Daredevil Comics # 5 (1941) Art by Frank M. Borth

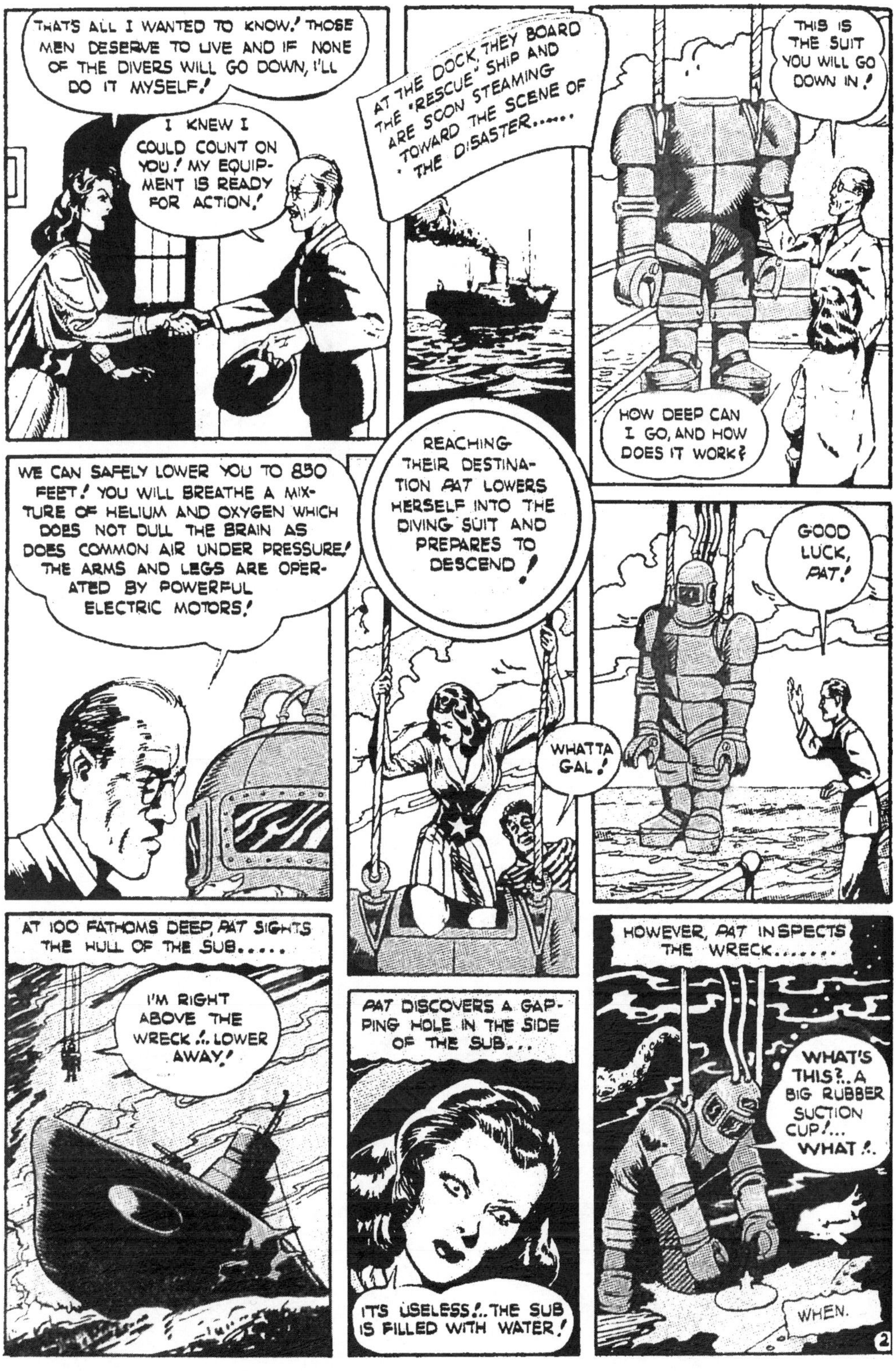
THAT'S ALL I WANTED TO KNOW! THOSE MEN DESERVE TO LIVE AND IF NONE OF THE DIVERS WILL GO DOWN, I'LL DO IT MYSELF!
I KNEW I COULD COUNT ON YOU! MY EQUIPMENT IS READY FOR ACTION!
AT THE DOCK, THEY BOARD THE "RESCUE" SHIP AND ARE SOON STEAMING TOWARD THE SCENE OF THE DISASTER......
THIS IS THE SUIT YOU WILL GO DOWN IN!
HOW DEEP CAN I GO, AND HOW DOES IT WORK?
WE CAN SAFELY LOWER YOU TO 850 FEET! YOU WILL BREATHE A MIXTURE OF HELIUM AND OXYGEN WHICH DOES NOT DULL THE BRAIN AS DOES COMMON AIR UNDER PRESSURE! THE ARMS AND LEGS ARE OPERATED BY POWERFUL ELECTRIC MOTORS!
REACHING THEIR DESTINATION PAT LOWERS HERSELF INTO THE DIVING SUIT AND PREPARES TO DESCEND!
WHATTA GAL!
GOOD LUCK, PAT!
AT 100 FATHOMS DEEP, PAT SIGHTS THE HULL OF THE SUB.....
I'M RIGHT ABOVE THE WRECK!.. LOWER AWAY!
PAT DISCOVERS A GAPING HOLE IN THE SIDE OF THE SUB...
IT'S USELESS!..THE SUB IS FILLED WITH WATER!
HOWEVER, PAT INSPECTS THE WRECK.......
WHAT'S THIS?..A BIG RUBBER SUCTION CUP!... WHAT!..
WHEN.
2

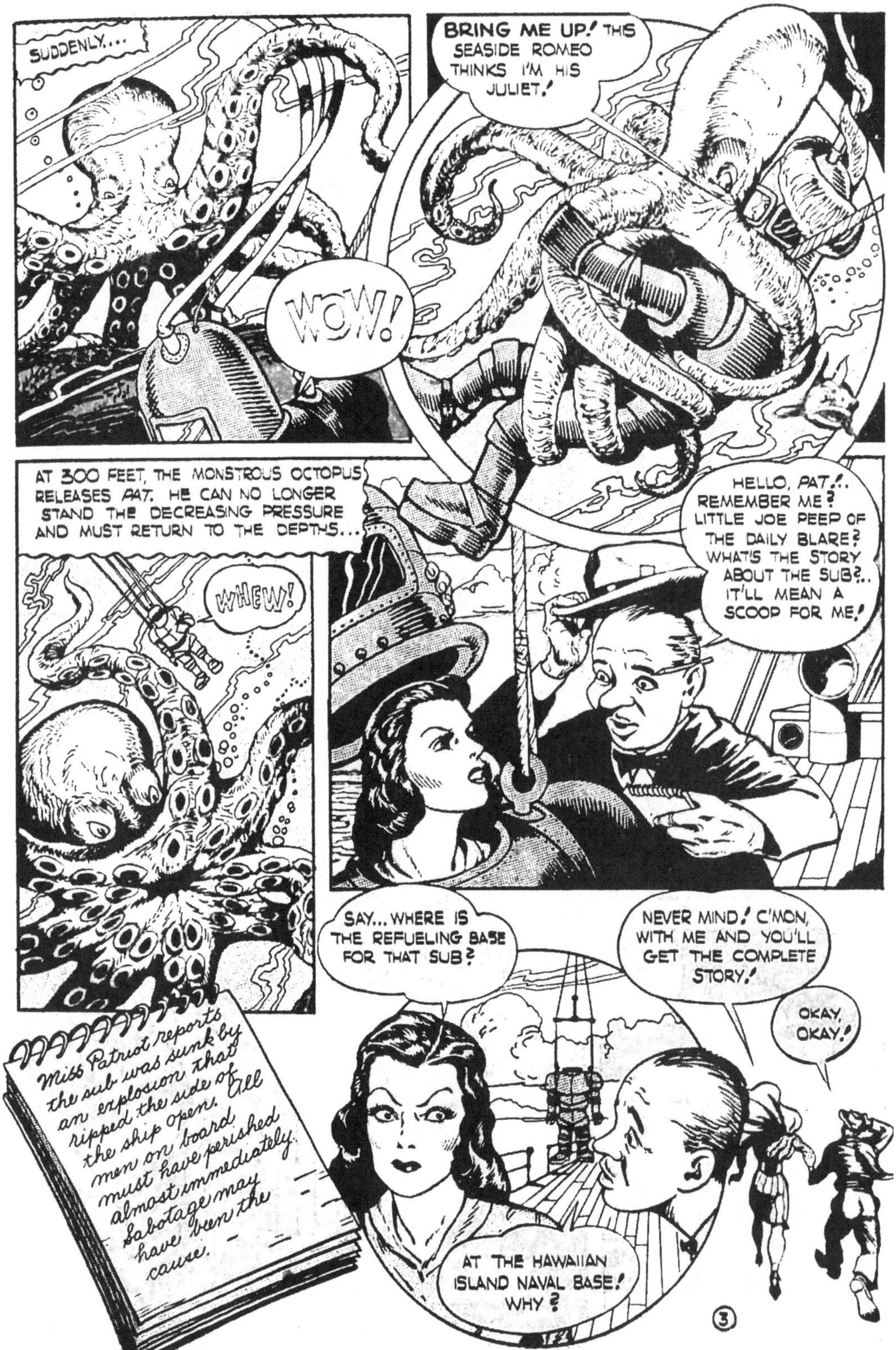
SUDDENLY....
WOW!
BRING ME UP! THIS SEASIDE ROMEO THINKS I'M HIS JULIET!
AT 300 FEET, THE MONSTROUS OCTOPUS RELEASES PAT. HE CAN NO LONGER STAND THE DECREASING PRESSURE AND MUST RETURN TO THE DEPTHS...
WHEW!
HELLO, PAT!.. REMEMBER ME? LITTLE JOE PEEP OF THE DAILY BLARE? WHAT'S THE STORY ABOUT THE SUB?.. IT'LL MEAN A SCOOP FOR ME!
Miss Patriot reports the sub was sunk by an explosion that ripped the side of the ship open. All men on board must have perished almost immediately. Sabotage may have been the cause.
SAY... WHERE IS THE REFUELING BASE FOR THAT SUB?
AT THE HAWAIIAN ISLAND NAVAL BASE! WHY?
NEVER MIND! C'MON, WITH ME AND YOU'LL GET THE COMPLETE STORY!
OKAY, OKAY!
3

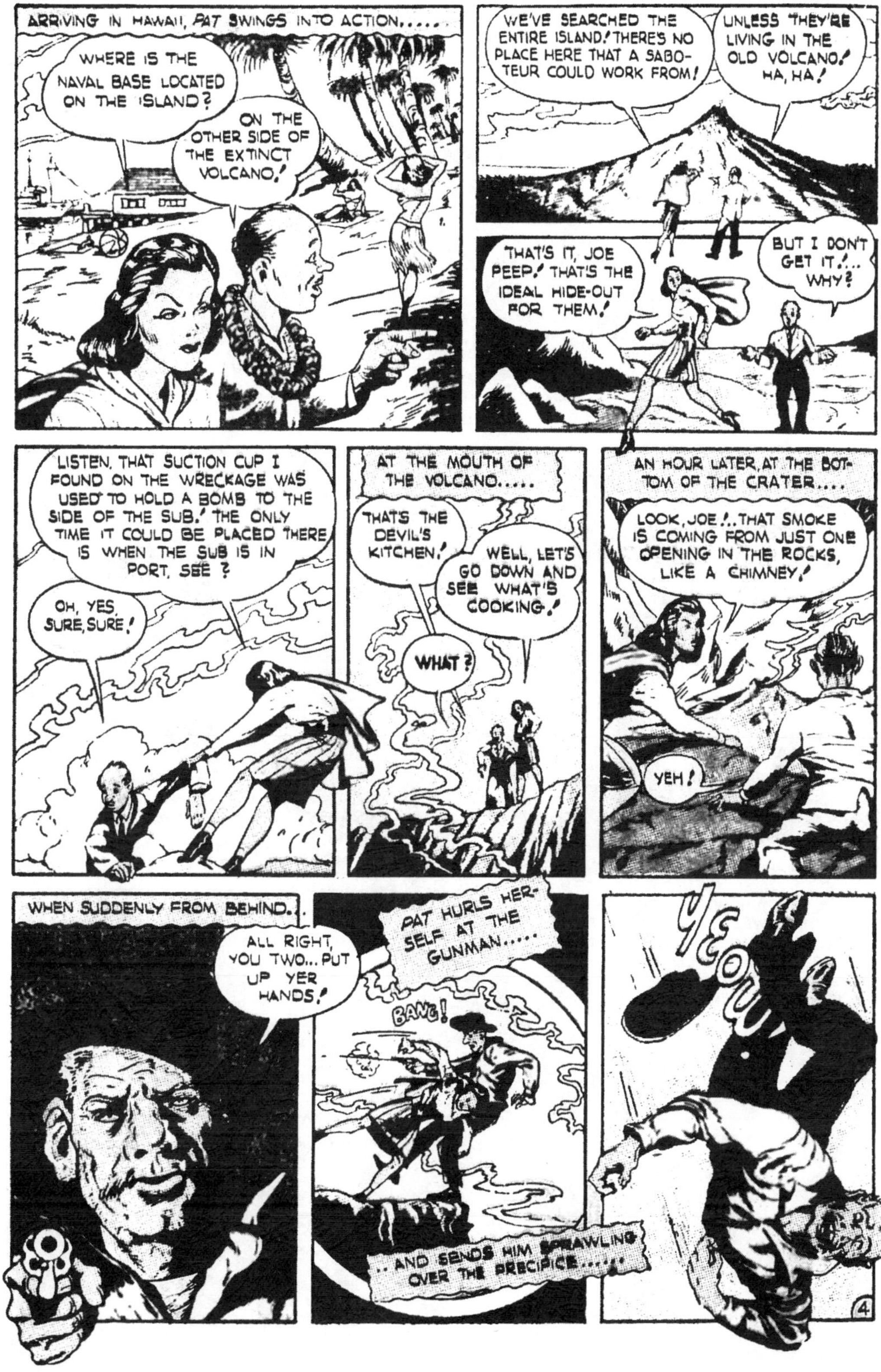
ARRIVING IN HAWAII, PAT SWINGS INTO ACTION.....
WHERE IS THE NAVAL BASE LOCATED ON THE ISLAND?
ON THE OTHER SIDE OF THE EXTINCT VOLCANO!
WE'VE SEARCHED THE ENTIRE ISLAND! THERE'S NO PLACE HERE THAT A SABOTEUR COULD WORK FROM!
UNLESS THEY'RE LIVING IN THE OLD VOLCANO! HA, HA!
THAT'S IT, JOE PEEP! THAT'S THE IDEAL HIDE-OUT FOR THEM!
BUT I DON'T GET IT!... WHY?
LISTEN. THAT SUCTION CUP I FOUND ON THE WRECKAGE WAS USED TO HOLD A BOMB TO THE SIDE OF THE SUB! THE ONLY TIME IT COULD BE PLACED THERE IS WHEN THE SUB IS IN PORT, SEE?
OH, YES, SURE, SURE!
AT THE MOUTH OF THE VOLCANO.....
THAT'S THE DEVIL'S KITCHEN!
WELL, LET'S GO DOWN AND SEE WHAT'S COOKING!
WHAT?
AN HOUR LATER, AT THE BOTTOM OF THE CRATER....
LOOK, JOE!..THAT SMOKE IS COMING FROM JUST ONE OPENING IN THE ROCKS, LIKE A CHIMNEY!
YEH!
WHEN SUDDENLY FROM BEHIND...
ALL RIGHT, YOU TWO...PUT UP YER HANDS!
PAT HURLS HERSELF AT THE GUNMAN.....
BANG!
..AND SENDS HIM SPRAWLING OVER THE PRECIPICE.....
YEOW!
4

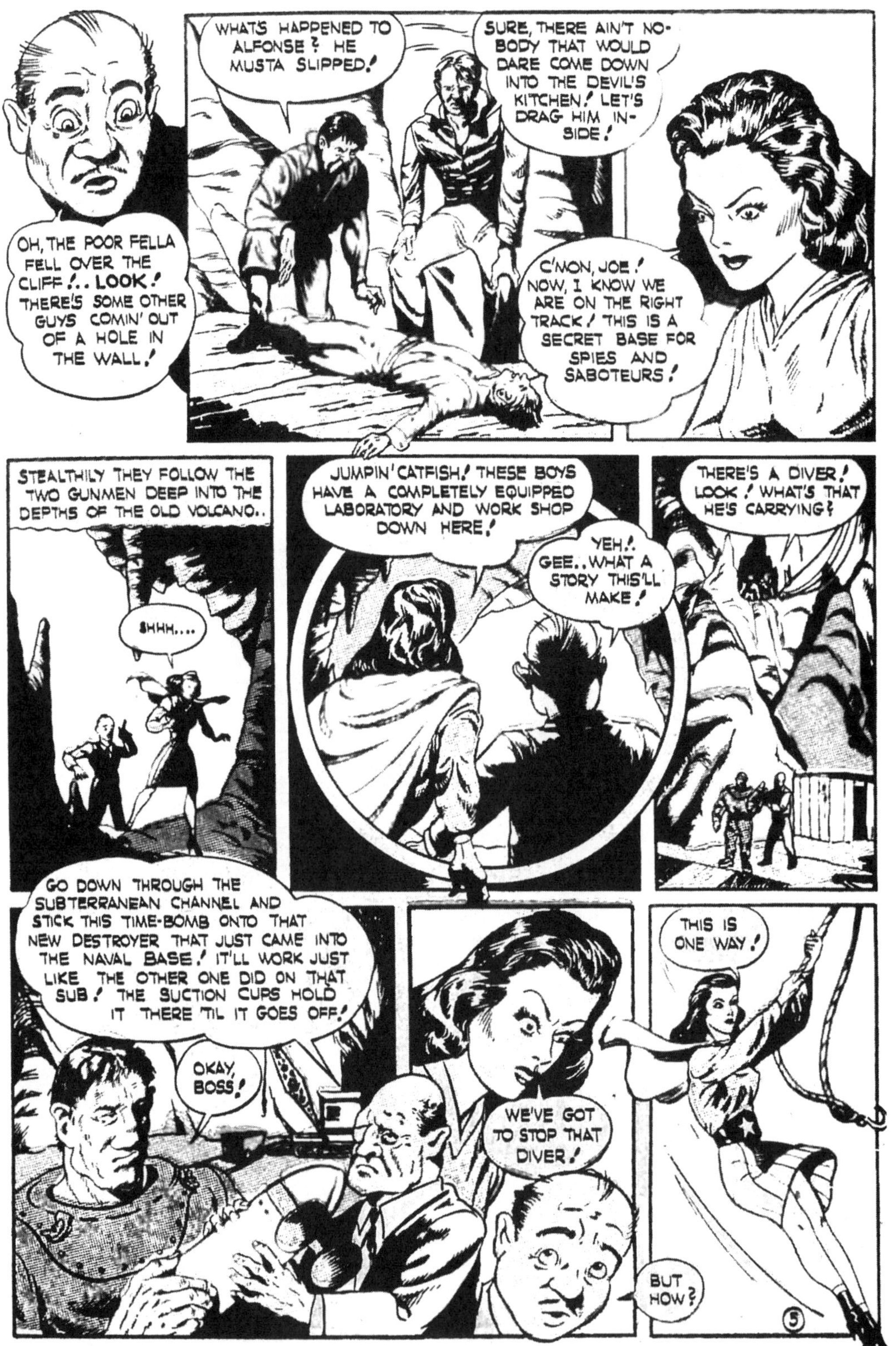
WHAT'S HAPPENED TO ALFONSE? HE MUSTA SLIPPED!
SURE, THERE AIN'T NOBODY THAT WOULD DARE COME DOWN INTO THE DEVIL'S KITCHEN! LET'S DRAG HIM INSIDE!
OH, THE POOR FELLA FELL OVER THE CLIFF!.. LOOK! THERE'S SOME OTHER GUYS COMIN' OUT OF A HOLE IN THE WALL!
C'MON, JOE! NOW, I KNOW WE ARE ON THE RIGHT TRACK! THIS IS A SECRET BASE FOR SPIES AND SABOTEURS!
STEALTHILY THEY FOLLOW THE TWO GUNMEN DEEP INTO THE DEPTHS OF THE OLD VOLCANO..
SHHH....
JUMPIN' CATFISH! THESE BOYS HAVE A COMPLETELY EQUIPPED LABORATORY AND WORK SHOP DOWN HERE!
YEH!. GEE..WHAT A STORY THIS'LL MAKE!
THERE'S A DIVER! LOOK! WHAT'S THAT HE'S CARRYING?
GO DOWN THROUGH THE SUBTERRANEAN CHANNEL AND STICK THIS TIME-BOMB ONTO THAT NEW DESTROYER THAT JUST CAME INTO THE NAVAL BASE! IT'LL WORK JUST LIKE THE OTHER ONE DID ON THAT SUB! THE SUCTION CUPS HOLD IT THERE 'TIL IT GOES OFF!
OKAY, BOSS!
WE'VE GOT TO STOP THAT DIVER!
BUT HOW?
THIS IS ONE WAY!
5

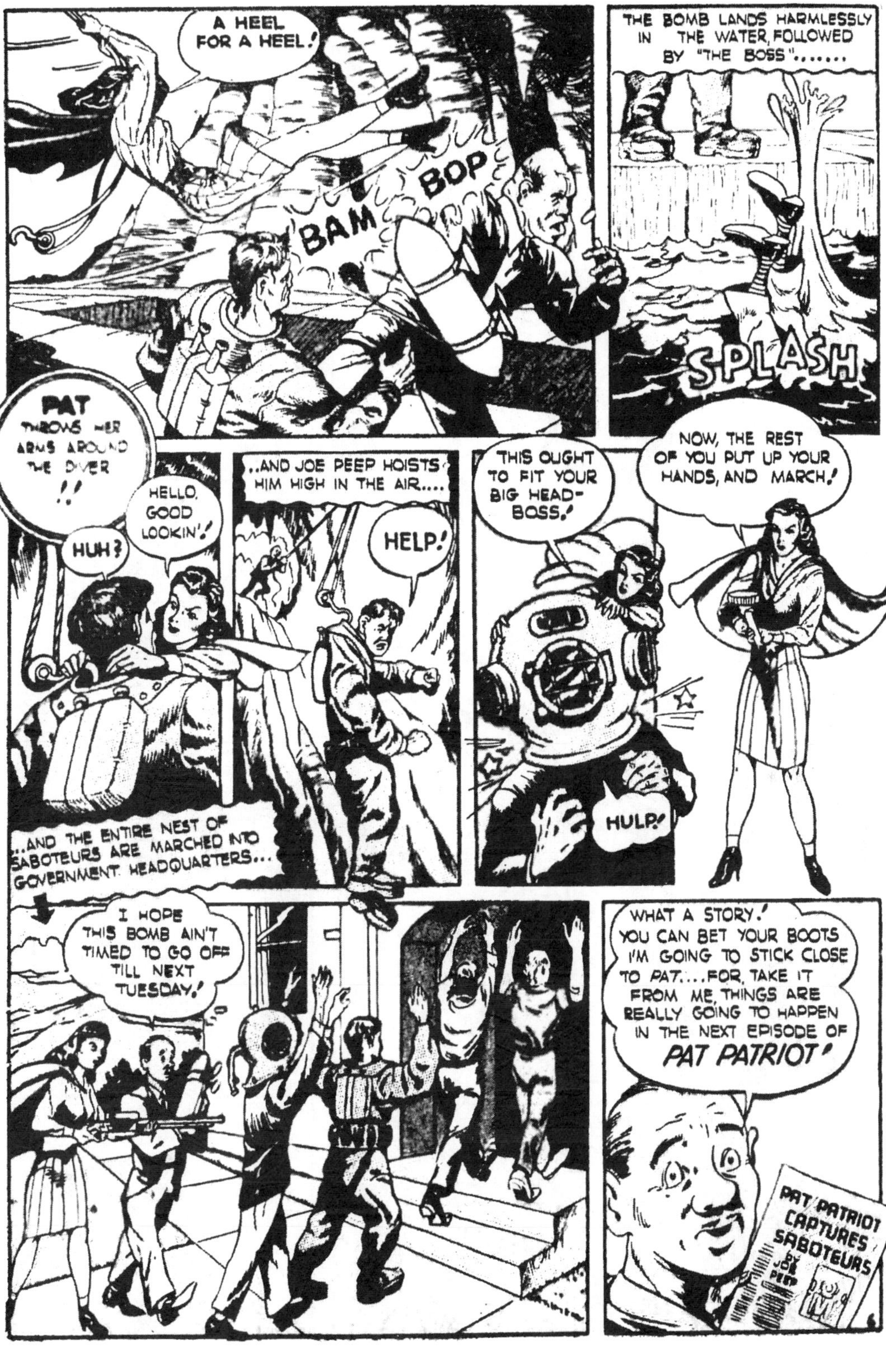
A HEEL FOR A HEEL!
BAM
BOP
THE BOMB LANDS HARMLESSLY IN THE WATER, FOLLOWED BY "THE BOSS".......
SPLASH
PAT THROWS HER ARMS AROUND THE DIVER !!
HELLO, GOOD LOOKIN'!
HUH?
..AND JOE PEEP HOISTS HIM HIGH IN THE AIR....
HELP!
THIS OUGHT TO FIT YOUR BIG HEAD- BOSS!
HULP!
NOW, THE REST OF YOU PUT UP YOUR HANDS, AND MARCH!
..AND THE ENTIRE NEST OF SABOTEURS ARE MARCHED INTO GOVERNMENT HEADQUARTERS...
I HOPE THIS BOMB AIN'T TIMED TO GO OFF TILL NEXT TUESDAY!
WHAT A STORY! YOU CAN BET YOUR BOOTS I'M GOING TO STICK CLOSE TO PAT....FOR, TAKE IT FROM ME, THINGS ARE REALLY GOING TO HAPPEN IN THE NEXT EPISODE OF PAT PATRIOT!
PAT PATRIOT CAPTURES SABOTEURS

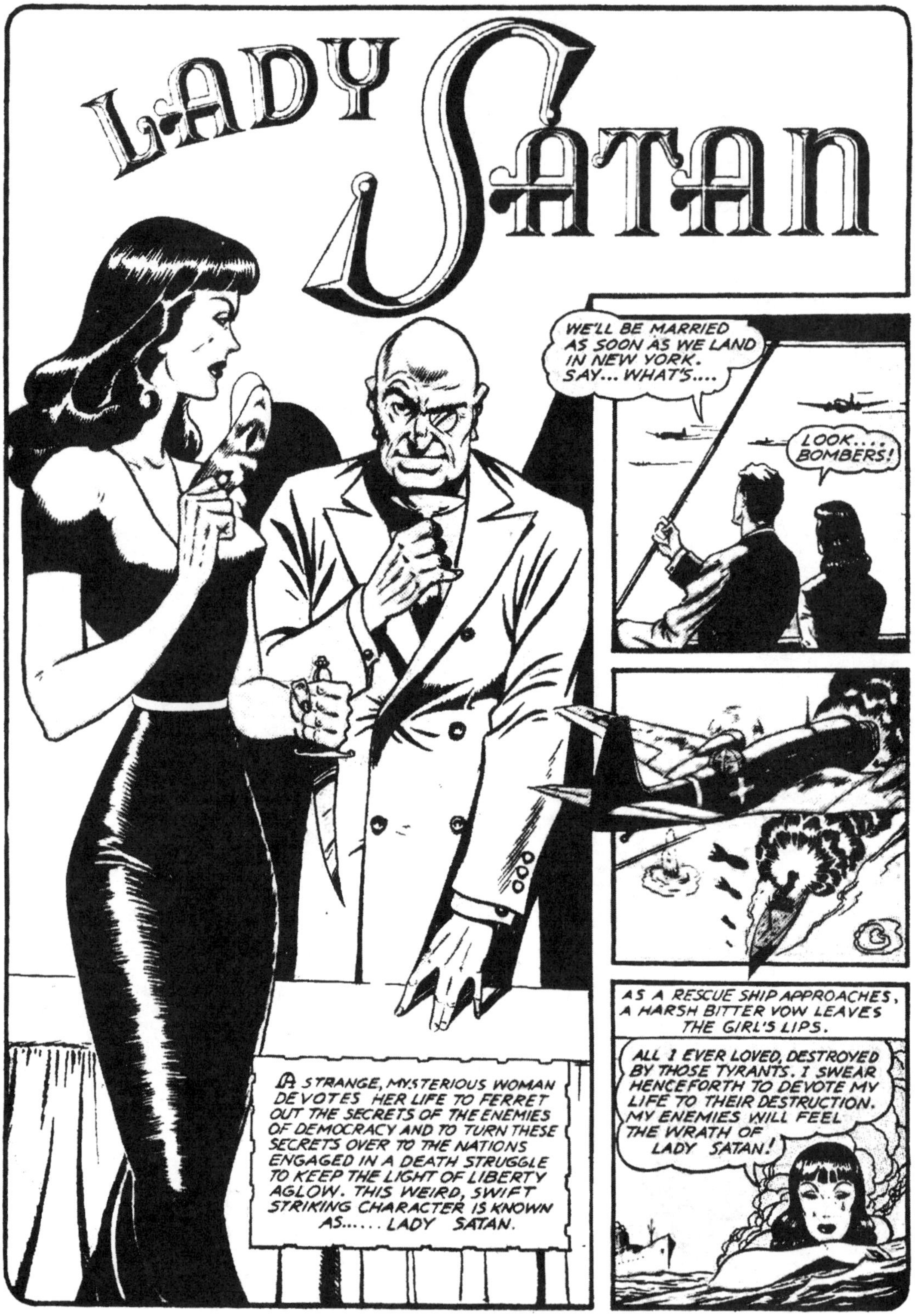
LADY SATAN
WE'LL BE MARRIED AS SOON AS WE LAND IN NEW YORK. SAY... WHAT'S....
LOOK.... BOMBERS!
AS A RESCUE SHIP APPROACHES, A HARSH BITTER VOW LEAVES THE GIRL'S LIPS.
ALL I EVER LOVED, DESTROYED BY THOSE TYRANTS. I SWEAR HENCEFORTH TO DEVOTE MY LIFE TO THEIR DESTRUCTION. MY ENEMIES WILL FEEL THE WRATH OF LADY SATAN!
A STRANGE, MYSTERIOUS WOMAN DEVOTES HER LIFE TO FERRET OUT THE SECRETS OF THE ENEMIES OF DEMOCRACY AND TO TURN THESE SECRETS OVER TO THE NATIONS ENGAGED IN A DEATH STRUGGLE TO KEEP THE LIGHT OF LIBERTY AGLOW. THIS WEIRD, SWIFT STRIKING CHARACTER IS KNOWN AS..... LADY SATAN.

From Dynamic Comics #2 (1941) Art by George Tuska

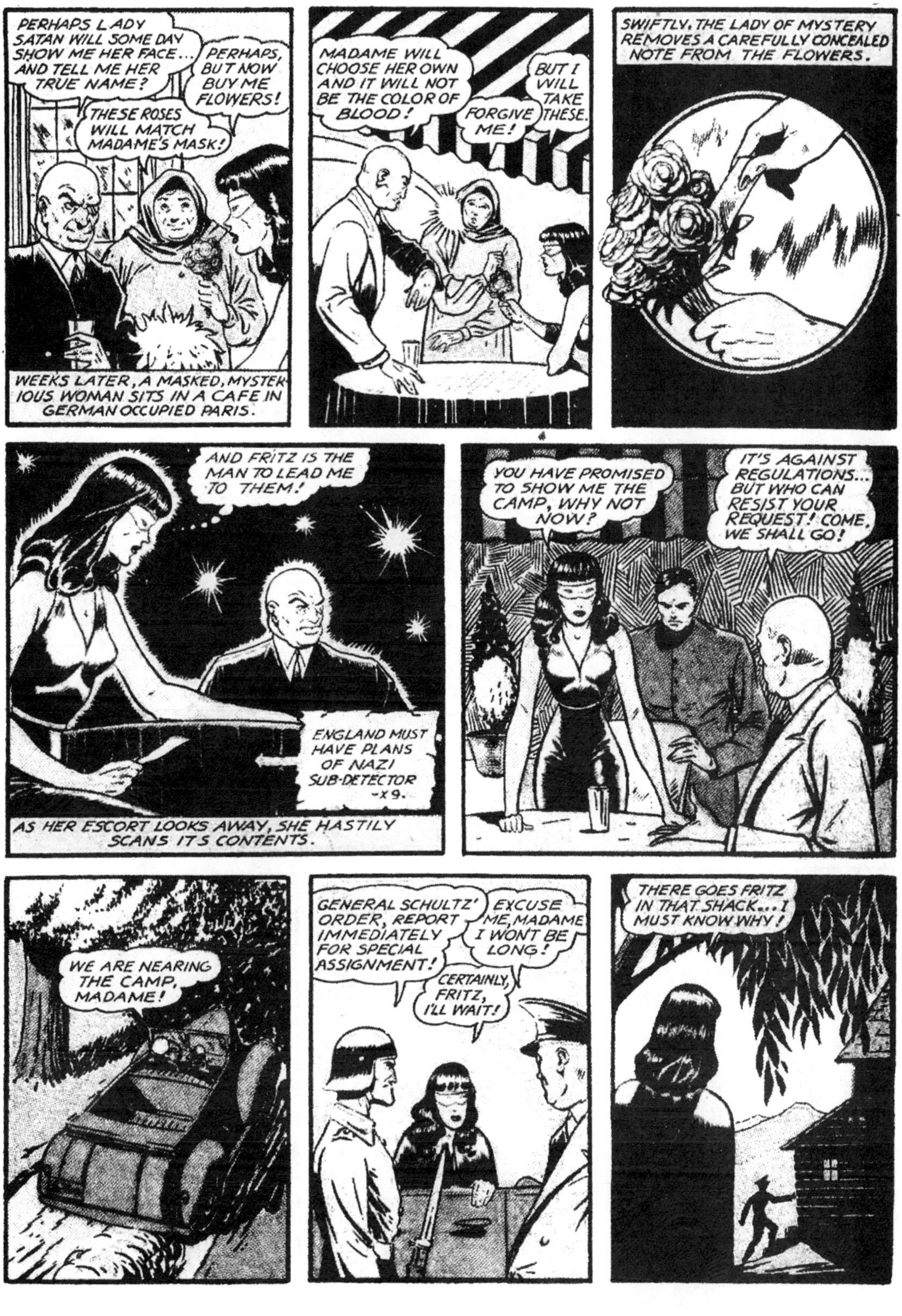
PERHAPS LADY SATAN WILL SOME DAY SHOW ME HER FACE... AND TELL ME HER TRUE NAME?
PERHAPS, BUT NOW BUY ME FLOWERS!
THESE ROSES WILL MATCH MADAME'S MASK!
WEEKS LATER, A MASKED, MYSTERIOUS WOMAN SITS IN A CAFE IN GERMAN OCCUPIED PARIS.
MADAME WILL CHOOSE HER OWN AND IT WILL NOT BE THE COLOR OF BLOOD!
FORGIVE ME!
BUT I WILL TAKE THESE.
SWIFTLY, THE LADY OF MYSTERY REMOVES A CAREFULLY CONCEALED NOTE FROM THE FLOWERS.
AND FRITZ IS THE MAN TO LEAD ME TO THEM!
ENGLAND MUST HAVE PLANS OF NAZI SUB-DETECTOR -X9.
AS HER ESCORT LOOKS AWAY, SHE HASTILY SCANS ITS CONTENTS.
YOU HAVE PROMISED TO SHOW ME THE CAMP, WHY NOT NOW?
IT'S AGAINST REGULATIONS... BUT WHO CAN RESIST YOUR REQUEST! COME, WE SHALL GO!
WE ARE NEARING THE CAMP, MADAME!
GENERAL SCHULTZ' ORDER, REPORT IMMEDIATELY FOR SPECIAL ASSIGNMENT!
EXCUSE ME, MADAME I WON'T BE LONG!
CERTAINLY, FRITZ, I'LL WAIT!
THERE GOES FRITZ IN THAT SHACK... I MUST KNOW WHY!

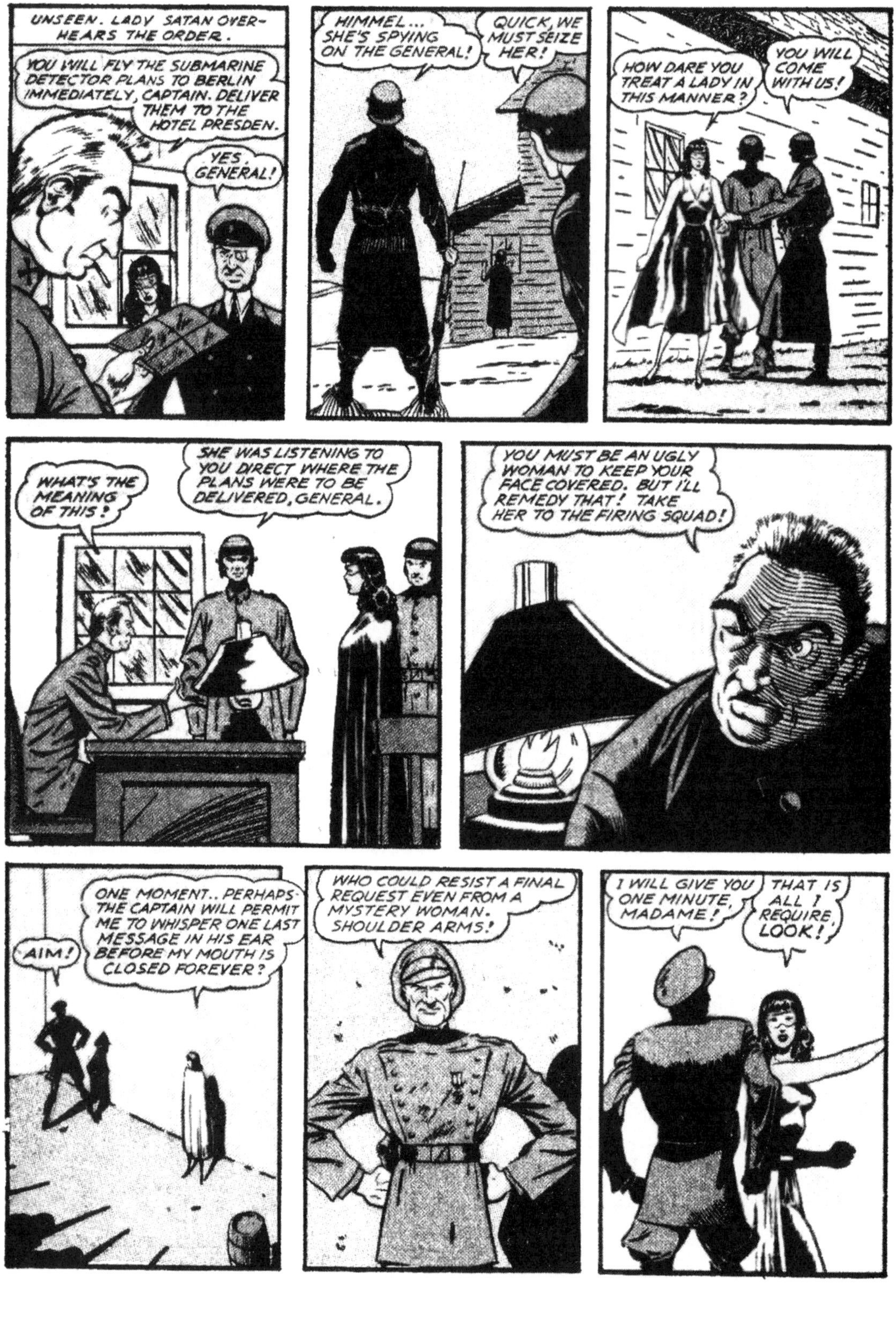
UNSEEN, LADY SATAN OVER-HEARS THE ORDER.
YOU WILL FLY THE SUBMARINE DETECTOR PLANS TO BERLIN IMMEDIATELY, CAPTAIN. DELIVER THEM TO THE HOTEL PRESDEN.
YES, GENERAL!
HIMMEL... SHE'S SPYING ON THE GENERAL!
QUICK, WE MUST SEIZE HER!
HOW DARE YOU TREAT A LADY IN THIS MANNER?
YOU WILL COME WITH US!
WHAT'S THE MEANING OF THIS?
SHE WAS LISTENING TO YOU DIRECT WHERE THE PLANS WERE TO BE DELIVERED, GENERAL.
YOU MUST BE AN UGLY WOMAN TO KEEP YOUR FACE COVERED. BUT I'LL REMEDY THAT! TAKE HER TO THE FIRING SQUAD!
AIM!
ONE MOMENT.. PERHAPS THE CAPTAIN WILL PERMIT ME TO WHISPER ONE LAST MESSAGE IN HIS EAR BEFORE MY MOUTH IS CLOSED FOREVER?
WHO COULD RESIST A FINAL REQUEST EVEN FROM A MYSTERY WOMAN. SHOULDER ARMS!
I WILL GIVE YOU ONE MINUTE, MADAME!
THAT IS ALL I REQUIRE, LOOK!

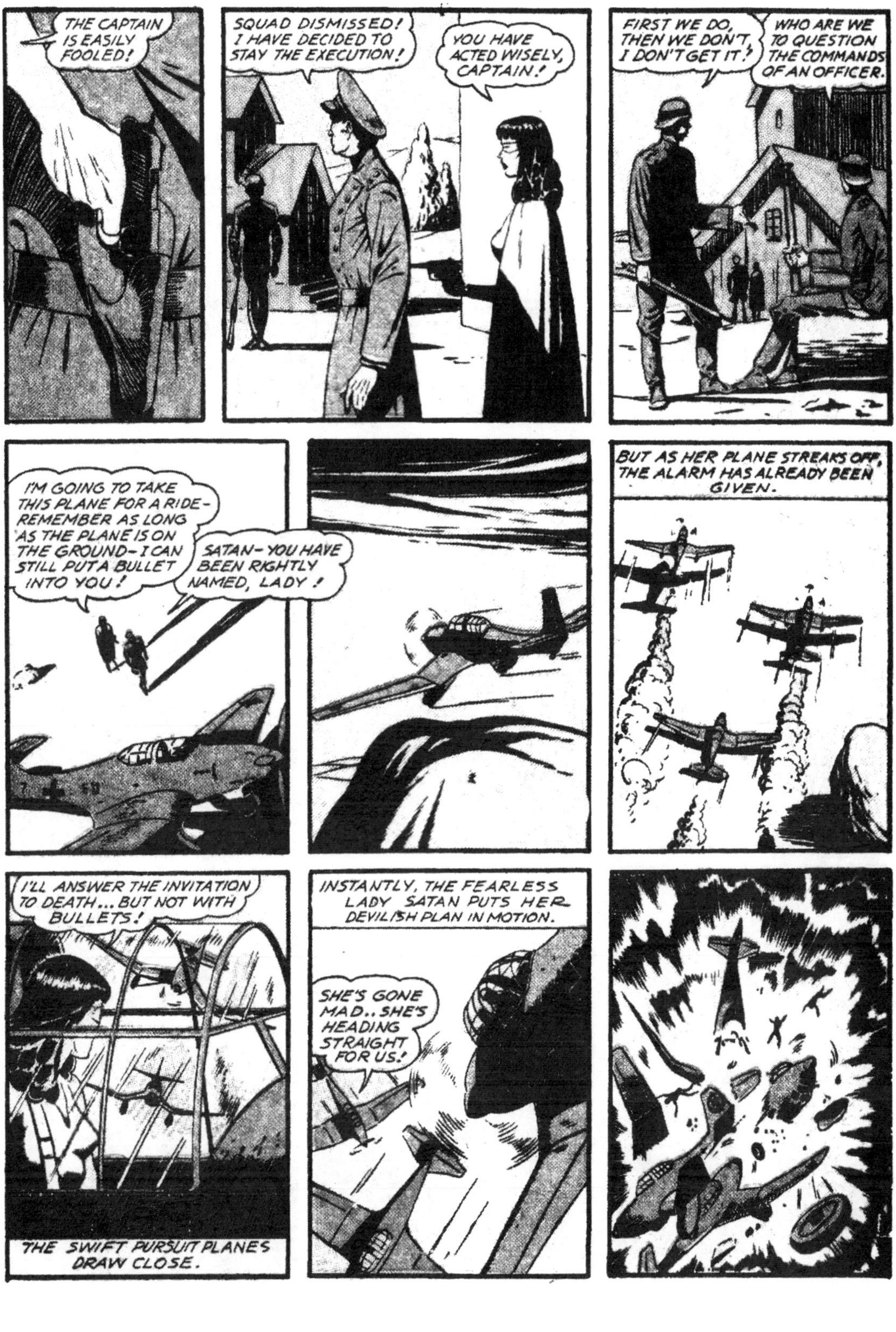
THE CAPTAIN IS EASILY FOOLED!
SQUAD DISMISSED! I HAVE DECIDED TO STAY THE EXECUTION!
YOU HAVE ACTED WISELY, CAPTAIN!
FIRST WE DO, THEN WE DON'T, I DON'T GET IT!
WHO ARE WE TO QUESTION THE COMMANDS OF AN OFFICER.
I'M GOING TO TAKE THIS PLANE FOR A RIDE- REMEMBER AS LONG AS THE PLANE IS ON THE GROUND- I CAN STILL PUT A BULLET INTO YOU!
SATAN- YOU HAVE BEEN RIGHTLY NAMED, LADY!
BUT AS HER PLANE STREAKS OFF, THE ALARM HAS ALREADY BEEN GIVEN.
I'LL ANSWER THE INVITATION TO DEATH... BUT NOT WITH BULLETS!
THE SWIFT PURSUIT PLANES DRAW CLOSE.
INSTANTLY, THE FEARLESS LADY SATAN PUTS HER DEVILISH PLAN IN MOTION.
SHE'S GONE MAD.. SHE'S HEADING STRAIGHT FOR US!

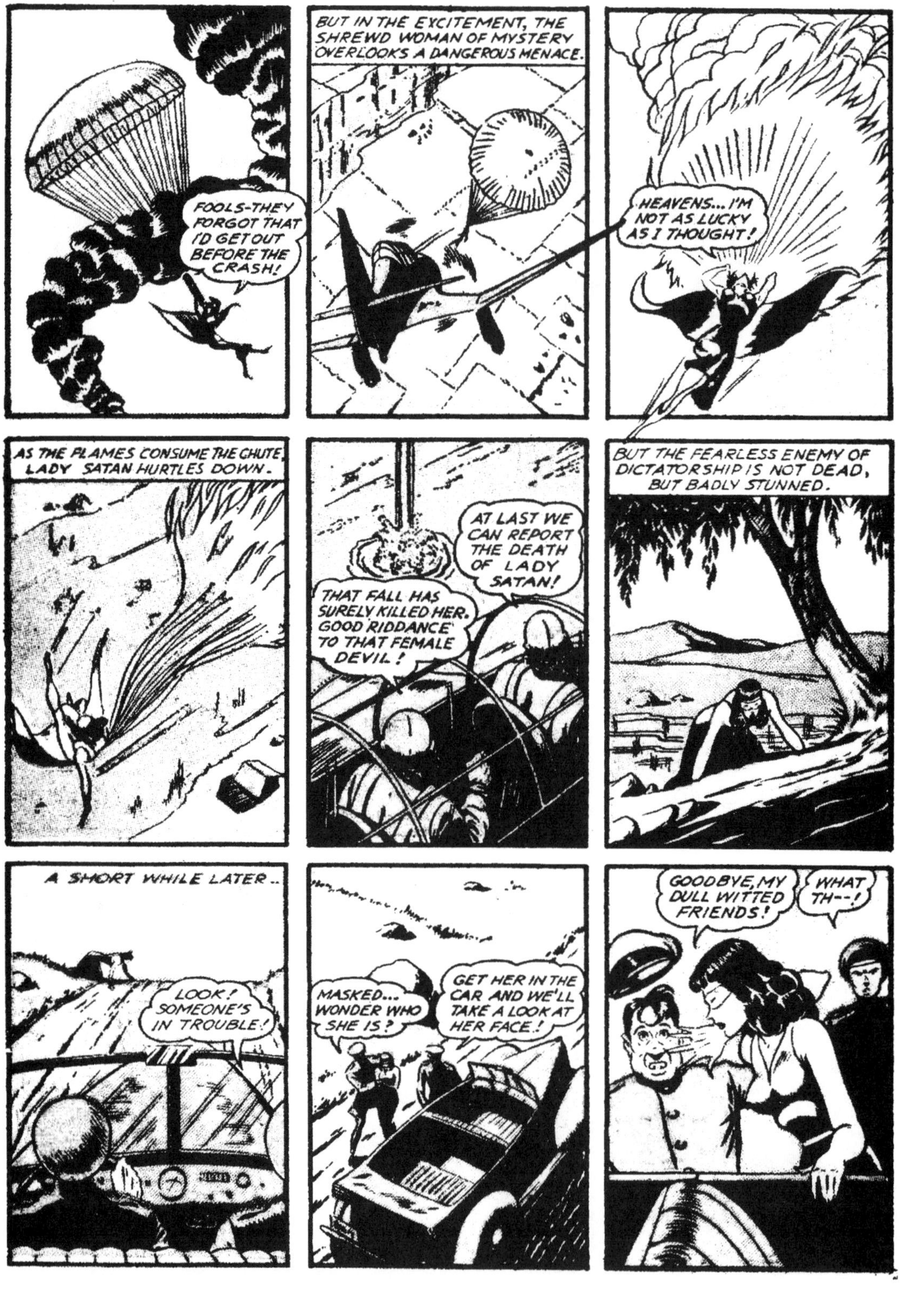
FOOLS-THEY FORGOT THAT I'D GET OUT BEFORE THE CRASH!
BUT IN THE EXCITEMENT, THE SHREWD WOMAN OF MYSTERY OVERLOOKS A DANGEROUS MENACE.
HEAVENS... I'M NOT AS LUCKY AS I THOUGHT!
AS THE FLAMES CONSUME THE CHUTE, LADY SATAN HURTLES DOWN.
AT LAST WE CAN REPORT THE DEATH OF LADY SATAN!
THAT FALL HAS SURELY KILLED HER. GOOD RIDDANCE TO THAT FEMALE DEVIL!
BUT THE FEARLESS ENEMY OF DICTATORSHIP IS NOT DEAD, BUT BADLY STUNNED.
A SHORT WHILE LATER..
LOOK! SOMEONE'S IN TROUBLE!
MASKED... WONDER WHO SHE IS?
GET HER IN THE CAR AND WE'LL TAKE A LOOK AT HER FACE!
GOODBYE, MY DULL WITTED FRIENDS!
WHAT TH--!

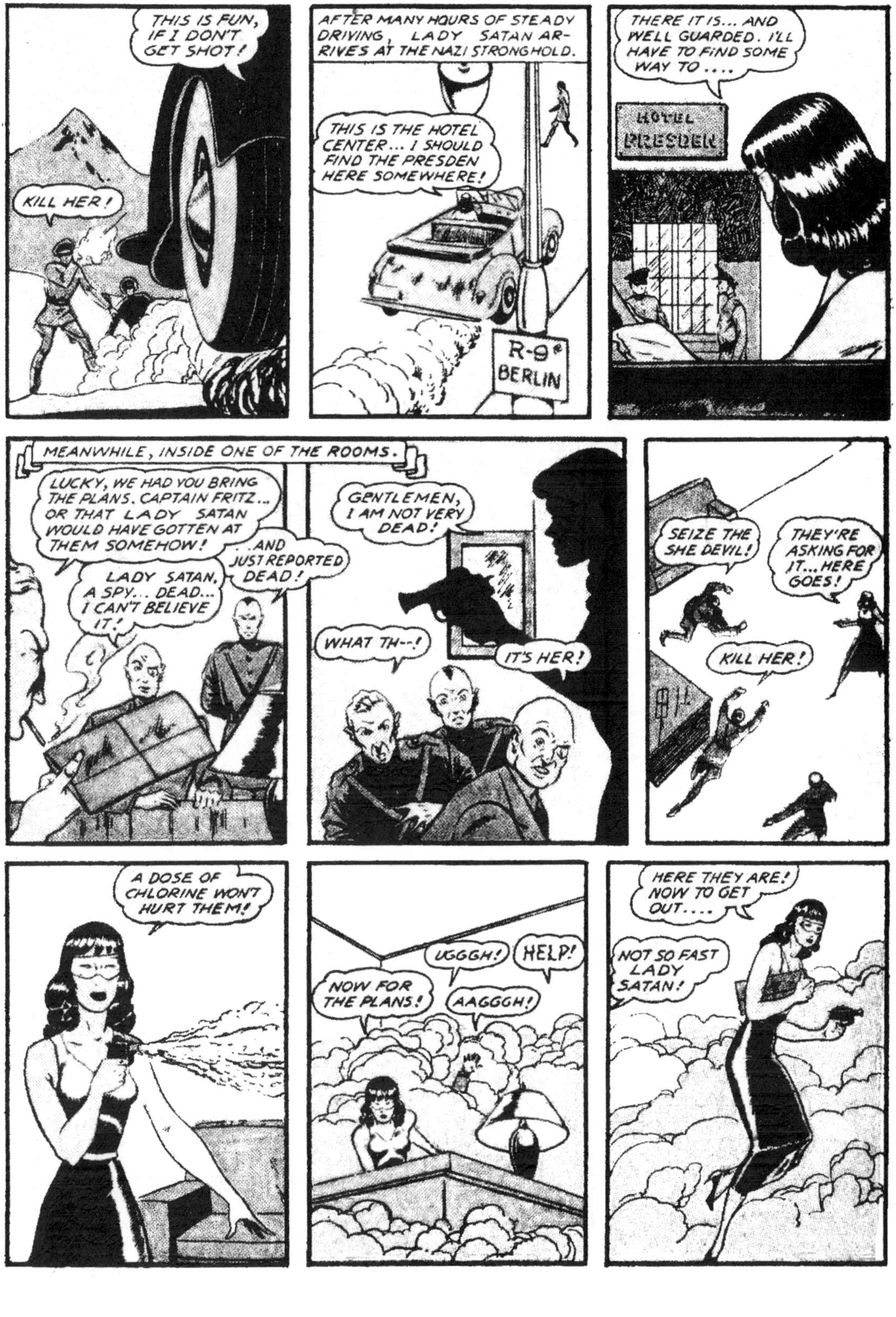
THIS IS FUN, IF I DON'T GET SHOT!
KILL HER!
AFTER MANY HOURS OF STEADY DRIVING, LADY SATAN ARRIVES AT THE NAZI STRONGHOLD.
THIS IS THE HOTEL CENTER... I SHOULD FIND THE PRESDEN HERE SOMEWHERE!
R-9
BERLIN
THERE IT IS... AND WELL GUARDED. I'LL HAVE TO FIND SOME WAY TO....
HOTEL PRESDEN
MEANWHILE, INSIDE ONE OF THE ROOMS.
LUCKY, WE HAD YOU BRING THE PLANS. CAPTAIN FRITZ... OR THAT LADY SATAN WOULD HAVE GOTTEN AT THEM SOMEHOW!
LADY SATAN, A SPY... DEAD... I CAN'T BELIEVE IT!
..AND JUST REPORTED DEAD!
GENTLEMEN, I AM NOT VERY DEAD!
WHAT TH--!
IT'S HER!
SEIZE THE SHE DEVIL!
THEY'RE ASKING FOR IT... HERE GOES!
KILL HER!
A DOSE OF CHLORINE WON'T HURT THEM!
UGGGH!
HELP!
NOW FOR THE PLANS!
AAGGGH!
HERE THEY ARE! NOW TO GET OUT....
NOT SO FAST LADY SATAN!

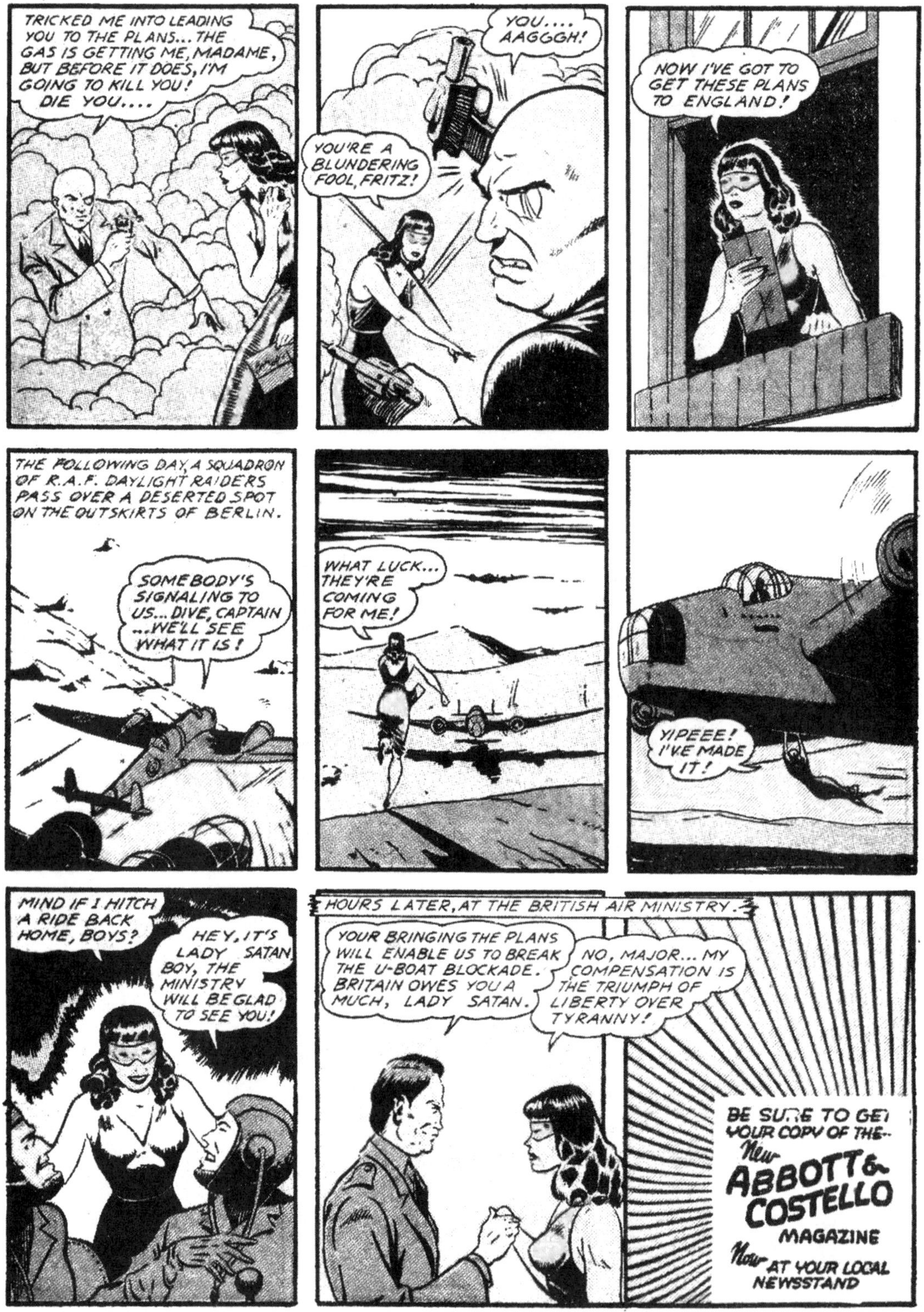
TRICKED ME INTO LEADING YOU TO THE PLANS... THE GAS IS GETTING ME, MADAME, BUT BEFORE IT DOES, I'M GOING TO KILL YOU! DIE YOU....
YOU.... AAGGGH!
YOU'RE A BLUNDERING FOOL, FRITZ!
NOW I'VE GOT TO GET THESE PLANS TO ENGLAND!
THE FOLLOWING DAY, A SQUADRON OF R.A.F. DAYLIGHT RAIDERS PASS OVER A DESERTED SPOT ON THE OUTSKIRTS OF BERLIN.
SOMEBODY'S SIGNALING TO US... DIVE, CAPTAIN ...WE'LL SEE WHAT IT IS!
WHAT LUCK... THEY'RE COMING FOR ME!
YIPEEE! I'VE MADE IT!
MIND IF I HITCH A RIDE BACK HOME, BOYS?
HEY, IT'S LADY SATAN BOY, THE MINISTRY WILL BE GLAD TO SEE YOU!
HOURS LATER, AT THE BRITISH AIR MINISTRY.
YOUR BRINGING THE PLANS WILL ENABLE US TO BREAK THE U-BOAT BLOCKADE. BRITAIN OWES YOU A MUCH, LADY SATAN.
NO, MAJOR... MY COMPENSATION IS THE TRIUMPH OF LIBERTY OVER TYRANNY!
BE SURE TO GET YOUR COPY OF THE-- New ABBOTT & COSTELLO MAGAZINE Now AT YOUR LOCAL NEWSSTAND

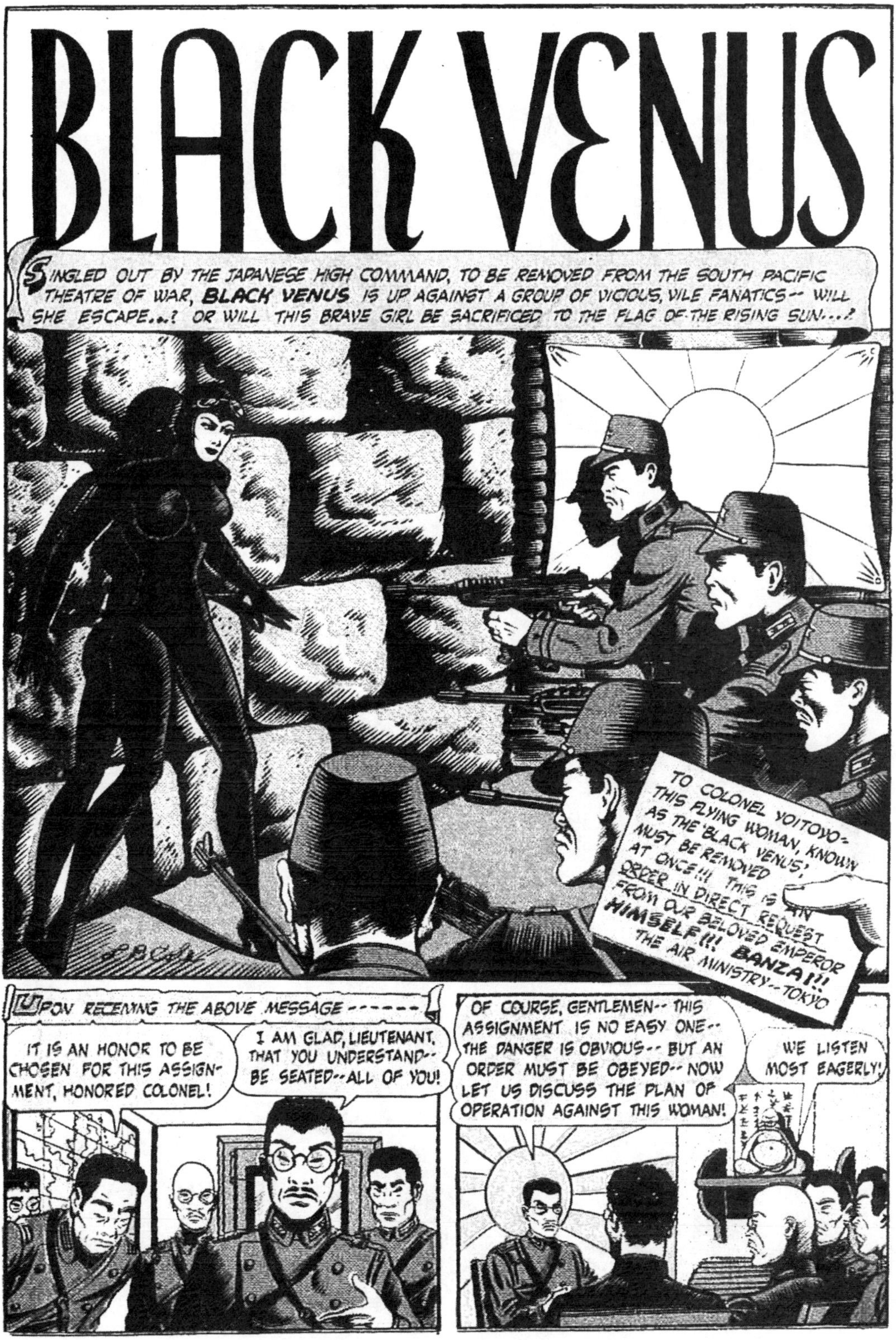
BLACK VENUS
SINGLED OUT BY THE JAPANESE HIGH COMMAND, TO BE REMOVED FROM THE SOUTH PACIFIC THEATRE OF WAR, BLACK VENUS IS UP AGAINST A GROUP OF VICIOUS, VILE FANATICS-- WILL SHE ESCAPE...? OR WILL THIS BRAVE GIRL BE SACRIFICED TO THE FLAG OF THE RISING SUN...?
TO COLONEL YOITOYO- THIS FLYING WOMAN, KNOWN AS THE 'BLACK VENUS,' MUST BE REMOVED AT ONCE!!! THIS IS AN ORDER IN DIRECT REQUEST FROM OUR BELOVED EMPEROR HIMSELF!!! BANZAI!!! THE AIR MINISTRY--TOKYO
UPON RECEIVING THE ABOVE MESSAGE ------
IT IS AN HONOR TO BE CHOSEN FOR THIS ASSIGNMENT, HONORED COLONEL!
I AM GLAD, LIEUTENANT, THAT YOU UNDERSTAND-- BE SEATED--ALL OF YOU!
OF COURSE, GENTLEMEN-- THIS ASSIGNMENT IS NO EASY ONE-- THE DANGER IS OBVIOUS-- BUT AN ORDER MUST BE OBEYED-- NOW LET US DISCUSS THE PLAN OF OPERATION AGAINST THIS WOMAN!
WE LISTEN MOST EAGERLY!

From Contact Comics #3 (1944) Art by L.B. Cole

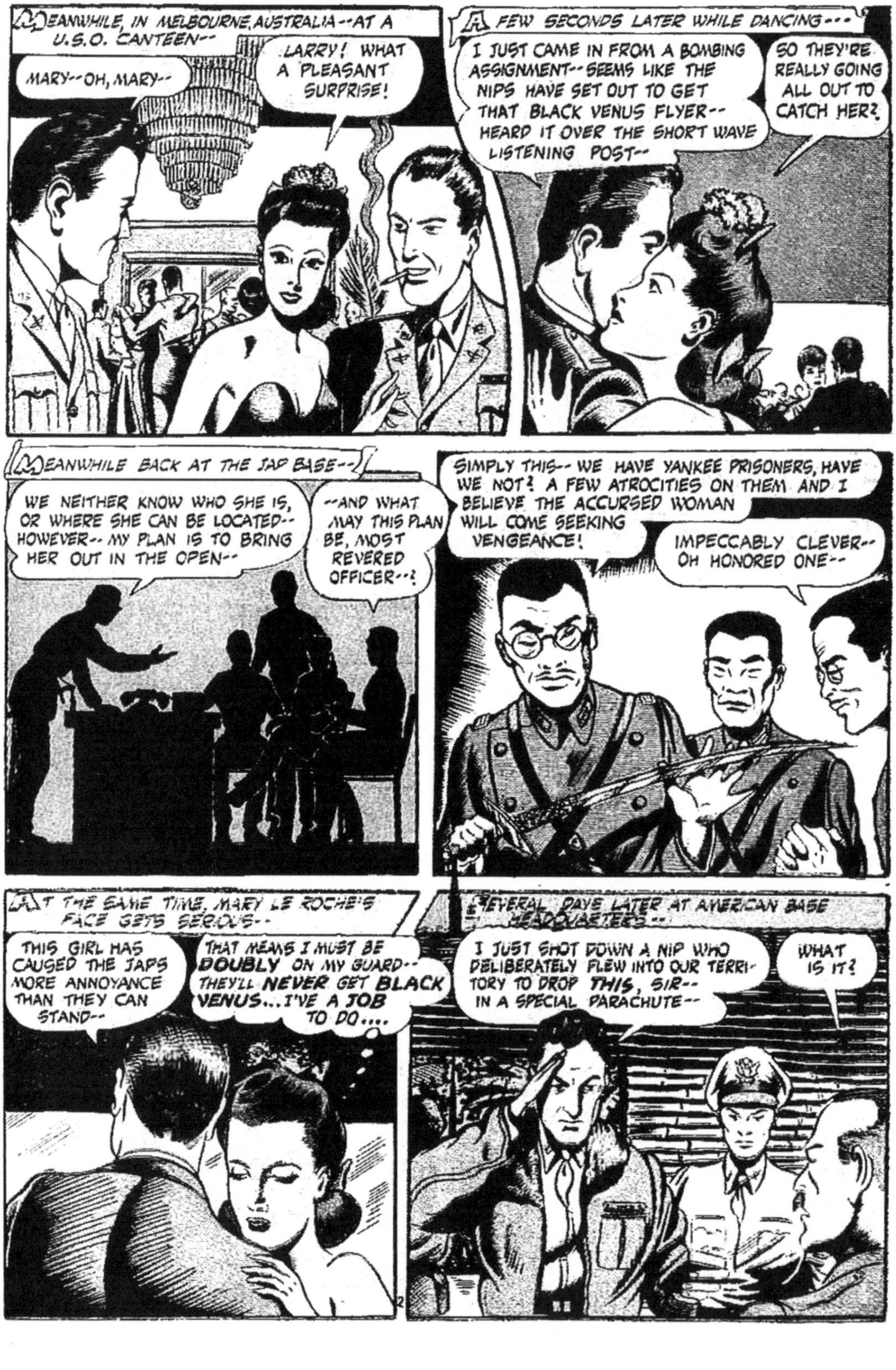
MEANWHILE, IN MELBOURNE, AUSTRALIA--AT A U.S.O. CANTEEN--
MARY--OH, MARY--
LARRY! WHAT A PLEASANT SURPRISE!
A FEW SECONDS LATER WHILE DANCING---
I JUST CAME IN FROM A BOMBING ASSIGNMENT--SEEMS LIKE THE NIPS HAVE SET OUT TO GET THAT BLACK VENUS FLYER--HEARD IT OVER THE SHORT WAVE LISTENING POST--
SO THEY'RE REALLY GOING ALL OUT TO CATCH HER?
MEANWHILE BACK AT THE JAP BASE--
WE NEITHER KNOW WHO SHE IS, OR WHERE SHE CAN BE LOCATED--HOWEVER--MY PLAN IS TO BRING HER OUT IN THE OPEN--
--AND WHAT MAY THIS PLAN BE, MOST REVERED OFFICER--?
SIMPLY THIS--WE HAVE YANKEE PRISONERS, HAVE WE NOT? A FEW ATROCITIES ON THEM AND I BELIEVE THE ACCURSED WOMAN WILL COME SEEKING VENGEANCE!
IMPECCABLY CLEVER--OH HONORED ONE--
AT THE SAME TIME, MARY LE ROCHE'S FACE GETS SERIOUS--
THIS GIRL HAS CAUSED THE JAPS MORE ANNOYANCE THAN THEY CAN STAND--
THAT MEANS I MUST BE DOUBLY ON MY GUARD--THEY'LL NEVER GET BLACK VENUS...I'VE A JOB TO DO....
SEVERAL DAYS LATER AT AMERICAN BASE HEADQUARTERS--
I JUST SHOT DOWN A NIP WHO DELIBERATELY FLEW INTO OUR TERRITORY TO DROP THIS, SIR--IN A SPECIAL PARACHUTE--
WHAT IS IT?

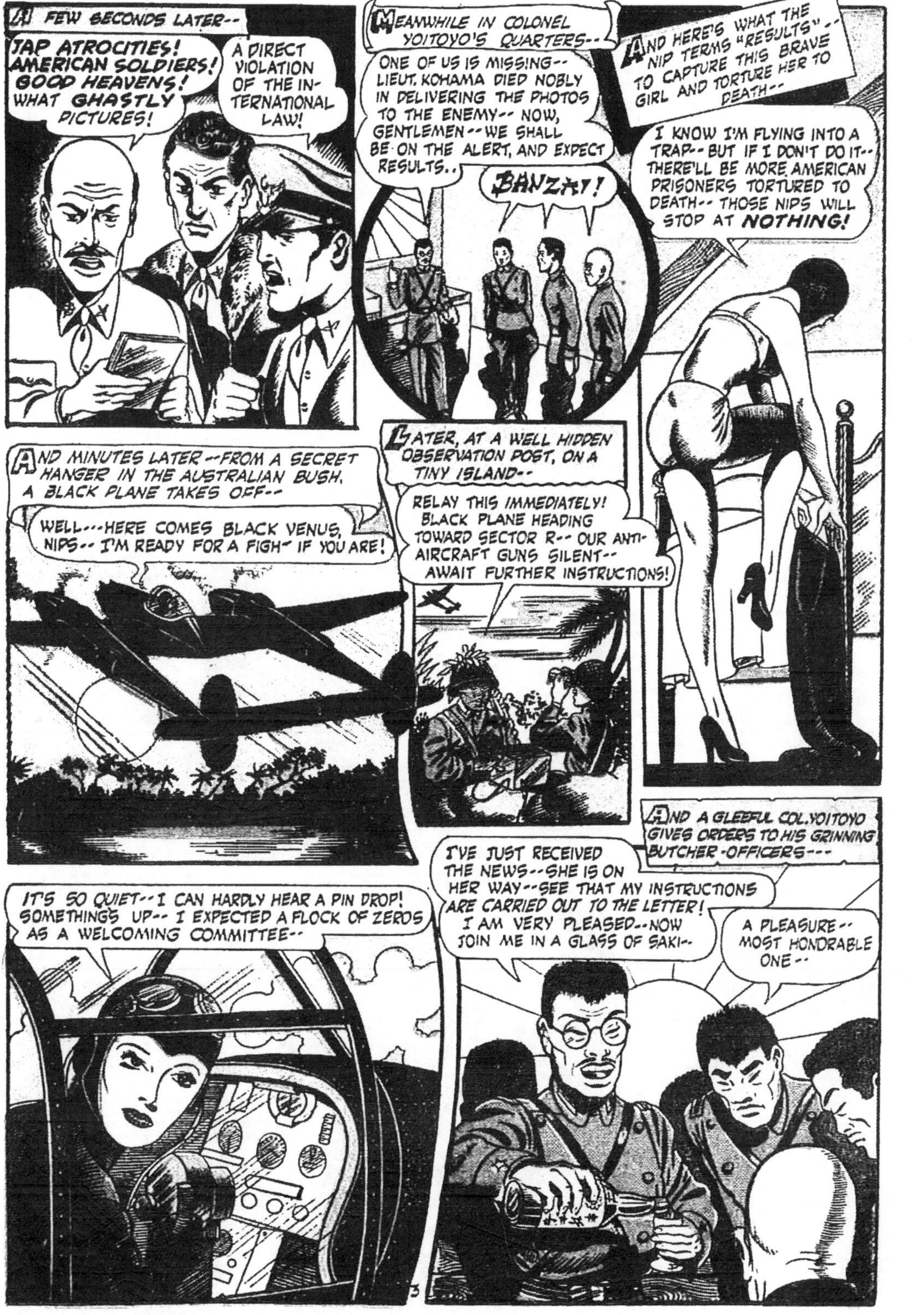
A FEW SECONDS LATER--
JAP ATROCITIES! AMERICAN SOLDIERS! GOOD HEAVENS! WHAT GHASTLY PICTURES!
A DIRECT VIOLATION OF THE INTERNATIONAL LAW!
MEANWHILE IN COLONEL YOITOYO'S QUARTERS--
ONE OF US IS MISSING-- LIEUT. KOHAMA DIED NOBLY IN DELIVERING THE PHOTOS TO THE ENEMY-- NOW, GENTLEMEN-- WE SHALL BE ON THE ALERT, AND EXPECT RESULTS..
BANZAI!
AND HERE'S WHAT THE NIP TERMS "RESULTS"-- TO CAPTURE THIS BRAVE GIRL AND TORTURE HER TO DEATH--
I KNOW I'M FLYING INTO A TRAP-- BUT IF I DON'T DO IT-- THERE'LL BE MORE AMERICAN PRISONERS TORTURED TO DEATH-- THOSE NIPS WILL STOP AT NOTHING!
AND MINUTES LATER--FROM A SECRET HANGER IN THE AUSTRALIAN BUSH, A BLACK PLANE TAKES OFF--
WELL---HERE COMES BLACK VENUS, NIPS-- I'M READY FOR A FIGHT IF YOU ARE!
LATER, AT A WELL HIDDEN OBSERVATION POST, ON A TINY ISLAND--
RELAY THIS IMMEDIATELY! BLACK PLANE HEADING TOWARD SECTOR R-- OUR ANTI-AIRCRAFT GUNS SILENT-- AWAIT FURTHER INSTRUCTIONS!
IT'S SO QUIET-- I CAN HARDLY HEAR A PIN DROP! SOMETHING'S UP-- I EXPECTED A FLOCK OF ZEROS AS A WELCOMING COMMITTEE--
AND A GLEEFUL COL. YOITOYO GIVES ORDERS TO HIS GRINNING BUTCHER-OFFICERS---
I'VE JUST RECEIVED THE NEWS--SHE IS ON HER WAY--SEE THAT MY INSTRUCTIONS ARE CARRIED OUT TO THE LETTER!
I AM VERY PLEASED--NOW JOIN ME IN A GLASS OF SAKI--
A PLEASURE-- MOST HONORABLE ONE--

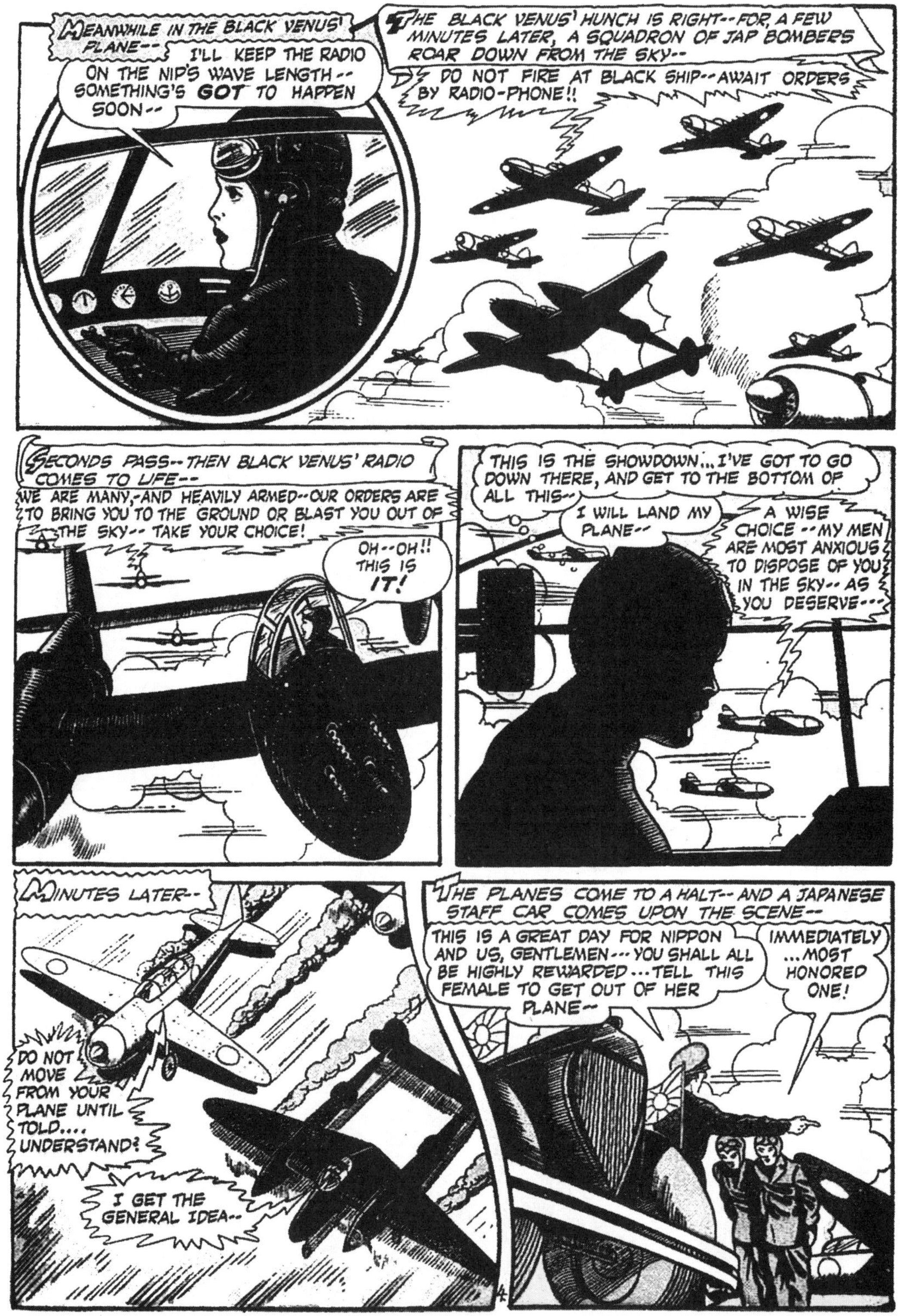
MEANWHILE IN THE BLACK VENUS' PLANE--
I'LL KEEP THE RADIO ON THE NIP'S WAVE LENGTH -- SOMETHING'S GOT TO HAPPEN SOON--
THE BLACK VENUS' HUNCH IS RIGHT--FOR A FEW MINUTES LATER, A SQUADRON OF JAP BOMBERS ROAR DOWN FROM THE SKY--
DO NOT FIRE AT BLACK SHIP--AWAIT ORDERS BY RADIO-PHONE!!
SECONDS PASS--THEN BLACK VENUS' RADIO COMES TO LIFE--
WE ARE MANY,-AND HEAVILY ARMED--OUR ORDERS ARE TO BRING YOU TO THE GROUND OR BLAST YOU OUT OF THE SKY-- TAKE YOUR CHOICE!
OH--OH!! THIS IS IT!
THIS IS THE SHOWDOWN...I'VE GOT TO GO DOWN THERE, AND GET TO THE BOTTOM OF ALL THIS--
I WILL LAND MY PLANE--
A WISE CHOICE --MY MEN ARE MOST ANXIOUS TO DISPOSE OF YOU IN THE SKY-- AS YOU DESERVE---
MINUTES LATER--
DO NOT MOVE FROM YOUR PLANE UNTIL TOLD.... UNDERSTAND?
I GET THE GENERAL IDEA--
THE PLANES COME TO A HALT-- AND A JAPANESE STAFF CAR COMES UPON THE SCENE--
THIS IS A GREAT DAY FOR NIPPON AND US, GENTLEMEN--- YOU SHALL ALL BE HIGHLY REWARDED ...TELL THIS FEMALE TO GET OUT OF HER PLANE--
IMMEDIATELY ...MOST HONORED ONE!

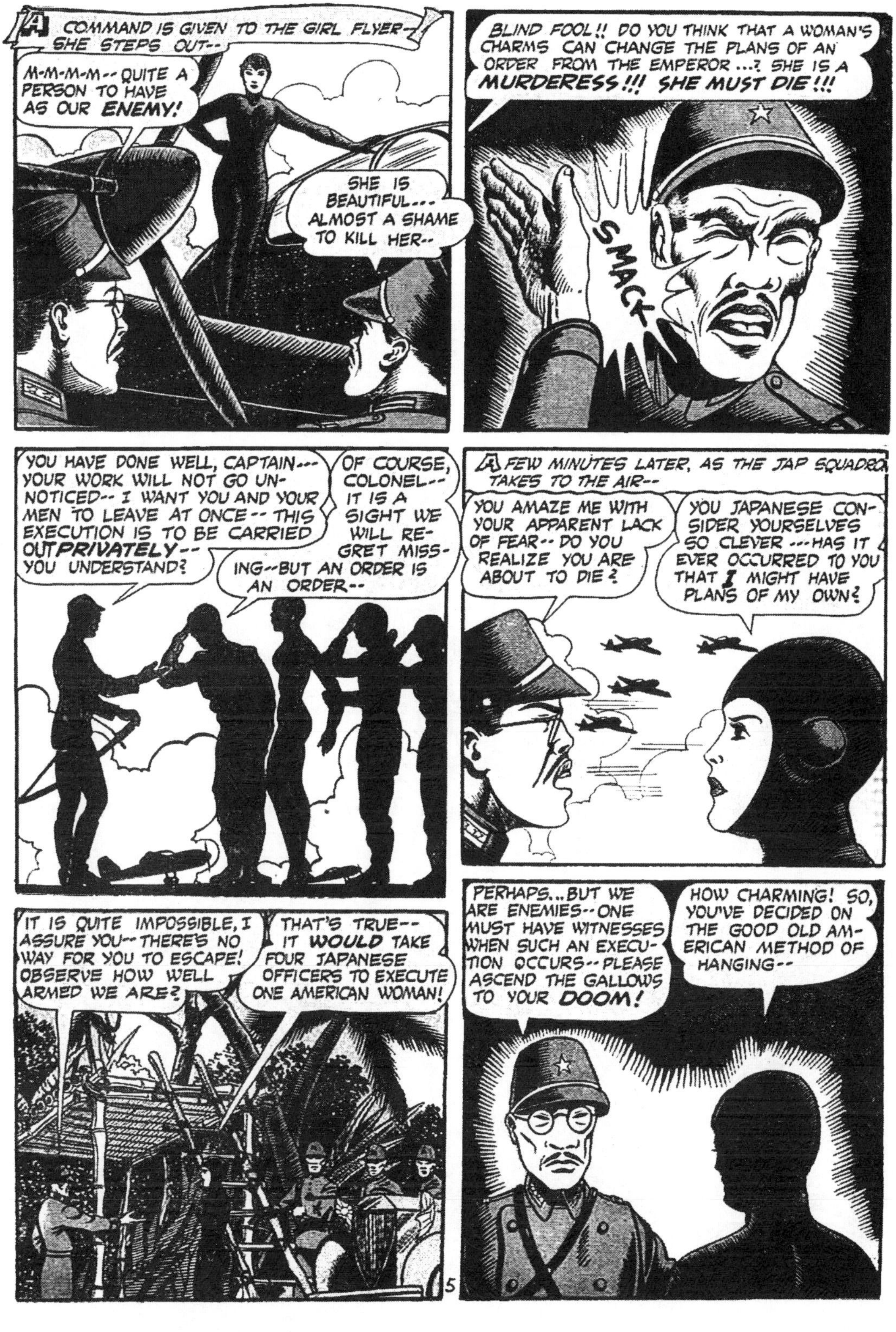
A COMMAND IS GIVEN TO THE GIRL FLYER-- SHE STEPS OUT--
M-M-M-M-- QUITE A PERSON TO HAVE AS OUR ENEMY!
SHE IS BEAUTIFUL--- ALMOST A SHAME TO KILL HER--
BLIND FOOL!! DO YOU THINK THAT A WOMAN'S CHARMS CAN CHANGE THE PLANS OF AN ORDER FROM THE EMPEROR ...? SHE IS A MURDERESS!!! SHE MUST DIE!!!
SMACK
YOU HAVE DONE WELL, CAPTAIN--- YOUR WORK WILL NOT GO UN-NOTICED-- I WANT YOU AND YOUR MEN TO LEAVE AT ONCE -- THIS EXECUTION IS TO BE CARRIED OUT PRIVATELY-- YOU UNDERSTAND?
OF COURSE, COLONEL-- IT IS A SIGHT WE WILL RE-GRET MISS-ING--BUT AN ORDER IS AN ORDER--
A FEW MINUTES LATER, AS THE JAP SQUADRON TAKES TO THE AIR--
YOU AMAZE ME WITH YOUR APPARENT LACK OF FEAR-- DO YOU REALIZE YOU ARE ABOUT TO DIE?
YOU JAPANESE CON-SIDER YOURSELVES SO CLEVER ---HAS IT EVER OCCURRED TO YOU THAT I MIGHT HAVE PLANS OF MY OWN?
IT IS QUITE IMPOSSIBLE, I ASSURE YOU-- THERE'S NO WAY FOR YOU TO ESCAPE! OBSERVE HOW WELL ARMED WE ARE?
THAT'S TRUE-- IT WOULD TAKE FOUR JAPANESE OFFICERS TO EXECUTE ONE AMERICAN WOMAN!
5
PERHAPS...BUT WE ARE ENEMIES--ONE MUST HAVE WITNESSES WHEN SUCH AN EXECU-TION OCCURS--PLEASE ASCEND THE GALLOWS TO YOUR DOOM!
HOW CHARMING! SO, YOU'VE DECIDED ON THE GOOD OLD AM-ERICAN METHOD OF HANGING--

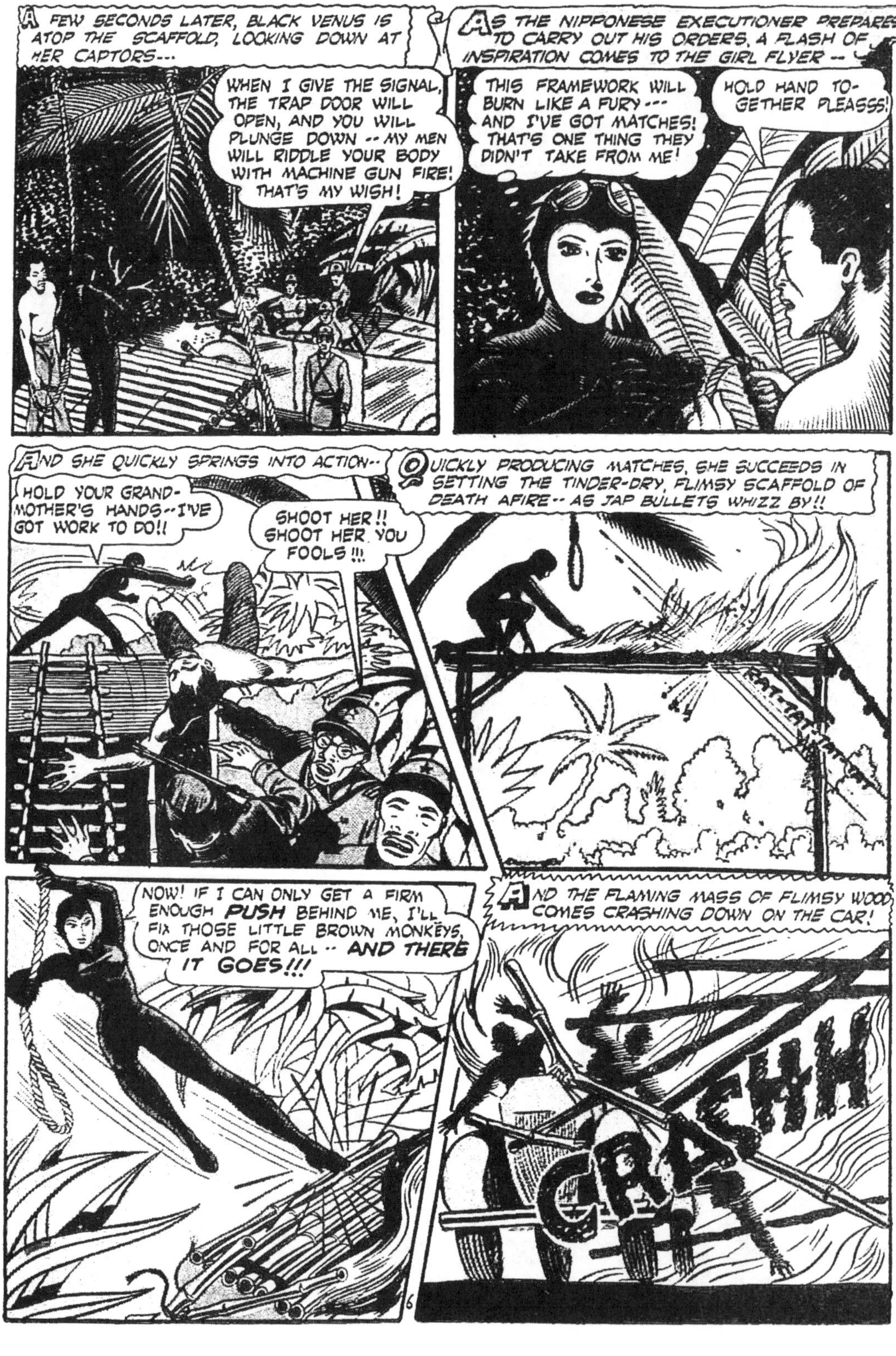
A FEW SECONDS LATER, BLACK VENUS IS ATOP THE SCAFFOLD, LOOKING DOWN AT HER CAPTORS---
WHEN I GIVE THE SIGNAL, THE TRAP DOOR WILL OPEN, AND YOU WILL PLUNGE DOWN -- MY MEN WILL RIDDLE YOUR BODY WITH MACHINE GUN FIRE! THAT'S MY WISH!
AS THE NIPPONESE EXECUTIONER PREPARES TO CARRY OUT HIS ORDERS, A FLASH OF INSPIRATION COMES TO THE GIRL FLYER --
THIS FRAMEWORK WILL BURN LIKE A FURY--- AND I'VE GOT MATCHES! THAT'S ONE THING THEY DIDN'T TAKE FROM ME!
HOLD HAND TO-GETHER PLEASSS!
AND SHE QUICKLY SPRINGS INTO ACTION--
HOLD YOUR GRAND-MOTHER'S HANDS--I'VE GOT WORK TO DO!!
SHOOT HER!! SHOOT HER YOU FOOLS!!!
QUICKLY PRODUCING MATCHES, SHE SUCCEEDS IN SETTING THE TINDER-DRY, FLIMSY SCAFFOLD OF DEATH AFIRE-- AS JAP BULLETS WHIZZ BY!!
RAT-TAT
NOW! IF I CAN ONLY GET A FIRM ENOUGH PUSH BEHIND ME, I'LL FIX THOSE LITTLE BROWN MONKEYS, ONCE AND FOR ALL -- AND THERE IT GOES!!!
AND THE FLAMING MASS OF FLIMSY WOOD COMES CRASHING DOWN ON THE CAR!
CRASHH

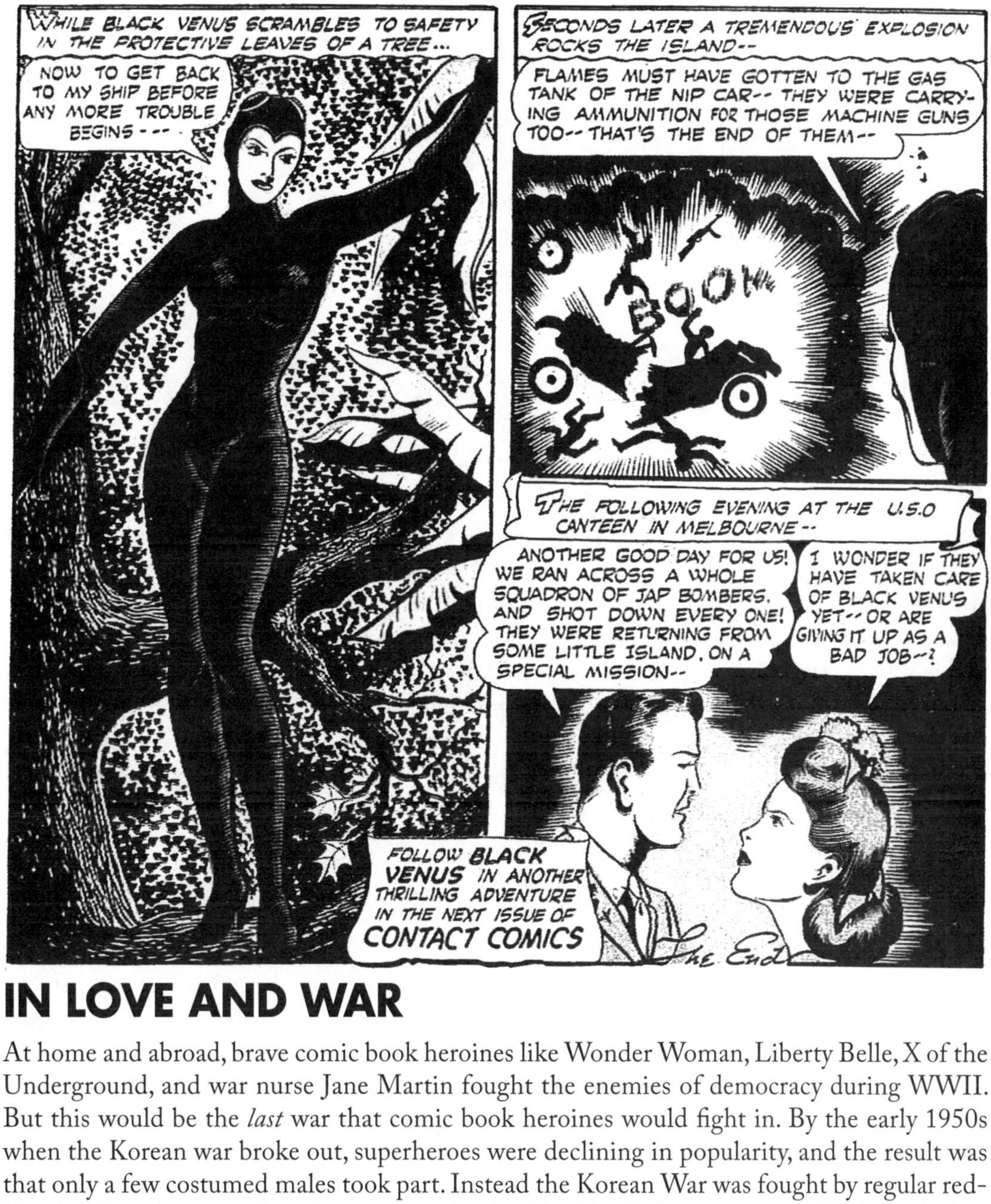
WHILE BLACK VENUS SCRAMBLES TO SAFETY IN THE PROTECTIVE LEAVES OF A TREE...
NOW TO GET BACK TO MY SHIP BEFORE ANY MORE TROUBLE BEGINS---
SECONDS LATER A TREMENDOUS EXPLOSION ROCKS THE ISLAND--
FLAMES MUST HAVE GOTTEN TO THE GAS TANK OF THE NIP CAR-- THEY WERE CARRYING AMMUNITION FOR THOSE MACHINE GUNS TOO-- THAT'S THE END OF THEM--
BOOM
THE FOLLOWING EVENING AT THE U.S.O CANTEEN IN MELBOURNE--
ANOTHER GOOD DAY FOR US! WE RAN ACROSS A WHOLE SQUADRON OF JAP BOMBERS. AND SHOT DOWN EVERY ONE! THEY WERE RETURNING FROM SOME LITTLE ISLAND, ON A SPECIAL MISSION--
I WONDER IF THEY HAVE TAKEN CARE OF BLACK VENUS YET-- OR ARE GIVING IT UP AS A BAD JOB--?
FOLLOW BLACK VENUS IN ANOTHER THRILLING ADVENTURE IN THE NEXT ISSUE OF CONTACT COMICS
The End

IN LOVE AND WAR

At home and abroad, brave comic book heroines like Wonder Woman, Liberty Belle, X of the Underground, and war nurse Jane Martin fought the enemies of democracy during WWII. But this would be the *last* war that comic book heroines would fight in. By the early 1950s when the Korean war broke out, superheroes were declining in popularity, and the result was that only a few costumed males took part. Instead the Korean War was fought by regular red-blooded American men in military themed series like *The Fighting Man* and *Warfront*. And in this new, more conservative era, women were mainly featured in comics like *G.I. Sweethearts* and *True Wartime Romances*. Now female characters were shown less on battlefields and more involved in romantic skirmishes with handsome soldiers.

When superheroes regained popularity in the early '60s, the Viet Nam war was being waged. But with opposition to the war growing among Americans, this time publishers had most of their superheroes—male or female—steer clear of the conflict.

MYSTERY WOMEN

A vigilante is defined as a "self-appointed doer of justice," someone who takes the law into his or her own hands. And America has had a complicated history with vigilantes. We think of our nation as a place that thrives on justice. So on the one hand we thrill to the *idea* of the vigilante. We think that the rugged individual on a single-minded quest for justice, against all odds, no matter what the cost, is typical of what made this country great. The problem is that the vigilante's definition of justice is subjective—it is *that* person's opinion of not only *who* is guilty, but also what the proper punishment should be, no matter how severe. America likes when vigilantes take up the seemingly thankless job of protecting their fellow citizens. For example, in 1979, the Guardian Angels began patrolling the streets of New York to fight violence and crime. They were vigilantes, and were seen as heroes. The Ku Klux Klan were also vigilantes. Two different groups, two different definitions of crime and punishment. So you see where the complication comes in.

After seven decades of superheroes, we have become so accustomed to the concept of the costumed crime fighter of comic books that we have forgotten that they too started out as vigilantes. Plain and simple, the superhero is a person who takes the law into his own hands. Bruce Wayne becomes Batman, Carter Hall becomes Hawkman, Dan Garrett becomes the Blue Beetle to do what they feel the law cannot or will not do—bring the guilty to justice. In the world of comic books, good and evil are generally black and white. But still, you are depending on the morality, and the mental stability, of a man hiding behind a false identity, dressed like a bat or a bird or an insect, to make the right decisions about punishing who *he* deems to be guilty.

TV shows, movies, and endless comic books have made the crusade of the costumed crime fighter a noble cause. But when you read these stories from the early days of comic books, you can still clearly see the vigilante roots of the superhero. We're reminded of what superheroes started out to be, before their images were cleaned up enough to be on a cereal box. And, it's not always pretty. The early vigilante superheroes were violent, scary, and often pitiless.

So, what happens when a woman takes the law into her own hands? The stories in this chapter will show you *what* happens when a woman becomes a vigilante, but they may not always tell you *why*. Of course there is a basic human motivation—the heroine sees there is evil in the world, and wants to do something about it. But we don't always get more detail, or motivation, than that. What events made secretary Ginny Spears adopt the guise of the Veiled Avenger? We don't know because we aren't told. She is already established in her role when we meet her. The Veiled Avenger and the other women in this chapter are such big heroic figures that we don't really ask too many questions. We're simply swept up in the action of the story. When there is an origin story, it is presented quickly, and we move on to the adventure at hand. Comic books of the 1960s began the trend of the more complex heroic origin story. This was further embellished in the 1970s and after with the addition of flashbacks, altered histories and untold tales that gave the reader a more detailed backstory on a character, and a more psychological understanding of the hero's motivation for donning a costume and fighting evil.

With these characters, you won't get the existential musings and introspection seen in modern comics. But you do get action and adventure. There is a perception among modern day readers that Golden Age comics were just cornball stories written for kids, and lack the edge and grittiness of modern day comics. While these stories lack the cynicism and sexuality of some modern comics, they are not sappy. Readers of today may think that the hero with questionable morals is a modern development. That's not the case in these stories. Make no mistake—these women are tough. They are vigilantes on a mission, and will not be deterred. They think nothing of taking a life if it means that justice will be served. The end justifies the means to them. They are modern day furies acting as judge, jury, and sometimes, executioner.

In these early days of comic books, before the term "superhero" became popular (and trademarked), masked vigilantes were often referred to as "mystery men." So, let's meet the Mystery *Women* in this chapter—

 **THE WOMAN IN RED**—Although Fantomah *(see 20th Century Goddesses)* is considered the first superpowered comic book heroine, The Woman in Red is regarded as the first female costumed crime fighter. Making her debut in 1940, Detective Peggy Allen was the police commissioner's secret weapon, assigned to handle his most baffling cases in her own way. A cool, confident, and consummate professional, Peggy is as quick with a gun as she is with a snappy remark—and she isn't afraid to dispense either. The Woman in Red's stories had the aura of old pulp magazine detective stories about them, complete with dark mansions, menacing butlers, and prisoners locked in attics. She battled the underworld, and later spies, in *Thrilling Comics* and *America's Best Comics* until 1946.

SPIDER QUEEN—A mysterious masked crime fighter weaves a web to ensnare evildoers. Is this the Spider-Man, star of comic books, TV, movies and the Broadway stage? No, it's the Spider Queen, who debuted in 1941 (more than twenty years *before* Spider-Man), and has almost the same powers as the mega popular Marvel Comics superhero. The story here is her origin, and tells how ingenious widow Shannon Hale devises special bracelets that shoot a "spider-web fluid." Like many heroines in the 1940s, crafty Shannon hid behind a meek exterior, and only (literally) let her hair down when she became Spider Queen. She made only three appearances in *The Eagle* before swinging into comic book limbo.

MOTHER HUBBARD— In nursery rhymes, Mother Hubbard went to her cupboard to fetch her dog a bone. In this comic book version, the old gal is stockpiling something else in her larder. "A pinch of this, a drop of that, all wicked crime, I will combat!" says Mother Hubbard, as she surveys the assortment of magic potions in her pantry. After centuries of fairy tales and legends, we have become accustomed to the image of the old witch as an evil figure. But as we learn in this origin tale of sorts, this most unlikely comic book crimefighter decides to use her black magic for good. At the end of this bizarre story, we feel sympathy for Mother Hubbard and her quest to change her ways. Everyone deserves a second chance. Mother Hubbard only made a few appearances in 1941's *Scoop Comics*, but she was not the only senior citizen to fight crime. The geriatric detective Granny Gumshoe solved crimes in *National Comics* from 1946-49.

THE SPIDER WIDOW— The concept of a beautiful woman transforming into an ugly hag to fight crime is a novelty in comic books. But this is what debutante Dianne Grayton did when she decided to battle the spies and criminals preying on the innocent. Donning a witch's mask and aided by her black widow spiders, Dianne becomes The Spider Widow, Grandmother of Terror. As "the most horrible dispenser of justice of all times," the witty Spider Widow used *fear* as her greatest weapon, and had fun doing it. In time, The Spider Widow got a male sidekick/love interest called The Raven. But The Spider Widow always got top billing, which was rare in a day when most male heroes had female sidekicks. The Spider Widow appeared in *Feature Comics* from 1942-43.

VEILED AVENGER— "Ginny Spears leads a double life. By day she's the district attorney's secretary. By night The Veiled Avenger, exotic enemy of evil." Thus were readers introduced to the lethal whip-wielding vigilante in 1944. They never learned why Ginny first took on the role of Veiled Avenger, or how she had learned mastery of the bullwhip. But one glimpse of Ginny in action told readers that she was deadly serious about her war on crime. "Drop that Roscoe or I'll rip you to ribbons!" Veiled Avenger shouts, as her bullwhip snares the arm of a gunman. This story presented here feels especially sordid, with criminals dealing in black market blood. Veiled Avenger seems to take pleasure in causing the crooks' deaths at the end of the story without actually getting her hands dirty. She made only four appearances, in *Spotlight Comics* and *Red Seal Comics*.

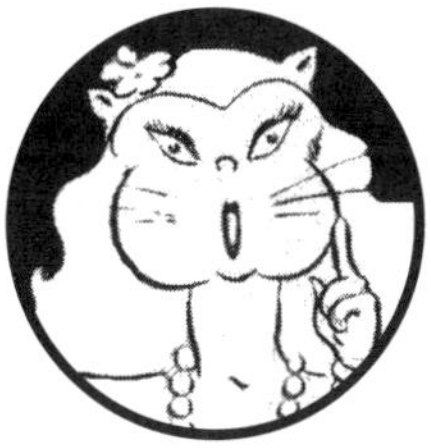

PUSSY KATNIP— There were a lot of funny animal characters in Golden Age Comics, but not many *sexy* ones. Pussy Katnip was the exception. This sultry feline was the proprietress of a café in Mut-Town, where she also entertained the crowds as a torch singer. A pack of criminal weasels and foxes was always cooking up trouble for Pussy, forcing her to take the law into her own…paws. Drinking a cocktail of the mysterious "Katnip Fizz" would result in a wild "katfit," after which Pussy transformed into a "crime-fighting feline" possessing superior strength, intelligence, detective skills and even clairvoyance. That was one powerful drink! Despite her many abilities, the intoxicating Pussy could never spark much of a hot romance with her boyfriend George, the town's canine fire chief. The bizarre exploits of Pussy Katnip appeared in titles such as *All Top Comics*, *Ribtickler*, and *Zoot Comics* between 1944-46.

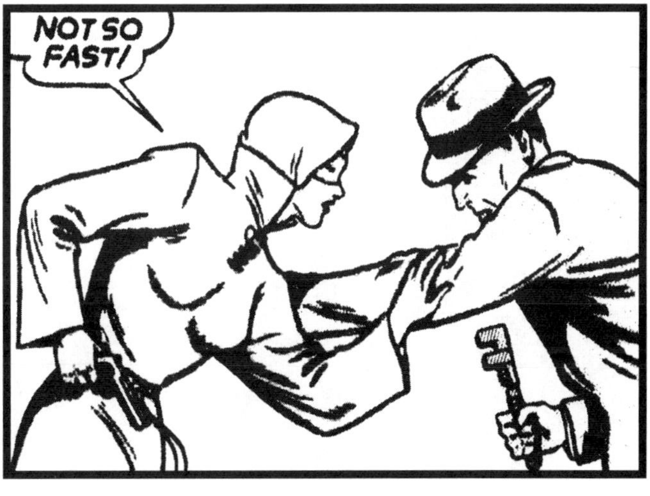
NOT SO FAST!

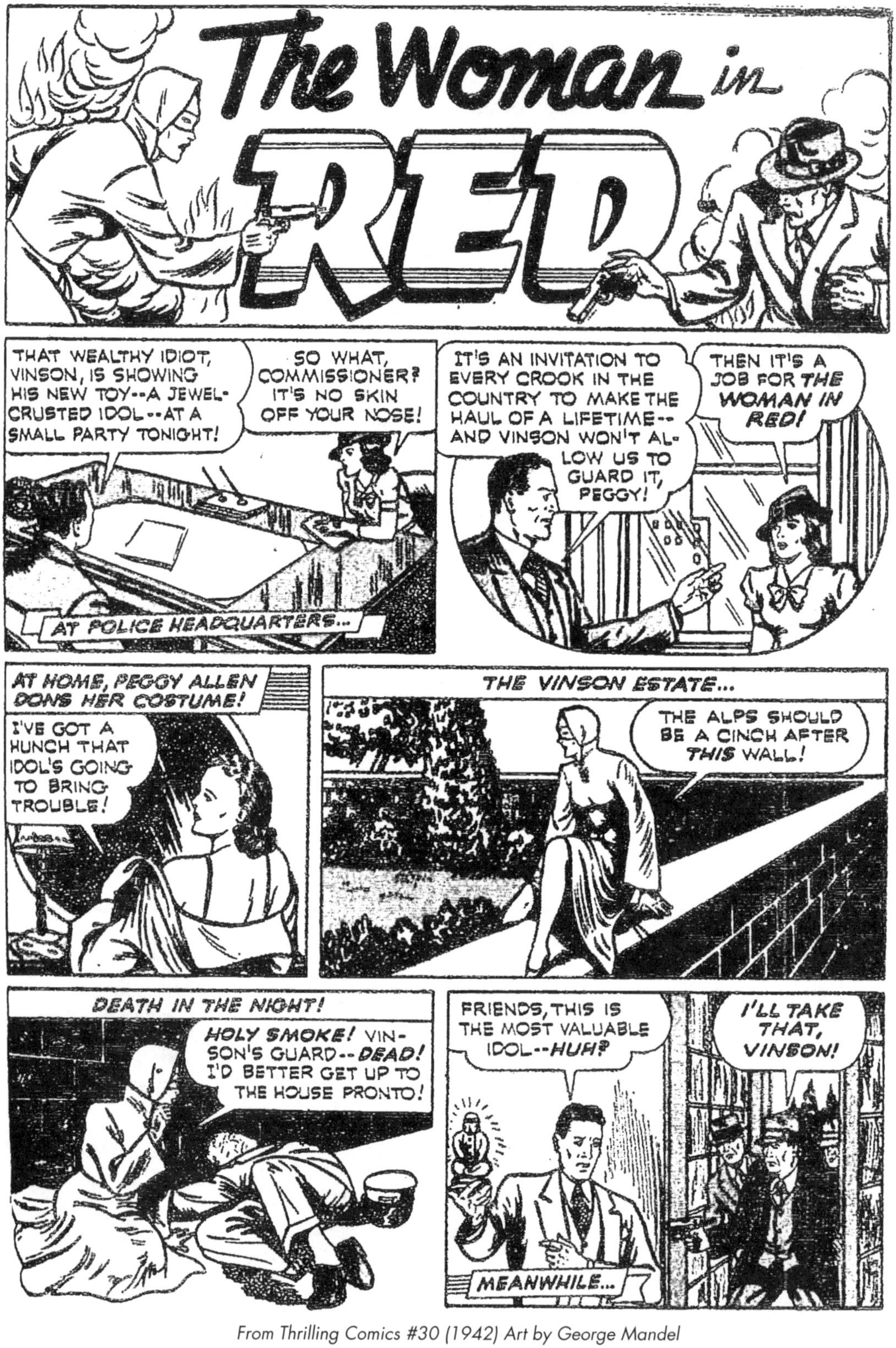
The Woman in RED
THAT WEALTHY IDIOT, VINSON, IS SHOWING HIS NEW TOY--A JEWEL-CRUSTED IDOL--AT A SMALL PARTY TONIGHT!
SO WHAT, COMMISSIONER? IT'S NO SKIN OFF YOUR NOSE!
AT POLICE HEADQUARTERS...
IT'S AN INVITATION TO EVERY CROOK IN THE COUNTRY TO MAKE THE HAUL OF A LIFETIME--AND VINSON WON'T ALLOW US TO GUARD IT, PEGGY!
THEN IT'S A JOB FOR THE WOMAN IN RED!
AT HOME, PEGGY ALLEN DONS HER COSTUME!
I'VE GOT A HUNCH THAT IDOL'S GOING TO BRING TROUBLE!
THE VINSON ESTATE...
THE ALPS SHOULD BE A CINCH AFTER THIS WALL!
DEATH IN THE NIGHT!
HOLY SMOKE! VINSON'S GUARD--DEAD! I'D BETTER GET UP TO THE HOUSE PRONTO!
FRIENDS, THIS IS THE MOST VALUABLE IDOL--HUH?
I'LL TAKE THAT, VINSON!
MEANWHILE...

From Thrilling Comics #30 (1942) Art by George Mandel

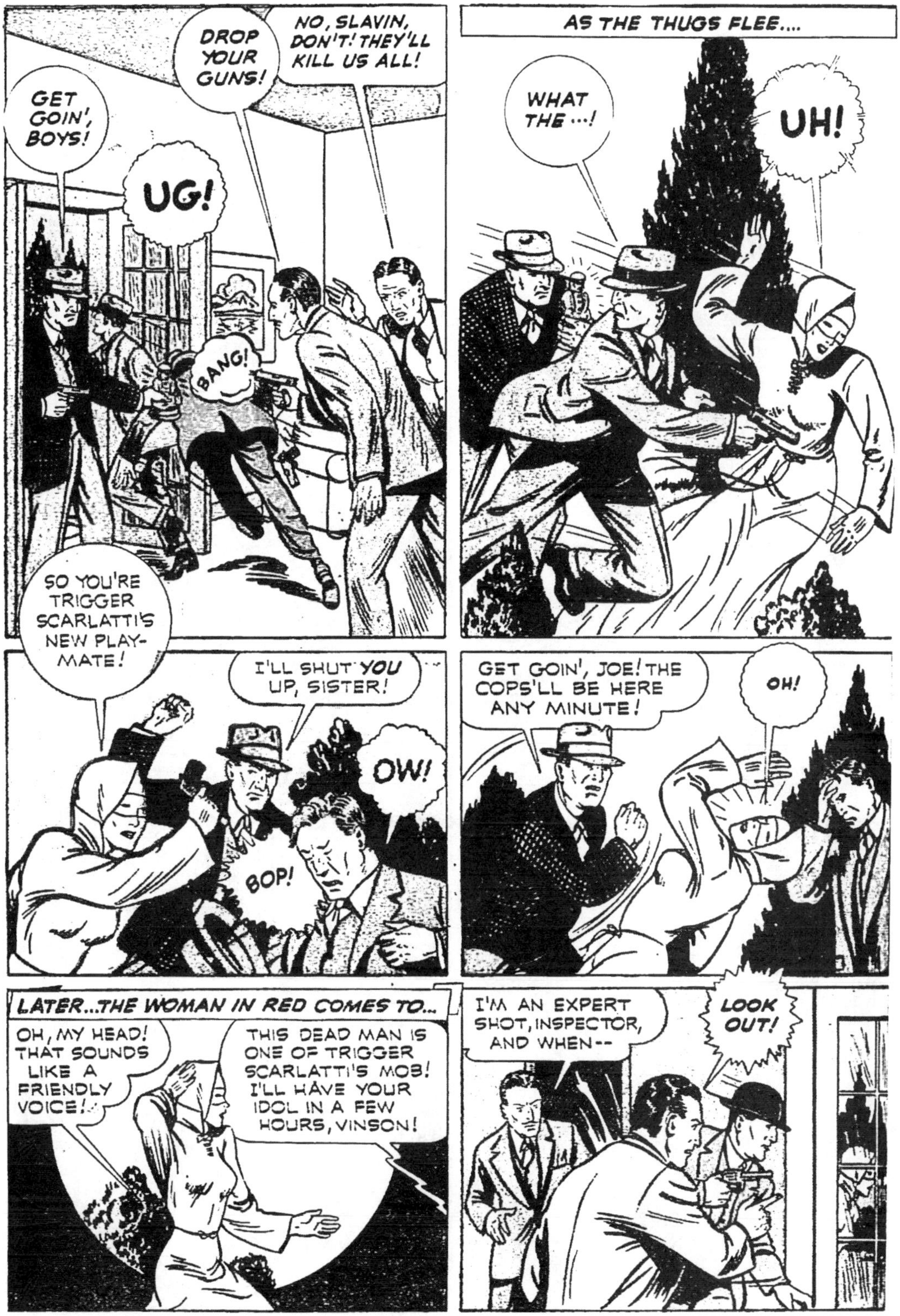
GET GOIN', BOYS!
UG!
DROP YOUR GUNS!
NO, SLAVIN, DON'T! THEY'LL KILL US ALL!
BANG!
AS THE THUGS FLEE....
WHAT THE ...!
UH!
SO YOU'RE TRIGGER SCARLATTI'S NEW PLAY-MATE!
I'LL SHUT YOU UP, SISTER!
OW!
BOP!
GET GOIN', JOE! THE COPS'LL BE HERE ANY MINUTE!
OH!
LATER...THE WOMAN IN RED COMES TO...
OH, MY HEAD! THAT SOUNDS LIKE A FRIENDLY VOICE!
THIS DEAD MAN IS ONE OF TRIGGER SCARLATTI'S MOB! I'LL HAVE YOUR IDOL IN A FEW HOURS, VINSON!
I'M AN EXPERT SHOT, INSPECTOR, AND WHEN --
LOOK OUT!

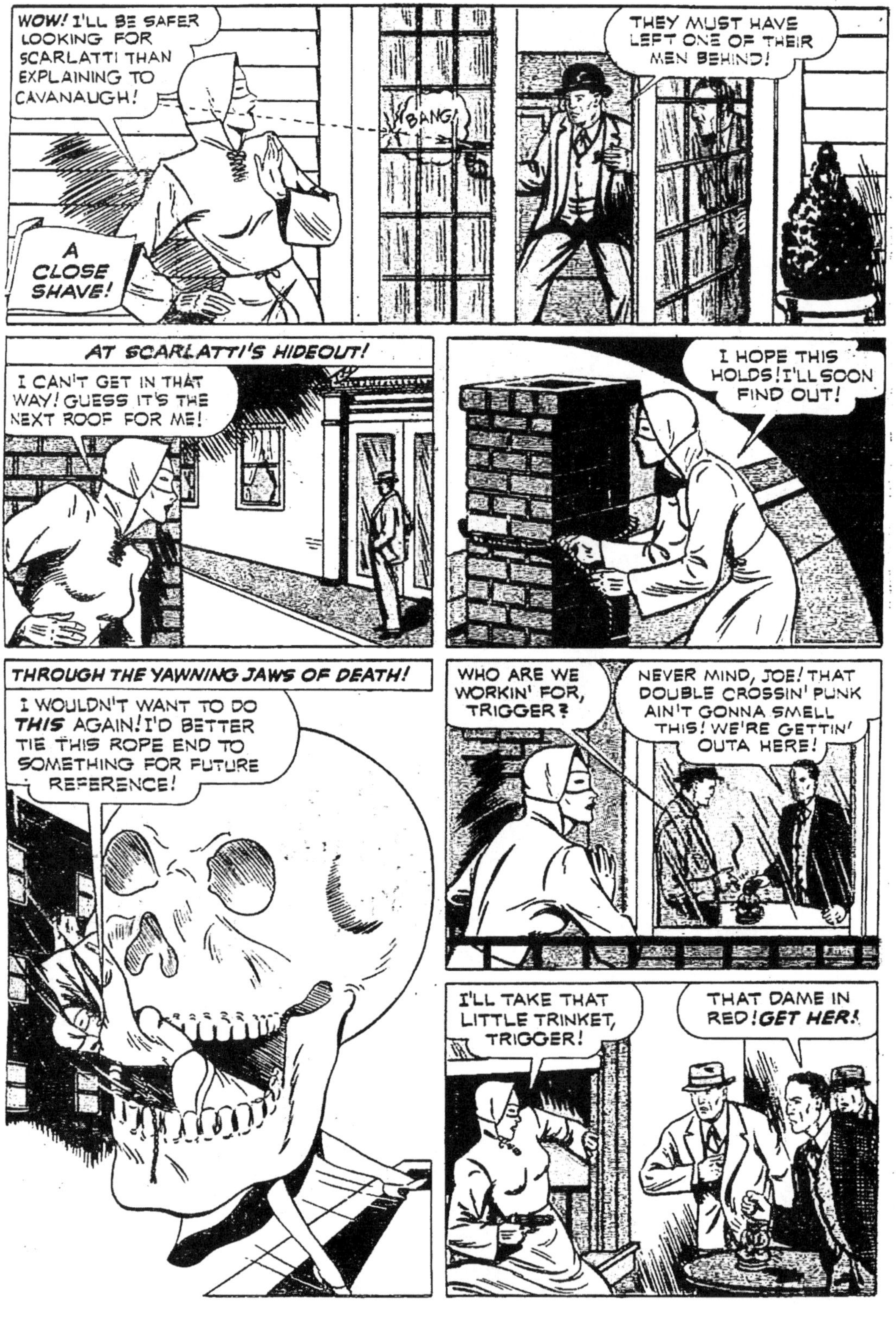
WOW! I'LL BE SAFER LOOKING FOR SCARLATTI THAN EXPLAINING TO CAVANAUGH!
A CLOSE SHAVE!
BANG!
THEY MUST HAVE LEFT ONE OF THEIR MEN BEHIND!
AT SCARLATTI'S HIDEOUT!
I CAN'T GET IN THAT WAY! GUESS IT'S THE NEXT ROOF FOR ME!
I HOPE THIS HOLDS! I'LL SOON FIND OUT!
THROUGH THE YAWNING JAWS OF DEATH!
I WOULDN'T WANT TO DO THIS AGAIN! I'D BETTER TIE THIS ROPE END TO SOMETHING FOR FUTURE REFERENCE!
WHO ARE WE WORKIN' FOR, TRIGGER?
NEVER MIND, JOE! THAT DOUBLE CROSSIN' PUNK AIN'T GONNA SMELL THIS! WE'RE GETTIN' OUTA HERE!
I'LL TAKE THAT LITTLE TRINKET, TRIGGER!
THAT DAME IN RED! GET HER!

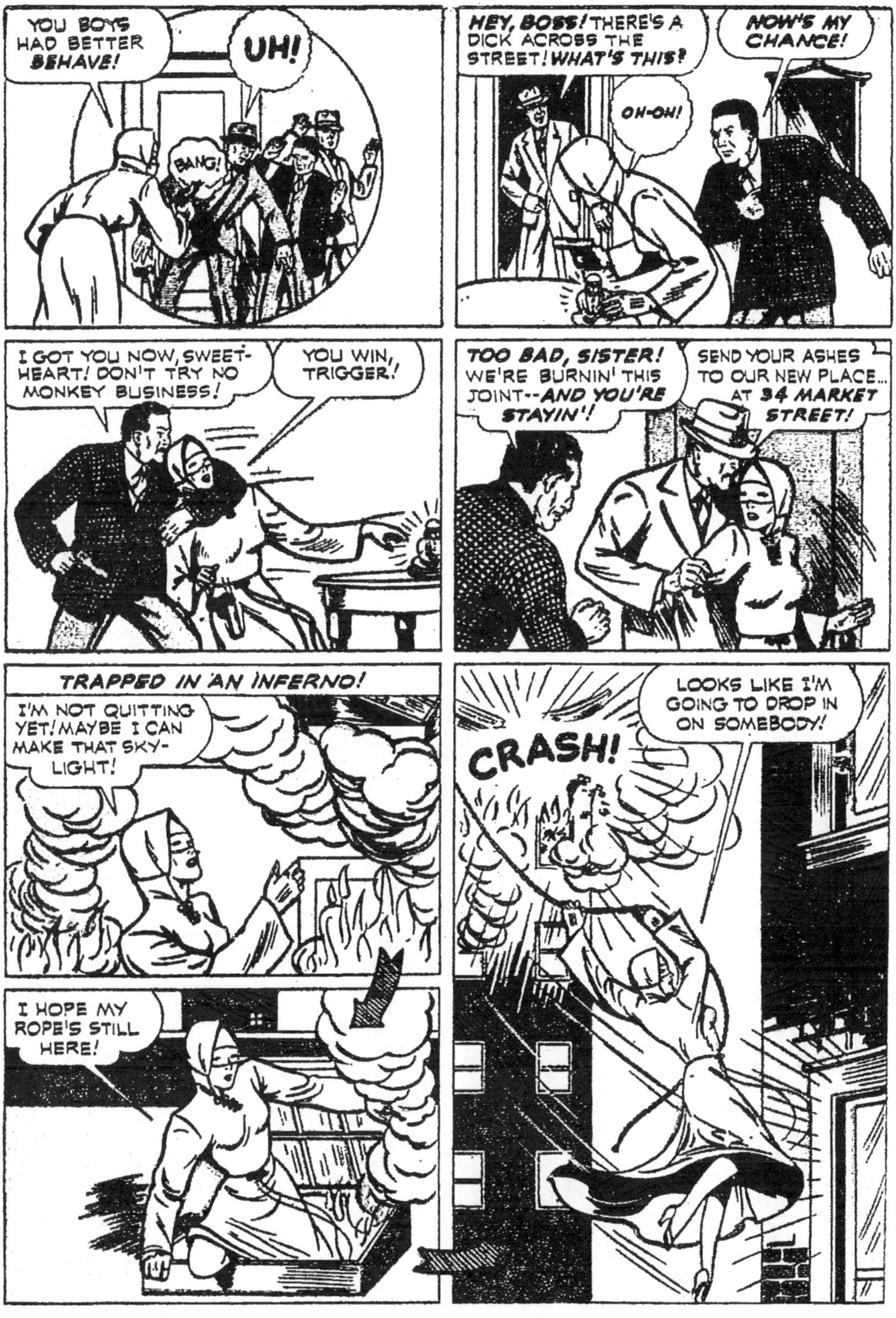

YOU BOYS HAD BETTER BEHAVE!
UH!
BANG!
HEY, BOSS! THERE'S A DICK ACROSS THE STREET! WHAT'S THIS?
NOW'S MY CHANCE!
OH-OH!
I GOT YOU NOW, SWEET-HEART! DON'T TRY NO MONKEY BUSINESS!
YOU WIN, TRIGGER!
TOO BAD, SISTER! WE'RE BURNIN' THIS JOINT--AND YOU'RE STAYIN'!
SEND YOUR ASHES TO OUR NEW PLACE... AT 34 MARKET STREET!
TRAPPED IN AN INFERNO!
I'M NOT QUITTING YET! MAYBE I CAN MAKE THAT SKY-LIGHT!
LOOKS LIKE I'M GOING TO DROP IN ON SOMEBODY!
CRASH!
I HOPE MY ROPE'S STILL HERE!

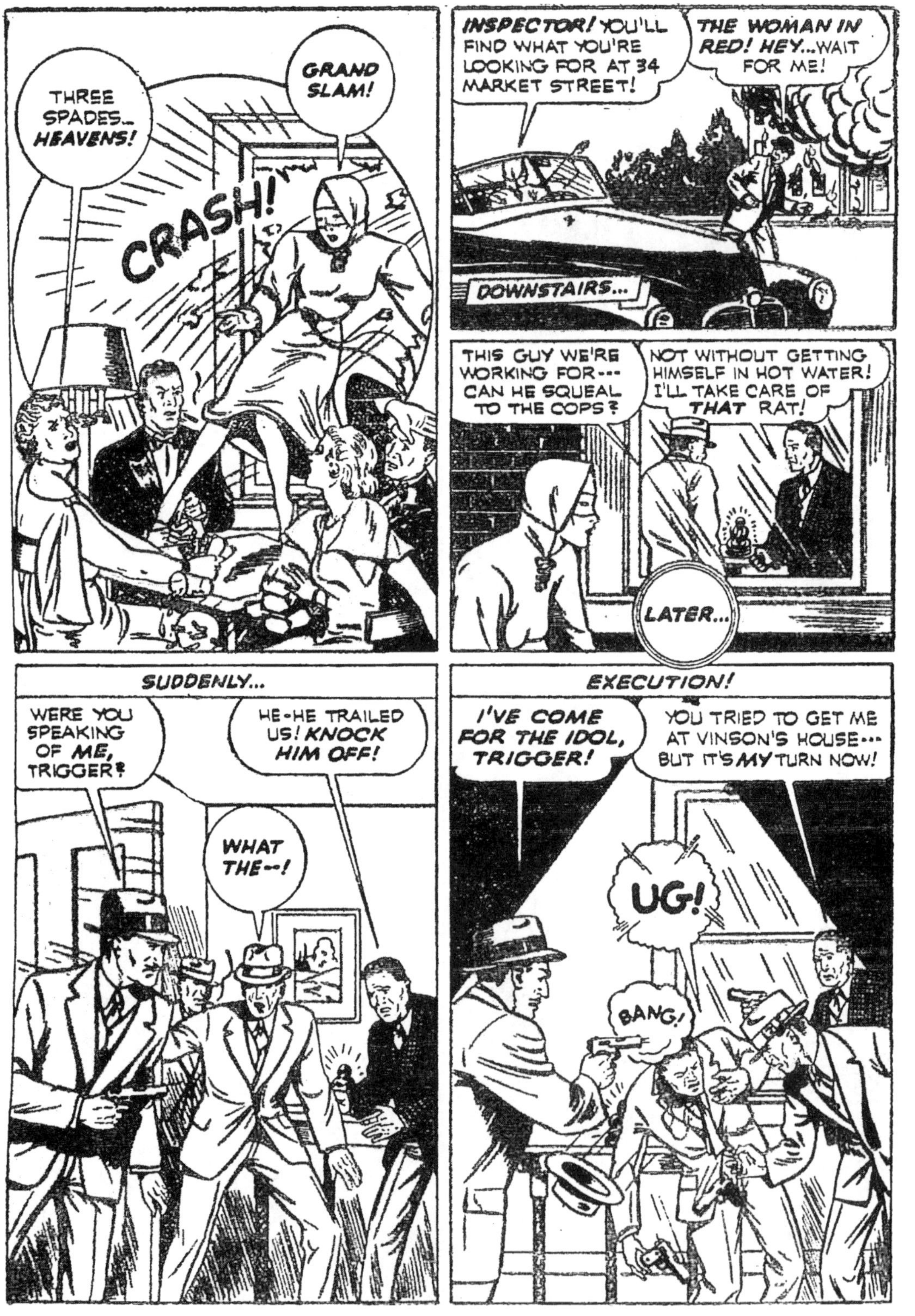
THREE SPADES... HEAVENS!
GRAND SLAM!
CRASH!
INSPECTOR! YOU'LL FIND WHAT YOU'RE LOOKING FOR AT 34 MARKET STREET!
THE WOMAN IN RED! HEY...WAIT FOR ME!
DOWNSTAIRS...
THIS GUY WE'RE WORKING FOR--- CAN HE SQUEAL TO THE COPS?
NOT WITHOUT GETTING HIMSELF IN HOT WATER! I'LL TAKE CARE OF THAT RAT!
LATER...
SUDDENLY...
WERE YOU SPEAKING OF ME, TRIGGER?
HE-HE TRAILED US! KNOCK HIM OFF!
WHAT THE--!
EXECUTION!
I'VE COME FOR THE IDOL, TRIGGER!
YOU TRIED TO GET ME AT VINSON'S HOUSE--- BUT IT'S MY TURN NOW!
UG!
BANG!

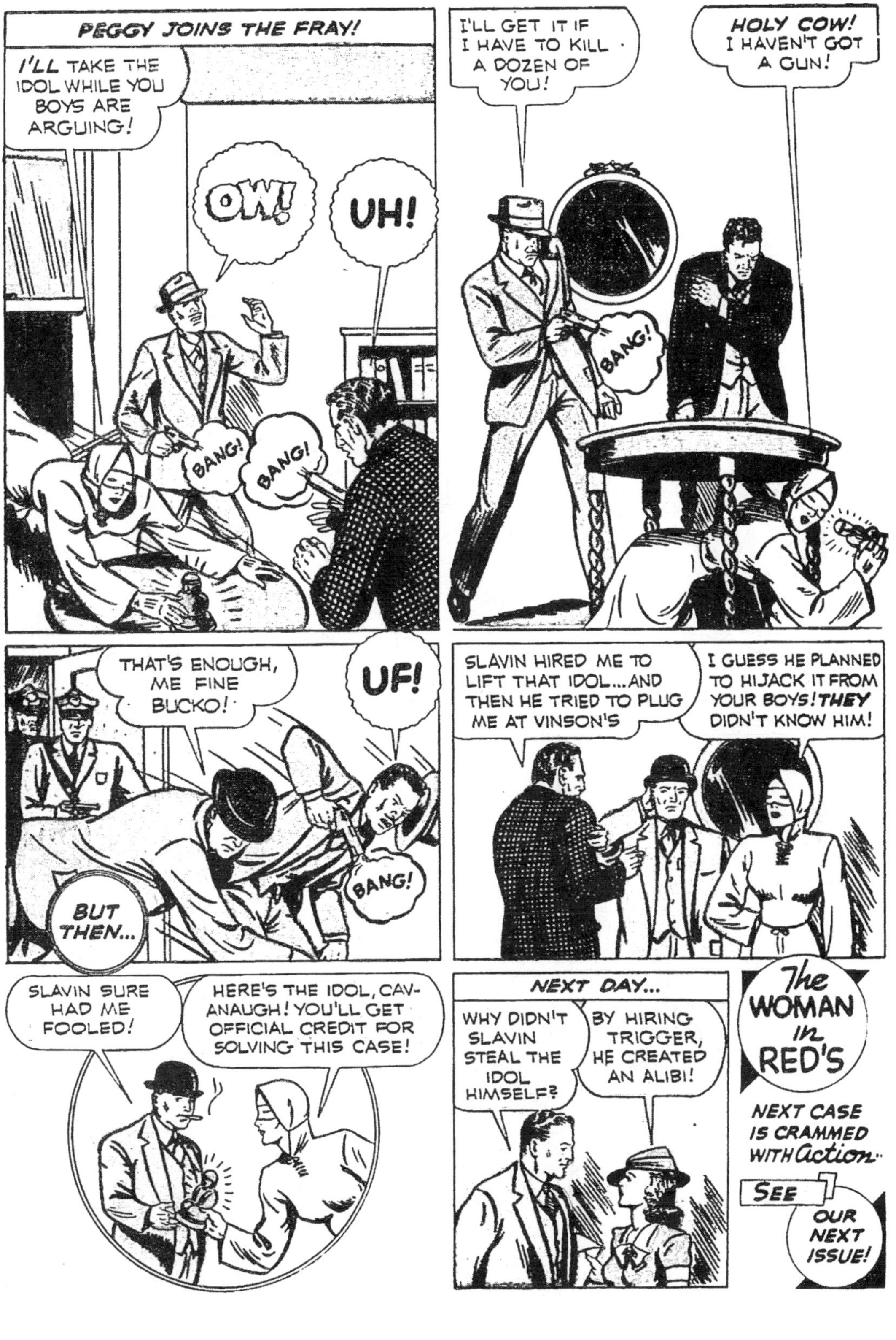
PEGGY JOINS THE FRAY!
I'LL TAKE THE IDOL WHILE YOU BOYS ARE ARGUING!
OW!
UH!
BANG!
BANG!
I'LL GET IT IF I HAVE TO KILL A DOZEN OF YOU!
HOLY COW! I HAVEN'T GOT A GUN!
BANG!
THAT'S ENOUGH, ME FINE BUCKO!
UF!
BANG!
BUT THEN...
SLAVIN HIRED ME TO LIFT THAT IDOL...AND THEN HE TRIED TO PLUG ME AT VINSON'S
I GUESS HE PLANNED TO HIJACK IT FROM YOUR BOYS! THEY DIDN'T KNOW HIM!
SLAVIN SURE HAD ME FOOLED!
HERE'S THE IDOL, CAV-ANAUGH! YOU'LL GET OFFICIAL CREDIT FOR SOLVING THIS CASE!
NEXT DAY...
WHY DIDN'T SLAVIN STEAL THE IDOL HIMSELF?
BY HIRING TRIGGER, HE CREATED AN ALIBI!
The WOMAN in RED'S
NEXT CASE IS CRAMMED WITH Action...
SEE OUR NEXT ISSUE!

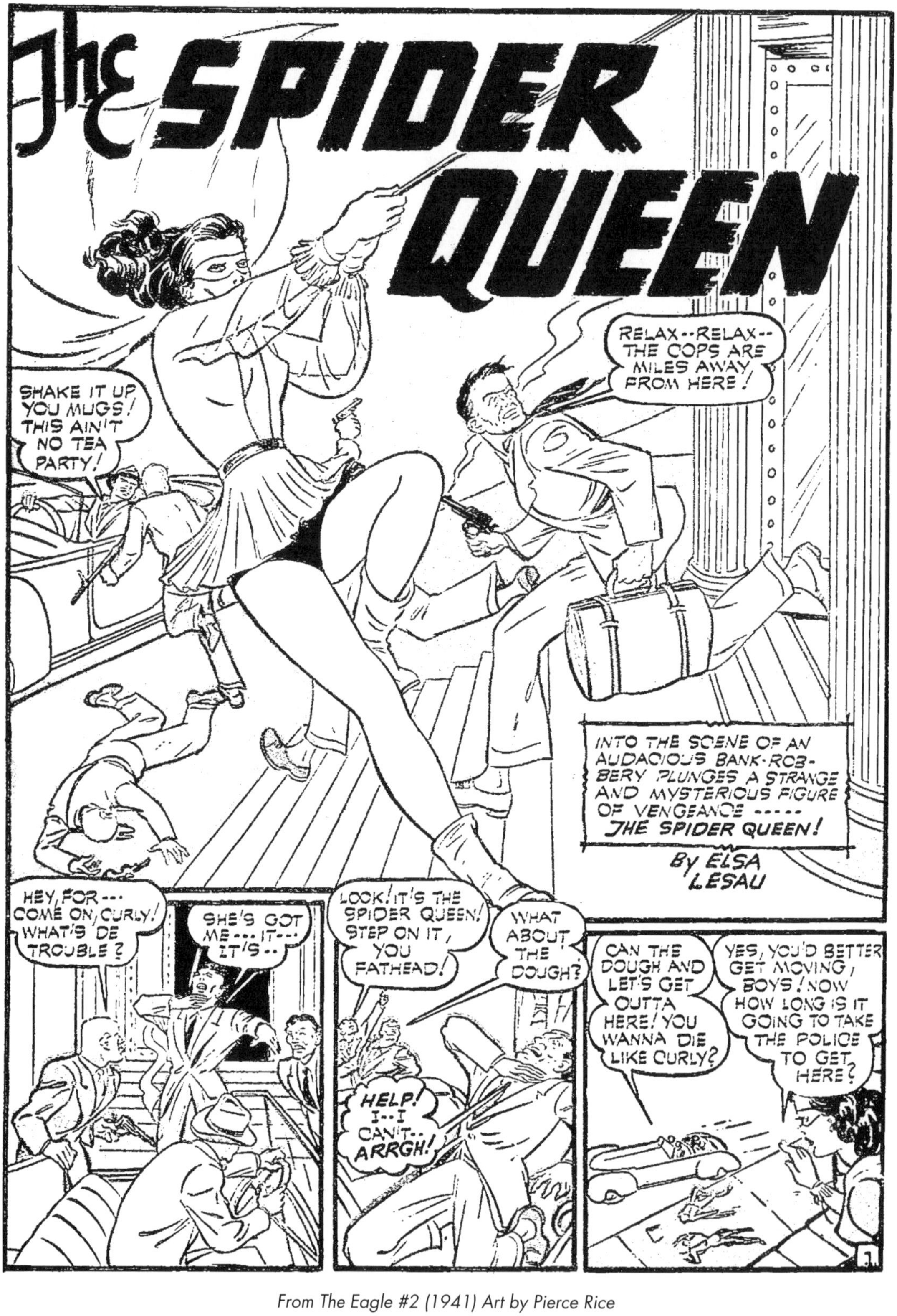
The SPIDER QUEEN
RELAX--RELAX--THE COPS ARE MILES AWAY FROM HERE!
SHAKE IT UP YOU MUGS! THIS AIN'T NO TEA PARTY!
INTO THE SCENE OF AN AUDACIOUS BANK-ROBBERY PLUNGES A STRANGE AND MYSTERIOUS FIGURE OF VENGEANCE ----- THE SPIDER QUEEN!
BY ELSA LESAU
HEY, FOR--- COME ON, CURLY! WHAT'S DE TROUBLE?
SHE'S GOT ME--- IT--- IT'S--
LOOK! IT'S THE SPIDER QUEEN! STEP ON IT, YOU FATHEAD!
WHAT ABOUT THE DOUGH?
HELP! I--I CAN'T.. ARRGH!
CAN THE DOUGH AND LET'S GET OUTTA HERE! YOU WANNA DIE LIKE CURLY?
YES, YOU'D BETTER GET MOVING, BOYS! NOW HOW LONG IS IT GOING TO TAKE THE POLICE TO GET HERE?

From The Eagle #2 (1941) Art by Pierce Rice

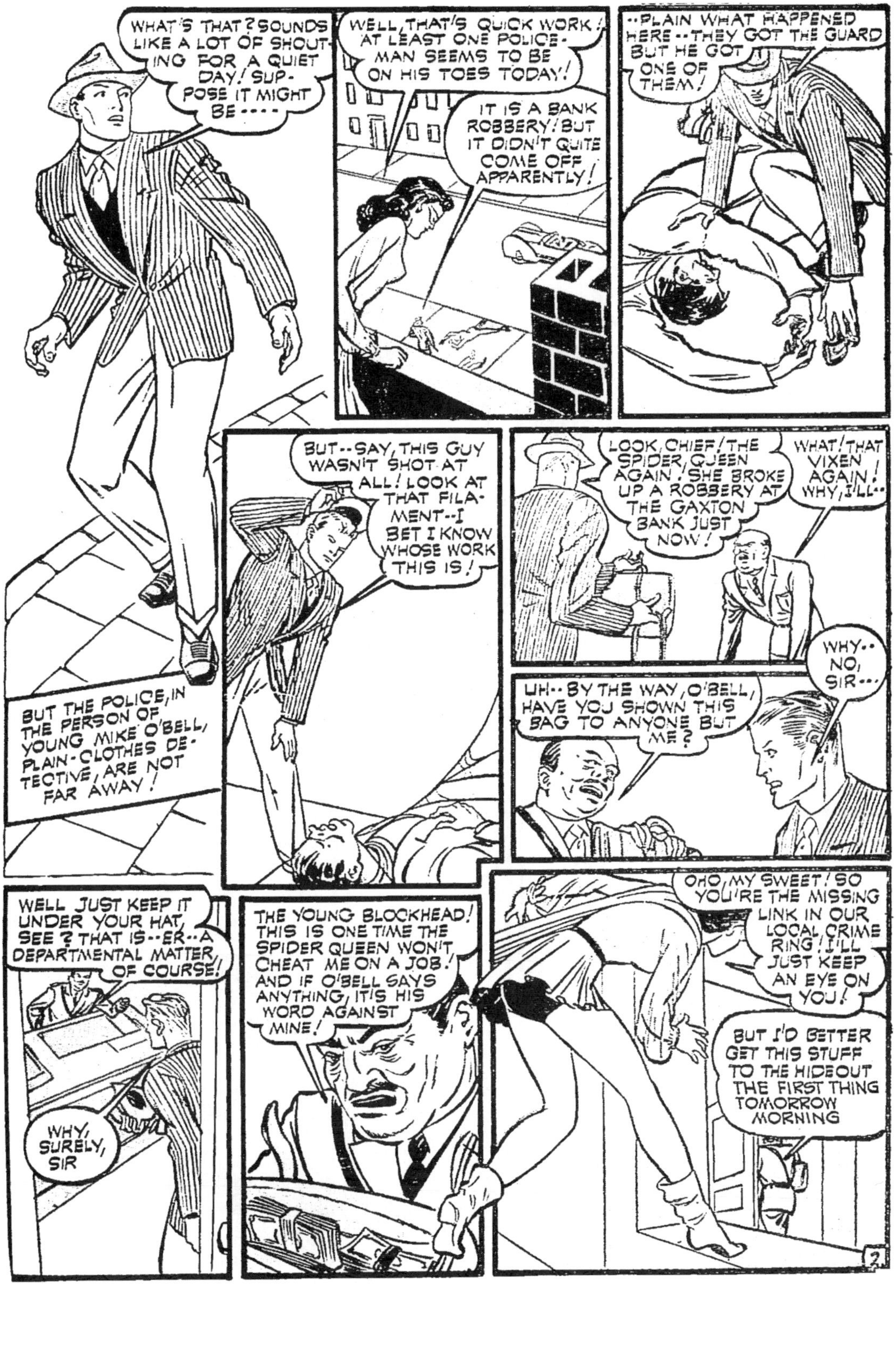
WHAT'S THAT? SOUNDS LIKE A LOT OF SHOUTING FOR A QUIET DAY! SUPPOSE IT MIGHT BE ----
WELL, THAT'S QUICK WORK! AT LEAST ONE POLICEMAN SEEMS TO BE ON HIS TOES TODAY!
IT IS A BANK ROBBERY! BUT IT DIDN'T QUITE COME OFF APPARENTLY!
..PLAIN WHAT HAPPENED HERE..THEY GOT THE GUARD BUT HE GOT ONE OF THEM!
BUT THE POLICE, IN THE PERSON OF YOUNG MIKE O'BELL, PLAIN-CLOTHES DETECTIVE, ARE NOT FAR AWAY!
BUT--SAY, THIS GUY WASN'T SHOT AT ALL! LOOK AT THAT FILAMENT--I BET I KNOW WHOSE WORK THIS IS!
LOOK, CHIEF! THE SPIDER QUEEN AGAIN! SHE BROKE UP A ROBBERY AT THE GAXTON BANK JUST NOW!
WHAT! THAT VIXEN AGAIN! WHY, I'LL..
UH..BY THE WAY, O'BELL, HAVE YOU SHOWN THIS BAG TO ANYONE BUT ME?
WHY.. NO, SIR...
WELL JUST KEEP IT UNDER YOUR HAT, SEE? THAT IS--ER--A DEPARTMENTAL MATTER, OF COURSE!
WHY, SURELY, SIR
THE YOUNG BLOCKHEAD! THIS IS ONE TIME THE SPIDER QUEEN WON'T CHEAT ME ON A JOB! AND IF O'BELL SAYS ANYTHING, IT'S HIS WORD AGAINST MINE!
OHO, MY SWEET! SO YOU'RE THE MISSING LINK IN OUR LOCAL CRIME RING! I'LL JUST KEEP AN EYE ON YOU!
BUT I'D BETTER GET THIS STUFF TO THE HIDEOUT THE FIRST THING TOMORROW MORNING
2

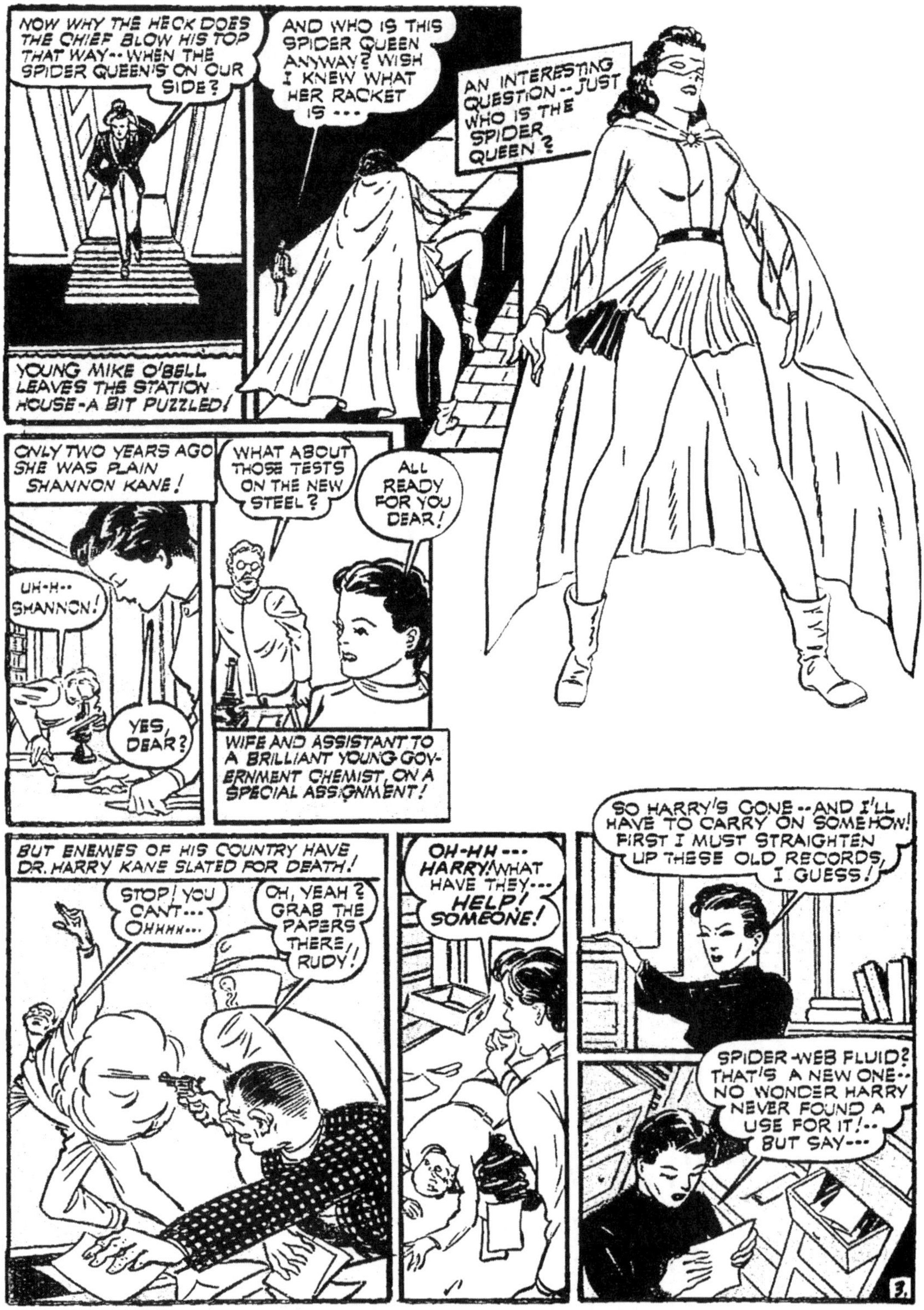
NOW WHY THE HECK DOES THE CHIEF BLOW HIS TOP THAT WAY-- WHEN THE SPIDER QUEEN'S ON OUR SIDE?
YOUNG MIKE O'BELL LEAVES THE STATION HOUSE-A BIT PUZZLED!
AND WHO IS THIS SPIDER QUEEN ANYWAY? WISH I KNEW WHAT HER RACKET IS ---
AN INTERESTING QUESTION -- JUST WHO IS THE SPIDER QUEEN?
ONLY TWO YEARS AGO SHE WAS PLAIN SHANNON KANE!
UH-H-- SHANNON!
YES, DEAR?
WHAT ABOUT THOSE TESTS ON THE NEW STEEL?
ALL READY FOR YOU DEAR!
WIFE AND ASSISTANT TO A BRILLIANT YOUNG GOVERNMENT CHEMIST, ON A SPECIAL ASSIGNMENT!
BUT ENEMIES OF HIS COUNTRY HAVE DR. HARRY KANE SLATED FOR DEATH!
STOP! YOU CANT--- OHHHH---
OH, YEAH? GRAB THE PAPERS THERE, RUDY!
OH-HH--- HARRY! WHAT HAVE THEY--- HELP! SOMEONE!
SO HARRY'S GONE -- AND I'LL HAVE TO CARRY ON SOMEHOW! FIRST I MUST STRAIGHTEN UP THESE OLD RECORDS, I GUESS!
SPIDER-WEB FLUID? THAT'S A NEW ONE-- NO WONDER HARRY NEVER FOUND A USE FOR IT!-- BUT SAY---
3.

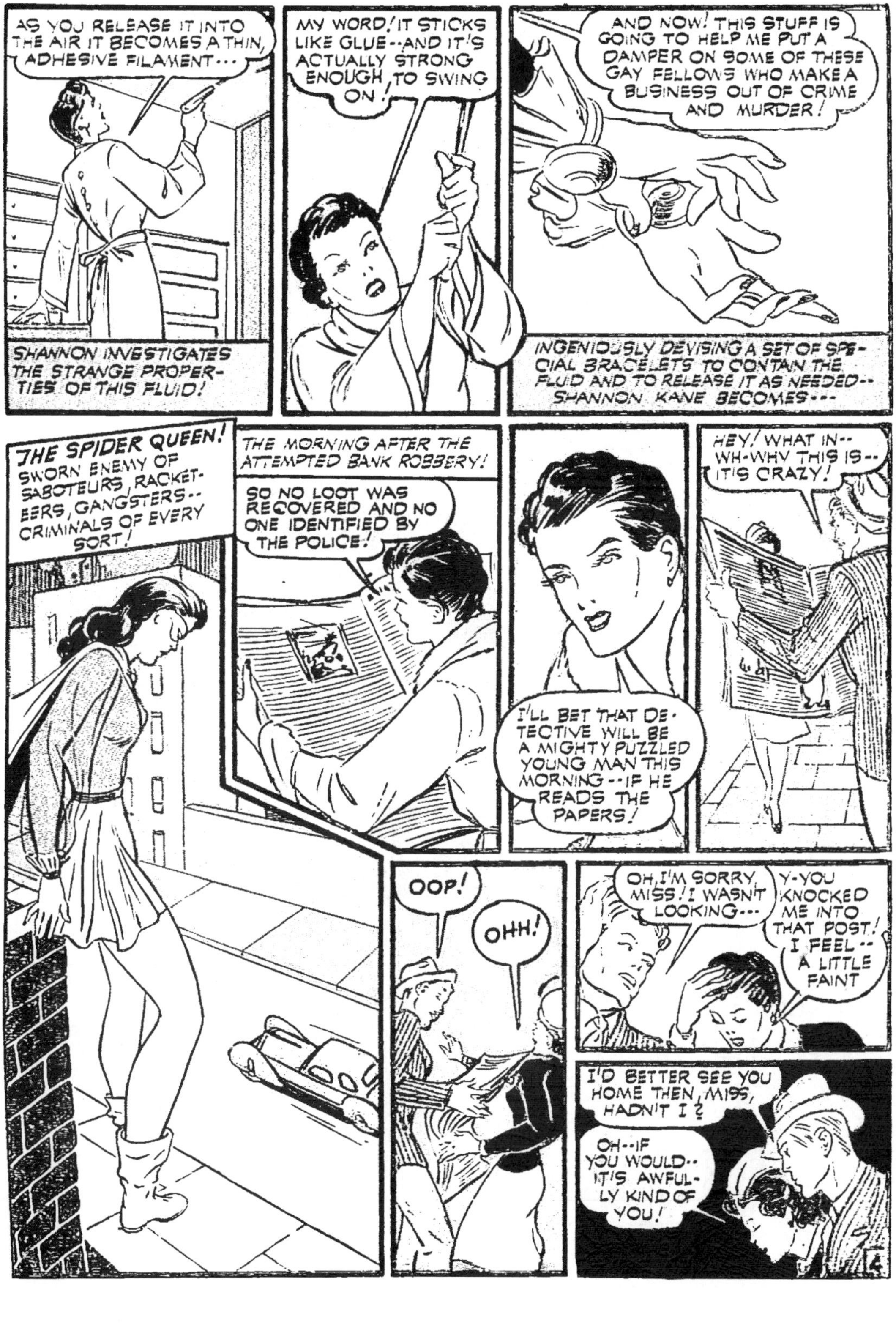
AS YOU RELEASE IT INTO THE AIR IT BECOMES A THIN, ADHESIVE FILAMENT...
SHANNON INVESTIGATES THE STRANGE PROPERTIES OF THIS FLUID!
MY WORD! IT STICKS LIKE GLUE--AND IT'S ACTUALLY STRONG ENOUGH TO SWING ON!
AND NOW! THIS STUFF IS GOING TO HELP ME PUT A DAMPER ON SOME OF THESE GAY FELLOWS WHO MAKE A BUSINESS OUT OF CRIME AND MURDER!
INGENIOUSLY DEVISING A SET OF SPECIAL BRACELETS TO CONTAN THE FLUID AND TO RELEASE IT AS NEEDED--SHANNON KANE BECOMES---
THE SPIDER QUEEN! SWORN ENEMY OF SABOTEURS, RACKETEERS, GANGSTERS--CRIMINALS OF EVERY SORT!
THE MORNING AFTER THE ATTEMPTED BANK ROBBERY!
SO NO LOOT WAS RECOVERED AND NO ONE IDENTIFIED BY THE POLICE!
I'LL BET THAT DETECTIVE WILL BE A MIGHTY PUZZLED YOUNG MAN THIS MORNING--IF HE READS THE PAPERS!
HEY! WHAT IN--WH-WHY THIS IS--IT'S CRAZY!
OOP!
OHH!
OH, I'M SORRY, MISS! I WASN'T LOOKING---
Y-YOU KNOCKED ME INTO THAT POST! I FEEL--A LITTLE FAINT
I'D BETTER SEE YOU HOME THEN, MISS, HADN'T I?
OH--IF YOU WOULD--IT'S AWFULLY KIND OF YOU!

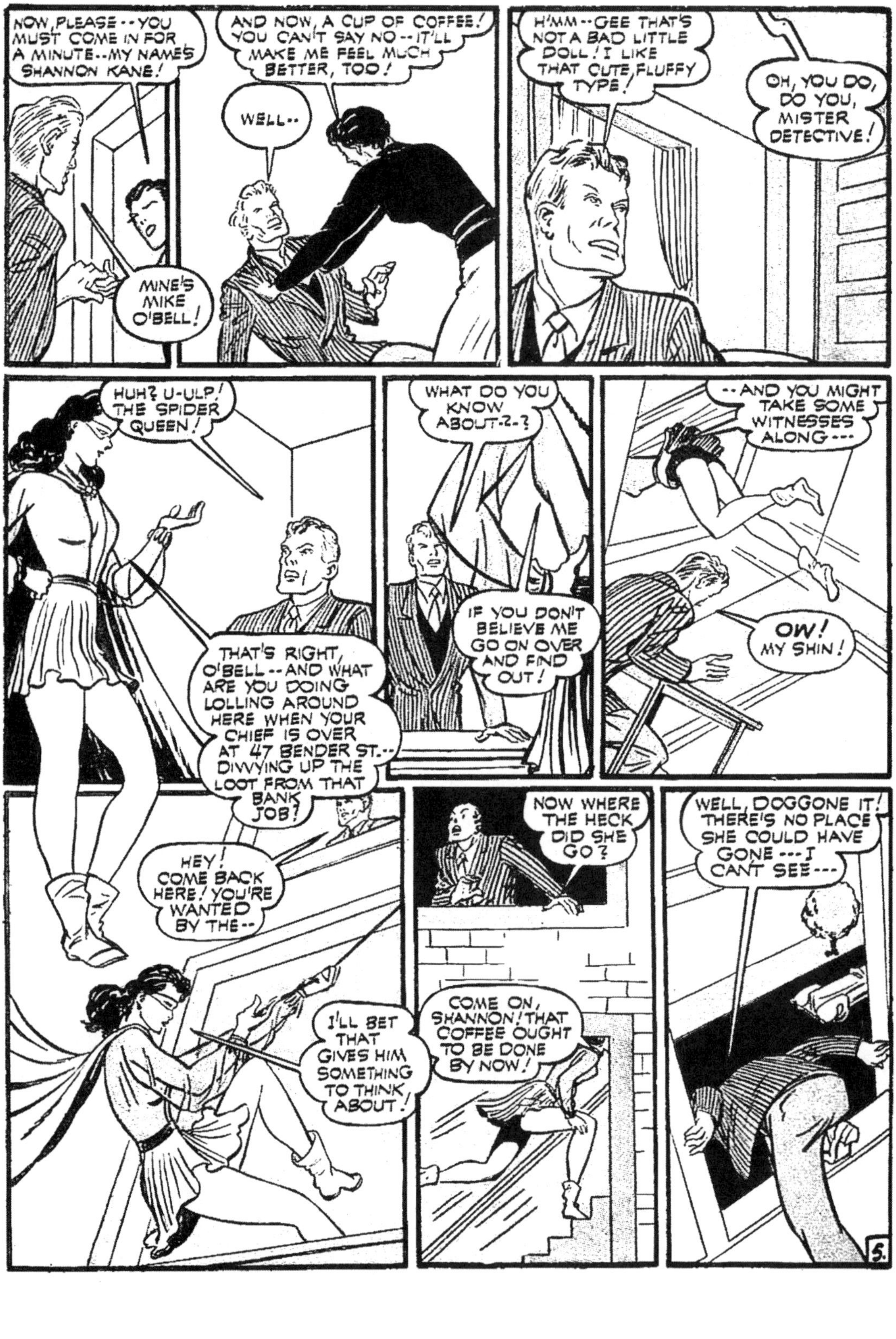
NOW, PLEASE--YOU MUST COME IN FOR A MINUTE--MY NAME'S SHANNON KANE!
MINE'S MIKE O'BELL!
AND NOW, A CUP OF COFFEE! YOU CAN'T SAY NO--IT'LL MAKE ME FEEL MUCH BETTER, TOO!
WELL--
H'MM--GEE THAT'S NOT A BAD LITTLE DOLL! I LIKE THAT CUTE, FLUFFY TYPE!
OH, YOU DO, DO YOU, MISTER DETECTIVE!
HUH? U-ULP! THE SPIDER QUEEN!
THAT'S RIGHT, O'BELL--AND WHAT ARE YOU DOING LOLLING AROUND HERE WHEN YOUR CHIEF IS OVER AT 47 BENDER ST.--DIVVYING UP THE LOOT FROM THAT BANK JOB?
WHAT DO YOU KNOW ABOUT-Z-?
IF YOU DON'T BELIEVE ME GO ON OVER AND FIND OUT!
--AND YOU MIGHT TAKE SOME WITNESSES ALONG---
OW! MY SHIN!
HEY! COME BACK HERE! YOU'RE WANTED BY THE--
I'LL BET THAT GIVES HIM SOMETHING TO THINK ABOUT!
NOW WHERE THE HECK DID SHE GO?
COME ON, SHANNON! THAT COFFEE OUGHT TO BE DONE BY NOW!
WELL, DOGGONE IT! THERE'S NO PLACE SHE COULD HAVE GONE---I CAN'T SEE---
5.

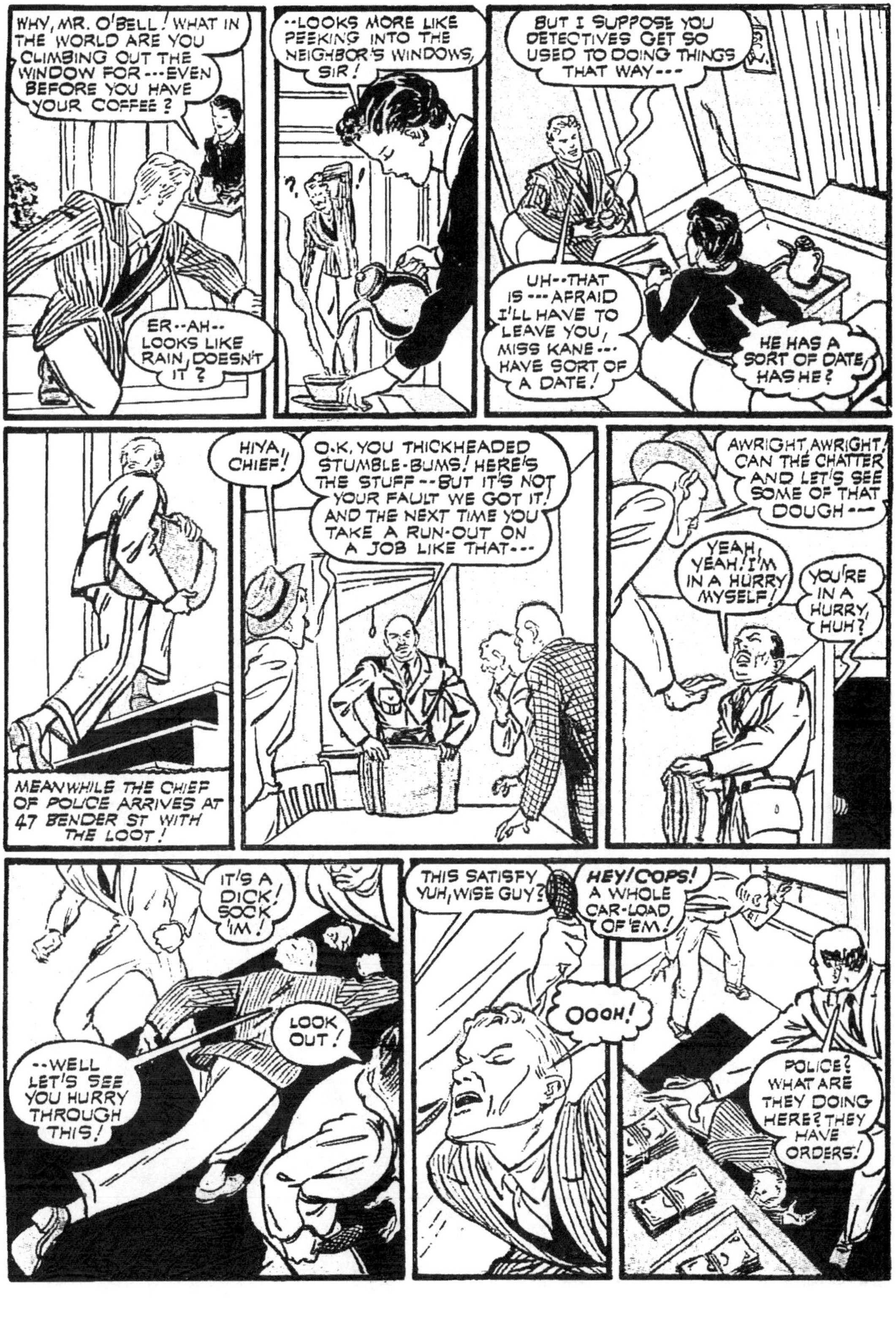
WHY, MR. O'BELL! WHAT IN THE WORLD ARE YOU CLIMBING OUT THE WINDOW FOR---EVEN BEFORE YOU HAVE YOUR COFFEE?
ER--AH--LOOKS LIKE RAIN, DOESN'T IT?
--LOOKS MORE LIKE PEEKING INTO THE NEIGHBOR'S WINDOWS, SIR!
?
!
BUT I SUPPOSE YOU DETECTIVES GET SO USED TO DOING THINGS THAT WAY---
UH--THAT IS---AFRAID I'LL HAVE TO LEAVE YOU, MISS KANE---HAVE SORT OF A DATE!
HE HAS A SORT OF DATE, HAS HE?
MEANWHILE THE CHIEF OF POLICE ARRIVES AT 47 BENDER ST WITH THE LOOT!
HIYA, CHIEF!
O.K. YOU THICKHEADED STUMBLE-BUMS! HERE'S THE STUFF--BUT IT'S NOT YOUR FAULT WE GOT IT! AND THE NEXT TIME YOU TAKE A RUN-OUT ON A JOB LIKE THAT---
AWRIGHT, AWRIGHT! CAN THE CHATTER AND LET'S SEE SOME OF THAT DOUGH--
YEAH, YEAH! I'M IN A HURRY MYSELF!
YOU'RE IN A HURRY, HUH?
IT'S A DICK! SOCK 'IM!
LOOK OUT!
--WELL LET'S SEE YOU HURRY THROUGH THIS!
THIS SATISFY YUH, WISE GUY?
OOOH!
HEY! COPS! A WHOLE CAR-LOAD OF 'EM!
POLICE? WHAT ARE THEY DOING HERE? THEY HAVE ORDERS!

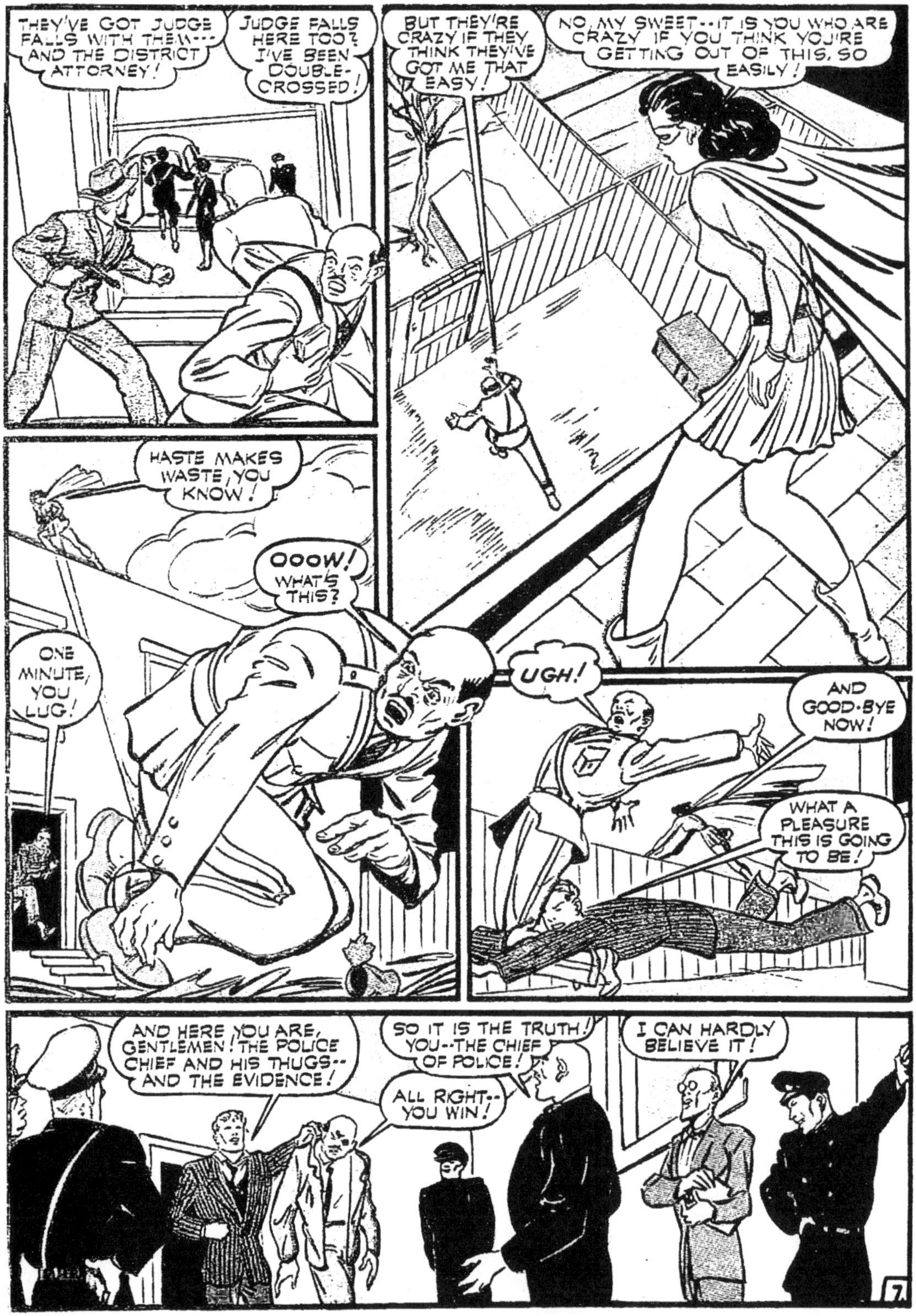
THEY'VE GOT JUDGE FALLS WITH THEM--- AND THE DISTRICT ATTORNEY!
JUDGE FALLS HERE TOO? I'VE BEEN DOUBLE-CROSSED!
BUT THEY'RE CRAZY IF THEY THINK THEY'VE GOT ME THAT EASY!
NO, MY SWEET--IT IS YOU WHO ARE CRAZY IF YOU THINK YOU'RE GETTING OUT OF THIS, SO EASILY!
HASTE MAKES WASTE, YOU KNOW!
OOOW! WHAT'S THIS?
ONE MINUTE, YOU LUG!
UGH!
AND GOOD-BYE NOW!
WHAT A PLEASURE THIS IS GOING TO BE!
AND HERE YOU ARE, GENTLEMEN! THE POLICE CHIEF AND HIS THUGS--AND THE EVIDENCE!
SO IT IS THE TRUTH! YOU--THE CHIEF OF POLICE!
ALL RIGHT--YOU WIN!
I CAN HARDLY BELIEVE IT!
7

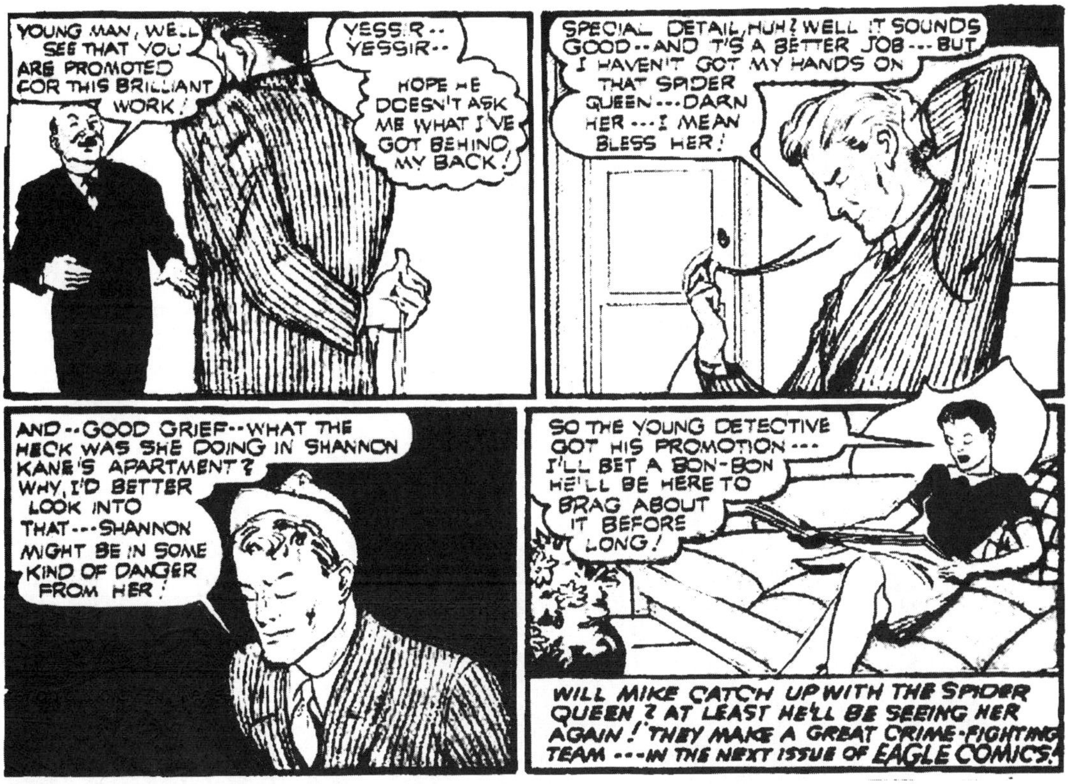
YOUNG MAN, WE'LL SEE THAT YOU ARE PROMOTED FOR THIS BRILLIANT WORK!
YESSIR-- YESSIR--
HOPE HE DOESN'T ASK ME WHAT I'VE GOT BEHIND MY BACK!
SPECIAL DETAIL, HUH? WELL IT SOUNDS GOOD--AND IT'S A BETTER JOB---BUT I HAVEN'T GOT MY HANDS ON THAT SPIDER QUEEN---DARN HER---I MEAN BLESS HER!
AND--GOOD GRIEF--WHAT THE HECK WAS SHE DOING IN SHANNON KANE'S APARTMENT? WHY, I'D BETTER LOOK INTO THAT---SHANNON MIGHT BE IN SOME KIND OF DANGER FROM HER!
SO THE YOUNG DETECTIVE GOT HIS PROMOTION--- I'LL BET A BON-BON HE'LL BE HERE TO BRAG ABOUT IT BEFORE LONG!
WILL MIKE CATCH UP WITH THE SPIDER QUEEN? AT LEAST HE'LL BE SEEING HER AGAIN! THEY MAKE A GREAT CRIME-FIGHTING TEAM---IN THE NEXT ISSUE OF EAGLE COMICS!

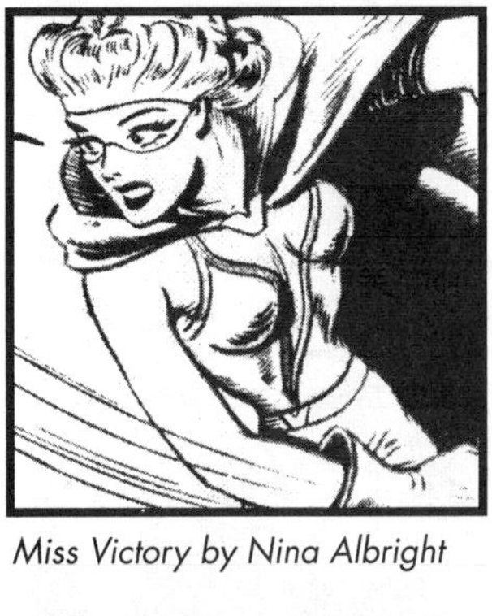

Miss Victory by Nina Albright

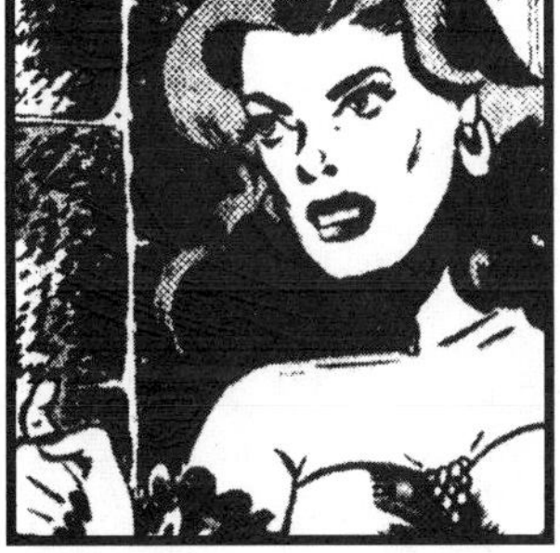

Senorita Rio by Lily Renée

WOMEN ARTISTS IN THE COMICS

Women had been working as cartoonists since the early years of the 20th century, often specializing in fanciful comic strips about children or pretty young flappers. When Tarpe Mills created her superheroine Miss Fury in 1941, it signaled a change for female comic artists. By the early 1940s, artists like Ruth Atkinson, Ann Brewster, Barbara Hall and Fran Hopper were drawing superhero stories for a number of different comic books. When male artists were drafted to serve in WWII, it provided even more opportunities for women to draw heroic stories in comics. Artists Lily Renée, Nina Albright, Pauline Loth, and Jill Elgin often illustrated the adventures of daring wartime heroines like Senorita Rio, Miss Victory, and the Girl Commandos. When male artists returned from the war, they took back the job of drawing adventure comics. The women moved on to draw romance comics, or left the industry entirely.

After twenty years most of these women artists' names would be largely forgotten, just like the heroines they had illustrated. It wasn't until the 1980s that female artists began to once more become a presence in mainstream superhero comics.

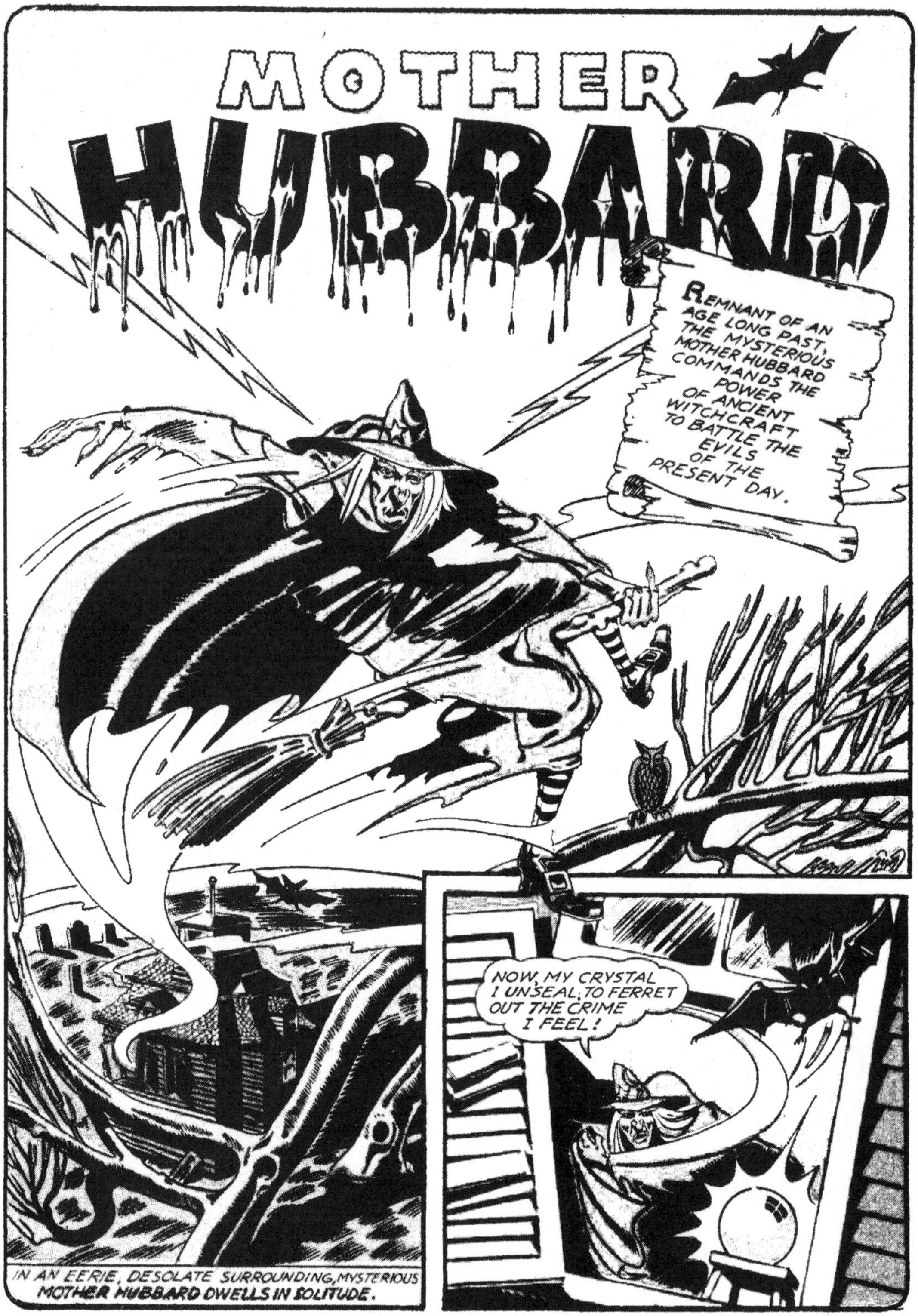
MOTHER HUBBARD
REMNANT OF AN AGE LONG PAST, THE MYSTERIOUS MOTHER HUBBARD COMMANDS THE POWER OF ANCIENT WITCHCRAFT TO BATTLE THE EVILS OF THE PRESENT DAY.
IN AN EERIE, DESOLATE SURROUNDING, MYSTERIOUS MOTHER HUBBARD DWELLS IN SOLITUDE.
NOW, MY CRYSTAL I UNSEAL, TO FERRET OUT THE CRIME I FEEL!

From Scoop Comics #1 (1941) Artist Unknown

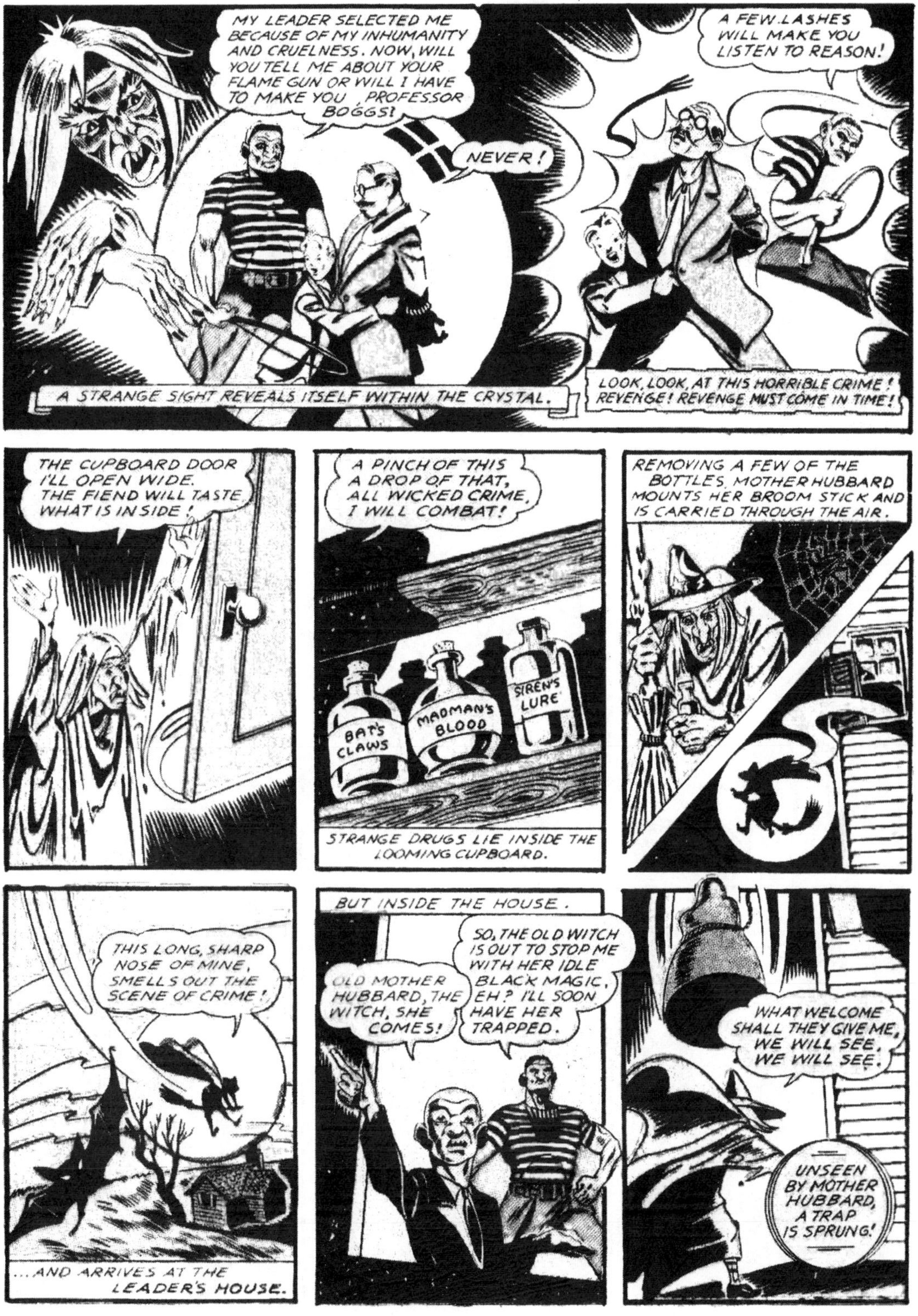
MY LEADER SELECTED ME BECAUSE OF MY INHUMANITY AND CRUELNESS. NOW, WILL YOU TELL ME ABOUT YOUR FLAME GUN OR WILL I HAVE TO MAKE YOU , PROFESSOR BOGGS!
NEVER!
A STRANGE SIGHT REVEALS ITSELF WITHIN THE CRYSTAL.
A FEW LASHES WILL MAKE YOU LISTEN TO REASON!
LOOK, LOOK, AT THIS HORRIBLE CRIME! REVENGE! REVENGE MUST COME IN TIME!
THE CUPBOARD DOOR I'LL OPEN WIDE. THE FIEND WILL TASTE WHAT IS INSIDE!
A PINCH OF THIS A DROP OF THAT, ALL WICKED CRIME, I WILL COMBAT!
BAT'S CLAWS
MADMAN'S BLOOD
SIREN'S LURE
STRANGE DRUGS LIE INSIDE THE LOOMING CUPBOARD.
REMOVING A FEW OF THE BOTTLES, MOTHER HUBBARD MOUNTS HER BROOM STICK AND IS CARRIED THROUGH THE AIR.
THIS LONG, SHARP NOSE OF MINE, SMELLS OUT THE SCENE OF CRIME!
...AND ARRIVES AT THE LEADER'S HOUSE.
BUT INSIDE THE HOUSE.
OLD MOTHER HUBBARD, THE WITCH, SHE COMES!
SO, THE OLD WITCH IS OUT TO STOP ME WITH HER IDLE BLACK MAGIC, EH? I'LL SOON HAVE HER TRAPPED.
WHAT WELCOME SHALL THEY GIVE ME, WE WILL SEE, WE WILL SEE.
UNSEEN BY MOTHER HUBBARD, A TRAP IS SPRUNG!

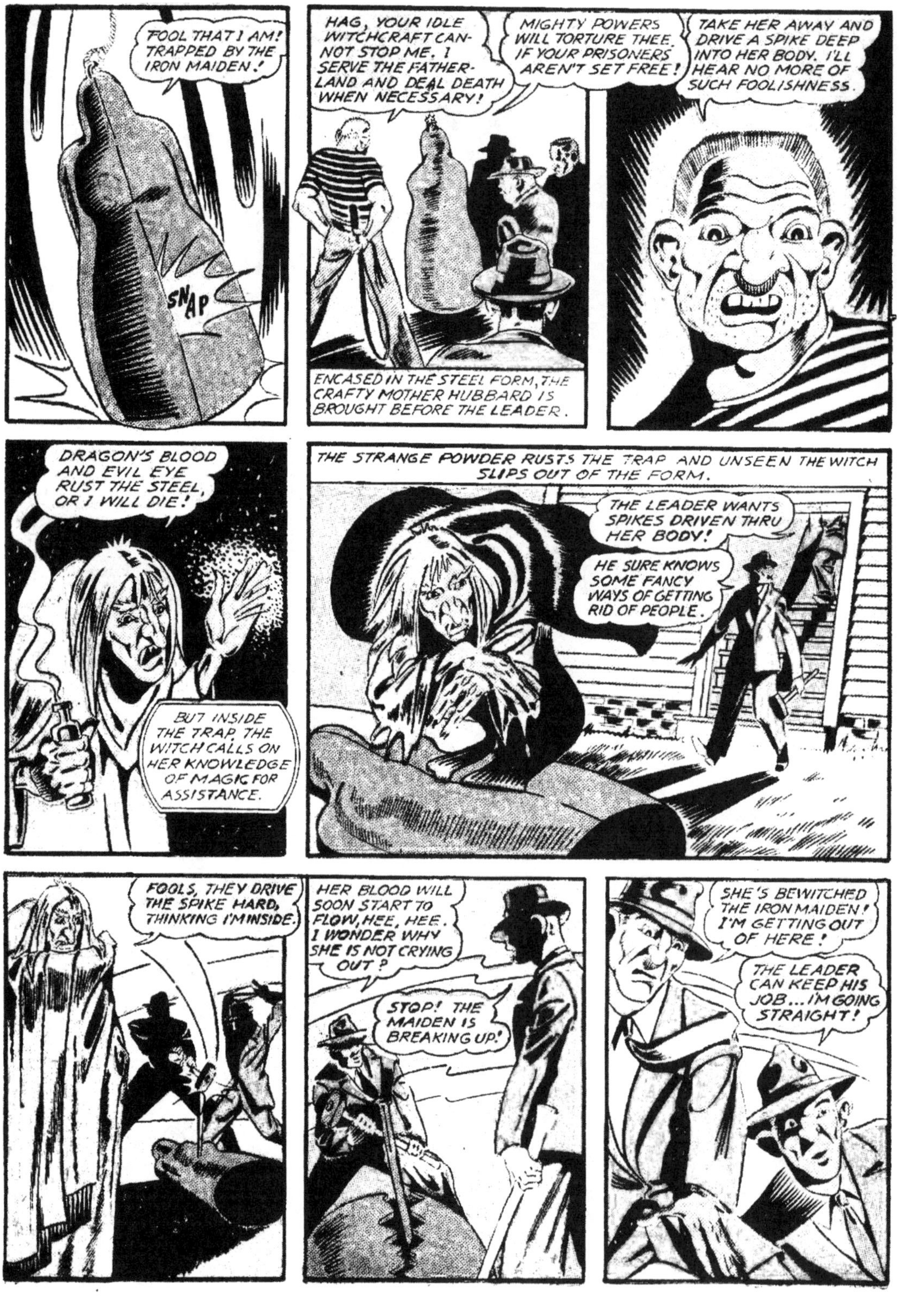
FOOL THAT I AM! TRAPPED BY THE IRON MAIDEN!
SNAP
HAG, YOUR IDLE WITCHCRAFT CAN-NOT STOP ME. I SERVE THE FATHER-LAND AND DEAL DEATH WHEN NECESSARY!
MIGHTY POWERS WILL TORTURE THEE IF YOUR PRISONERS AREN'T SET FREE!
ENCASED IN THE STEEL FORM, THE CRAFTY MOTHER HUBBARD IS BROUGHT BEFORE THE LEADER.
TAKE HER AWAY AND DRIVE A SPIKE DEEP INTO HER BODY. I'LL HEAR NO MORE OF SUCH FOOLISHNESS.
DRAGON'S BLOOD AND EVIL EYE RUST THE STEEL, OR I WILL DIE!
BUT INSIDE THE TRAP, THE WITCH CALLS ON HER KNOWLEDGE OF MAGIC FOR ASSISTANCE.
THE STRANGE POWDER RUSTS THE TRAP AND UNSEEN THE WITCH SLIPS OUT OF THE FORM.
THE LEADER WANTS SPIKES DRIVEN THRU HER BODY!
HE SURE KNOWS SOME FANCY WAYS OF GETTING RID OF PEOPLE.
FOOLS, THEY DRIVE THE SPIKE HARD, THINKING I'M INSIDE.
HER BLOOD WILL SOON START TO FLOW, HEE, HEE. I WONDER WHY SHE IS NOT CRYING OUT?
STOP! THE MAIDEN IS BREAKING UP!
SHE'S BEWITCHED THE IRON MAIDEN! I'M GETTING OUT OF HERE!
THE LEADER CAN KEEP HIS JOB... I'M GOING STRAIGHT!

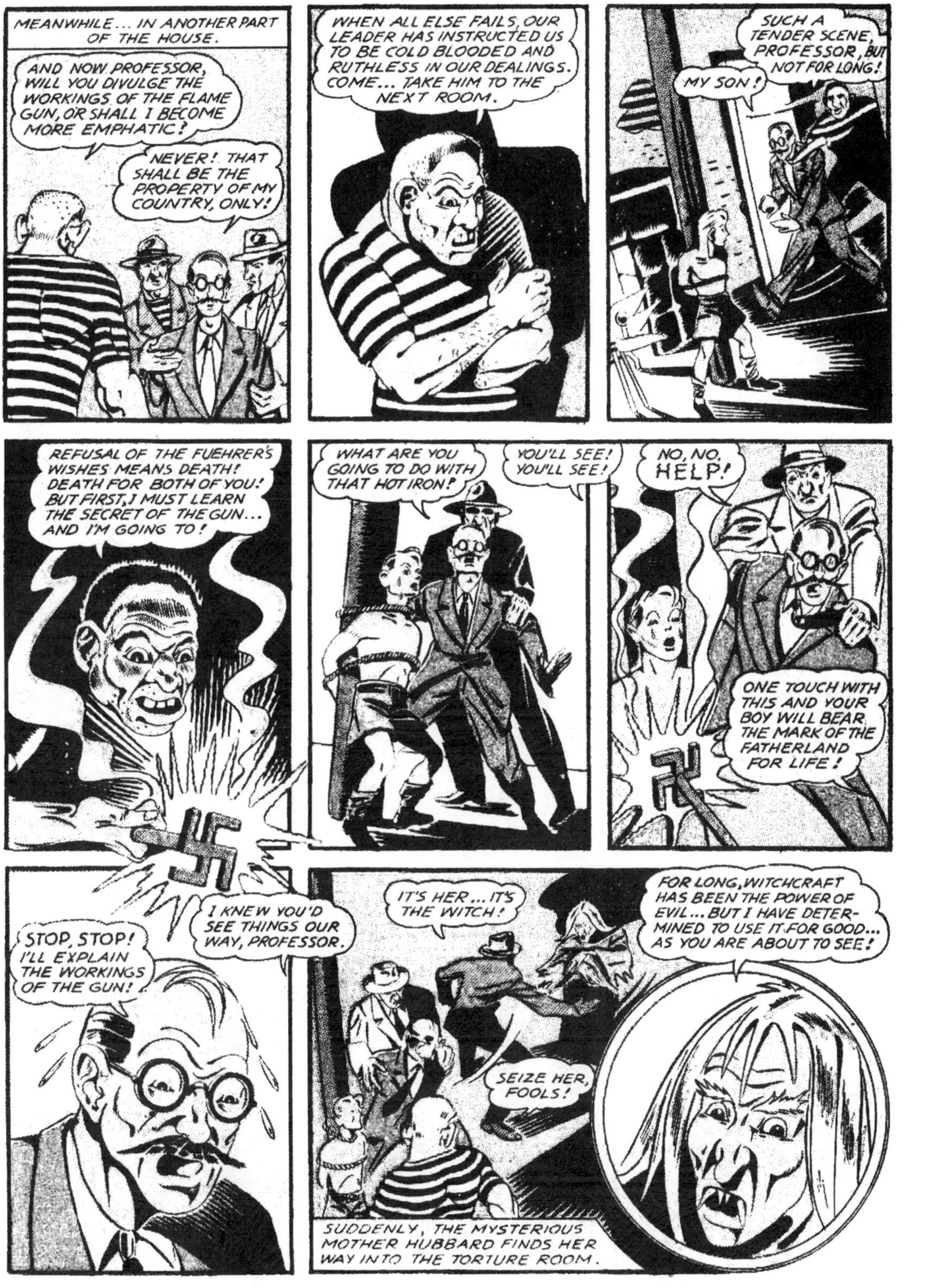
MEANWHILE... IN ANOTHER PART OF THE HOUSE.
AND NOW PROFESSOR, WILL YOU DIVULGE THE WORKINGS OF THE FLAME GUN, OR SHALL I BECOME MORE EMPHATIC?
NEVER! THAT SHALL BE THE PROPERTY OF MY COUNTRY, ONLY!
WHEN ALL ELSE FAILS, OUR LEADER HAS INSTRUCTED US TO BE COLD BLOODED AND RUTHLESS IN OUR DEALINGS. COME... TAKE HIM TO THE NEXT ROOM.
MY SON!
SUCH A TENDER SCENE, PROFESSOR, BUT NOT FOR LONG!
REFUSAL OF THE FUEHRER'S WISHES MEANS DEATH! DEATH FOR BOTH OF YOU! BUT FIRST, I MUST LEARN THE SECRET OF THE GUN... AND I'M GOING TO!
WHAT ARE YOU GOING TO DO WITH THAT HOT IRON?
YOU'LL SEE! YOU'LL SEE!
NO, NO. HELP!
ONE TOUCH WITH THIS AND YOUR BOY WILL BEAR THE MARK OF THE FATHERLAND FOR LIFE!
STOP, STOP! I'LL EXPLAIN THE WORKINGS OF THE GUN!
I KNEW YOU'D SEE THINGS OUR WAY, PROFESSOR.
IT'S HER... IT'S THE WITCH!
FOR LONG, WITCHCRAFT HAS BEEN THE POWER OF EVIL... BUT I HAVE DETERMINED TO USE IT FOR GOOD... AS YOU ARE ABOUT TO SEE!
SEIZE HER, FOOLS!
SUDDENLY, THE MYSTERIOUS MOTHER HUBBARD FINDS HER WAY INTO THE TORTURE ROOM.

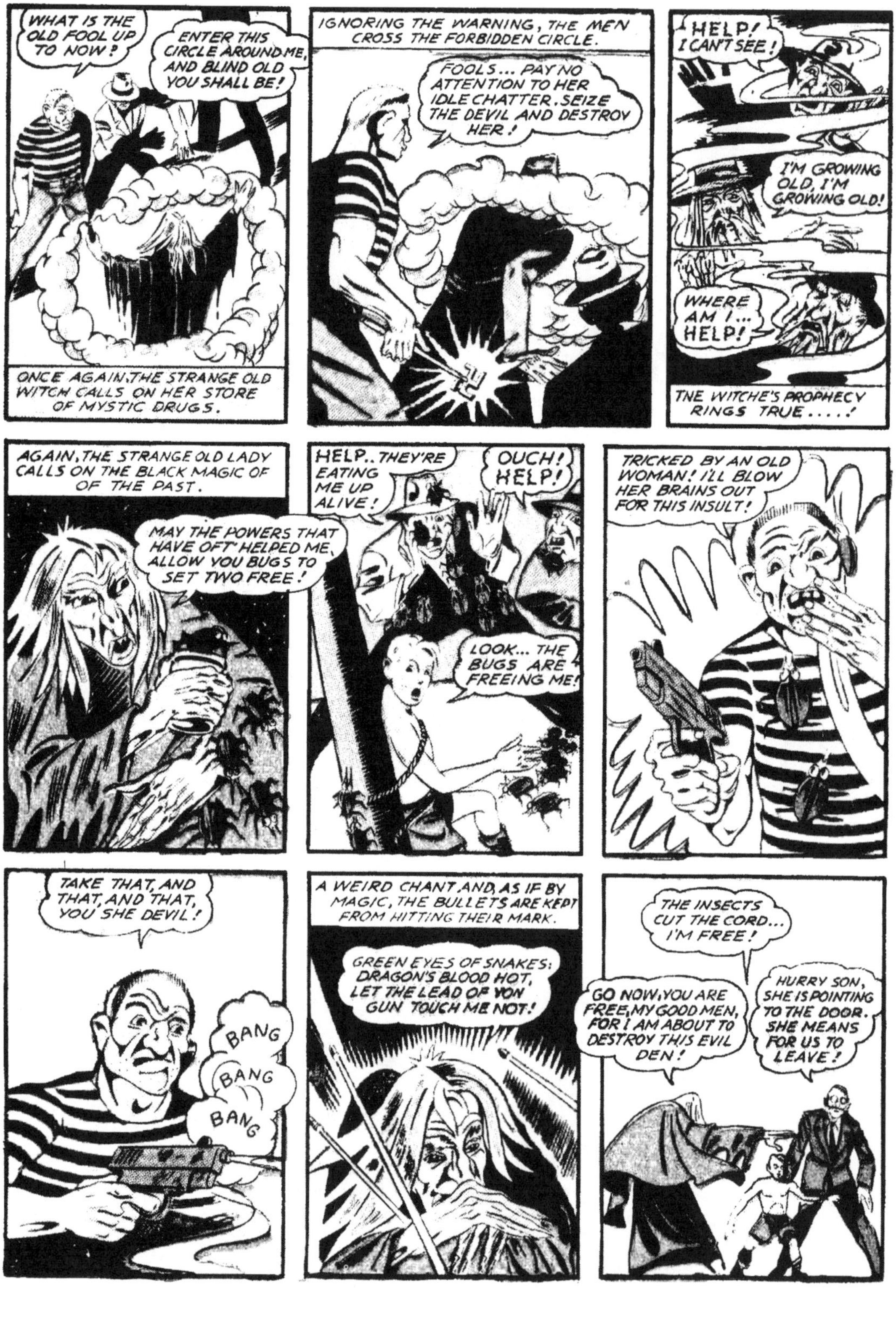
WHAT IS THE OLD FOOL UP TO NOW?
ENTER THIS CIRCLE AROUND ME, AND BLIND OLD YOU SHALL BE!
ONCE AGAIN, THE STRANGE OLD WITCH CALLS ON HER STORE OF MYSTIC DRUGS.
IGNORING THE WARNING, THE MEN CROSS THE FORBIDDEN CIRCLE.
FOOLS... PAY NO ATTENTION TO HER IDLE CHATTER. SEIZE THE DEVIL AND DESTROY HER!
HELP! I CAN'T SEE!
I'M GROWING OLD, I'M GROWING OLD!
WHERE AM I... HELP!
TNE WITCHE'S PROPHECY RINGS TRUE.....!
AGAIN, THE STRANGE OLD LADY CALLS ON THE BLACK MAGIC OF OF THE PAST.
MAY THE POWERS THAT HAVE OFT' HELPED ME, ALLOW YOU BUGS TO SET TWO FREE!
HELP.. THEY'RE EATING ME UP ALIVE!
OUCH! HELP!
LOOK... THE BUGS ARE FREEING ME!
TRICKED BY AN OLD WOMAN! I'LL BLOW HER BRAINS OUT FOR THIS INSULT!
TAKE THAT, AND THAT, AND THAT, YOU SHE DEVIL!
BANG
BANG
BANG
A WEIRD CHANT, AND, AS IF BY MAGIC, THE BULLETS ARE KEPT FROM HITTING THEIR MARK.
GREEN EYES OF SNAKES: DRAGON'S BLOOD HOT, LET THE LEAD OF YON GUN TOUCH ME NOT!
THE INSECTS CUT THE CORD... I'M FREE!
GO NOW, YOU ARE FREE, MY GOOD MEN, FOR I AM ABOUT TO DESTROY THIS EVIL DEN!
HURRY SON, SHE IS POINTING TO THE DOOR. SHE MEANS FOR US TO LEAVE!

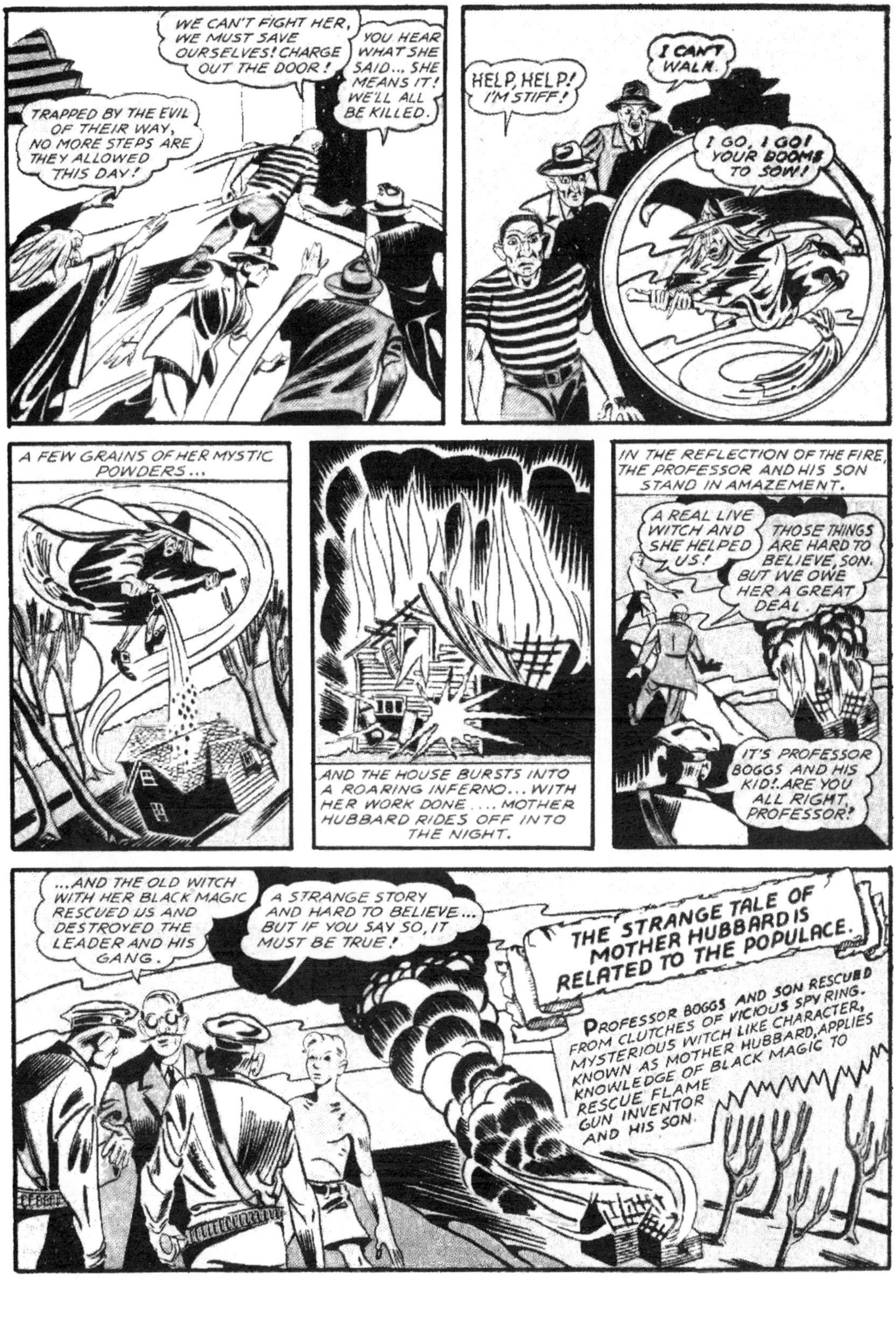

TRAPPED BY THE EVIL OF THEIR WAY, NO MORE STEPS ARE THEY ALLOWED THIS DAY!
WE CAN'T FIGHT HER, WE MUST SAVE OURSELVES! CHARGE OUT THE DOOR!
YOU HEAR WHAT SHE SAID... SHE MEANS IT! WE'LL ALL BE KILLED.
HELP, HELP! I'M STIFF!
I CAN'T WALK.
I GO, I GO! YOUR DOOMS TO SOW!
A FEW GRAINS OF HER MYSTIC POWDERS...
AND THE HOUSE BURSTS INTO A ROARING INFERNO... WITH HER WORK DONE.... MOTHER HUBBARD RIDES OFF INTO THE NIGHT.
IN THE REFLECTION OF THE FIRE, THE PROFESSOR AND HIS SON STAND IN AMAZEMENT.
A REAL LIVE WITCH AND SHE HELPED US!
THOSE THINGS ARE HARD TO BELIEVE, SON. BUT WE OWE HER A GREAT DEAL
IT'S PROFESSOR BOGGS AND HIS KID!. ARE YOU ALL RIGHT, PROFESSOR?
...AND THE OLD WITCH WITH HER BLACK MAGIC RESCUED US AND DESTROYED THE LEADER AND HIS GANG.
A STRANGE STORY AND HARD TO BELIEVE... BUT IF YOU SAY SO, IT MUST BE TRUE!
THE STRANGE TALE OF MOTHER HUBBARD IS RELATED TO THE POPULACE.
PROFESSOR BOGGS AND SON RESCUED FROM CLUTCHES OF VICIOUS SPY RING. MYSTERIOUS WITCH LIKE CHARACTER, KNOWN AS MOTHER HUBBARD, APPLIES KNOWLEDGE OF BLACK MAGIC TO RESCUE FLAME GUN INVENTOR AND HIS SON.

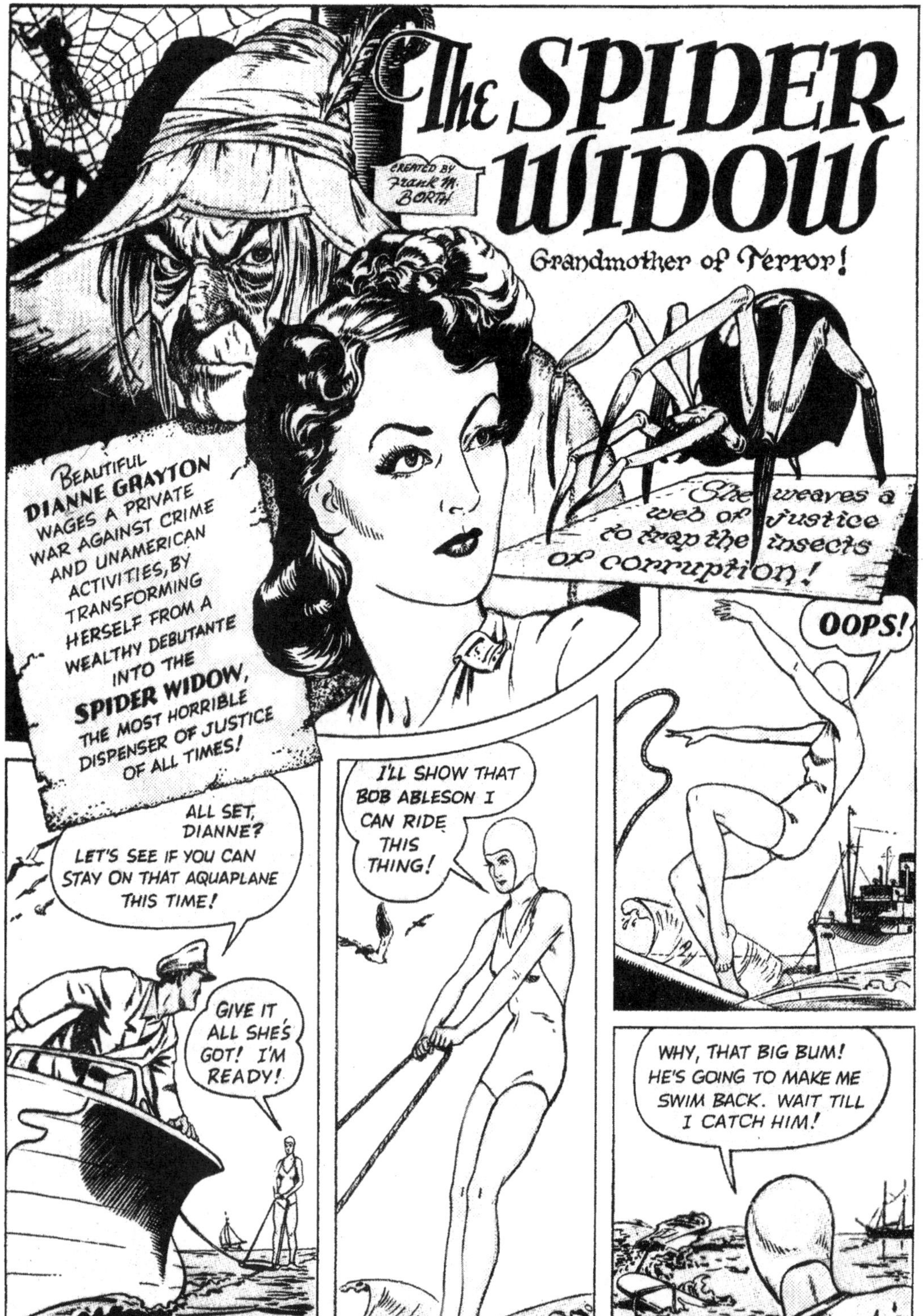
The SPIDER WIDOW
CREATED BY Frank M. BORTH
Grandmother of Terror!
BEAUTIFUL DIANNE GRAYTON WAGES A PRIVATE WAR AGAINST CRIME AND UNAMERICAN ACTIVITIES, BY TRANSFORMING HERSELF FROM A WEALTHY DEBUTANTE INTO THE SPIDER WIDOW, THE MOST HORRIBLE DISPENSER OF JUSTICE OF ALL TIMES!
She weaves a web of justice to trap the insects of corruption!
ALL SET, DIANNE? LET'S SEE IF YOU CAN STAY ON THAT AQUAPLANE THIS TIME!
GIVE IT ALL SHE'S GOT! I'M READY!
I'LL SHOW THAT BOB ABLESON I CAN RIDE THIS THING!
OOPS!
WHY, THAT BIG BUM! HE'S GOING TO MAKE ME SWIM BACK. WAIT TILL I CATCH HIM!

From Feature Comics #58 (1942) Art by Frank M. Borth

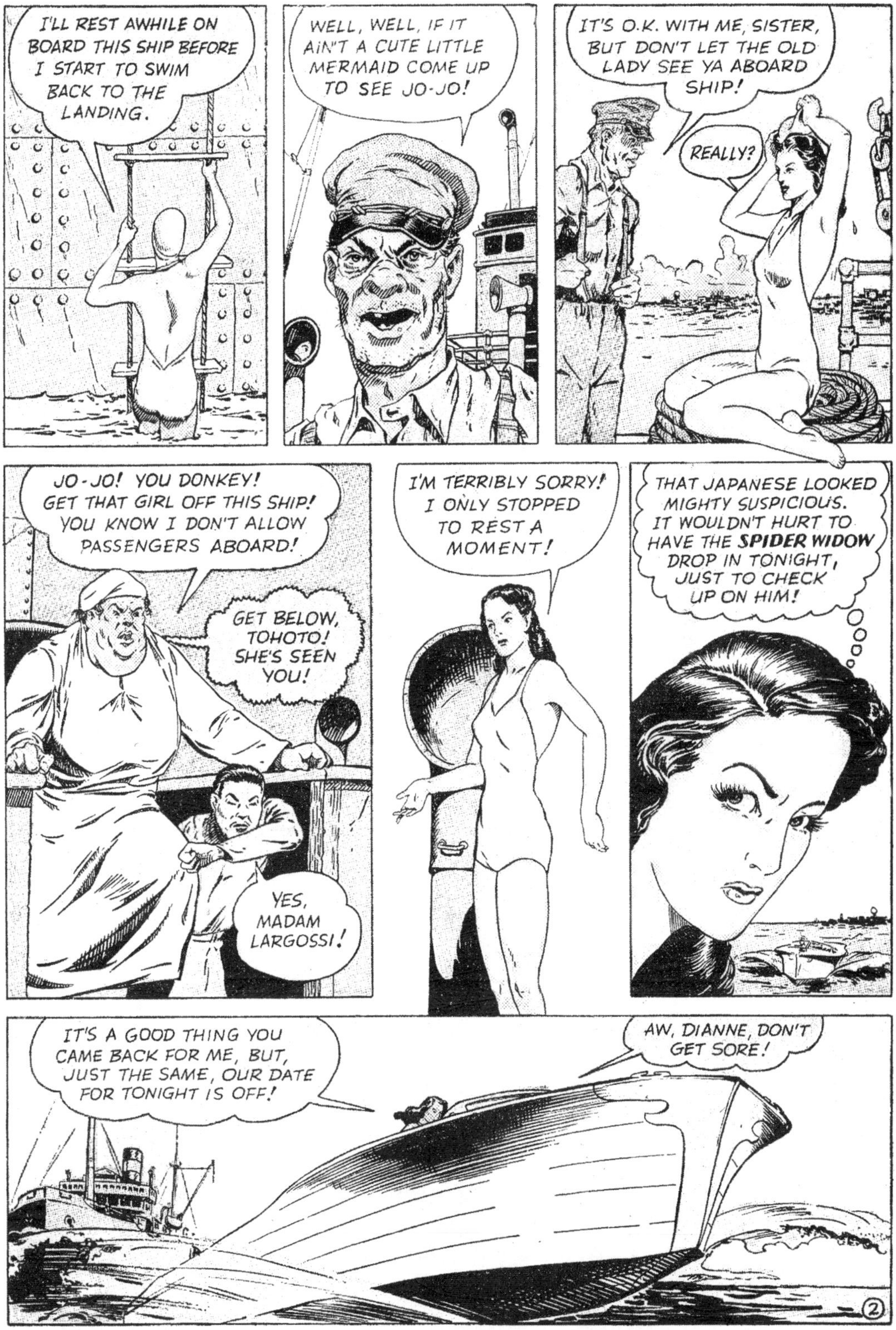
I'LL REST AWHILE ON BOARD THIS SHIP BEFORE I START TO SWIM BACK TO THE LANDING.
WELL, WELL, IF IT AIN'T A CUTE LITTLE MERMAID COME UP TO SEE JO-JO!
IT'S O.K. WITH ME, SISTER, BUT DON'T LET THE OLD LADY SEE YA ABOARD SHIP!
REALLY?
JO-JO! YOU DONKEY! GET THAT GIRL OFF THIS SHIP! YOU KNOW I DON'T ALLOW PASSENGERS ABOARD!
GET BELOW, TOHOTO! SHE'S SEEN YOU!
YES, MADAM LARGOSSI!
I'M TERRIBLY SORRY! I ONLY STOPPED TO REST A MOMENT!
THAT JAPANESE LOOKED MIGHTY SUSPICIOUS. IT WOULDN'T HURT TO HAVE THE SPIDER WIDOW DROP IN TONIGHT, JUST TO CHECK UP ON HIM!
IT'S A GOOD THING YOU CAME BACK FOR ME, BUT, JUST THE SAME, OUR DATE FOR TONIGHT IS OFF!
AW, DIANNE, DON'T GET SORE!
2

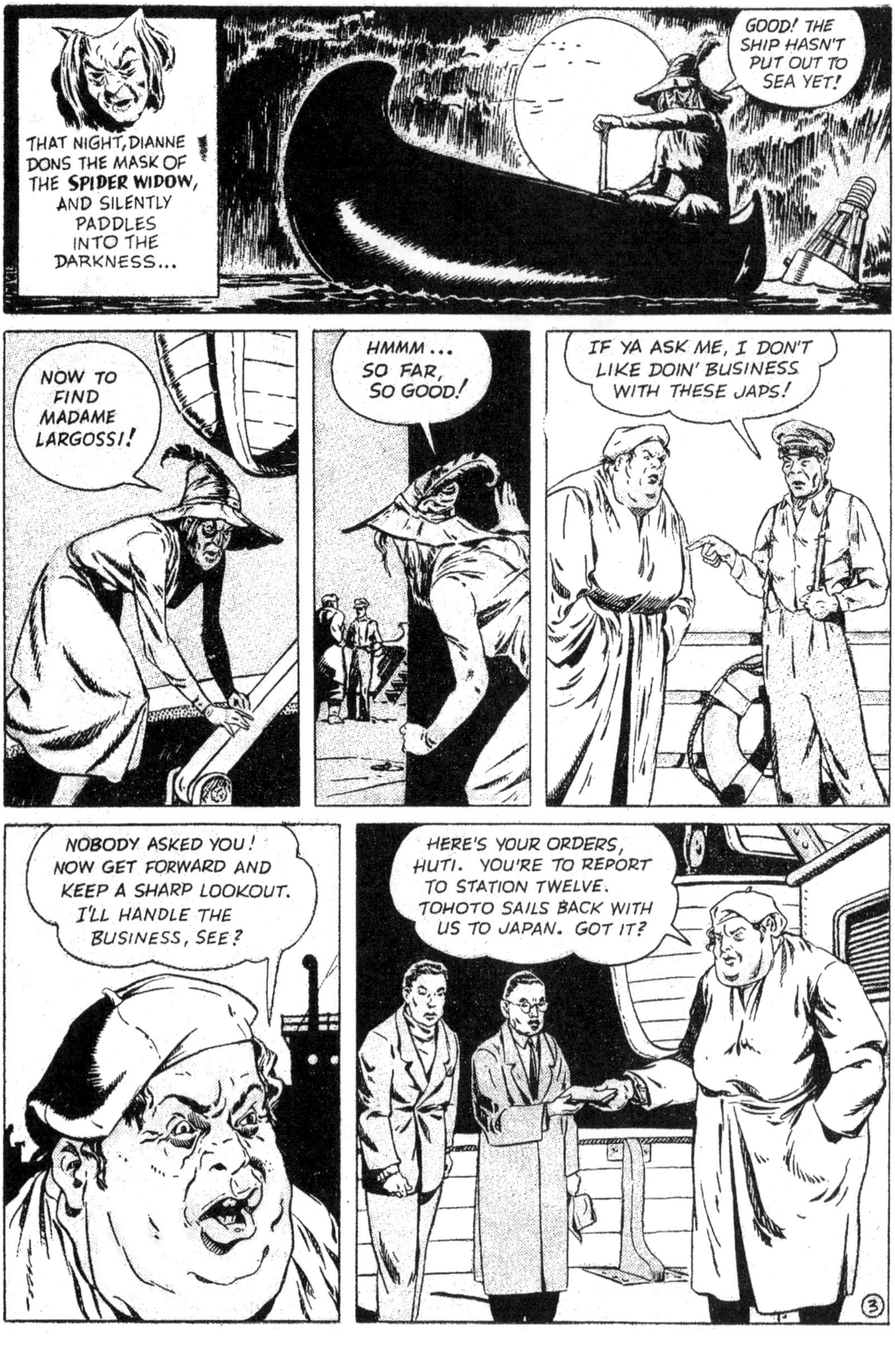
THAT NIGHT, DIANNE DONS THE MASK OF THE SPIDER WIDOW, AND SILENTLY PADDLES INTO THE DARKNESS...
GOOD! THE SHIP HASN'T PUT OUT TO SEA YET!
NOW TO FIND MADAME LARGOSSI!
HMMM... SO FAR, SO GOOD!
IF YA ASK ME, I DON'T LIKE DOIN' BUSINESS WITH THESE JAPS!
NOBODY ASKED YOU! NOW GET FORWARD AND KEEP A SHARP LOOKOUT. I'LL HANDLE THE BUSINESS, SEE?
HERE'S YOUR ORDERS, HUTI. YOU'RE TO REPORT TO STATION TWELVE. TOHOTO SAILS BACK WITH US TO JAPAN. GOT IT?
3

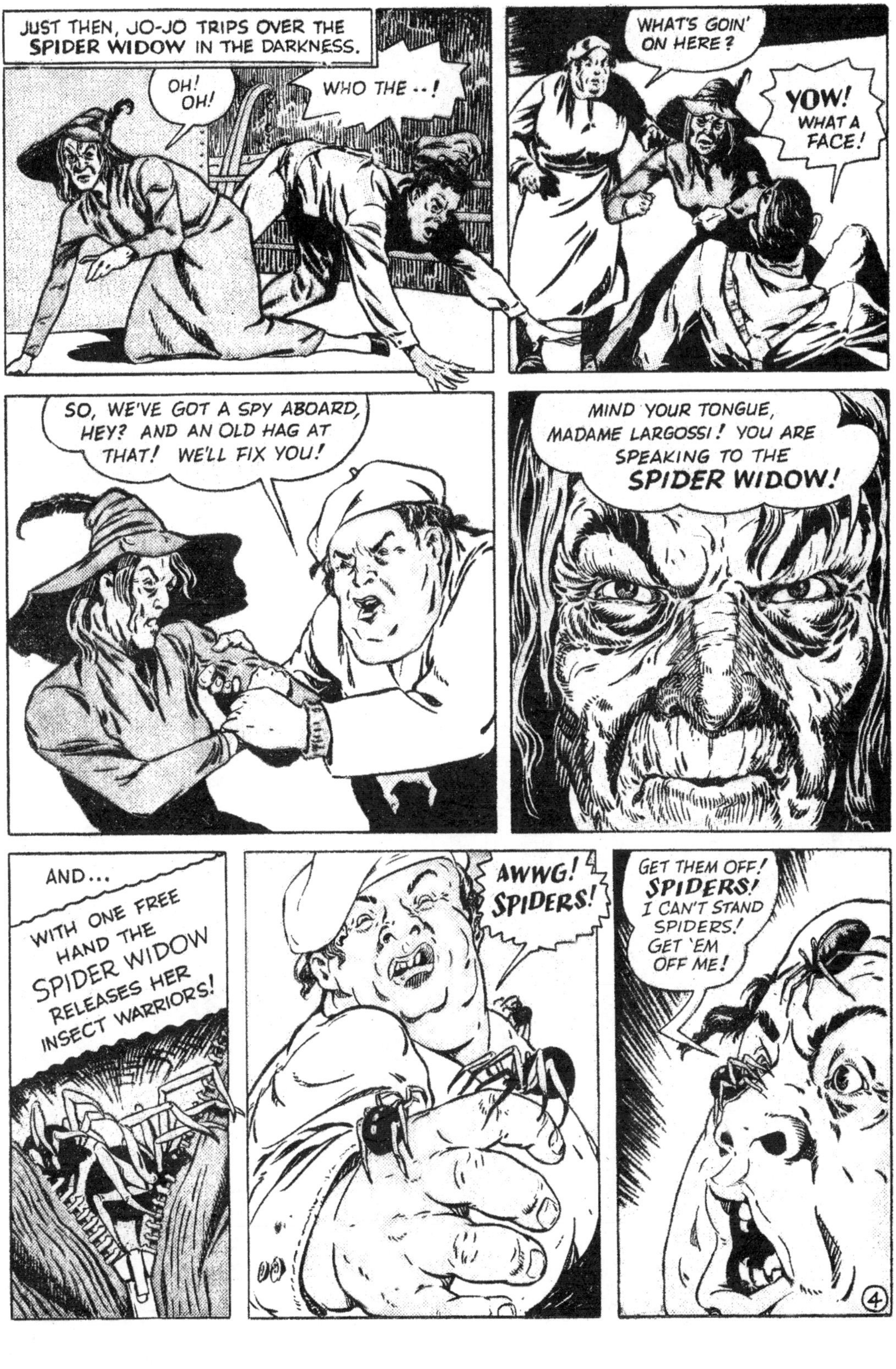
JUST THEN, JO-JO TRIPS OVER THE SPIDER WIDOW IN THE DARKNESS.
OH! OH!
WHO THE --!
WHAT'S GOIN' ON HERE?
YOW! WHAT A FACE!
SO, WE'VE GOT A SPY ABOARD, HEY? AND AN OLD HAG AT THAT! WE'LL FIX YOU!
MIND YOUR TONGUE, MADAME LARGOSSI! YOU ARE SPEAKING TO THE SPIDER WIDOW!
AND...
WITH ONE FREE HAND THE SPIDER WIDOW RELEASES HER INSECT WARRIORS!
AWWG! SPIDERS!
GET THEM OFF! SPIDERS! I CAN'T STAND SPIDERS! GET 'EM OFF ME!
4

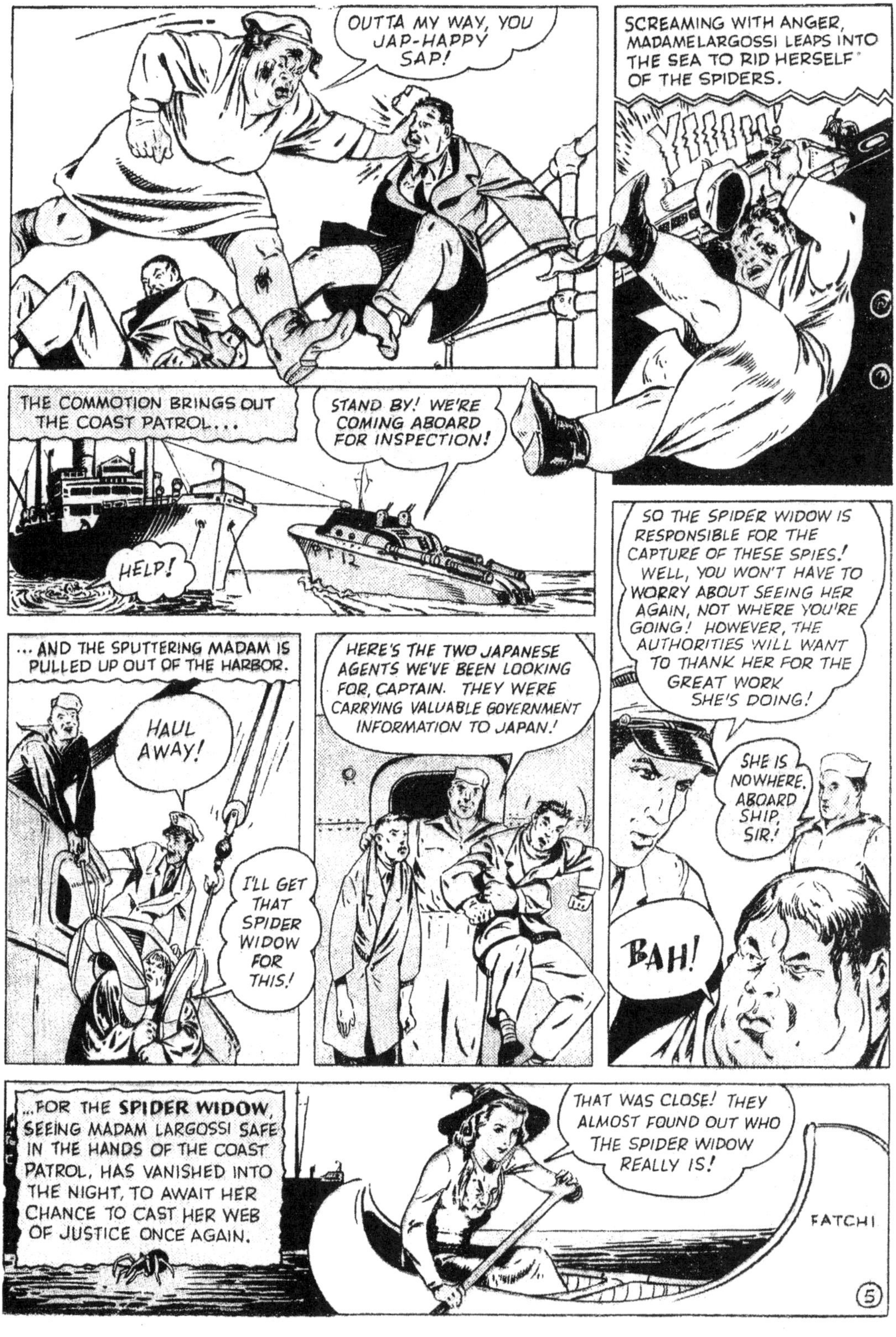
OUTTA MY WAY, YOU JAP-HAPPY SAP!
SCREAMING WITH ANGER, MADAMELARGOSSI LEAPS INTO THE SEA TO RID HERSELF OF THE SPIDERS.
YIIIII!
THE COMMOTION BRINGS OUT THE COAST PATROL...
STAND BY! WE'RE COMING ABOARD FOR INSPECTION!
HELP!
PT 12
SO THE SPIDER WIDOW IS RESPONSIBLE FOR THE CAPTURE OF THESE SPIES! WELL, YOU WON'T HAVE TO WORRY ABOUT SEEING HER AGAIN, NOT WHERE YOU'RE GOING! HOWEVER, THE AUTHORITIES WILL WANT TO THANK HER FOR THE GREAT WORK SHE'S DOING!
...AND THE SPUTTERING MADAM IS PULLED UP OUT OF THE HARBOR.
HAUL AWAY!
I'LL GET THAT SPIDER WIDOW FOR THIS!
HERE'S THE TWO JAPANESE AGENTS WE'VE BEEN LOOKING FOR, CAPTAIN. THEY WERE CARRYING VALUABLE GOVERNMENT INFORMATION TO JAPAN!
SHE IS NOWHERE ABOARD SHIP, SIR!
BAH!
...FOR THE SPIDER WIDOW, SEEING MADAM LARGOSSI SAFE IN THE HANDS OF THE COAST PATROL, HAS VANISHED INTO THE NIGHT, TO AWAIT HER CHANCE TO CAST HER WEB OF JUSTICE ONCE AGAIN.
THAT WAS CLOSE! THEY ALMOST FOUND OUT WHO THE SPIDER WIDOW REALLY IS!
FATCHI
5

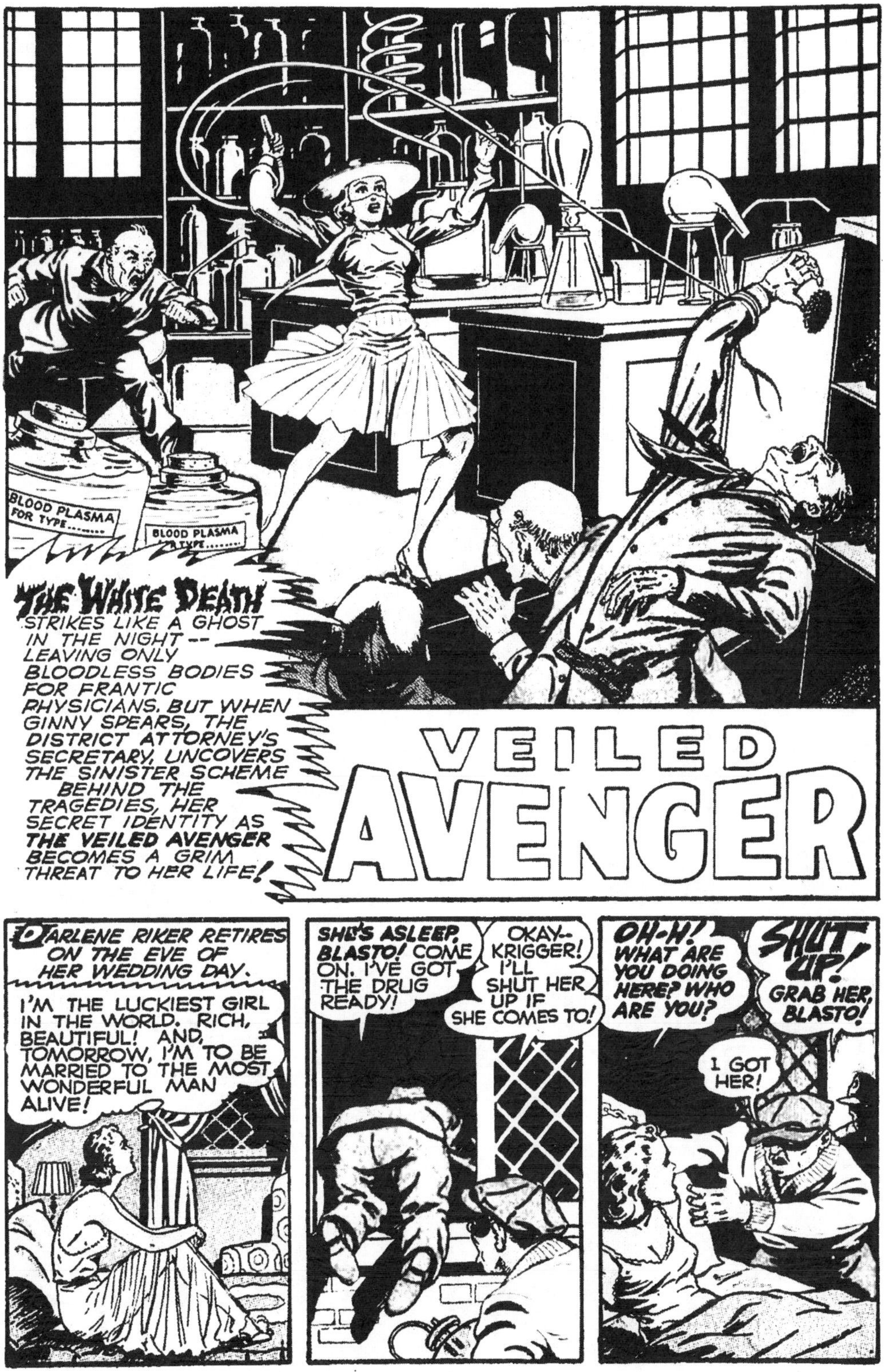
BLOOD PLASMA FOR TYPE.......
BLOOD PLASMA FOR TYPE........
THE WHITE DEATH STRIKES LIKE A GHOST IN THE NIGHT -- LEAVING ONLY BLOODLESS BODIES FOR FRANTIC PHYSICIANS. BUT WHEN GINNY SPEARS, THE DISTRICT ATTORNEY'S SECRETARY, UNCOVERS THE SINISTER SCHEME BEHIND THE TRAGEDIES, HER SECRET IDENTITY AS THE VEILED AVENGER BECOMES A GRIM THREAT TO HER LIFE!
VEILED AVENGER
DARLENE RIKER RETIRES ON THE EVE OF HER WEDDING DAY.
I'M THE LUCKIEST GIRL IN THE WORLD. RICH, BEAUTIFUL! AND, TOMORROW, I'M TO BE MARRIED TO THE MOST WONDERFUL MAN ALIVE!
SHE'S ASLEEP, BLASTO! COME ON. I'VE GOT THE DRUG READY!
OKAY-- KRIGGER! I'LL SHUT HER UP IF SHE COMES TO!
OH-H! WHAT ARE YOU DOING HERE? WHO ARE YOU?
SHUT UP! GRAB HER, BLASTO!
I GOT HER!

From Red Seal Comics #16 (1946) Art by Gus Ricca

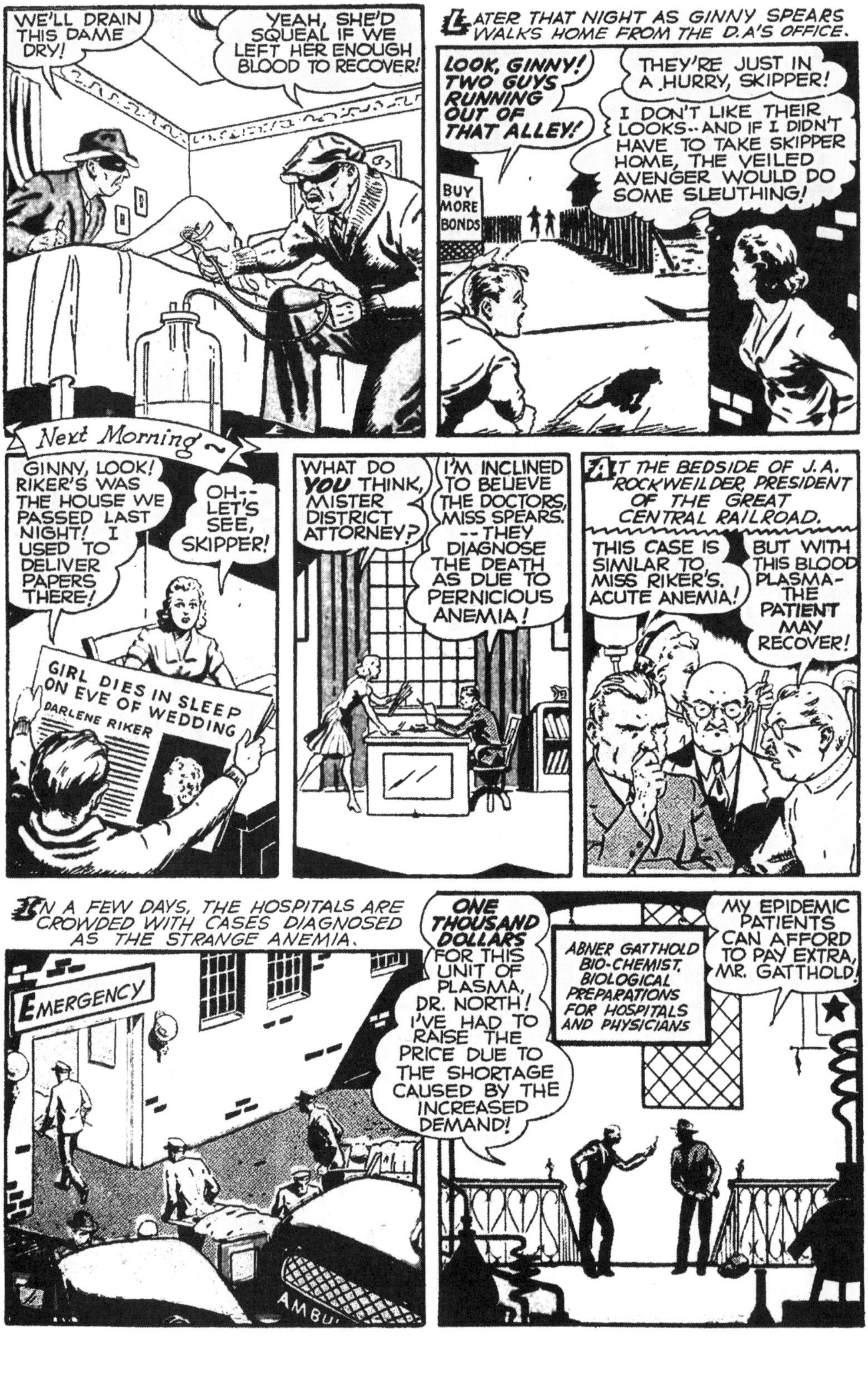
WE'LL DRAIN THIS DAME DRY!
YEAH, SHE'D SQUEAL IF WE LEFT HER ENOUGH BLOOD TO RECOVER!
LATER THAT NIGHT AS GINNY SPEARS WALKS HOME FROM THE D.A'S OFFICE.
LOOK, GINNY! TWO GUYS RUNNING OUT OF THAT ALLEY!
THEY'RE JUST IN A HURRY, SKIPPER!
I DON'T LIKE THEIR LOOKS--AND IF I DIDN'T HAVE TO TAKE SKIPPER HOME, THE VEILED AVENGER WOULD DO SOME SLEUTHING!
BUY MORE BONDS
Next Morning~
GINNY, LOOK! RIKER'S WAS THE HOUSE WE PASSED LAST NIGHT! I USED TO DELIVER PAPERS THERE!
OH--LET'S SEE, SKIPPER!
GIRL DIES IN SLEEP ON EVE OF WEDDING
DARLENE RIKER
WHAT DO YOU THINK, MISTER DISTRICT ATTORNEY?
I'M INCLINED TO BELIEVE THE DOCTORS, MISS SPEARS. --THEY DIAGNOSE THE DEATH AS DUE TO PERNICIOUS ANEMIA!
AT THE BEDSIDE OF J.A. ROCKWEILDER, PRESIDENT OF THE GREAT CENTRAL RAILROAD.
THIS CASE IS SIMILAR TO MISS RIKER'S. ACUTE ANEMIA!
BUT WITH THIS BLOOD PLASMA-THE PATIENT MAY RECOVER!
IN A FEW DAYS, THE HOSPITALS ARE CROWDED WITH CASES DIAGNOSED AS THE STRANGE ANEMIA.
EMERGENCY
AMBU
ONE THOUSAND DOLLARS FOR THIS UNIT OF PLASMA, DR. NORTH! I'VE HAD TO RAISE THE PRICE DUE TO THE SHORTAGE CAUSED BY THE INCREASED DEMAND!
ABNER GATTHOLD BIO-CHEMIST, BIOLOGICAL PREPARATIONS FOR HOSPITALS AND PHYSICIANS
MY EPIDEMIC PATIENTS CAN AFFORD TO PAY EXTRA, MR. GATTHOLD!

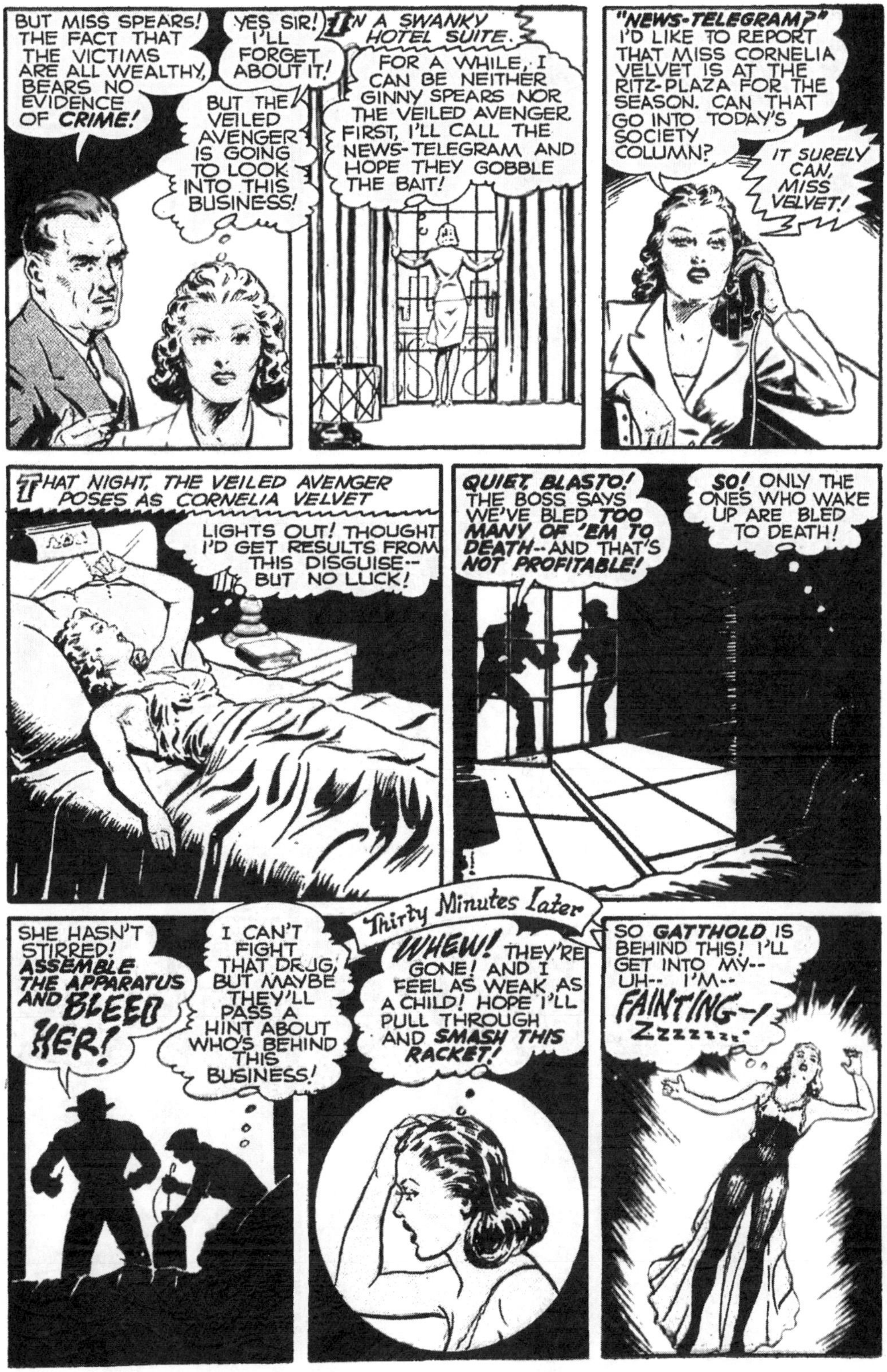
BUT MISS SPEARS! THE FACT THAT THE VICTIMS ARE ALL WEALTHY, BEARS NO EVIDENCE OF CRIME!
YES SIR! I'LL FORGET ABOUT IT!
BUT THE VEILED AVENGER IS GOING TO LOOK INTO THIS BUSINESS!
IN A SWANKY HOTEL SUITE.
FOR A WHILE, I CAN BE NEITHER GINNY SPEARS NOR THE VEILED AVENGER. FIRST, I'LL CALL THE NEWS-TELEGRAM AND HOPE THEY GOBBLE THE BAIT!
"NEWS-TELEGRAM?" I'D LIKE TO REPORT THAT MISS CORNELIA VELVET IS AT THE RITZ-PLAZA FOR THE SEASON. CAN THAT GO INTO TODAY'S SOCIETY COLUMN?
IT SURELY CAN, MISS VELVET!
THAT NIGHT, THE VEILED AVENGER POSES AS CORNELIA VELVET
LIGHTS OUT! THOUGHT I'D GET RESULTS FROM THIS DISGUISE-- BUT NO LUCK!
QUIET, BLASTO! THE BOSS SAYS WE'VE BLED TOO MANY OF 'EM TO DEATH--AND THAT'S NOT PROFITABLE!
SO! ONLY THE ONES WHO WAKE UP ARE BLED TO DEATH!
SHE HASN'T STIRRED! ASSEMBLE THE APPARATUS AND BLEED HER!
I CAN'T FIGHT THAT DRUG, BUT MAYBE THEY'LL PASS A HINT ABOUT WHO'S BEHIND THIS BUSINESS!
Thirty Minutes Later
WHEW! THEY'RE GONE! AND I FEEL AS WEAK AS A CHILD! HOPE I'LL PULL THROUGH AND SMASH THIS RACKET!
SO GATTHOLD IS BEHIND THIS! I'LL GET INTO MY-- UH-- I'M-- FAINTING--!
Zzzzzzz

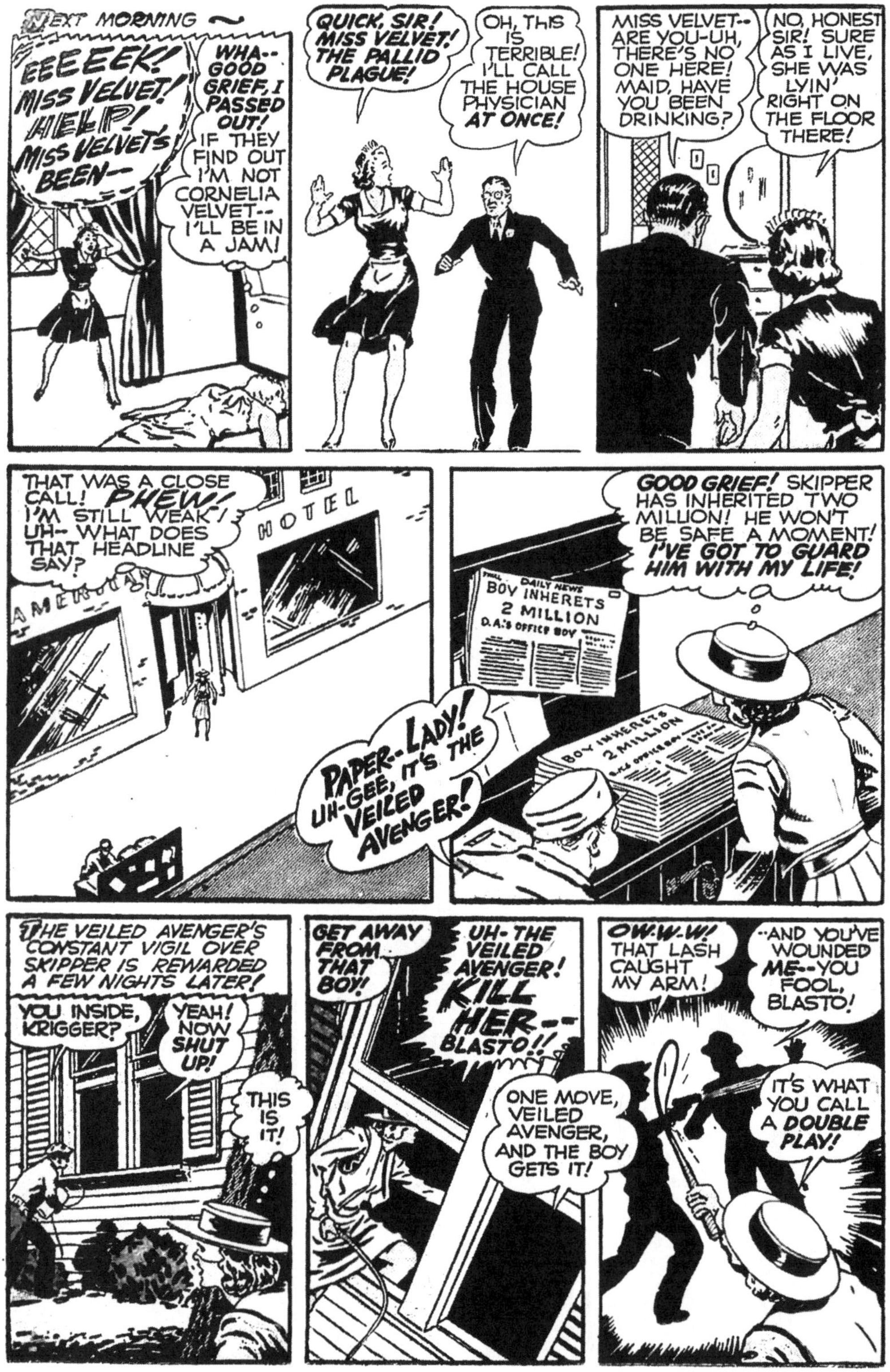
NEXT MORNING ~
EEEEEK! MISS VELVET! HELP! MISS VELVET'S BEEN--
WHA-- GOOD GRIEF, I PASSED OUT! IF THEY FIND OUT I'M NOT CORNELIA VELVET-- I'LL BE IN A JAM!
QUICK, SIR! MISS VELVET! THE PALLID PLAGUE!
OH, THIS IS TERRIBLE! I'LL CALL THE HOUSE PHYSICIAN AT ONCE!
MISS VELVET-- ARE YOU-UH, THERE'S NO ONE HERE! MAID, HAVE YOU BEEN DRINKING?
NO, HONEST SIR! SURE AS I LIVE, SHE WAS LYIN' RIGHT ON THE FLOOR THERE!
THAT WAS A CLOSE CALL! PHEW! I'M STILL WEAK! UH-- WHAT DOES THAT HEADLINE SAY?
HOTEL
AMERICAN
GOOD GRIEF! SKIPPER HAS INHERITED TWO MILLION! HE WON'T BE SAFE A MOMENT! I'VE GOT TO GUARD HIM WITH MY LIFE!
DAILY NEWS
BOY INHERETS 2 MILLION
D.A.'S OFFICE BOY
PAPER-- LADY! UH-GEE, IT'S THE VEILED AVENGER!
THE VEILED AVENGER'S CONSTANT VIGIL OVER SKIPPER IS REWARDED A FEW NIGHTS LATER!
YOU INSIDE, KRIGGER?
YEAH! NOW SHUT UP!
THIS IS IT!
GET AWAY FROM THAT BOY!
UH- THE VEILED AVENGER! KILL HER-- BLASTO!!
ONE MOVE, VEILED AVENGER, AND THE BOY GETS IT!
OW-W-W! THAT LASH CAUGHT MY ARM!
--AND YOU'VE WOUNDED ME-- YOU FOOL, BLASTO!
IT'S WHAT YOU CALL A DOUBLE PLAY!

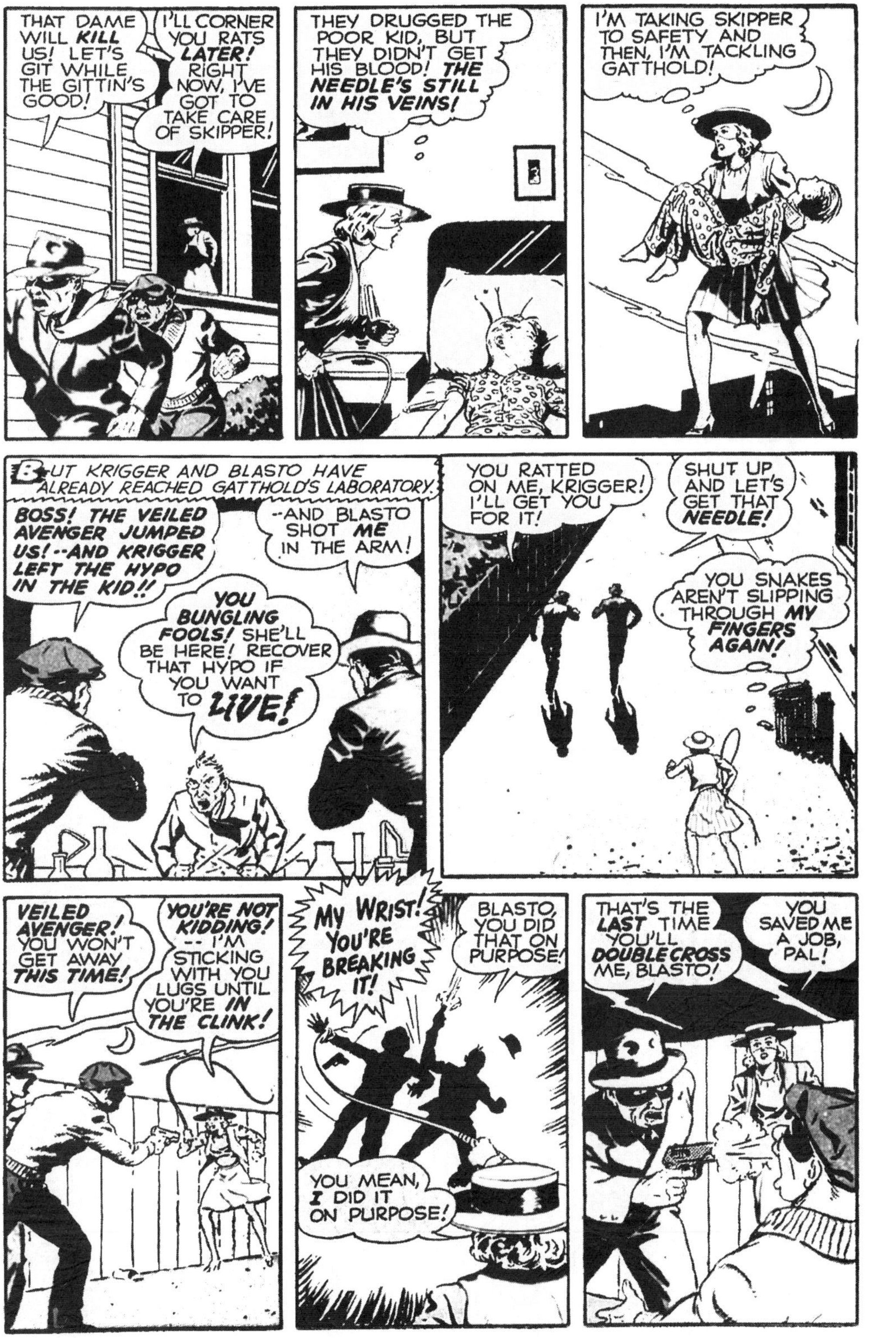

THAT DAME WILL KILL US! LET'S GIT WHILE THE GITTIN'S GOOD!
I'LL CORNER YOU RATS LATER! RIGHT NOW, I'VE GOT TO TAKE CARE OF SKIPPER!
THEY DRUGGED THE POOR KID, BUT THEY DIDN'T GET HIS BLOOD! THE NEEDLE'S STILL IN HIS VEINS!
I'M TAKING SKIPPER TO SAFETY AND THEN, I'M TACKLING GATTHOLD!
BUT KRIGGER AND BLASTO HAVE ALREADY REACHED GATTHOLD'S LABORATORY.
BOSS! THE VEILED AVENGER JUMPED US! --AND KRIGGER LEFT THE HYPO IN THE KID!!
--AND BLASTO SHOT ME IN THE ARM!
YOU BUNGLING FOOLS! SHE'LL BE HERE! RECOVER THAT HYPO IF YOU WANT TO LIVE!
YOU RATTED ON ME, KRIGGER! I'LL GET YOU FOR IT!
SHUT UP AND LET'S GET THAT NEEDLE!
YOU SNAKES AREN'T SLIPPING THROUGH MY FINGERS AGAIN!
VEILED AVENGER! YOU WON'T GET AWAY THIS TIME!
YOU'RE NOT KIDDING! -- I'M STICKING WITH YOU LUGS UNTIL YOU'RE IN THE CLINK!
MY WRIST! YOU'RE BREAKING IT!
BLASTO, YOU DID THAT ON PURPOSE!
YOU MEAN, I DID IT ON PURPOSE!
THAT'S THE LAST TIME YOU'LL DOUBLE CROSS ME, BLASTO!
YOU SAVED ME A JOB, PAL!

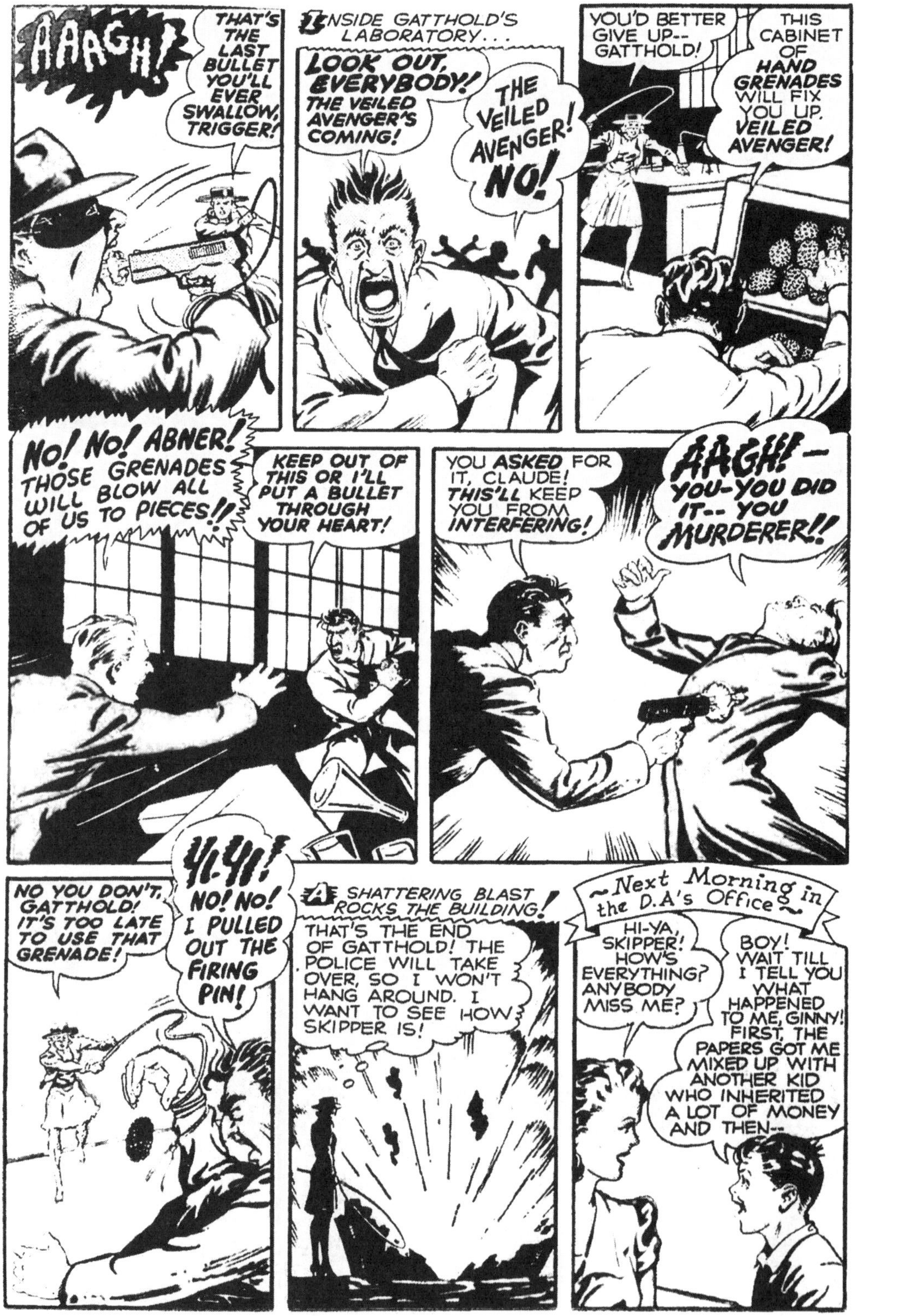
AAAGH!
THAT'S THE LAST BULLET YOU'LL EVER SWALLOW, TRIGGER!
INSIDE GATTHOLD'S LABORATORY...
LOOK OUT, EVERYBODY! THE VEILED AVENGER'S COMING!
THE VEILED AVENGER! NO!
YOU'D BETTER GIVE UP-- GATTHOLD!
THIS CABINET OF HAND GRENADES WILL FIX YOU UP, VEILED AVENGER!
NO! NO! ABNER! THOSE GRENADES WILL BLOW ALL OF US TO PIECES!!
KEEP OUT OF THIS OR I'LL PUT A BULLET THROUGH YOUR HEART!
YOU ASKED FOR IT, CLAUDE! THIS'LL KEEP YOU FROM INTERFERING!
AAGH! -- YOU-YOU DID IT-- YOU MURDERER!!
NO YOU DON'T, GATTHOLD! IT'S TOO LATE TO USE THAT GRENADE!
YI-YI! NO! NO! I PULLED OUT THE FIRING PIN!
A SHATTERING BLAST ROCKS THE BUILDING!
THAT'S THE END OF GATTHOLD! THE POLICE WILL TAKE OVER, SO I WON'T HANG AROUND. I WANT TO SEE HOW SKIPPER IS!
~Next Morning in the D.A's Office~
HI-YA, SKIPPER! HOW'S EVERYTHING? ANYBODY MISS ME?
BOY! WAIT TILL I TELL YOU WHAT HAPPENED TO ME, GINNY! FIRST, THE PAPERS GOT ME MIXED UP WITH ANOTHER KID WHO INHERITED A LOT OF MONEY AND THEN--

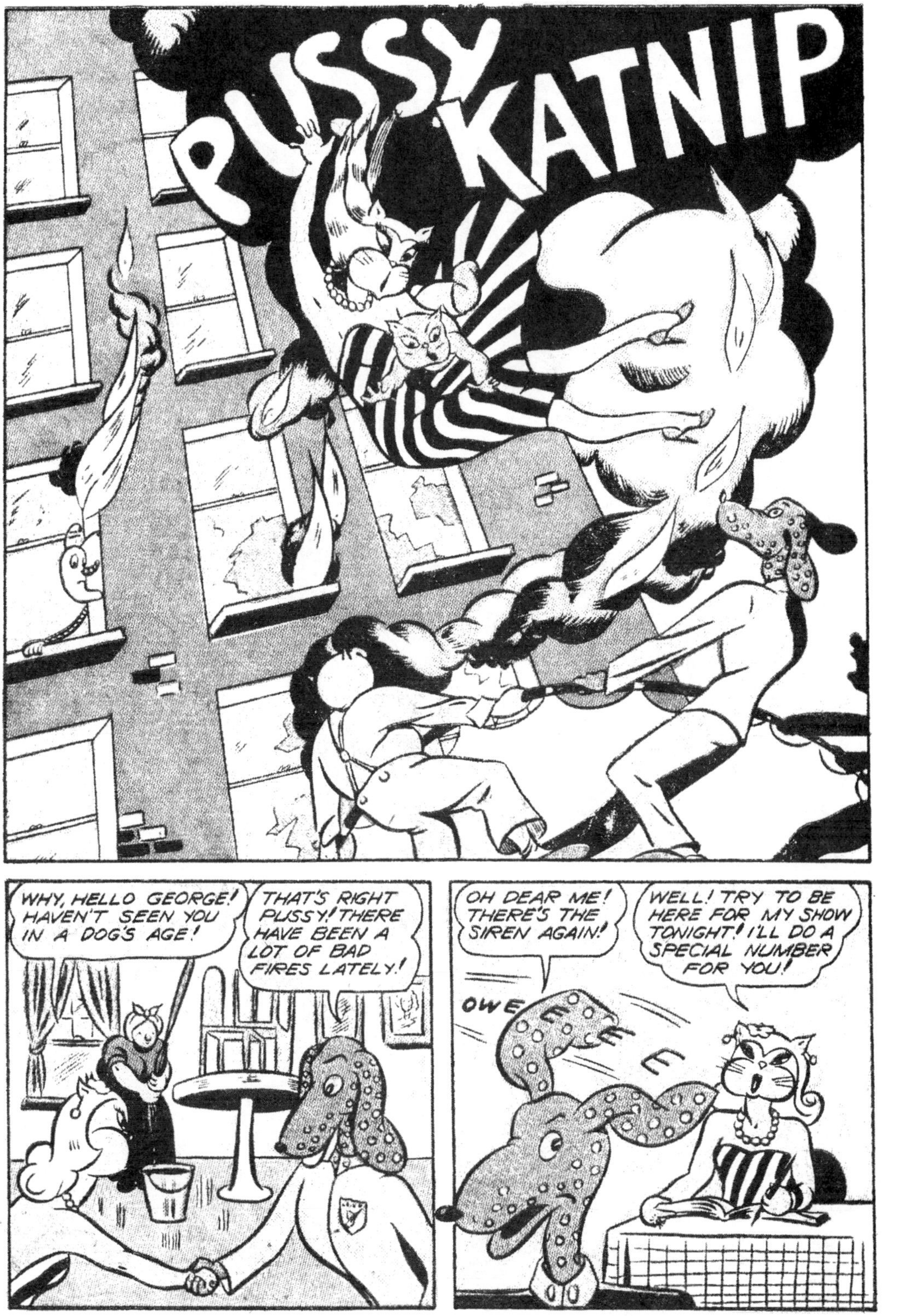
PUSSY KATNIP
WHY, HELLO GEORGE! HAVEN'T SEEN YOU IN A DOG'S AGE!
THAT'S RIGHT PUSSY! THERE HAVE BEEN A LOT OF BAD FIRES LATELY!
OH DEAR ME! THERE'S THE SIREN AGAIN!
OWE E E E
WELL! TRY TO BE HERE FOR MY SHOW TONIGHT! I'LL DO A SPECIAL NUMBER FOR YOU!

From All Top Comics (1944) Art by Len Short

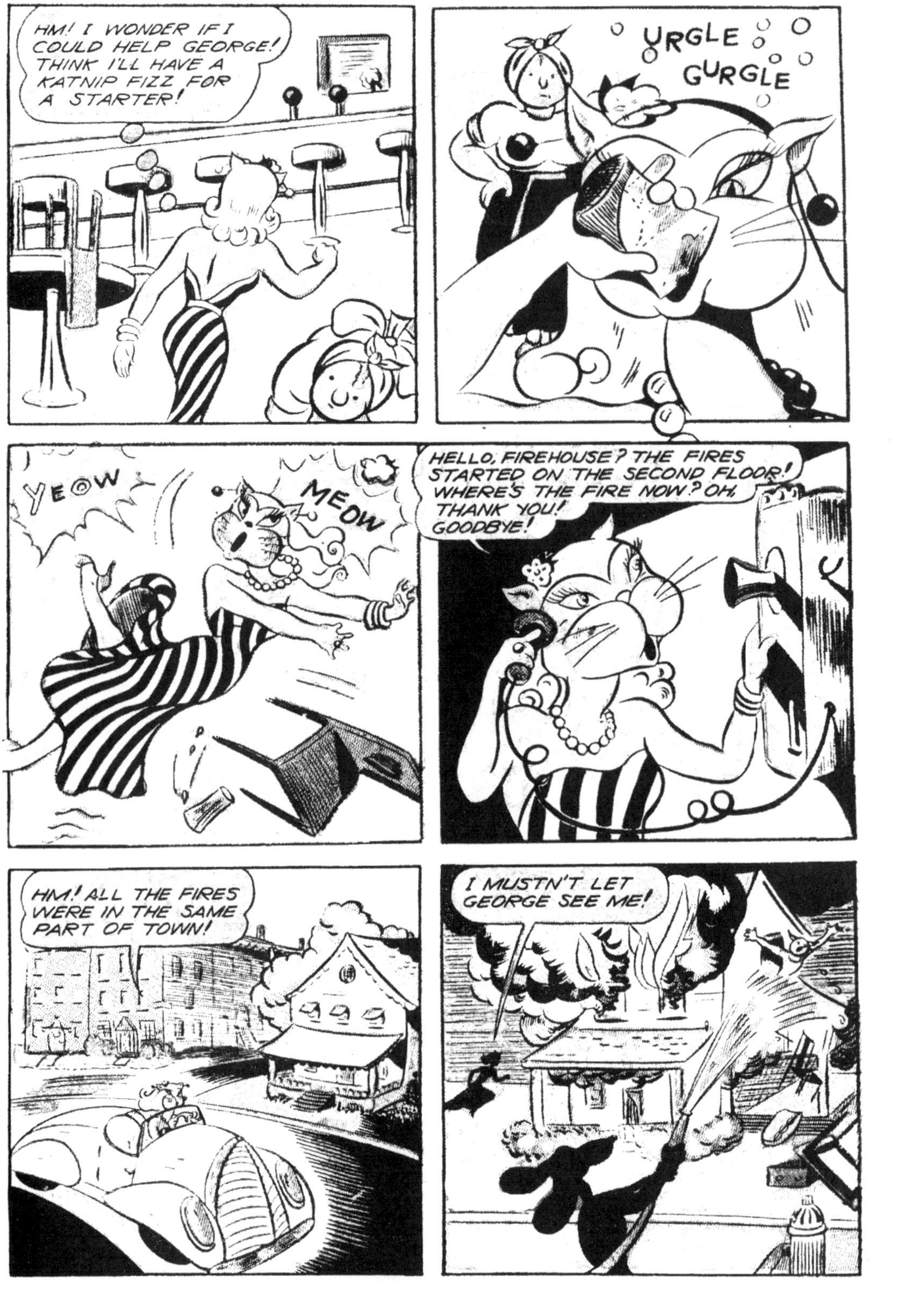
HM! I WONDER IF I COULD HELP GEORGE! THINK I'LL HAVE A KATNIP FIZZ FOR A STARTER!
URGLE GURGLE
YEOW
MEOW
HELLO, FIREHOUSE? THE FIRES STARTED ON THE SECOND FLOOR! WHERE'S THE FIRE NOW? OH, THANK YOU! GOODBYE!
HM! ALL THE FIRES WERE IN THE SAME PART OF TOWN!
I MUSTN'T LET GEORGE SEE ME!

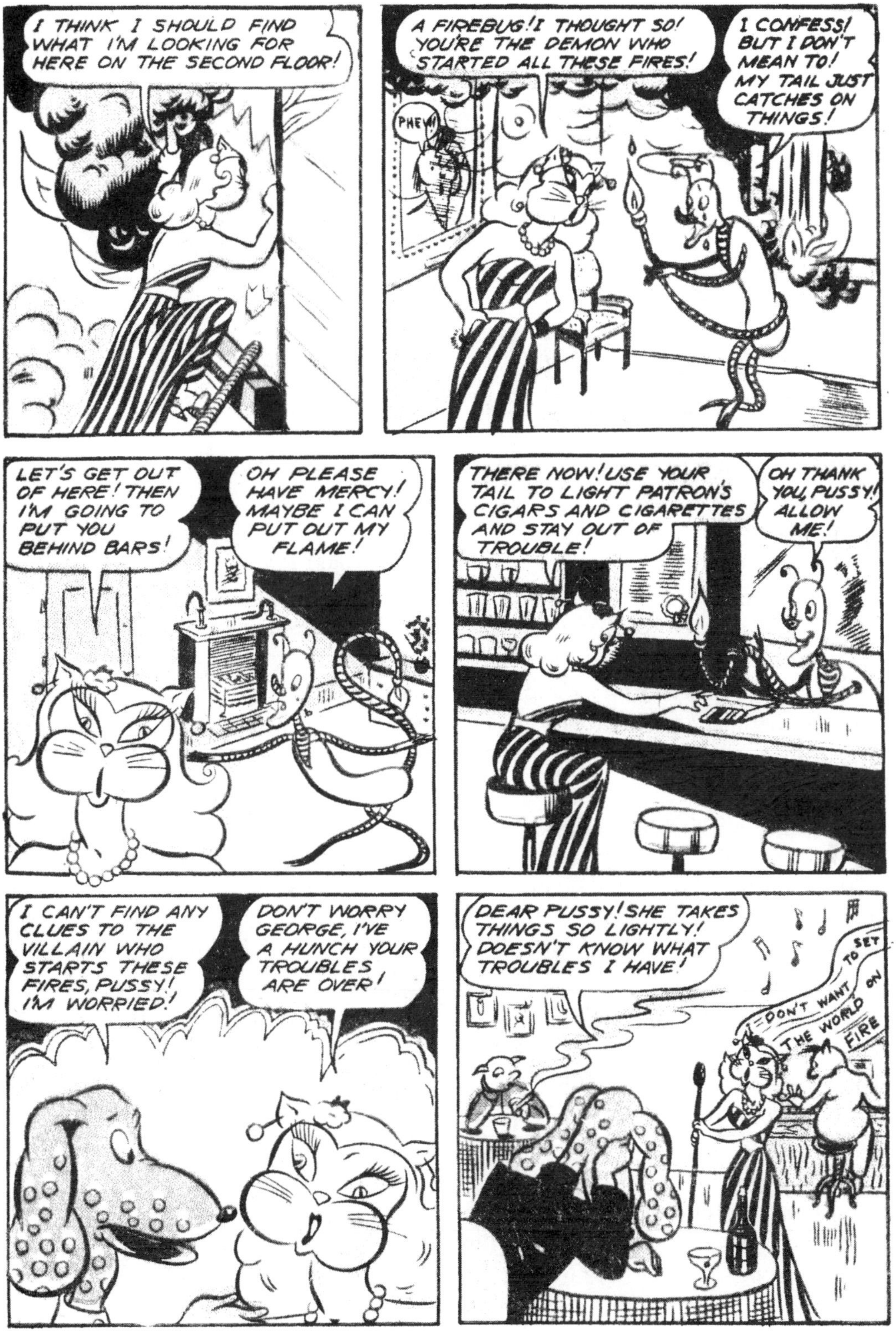
I THINK I SHOULD FIND WHAT I'M LOOKING FOR HERE ON THE SECOND FLOOR!
A FIREBUG! I THOUGHT SO! YOU'RE THE DEMON WHO STARTED ALL THESE FIRES!
I CONFESS! BUT I DON'T MEAN TO! MY TAIL JUST CATCHES ON THINGS!
LET'S GET OUT OF HERE! THEN I'M GOING TO PUT YOU BEHIND BARS!
OH PLEASE HAVE MERCY! MAYBE I CAN PUT OUT MY FLAME!
THERE NOW! USE YOUR TAIL TO LIGHT PATRON'S CIGARS AND CIGARETTES AND STAY OUT OF TROUBLE!
OH THANK YOU, PUSSY! ALLOW ME!
I CAN'T FIND ANY CLUES TO THE VILLAIN WHO STARTS THESE FIRES, PUSSY! I'M WORRIED!
DON'T WORRY GEORGE, I'VE A HUNCH YOUR TROUBLES ARE OVER!
DEAR PUSSY! SHE TAKES THINGS SO LIGHTLY! DOESN'T KNOW WHAT TROUBLES I HAVE!
DON'T WANT TO SET THE WORLD ON FIRE

DARING DAMES

Is the 20th century career woman an American invention? If not, she still is clearly a symbol of the nation's move into the future in the wake of WWI. Beginning in the 1920s, women began entering the workforce in greater numbers. As the focus of American life shifted from rural to urban areas, big city "working girls" would replace doe-eyed farm lasses as the heroines in popular entertainment. The feisty career women of '30s Hollywood movies played by Barbara Stanwyck and Rosalind Russell had quick wits and sharp tongues, and needed both to compete with men and prove their worth. Newspaper comic strips like *Winnie Winkle the Breadwinner* and *Brenda Starr, Reporter* featured the new heroines of the day—smart, independent, and emancipated. Their high-heeled feet walked magnificent avenues lined with towering skyscrapers, as they scanned the horizon in search of their destinies.

Lois Lane is the original career woman of the comic book world. She made her debut in 1938 as a Hollywood style dame with brains, guts and beauty. But aside from Lois Lane, the common perception of the comic book female is that of the scantily clad, masked superheroine. So, it might be surprising to many that in the early years of comics, there were a large number of career woman, from all walks of life, who starred in their own features in anthology titles.

Many of the masked female crimefighters of the Golden Age were wealthy debutantes who had the time and money to go running across rooftops in a costume in search of adventure. Even their names indicated their upper crust pedigrees—Sandra Knight was the Phantom Lady, Marla Drake was Miss Fury, Anita Morgan was The Purple Tigress. The working girls of the comics were strictly working class, and their names showed it— Sally O'Neil, Penny Wright, Betty Bates, Patty O'Day. These women didn't have the luxury of maintaining a secret identity. They needed to earn a living. That's not to say that they didn't have adventures or right wrongs. These flinty dames sent their share of evildoers to jail, but they didn't use magic rings or ray projectors or antigravity helmets. They used their brains, and a good right hook.

Unlike the secretaries that populated the newspaper comic strips, the working girls of comic books had professions that provided danger and intrigue as story fodder. Following in the mold of Lois Lane, there were a number of lady reporters—Penny Wright, Betty Boyd, Joan Mason, Molly O'Moore. There were also a slew of intrepid news photographers like Fran Frazer, Gail Porter, Patty O'Day and the Blonde Bomber who risked death to get a scoop. Sally O'Neil, Jeanette Copeland, and Lucky Dale were all policewomen, while Bonnie Hawks and Calamity Jane ran detective agencies. The most unexpected comic book heroine was Betty Bates, Lady at Law, a shrewd attorney with jiu jitsu skills.

In the world of superhero comics, male heroes have often said that fighting evil is no job for a woman. In the 1940s, even the all-powerful Wonder Woman was only allowed to be the Justice Society's secretary, while her male teammates had all of the adventures. The career women in these stories don't take a backseat to anyone. They are portrayed as competent and professional, never as hapless females trying to do a man's job and failing miserably. Simply, they aren't treated as jokes. They're resourceful and don't need a man to rescue them. And these women didn't balk at the idea of competing with a man, either. Some of them were even the bosses of men. The focus of their stories was action and adventure, not romance. These heroines are not shown biding their time waiting for a marriage proposal so that they can retire.

So what happened to these daring career women? Well, times changed, and tastes changed. When superheroes fell out of the fashion in the late '40s and early '50s, many of the anthology titles folded, or were changed into other genres that were becoming more popular, like westerns, horror, and romance. There was no longer a place for clever career women. By the 1950s, there were only two career women in comics. Marvel Comics published *Millie the Model*, which focused on humor, romance, and glamour. And Lois Lane was still around. Starting in 1958, she starred in her own title, *Superman's Girlfriend Lois Lane*. But these stories focused less on Lois as a reporter and more on her ongoing efforts to trap Superman into marriage. A moment in time had ended. It wasn't until the 1980s, and heroines like the tough private detective Ms. Tree, that regular women who didn't wear costumes would make a comeback in comics.

So now, let's take a look at the women who didn't need to wear a mask to fight the bad guys—

PENNY WRIGHT, FEATURE WRITER— Newspaper reporter Penny Wright's quest for her next big story took her all over the globe. She was a take-charge woman who tangled with Latin American revolutionaries and European spies. Like many of the pre-WWII comics, Penny's rollicking stories were reminiscent of the pulp magazines. As soon as daredevil Penny had managed to get herself out of a scrape, she was back at her typewriter, banging out her latest scoop that would send an evildoer to jail.

Penny Wright represents that early 20th century image of the American woman as the modern and independent firebrand, committed to exposing the truth. "Miss Wright, you American girls certainly have spunk and brains," says a gendarme at the end of the story presented here. Penny Wright appeared in only three stories in 1940s *Champion Comics*.

BETTY BATES, LADY AT LAW— Despite being an attorney, Betty Bates often wound up taking the law into her own hands. The lady lawyer seemed to spend more time investigating cases than she did in the courtroom. Even though educated Betty had her law degree, readers knew that this tough dame hadn't completely left her working class roots behind. "Listen sister…law isn't the only subject I've mastered!" snaps Betty, as she swats the face of a gun moll. "I may be a Portia, but my middle name's Dempsey!" Eventually Betty became district attorney, and gained a sidekick in the form of Larry, a reporter. But even with a male sidekick, Betty remained the star of the show, appearing in *Hit Comics* for an impressive run from 1940-50.

THE BLONDE BOMBER— Honey Blake was a blonde, but she was no dummy. As an intrepid camerawoman for Acme Newsreels, Honey combined "glamour and daring" in her pursuit of the biggest new stories, aided by her tubby assistant Jimmy Slapso. As the "fotographic furies," Honey and Slapso's assignments took them around the world; the two encountering criminals and Nazi spies along the way. Daredevil Honey was as quick with her fists as she was with her camera. But as the story presented here also points out, "Honey's character has many facets—in her laboratory she's an expert chemist…" The Blonde Bombers was a regular feature in *Green Hornet Comics* from 1942-47. In their final adventures, Honey and Slapso, no longer content to merely travel the world, now travelled through time in search of adventure. The Blonde Bomber also appeared in *All-New Comics* and *Speed Comics*. This story was drawn by artist Barbara Hall.

JILL TRENT, SCIENCE SLEUTH— Jill Trent may have been ahead of her time. First off, she was the proto girl geek of comics—a scientist who spent her time in the lab happily concocting fantastic creations like x-ray glasses and indestructible cloth. Second, Jill didn't have a boyfriend, but she did have her best friend and trusty assistant Daisy. On occasion, the girls were shown sharing a bed, suggesting this series may have been forward thinking in more ways than one. Jill and Daisy were always getting mixed up in criminal cases, which they solved using Jill's inventions, along with the pistols they always seemed to be packing. In this story, Jill whips up the instruments of her and Daisy's salvation from odds and ends, à la '80s TV hero "MacGyver." Jill Trent, Science Sleuth appeared in *Fighting Yank* and *Wonder Comics* from 1943-48.

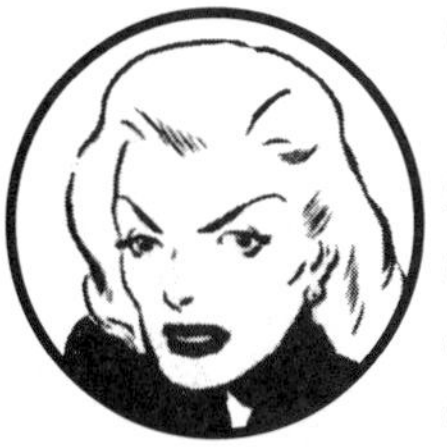

CALAMITY JANE— When you think of the hard-boiled detectives of 1940s noir stories, you picture a guy who's rough around the edges, maybe a little down on his luck, quick to get into a fight, cigarette dangling from the corner of his mouth. But you don't necessarily think of a woman. If that's the case, meet Calamity Jane. "I'm a detective in skirts! In the books I'm Jane Janis, private investigator...but to the cops I'm misery—so they call me Calamity..." No doubt about it, Calamity was a tough cookie. Her stories reflect the film noir inspired comics of the postwar era that had a cynicism not seen a few years earlier. Artist Bill Draut appeared in each story, as Calamity herself recounted her latest adventure for him to use in his next comic book. Calamity's assistant was a dim-witted cab driver named Hack who chauffeured her around town. The dialogue in this story is superb, with Calamity Jane dispensing one acid tongued barb after another. Calamity Jane appeared in *Boy Explorers Comics* and *Green Hornet Comics* from 1946-47.

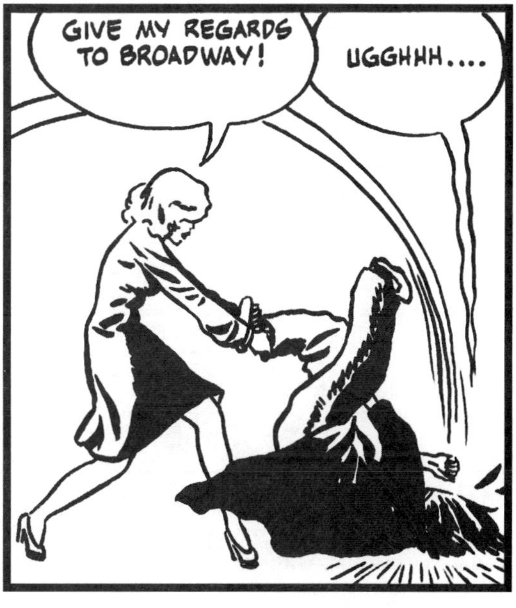
GIVE MY REGARDS TO BROADWAY!
UGGHHH....

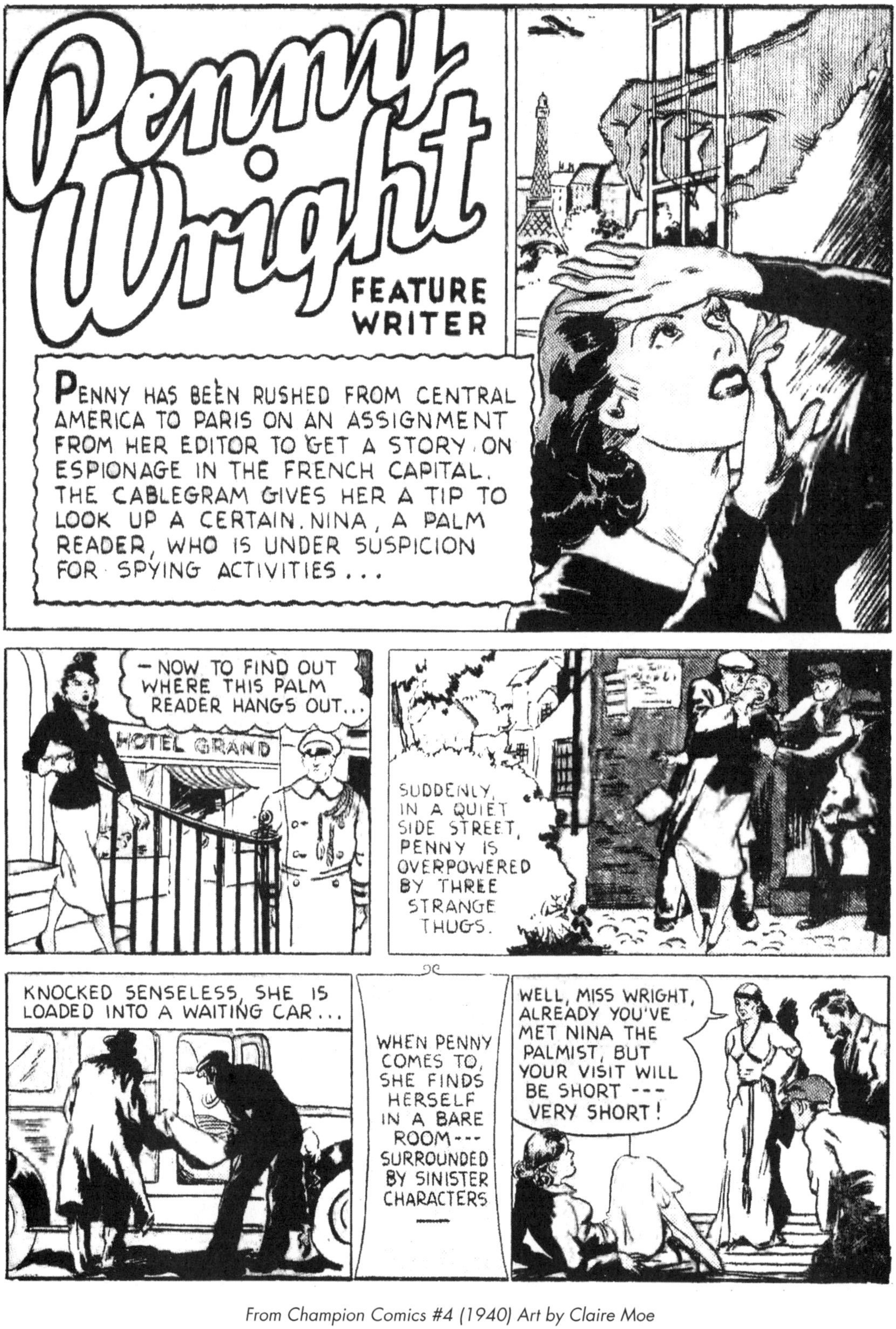
Penny Wright
FEATURE WRITER
PENNY HAS BEEN RUSHED FROM CENTRAL AMERICA TO PARIS ON AN ASSIGNMENT FROM HER EDITOR TO GET A STORY ON ESPIONAGE IN THE FRENCH CAPITAL. THE CABLEGRAM GIVES HER A TIP TO LOOK UP A CERTAIN. NINA, A PALM READER, WHO IS UNDER SUSPICION FOR SPYING ACTIVITIES...
—NOW TO FIND OUT WHERE THIS PALM READER HANGS OUT...
HOTEL GRAND
SUDDENLY, IN A QUIET SIDE STREET, PENNY IS OVERPOWERED BY THREE STRANGE THUGS.
KNOCKED SENSELESS, SHE IS LOADED INTO A WAITING CAR...
WHEN PENNY COMES TO, SHE FINDS HERSELF IN A BARE ROOM--- SURROUNDED BY SINISTER CHARACTERS
WELL, MISS WRIGHT, ALREADY YOU'VE MET NINA THE PALMIST, BUT YOUR VISIT WILL BE SHORT --- VERY SHORT!

From Champion Comics #4 (1940) Art by Claire Moe

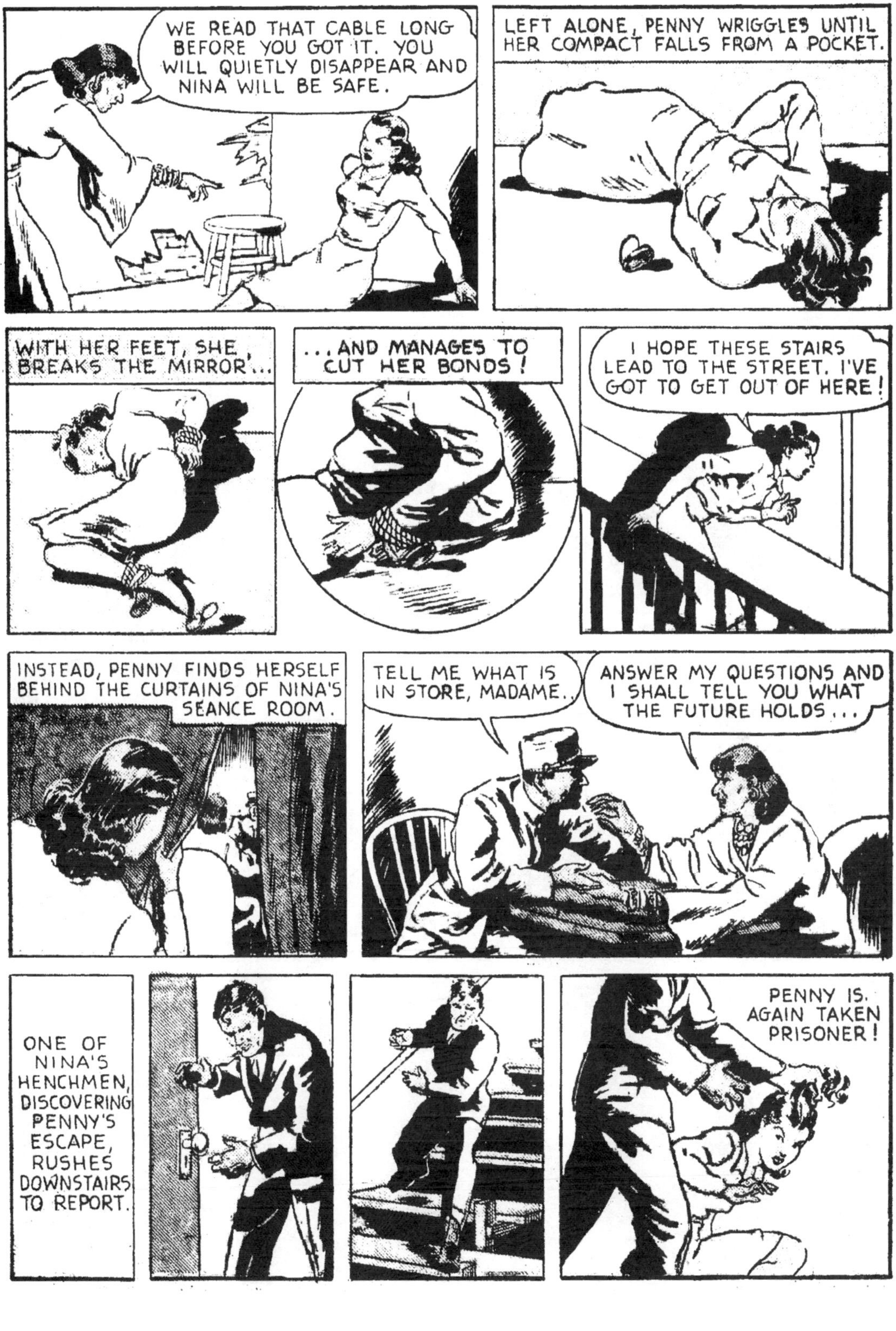
WE READ THAT CABLE LONG BEFORE YOU GOT IT. YOU WILL QUIETLY DISAPPEAR AND NINA WILL BE SAFE.
LEFT ALONE, PENNY WRIGGLES UNTIL HER COMPACT FALLS FROM A POCKET.
WITH HER FEET, SHE BREAKS THE MIRROR...
...AND MANAGES TO CUT HER BONDS!
I HOPE THESE STAIRS LEAD TO THE STREET. I'VE GOT TO GET OUT OF HERE!
INSTEAD, PENNY FINDS HERSELF BEHIND THE CURTAINS OF NINA'S SEANCE ROOM.
TELL ME WHAT IS IN STORE, MADAME.
ANSWER MY QUESTIONS AND I SHALL TELL YOU WHAT THE FUTURE HOLDS...
ONE OF NINA'S HENCHMEN, DISCOVERING PENNY'S ESCAPE, RUSHES DOWNSTAIRS TO REPORT.
PENNY IS AGAIN TAKEN PRISONER!

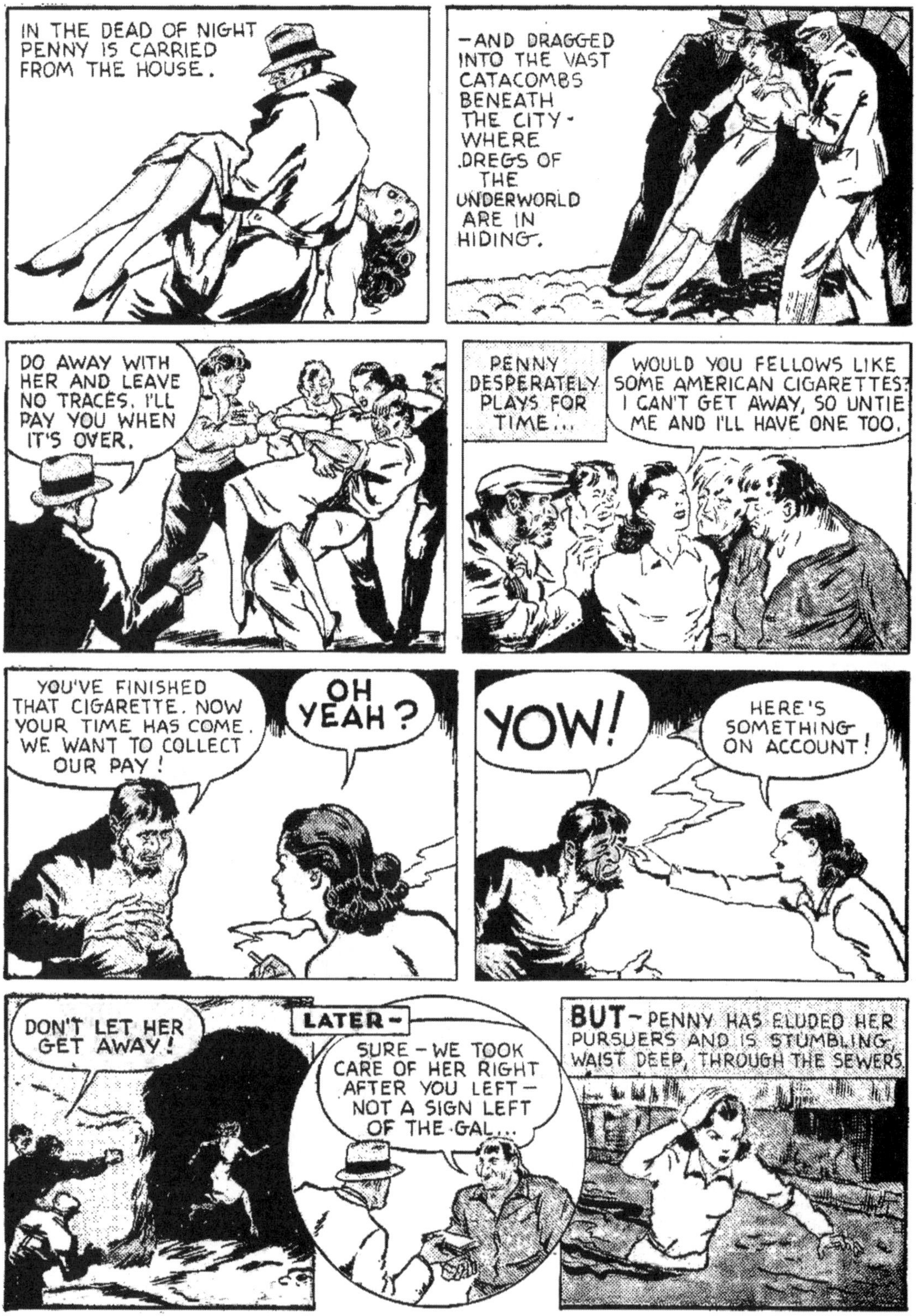
IN THE DEAD OF NIGHT PENNY IS CARRIED FROM THE HOUSE.
—AND DRAGGED INTO THE VAST CATACOMBS BENEATH THE CITY - WHERE DREGS OF THE UNDERWORLD ARE IN HIDING.
DO AWAY WITH HER AND LEAVE NO TRACES. I'LL PAY YOU WHEN IT'S OVER.
PENNY DESPERATELY PLAYS FOR TIME...
WOULD YOU FELLOWS LIKE SOME AMERICAN CIGARETTES? I CAN'T GET AWAY, SO UNTIE ME AND I'LL HAVE ONE TOO.
YOU'VE FINISHED THAT CIGARETTE. NOW YOUR TIME HAS COME. WE WANT TO COLLECT OUR PAY!
OH YEAH?
YOW!
HERE'S SOMETHING ON ACCOUNT!
DON'T LET HER GET AWAY!
LATER-
SURE—WE TOOK CARE OF HER RIGHT AFTER YOU LEFT— NOT A SIGN LEFT OF THE GAL...
BUT—PENNY HAS ELUDED HER PURSUERS AND IS STUMBLING, WAIST DEEP, THROUGH THE SEWERS.

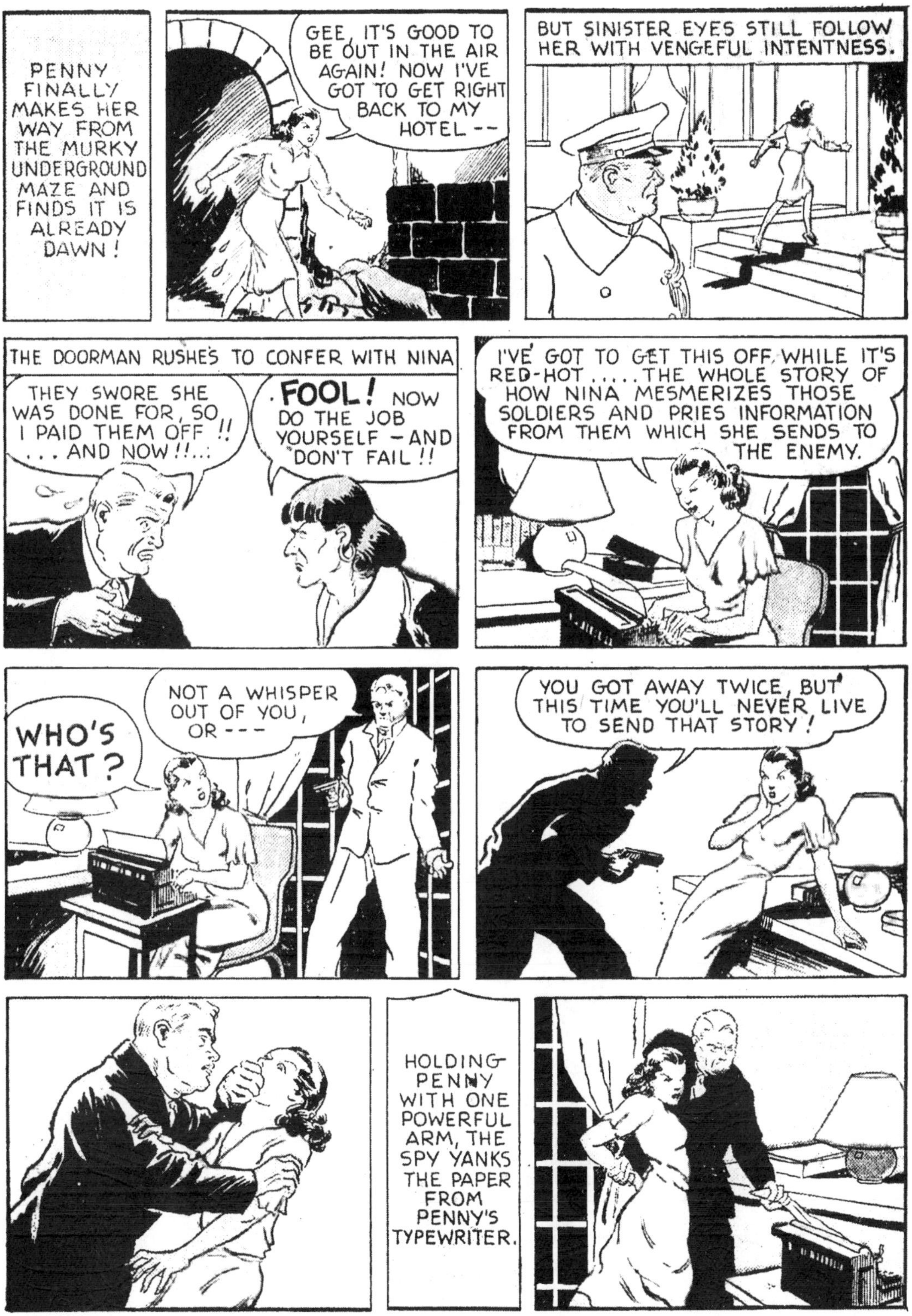
PENNY FINALLY MAKES HER WAY FROM THE MURKY UNDERGROUND MAZE AND FINDS IT IS ALREADY DAWN!
GEE, IT'S GOOD TO BE OUT IN THE AIR AGAIN! NOW I'VE GOT TO GET RIGHT BACK TO MY HOTEL --
BUT SINISTER EYES STILL FOLLOW HER WITH VENGEFUL INTENTNESS.
THE DOORMAN RUSHES TO CONFER WITH NINA
THEY SWORE SHE WAS DONE FOR, SO I PAID THEM OFF !! ... AND NOW!!...
FOOL! NOW DO THE JOB YOURSELF - AND DON'T FAIL!!
I'VE GOT TO GET THIS OFF WHILE IT'S RED-HOT ..... THE WHOLE STORY OF HOW NINA MESMERIZES THOSE SOLDIERS AND PRIES INFORMATION FROM THEM WHICH SHE SENDS TO THE ENEMY.
WHO'S THAT?
NOT A WHISPER OUT OF YOU, OR ---
YOU GOT AWAY TWICE, BUT THIS TIME YOU'LL NEVER LIVE TO SEND THAT STORY!
HOLDING PENNY WITH ONE POWERFUL ARM, THE SPY YANKS THE PAPER FROM PENNY'S TYPEWRITER.

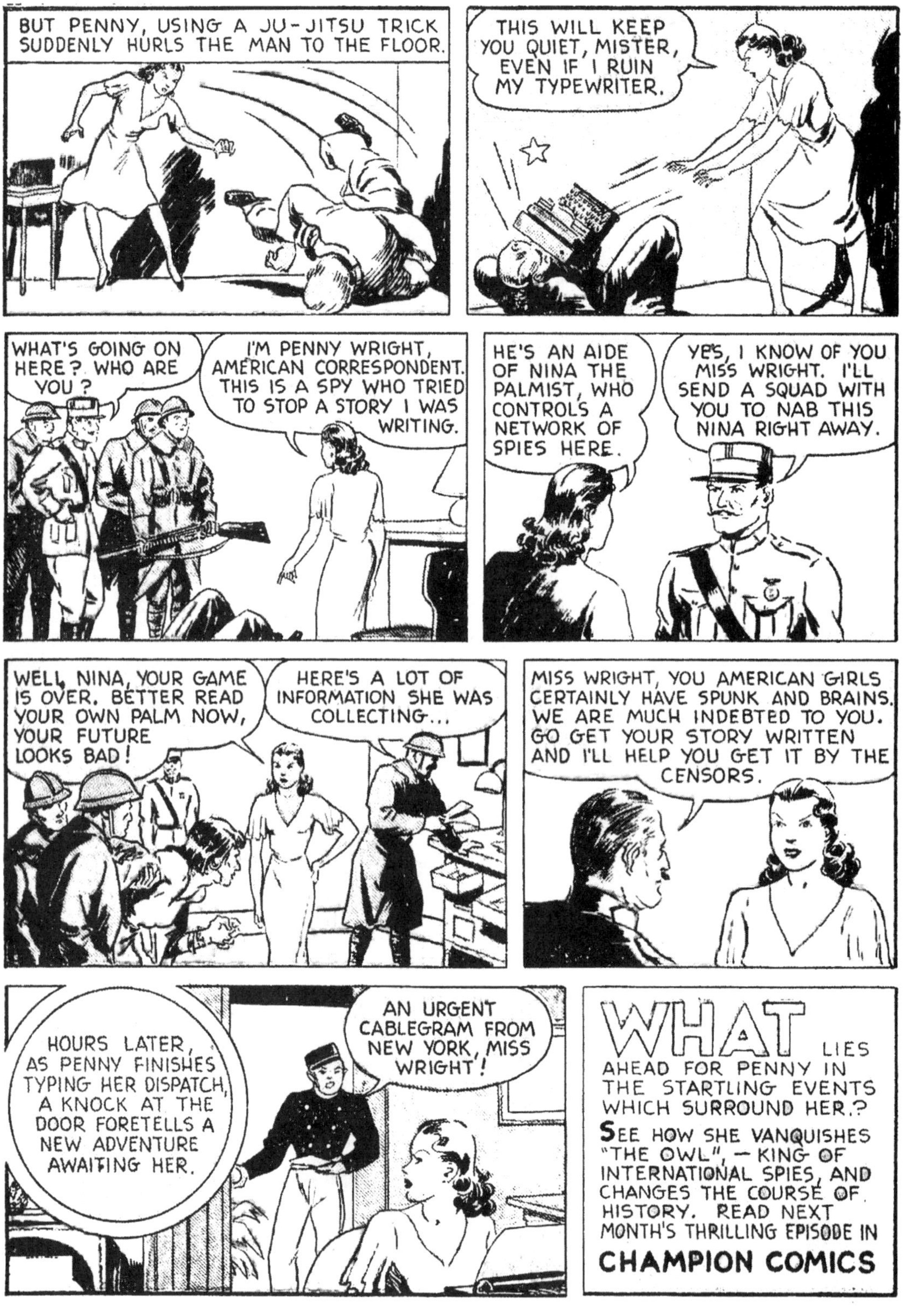
BUT PENNY, USING A JU-JITSU TRICK SUDDENLY HURLS THE MAN TO THE FLOOR.
THIS WILL KEEP YOU QUIET, MISTER, EVEN IF I RUIN MY TYPEWRITER.
WHAT'S GOING ON HERE? WHO ARE YOU?
I'M PENNY WRIGHT, AMERICAN CORRESPONDENT. THIS IS A SPY WHO TRIED TO STOP A STORY I WAS WRITING.
HE'S AN AIDE OF NINA THE PALMIST, WHO CONTROLS A NETWORK OF SPIES HERE.
YES, I KNOW OF YOU MISS WRIGHT. I'LL SEND A SQUAD WITH YOU TO NAB THIS NINA RIGHT AWAY.
WELL, NINA, YOUR GAME IS OVER. BETTER READ YOUR OWN PALM NOW, YOUR FUTURE LOOKS BAD!
HERE'S A LOT OF INFORMATION SHE WAS COLLECTING...
MISS WRIGHT, YOU AMERICAN GIRLS CERTAINLY HAVE SPUNK AND BRAINS. WE ARE MUCH INDEBTED TO YOU. GO GET YOUR STORY WRITTEN AND I'LL HELP YOU GET IT BY THE CENSORS.
HOURS LATER, AS PENNY FINISHES TYPING HER DISPATCH, A KNOCK AT THE DOOR FORETELLS A NEW ADVENTURE AWAITING HER.
AN URGENT CABLEGRAM FROM NEW YORK, MISS WRIGHT!
WHAT LIES AHEAD FOR PENNY IN THE STARTLING EVENTS WHICH SURROUND HER.?
SEE HOW SHE VANQUISHES "THE OWL", — KING OF INTERNATIONAL SPIES, AND CHANGES THE COURSE OF HISTORY. READ NEXT MONTH'S THRILLING EPISODE IN
CHAMPION COMICS

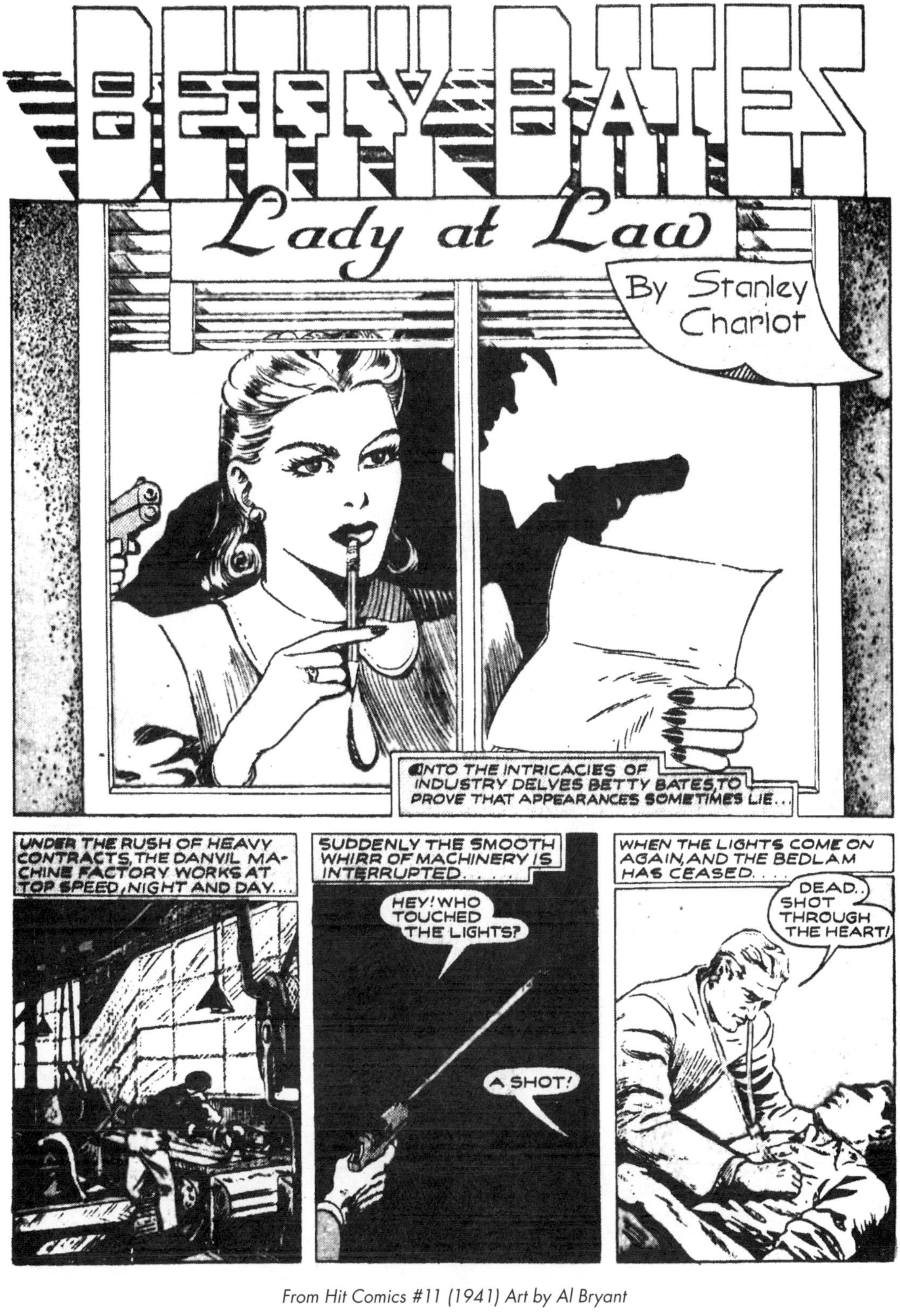
BETTY BATES
Lady at Law
By Stanley Charlot
INTO THE INTRICACIES OF INDUSTRY DELVES BETTY BATES,TO PROVE THAT APPEARANCES SOMETIMES LIE...
UNDER THE RUSH OF HEAVY CONTRACTS,THE DANVIL MACHINE FACTORY WORKS AT TOP SPEED,NIGHT AND DAY...
SUDDENLY THE SMOOTH WHIRR OF MACHINERY IS INTERRUPTED. . .
HEY! WHO TOUCHED THE LIGHTS?
A SHOT!
WHEN THE LIGHTS COME ON AGAIN,AND THE BEDLAM HAS CEASED. . . .
DEAD.. SHOT THROUGH THE HEART!

From Hit Comics #11 (1941) Art by Al Bryant

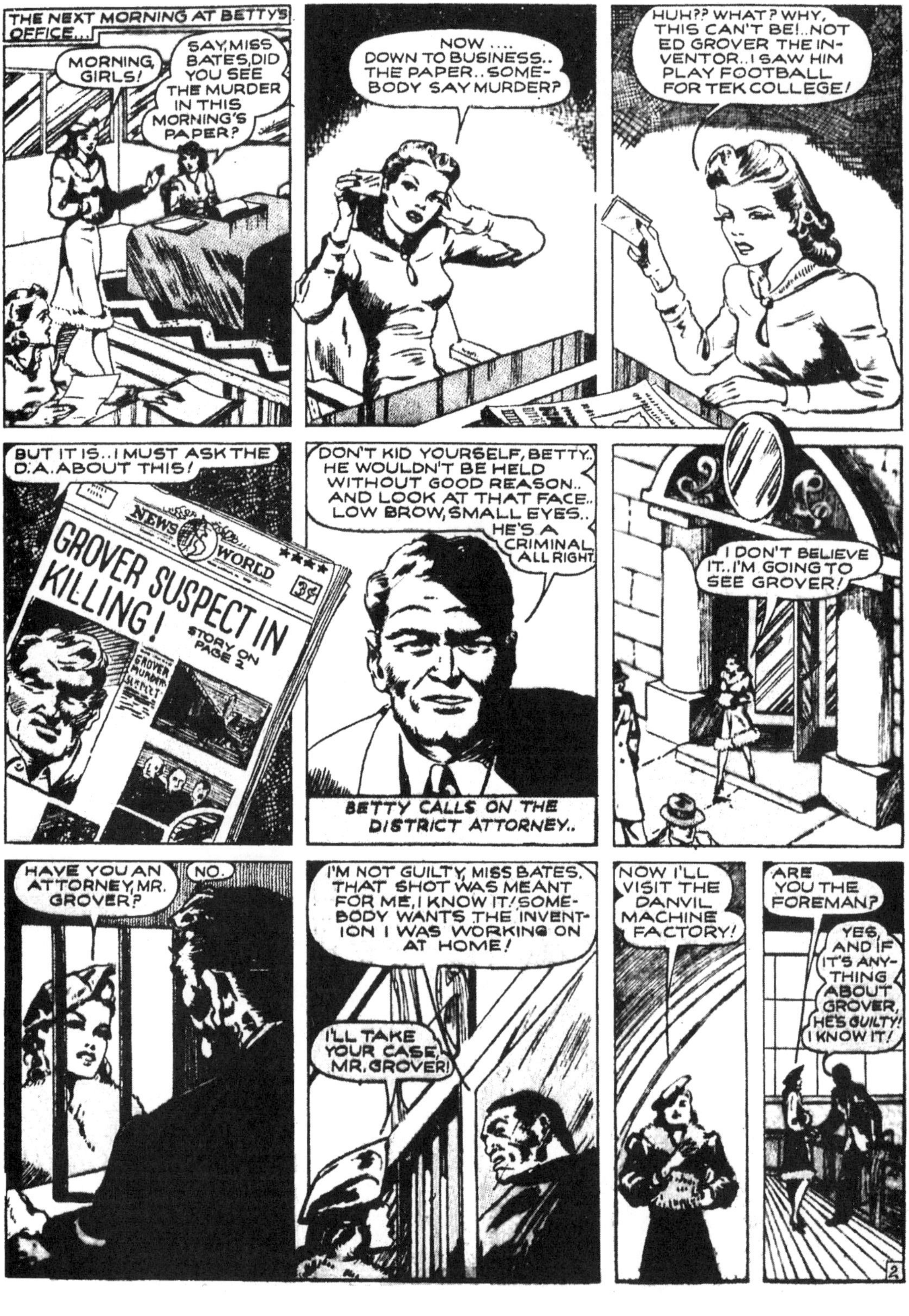
THE NEXT MORNING AT BETTY'S OFFICE...
MORNING, GIRLS!
SAY, MISS BATES, DID YOU SEE THE MURDER IN THIS MORNING'S PAPER?
NOW .... DOWN TO BUSINESS.. THE PAPER.. SOMEBODY SAY MURDER?
HUH?? WHAT? WHY, THIS CAN'T BE!..NOT ED GROVER THE INVENTOR..I SAW HIM PLAY FOOTBALL FOR TEK COLLEGE!
BUT IT IS..I MUST ASK THE D.A. ABOUT THIS!
NEWS WORLD
GROVER SUSPECT IN KILLING!
STORY ON PAGE 2
3¢
GROVER MURDER SUSPECT
DON'T KID YOURSELF, BETTY.. HE WOULDN'T BE HELD WITHOUT GOOD REASON.. AND LOOK AT THAT FACE.. LOW BROW, SMALL EYES..
HE'S A CRIMINAL ALL RIGHT.
BETTY CALLS ON THE DISTRICT ATTORNEY..
I DON'T BELIEVE IT..I'M GOING TO SEE GROVER!
HAVE YOU AN ATTORNEY, MR. GROVER?
NO.
I'M NOT GUILTY, MISS BATES. THAT SHOT WAS MEANT FOR ME, I KNOW IT! SOMEBODY WANTS THE INVENTION I WAS WORKING ON AT HOME!
I'LL TAKE YOUR CASE, MR. GROVER!
NOW I'LL VISIT THE DANVIL MACHINE FACTORY!
ARE YOU THE FOREMAN?
YES, AND IF IT'S ANYTHING ABOUT GROVER, HE'S GUILTY! I KNOW IT!
2

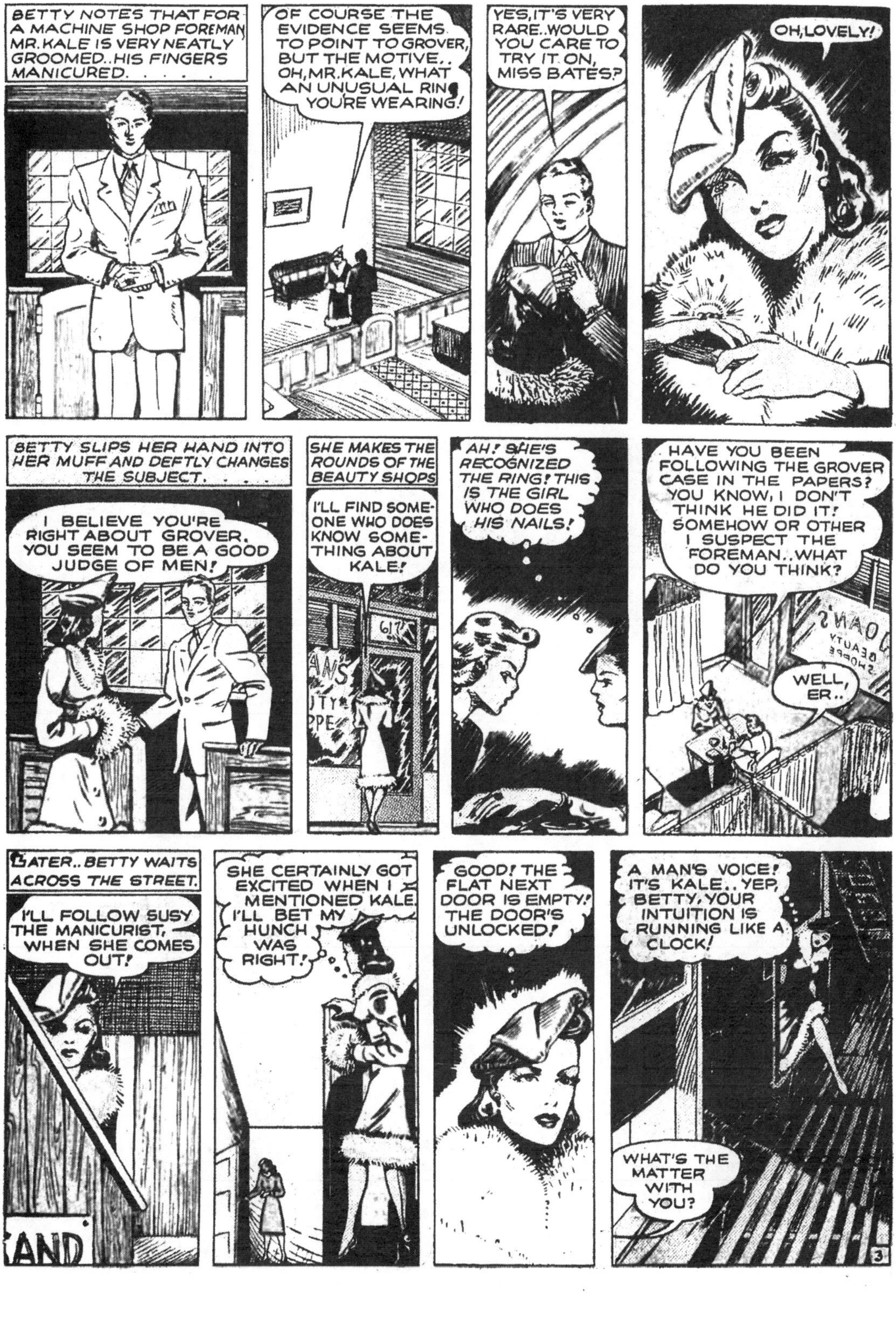
BETTY NOTES THAT FOR A MACHINE SHOP FOREMAN MR. KALE IS VERY NEATLY GROOMED..HIS FINGERS MANICURED. . . . .
OF COURSE THE EVIDENCE SEEMS TO POINT TO GROVER, BUT THE MOTIVE.. OH, MR. KALE, WHAT AN UNUSUAL RING YOU'RE WEARING!
YES, IT'S VERY RARE..WOULD YOU CARE TO TRY IT ON, MISS BATES?
OH, LOVELY!
BETTY SLIPS HER HAND INTO HER MUFF AND DEFTLY CHANGES THE SUBJECT. . . .
I BELIEVE YOU'RE RIGHT ABOUT GROVER. YOU SEEM TO BE A GOOD JUDGE OF MEN!
SHE MAKES THE ROUNDS OF THE BEAUTY SHOPS
I'LL FIND SOMEONE WHO DOES KNOW SOMETHING ABOUT KALE!
AH! SHE'S RECOGNIZED THE RING! THIS IS THE GIRL WHO DOES HIS NAILS!
HAVE YOU BEEN FOLLOWING THE GROVER CASE IN THE PAPERS? YOU KNOW, I DON'T THINK HE DID IT! SOMEHOW OR OTHER I SUSPECT THE FOREMAN..WHAT DO YOU THINK?
WELL, ER..
LATER..BETTY WAITS ACROSS THE STREET.
I'LL FOLLOW SUSY THE MANICURIST, WHEN SHE COMES OUT!
SHE CERTAINLY GOT EXCITED WHEN I MENTIONED KALE. I'LL BET MY HUNCH WAS RIGHT!
GOOD! THE FLAT NEXT DOOR IS EMPTY! THE DOOR'S UNLOCKED!
A MAN'S VOICE! IT'S KALE..YEP, BETTY, YOUR INTUITION IS RUNNING LIKE A CLOCK!
WHAT'S THE MATTER WITH YOU?
3

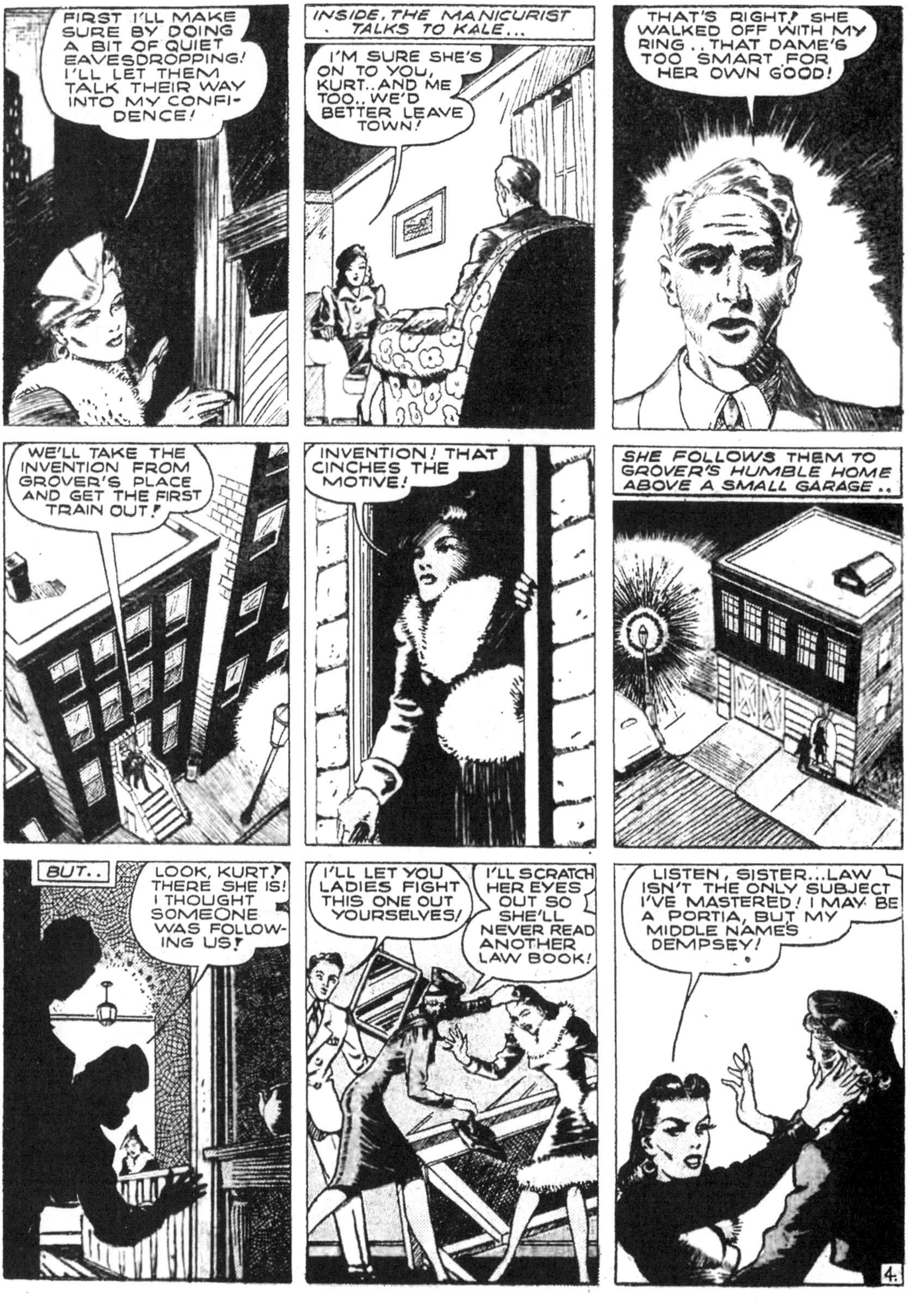
FIRST I'LL MAKE SURE BY DOING A BIT OF QUIET EAVESDROPPING! I'LL LET THEM TALK THEIR WAY INTO MY CONFI-DENCE!
INSIDE, THE MANICURIST TALKS TO KALE...
I'M SURE SHE'S ON TO YOU, KURT.. AND ME TOO.. WE'D BETTER LEAVE TOWN!
THAT'S RIGHT! SHE WALKED OFF WITH MY RING.. THAT DAME'S TOO SMART FOR HER OWN GOOD!
WE'LL TAKE THE INVENTION FROM GROVER'S PLACE AND GET THE FIRST TRAIN OUT!
INVENTION! THAT CINCHES THE MOTIVE!
SHE FOLLOWS THEM TO GROVER'S HUMBLE HOME ABOVE A SMALL GARAGE..
BUT..
LOOK, KURT! THERE SHE IS! I THOUGHT SOMEONE WAS FOLLOW-ING US!
I'LL LET YOU LADIES FIGHT THIS ONE OUT YOURSELVES!
I'LL SCRATCH HER EYES OUT SO SHE'LL NEVER READ ANOTHER LAW BOOK!
LISTEN, SISTER...LAW ISN'T THE ONLY SUBJECT I'VE MASTERED! I MAY BE A PORTIA, BUT MY MIDDLE NAME'S DEMPSEY!
4.

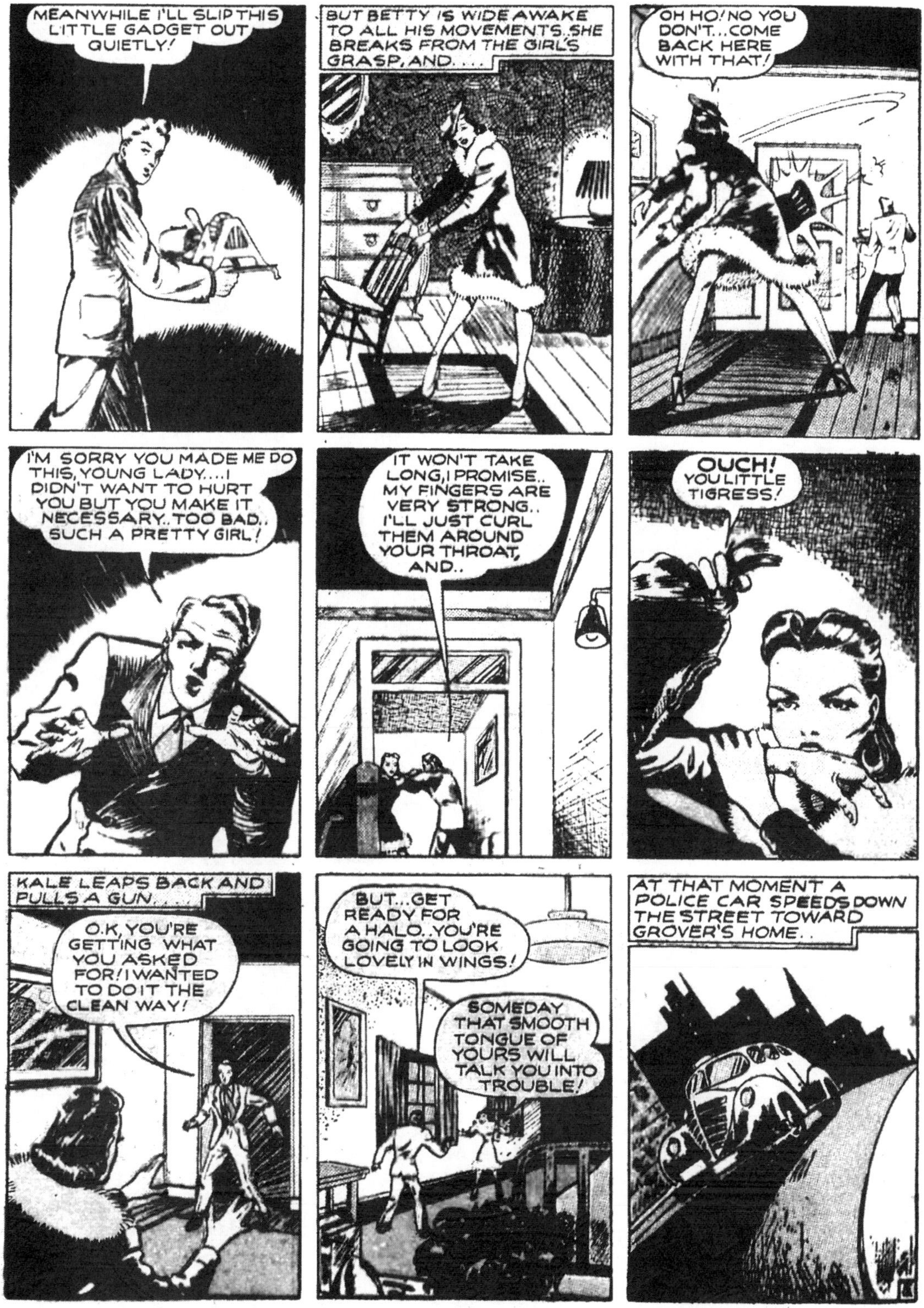
MEANWHILE I'LL SLIP THIS LITTLE GADGET OUT QUIETLY!
BUT BETTY IS WIDE AWAKE TO ALL HIS MOVEMENTS..SHE BREAKS FROM THE GIRL'S GRASP, AND. . . .
OH HO! NO YOU DON'T...COME BACK HERE WITH THAT!
I'M SORRY YOU MADE ME DO THIS, YOUNG LADY....I DIDN'T WANT TO HURT YOU BUT YOU MAKE IT NECESSARY..TOO BAD.. SUCH A PRETTY GIRL!
IT WON'T TAKE LONG, I PROMISE.. MY FINGERS ARE VERY STRONG.. I'LL JUST CURL THEM AROUND YOUR THROAT, AND..
OUCH! YOU LITTLE TIGRESS!
KALE LEAPS BACK AND PULLS A GUN. . .
O.K, YOU'RE GETTING WHAT YOU ASKED FOR! I WANTED TO DO IT THE CLEAN WAY!
BUT...GET READY FOR A HALO..YOU'RE GOING TO LOOK LOVELY IN WINGS!
SOMEDAY THAT SMOOTH TONGUE OF YOURS WILL TALK YOU INTO TROUBLE!
AT THAT MOMENT A POLICE CAR SPEEDS DOWN THE STREET TOWARD GROVER'S HOME. .

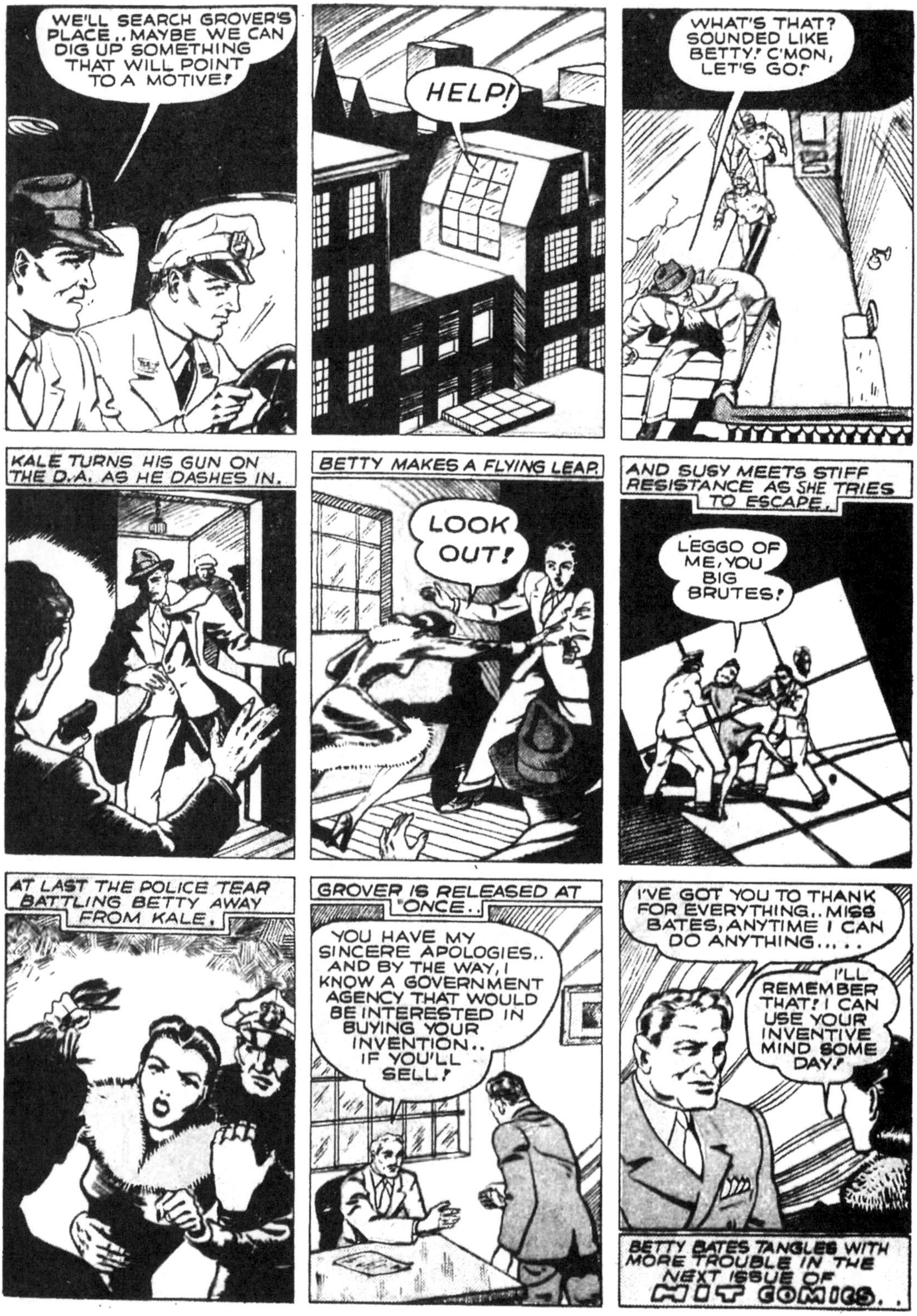
WE'LL SEARCH GROVER'S PLACE.. MAYBE WE CAN DIG UP SOMETHING THAT WILL POINT TO A MOTIVE!
HELP!
WHAT'S THAT? SOUNDED LIKE BETTY! C'MON, LET'S GO!
KALE TURNS HIS GUN ON THE D.A. AS HE DASHES IN.
BETTY MAKES A FLYING LEAP.
LOOK OUT!
AND SUSY MEETS STIFF RESISTANCE AS SHE TRIES TO ESCAPE.
LEGGO OF ME, YOU BIG BRUTES!
AT LAST THE POLICE TEAR BATTLING BETTY AWAY FROM KALE.
GROVER IS RELEASED AT ONCE.
YOU HAVE MY SINCERE APOLOGIES.. AND BY THE WAY, I KNOW A GOVERNMENT AGENCY THAT WOULD BE INTERESTED IN BUYING YOUR INVENTION.. IF YOU'LL SELL!
I'VE GOT YOU TO THANK FOR EVERYTHING.. MISS BATES, ANYTIME I CAN DO ANYTHING.....
I'LL REMEMBER THAT! I CAN USE YOUR INVENTIVE MIND SOME DAY!
BETTY BATES TANGLES WITH MORE TROUBLE IN THE NEXT ISSUE OF HIT COMICS..

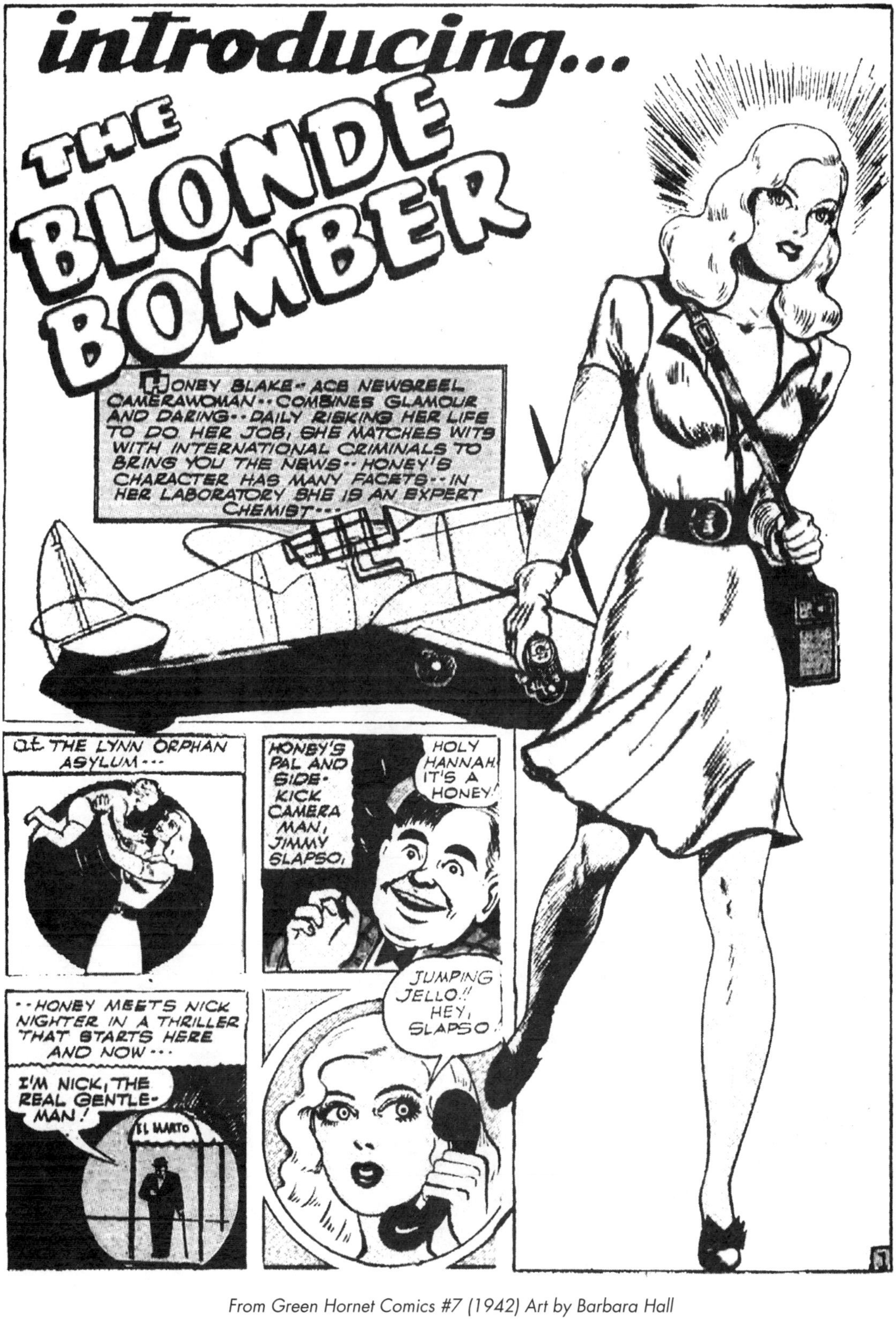
introducing...
THE BLONDE BOMBER
HONEY BLAKE -- ACE NEWSREEL CAMERAWOMAN -- COMBINES GLAMOUR AND DARING -- DAILY RISKING HER LIFE TO DO HER JOB, SHE MATCHES WITS WITH INTERNATIONAL CRIMINALS TO BRING YOU THE NEWS -- HONEY'S CHARACTER HAS MANY FACETS -- IN HER LABORATORY SHE IS AN EXPERT CHEMIST ---
AT THE LYNN ORPHAN ASYLUM ---
HONEY'S PAL AND SIDE-KICK CAMERA MAN, JIMMY SLAPSO,
HOLY HANNAH! IT'S A HONEY!
-- HONEY MEETS NICK NIGHTER IN A THRILLER THAT STARTS HERE AND NOW ---
I'M NICK, THE REAL GENTLE-MAN!
JUMPING JELLO!! HEY, SLAPSO!

From Green Hornet Comics #7 (1942) Art by Barbara Hall

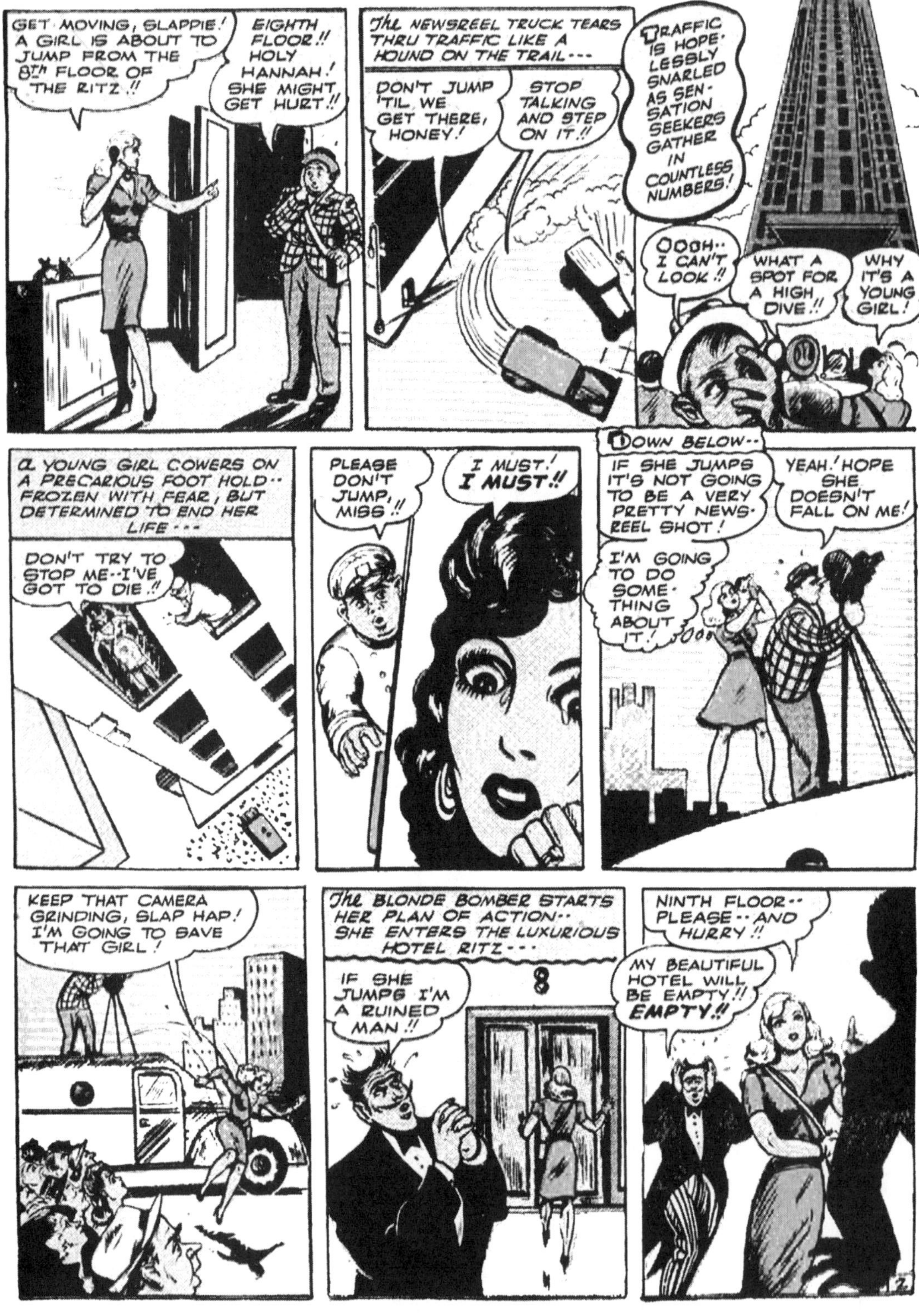
GET MOVING, SLAPPIE! A GIRL IS ABOUT TO JUMP FROM THE 8TH FLOOR OF THE RITZ !!
EIGHTH FLOOR !! HOLY HANNAH! SHE MIGHT GET HURT !!
THE NEWSREEL TRUCK TEARS THRU TRAFFIC LIKE A HOUND ON THE TRAIL---
DON'T JUMP 'TIL WE GET THERE, HONEY!
STOP TALKING AND STEP ON IT !!
TRAFFIC IS HOPELESSLY SNARLED AS SENSATION SEEKERS GATHER IN COUNTLESS NUMBERS!
OOOH.. I CAN'T LOOK !!
WHAT A SPOT FOR A HIGH DIVE !!
WHY IT'S A YOUNG GIRL!
A YOUNG GIRL COWERS ON A PRECARIOUS FOOT HOLD.. FROZEN WITH FEAR, BUT DETERMINED TO END HER LIFE---
DON'T TRY TO STOP ME--I'VE GOT TO DIE !!
PLEASE DON'T JUMP, MISS !!
I MUST! I MUST!!
DOWN BELOW..
IF SHE JUMPS IT'S NOT GOING TO BE A VERY PRETTY NEWSREEL SHOT!
YEAH! HOPE SHE DOESN'T FALL ON ME!
I'M GOING TO DO SOMETHING ABOUT IT!
KEEP THAT CAMERA GRINDING, SLAP HAP! I'M GOING TO SAVE THAT GIRL!
THE BLONDE BOMBER STARTS HER PLAN OF ACTION.. SHE ENTERS THE LUXURIOUS HOTEL RITZ---
IF SHE JUMPS I'M A RUINED MAN !!
8
NINTH FLOOR.. PLEASE--AND HURRY !!
MY BEAUTIFUL HOTEL WILL BE EMPTY !! EMPTY !!
7

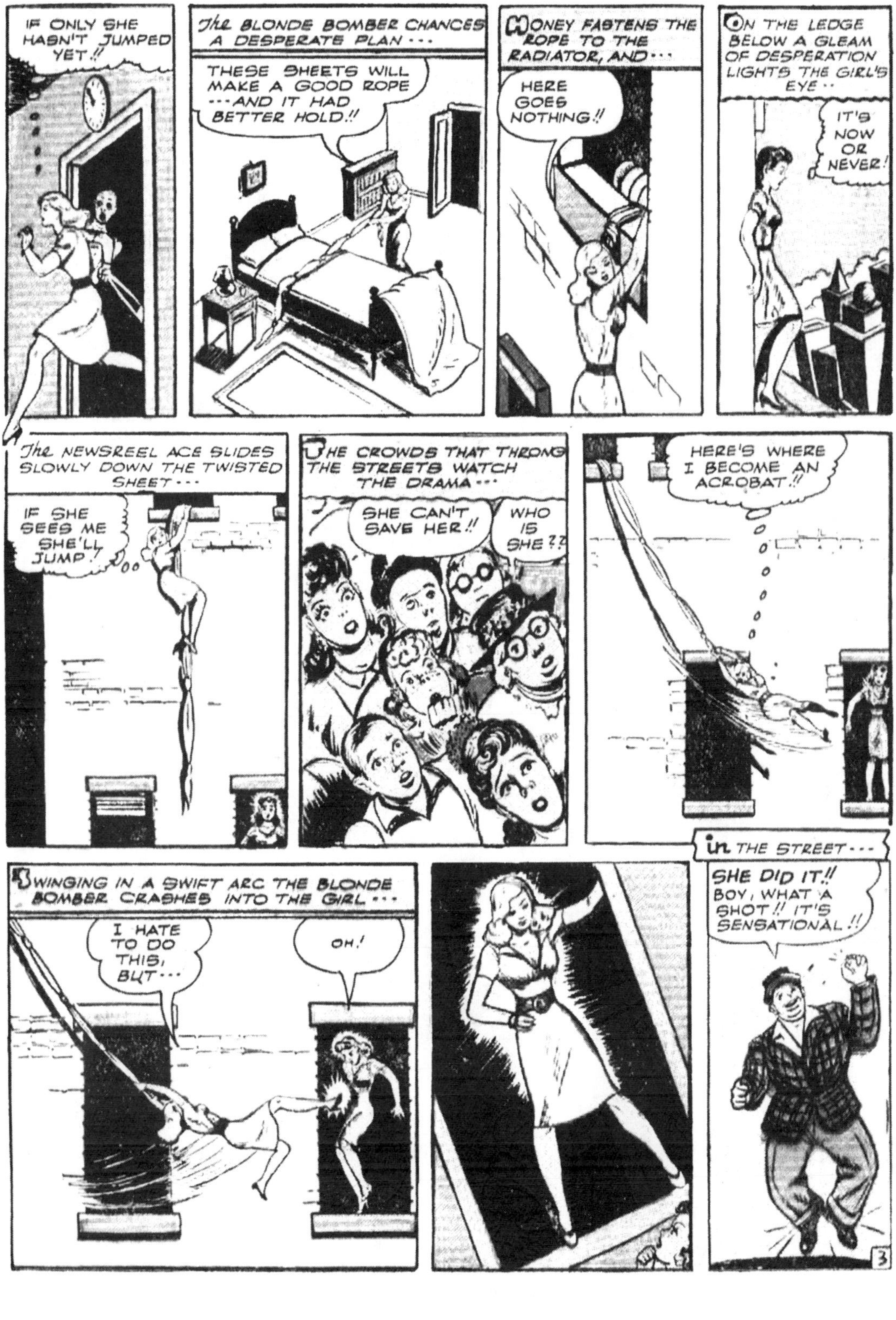
IF ONLY SHE HASN'T JUMPED YET!!
The BLONDE BOMBER CHANCES A DESPERATE PLAN ···
THESE SHEETS WILL MAKE A GOOD ROPE ···AND IT HAD BETTER HOLD!!
HONEY FASTENS THE ROPE TO THE RADIATOR, AND···
HERE GOES NOTHING!!
ON THE LEDGE BELOW A GLEAM OF DESPERATION LIGHTS THE GIRL'S EYE··
IT'S NOW OR NEVER!
The NEWSREEL ACE SLIDES SLOWLY DOWN THE TWISTED SHEET···
IF SHE SEES ME SHE'LL JUMP!
THE CROWDS THAT THRONG THE STREETS WATCH THE DRAMA···
SHE CAN'T SAVE HER!!
WHO IS SHE??
HERE'S WHERE I BECOME AN ACROBAT!!
SWINGING IN A SWIFT ARC THE BLONDE BOMBER CRASHES INTO THE GIRL···
I HATE TO DO THIS, BUT···
OH!
in THE STREET···
SHE DID IT!! BOY, WHAT A SHOT!! IT'S SENSATIONAL!!
3

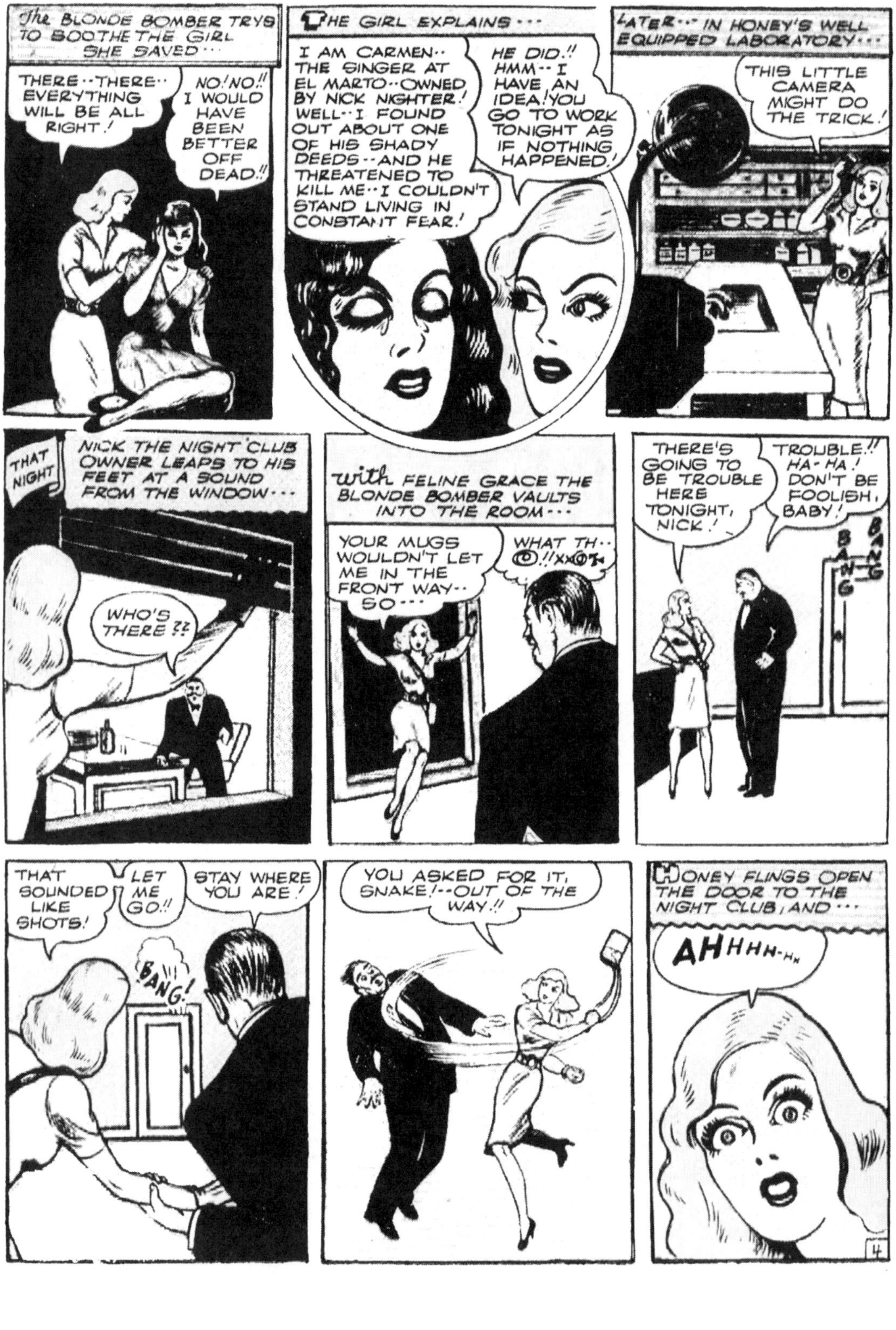
The BLONDE BOMBER TRYS TO SOOTHE THE GIRL SHE SAVED···
THERE··THERE·· EVERYTHING WILL BE ALL RIGHT!
NO! NO!! I WOULD HAVE BEEN BETTER OFF DEAD!!
THE GIRL EXPLAINS···
I AM CARMEN·· THE SINGER AT EL MARTO··OWNED BY NICK NIGHTER! WELL··I FOUND OUT ABOUT ONE OF HIS SHADY DEEDS··AND HE THREATENED TO KILL ME··I COULDN'T STAND LIVING IN CONSTANT FEAR!
HE DID!! HMM··I HAVE AN IDEA! YOU GO TO WORK TONIGHT AS IF NOTHING HAPPENED!
LATER··· IN HONEY'S WELL EQUIPPED LABORATORY···
THIS LITTLE CAMERA MIGHT DO THE TRICK!
THAT NIGHT
NICK THE NIGHT CLUB OWNER LEAPS TO HIS FEET AT A SOUND FROM THE WINDOW···
WHO'S THERE??
with FELINE GRACE THE BLONDE BOMBER VAULTS INTO THE ROOM···
YOUR MUGS WOULDN'T LET ME IN THE FRONT WAY·· SO···
WHAT TH··
THERE'S GOING TO BE TROUBLE HERE TONIGHT, NICK!
TROUBLE!! HA-HA! DON'T BE FOOLISH, BABY!
BANG
BANG
THAT SOUNDED LIKE SHOTS!
LET ME GO!!
STAY WHERE YOU ARE!
BANG!
YOU ASKED FOR IT, SNAKE!--OUT OF THE WAY!!
HONEY FLINGS OPEN THE DOOR TO THE NIGHT CLUB, AND···
AHHHH-HH
4

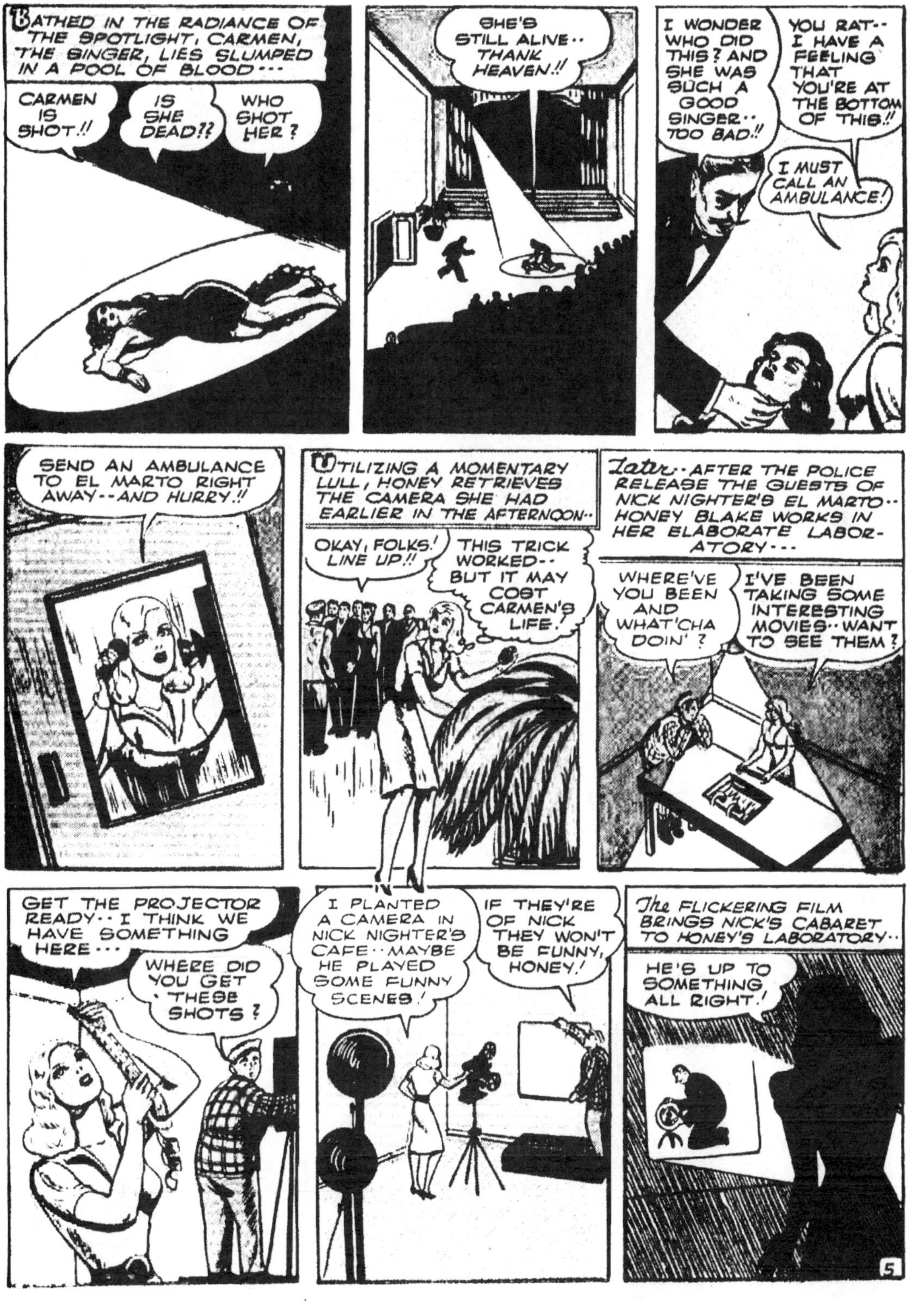
BATHED IN THE RADIANCE OF THE SPOTLIGHT, CARMEN, THE SINGER, LIES SLUMPED IN A POOL OF BLOOD---
CARMEN IS SHOT!!
IS SHE DEAD??
WHO SHOT HER?
SHE'S STILL ALIVE.. THANK HEAVEN!!
I WONDER WHO DID THIS? AND SHE WAS SUCH A GOOD SINGER.. TOO BAD!!
YOU RAT-- I HAVE A FEELING THAT YOU'RE AT THE BOTTOM OF THIS!!
I MUST CALL AN AMBULANCE!
SEND AN AMBULANCE TO EL MARTO RIGHT AWAY--AND HURRY!!
UTILIZING A MOMENTARY LULL, HONEY RETRIEVES THE CAMERA SHE HAD EARLIER IN THE AFTERNOON..
OKAY, FOLKS! LINE UP!!
THIS TRICK WORKED-- BUT IT MAY COST CARMEN'S LIFE!
Later.. AFTER THE POLICE RELEASE THE GUESTS OF NICK NIGHTER'S EL MARTO.. HONEY BLAKE WORKS IN HER ELABORATE LABORATORY---
WHERE'VE YOU BEEN AND WHAT'CHA DOIN'?
I'VE BEEN TAKING SOME INTERESTING MOVIES.. WANT TO SEE THEM?
GET THE PROJECTOR READY.. I THINK WE HAVE SOMETHING HERE---
WHERE DID YOU GET THESE SHOTS?
I PLANTED A CAMERA IN NICK NIGHTER'S CAFE.. MAYBE HE PLAYED SOME FUNNY SCENES!
IF THEY'RE OF NICK THEY WON'T BE FUNNY, HONEY!
The FLICKERING FILM BRINGS NICK'S CABARET TO HONEY'S LABORATORY..
HE'S UP TO SOMETHING ALL RIGHT!
5

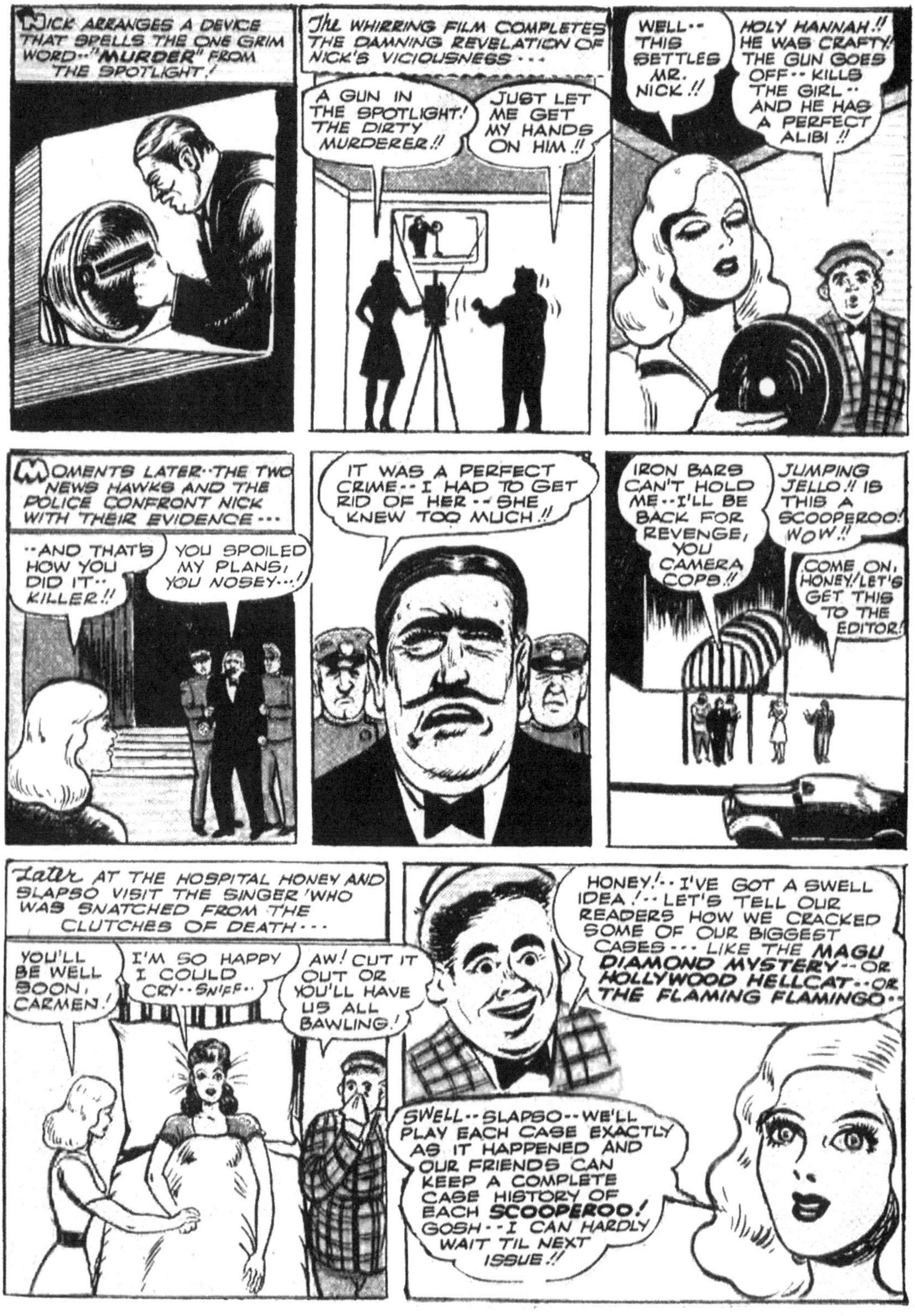
NICK ARRANGES A DEVICE THAT SPELLS THE ONE GRIM WORD--"MURDER" FROM THE SPOTLIGHT!
THE WHIRRING FILM COMPLETES THE DAMNING REVELATION OF NICK'S VICIOUSNESS ---
A GUN IN THE SPOTLIGHT! THE DIRTY MURDERER!!
JUST LET ME GET MY HANDS ON HIM!!
WELL-- THIS SETTLES MR. NICK!!
HOLY HANNAH!! HE WAS CRAFTY! THE GUN GOES OFF--KILLS THE GIRL-- AND HE HAS A PERFECT ALIBI!!
MOMENTS LATER--THE TWO NEWS HAWKS AND THE POLICE CONFRONT NICK WITH THEIR EVIDENCE ---
--AND THAT'S HOW YOU DID IT-- KILLER!!
YOU SPOILED MY PLANS, YOU NOSEY---!
IT WAS A PERFECT CRIME--I HAD TO GET RID OF HER--SHE KNEW TOO MUCH!!
IRON BARS CAN'T HOLD ME--I'LL BE BACK FOR REVENGE, YOU CAMERA COPS!!
JUMPING JELLO!! IS THIS A SCOOPEROO! WOW!!
COME ON, HONEY! LET'S GET THIS TO THE EDITOR!
LATER AT THE HOSPITAL HONEY AND SLAPSO VISIT THE SINGER WHO WAS SNATCHED FROM THE CLUTCHES OF DEATH ---
YOU'LL BE WELL SOON, CARMEN!
I'M SO HAPPY I COULD CRY--SNIFF--
AW! CUT IT OUT OR YOU'LL HAVE US ALL BAWLING!
HONEY!--I'VE GOT A SWELL IDEA!--LET'S TELL OUR READERS HOW WE CRACKED SOME OF OUR BIGGEST CASES --- LIKE THE MAGU DIAMOND MYSTERY--OR HOLLYWOOD HELLCAT--OR THE FLAMING FLAMINGO--
SWELL--SLAPSO--WE'LL PLAY EACH CASE EXACTLY AS IT HAPPENED AND OUR FRIENDS CAN KEEP A COMPLETE CASE HISTORY OF EACH SCOOPEROO! GOSH--I CAN HARDLY WAIT TIL NEXT ISSUE!!

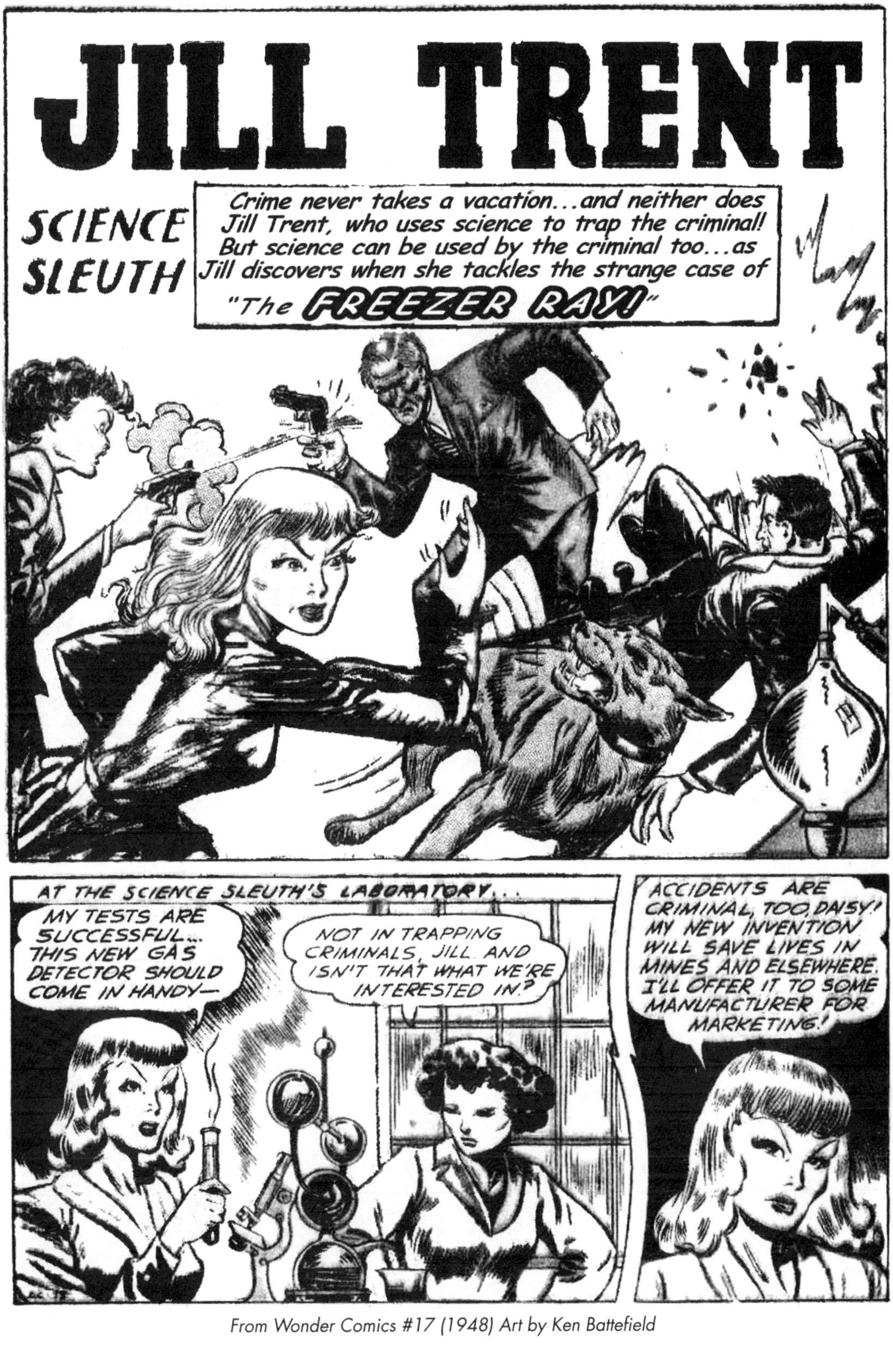
JILL TRENT
SCIENCE SLEUTH
Crime never takes a vacation...and neither does Jill Trent, who uses science to trap the criminal! But science can be used by the criminal too...as Jill discovers when she tackles the strange case of
"The FREEZER RAY!"
AT THE SCIENCE SLEUTH'S LABORATORY...
MY TESTS ARE SUCCESSFUL... THIS NEW GAS DETECTOR SHOULD COME IN HANDY—
NOT IN TRAPPING CRIMINALS, JILL. AND ISN'T THAT WHAT WE'RE INTERESTED IN?
ACCIDENTS ARE CRIMINAL, TOO, DAISY! MY NEW INVENTION WILL SAVE LIVES IN MINES AND ELSEWHERE. I'LL OFFER IT TO SOME MANUFACTURER FOR MARKETING!

From Wonder Comics #17 (1948) Art by Ken Battefield

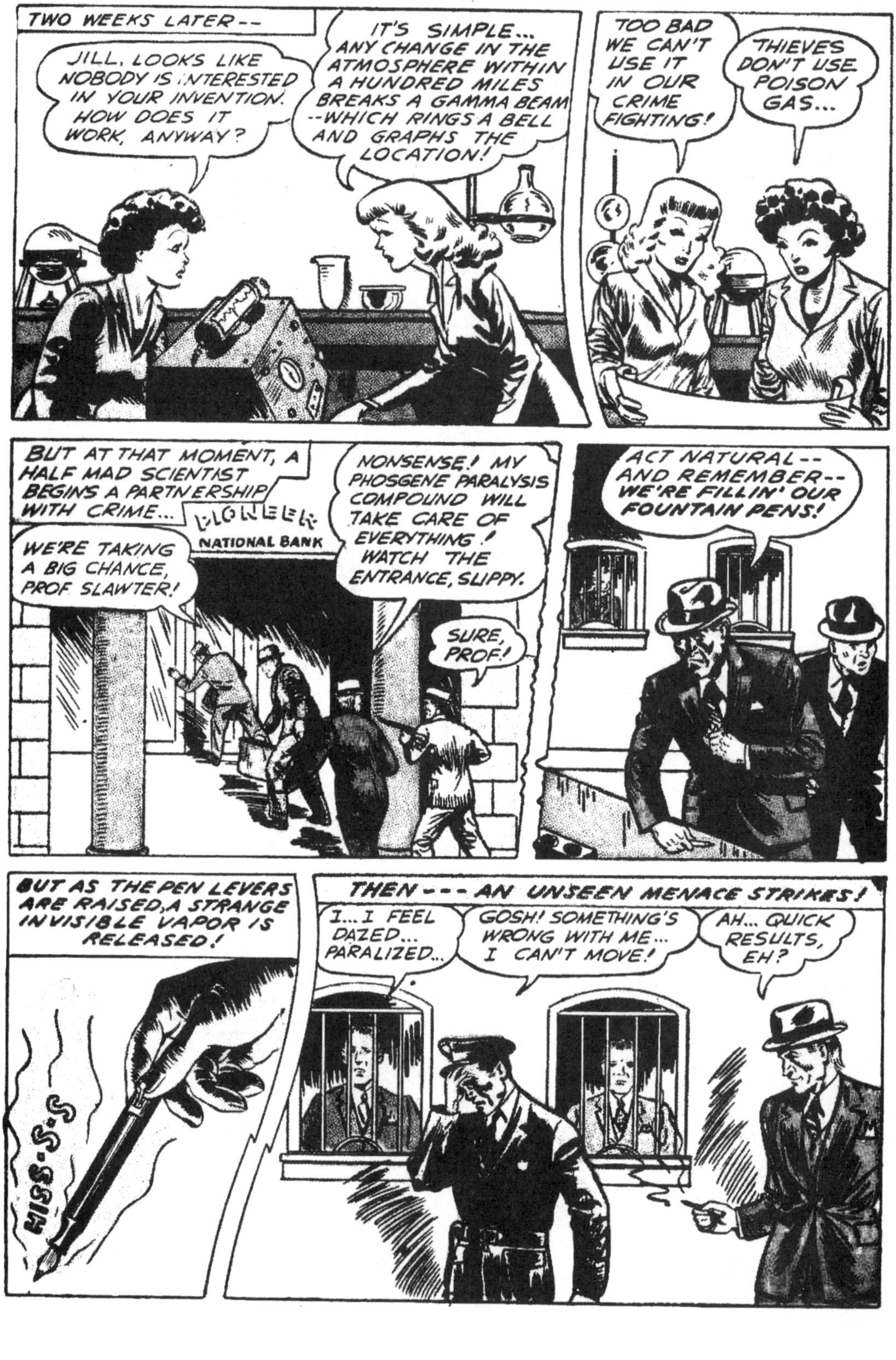
TWO WEEKS LATER--
JILL, LOOKS LIKE NOBODY IS INTERESTED IN YOUR INVENTION. HOW DOES IT WORK, ANYWAY?
IT'S SIMPLE... ANY CHANGE IN THE ATMOSPHERE WITHIN A HUNDRED MILES BREAKS A GAMMA BEAM --WHICH RINGS A BELL AND GRAPHS THE LOCATION!
TOO BAD WE CAN'T USE IT IN OUR CRIME FIGHTING!
THIEVES DON'T USE POISON GAS...
BUT AT THAT MOMENT, A HALF MAD SCIENTIST BEGINS A PARTNERSHIP WITH CRIME...
PIONEER NATIONAL BANK
WE'RE TAKING A BIG CHANCE, PROF SLAWTER!
NONSENSE! MY PHOSGENE PARALYSIS COMPOUND WILL TAKE CARE OF EVERYTHING! WATCH THE ENTRANCE, SLIPPY.
SURE, PROF!
ACT NATURAL-- AND REMEMBER-- WE'RE FILLIN' OUR FOUNTAIN PENS!
BUT AS THE PEN LEVERS ARE RAISED, A STRANGE INVISIBLE VAPOR IS RELEASED!
HISS-S-S
THEN --- AN UNSEEN MENACE STRIKES!
I... I FEEL DAZED... PARALIZED...
GOSH! SOMETHING'S WRONG WITH ME... I CAN'T MOVE!
AH... QUICK RESULTS, EH?

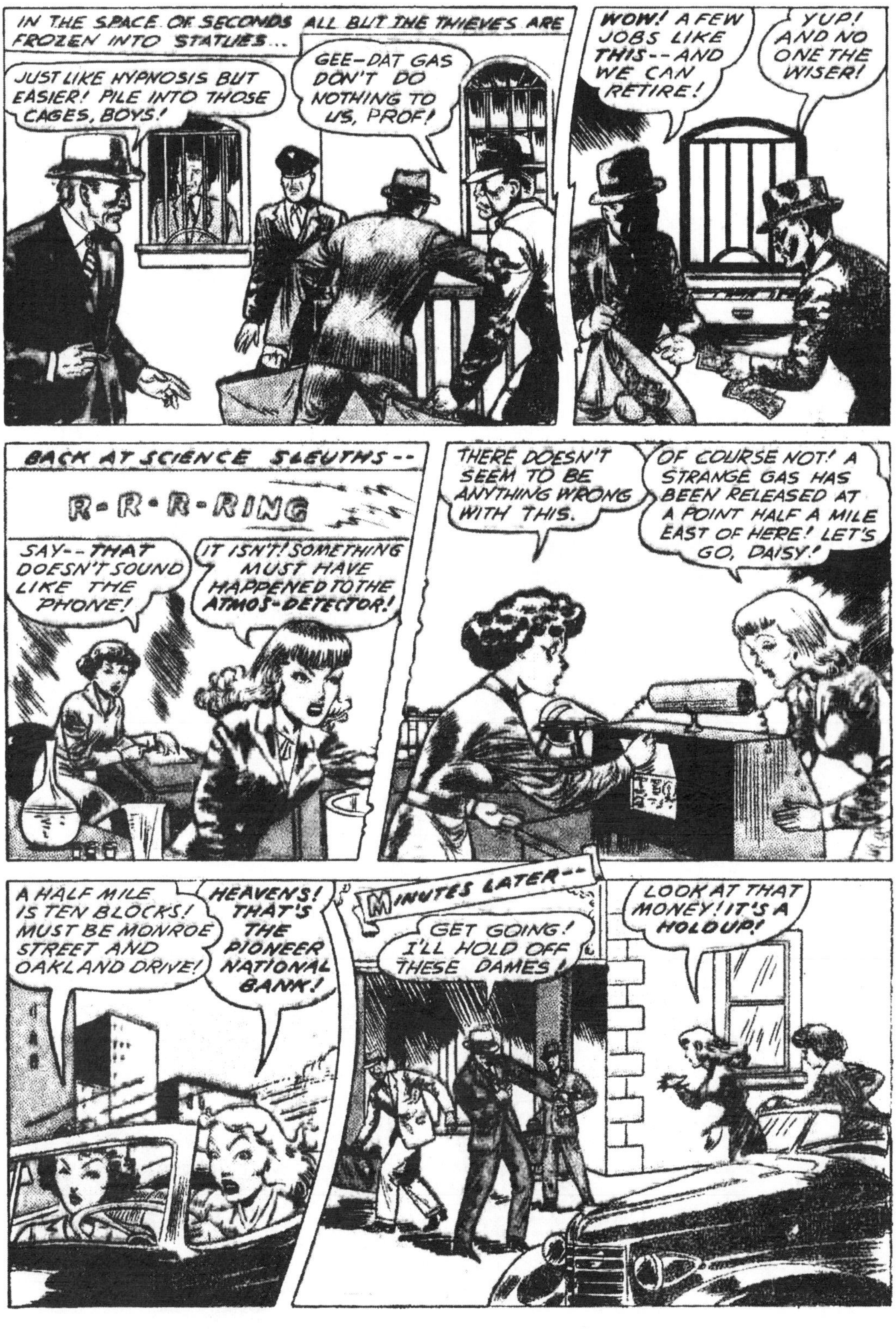
IN THE SPACE OF SECONDS ALL BUT THE THIEVES ARE FROZEN INTO STATUES...
JUST LIKE HYPNOSIS BUT EASIER! PILE INTO THOSE CAGES, BOYS!
GEE-DAT GAS DON'T DO NOTHING TO US, PROF!
WOW! A FEW JOBS LIKE THIS--AND WE CAN RETIRE!
YUP! AND NO ONE THE WISER!
BACK AT SCIENCE SLEUTHS--
R-R-R-RING
SAY--THAT DOESN'T SOUND LIKE THE PHONE!
IT ISN'T! SOMETHING MUST HAVE HAPPENED TO THE ATMOS-DETECTOR!
THERE DOESN'T SEEM TO BE ANYTHING WRONG WITH THIS.
OF COURSE NOT! A STRANGE GAS HAS BEEN RELEASED AT A POINT HALF A MILE EAST OF HERE! LET'S GO, DAISY!
A HALF MILE IS TEN BLOCKS! MUST BE MONROE STREET AND OAKLAND DRIVE!
HEAVENS! THAT'S THE PIONEER NATIONAL BANK!
MINUTES LATER--
GET GOING! I'LL HOLD OFF THESE DAMES!
LOOK AT THAT MONEY! IT'S A HOLDUP!

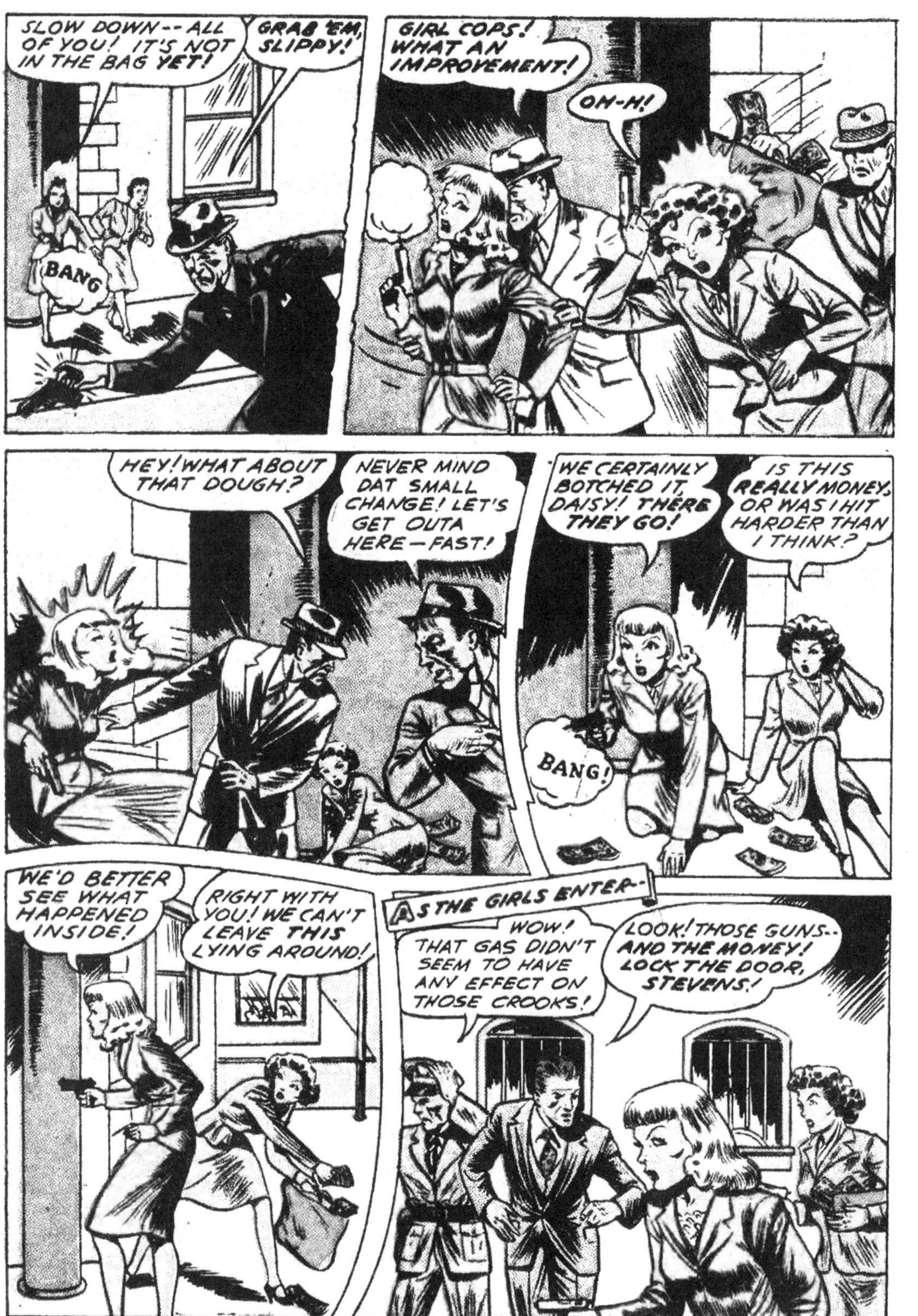
SLOW DOWN-- ALL OF YOU! IT'S NOT IN THE BAG YET!
GRAB 'EM, SLIPPY!
BANG
GIRL COPS! WHAT AN IMPROVEMENT!
OH-H!
HEY! WHAT ABOUT THAT DOUGH?
NEVER MIND DAT SMALL CHANGE! LET'S GET OUTA HERE—FAST!
WE CERTAINLY BOTCHED IT, DAISY! THERE THEY GO!
IS THIS REALLY MONEY, OR WAS I HIT HARDER THAN I THINK?
BANG!
WE'D BETTER SEE WHAT HAPPENED INSIDE!
RIGHT WITH YOU! WE CAN'T LEAVE THIS LYING AROUND!
AS THE GIRLS ENTER--
WOW! THAT GAS DIDN'T SEEM TO HAVE ANY EFFECT ON THOSE CROOKS!
LOOK! THOSE GUNS-- AND THE MONEY! LOCK THE DOOR, STEVENS!

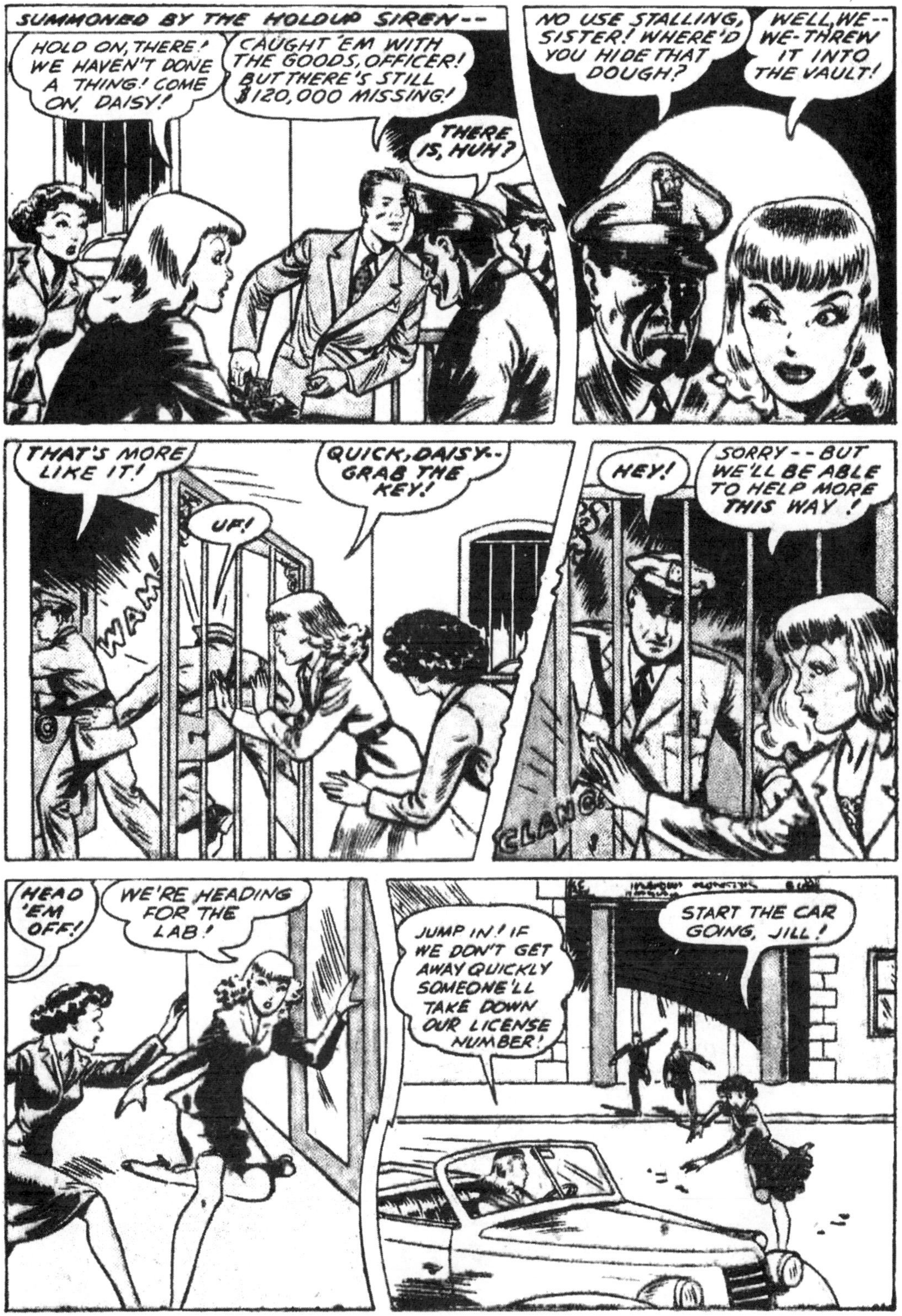
SUMMONED BY THE HOLDUP SIREN--
HOLD ON, THERE! WE HAVEN'T DONE A THING! COME ON, DAISY!
CAUGHT 'EM WITH THE GOODS, OFFICER! BUT THERE'S STILL $120,000 MISSING!
THERE IS, HUH?
NO USE STALLING, SISTER! WHERE'D YOU HIDE THAT DOUGH?
WELL, WE-- WE-THREW IT INTO THE VAULT!
THAT'S MORE LIKE IT!
WAM!
UF!
QUICK, DAISY-- GRAB THE KEY!
HEY!
SORRY--BUT WE'LL BE ABLE TO HELP MORE THIS WAY!
CLANG!
HEAD 'EM OFF!
WE'RE HEADING FOR THE LAB!
JUMP IN! IF WE DON'T GET AWAY QUICKLY SOMEONE'LL TAKE DOWN OUR LICENSE NUMBER!
START THE CAR GOING, JILL!

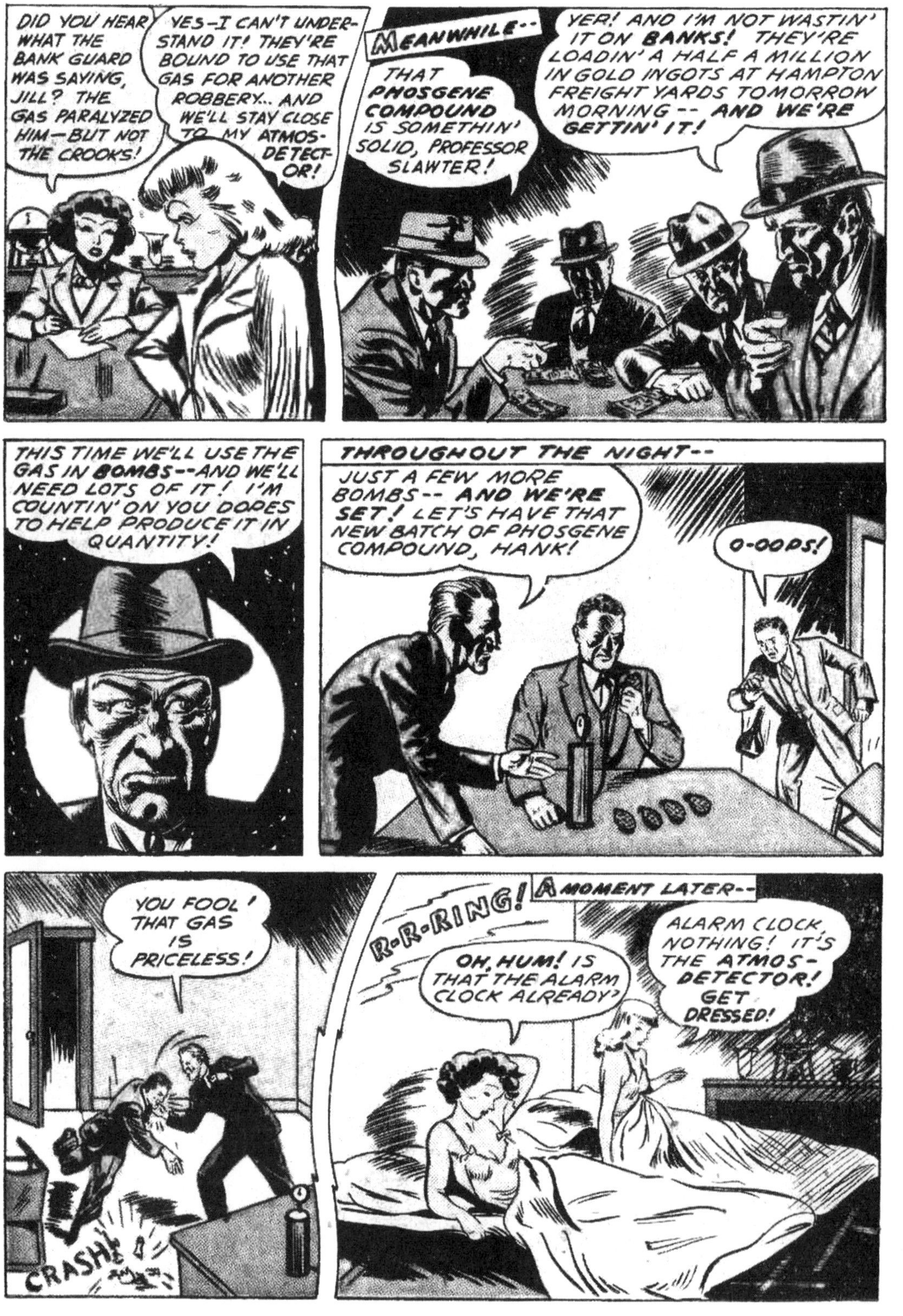
DID YOU HEAR WHAT THE BANK GUARD WAS SAYING, JILL? THE GAS PARALYZED HIM—BUT NOT THE CROOKS!
YES—I CAN'T UNDERSTAND IT! THEY'RE BOUND TO USE THAT GAS FOR ANOTHER ROBBERY... AND WE'LL STAY CLOSE TO MY ATMOS-DETECTOR!
MEANWHILE--
THAT PHOSGENE COMPOUND IS SOMETHIN' SOLID, PROFESSOR SLAWTER!
YEP! AND I'M NOT WASTIN' IT ON BANKS! THEY'RE LOADIN' A HALF A MILLION IN GOLD INGOTS AT HAMPTON FREIGHT YARDS TOMORROW MORNING -- AND WE'RE GETTIN' IT!
THIS TIME WE'LL USE THE GAS IN BOMBS--AND WE'LL NEED LOTS OF IT! I'M COUNTIN' ON YOU DOPES TO HELP PRODUCE IT IN QUANTITY!
THROUGHOUT THE NIGHT--
JUST A FEW MORE BOMBS-- AND WE'RE SET! LET'S HAVE THAT NEW BATCH OF PHOSGENE COMPOUND, HANK!
O-OOPS!
YOU FOOL! THAT GAS IS PRICELESS!
CRASH!
R-R-RING!
A MOMENT LATER--
OH, HUM! IS THAT THE ALARM CLOCK ALREADY?
ALARM CLOCK, NOTHING! IT'S THE ATMOS-DETECTOR! GET DRESSED!

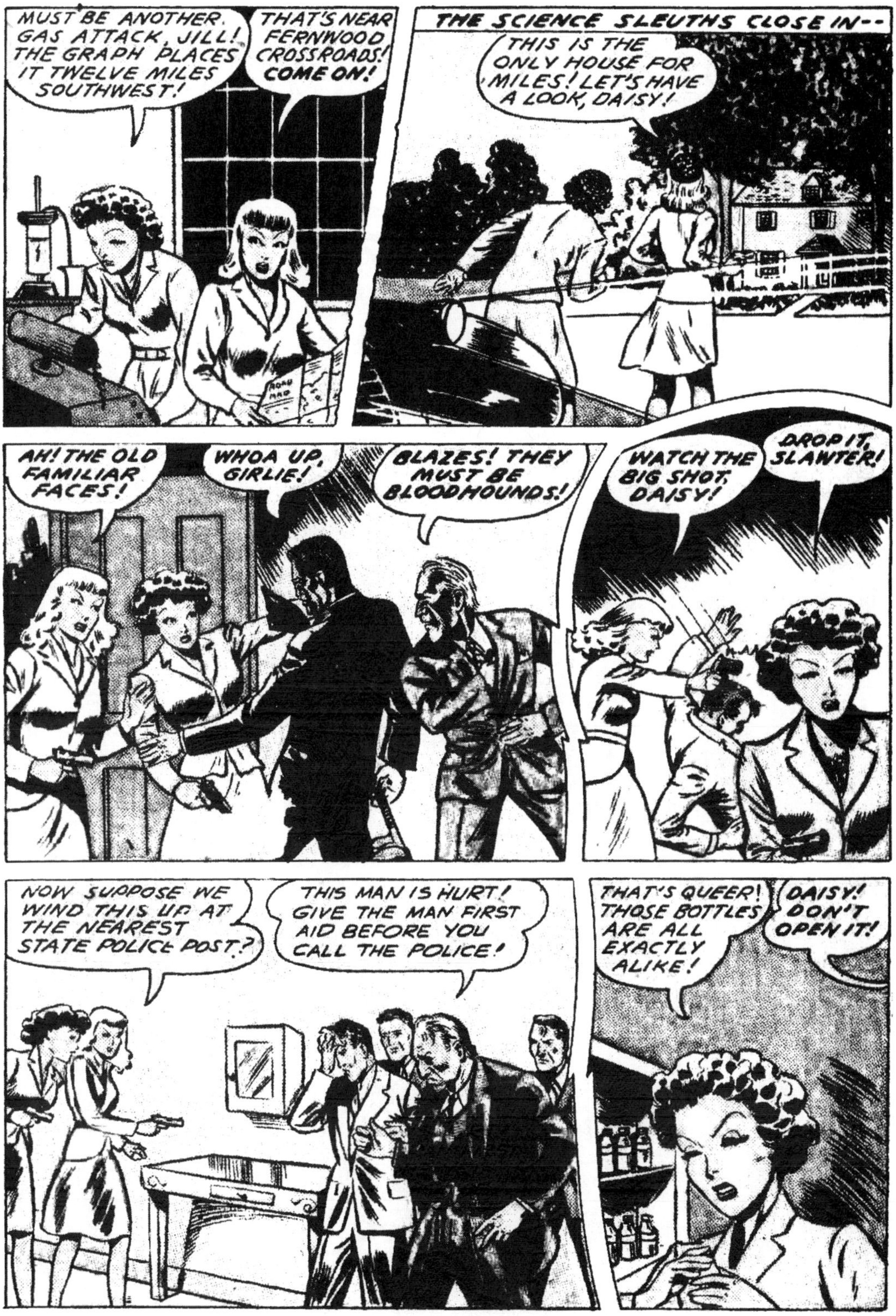
MUST BE ANOTHER GAS ATTACK, JILL! THE GRAPH PLACES IT TWELVE MILES SOUTHWEST!
THAT'S NEAR FERNWOOD CROSSROADS! COME ON!
THE SCIENCE SLEUTHS CLOSE IN--
THIS IS THE ONLY HOUSE FOR MILES! LET'S HAVE A LOOK, DAISY!
AH! THE OLD FAMILIAR FACES!
WHOA UP, GIRLIE!
BLAZES! THEY MUST BE BLOODHOUNDS!
WATCH THE BIG SHOT, DAISY!
DROP IT, SLAWTER!
NOW SUPPOSE WE WIND THIS UP AT THE NEAREST STATE POLICE POST?
THIS MAN IS HURT! GIVE THE MAN FIRST AID BEFORE YOU CALL THE POLICE!
THAT'S QUEER! THOSE BOTTLES ARE ALL EXACTLY ALIKE!
DAISY! DON'T OPEN IT!

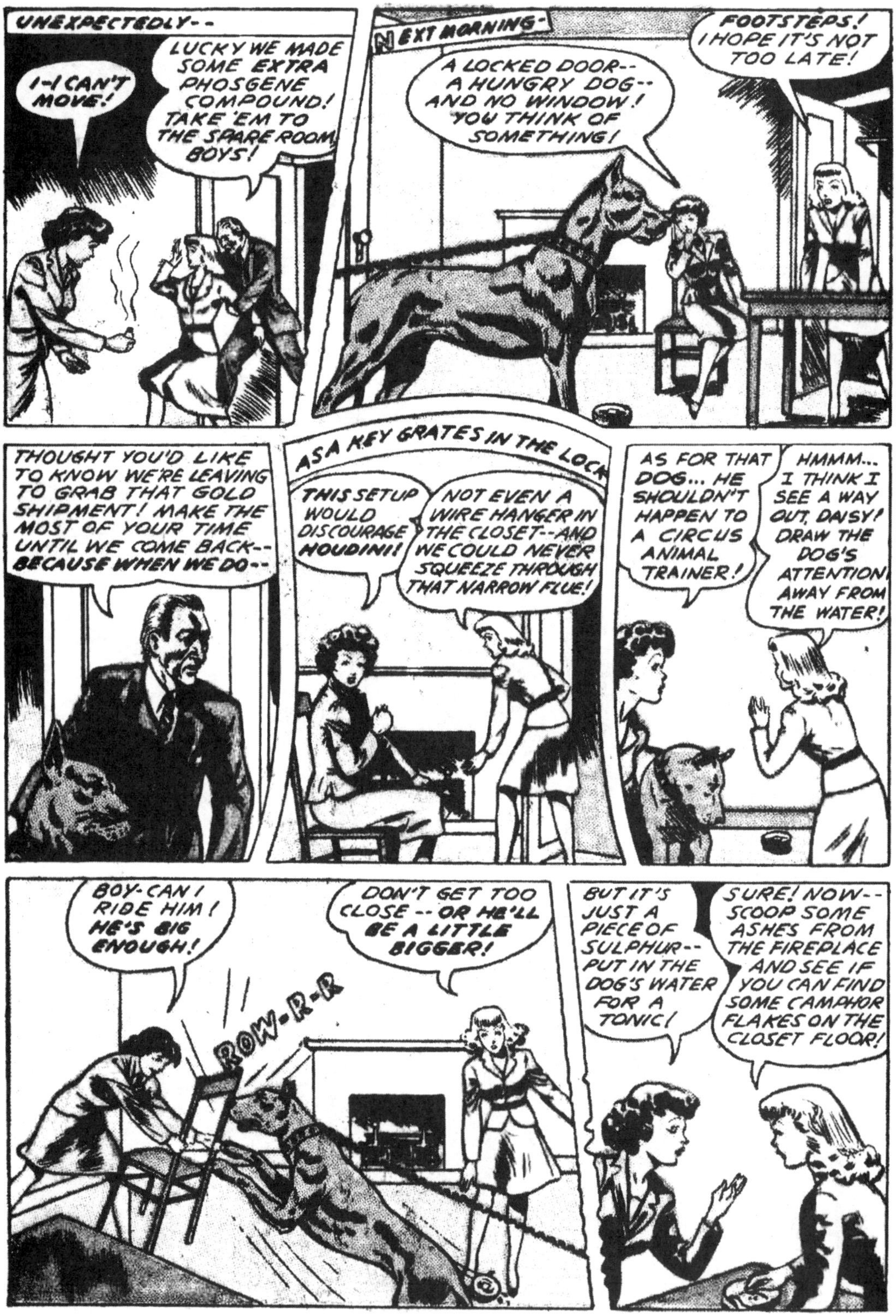
UNEXPECTEDLY--
I-I CAN'T MOVE!
LUCKY WE MADE SOME EXTRA PHOSGENE COMPOUND! TAKE 'EM TO THE SPARE ROOM, BOYS!
NEXT MORNING-
A LOCKED DOOR-- A HUNGRY DOG-- AND NO WINDOW! YOU THINK OF SOMETHING!
FOOTSTEPS! I HOPE IT'S NOT TOO LATE!
THOUGHT YOU'D LIKE TO KNOW WE'RE LEAVING TO GRAB THAT GOLD SHIPMENT! MAKE THE MOST OF YOUR TIME UNTIL WE COME BACK-- BECAUSE WHEN WE DO--
AS A KEY GRATES IN THE LOCK
THIS SETUP WOULD DISCOURAGE HOUDINI!
NOT EVEN A WIRE HANGER IN THE CLOSET--AND WE COULD NEVER SQUEEZE THROUGH THAT NARROW FLUE!
AS FOR THAT DOG... HE SHOULDN'T HAPPEN TO A CIRCUS ANIMAL TRAINER!
HMMM... I THINK I SEE A WAY OUT, DAISY! DRAW THE DOG'S ATTENTION AWAY FROM THE WATER!
BOY-CAN I RIDE HIM! HE'S BIG ENOUGH!
DON'T GET TOO CLOSE -- OR HE'LL BE A LITTLE BIGGER!
ROW-R-R
BUT IT'S JUST A PIECE OF SULPHUR-- PUT IN THE DOG'S WATER FOR A TONIC!
SURE! NOW-- SCOOP SOME ASHES FROM THE FIREPLACE AND SEE IF YOU CAN FIND SOME CAMPHOR FLAKES ON THE CLOSET FLOOR!

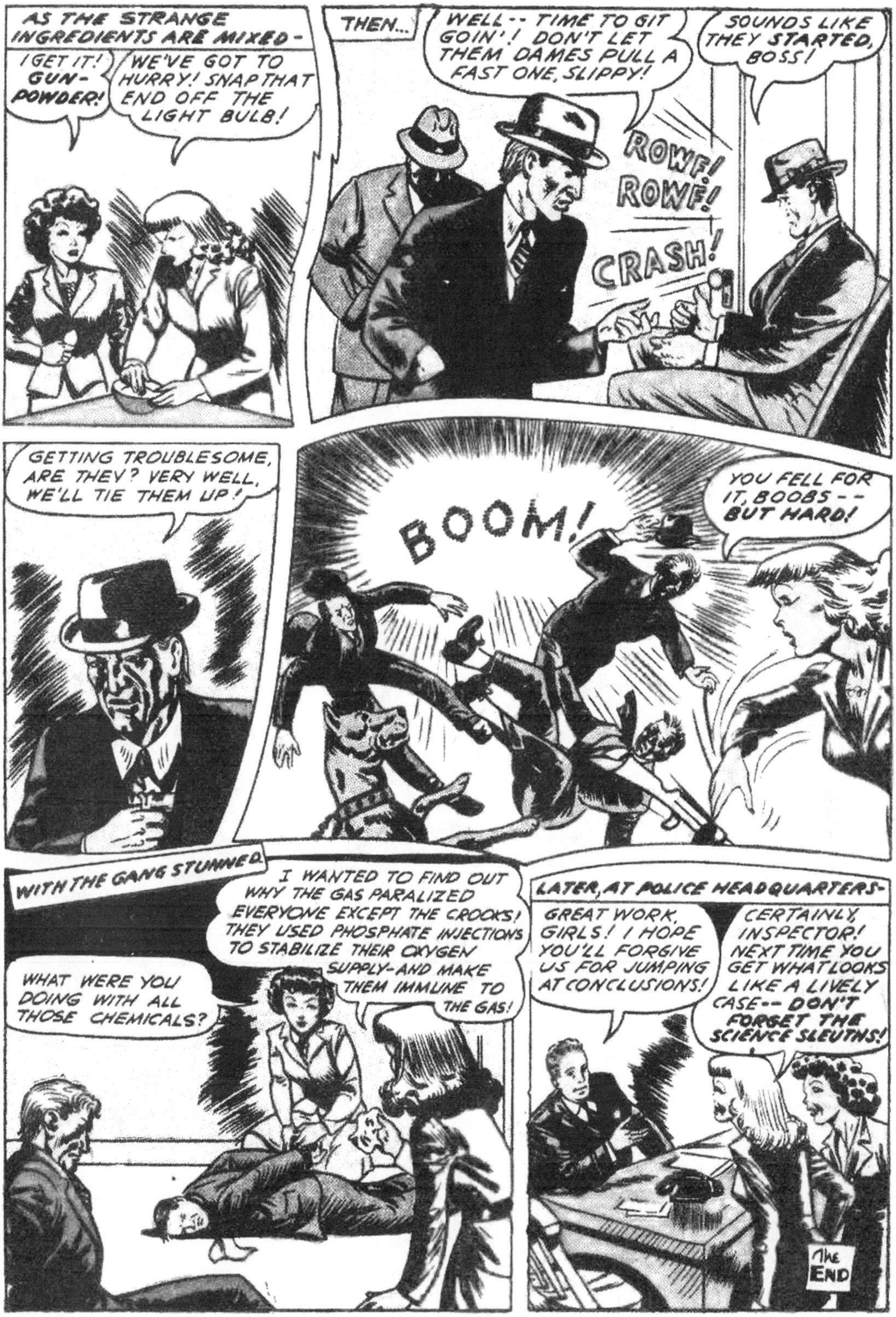
AS THE STRANGE INGREDIENTS ARE MIXED -
I GET IT! GUN-POWDER!
WE'VE GOT TO HURRY! SNAP THAT END OFF THE LIGHT BULB!
THEN...
WELL -- TIME TO GIT GOIN'! DON'T LET THEM DAMES PULL A FAST ONE, SLIPPY!
SOUNDS LIKE THEY STARTED, BOSS!
ROWF! ROWF!
CRASH!
GETTING TROUBLESOME, ARE THEY? VERY WELL. WE'LL TIE THEM UP!
BOOM!
YOU FELL FOR IT, BOOBS -- BUT HARD!
WITH THE GANG STUNNED
WHAT WERE YOU DOING WITH ALL THOSE CHEMICALS?
I WANTED TO FIND OUT WHY THE GAS PARALIZED EVERYONE EXCEPT THE CROOKS! THEY USED PHOSPHATE INJECTIONS TO STABILIZE THEIR OXYGEN SUPPLY - AND MAKE THEM IMMUNE TO THE GAS!
LATER, AT POLICE HEADQUARTERS -
GREAT WORK, GIRLS! I HOPE YOU'LL FORGIVE US FOR JUMPING AT CONCLUSIONS!
CERTAINLY, INSPECTOR! NEXT TIME YOU GET WHAT LOOKS LIKE A LIVELY CASE -- DON'T FORGET THE SCIENCE SLEUTHS!
THE END

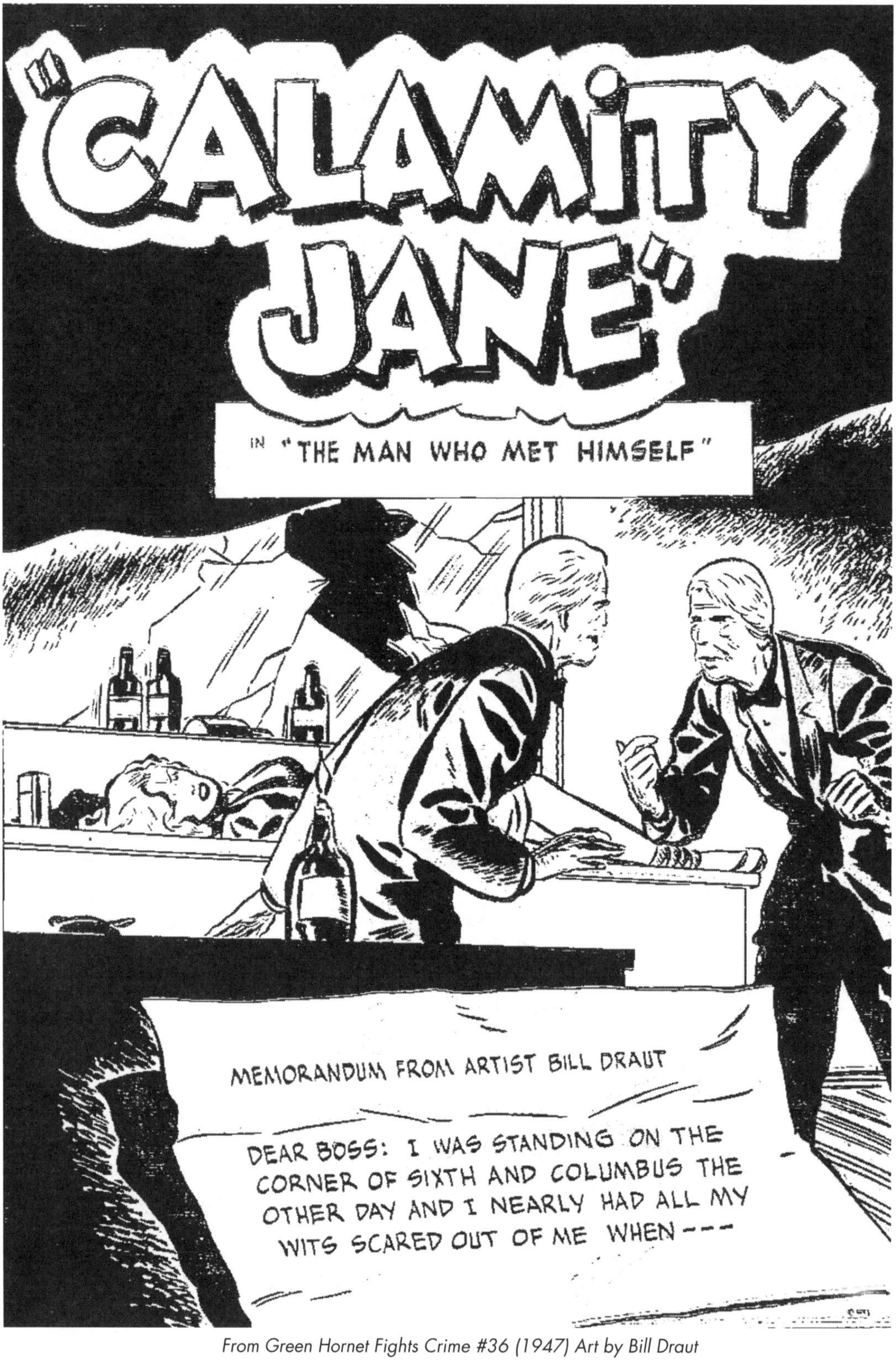
"CALAMITY JANE"
IN "THE MAN WHO MET HIMSELF"
MEMORANDUM FROM ARTIST BILL DRAUT
DEAR BOSS: I WAS STANDING ON THE CORNER OF SIXTH AND COLUMBUS THE OTHER DAY AND I NEARLY HAD ALL MY WITS SCARED OUT OF ME WHEN---

From Green Hornet Fights Crime #36 (1947) Art by Bill Draut

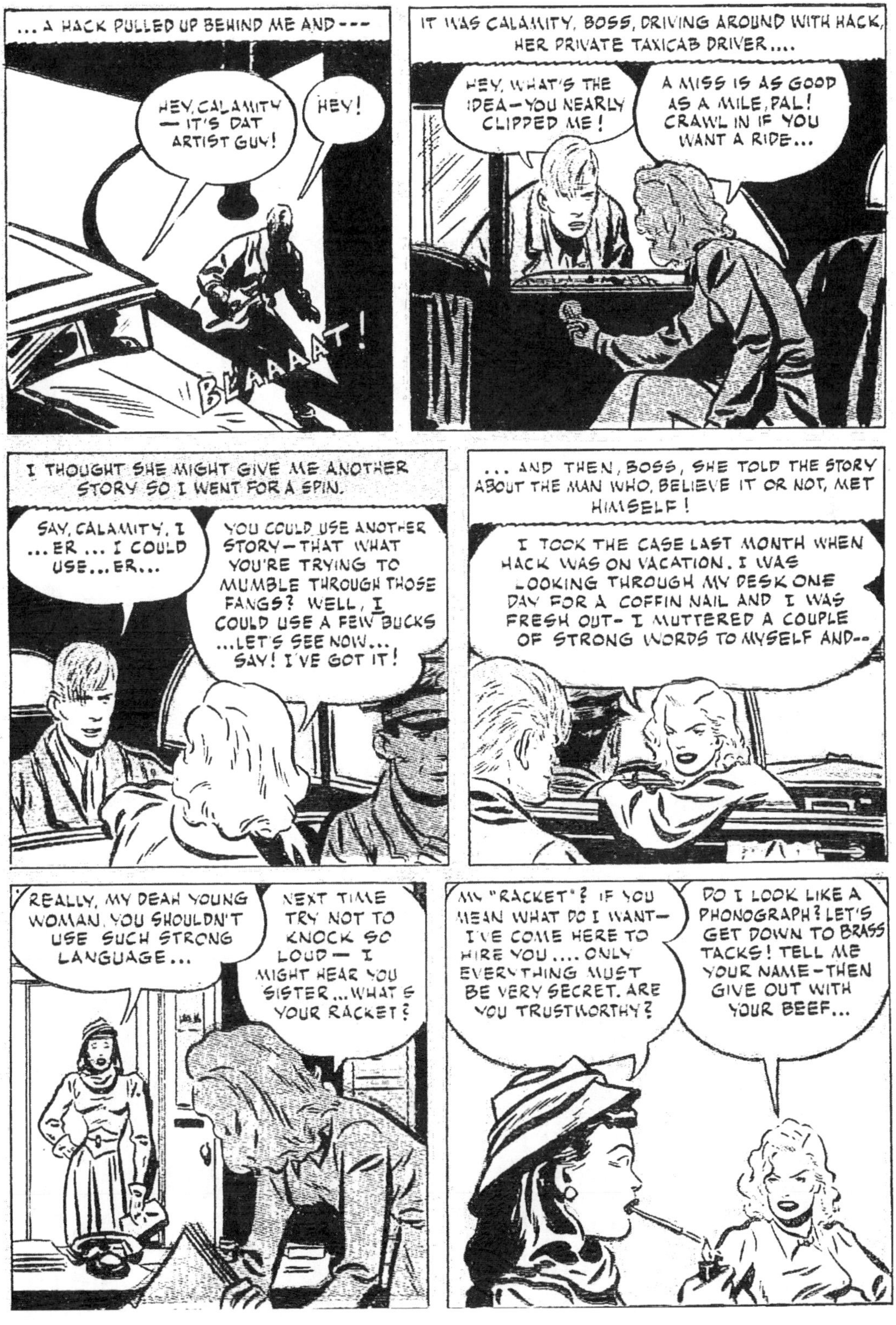

... A HACK PULLED UP BEHIND ME AND ---
HEY, CALAMITY — IT'S DAT ARTIST GUY!
HEY!
BLAAAAT!
IT WAS CALAMITY, BOSS, DRIVING AROUND WITH HACK, HER PRIVATE TAXICAB DRIVER....
HEY, WHAT'S THE IDEA—YOU NEARLY CLIPPED ME!
A MISS IS AS GOOD AS A MILE, PAL! CRAWL IN IF YOU WANT A RIDE...
I THOUGHT SHE MIGHT GIVE ME ANOTHER STORY SO I WENT FOR A SPIN.
SAY, CALAMITY, I ...ER ... I COULD USE...ER...
YOU COULD USE ANOTHER STORY—THAT WHAT YOU'RE TRYING TO MUMBLE THROUGH THOSE FANGS? WELL, I COULD USE A FEW BUCKS ...LET'S SEE NOW... SAY! I'VE GOT IT!
... AND THEN, BOSS, SHE TOLD THE STORY ABOUT THE MAN WHO, BELIEVE IT OR NOT, MET HIMSELF!
I TOOK THE CASE LAST MONTH WHEN HACK WAS ON VACATION. I WAS LOOKING THROUGH MY DESK ONE DAY FOR A COFFIN NAIL AND I WAS FRESH OUT- I MUTTERED A COUPLE OF STRONG WORDS TO MYSELF AND--
REALLY, MY DEAH YOUNG WOMAN, YOU SHOULDN'T USE SUCH STRONG LANGUAGE...
NEXT TIME TRY NOT TO KNOCK SO LOUD— I MIGHT HEAR YOU SISTER...WHAT'S YOUR RACKET?
MY "RACKET"? IF YOU MEAN WHAT DO I WANT— I'VE COME HERE TO HIRE YOU.... ONLY EVERYTHING MUST BE VERY SECRET. ARE YOU TRUSTWORTHY?
DO I LOOK LIKE A PHONOGRAPH? LET'S GET DOWN TO BRASS TACKS! TELL ME YOUR NAME—THEN GIVE OUT WITH YOUR BEEF...

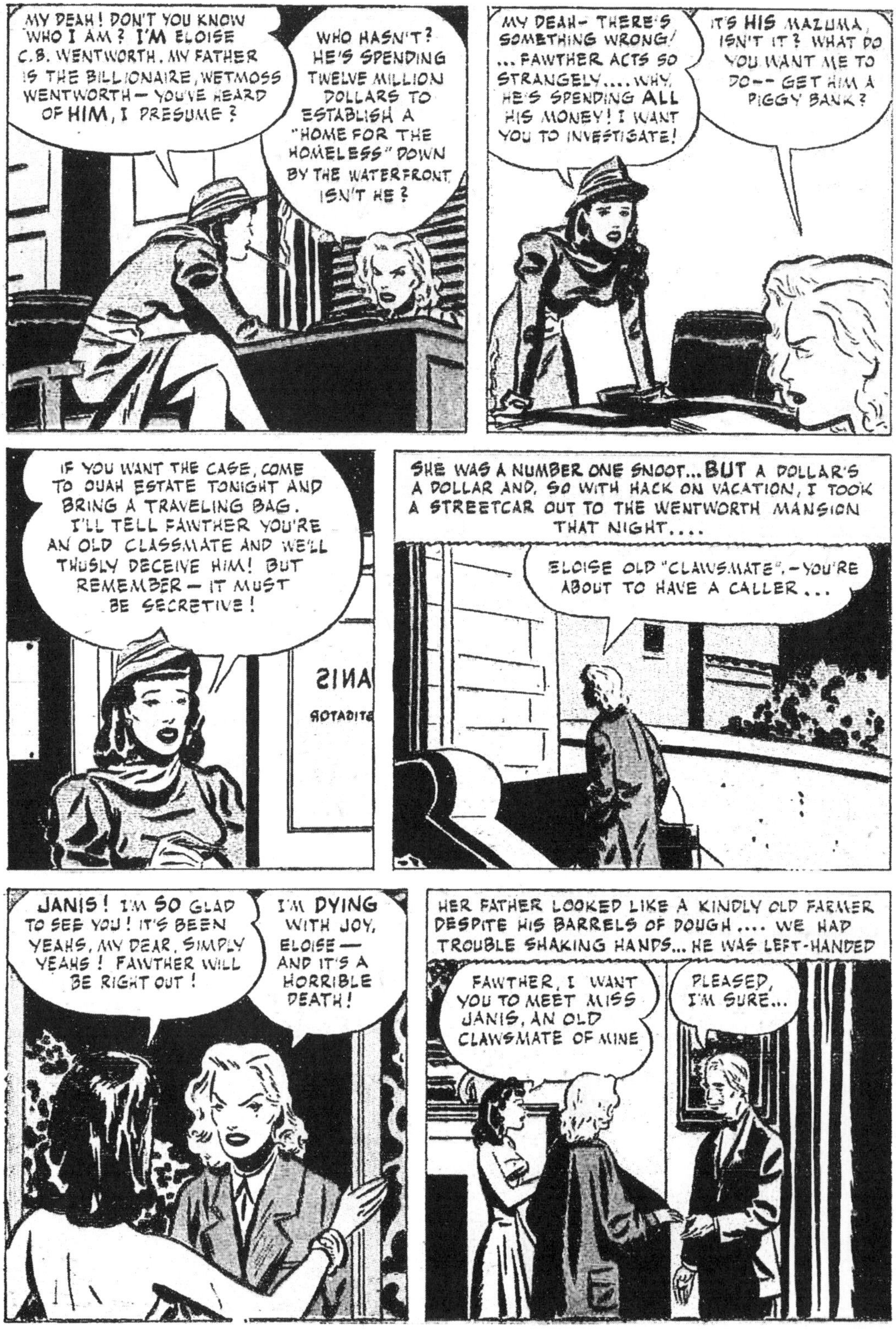
MY DEAH! DON'T YOU KNOW WHO I AM? I'M ELOISE C.B. WENTWORTH. MY FATHER IS THE BILLIONAIRE, WETMOSS WENTWORTH — YOU'VE HEARD OF HIM, I PRESUME?
WHO HASN'T? HE'S SPENDING TWELVE MILLION DOLLARS TO ESTABLISH A "HOME FOR THE HOMELESS" DOWN BY THE WATERFRONT, ISN'T HE?
MY DEAH— THERE'S SOMETHING WRONG! ...FAWTHER ACTS SO STRANGELY.... WHY, HE'S SPENDING ALL HIS MONEY! I WANT YOU TO INVESTIGATE!
IT'S HIS MAZUMA, ISN'T IT? WHAT DO YOU WANT ME TO DO-- GET HIM A PIGGY BANK?
IF YOU WANT THE CASE, COME TO OUAH ESTATE TONIGHT AND BRING A TRAVELING BAG. I'LL TELL FAWTHER YOU'RE AN OLD CLASSMATE AND WE'LL THUSLY DECEIVE HIM! BUT REMEMBER — IT MUST BE SECRETIVE!
SINA
ROTADIT
SHE WAS A NUMBER ONE SNOOT...BUT A DOLLAR'S A DOLLAR AND, SO WITH HACK ON VACATION, I TOOK A STREETCAR OUT TO THE WENTWORTH MANSION THAT NIGHT....
ELOISE OLD "CLAWSMATE". — YOU'RE ABOUT TO HAVE A CALLER...
JANIS! I'M SO GLAD TO SEE YOU! IT'S BEEN YEAHS, MY DEAR, SIMPLY YEAHS! FAWTHER WILL BE RIGHT OUT!
I'M DYING WITH JOY, ELOISE — AND IT'S A HORRIBLE DEATH!
HER FATHER LOOKED LIKE A KINDLY OLD FARMER DESPITE HIS BARRELS OF DOUGH.... WE HAD TROUBLE SHAKING HANDS... HE WAS LEFT-HANDED
FAWTHER, I WANT YOU TO MEET MISS JANIS, AN OLD CLAWSMATE OF MINE
PLEASED, I'M SURE...

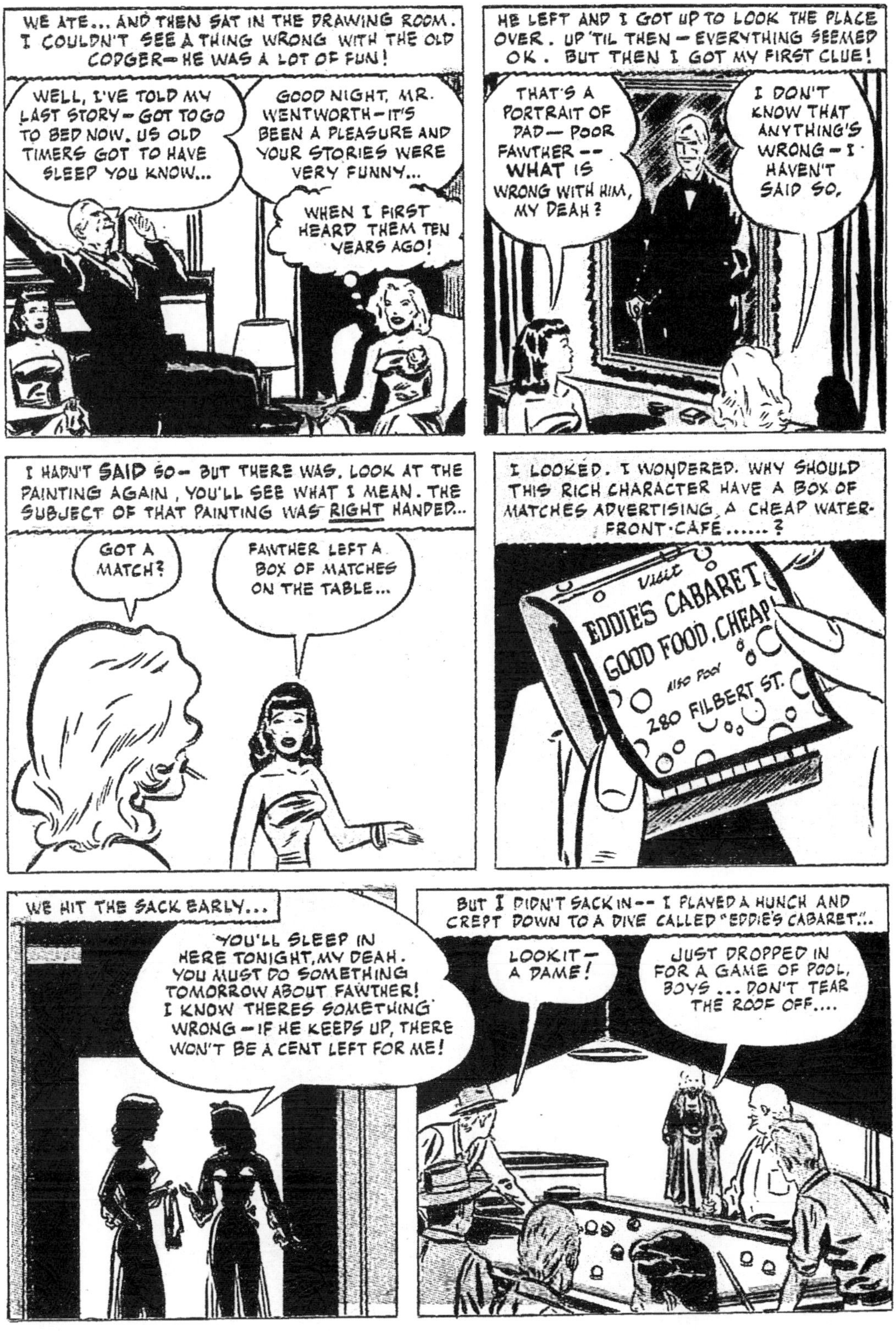
WE ATE... AND THEN SAT IN THE DRAWING ROOM. I COULDN'T SEE A THING WRONG WITH THE OLD CODGER—HE WAS A LOT OF FUN!
WELL, I'VE TOLD MY LAST STORY—GOT TO GO TO BED NOW. US OLD TIMERS GOT TO HAVE SLEEP YOU KNOW...
GOOD NIGHT, MR. WENTWORTH—IT'S BEEN A PLEASURE AND YOUR STORIES WERE VERY FUNNY...
WHEN I FIRST HEARD THEM TEN YEARS AGO!
HE LEFT AND I GOT UP TO LOOK THE PLACE OVER. UP 'TIL THEN—EVERYTHING SEEMED OK. BUT THEN I GOT MY FIRST CLUE!
THAT'S A PORTRAIT OF DAD— POOR FAWTHER -- WHAT IS WRONG WITH HIM, MY DEAH?
I DON'T KNOW THAT ANYTHING'S WRONG—I HAVEN'T SAID SO.
I HADN'T SAID SO— BUT THERE WAS. LOOK AT THE PAINTING AGAIN, YOU'LL SEE WHAT I MEAN. THE SUBJECT OF THAT PAINTING WAS RIGHT HANDED...
GOT A MATCH?
FAWTHER LEFT A BOX OF MATCHES ON THE TABLE...
I LOOKED. I WONDERED. WHY SHOULD THIS RICH CHARACTER HAVE A BOX OF MATCHES ADVERTISING A CHEAP WATER-FRONT CAFÉ......?
Visit EDDIE'S CABARET GOOD FOOD, CHEAP Also Pool 280 FILBERT ST.
WE HIT THE SACK EARLY...
YOU'LL SLEEP IN HERE TONIGHT, MY DEAH. YOU MUST DO SOMETHING TOMORROW ABOUT FAWTHER! I KNOW THERES SOMETHING WRONG—IF HE KEEPS UP, THERE WON'T BE A CENT LEFT FOR ME!
BUT I DIDN'T SACK IN-- I PLAYED A HUNCH AND CREPT DOWN TO A DIVE CALLED "EDDIE'S CABARET"...
LOOKIT— A DAME!
JUST DROPPED IN FOR A GAME OF POOL, BOYS ... DON'T TEAR THE ROOF OFF....

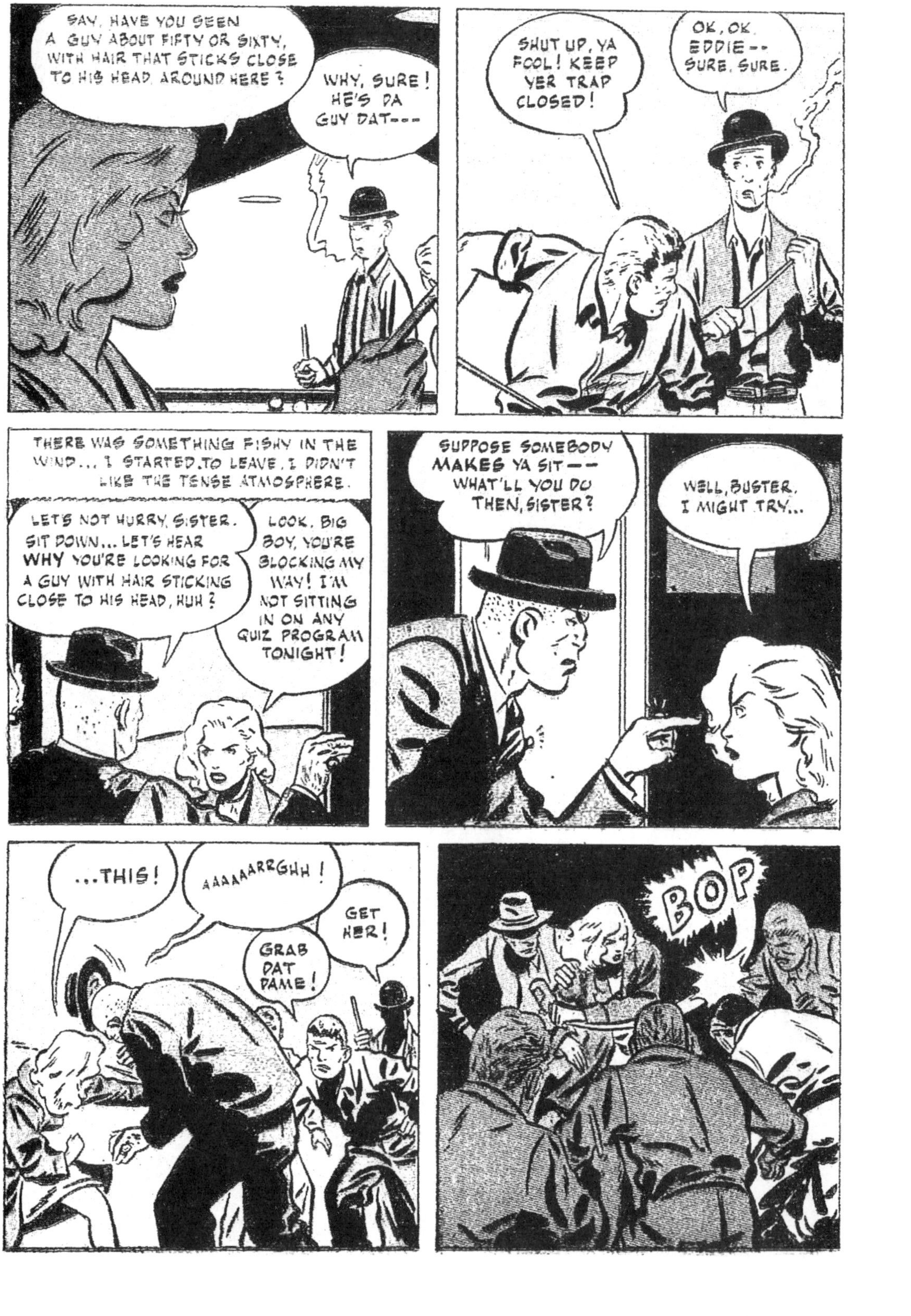
SAY, HAVE YOU SEEN A GUY ABOUT FIFTY OR SIXTY, WITH HAIR THAT STICKS CLOSE TO HIS HEAD AROUND HERE ?
WHY, SURE! HE'S DA GUY DAT---
SHUT UP, YA FOOL! KEEP YER TRAP CLOSED!
OK, OK. EDDIE-- SURE, SURE.
THERE WAS SOMETHING FISHY IN THE WIND... I STARTED TO LEAVE. I DIDN'T LIKE THE TENSE ATMOSPHERE.
LET'S NOT HURRY, SISTER. SIT DOWN... LET'S HEAR WHY YOU'RE LOOKING FOR A GUY WITH HAIR STICKING CLOSE TO HIS HEAD, HUH ?
LOOK, BIG BOY, YOU'RE BLOCKING MY WAY! I'M NOT SITTING IN ON ANY QUIZ PROGRAM TONIGHT!
SUPPOSE SOMEBODY MAKES YA SIT -- WHAT'LL YOU DO THEN, SISTER?
WELL, BUSTER, I MIGHT TRY...
...THIS!
AAAAAARRGHH !
GET HER!
GRAB DAT DAME!
BOP

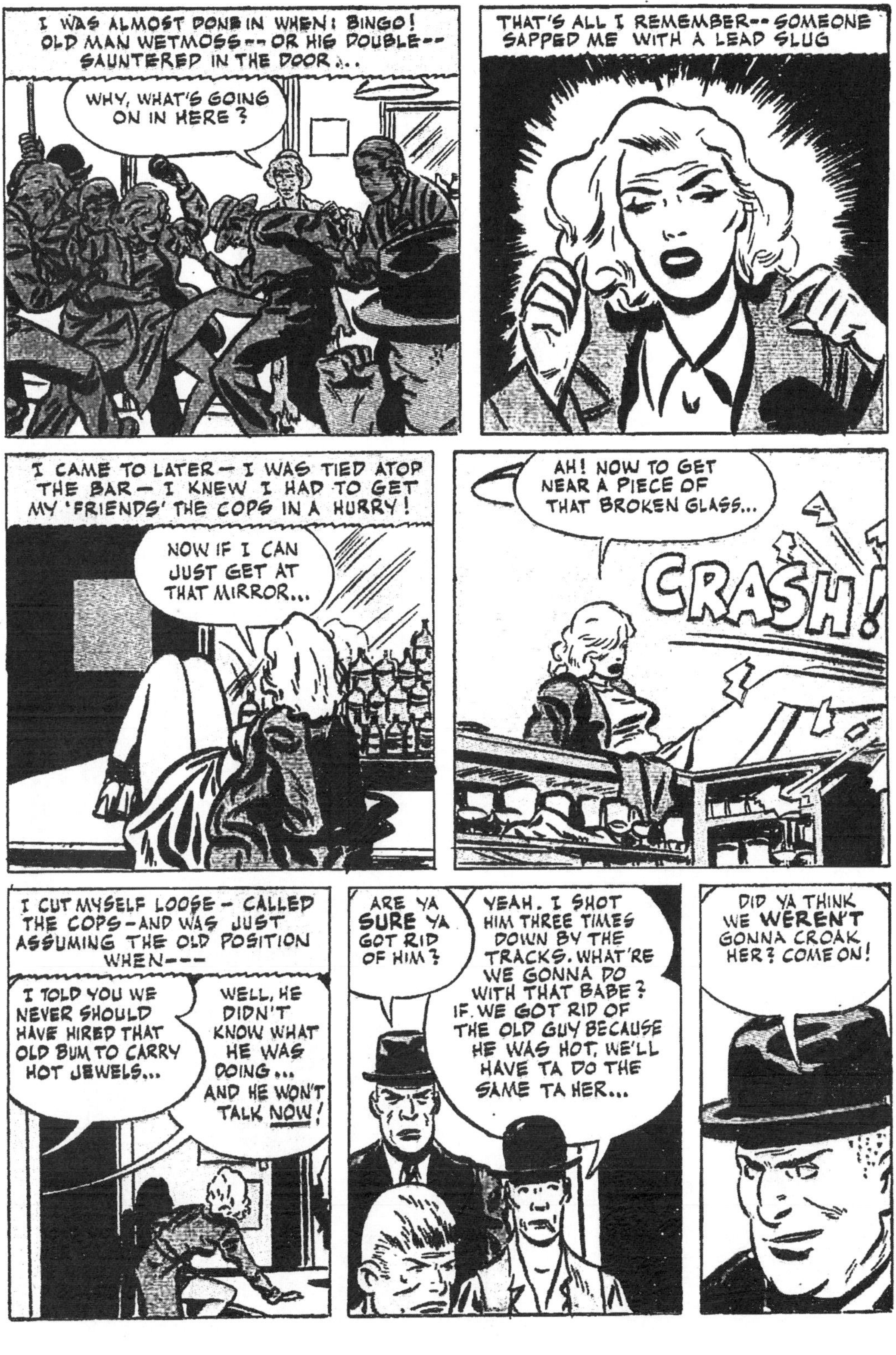
I WAS ALMOST DONE IN WHEN: BINGO! OLD MAN WETMOSS -- OR HIS DOUBLE -- SAUNTERED IN THE DOOR ...
WHY, WHAT'S GOING ON IN HERE ?
THAT'S ALL I REMEMBER -- SOMEONE SAPPED ME WITH A LEAD SLUG
I CAME TO LATER — I WAS TIED ATOP THE BAR — I KNEW I HAD TO GET MY 'FRIENDS' THE COPS IN A HURRY!
NOW IF I CAN JUST GET AT THAT MIRROR...
AH! NOW TO GET NEAR A PIECE OF THAT BROKEN GLASS...
CRASH!
I CUT MYSELF LOOSE — CALLED THE COPS — AND WAS JUST ASSUMING THE OLD POSITION WHEN---
I TOLD YOU WE NEVER SHOULD HAVE HIRED THAT OLD BUM TO CARRY HOT JEWELS...
WELL, HE DIDN'T KNOW WHAT HE WAS DOING... AND HE WON'T TALK NOW!
ARE YA SURE YA GOT RID OF HIM?
YEAH. I SHOT HIM THREE TIMES DOWN BY THE TRACKS. WHAT'RE WE GONNA DO WITH THAT BABE? IF WE GOT RID OF THE OLD GUY BECAUSE HE WAS HOT, WE'LL HAVE TA DO THE SAME TA HER...
DID YA THINK WE WEREN'T GONNA CROAK HER? COME ON!

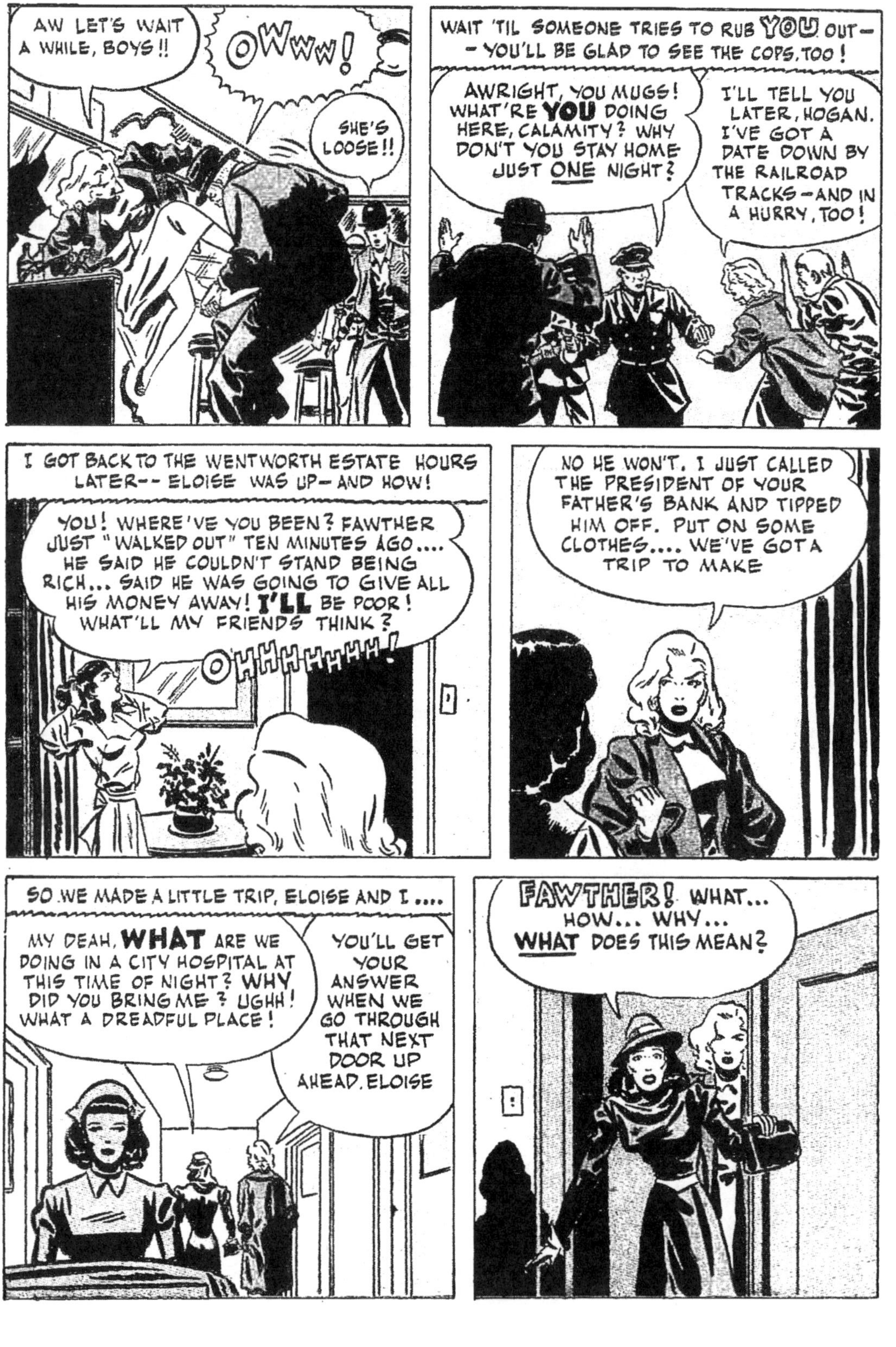
AW LET'S WAIT A WHILE, BOYS!!
OWWW!
SHE'S LOOSE!!
WAIT 'TIL SOMEONE TRIES TO RUB YOU OUT-- YOU'LL BE GLAD TO SEE THE COPS, TOO!
AWRIGHT, YOU MUGS! WHAT'RE YOU DOING HERE, CALAMITY? WHY DON'T YOU STAY HOME JUST ONE NIGHT?
I'LL TELL YOU LATER, HOGAN. I'VE GOT A DATE DOWN BY THE RAILROAD TRACKS--AND IN A HURRY, TOO!
I GOT BACK TO THE WENTWORTH ESTATE HOURS LATER-- ELOISE WAS UP-- AND HOW!
YOU! WHERE'VE YOU BEEN? FAWTHER JUST "WALKED OUT" TEN MINUTES AGO.... HE SAID HE COULDN'T STAND BEING RICH... SAID HE WAS GOING TO GIVE ALL HIS MONEY AWAY! I'LL BE POOR! WHAT'LL MY FRIENDS THINK?
OHHHHHHH!
NO HE WON'T. I JUST CALLED THE PRESIDENT OF YOUR FATHER'S BANK AND TIPPED HIM OFF. PUT ON SOME CLOTHES.... WE'VE GOT A TRIP TO MAKE
SO WE MADE A LITTLE TRIP, ELOISE AND I....
MY DEAH, WHAT ARE WE DOING IN A CITY HOSPITAL AT THIS TIME OF NIGHT? WHY DID YOU BRING ME? UGHH! WHAT A DREADFUL PLACE!
YOU'LL GET YOUR ANSWER WHEN WE GO THROUGH THAT NEXT DOOR UP AHEAD, ELOISE
FAWTHER! WHAT... HOW... WHY... WHAT DOES THIS MEAN?

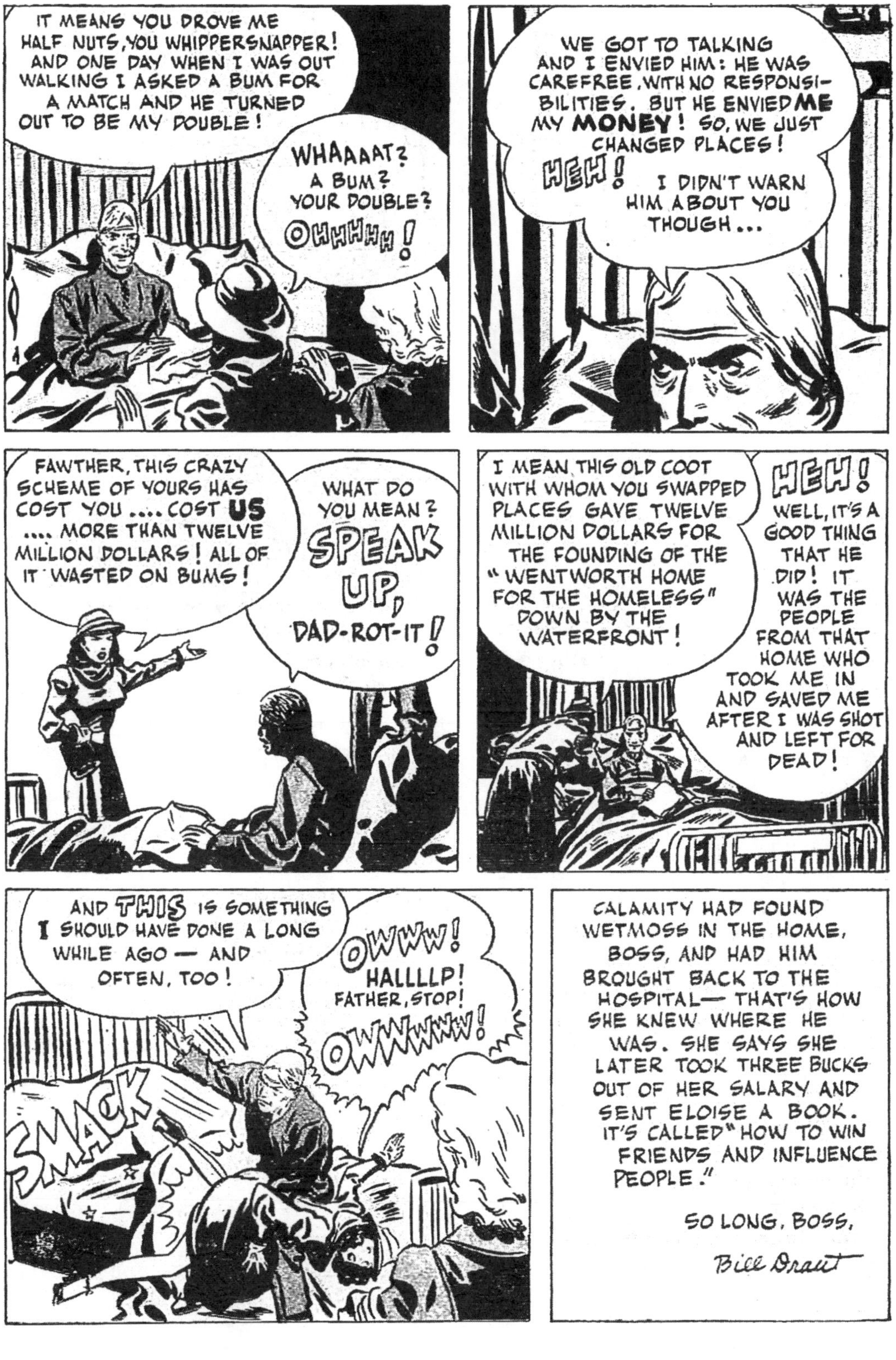
IT MEANS YOU DROVE ME HALF NUTS, YOU WHIPPERSNAPPER! AND ONE DAY WHEN I WAS OUT WALKING I ASKED A BUM FOR A MATCH AND HE TURNED OUT TO BE MY DOUBLE!
WHAAAAT? A BUM? YOUR DOUBLE? OHHHHH!
WE GOT TO TALKING AND I ENVIED HIM: HE WAS CAREFREE, WITH NO RESPONSIBILITIES. BUT HE ENVIED ME MY MONEY! SO, WE JUST CHANGED PLACES!
HEH! I DIDN'T WARN HIM ABOUT YOU THOUGH...
FAWTHER, THIS CRAZY SCHEME OF YOURS HAS COST YOU .... COST US .... MORE THAN TWELVE MILLION DOLLARS! ALL OF IT WASTED ON BUMS!
WHAT DO YOU MEAN? SPEAK UP, DAD-ROT-IT!
I MEAN THIS OLD COOT WITH WHOM YOU SWAPPED PLACES GAVE TWELVE MILLION DOLLARS FOR THE FOUNDING OF THE "WENTWORTH HOME FOR THE HOMELESS" DOWN BY THE WATERFRONT!
HEH! WELL, IT'S A GOOD THING THAT HE DID! IT WAS THE PEOPLE FROM THAT HOME WHO TOOK ME IN AND SAVED ME AFTER I WAS SHOT AND LEFT FOR DEAD!
AND THIS IS SOMETHING I SHOULD HAVE DONE A LONG WHILE AGO — AND OFTEN, TOO!
OWWW! HALLLLP! FATHER, STOP! OWWWWW!
SMACK
CALAMITY HAD FOUND WETMOSS IN THE HOME, BOSS, AND HAD HIM BROUGHT BACK TO THE HOSPITAL— THAT'S HOW SHE KNEW WHERE HE WAS. SHE SAYS SHE LATER TOOK THREE BUCKS OUT OF HER SALARY AND SENT ELOISE A BOOK. IT'S CALLED "HOW TO WIN FRIENDS AND INFLUENCE PEOPLE."
SO LONG, BOSS,
Bill Draut

20th CENTURY  GODDESSES

When Superman first leapt across the comic book page in 1938, he embodied an ideal that humans had revered for thousands of years—handsome, physically perfect, literally descended from the heavens. He was, in a word, godlike. He flew like a bird, bent steel in his hands, and weapons bounced harmlessly off his indestructible chest. However, Superman couldn't command wild animals to do his bidding, transform men into monsters, destroy squadrons of airplanes with a single thought, or reshape reality. But Fantomah could.

Making her debut in 1940, Fantomah is considered to be the first female with extraordinary powers to appear in comics—the Eve to Superman's Adam. But while Superman chose to live among humanity, Fantomah set herself apart from it. She was a beautiful white woman who lived in a "secret observatory" deep in the heart of the African jungle. From there, readers were told, through her "strange wizardry, she guards the jungle's secrets and avenges the evil deeds against the jungle-born." Fantomah is described as "the most remarkable woman in the universe," which sounds less like a superhero, and more like a goddess. Fantomah best fits that ancient image of the goddess who could be both benevolent *and* terrifying. Like all deities, Fantomah is all-knowing and all-seeing, and has established a set of laws. And woe unto anyone who breaks those laws! Fantomah possessed a seemingly endless array of powers, which she used to smite those who dared threaten the peace of the jungle. "Now you will pay a dreadful penalty!" Fantomah would announce, as she transformed herself from a lovely blonde into a hideous, skull-faced angel of destruction. With her boundless powers, Fantomah could have simply destroyed her foes. But like a true goddess, she used her magnificent abilities to pass judgment on her enemies, and punish them with divine fury. "Farewell, you fool!" Fantomah would say, after sentencing a fallen foe to spend the rest of his days deep within the bowels of the earth.

To call Fantomah a "goddess" is not to say that she is literally from a pantheon of divinities. The comic book goddess is simply a woman who is *other* than a mere human. *More* than human. Sheena, the Queen of the Jungle, arguably the first heroine of comics, first appeared in 1937. Sheena established the image of the woman as goddess who is both an object of desire and fear. Powerful, beautiful, unattainable. She is like a force of nature, and can't always be held to follow the same laws that mere mortals must adhere to. Of the women we will meet in this chapter, only Diana the Huntress is a familiar goddess of antiquity. Others, like Maureen Marine and Wildfire were humans who were granted powers by ancient gods. Fantomah and Amazona both have mysterious origins, while Marga the Panther Woman is a primal being that is just not like other humans.

In the wake of Superman's arrival, publishers scrambled to jump on the superhero bandwagon. Obvious choices to fill the pages of comic books were the mythological figures of antiquity. Soon, a parade of deities and demigods and heroes of the past made their way into the comic to fight evil—Hercules and Samson, Mercury, Thor and Vulcan, Diana and Venus. But there were some interesting cultural, or even theological, clashes that arose when the ancient pagan gods appeared in comic books in the modern world, circa the 1940s. In 1944's *Yellowjacket Comics*, Zeus sends his daughter Diana, the goddess of the hunt, to modern day Greece to fight the Nazi invaders. Diana arrives to learn the Nazis have stolen an icon from a Greek Orthodox Church. "Here is a chance for me to do my first kindness for my people! I'll find their sacred picture!" Diana declares, as she sets off, an ancient Olympian *pagan* goddess on a mission to save an image of a *Christian* saint. Ironic when you consider that it was Christianity that toppled the worship of the Olympian gods. A few months later we see Diana, in her short Grecian chiton, fire a deadly arrow at a Turk bandit who begs, "No! In Allah's name, spare me!" That same year in *Red Circle Comics*, young fisherman's daughter Maureen drowns in a shipwreck. "W-where am I? Is this Heaven?" she asks, when she awakes in the arms of a white bearded gentleman. But God the Father is not Maureen's savior, but rather Father Neptune, the ancient *pagan* god of the sea. One wonders if Maureen, presumably a good Catholic girl, felt like she'd wasted her time saying the rosary all those years.

Then there is the question of morality and the goddess. Gods have always established laws—morals—by which mortals must live their lives. But does a goddess have to abide by the rules of humanity, when she is *apart* from humanity? To readers of modern comic books, the "Dark Phoenix Saga" in Marvel Comics' *X-Men* is considered to be a classic. It is the tale of mutant heroine Jean Grey's transformation into the all-powerful Phoenix, a goddess-like being—a fiery angel of death who killed billions. Phoenix ultimately sacrifices herself to atone for her sins: her *human* soul can't live with her *godly* deeds. But forty years earlier, Fantomah wielded infinite powers that rivaled those of the Phoenix, and she had no qualms about wreaking havoc on a humanity that broke *her* laws. Similarly, Marga the Panther Woman's "primitive emotions" result in bloody carnage in the story presented here. But she isn't punished because she doesn't follow the same rules humans do. Humans can't hold the goddess accountable for her actions because she is above humans.

Now, in this chapter, let us worship at the altar of the 20th Century Goddesses—

FANTOMAH, MYSTERY WOMAN OF THE JUNGLE— As the first superheroine of comics, Fantomah's story reflects how experimental the early comics were. Created by artist Fletcher Hanks (drawing as Barclay Flagg) Fantomah was a godlike creature with almost limitless powers. Hanks' tales are truly among the most bizarre of their day. When he left the series in 1941, Fantomah became more of a typical jungle queen à la Sheena, still possessing some magic but not the infinite power she'd had earlier. By 1942, Fantomah became the ruler of a lost Egyptian city, and her fantastic powers were all gone. Her adventures in *Jungle Comics* came to an end in 1944, bringing a rather lackluster close to the story of this first powerful superwoman of comics.

AMAZONA, THE MIGHTY WOMAN— A beautiful and powerful young woman from a lost race falls in love with a man from the modern world, and leaves her faraway homeland to travel to America. Is this Wonder Woman? No, it's Amazona, who made her debut in 1940, over a year *before* Wonder Woman, but whose story is remarkably similar. Besides arriving in comics earlier, Amazona was also a bit more "untamed" than Wonder Woman. Wonder Woman extolled the virtues of peace and love; Amazona hit first and asked questions later. And while Wonder Woman is seen as a symbol of feminism, in this story we see Amazona stand up for her rights in a highly aggressive, no nonsense manner. One feels pity for her boyfriend Blake, who finds himself on one of the worst first dates in history. Amazona seemed like a mythical creature that was too imposing to fit into the world of mortals. Maybe that's why she only made this one appearance in *Planet Comics*.

MARGA THE PANTHER WOMAN— Comic book jungle queens were a dime a dozen in the '40s and '50s. Marga was unique. As a girl, Marga had been nursed by panthers, which gave her the strength, speed, and agility of the great jungle cat. She also had the claws and savage nature of a panther. For years, modern day comic book fans have been thrilled by the savage temperament and killer instinct of Wolverine, the sharp-clawed member of Marvel's X-Men. Judging by this story, Marga could have given Wolverine a run for his money. Here, Marga leaves the jungle and tries living in the civilized world, with dire results. This story represents the peak of Marga's animalistic side. After this, she became steadily tamer. Marga the Panther Woman appeared in *Science Comics* and *Weird Comics* between 1940-42.

WILDFIRE— When a forest fire orphaned young Carol Vance, the God of Fire granted the child mastery over flame. Adopted by a wealthy couple, she grew up to become yet another of the many beautiful debutantes of comic books. "I'm happiest when using my powers to help others!" Carol said, as she became Wildfire, "princess of flame, and nemesis of all who break man's laws." In an era when few heroines wielded mighty powers, Wildfire's fiery abilities were unique. She also sported one of the most racy costumes of her day. This story introduces readers to Wildfire, who conjures giant flaming hands to pass judgment on Nazi evildoers in true goddess-like fashion. Wildfire appeared in *Smash Comics* from 1941-42.

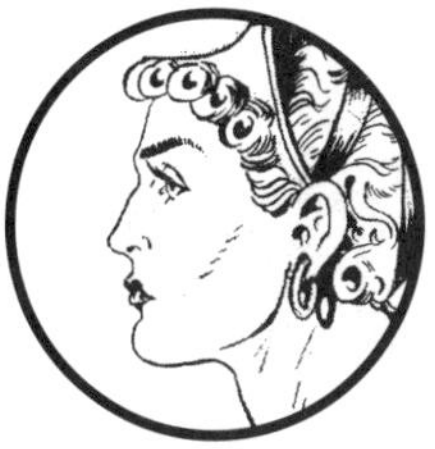

DIANA THE HUNTRESS— In Homer's *Iliad*, the gods of Olympus interfered in the battles of the mortal Trojan War. So it seems fitting that they would do the same in WWII. When Zeus orders the gods to protect their beloved Greece from the Nazis, his daughter Diana, the goddess of the hunt, takes aim at the Axis invaders. In this story, the sight of a vengeful Diana and her fellow Olympians destroying German battleships is certainly frightening. But it is the cold look in Diana's eyes as she instructs the gods to show the mortals no mercy that reminds us of the perils of incurring the wrath of a goddess. These stories also remind us of the reassuring quality that deities have on mere mortals. "Always remember: we are with you in your time of need!" Diana tells a group of Greek freedom fighters, as she and Zeus ascend once more into the heavens. Diana the Huntress appeared in *Yellowjacket Comics* between 1944-46.

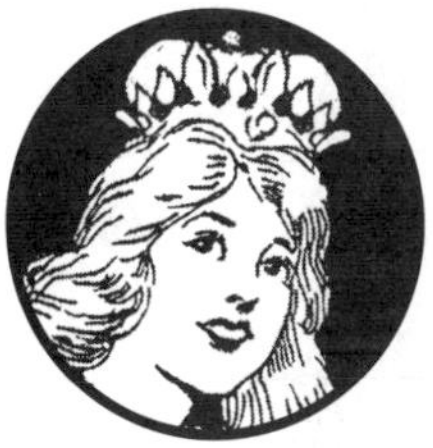

MAUREEN MARINE— Young Maureen thought it would be fun to stow away on her father's fishing boat, never dreaming a Nazi U-boat would sink it. Father Neptune rescues the drowned girl and transforms her into a water breather. He then takes Maureen to Atlantis, where she is crowned queen of the undersea kingdom. There'll be no competition for the title of prettiest girl under the sea, since Maureen is the sole female in an all-male population. Even godly father Neptune must bow to the authority of the girl ruler, who in this story proves that she is a good military strategist. Maureen never seemed to miss the surface world she left behind, as she had fanciful fairy tale style adventures beneath the waves. Maureen Marine ruled Atlantis between 1944-45 in the pages of *Blue Circle Comics*.

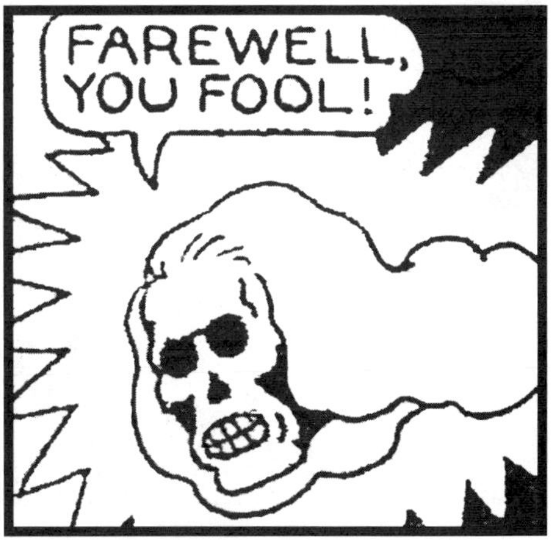
FAREWELL, YOU FOOL!

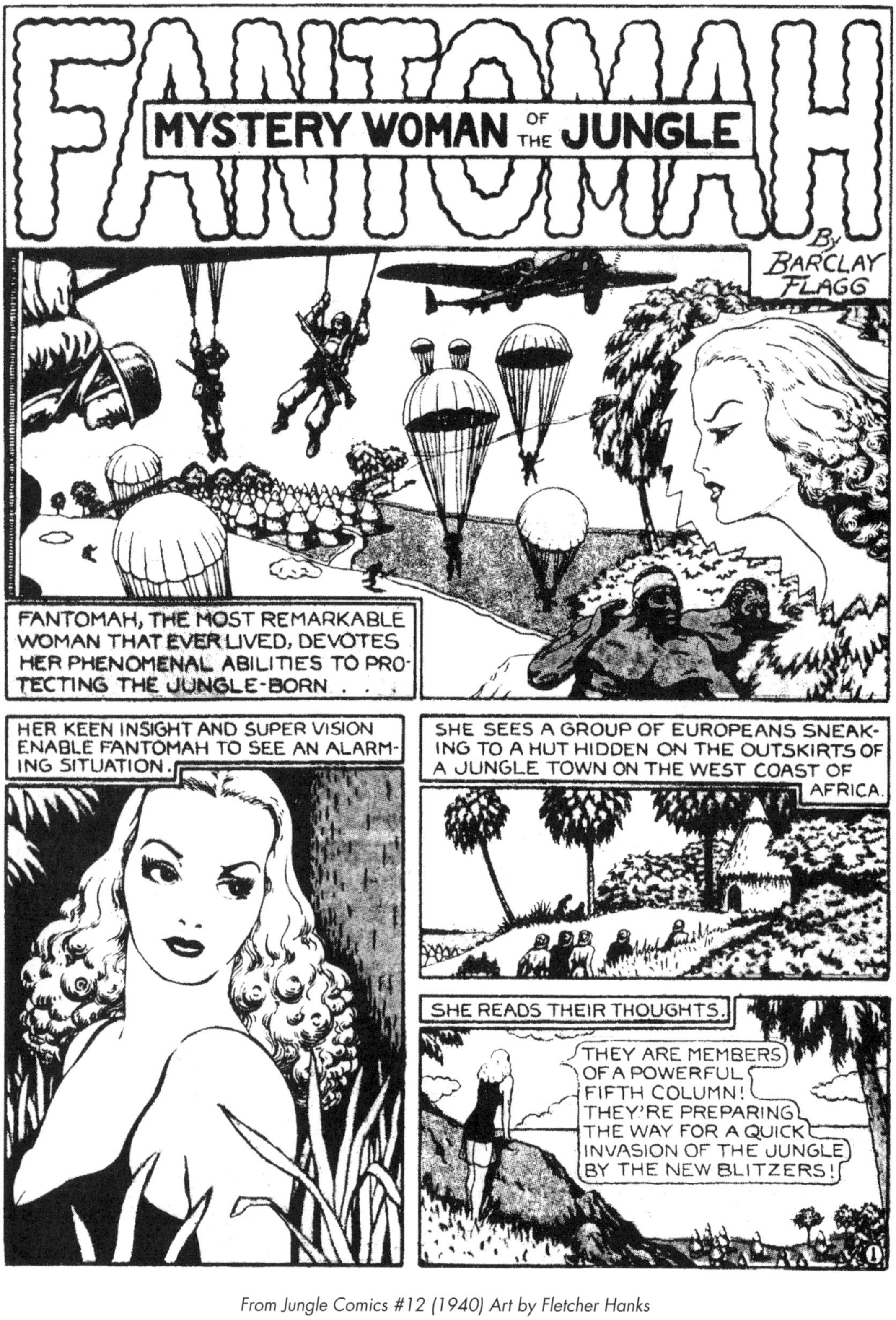
FANTOMAH
MYSTERY WOMAN OF THE JUNGLE
BY BARCLAY FLAGG
FANTOMAH, THE MOST REMARKABLE WOMAN THAT EVER LIVED, DEVOTES HER PHENOMENAL ABILITIES TO PROTECTING THE JUNGLE-BORN . . .
HER KEEN INSIGHT AND SUPER VISION ENABLE FANTOMAH TO SEE AN ALARMING SITUATION.
SHE SEES A GROUP OF EUROPEANS SNEAKING TO A HUT HIDDEN ON THE OUTSKIRTS OF A JUNGLE TOWN ON THE WEST COAST OF AFRICA.
SHE READS THEIR THOUGHTS.
THEY ARE MEMBERS OF A POWERFUL FIFTH COLUMN! THEY'RE PREPARING THE WAY FOR A QUICK INVASION OF THE JUNGLE BY THE NEW BLITZERS!
1

From Jungle Comics #12 (1940) Art by Fletcher Hanks

INSIDE THE HUT, THE FIFTH COLUMN IS RUSHING ITS PREPARATIONS.

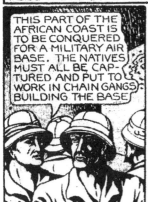

THIS PART OF THE AFRICAN COAST IS TO BE CONQUERED FOR A MILITARY AIR BASE. THE NATIVES MUST ALL BE CAPTURED AND PUT TO WORK IN CHAIN GANGS BUILDING THE BASE.

YES! AND AS SOON AS THE BASE IS ESTABLISHED, WE CAN SEND ALL OF OUR WARPLANES ACROSS TO SOUTH AMERICA.

WE'LL ESTABLISH ANOTHER BASE IN BRAZIL, AND FROM THERE, WE'LL INVADE THE UNITED STATES. THAT WILL MEAN THE END OF DEMOCRACY AND FREEDOM!

THE INVADING BARBARIANS PLAN TO ENSLAVE THE REST OF THE WORLD!... THAT WILL MEAN TORTURE AND BRUTAL DEATH FOR INNOCENT JUNGLE PEOPLE!

THE FIFTH COLUMN HAS ALREADY SPREAD TERROR AMONG COASTAL NATIVES..

THE WHITE GODS SAY THE DEVIL-BIRDS ARE COMING! IF WE RUN, WE DIE! IF WE FIGHT, WE DIE!

THE FIFTH COLUMN SOON COMPLETES ITS PREPARATIONS FOR THE INVASION.

EVERY LINE OF COMMUNICATION IS NOW UNDER OUR CONTROL! THE BLITZ WILL BEGIN AT DAWN!

ALL DURING THE NIGHT, IN THE THICK OF THE JUNGLE, THE NATIVES, HUDDLE IN DREAD.

AT LAST, THE DAWN COMES.

IN RAPID SUCCESSION, THE COAST TOWNS FALL INTO THE HANDS OF INVADERS..

THE FIFTH COLUMN MEMBERS GLOAT. . . . .

WE HAVE TIMED EVERYTHING PERFECTLY!

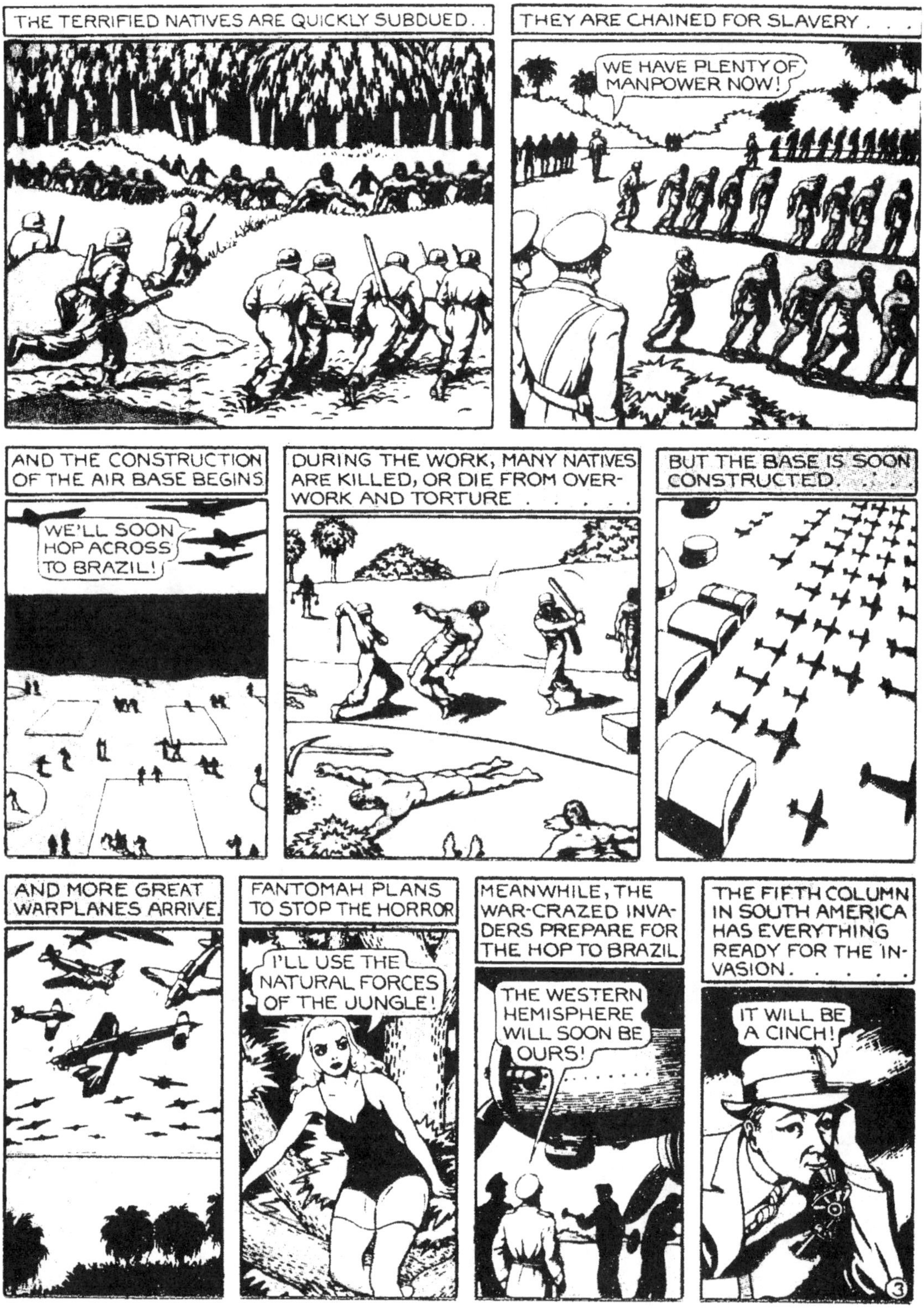
THE TERRIFIED NATIVES ARE QUICKLY SUBDUED . .
THEY ARE CHAINED FOR SLAVERY . . .
WE HAVE PLENTY OF MANPOWER NOW!
AND THE CONSTRUCTION OF THE AIR BASE BEGINS
WE'LL SOON HOP ACROSS TO BRAZIL!
DURING THE WORK, MANY NATIVES ARE KILLED, OR DIE FROM OVER-WORK AND TORTURE . . . . .
BUT THE BASE IS SOON CONSTRUCTED. . . .
AND MORE GREAT WARPLANES ARRIVE.
FANTOMAH PLANS TO STOP THE HORROR
I'LL USE THE NATURAL FORCES OF THE JUNGLE!
MEANWHILE, THE WAR-CRAZED INVADERS PREPARE FOR THE HOP TO BRAZIL
THE WESTERN HEMISPHERE WILL SOON BE OURS!
THE FIFTH COLUMN IN SOUTH AMERICA HAS EVERYTHING READY FOR THE INVASION . . . . .
IT WILL BE A CINCH!
3

FANTOMAH, TRANSPORTING HERSELF ON CONCENTRATED WILL-POWER WAVES, SETS OUT TO DEFEAT THEIR PLANS . . .

THEY'LL LEARN THE POWER OF THE JUNGLE!

SHE THEN EXERTS HER SECRET POWER OVER CERTAIN JUNGLE BEASTS, IN BOTH AFRICA AND SOUTH AMERICA . . . .

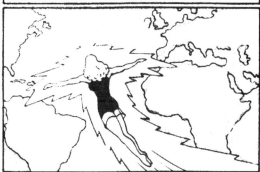

THE BEASTS IMMEDIATELY RESPOND TO HER WIZARDRY.

IN AFRICA, HUGE JUNGLE CATS BEGIN MOVING TO A POINT NEAR THE INVADERS MILITARY BASE . . . . .

IN SOUTH AMERICA, BEASTS UNKNOWN TO WHITE MEN MOVE OUT UPON AN UNCHARTED PLATEAU IN THE WILDS OF BRAZIL . . . .

MEANWHILE, FANTOMAH EXERTS HER POWER OVER THE ATMOSPHERIC ELEMENTS.

PECULIAR STORM-CLOUDS START FORMING OUT AT SEA . . .

AT THE SAME TIME, THE GREAT PLANES LINE UP FOR THEIR HOP TO BRAZIL . .

IT'S ONLY 1700 MILES! OUR SUPERS CAN MAKE IT IN FOUR HOURS!

THEY TAKE OFF IN FORMATION WAVES.

AS THEY GET OUT TO SEA, THE PECULIAR STORM-CLOUDS BEGIN TO TAKE VIOLENT MOTION AND DEVELOP INTO A SIROCCO. . .

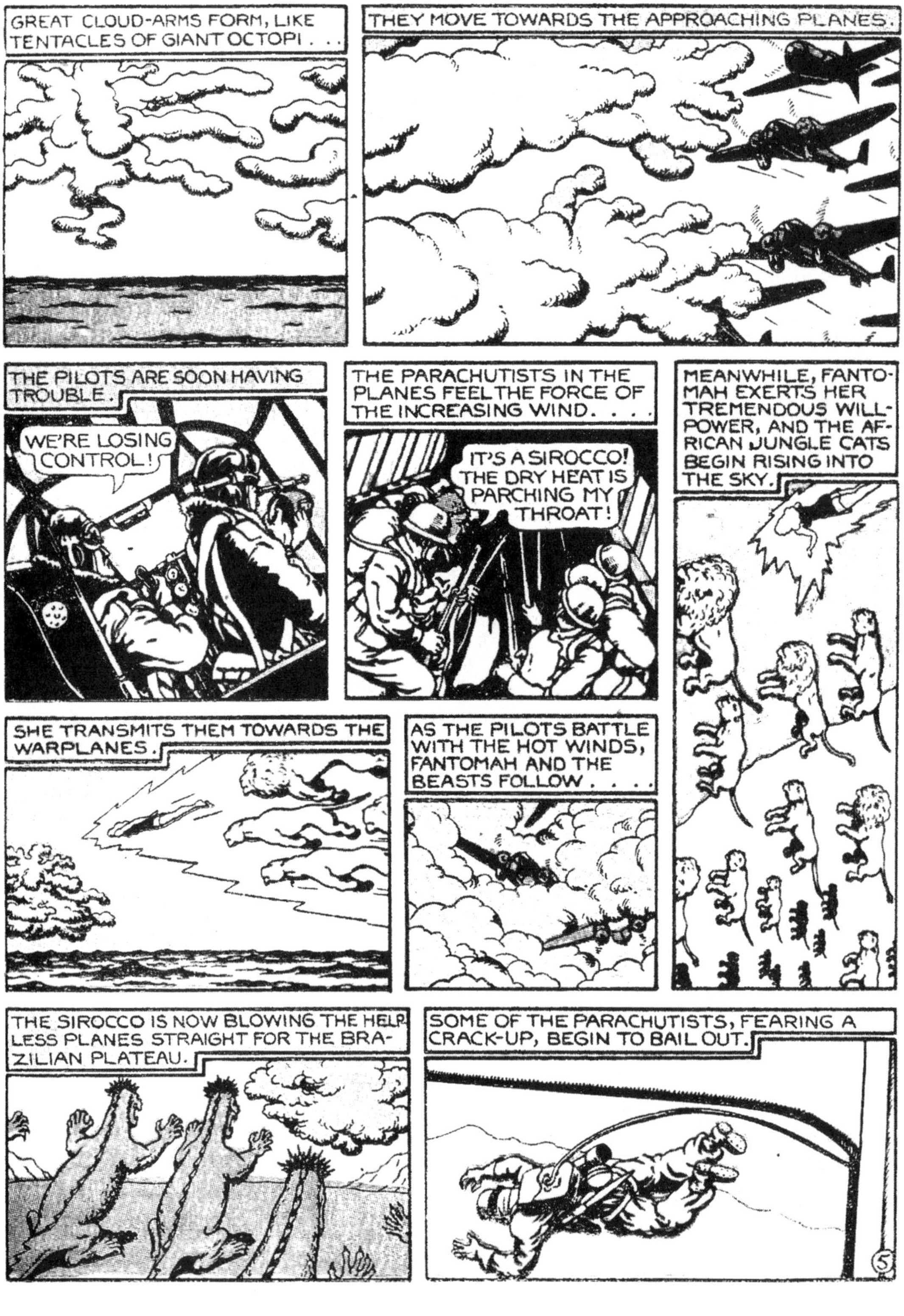
GREAT CLOUD-ARMS FORM, LIKE TENTACLES OF GIANT OCTOPI . . .
THEY MOVE TOWARDS THE APPROACHING PLANES.
THE PILOTS ARE SOON HAVING TROUBLE.
WE'RE LOSING CONTROL!
THE PARACHUTISTS IN THE PLANES FEEL THE FORCE OF THE INCREASING WIND. . . .
IT'S A SIROCCO! THE DRY HEAT IS PARCHING MY THROAT!
MEANWHILE, FANTOMAH EXERTS HER TREMENDOUS WILL-POWER, AND THE AFRICAN JUNGLE CATS BEGIN RISING INTO THE SKY.
SHE TRANSMITS THEM TOWARDS THE WARPLANES.
AS THE PILOTS BATTLE WITH THE HOT WINDS, FANTOMAH AND THE BEASTS FOLLOW . . . .
THE SIROCCO IS NOW BLOWING THE HELPLESS PLANES STRAIGHT FOR THE BRAZILIAN PLATEAU.
SOME OF THE PARACHUTISTS, FEARING A CRACK-UP, BEGIN TO BAIL OUT.
5

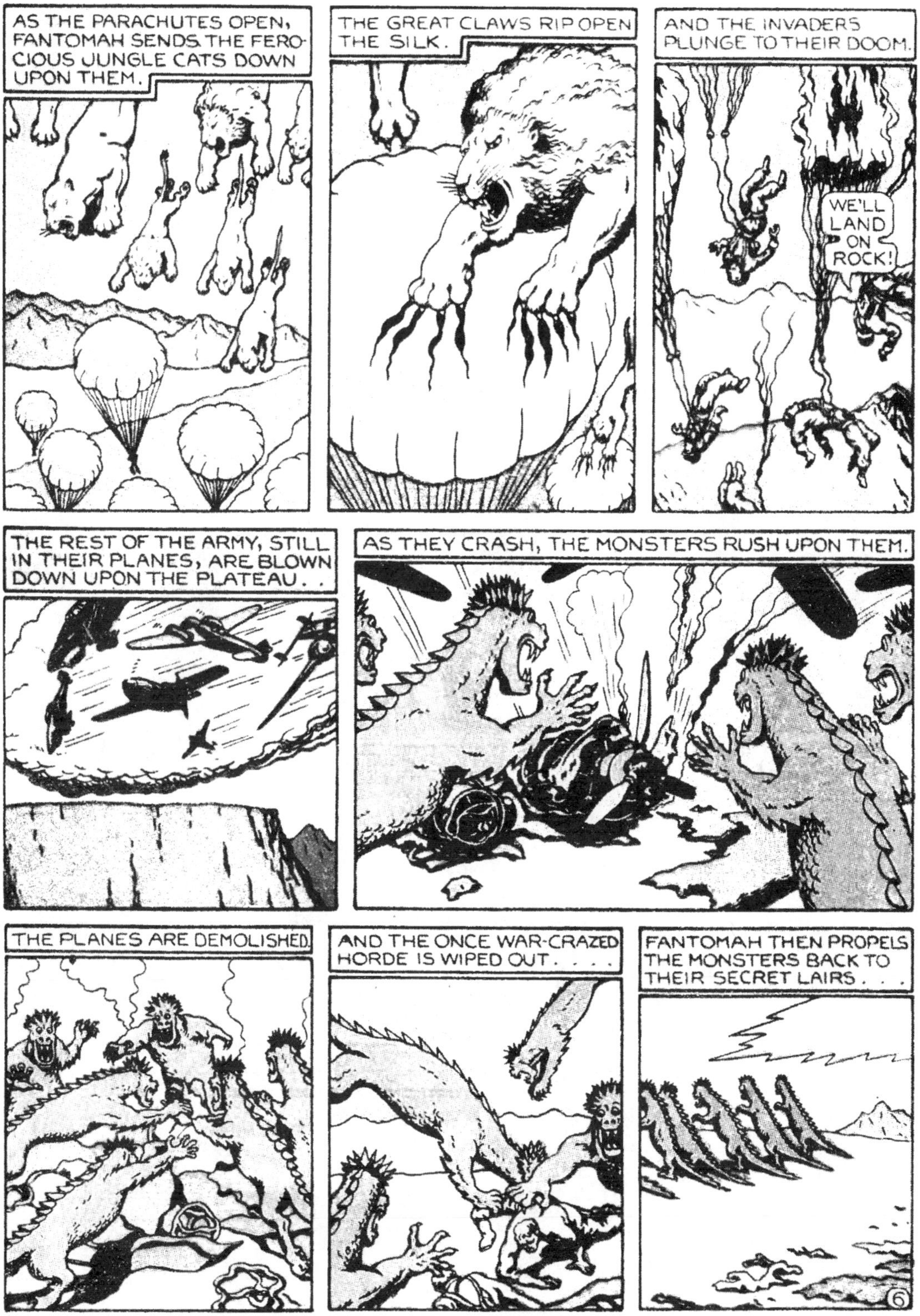
AS THE PARACHUTES OPEN, FANTOMAH SENDS THE FEROCIOUS JUNGLE CATS DOWN UPON THEM.
THE GREAT CLAWS RIP OPEN THE SILK.
AND THE INVADERS PLUNGE TO THEIR DOOM.
WE'LL LAND ON ROCK!
THE REST OF THE ARMY, STILL IN THEIR PLANES, ARE BLOWN DOWN UPON THE PLATEAU . .
AS THEY CRASH, THE MONSTERS RUSH UPON THEM.
THE PLANES ARE DEMOLISHED.
AND THE ONCE WAR-CRAZED HORDE IS WIPED OUT . . . .
FANTOMAH THEN PROPELS THE MONSTERS BACK TO THEIR SECRET LAIRS . . .
6

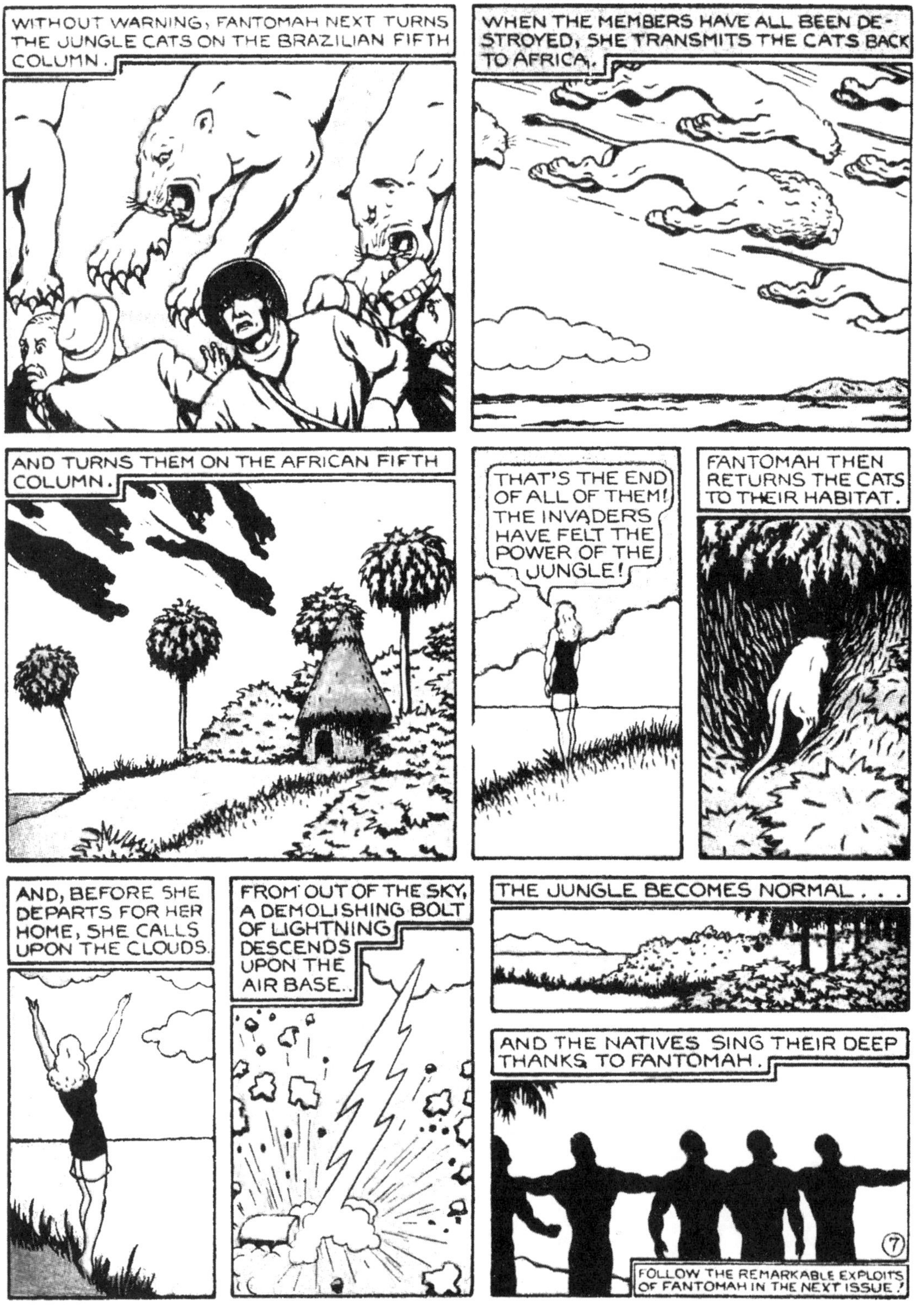
WITHOUT WARNING, FANTOMAH NEXT TURNS THE JUNGLE CATS ON THE BRAZILIAN FIFTH COLUMN.
WHEN THE MEMBERS HAVE ALL BEEN DESTROYED, SHE TRANSMITS THE CATS BACK TO AFRICA,
AND TURNS THEM ON THE AFRICAN FIFTH COLUMN.
THAT'S THE END OF ALL OF THEM! THE INVADERS HAVE FELT THE POWER OF THE JUNGLE!
FANTOMAH THEN RETURNS THE CATS TO THEIR HABITAT.
AND, BEFORE SHE DEPARTS FOR HER HOME, SHE CALLS UPON THE CLOUDS.
FROM OUT OF THE SKY, A DEMOLISHING BOLT OF LIGHTNING DESCENDS UPON THE AIR BASE..
THE JUNGLE BECOMES NORMAL . . .
AND THE NATIVES SING THEIR DEEP THANKS TO FANTOMAH.
7
FOLLOW THE REMARKABLE EXPLOITS OF FANTOMAH IN THE NEXT ISSUE!

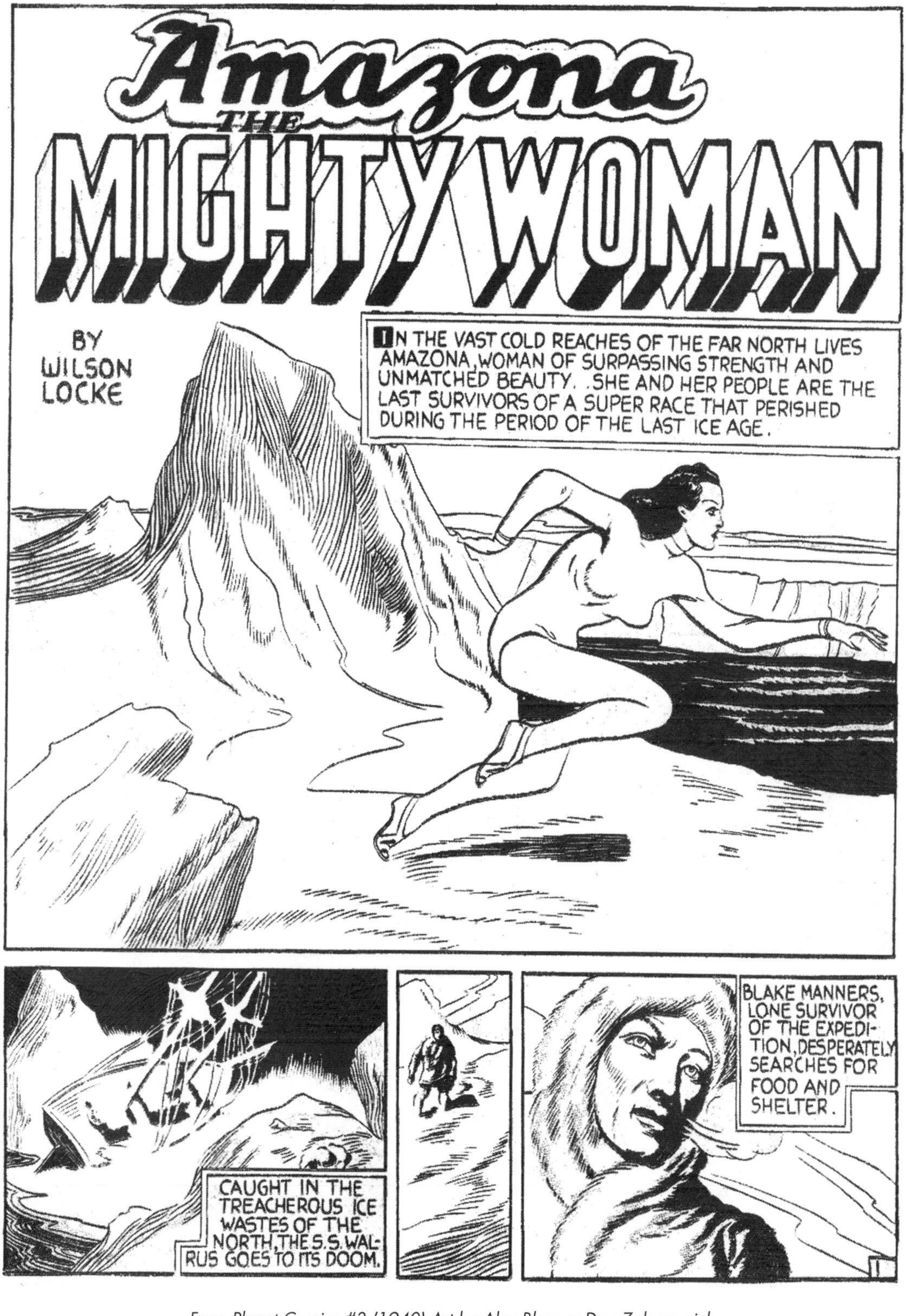
Amazona
THE
MIGHTY WOMAN
BY
WILSON
LOCKE
IN THE VAST COLD REACHES OF THE FAR NORTH LIVES AMAZONA, WOMAN OF SURPASSING STRENGTH AND UNMATCHED BEAUTY. .SHE AND HER PEOPLE ARE THE LAST SURVIVORS OF A SUPER RACE THAT PERISHED DURING THE PERIOD OF THE LAST ICE AGE.
CAUGHT IN THE TREACHEROUS ICE WASTES OF THE NORTH, THE S.S. WALRUS GOES TO ITS DOOM.
BLAKE MANNERS, LONE SURVIVOR OF THE EXPEDITION, DESPERATELY SEARCHES FOR FOOD AND SHELTER.

From Planet Comics #3 (1940) Art by Alex Blum or Dan Zolnerowich

154

SUDDENLY, HE COMES UPON A STRANGE STRUCTURE...

HE ENTERS.

WHITE MEN! I-I THOUGHT I'D NEVER SEE ONE AGAIN.

WELCOME, MY SON!

QUIETLY, THE ELDERLY MAN TELLS BLAKE OF HIS STRANGE ANCESTORS . . . . . .

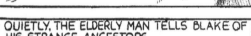

WE ARE DESCENDANTS OF AN ANCIENT PEOPLE. ONLY THE HARDIEST OF THEM SURVIVED THE RIGORS OF THIS VAST ARCTIC LAND!

HOW INTERESTING

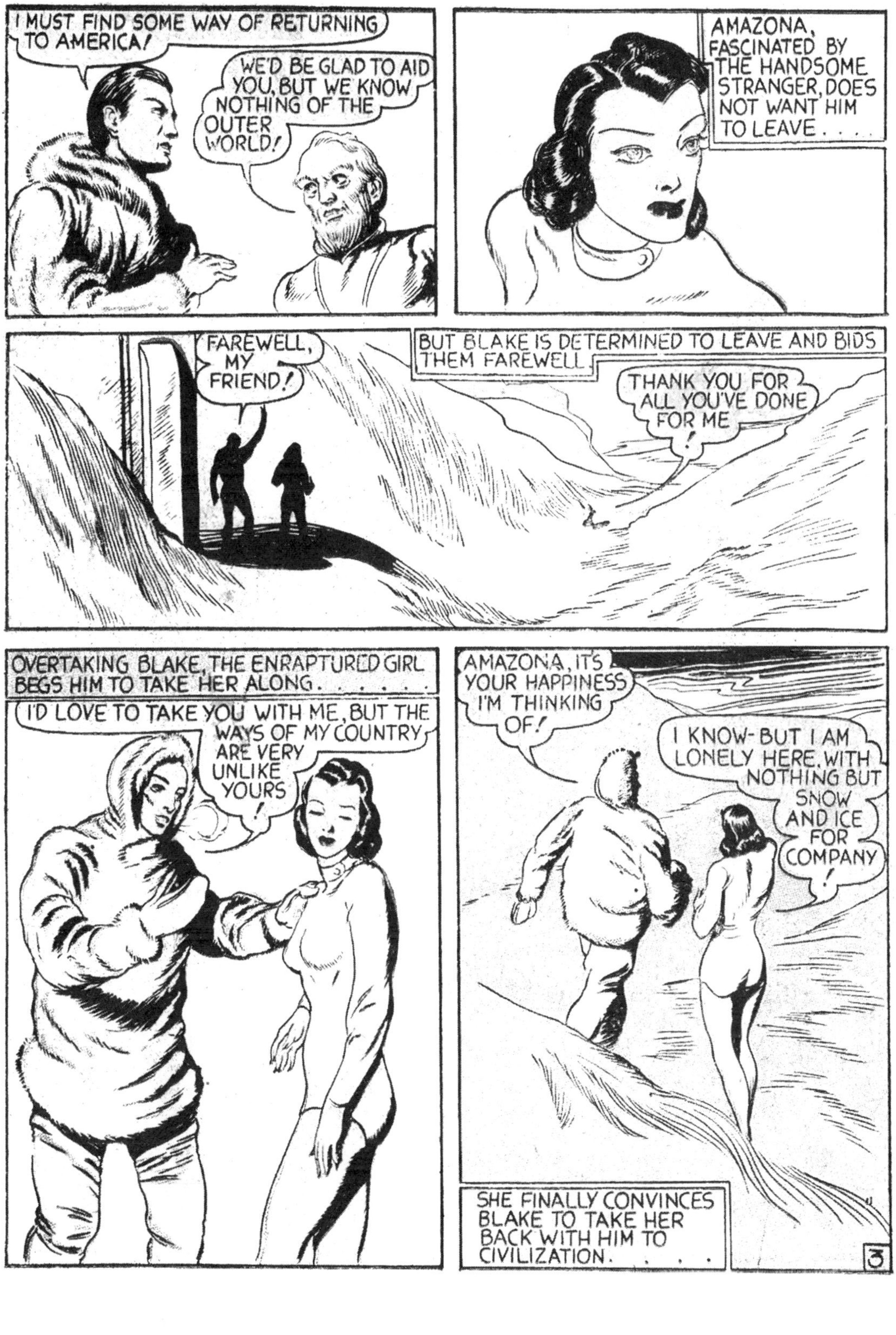
I MUST FIND SOME WAY OF RETURNING TO AMERICA!
WE'D BE GLAD TO AID YOU, BUT WE KNOW NOTHING OF THE OUTER WORLD!
AMAZONA, FASCINATED BY THE HANDSOME STRANGER, DOES NOT WANT HIM TO LEAVE . . .
FAREWELL, MY FRIEND!
BUT BLAKE IS DETERMINED TO LEAVE AND BIDS THEM FAREWELL
THANK YOU FOR ALL YOU'VE DONE FOR ME!
OVERTAKING BLAKE, THE ENRAPTURED GIRL BEGS HIM TO TAKE HER ALONG . . . . .
I'D LOVE TO TAKE YOU WITH ME, BUT THE WAYS OF MY COUNTRY ARE VERY UNLIKE YOURS!
AMAZONA, IT'S YOUR HAPPINESS I'M THINKING OF!
I KNOW- BUT I AM LONELY HERE, WITH NOTHING BUT SNOW AND ICE FOR COMPANY!
SHE FINALLY CONVINCES BLAKE TO TAKE HER BACK WITH HIM TO CIVILIZATION . . .
3

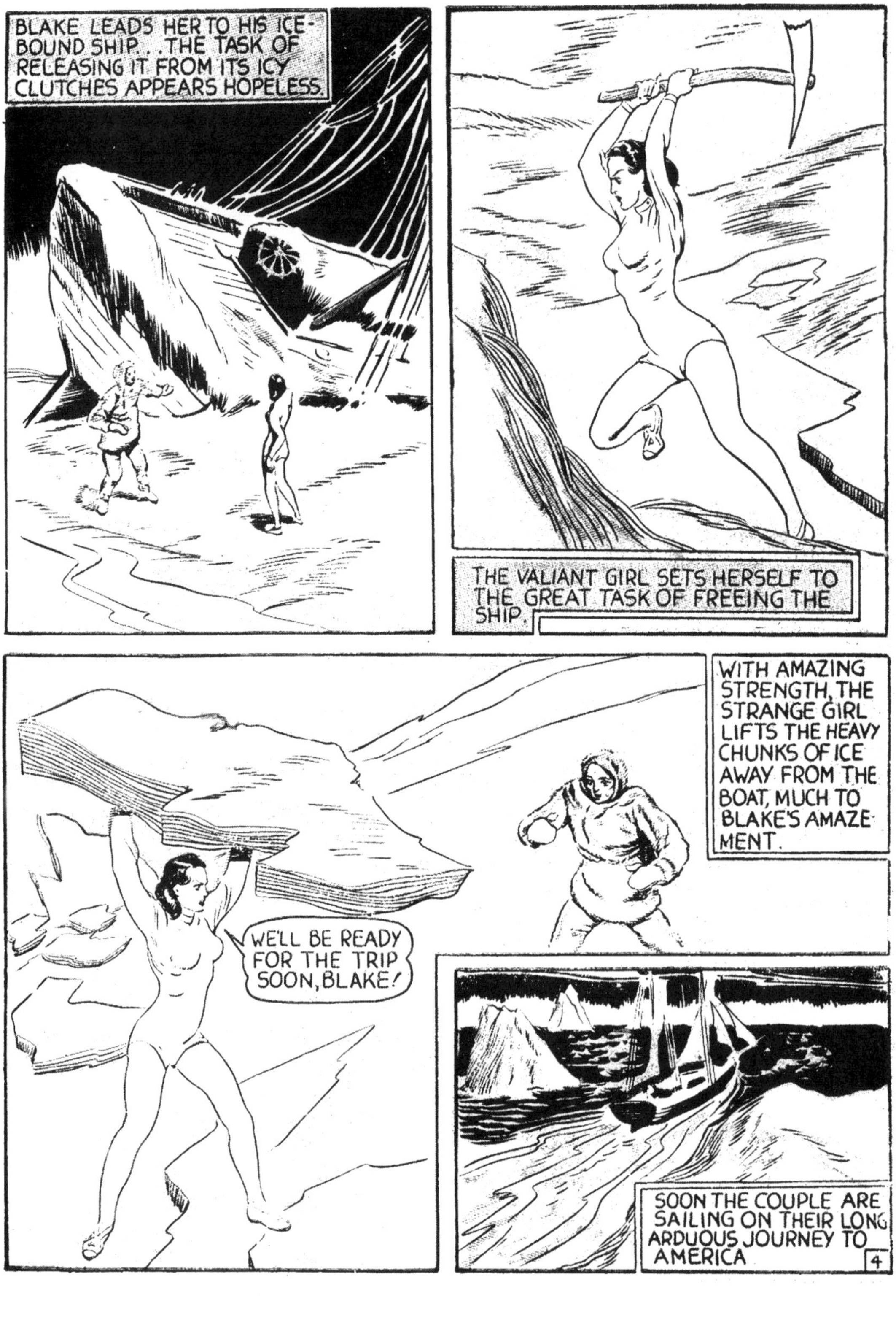
BLAKE LEADS HER TO HIS ICE-BOUND SHIP. . THE TASK OF RELEASING IT FROM ITS ICY CLUTCHES APPEARS HOPELESS.
THE VALIANT GIRL SETS HERSELF TO THE GREAT TASK OF FREEING THE SHIP.
WITH AMAZING STRENGTH, THE STRANGE GIRL LIFTS THE HEAVY CHUNKS OF ICE AWAY FROM THE BOAT, MUCH TO BLAKE'S AMAZEMENT.
WE'LL BE READY FOR THE TRIP SOON, BLAKE!
SOON THE COUPLE ARE SAILING ON THEIR LONG ARDUOUS JOURNEY TO AMERICA
4

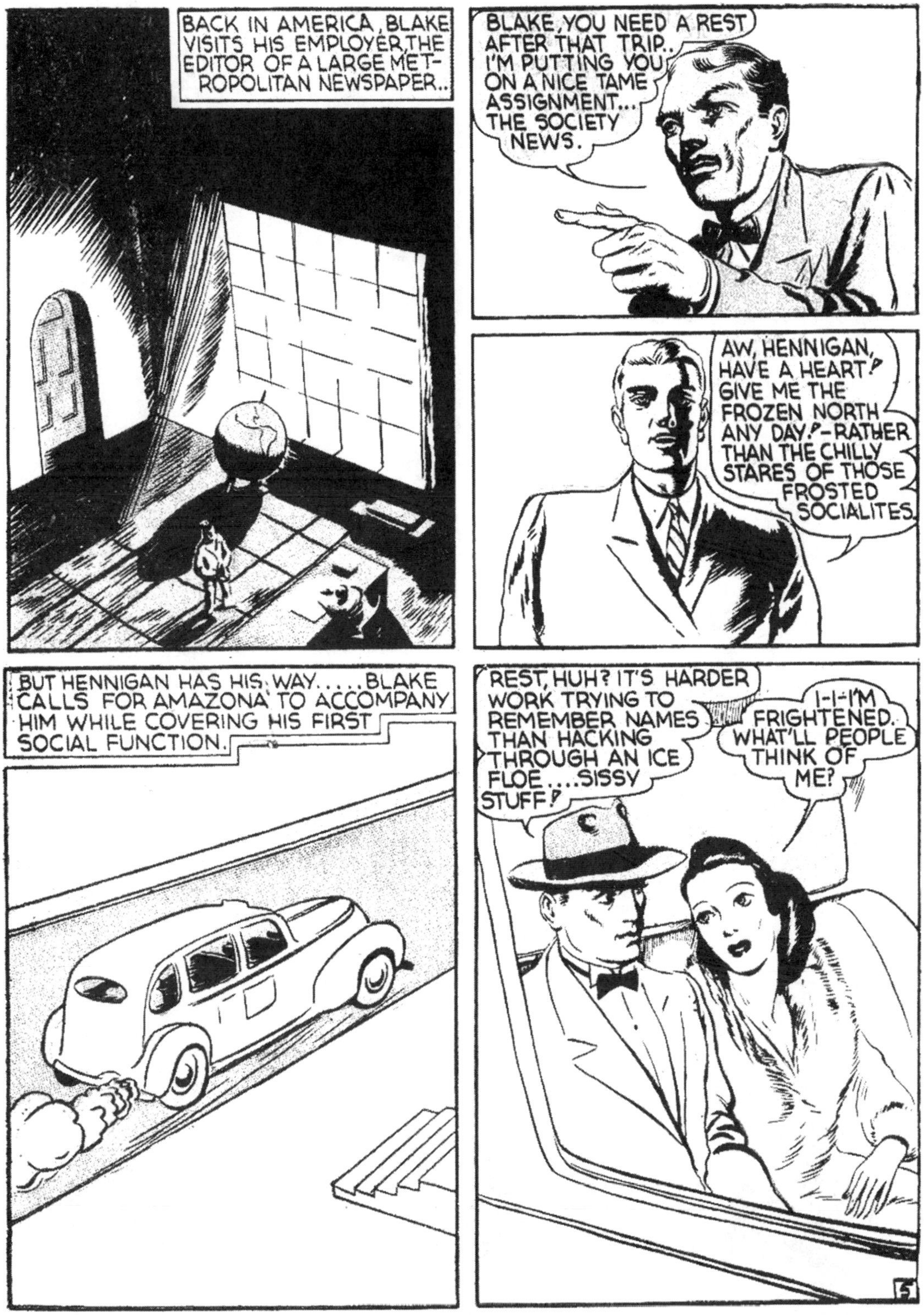
BACK IN AMERICA, BLAKE VISITS HIS EMPLOYER, THE EDITOR OF A LARGE METROPOLITAN NEWSPAPER..
BLAKE, YOU NEED A REST AFTER THAT TRIP.. I'M PUTTING YOU ON A NICE TAME ASSIGNMENT... THE SOCIETY NEWS.
AW, HENNIGAN, HAVE A HEART! GIVE ME THE FROZEN NORTH ANY DAY! - RATHER THAN THE CHILLY STARES OF THOSE FROSTED SOCIALITES.
BUT HENNIGAN HAS HIS WAY.....BLAKE CALLS FOR AMAZONA TO ACCOMPANY HIM WHILE COVERING HIS FIRST SOCIAL FUNCTION.
REST, HUH? IT'S HARDER WORK TRYING TO REMEMBER NAMES THAN HACKING THROUGH AN ICE FLOE....SISSY STUFF!
I-I-I'M FRIGHTENED. WHAT'LL PEOPLE THINK OF ME?
5

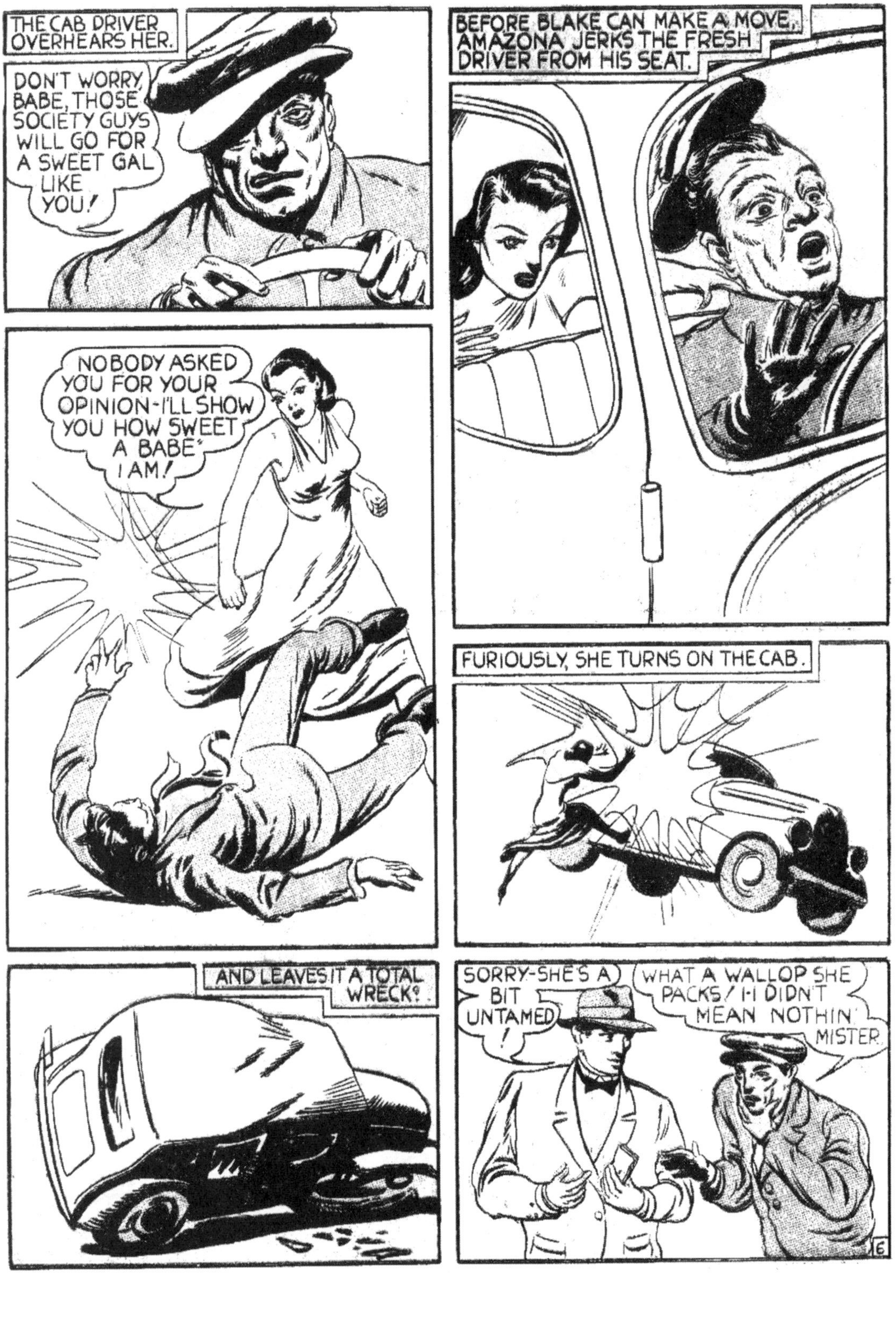
THE CAB DRIVER OVERHEARS HER.
DON'T WORRY, BABE, THOSE SOCIETY GUYS WILL GO FOR A SWEET GAL LIKE YOU!
BEFORE BLAKE CAN MAKE A MOVE, AMAZONA JERKS THE FRESH DRIVER FROM HIS SEAT.
NOBODY ASKED YOU FOR YOUR OPINION-I'LL SHOW YOU HOW SWEET A BABE I AM!
FURIOUSLY, SHE TURNS ON THE CAB.
AND LEAVES IT A TOTAL WRECK!
SORRY-SHE'S A BIT UNTAMED!
WHAT A WALLOP SHE PACKS! I-I DIDN'T MEAN NOTHIN' MISTER
6

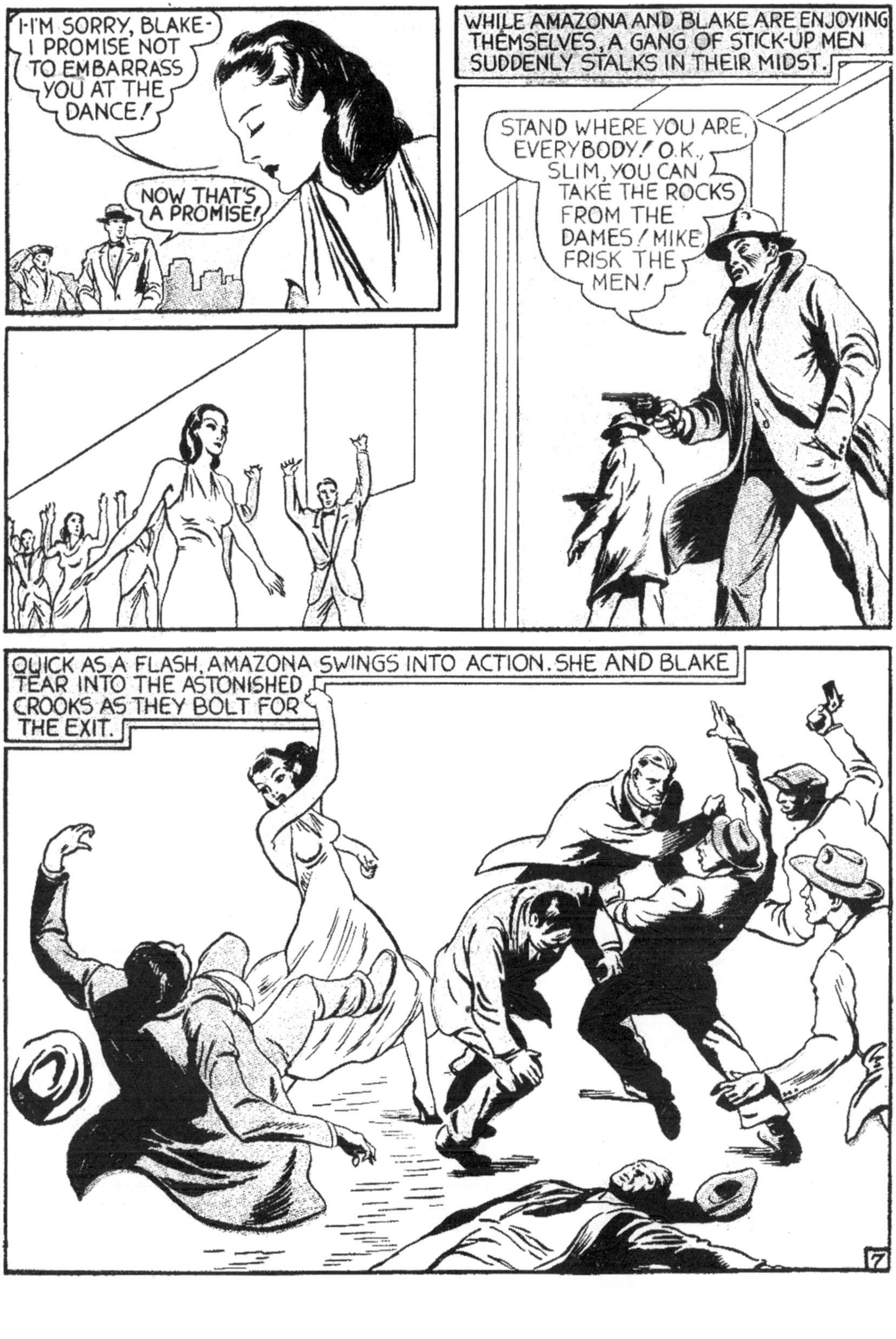
I-I'M SORRY, BLAKE- I PROMISE NOT TO EMBARRASS YOU AT THE DANCE!
NOW THAT'S A PROMISE!
WHILE AMAZONA AND BLAKE ARE ENJOYING THEMSELVES, A GANG OF STICK-UP MEN SUDDENLY STALKS IN THEIR MIDST.
STAND WHERE YOU ARE, EVERYBODY! O.K., SLIM, YOU CAN TAKE THE ROCKS FROM THE DAMES! MIKE, FRISK THE MEN!
QUICK AS A FLASH, AMAZONA SWINGS INTO ACTION. SHE AND BLAKE TEAR INTO THE ASTONISHED CROOKS AS THEY BOLT FOR THE EXIT.
7

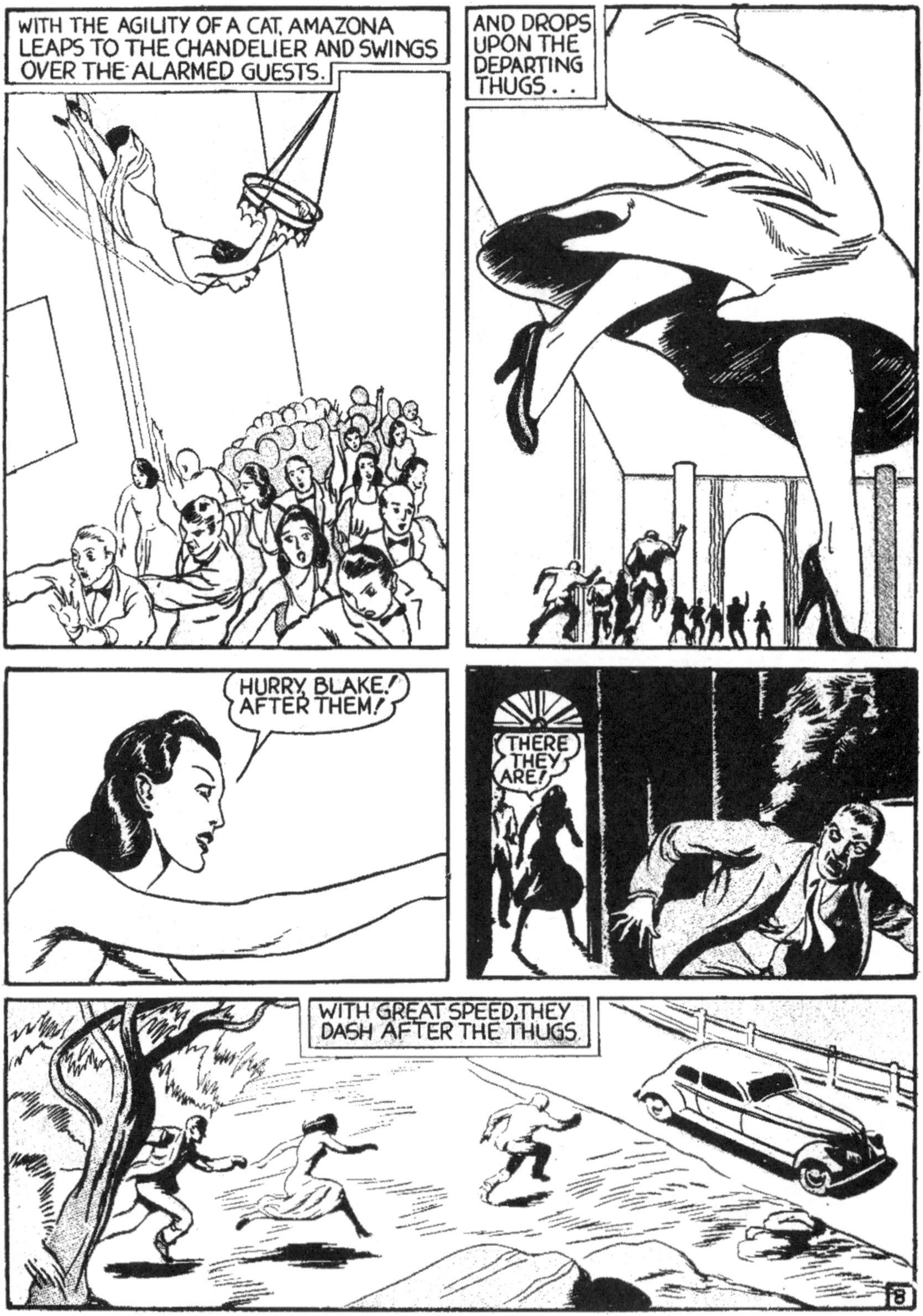
WITH THE AGILITY OF A CAT, AMAZONA LEAPS TO THE CHANDELIER AND SWINGS OVER THE ALARMED GUESTS.
AND DROPS UPON THE DEPARTING THUGS . .
HURRY, BLAKE! AFTER THEM!
THERE THEY ARE!
WITH GREAT SPEED, THEY DASH AFTER THE THUGS.
8

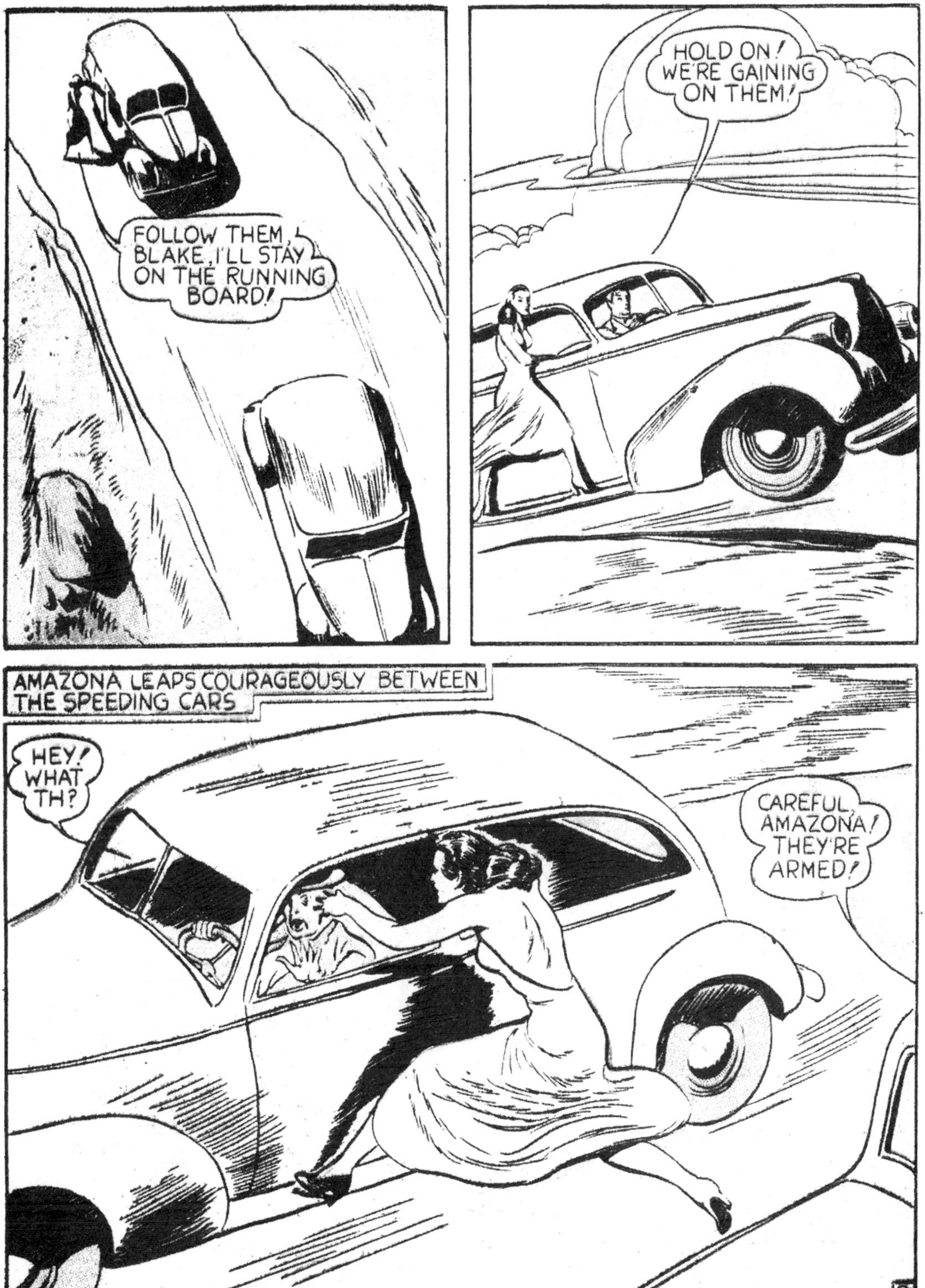
FOLLOW THEM, BLAKE, I'LL STAY ON THE RUNNING BOARD!
HOLD ON! WE'RE GAINING ON THEM!
AMAZONA LEAPS COURAGEOUSLY BETWEEN THE SPEEDING CARS
HEY! WHAT TH?
CAREFUL, AMAZONA! THEY'RE ARMED!
9

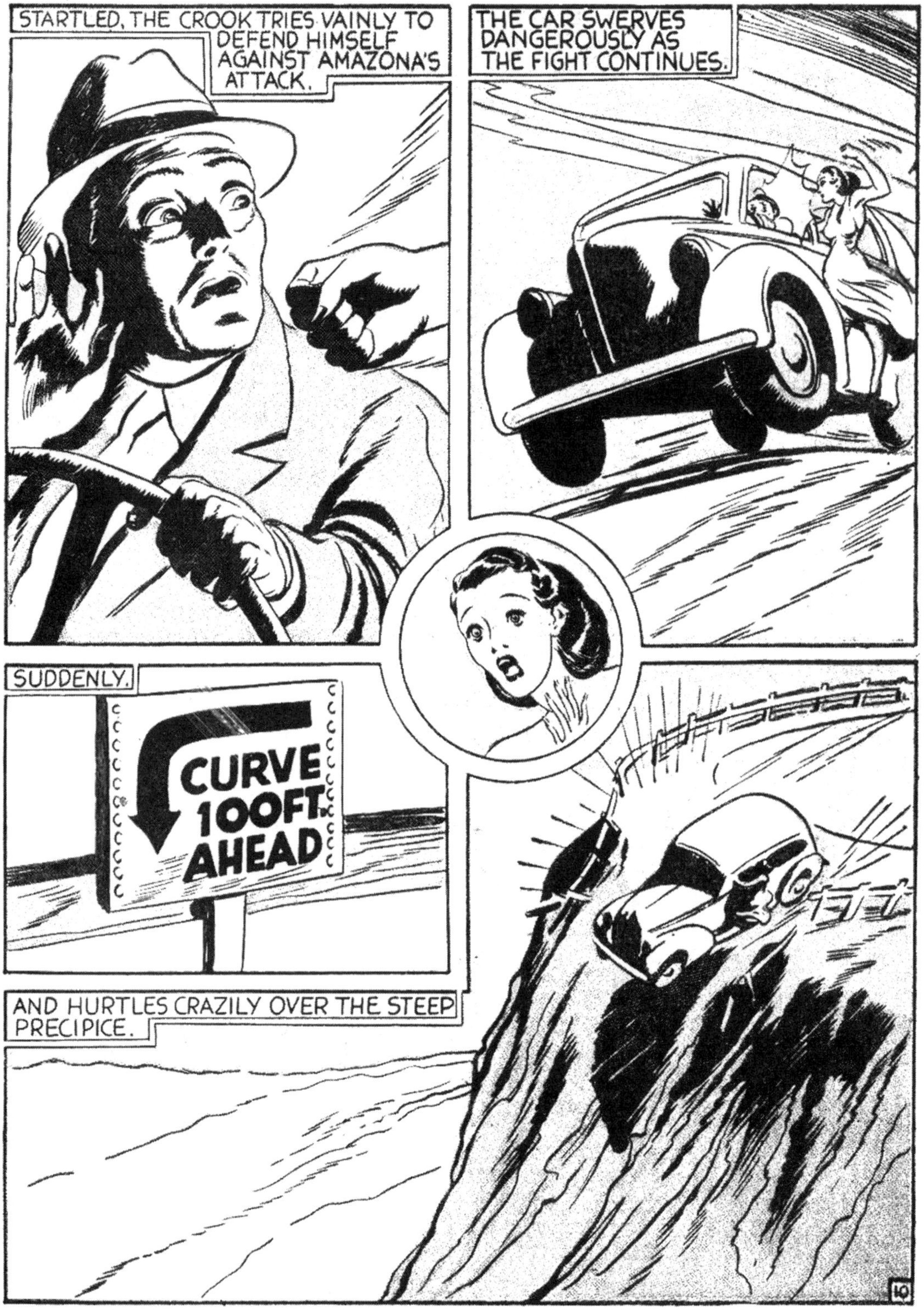
STARTLED, THE CROOK TRIES VAINLY TO DEFEND HIMSELF AGAINST AMAZONA'S ATTACK.
THE CAR SWERVES DANGEROUSLY AS THE FIGHT CONTINUES.
SUDDENLY.
CURVE 100FT. AHEAD
AND HURTLES CRAZILY OVER THE STEEP PRECIPICE.
10

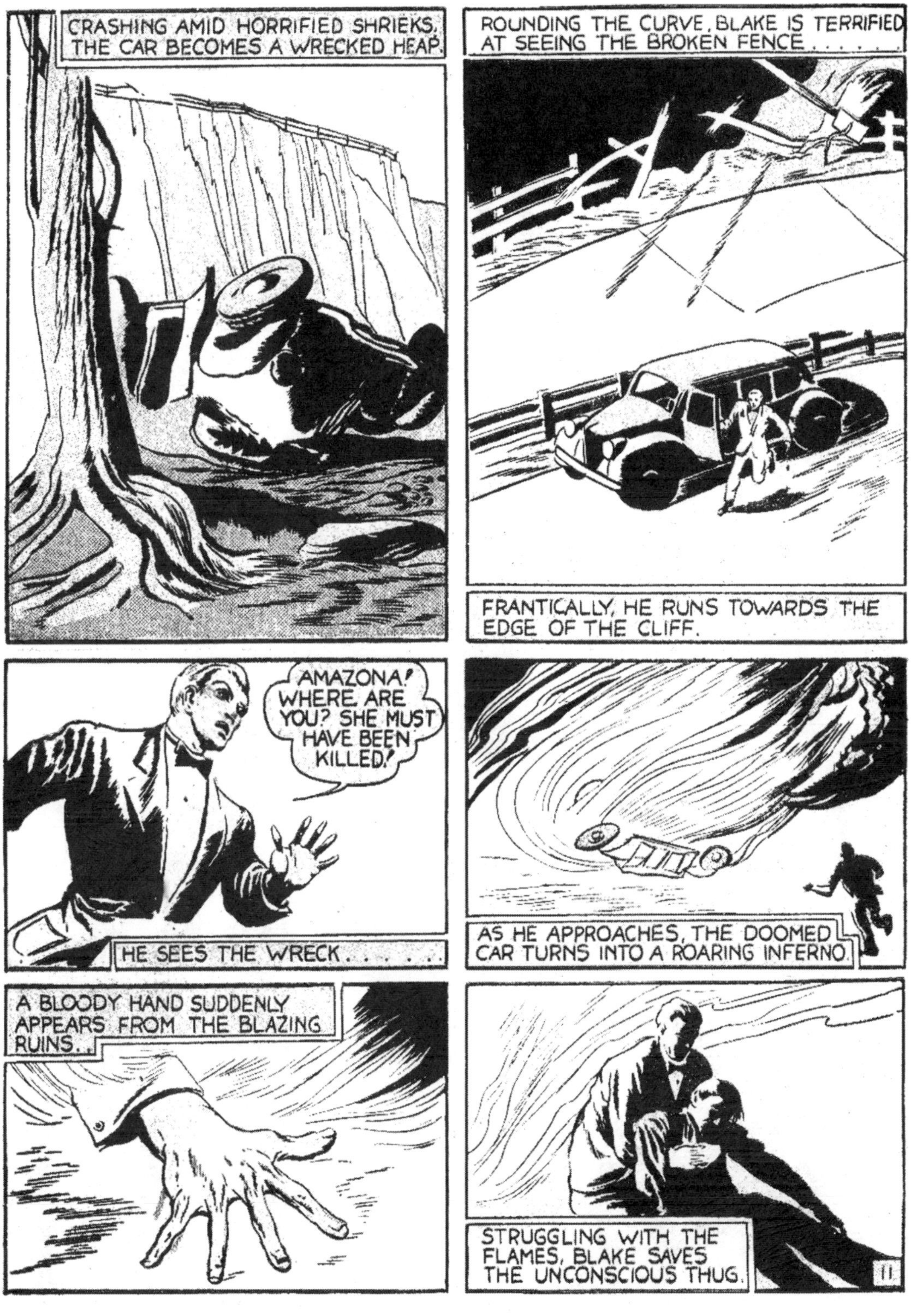
CRASHING AMID HORRIFIED SHRIEKS, THE CAR BECOMES A WRECKED HEAP.
ROUNDING THE CURVE, BLAKE IS TERRIFIED AT SEEING THE BROKEN FENCE . . . . .
FRANTICALLY, HE RUNS TOWARDS THE EDGE OF THE CLIFF.
AMAZONA! WHERE ARE YOU? SHE MUST HAVE BEEN KILLED!
HE SEES THE WRECK . . . . .
AS HE APPROACHES, THE DOOMED CAR TURNS INTO A ROARING INFERNO.
A BLOODY HAND SUDDENLY APPEARS FROM THE BLAZING RUINS. .
STRUGGLING WITH THE FLAMES, BLAKE SAVES THE UNCONSCIOUS THUG.
11

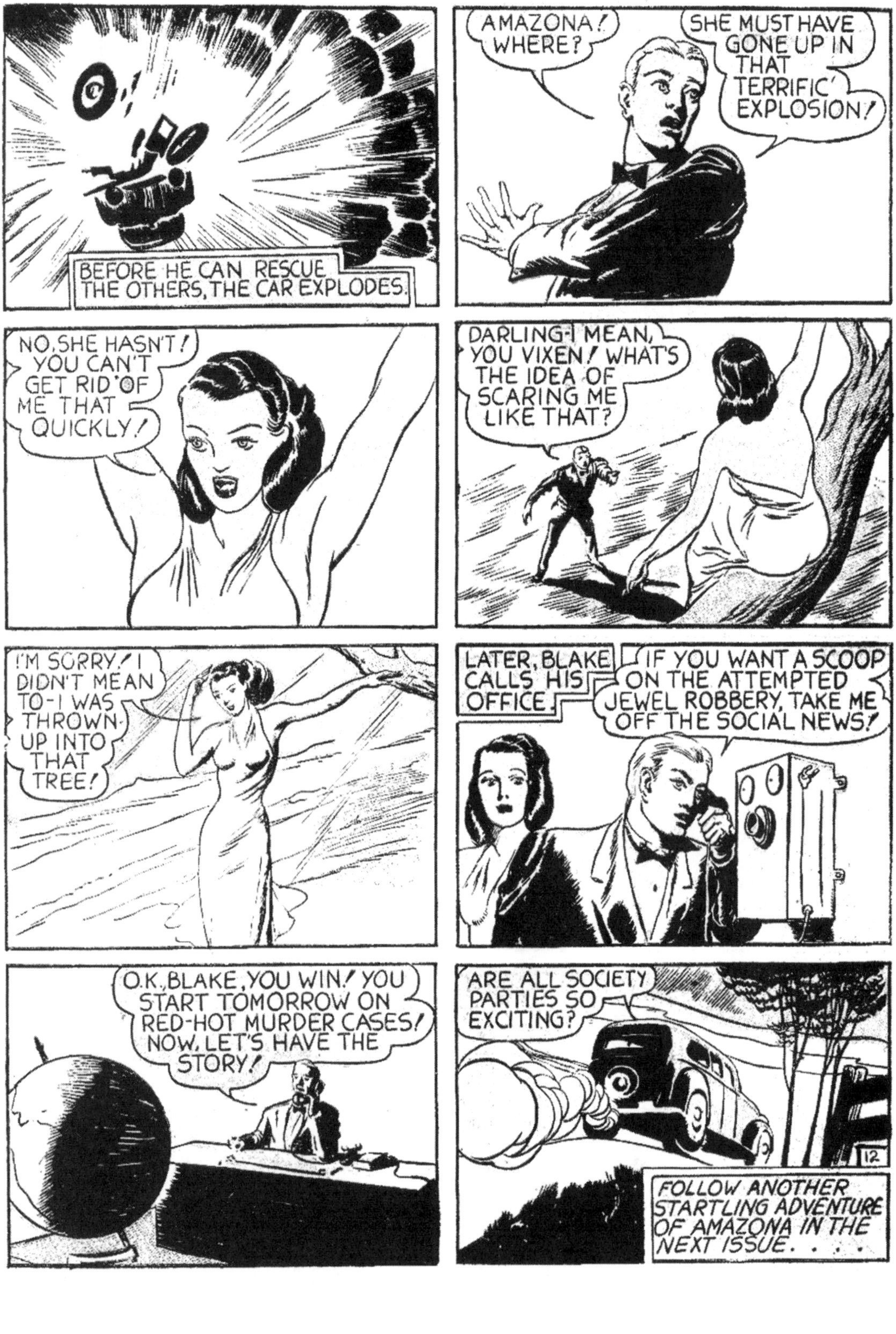
BEFORE HE CAN RESCUE THE OTHERS, THE CAR EXPLODES.
AMAZONA! WHERE?
SHE MUST HAVE GONE UP IN THAT TERRIFIC EXPLOSION!
NO, SHE HASN'T! YOU CAN'T GET RID OF ME THAT QUICKLY!
DARLING-I MEAN, YOU VIXEN! WHAT'S THE IDEA OF SCARING ME LIKE THAT?
I'M SORRY! I DIDN'T MEAN TO-I WAS THROWN UP INTO THAT TREE!
LATER, BLAKE CALLS HIS OFFICE.
IF YOU WANT A SCOOP ON THE ATTEMPTED JEWEL ROBBERY, TAKE ME OFF THE SOCIAL NEWS!
O.K., BLAKE, YOU WIN! YOU START TOMORROW ON RED-HOT MURDER CASES! NOW, LET'S HAVE THE STORY!
ARE ALL SOCIETY PARTIES SO EXCITING?
12
FOLLOW ANOTHER STARTLING ADVENTURE OF AMAZONA IN THE NEXT ISSUE. . . .

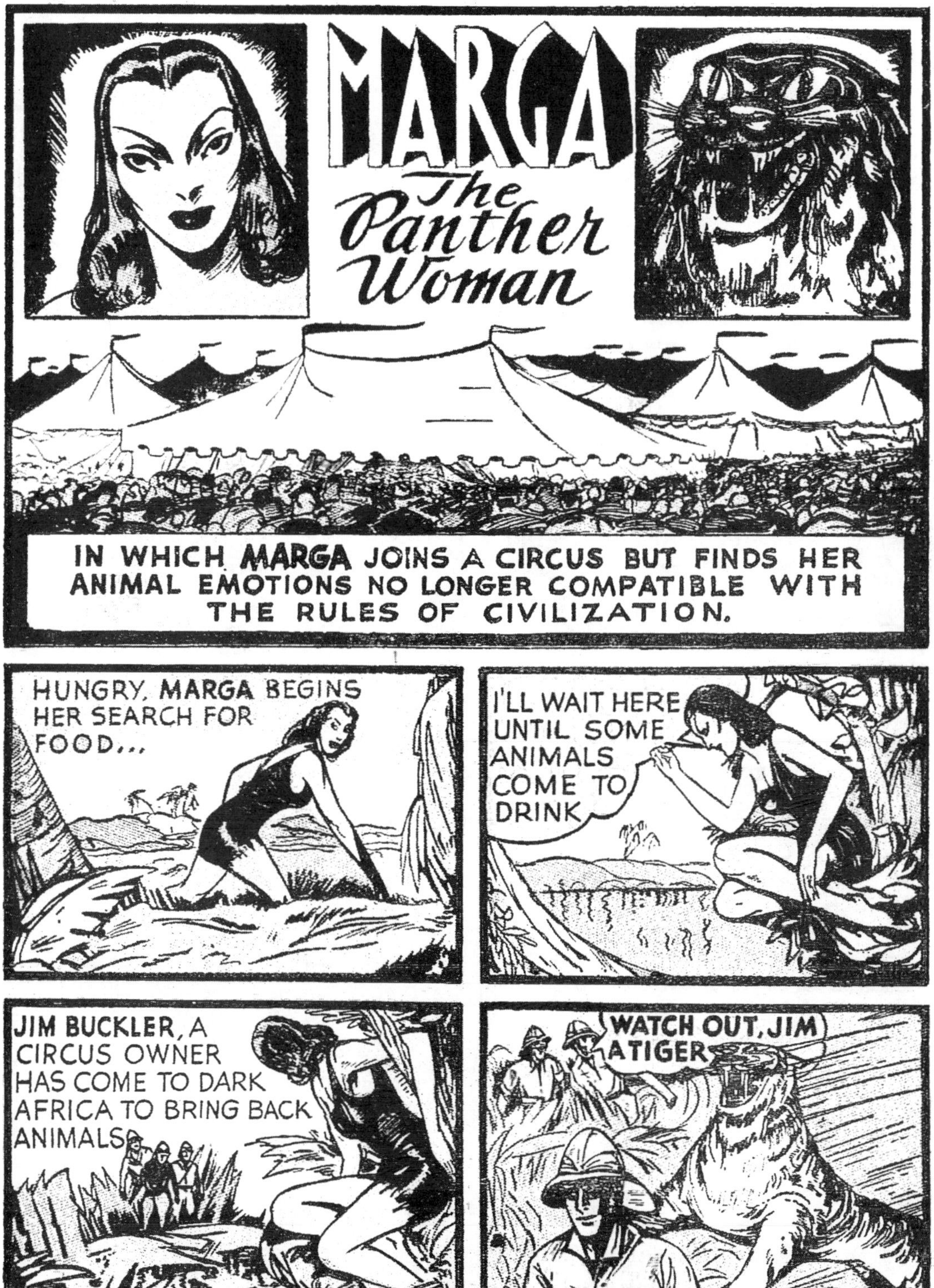
MARGA
The Panther Woman
IN WHICH MARGA JOINS A CIRCUS BUT FINDS HER ANIMAL EMOTIONS NO LONGER COMPATIBLE WITH THE RULES OF CIVILIZATION.
HUNGRY, MARGA BEGINS HER SEARCH FOR FOOD...
I'LL WAIT HERE UNTIL SOME ANIMALS COME TO DRINK
JIM BUCKLER, A CIRCUS OWNER HAS COME TO DARK AFRICA TO BRING BACK ANIMALS
WATCH OUT, JIM A TIGER

From Science Comics #6 (1940) Artist Unknown

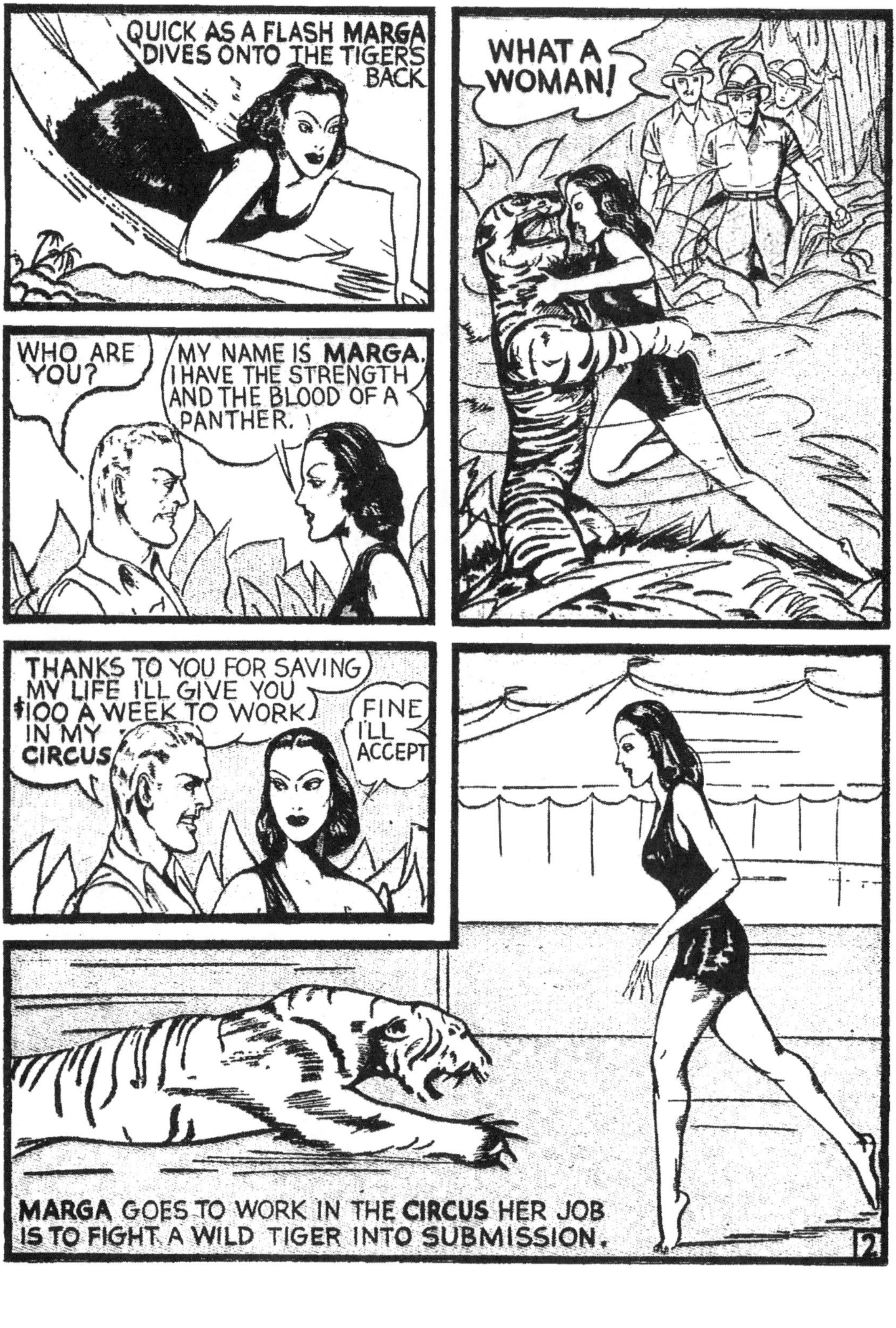
QUICK AS A FLASH MARGA DIVES ONTO THE TIGERS BACK
WHAT A WOMAN!
WHO ARE YOU?
MY NAME IS MARGA. I HAVE THE STRENGTH AND THE BLOOD OF A PANTHER.
THANKS TO YOU FOR SAVING MY LIFE I'LL GIVE YOU $100 A WEEK TO WORK IN MY CIRCUS
FINE I'LL ACCEPT
MARGA GOES TO WORK IN THE CIRCUS HER JOB IS TO FIGHT A WILD TIGER INTO SUBMISSION.
12

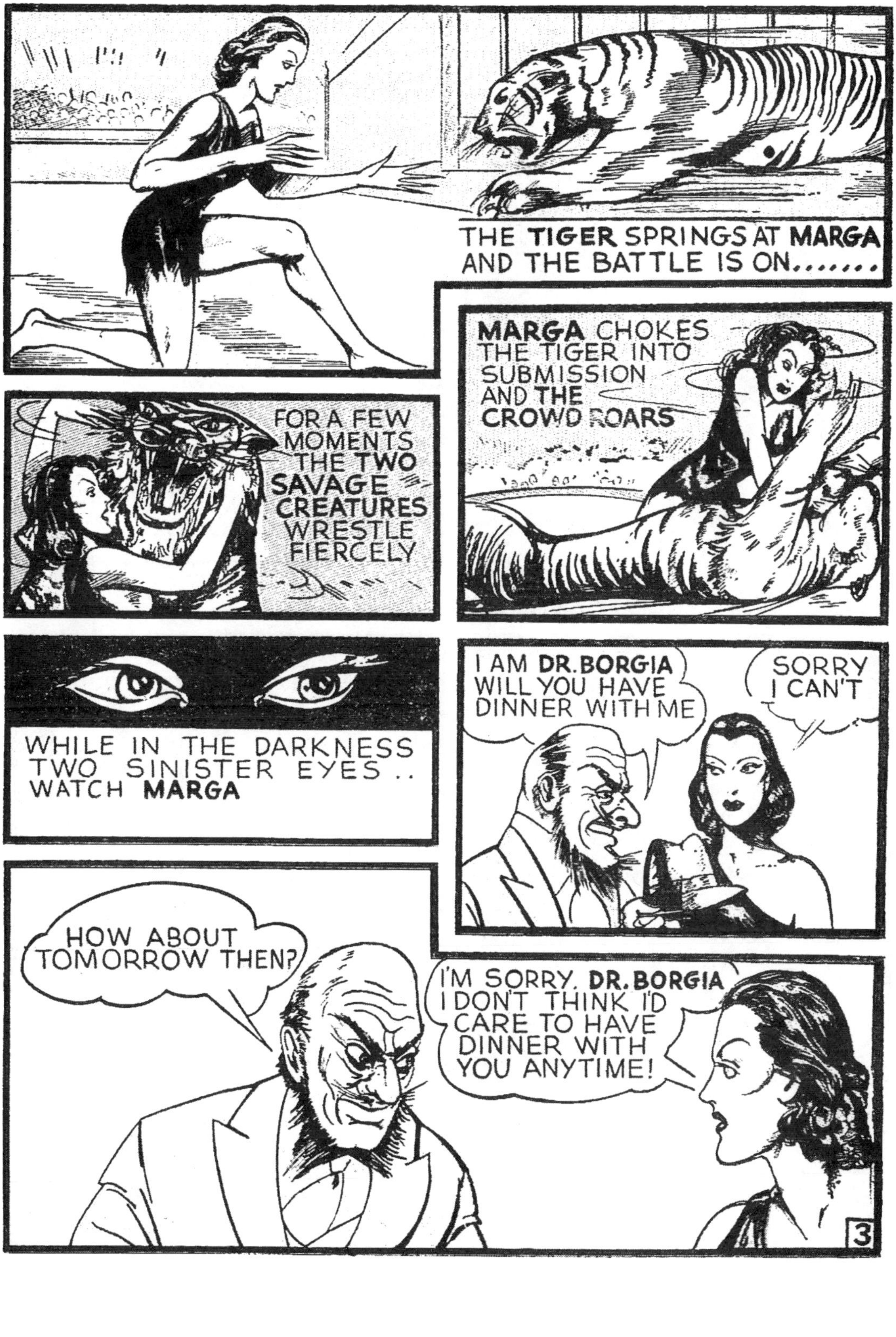
THE TIGER SPRINGS AT MARGA AND THE BATTLE IS ON.......
MARGA CHOKES THE TIGER INTO SUBMISSION AND THE CROWD ROARS
FOR A FEW MOMENTS THE TWO SAVAGE CREATURES WRESTLE FIERCELY
WHILE IN THE DARKNESS TWO SINISTER EYES .. WATCH MARGA
I AM DR. BORGIA WILL YOU HAVE DINNER WITH ME
SORRY I CAN'T
HOW ABOUT TOMORROW THEN?
I'M SORRY, DR. BORGIA I DON'T THINK I'D CARE TO HAVE DINNER WITH YOU ANYTIME!
3

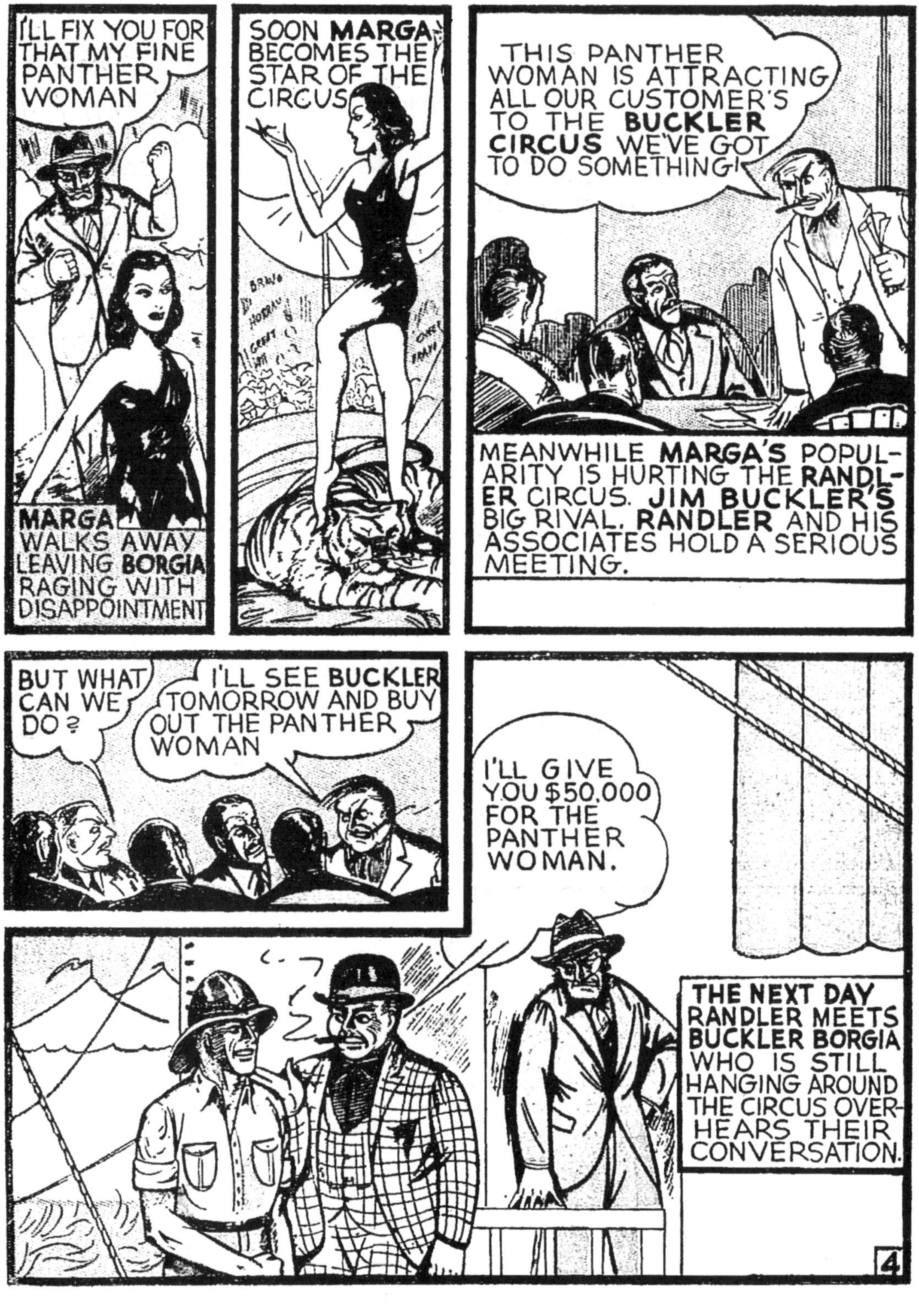
I'LL FIX YOU FOR THAT MY FINE PANTHER WOMAN
MARGA WALKS AWAY LEAVING BORGIA RAGING WITH DISAPPOINTMENT
SOON MARGA BECOMES THE STAR OF THE CIRCUS
THIS PANTHER WOMAN IS ATTRACTING ALL OUR CUSTOMER'S TO THE BUCKLER CIRCUS WE'VE GOT TO DO SOMETHING!
MEANWHILE MARGA'S POPULARITY IS HURTING THE RANDLER CIRCUS. JIM BUCKLER'S BIG RIVAL. RANDLER AND HIS ASSOCIATES HOLD A SERIOUS MEETING.
BUT WHAT CAN WE DO?
I'LL SEE BUCKLER TOMORROW AND BUY OUT THE PANTHER WOMAN
I'LL GIVE YOU $50,000 FOR THE PANTHER WOMAN.
THE NEXT DAY RANDLER MEETS BUCKLER BORGIA WHO IS STILL HANGING AROUND THE CIRCUS OVERHEARS THEIR CONVERSATION.
4

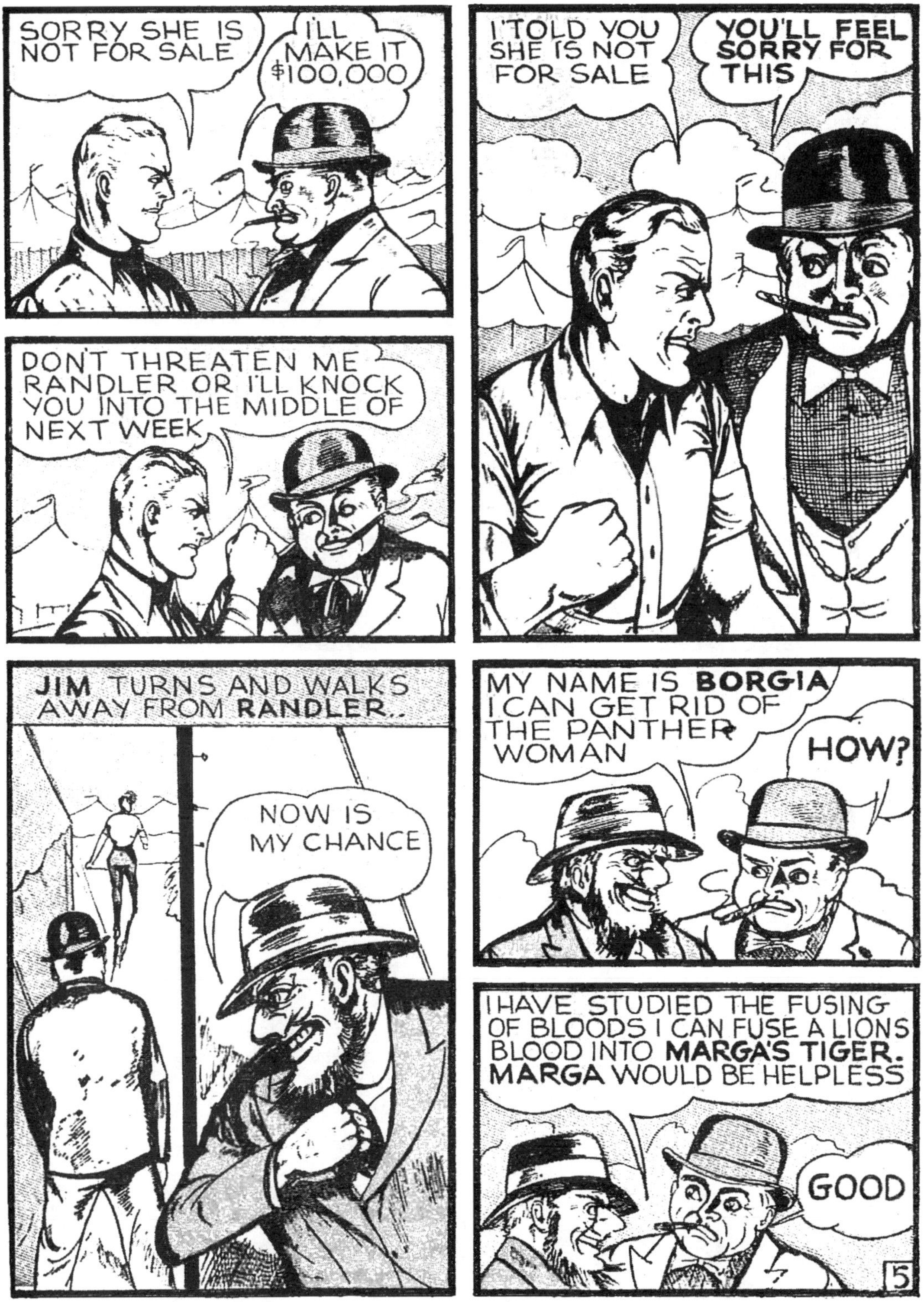
SORRY SHE IS NOT FOR SALE
I'LL MAKE IT $100,000
I'TOLD YOU SHE IS NOT FOR SALE
YOU'LL FEEL SORRY FOR THIS
DON'T THREATEN ME RANDLER OR I'LL KNOCK YOU INTO THE MIDDLE OF NEXT WEEK
JIM TURNS AND WALKS AWAY FROM RANDLER..
NOW IS MY CHANCE
MY NAME IS BORGIA I CAN GET RID OF THE PANTHER WOMAN
HOW?
I HAVE STUDIED THE FUSING OF BLOODS I CAN FUSE A LIONS BLOOD INTO MARGA'S TIGER. MARGA WOULD BE HELPLESS
GOOD
5

THE SAME NIGHT **BORGIA** AND **RANDLER** STEAL **MARGA'S** TIGER FROM HIS CAGE

THE NEXT DAY— **MARGA** SITTING IN HER TENT, IS TROUBLED. HER ANIMAL INSTINCT TELLS HER OF DANGER AND SHE WONDERS WHAT IT CAN BE....

MEANWHILE IN **DR. BORGIA'S** LABORATORY

I WILL INJECT THE BLOOD OF ONE OF **RANDLER'S** LIONS INTO **MARGA'S.** TIGER.....

WHAT'S THIS?

MARGA OVERHEARS **BORGIA** AND **RANDLER'S** CONVERSATION

WITH THE LION'S BLOOD INSIDE THE TIGER **MARGA** WON'T HAVE A CHANCE

AT THE SAME TIME JIM CALLS!

MARGA WHERE ARE YOU?

UNCERTAIN WHICH WAY TO TURN— **MARGA** HESITATES AND IN THE MEANTIME **RANDLER** AND **BORGIA** WALK AWAY

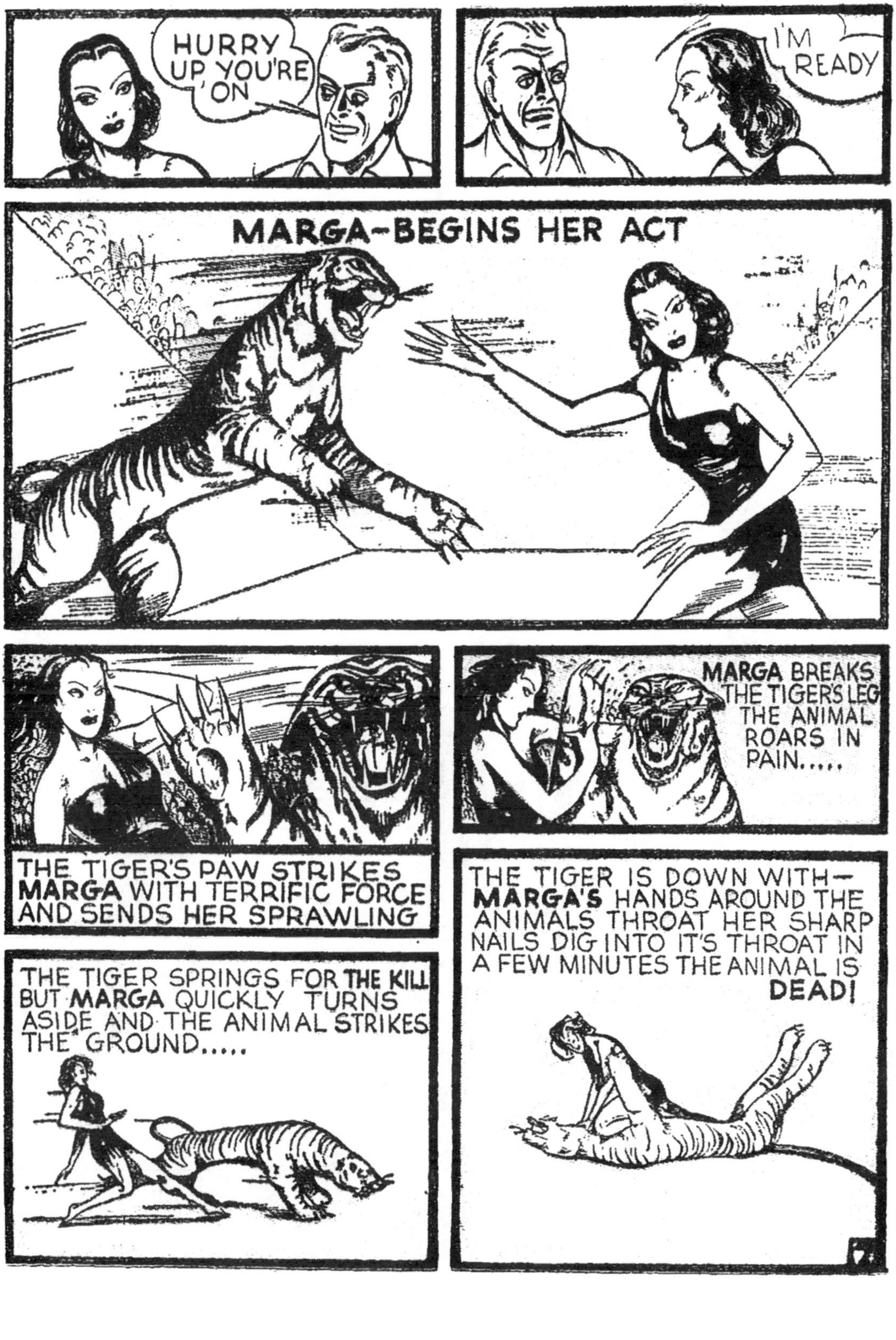
HURRY UP YOU'RE ON
I'M READY
MARGA-BEGINS HER ACT
THE TIGER'S PAW STRIKES MARGA WITH TERRIFIC FORCE AND SENDS HER SPRAWLING
MARGA BREAKS THE TIGER'S LEG THE ANIMAL ROARS IN PAIN.....
THE TIGER SPRINGS FOR THE KILL BUT MARGA QUICKLY TURNS ASIDE AND THE ANIMAL STRIKES THE GROUND.....
THE TIGER IS DOWN WITH— MARGA'S HANDS AROUND THE ANIMALS THROAT HER SHARP NAILS DIG INTO IT'S THROAT IN A FEW MINUTES THE ANIMAL IS DEAD!
7

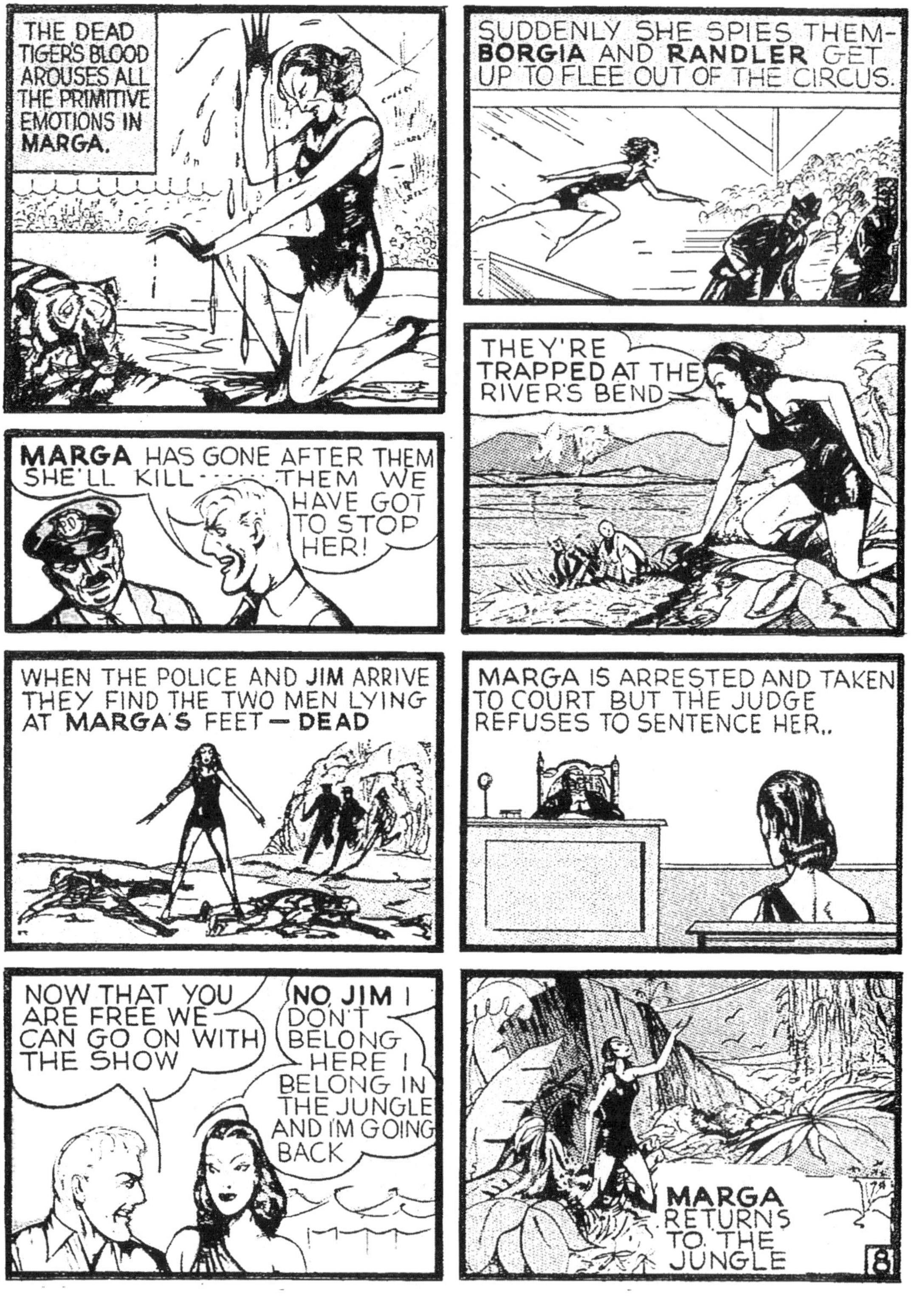
THE DEAD TIGER'S BLOOD AROUSES ALL THE PRIMITIVE EMOTIONS IN MARGA.
SUDDENLY SHE SPIES THEM- BORGIA AND RANDLER GET UP TO FLEE OUT OF THE CIRCUS.
MARGA HAS GONE AFTER THEM SHE'LL KILL ..... THEM WE HAVE GOT TO STOP HER!
THEY'RE TRAPPED AT THE RIVER'S BEND
WHEN THE POLICE AND JIM ARRIVE THEY FIND THE TWO MEN LYING AT MARGA'S FEET — DEAD
MARGA IS ARRESTED AND TAKEN TO COURT BUT THE JUDGE REFUSES TO SENTENCE HER..
NOW THAT YOU ARE FREE WE CAN GO ON WITH THE SHOW
NO JIM I DON'T BELONG HERE I BELONG IN THE JUNGLE AND I'M GOING BACK
MARGA RETURNS TO THE JUNGLE
8

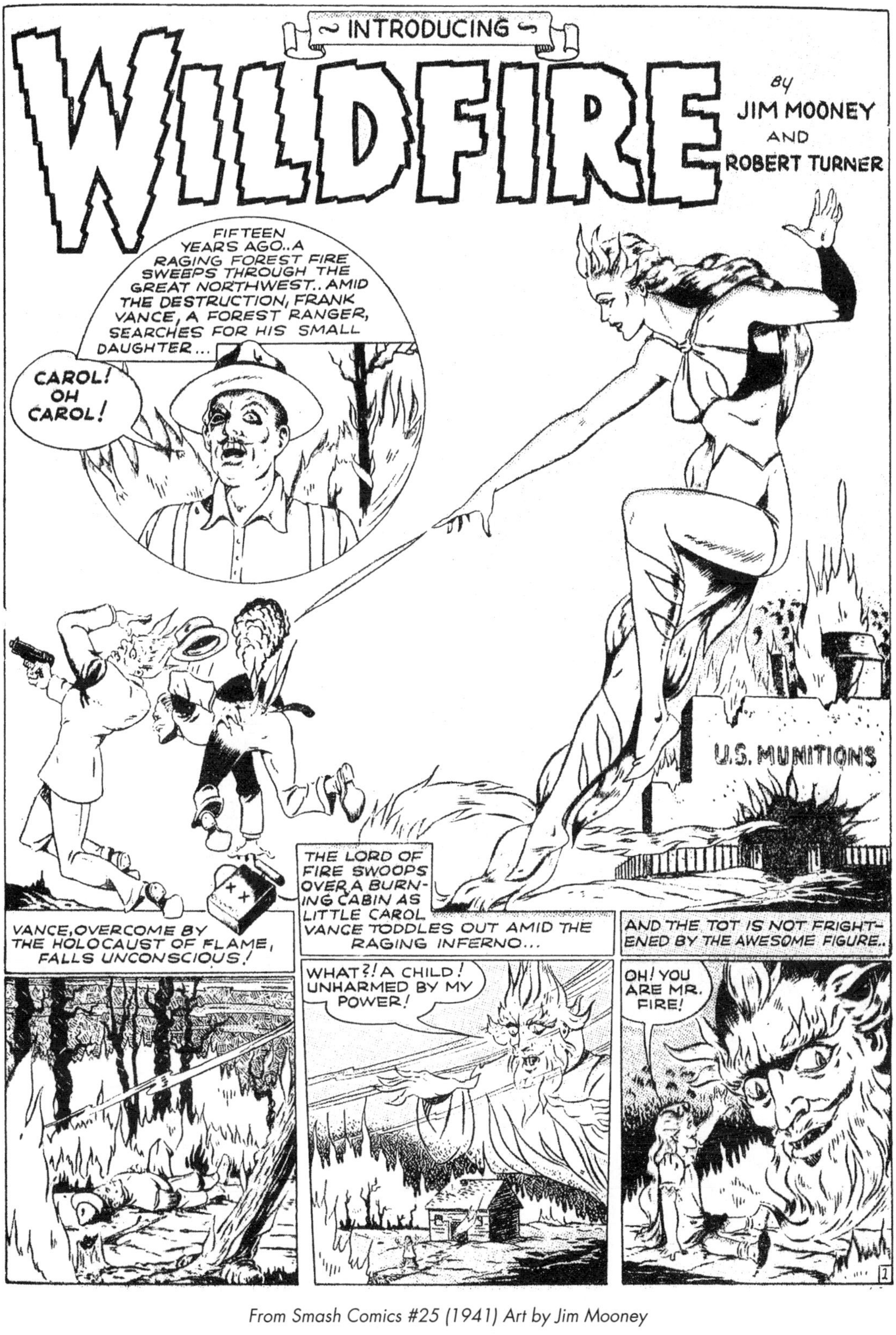
INTRODUCING
WILDFIRE
BY JIM MOONEY AND ROBERT TURNER
FIFTEEN YEARS AGO..A RAGING FOREST FIRE SWEEPS THROUGH THE GREAT NORTHWEST..AMID THE DESTRUCTION, FRANK VANCE, A FOREST RANGER, SEARCHES FOR HIS SMALL DAUGHTER...
CAROL! OH CAROL!
U.S. MUNITIONS
VANCE, OVERCOME BY THE HOLOCAUST OF FLAME, FALLS UNCONSCIOUS!
THE LORD OF FIRE SWOOPS OVER A BURNING CABIN AS LITTLE CAROL VANCE TODDLES OUT AMID THE RAGING INFERNO...
WHAT?! A CHILD! UNHARMED BY MY POWER!
AND THE TOT IS NOT FRIGHTENED BY THE AWESOME FIGURE..
OH! YOU ARE MR. FIRE!
1

From Smash Comics #25 (1941) Art by Jim Mooney

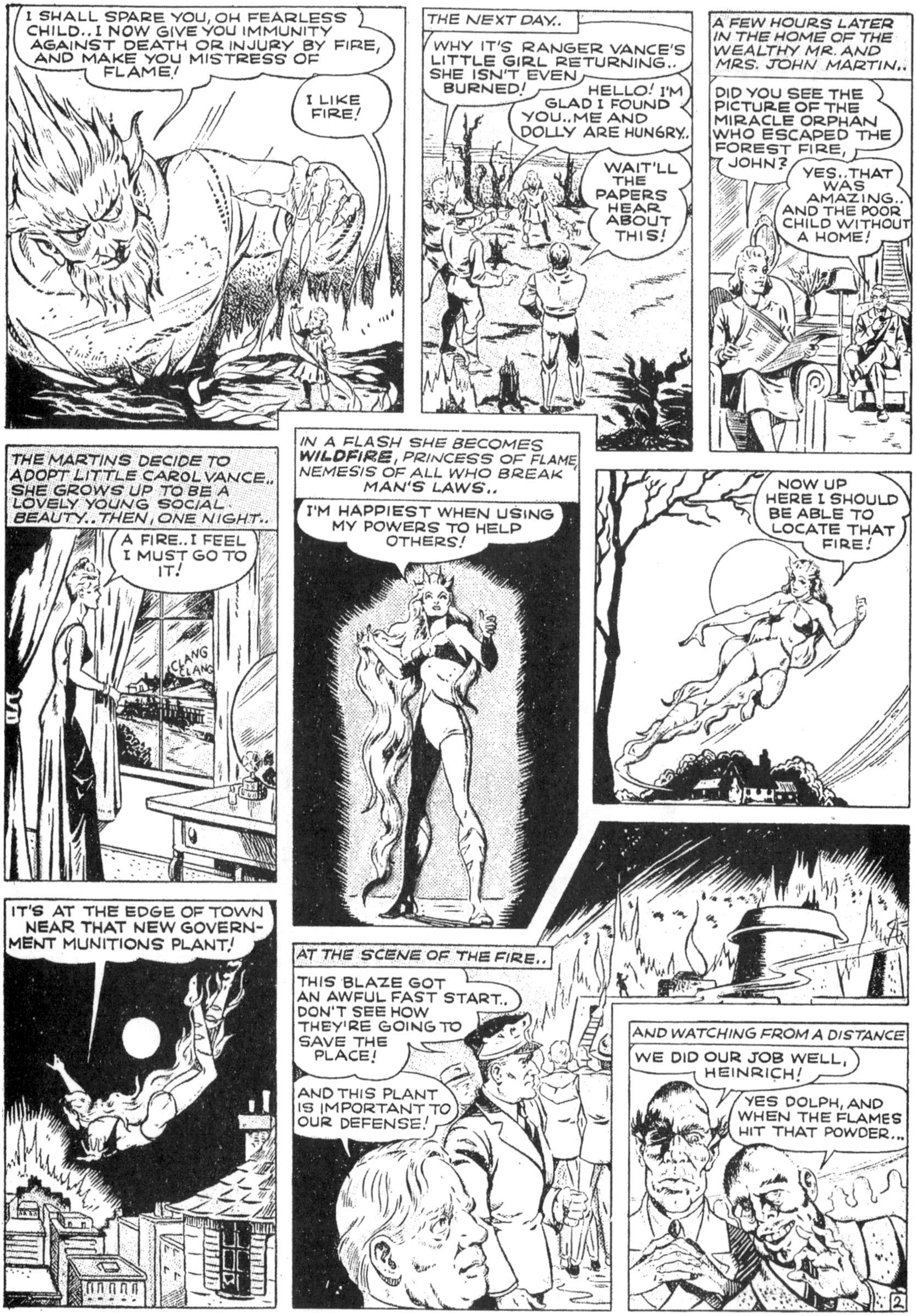
I SHALL SPARE YOU, OH FEARLESS CHILD.. I NOW GIVE YOU IMMUNITY AGAINST DEATH OR INJURY BY FIRE, AND MAKE YOU MISTRESS OF FLAME!
I LIKE FIRE!
THE NEXT DAY..
WHY IT'S RANGER VANCE'S LITTLE GIRL RETURNING.. SHE ISN'T EVEN BURNED!
HELLO! I'M GLAD I FOUND YOU..ME AND DOLLY ARE HUNGRY..
WAIT'LL THE PAPERS HEAR ABOUT THIS!
A FEW HOURS LATER IN THE HOME OF THE WEALTHY MR. AND MRS. JOHN MARTIN..
DID YOU SEE THE PICTURE OF THE MIRACLE ORPHAN WHO ESCAPED THE FOREST FIRE, JOHN?
YES.. THAT WAS AMAZING.. AND THE POOR CHILD WITHOUT A HOME!
THE MARTINS DECIDE TO ADOPT LITTLE CAROL VANCE.. SHE GROWS UP TO BE A LOVELY YOUNG SOCIAL BEAUTY.. THEN, ONE NIGHT..
A FIRE.. I FEEL I MUST GO TO IT!
CLANG CLANG
IN A FLASH SHE BECOMES WILDFIRE, PRINCESS OF FLAME, NEMESIS OF ALL WHO BREAK MAN'S LAWS..
I'M HAPPIEST WHEN USING MY POWERS TO HELP OTHERS!
NOW UP HERE I SHOULD BE ABLE TO LOCATE THAT FIRE!
IT'S AT THE EDGE OF TOWN NEAR THAT NEW GOVERNMENT MUNITIONS PLANT!
AT THE SCENE OF THE FIRE..
THIS BLAZE GOT AN AWFUL FAST START.. DON'T SEE HOW THEY'RE GOING TO SAVE THE PLACE!
AND THIS PLANT IS IMPORTANT TO OUR DEFENSE!
AND WATCHING FROM A DISTANCE
WE DID OUR JOB WELL, HEINRICH!
YES DOLPH, AND WHEN THE FLAMES HIT THAT POWDER...
2

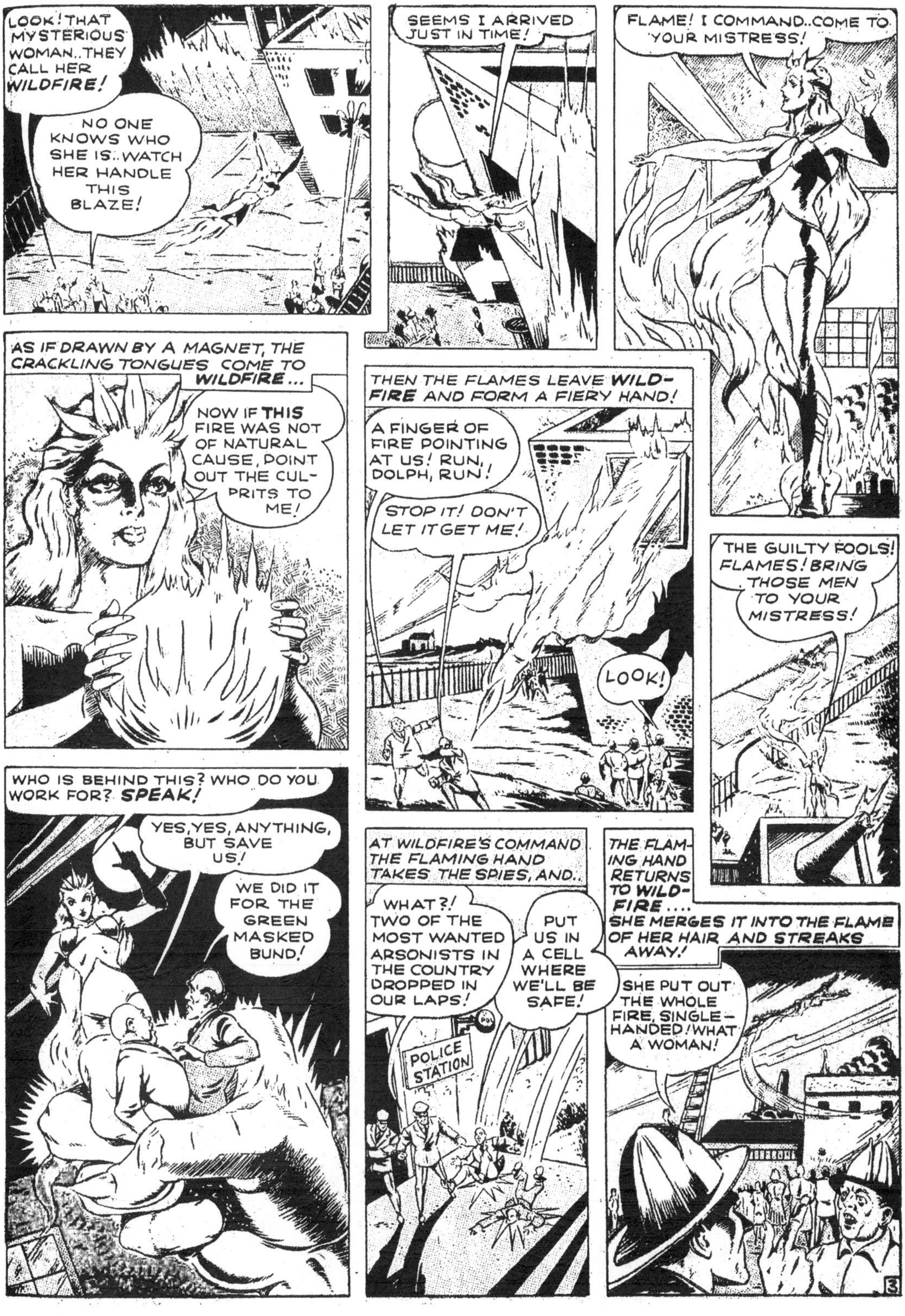
LOOK! THAT MYSTERIOUS WOMAN..THEY CALL HER WILDFIRE!
NO ONE KNOWS WHO SHE IS..WATCH HER HANDLE THIS BLAZE!
SEEMS I ARRIVED JUST IN TIME!
FLAME! I COMMAND..COME TO YOUR MISTRESS!
AS IF DRAWN BY A MAGNET, THE CRACKLING TONGUES COME TO WILDFIRE...
NOW IF THIS FIRE WAS NOT OF NATURAL CAUSE, POINT OUT THE CUL-PRITS TO ME!
THEN THE FLAMES LEAVE WILD-FIRE AND FORM A FIERY HAND!
A FINGER OF FIRE POINTING AT US! RUN, DOLPH, RUN!
STOP IT! DON'T LET IT GET ME!
LOOK!
THE GUILTY FOOLS! FLAMES! BRING THOSE MEN TO YOUR MISTRESS!
WHO IS BEHIND THIS? WHO DO YOU WORK FOR? SPEAK!
YES, YES, ANYTHING, BUT SAVE US!
WE DID IT FOR THE GREEN MASKED BUND!
AT WILDFIRE'S COMMAND THE FLAMING HAND TAKES THE SPIES, AND..
WHAT?! TWO OF THE MOST WANTED ARSONISTS IN THE COUNTRY DROPPED IN OUR LAPS!
PUT US IN A CELL WHERE WE'LL BE SAFE!
POLICE STATION
THE FLAM-ING HAND RETURNS TO WILD-FIRE.... SHE MERGES IT INTO THE FLAME OF HER HAIR AND STREAKS AWAY!
SHE PUT OUT THE WHOLE FIRE, SINGLE-HANDED! WHAT A WOMAN!
3

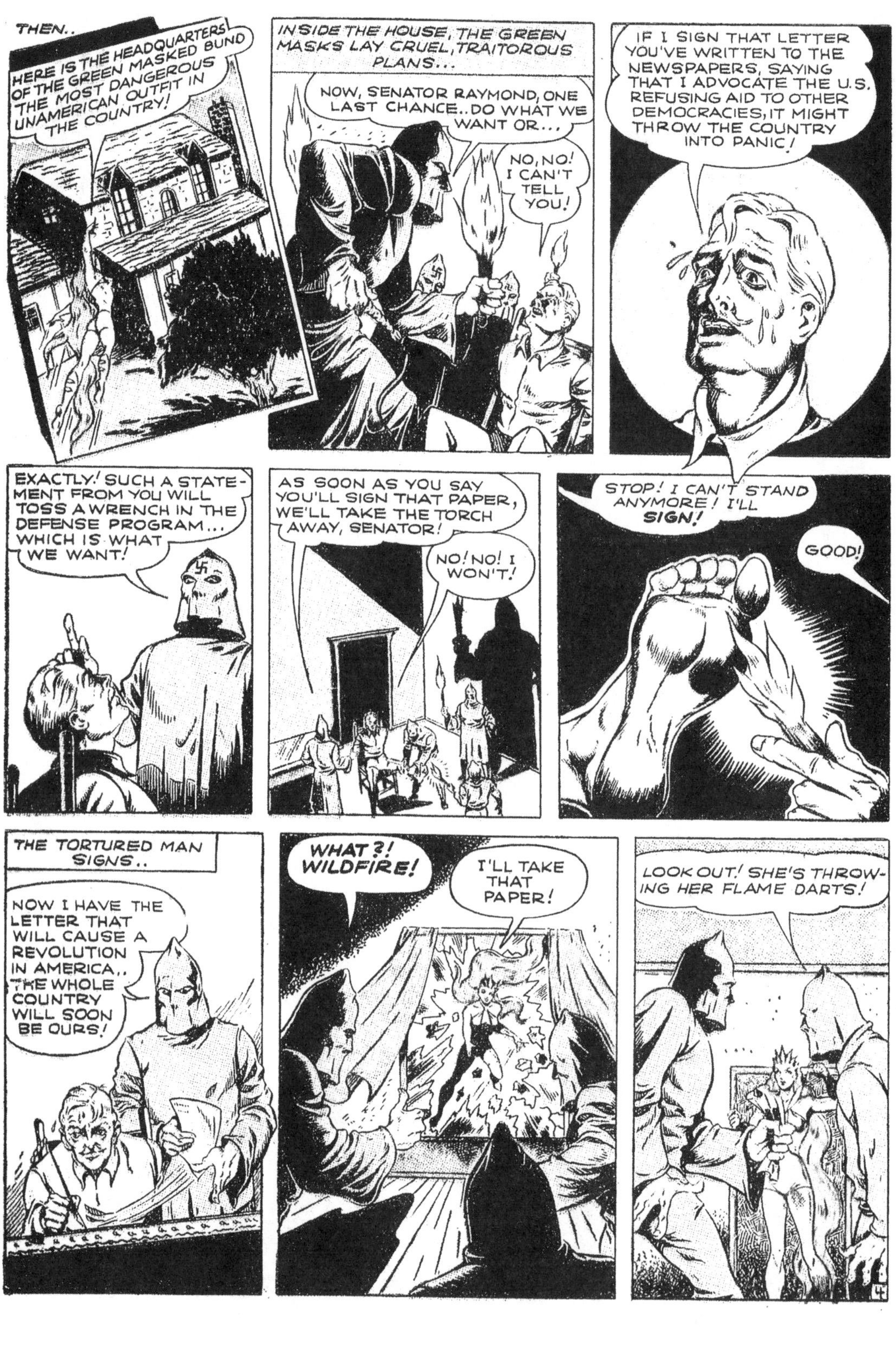
THEN..
HERE IS THE HEADQUARTERS OF THE GREEN MASKED BUND THE MOST DANGEROUS UNAMERICAN OUTFIT IN THE COUNTRY!
INSIDE THE HOUSE, THE GREEN MASKS LAY CRUEL, TRAITOROUS PLANS...
NOW, SENATOR RAYMOND, ONE LAST CHANCE..DO WHAT WE WANT OR...
NO, NO! I CAN'T TELL YOU!
IF I SIGN THAT LETTER YOU'VE WRITTEN TO THE NEWSPAPERS, SAYING THAT I ADVOCATE THE U.S. REFUSING AID TO OTHER DEMOCRACIES, IT MIGHT THROW THE COUNTRY INTO PANIC!
EXACTLY! SUCH A STATEMENT FROM YOU WILL TOSS A WRENCH IN THE DEFENSE PROGRAM... WHICH IS WHAT WE WANT!
AS SOON AS YOU SAY YOU'LL SIGN THAT PAPER, WE'LL TAKE THE TORCH AWAY, SENATOR!
NO! NO! I WON'T!
STOP! I CAN'T STAND ANYMORE! I'LL SIGN!
GOOD!
THE TORTURED MAN SIGNS..
NOW I HAVE THE LETTER THAT WILL CAUSE A REVOLUTION IN AMERICA.. THE WHOLE COUNTRY WILL SOON BE OURS!
WHAT?! WILDFIRE!
I'LL TAKE THAT PAPER!
LOOK OUT! SHE'S THROWING HER FLAME DARTS!
4

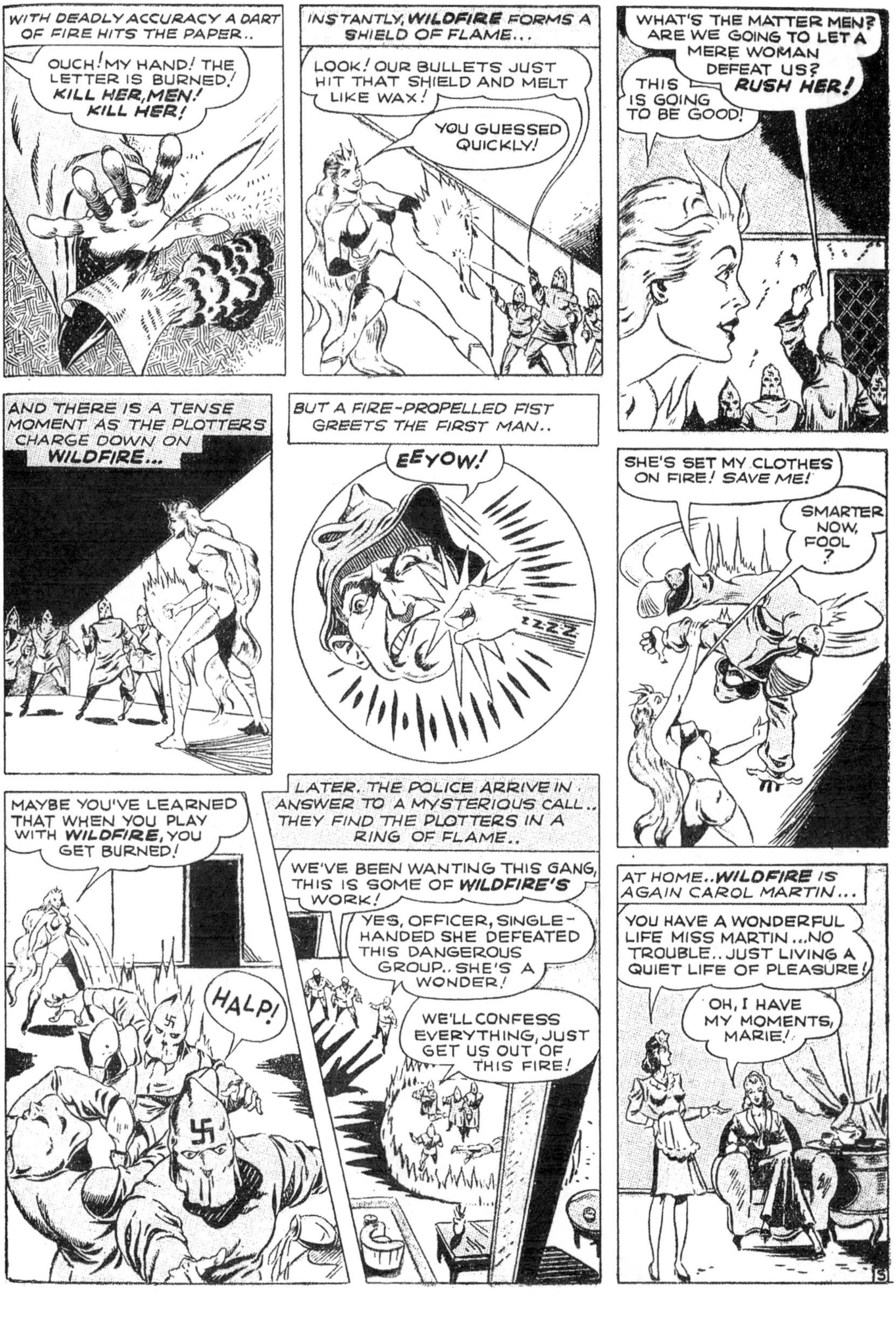
WITH DEADLY ACCURACY A DART OF FIRE HITS THE PAPER..
OUCH! MY HAND! THE LETTER IS BURNED! KILL HER, MEN! KILL HER!
INSTANTLY, WILDFIRE FORMS A SHIELD OF FLAME...
LOOK! OUR BULLETS JUST HIT THAT SHIELD AND MELT LIKE WAX!
YOU GUESSED QUICKLY!
WHAT'S THE MATTER MEN? ARE WE GOING TO LET A MERE WOMAN DEFEAT US? RUSH HER!
THIS IS GOING TO BE GOOD!
AND THERE IS A TENSE MOMENT AS THE PLOTTERS CHARGE DOWN ON WILDFIRE...
BUT A FIRE-PROPELLED FIST GREETS THE FIRST MAN..
EEYOW!
Z-Z-Z-Z
SHE'S SET MY CLOTHES ON FIRE! SAVE ME!
SMARTER NOW, FOOL?
MAYBE YOU'VE LEARNED THAT WHEN YOU PLAY WITH WILDFIRE, YOU GET BURNED!
HALP!
LATER, THE POLICE ARRIVE IN ANSWER TO A MYSTERIOUS CALL.. THEY FIND THE PLOTTERS IN A RING OF FLAME..
WE'VE BEEN WANTING THIS GANG, THIS IS SOME OF WILDFIRE'S WORK!
YES, OFFICER, SINGLE-HANDED SHE DEFEATED THIS DANGEROUS GROUP.. SHE'S A WONDER!
WE'LL CONFESS EVERYTHING, JUST GET US OUT OF THIS FIRE!
AT HOME.. WILDFIRE IS AGAIN CAROL MARTIN...
YOU HAVE A WONDERFUL LIFE MISS MARTIN...NO TROUBLE.. JUST LIVING A QUIET LIFE OF PLEASURE!
OH, I HAVE MY MOMENTS, MARIE!
5

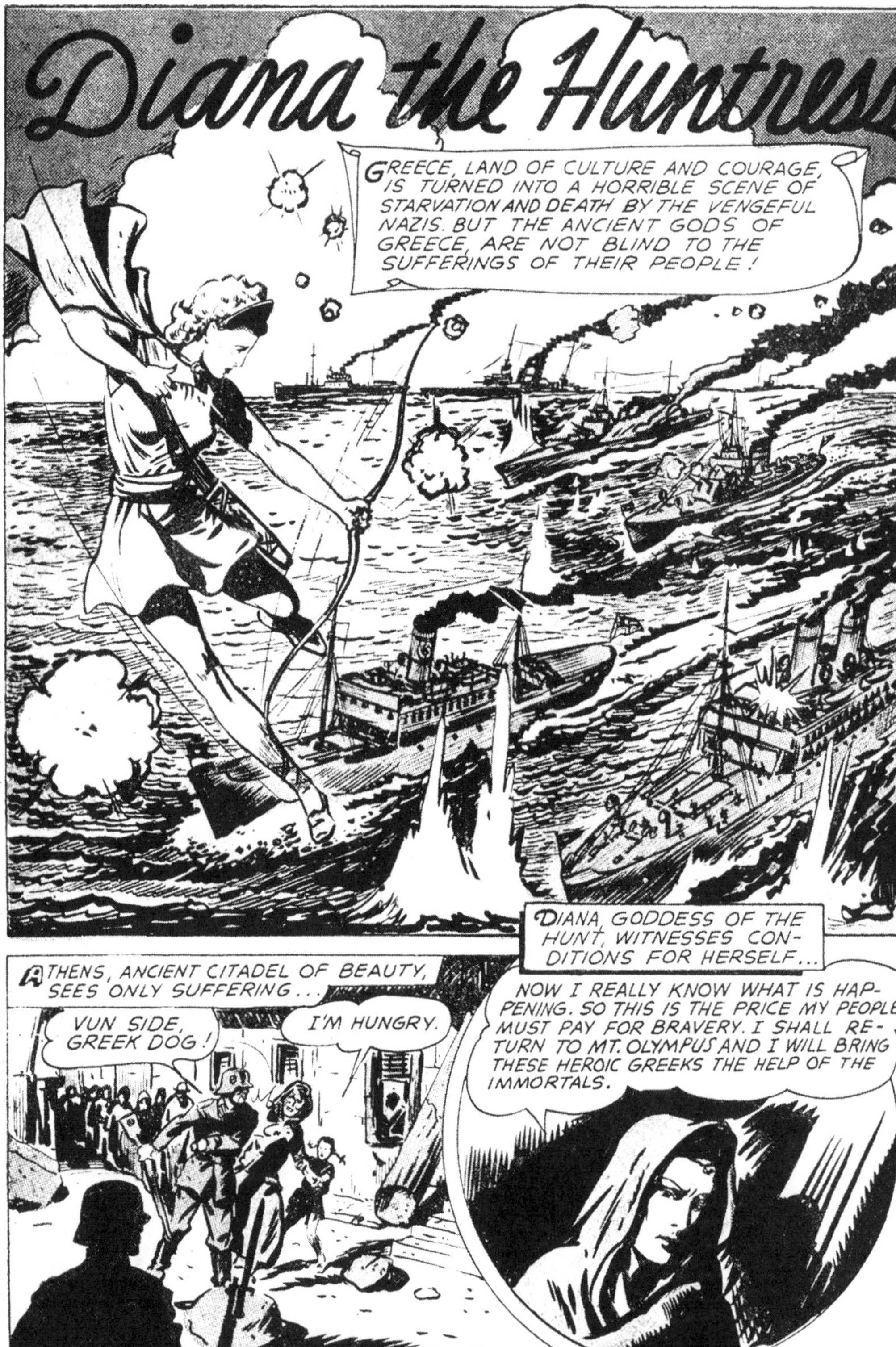
Diana the Huntress
GREECE, LAND OF CULTURE AND COURAGE, IS TURNED INTO A HORRIBLE SCENE OF STARVATION AND DEATH BY THE VENGEFUL NAZIS. BUT THE ANCIENT GODS OF GREECE, ARE NOT BLIND TO THE SUFFERINGS OF THEIR PEOPLE!
ATHENS, ANCIENT CITADEL OF BEAUTY, SEES ONLY SUFFERING...
VUN SIDE, GREEK DOG!
I'M HUNGRY.
DIANA, GODDESS OF THE HUNT, WITNESSES CONDITIONS FOR HERSELF...
NOW I REALLY KNOW WHAT IS HAPPENING. SO THIS IS THE PRICE MY PEOPLE MUST PAY FOR BRAVERY. I SHALL RETURN TO MT. OLYMPUS AND I WILL BRING THESE HEROIC GREEKS THE HELP OF THE IMMORTALS.

From Yellowjacket Comics #3 (1944) Art by Leo Morey

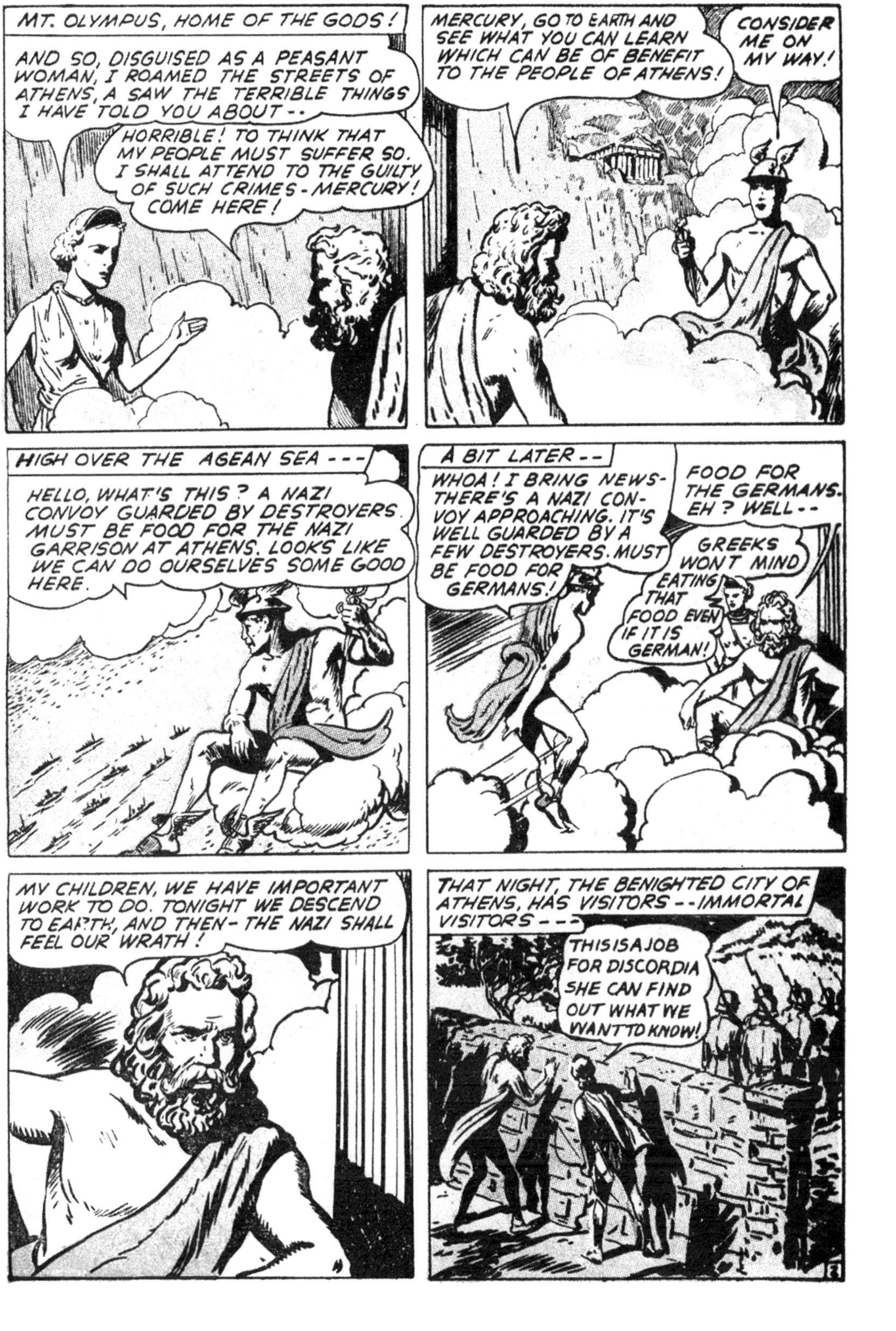
MT. OLYMPUS, HOME OF THE GODS!
AND SO, DISGUISED AS A PEASANT WOMAN, I ROAMED THE STREETS OF ATHENS, A SAW THE TERRIBLE THINGS I HAVE TOLD YOU ABOUT --
HORRIBLE! TO THINK THAT MY PEOPLE MUST SUFFER SO. I SHALL ATTEND TO THE GUILTY OF SUCH CRIMES - MERCURY! COME HERE!
MERCURY, GO TO EARTH AND SEE WHAT YOU CAN LEARN WHICH CAN BE OF BENEFIT TO THE PEOPLE OF ATHENS!
CONSIDER ME ON MY WAY!
HIGH OVER THE AGEAN SEA ---
HELLO, WHAT'S THIS? A NAZI CONVOY GUARDED BY DESTROYERS. MUST BE FOOD FOR THE NAZI GARRISON AT ATHENS. LOOKS LIKE WE CAN DO OURSELVES SOME GOOD HERE.
A BIT LATER --
WHOA! I BRING NEWS- THERE'S A NAZI CONVOY APPROACHING. IT'S WELL GUARDED BY A FEW DESTROYERS. MUST BE FOOD FOR GERMANS!
FOOD FOR THE GERMANS. EH? WELL --
GREEKS WON'T MIND EATING THAT FOOD EVEN IF IT IS GERMAN!
MY CHILDREN, WE HAVE IMPORTANT WORK TO DO. TONIGHT WE DESCEND TO EARTH, AND THEN - THE NAZI SHALL FEEL OUR WRATH!
THAT NIGHT, THE BENIGHTED CITY OF ATHENS, HAS VISITORS -- IMMORTAL VISITORS ---
THIS IS A JOB FOR DISCORDIA SHE CAN FIND OUT WHAT WE WANT TO KNOW!

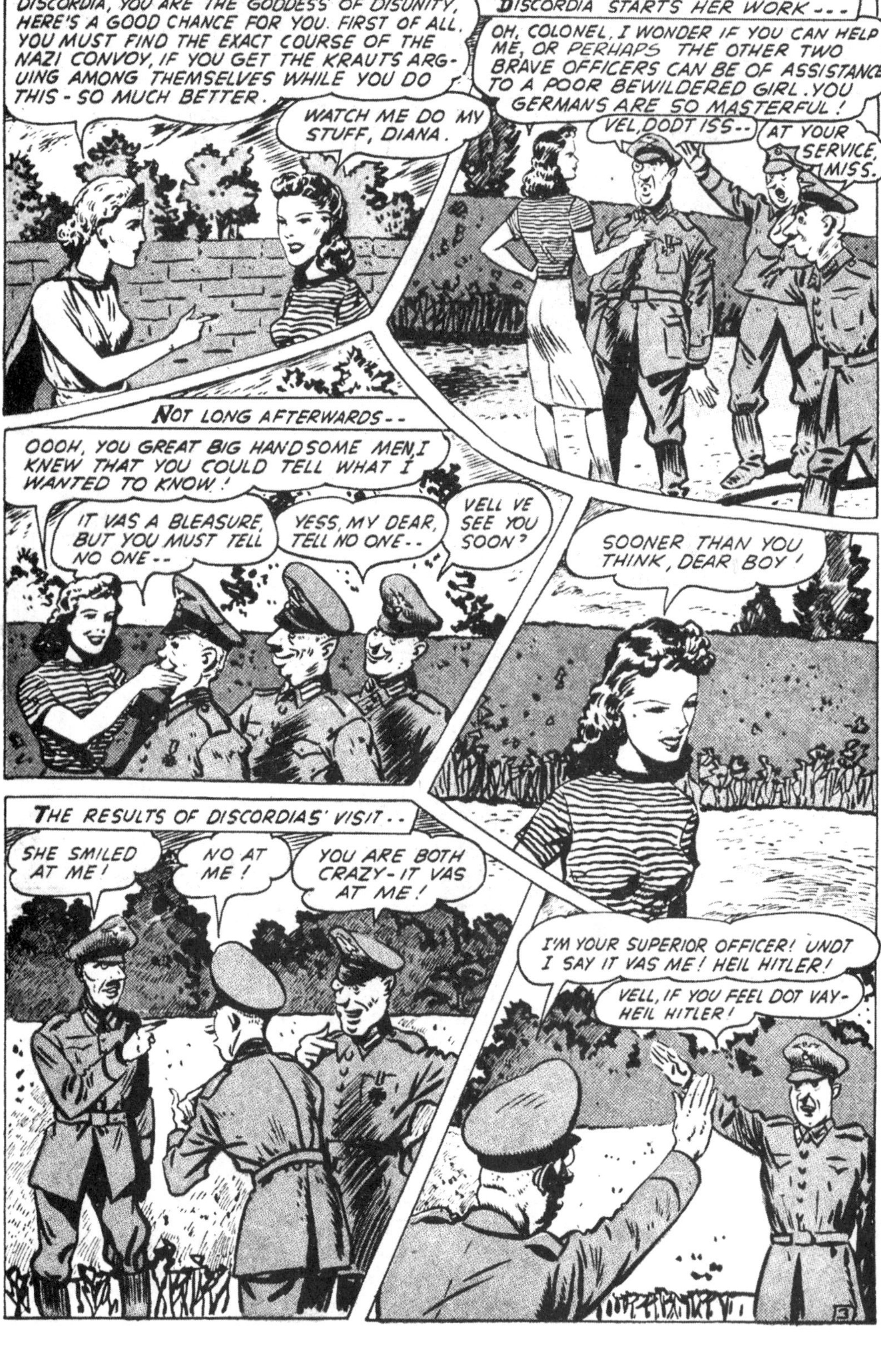
DISCORDIA, YOU ARE THE GODDESS OF DISUNITY, HERE'S A GOOD CHANCE FOR YOU. FIRST OF ALL, YOU MUST FIND THE EXACT COURSE OF THE NAZI CONVOY, IF YOU GET THE KRAUTS ARGUING AMONG THEMSELVES WHILE YOU DO THIS - SO MUCH BETTER.
WATCH ME DO MY STUFF, DIANA.
DISCORDIA STARTS HER WORK - - -
OH, COLONEL, I WONDER IF YOU CAN HELP ME, OR PERHAPS THE OTHER TWO BRAVE OFFICERS CAN BE OF ASSISTANCE TO A POOR BEWILDERED GIRL. YOU GERMANS ARE SO MASTERFUL!
VEL, DODT ISS--
AT YOUR SERVICE, MISS.
NOT LONG AFTERWARDS--
OOOH, YOU GREAT BIG HANDSOME MEN, I KNEW THAT YOU COULD TELL WHAT I WANTED TO KNOW!
IT VAS A BLEASURE, BUT YOU MUST TELL NO ONE--
YESS, MY DEAR, TELL NO ONE--
VELL VE SEE YOU SOON?
SOONER THAN YOU THINK, DEAR BOY!
THE RESULTS OF DISCORDIAS' VISIT--
SHE SMILED AT ME!
NO AT ME!
YOU ARE BOTH CRAZY- IT VAS AT ME!
I'M YOUR SUPERIOR OFFICER! UNDT I SAY IT VAS ME! HEIL HITLER!
VELL, IF YOU FEEL DOT VAY- HEIL HITLER!
3

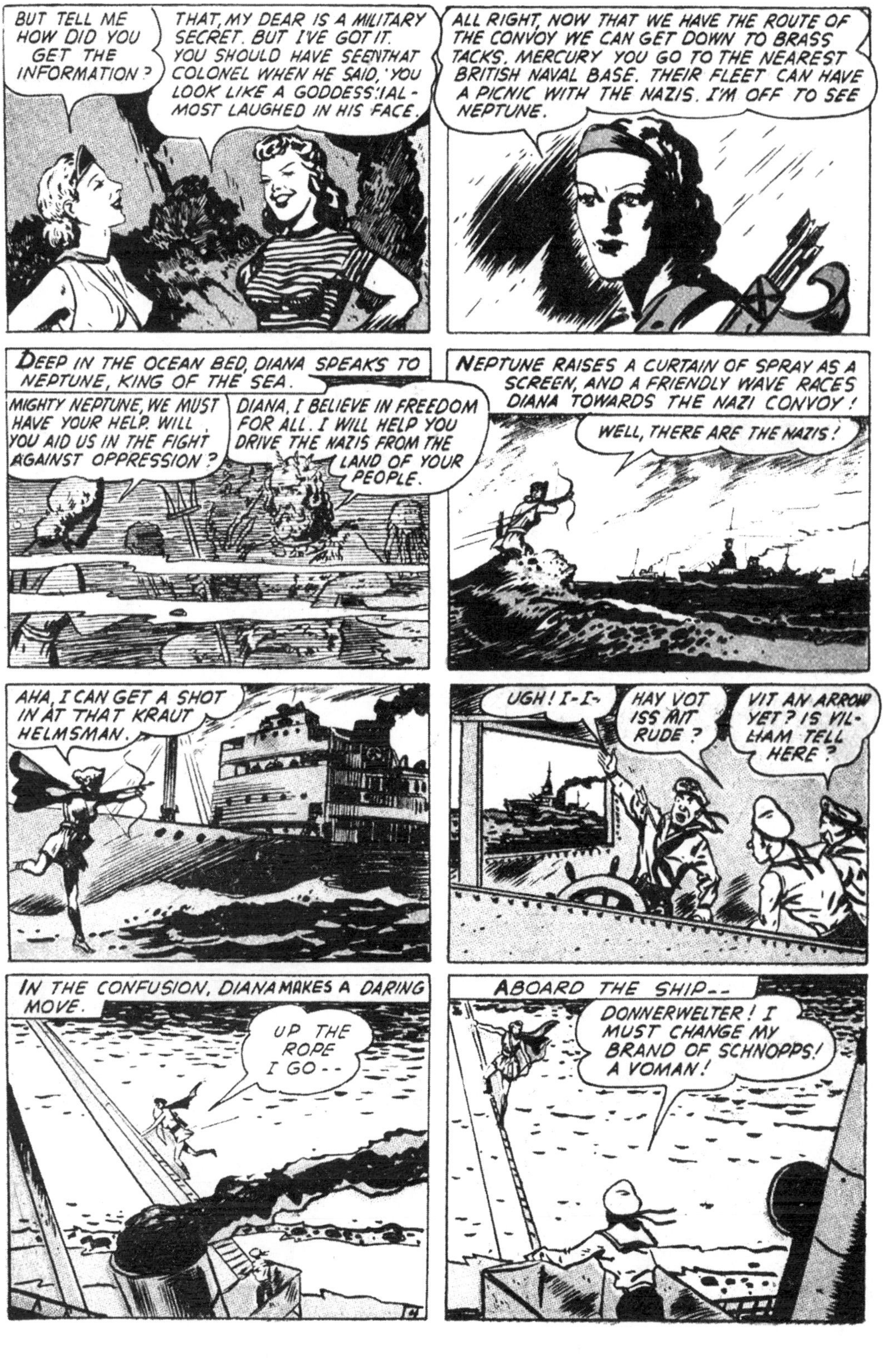
BUT TELL ME HOW DID YOU GET THE INFORMATION?
THAT, MY DEAR IS A MILITARY SECRET. BUT I'VE GOT IT. YOU SHOULD HAVE SEENTHAT COLONEL WHEN HE SAID, 'YOU LOOK LIKE A GODDESS:'IAL-MOST LAUGHED IN HIS FACE.
ALL RIGHT, NOW THAT WE HAVE THE ROUTE OF THE CONVOY WE CAN GET DOWN TO BRASS TACKS. MERCURY YOU GO TO THE NEAREST BRITISH NAVAL BASE. THEIR FLEET CAN HAVE A PICNIC WITH THE NAZIS. I'M OFF TO SEE NEPTUNE.
DEEP IN THE OCEAN BED, DIANA SPEAKS TO NEPTUNE, KING OF THE SEA.
MIGHTY NEPTUNE, WE MUST HAVE YOUR HELP. WILL YOU AID US IN THE FIGHT AGAINST OPPRESSION?
DIANA, I BELIEVE IN FREEDOM FOR ALL. I WILL HELP YOU DRIVE THE NAZIS FROM THE LAND OF YOUR PEOPLE.
NEPTUNE RAISES A CURTAIN OF SPRAY AS A SCREEN, AND A FRIENDLY WAVE RACES DIANA TOWARDS THE NAZI CONVOY!
WELL, THERE ARE THE NAZIS!
AHA, I CAN GET A SHOT IN AT THAT KRAUT HELMSMAN.
UGH! I-I-
HAY VOT ISS MIT RUDE?
VIT AN ARROW YET? IS VIL-LIAM TELL HERE?
IN THE CONFUSION, DIANA MAKES A DARING MOVE.
UP THE ROPE I GO--
ABOARD THE SHIP--
DONNERWELTER! I MUST CHANGE MY BRAND OF SCHNOPPS! A VOMAN!

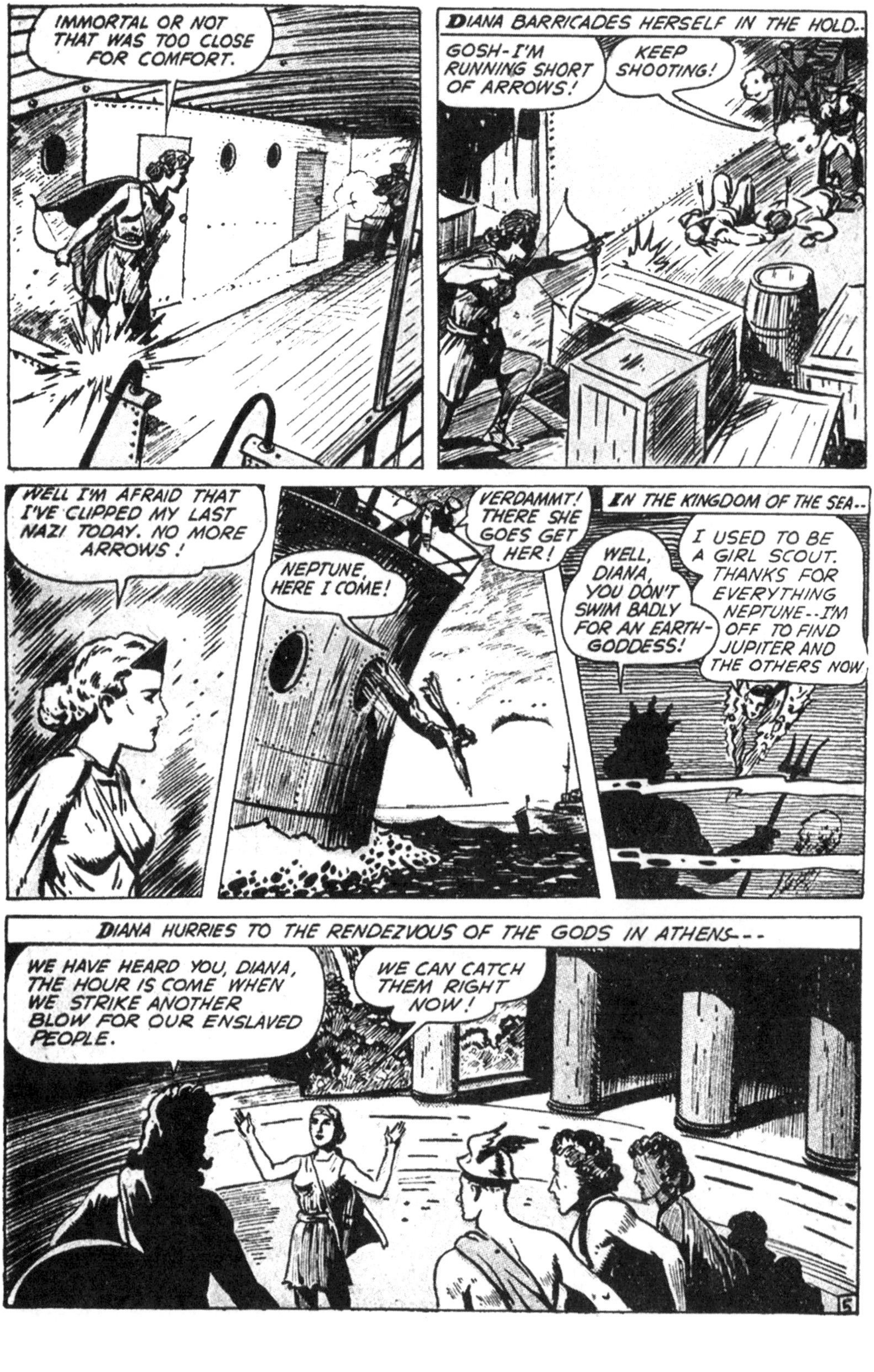
IMMORTAL OR NOT THAT WAS TOO CLOSE FOR COMFORT.
DIANA BARRICADES HERSELF IN THE HOLD..
GOSH-I'M RUNNING SHORT OF ARROWS!
KEEP SHOOTING!
WELL I'M AFRAID THAT I'VE CLIPPED MY LAST NAZI TODAY. NO MORE ARROWS!
VERDAMMT! THERE SHE GOES GET HER!
NEPTUNE, HERE I COME!
IN THE KINGDOM OF THE SEA..
WELL, DIANA, YOU DON'T SWIM BADLY FOR AN EARTH-GODDESS!
I USED TO BE A GIRL SCOUT. THANKS FOR EVERYTHING NEPTUNE--I'M OFF TO FIND JUPITER AND THE OTHERS NOW
DIANA HURRIES TO THE RENDEZVOUS OF THE GODS IN ATHENS---
WE HAVE HEARD YOU, DIANA, THE HOUR IS COME WHEN WE STRIKE ANOTHER BLOW FOR OUR ENSLAVED PEOPLE.
WE CAN CATCH THEM RIGHT NOW!
5

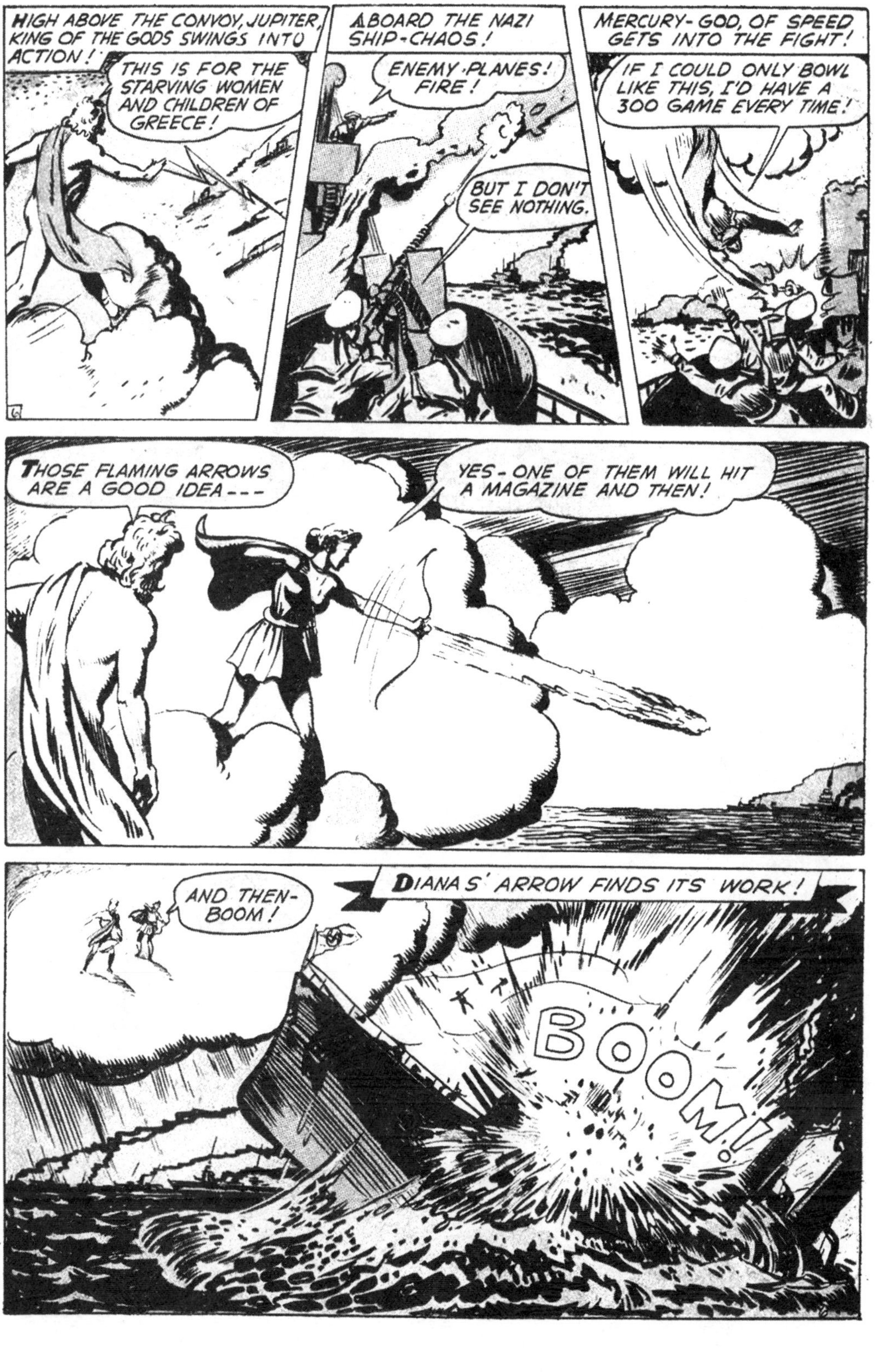
HIGH ABOVE THE CONVOY, JUPITER, KING OF THE GODS SWINGS INTO ACTION!
THIS IS FOR THE STARVING WOMEN AND CHILDREN OF GREECE!
ABOARD THE NAZI SHIP-CHAOS!
ENEMY PLANES! FIRE!
BUT I DON'T SEE NOTHING.
MERCURY-GOD OF SPEED GETS INTO THE FIGHT!
IF I COULD ONLY BOWL LIKE THIS, I'D HAVE A 300 GAME EVERY TIME!
THOSE FLAMING ARROWS ARE A GOOD IDEA---
YES-ONE OF THEM WILL HIT A MAGAZINE AND THEN!
DIANAS' ARROW FINDS ITS WORK!
AND THEN-BOOM!
BOOM!

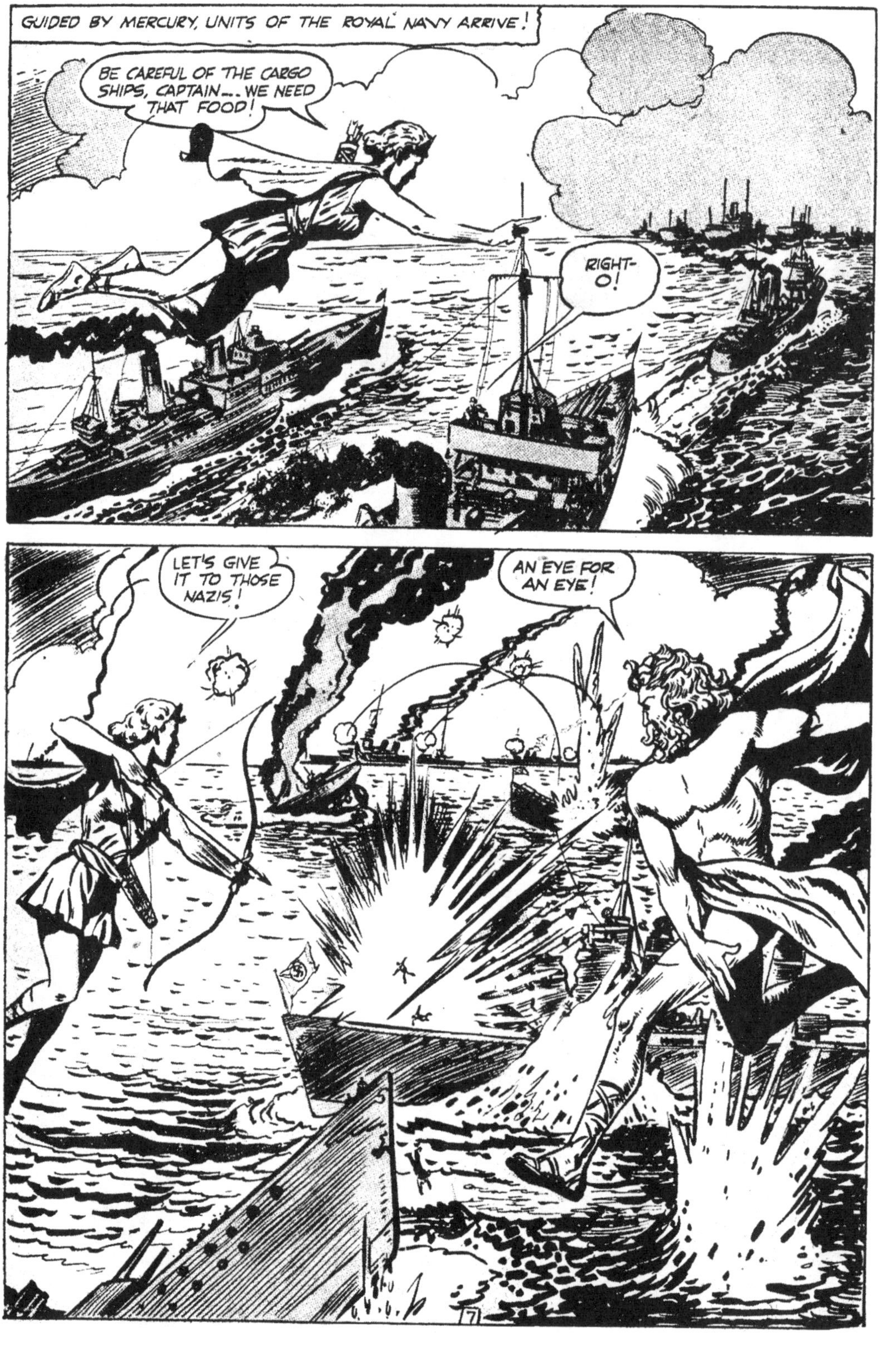
GUIDED BY MERCURY, UNITS OF THE ROYAL NAVY ARRIVE!
BE CAREFUL OF THE CARGO SHIPS, CAPTAIN... WE NEED THAT FOOD!
RIGHT-O!
LET'S GIVE IT TO THOSE NAZIS!
AN EYE FOR AN EYE!
7

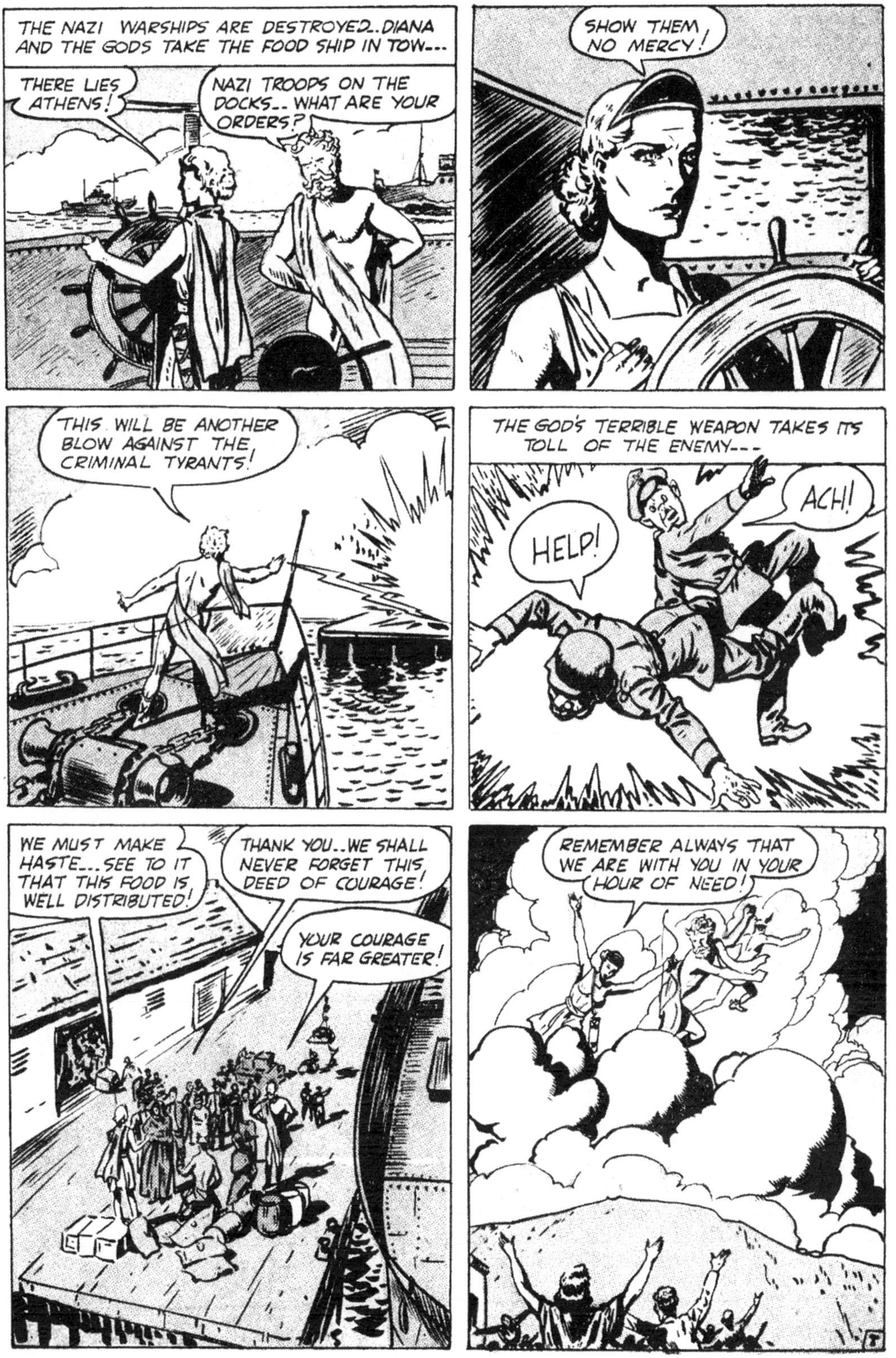
THE NAZI WARSHIPS ARE DESTROYED..DIANA AND THE GODS TAKE THE FOOD SHIP IN TOW---
THERE LIES ATHENS!
NAZI TROOPS ON THE DOCKS.. WHAT ARE YOUR ORDERS?
SHOW THEM NO MERCY!
THIS WILL BE ANOTHER BLOW AGAINST THE CRIMINAL TYRANTS!
THE GOD'S TERRIBLE WEAPON TAKES ITS TOLL OF THE ENEMY---
HELP!
ACH!
WE MUST MAKE HASTE...SEE TO IT THAT THIS FOOD IS WELL DISTRIBUTED!
THANK YOU..WE SHALL NEVER FORGET THIS DEED OF COURAGE!
YOUR COURAGE IS FAR GREATER!
REMEMBER ALWAYS THAT WE ARE WITH YOU IN YOUR HOUR OF NEED!

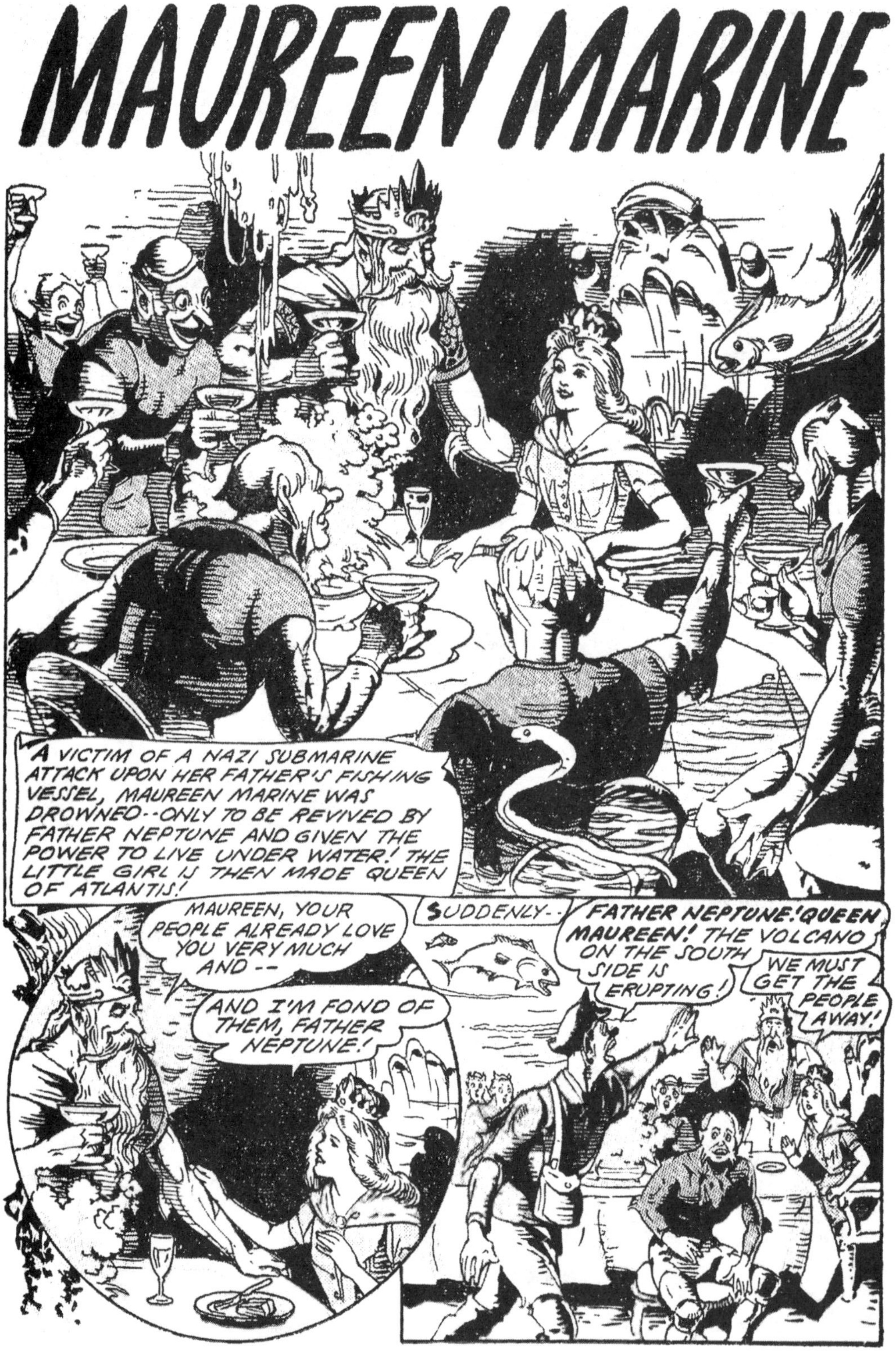
MAUREEN MARINE
A VICTIM OF A NAZI SUBMARINE ATTACK UPON HER FATHER'S FISHING VESSEL, MAUREEN MARINE WAS DROWNED--ONLY TO BE REVIVED BY FATHER NEPTUNE AND GIVEN THE POWER TO LIVE UNDER WATER! THE LITTLE GIRL IS THEN MADE QUEEN OF ATLANTIS!
MAUREEN, YOUR PEOPLE ALREADY LOVE YOU VERY MUCH AND --
AND I'M FOND OF THEM, FATHER NEPTUNE!
SUDDENLY--
FATHER NEPTUNE! QUEEN MAUREEN! THE VOLCANO ON THE SOUTH SIDE IS ERUPTING!
WE MUST GET THE PEOPLE AWAY!

From Blue Circle Comics #2 (1944) Art by Harold DeLay

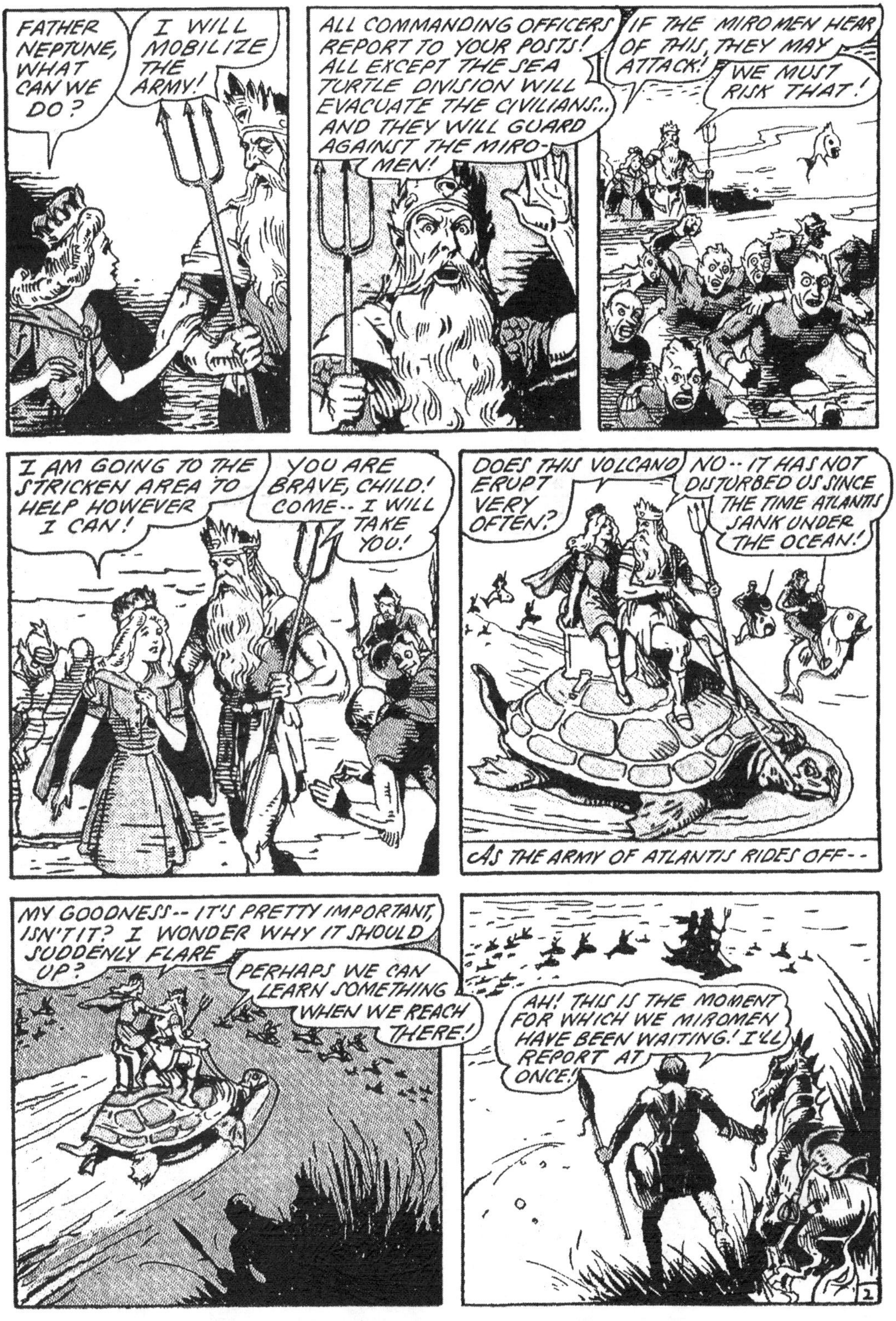
FATHER NEPTUNE, WHAT CAN WE DO?
I WILL MOBILIZE THE ARMY!
ALL COMMANDING OFFICERS REPORT TO YOUR POSTS! ALL EXCEPT THE SEA TURTLE DIVISION WILL EVACUATE THE CIVILIANS... AND THEY WILL GUARD AGAINST THE MIRO-MEN!
IF THE MIROMEN HEAR OF THIS, THEY MAY ATTACK!
WE MUST RISK THAT!
I AM GOING TO THE STRICKEN AREA TO HELP HOWEVER I CAN!
YOU ARE BRAVE, CHILD! COME-- I WILL TAKE YOU!
DOES THIS VOLCANO ERUPT VERY OFTEN?
NO-- IT HAS NOT DISTURBED US SINCE THE TIME ATLANTIS SANK UNDER THE OCEAN!
AS THE ARMY OF ATLANTIS RIDES OFF--
MY GOODNESS-- IT'S PRETTY IMPORTANT, ISN'T IT? I WONDER WHY IT SHOULD SUDDENLY FLARE UP?
PERHAPS WE CAN LEARN SOMETHING WHEN WE REACH THERE!
AH! THIS IS THE MOMENT FOR WHICH WE MIROMEN HAVE BEEN WAITING! I'LL REPORT AT ONCE!
2

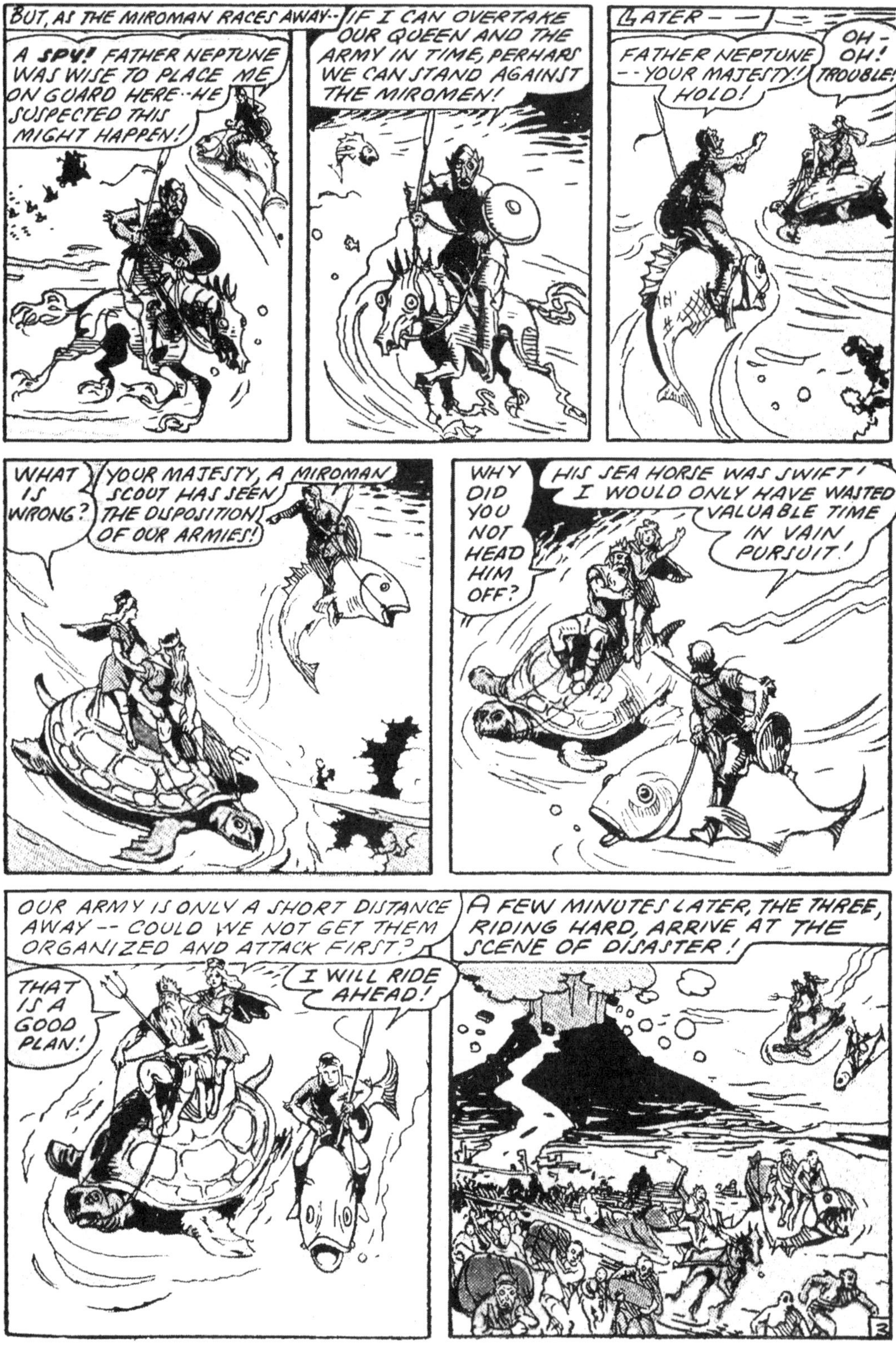

BUT, AS THE MIROMAN RACES AWAY--
A SPY! FATHER NEPTUNE WAS WISE TO PLACE ME ON GUARD HERE--HE SUSPECTED THIS MIGHT HAPPEN!
IF I CAN OVERTAKE OUR QUEEN AND THE ARMY IN TIME, PERHAPS WE CAN STAND AGAINST THE MIROMEN!
LATER---
FATHER NEPTUNE --YOUR MAJESTY! HOLD!
OH-OH! TROUBLE!
WHAT IS WRONG?
YOUR MAJESTY, A MIROMAN SCOUT HAS SEEN THE DISPOSITION OF OUR ARMIES!
WHY DID YOU NOT HEAD HIM OFF?
HIS SEA HORSE WAS SWIFT! I WOULD ONLY HAVE WASTED VALUABLE TIME IN VAIN PURSUIT!
OUR ARMY IS ONLY A SHORT DISTANCE AWAY -- COULD WE NOT GET THEM ORGANIZED AND ATTACK FIRST?
THAT IS A GOOD PLAN!
I WILL RIDE AHEAD!
A FEW MINUTES LATER, THE THREE, RIDING HARD, ARRIVE AT THE SCENE OF DISASTER!
3

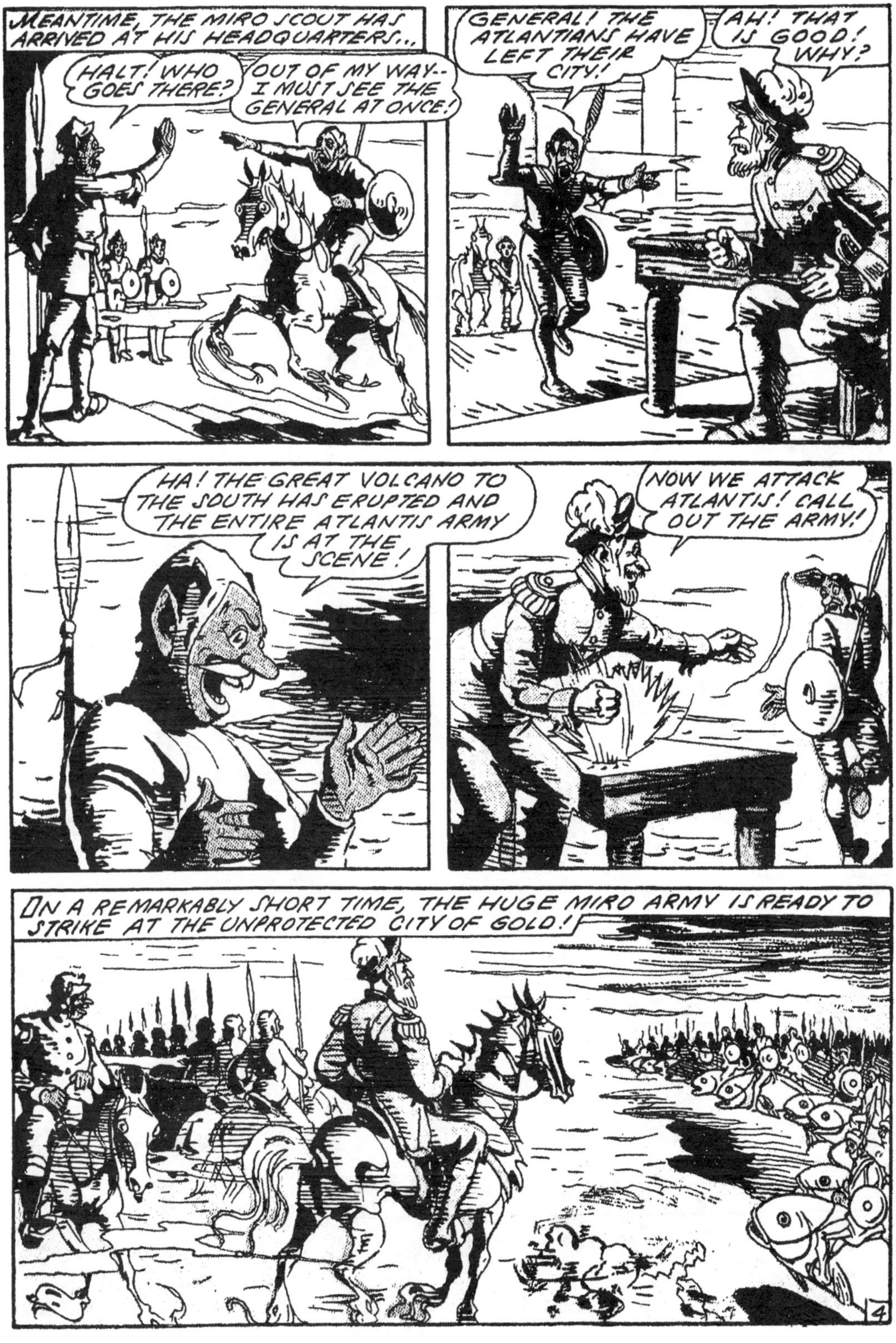
MEANTIME, THE MIRO SCOUT HAS ARRIVED AT HIS HEADQUARTERS...
HALT! WHO GOES THERE?
OUT OF MY WAY-- I MUST SEE THE GENERAL AT ONCE!
GENERAL! THE ATLANTIANS HAVE LEFT THEIR CITY!
AH! THAT IS GOOD! WHY?
HA! THE GREAT VOLCANO TO THE SOUTH HAS ERUPTED AND THE ENTIRE ATLANTIS ARMY IS AT THE SCENE!
NOW WE ATTACK ATLANTIS! CALL OUT THE ARMY!
IN A REMARKABLY SHORT TIME, THE HUGE MIRO ARMY IS READY TO STRIKE AT THE UNPROTECTED CITY OF GOLD!
4

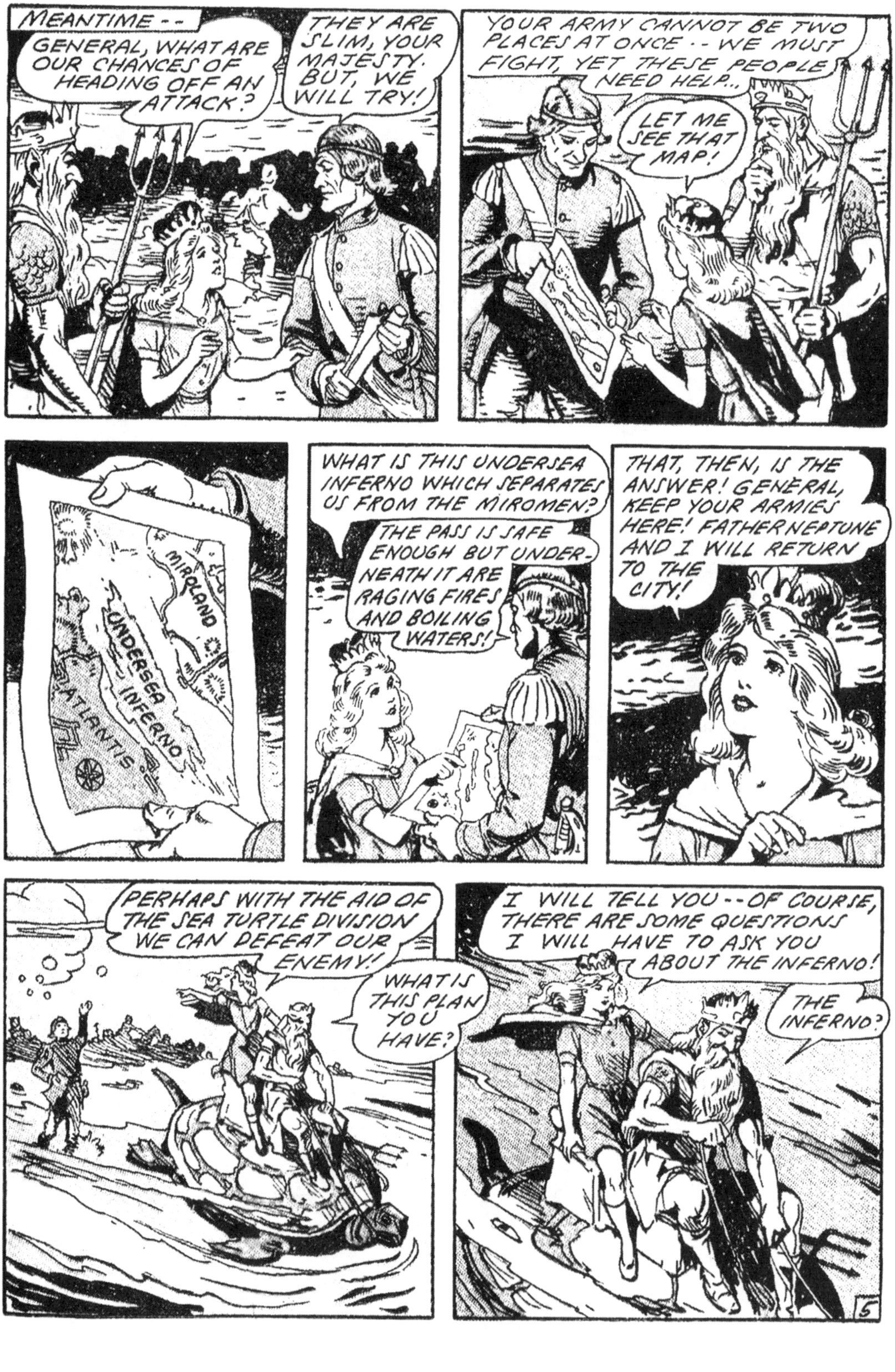
MEANTIME --
GENERAL, WHAT ARE OUR CHANCES OF HEADING OFF AN ATTACK?
THEY ARE SLIM, YOUR MAJESTY. BUT, WE WILL TRY!
YOUR ARMY CANNOT BE TWO PLACES AT ONCE -- WE MUST FIGHT, YET THESE PEOPLE NEED HELP..
LET ME SEE THAT MAP!
MIROLAND
UNDERSEA INFERNO
ATLANTIS
WHAT IS THIS UNDERSEA INFERNO WHICH SEPARATES US FROM THE MIROMEN?
THE PASS IS SAFE ENOUGH BUT UNDERNEATH IT ARE RAGING FIRES AND BOILING WATERS!
THAT, THEN, IS THE ANSWER! GENERAL, KEEP YOUR ARMIES HERE! FATHER NEPTUNE AND I WILL RETURN TO THE CITY!
PERHAPS WITH THE AID OF THE SEA TURTLE DIVISION WE CAN DEFEAT OUR ENEMY!
WHAT IS THIS PLAN YOU HAVE?
I WILL TELL YOU -- OF COURSE, THERE ARE SOME QUESTIONS I WILL HAVE TO ASK YOU ABOUT THE INFERNO!
THE INFERNO?
5

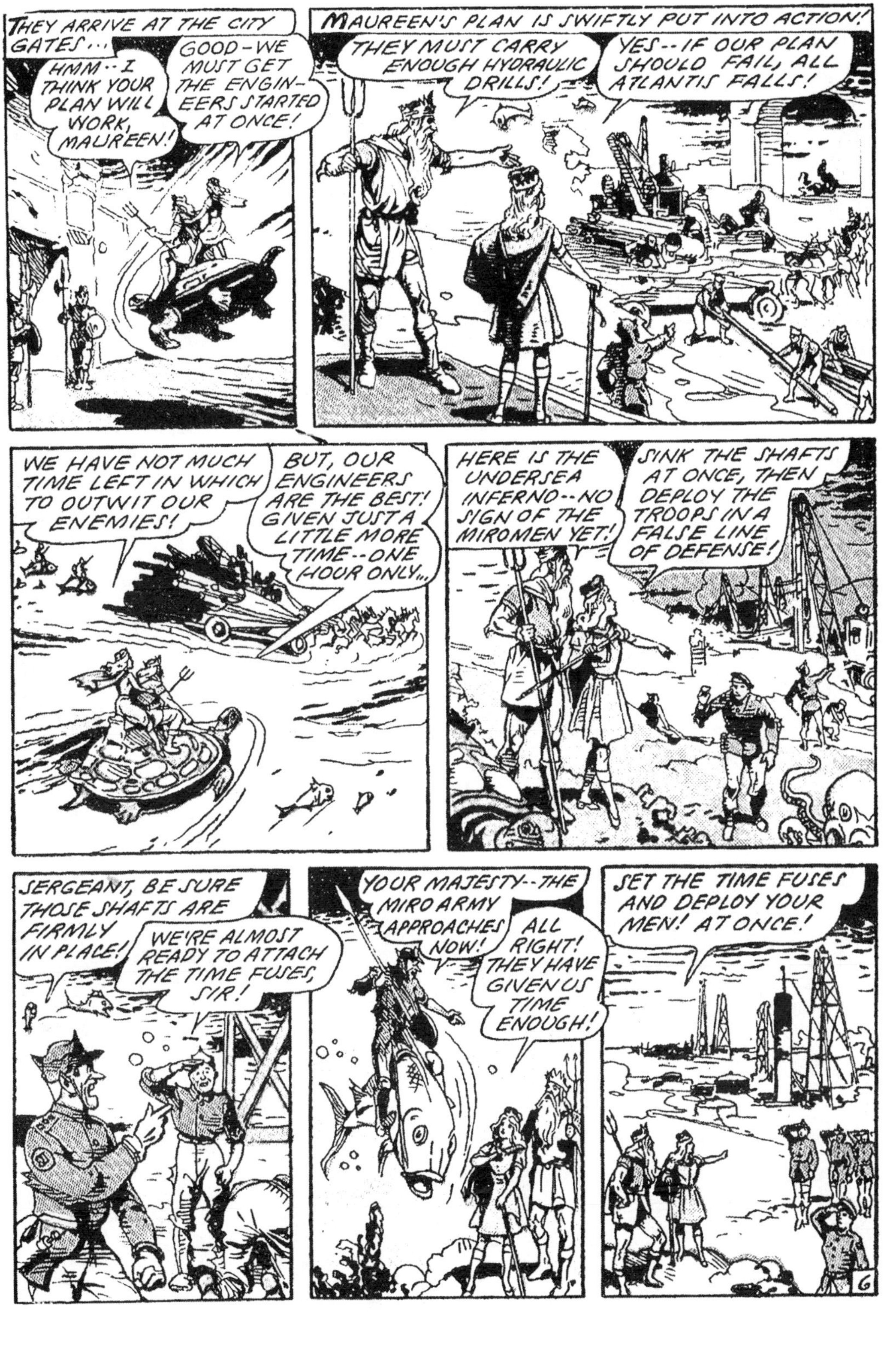
THEY ARRIVE AT THE CITY GATES...
HMM--I THINK YOUR PLAN WILL WORK, MAUREEN!
GOOD-WE MUST GET THE ENGINEERS STARTED AT ONCE!
MAUREEN'S PLAN IS SWIFTLY PUT INTO ACTION!
THEY MUST CARRY ENOUGH HYDRAULIC DRILLS!
YES--IF OUR PLAN SHOULD FAIL, ALL ATLANTIS FALLS!
WE HAVE NOT MUCH TIME LEFT IN WHICH TO OUTWIT OUR ENEMIES!
BUT, OUR ENGINEERS ARE THE BEST! GIVEN JUST A LITTLE MORE TIME--ONE HOUR ONLY...
HERE IS THE UNDERSEA INFERNO--NO SIGN OF THE MIROMEN YET!
SINK THE SHAFTS AT ONCE, THEN DEPLOY THE TROOPS IN A FALSE LINE OF DEFENSE!
SERGEANT, BE SURE THOSE SHAFTS ARE FIRMLY IN PLACE!
WE'RE ALMOST READY TO ATTACH THE TIME FUSES, SIR!
YOUR MAJESTY--THE MIRO ARMY APPROACHES NOW!
ALL RIGHT! THEY HAVE GIVEN US TIME ENOUGH!
SET THE TIME FUSES AND DEPLOY YOUR MEN! AT ONCE!
6

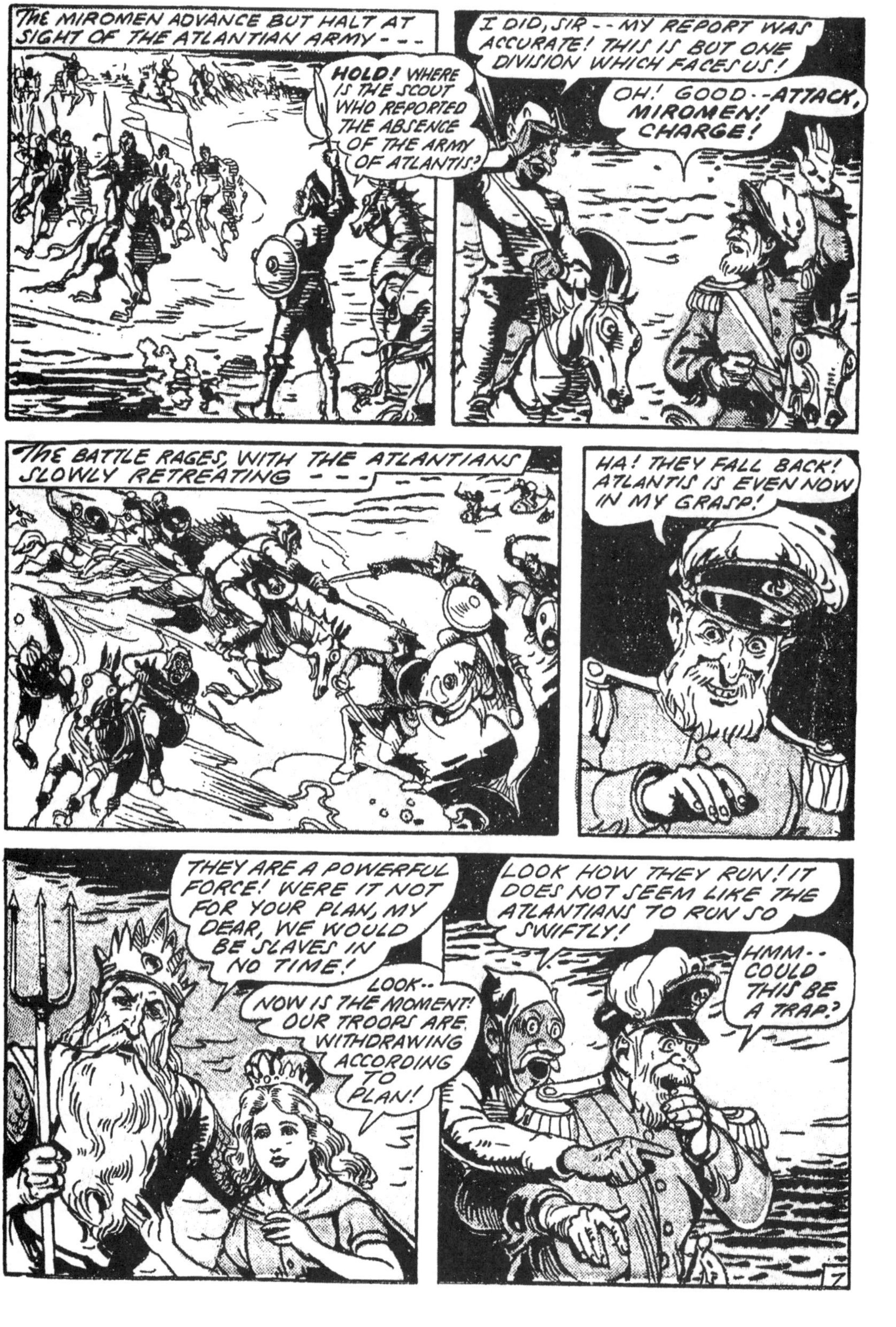
THE MIROMEN ADVANCE BUT HALT AT SIGHT OF THE ATLANTIAN ARMY---
HOLD! WHERE IS THE SCOUT WHO REPORTED THE ABSENCE OF THE ARMY OF ATLANTIS?
I DID, SIR--MY REPORT WAS ACCURATE! THIS IS BUT ONE DIVISION WHICH FACES US!
OH! GOOD--ATTACK, MIROMEN! CHARGE!
THE BATTLE RAGES, WITH THE ATLANTIANS SLOWLY RETREATING---
HA! THEY FALL BACK! ATLANTIS IS EVEN NOW IN MY GRASP!
THEY ARE A POWERFUL FORCE! WERE IT NOT FOR YOUR PLAN, MY DEAR, WE WOULD BE SLAVES IN NO TIME!
LOOK.. NOW IS THE MOMENT! OUR TROOPS ARE WITHDRAWING ACCORDING TO PLAN!
LOOK HOW THEY RUN! IT DOES NOT SEEM LIKE THE ATLANTIANS TO RUN SO SWIFTLY!
HMM-- COULD THIS BE A TRAP?
7

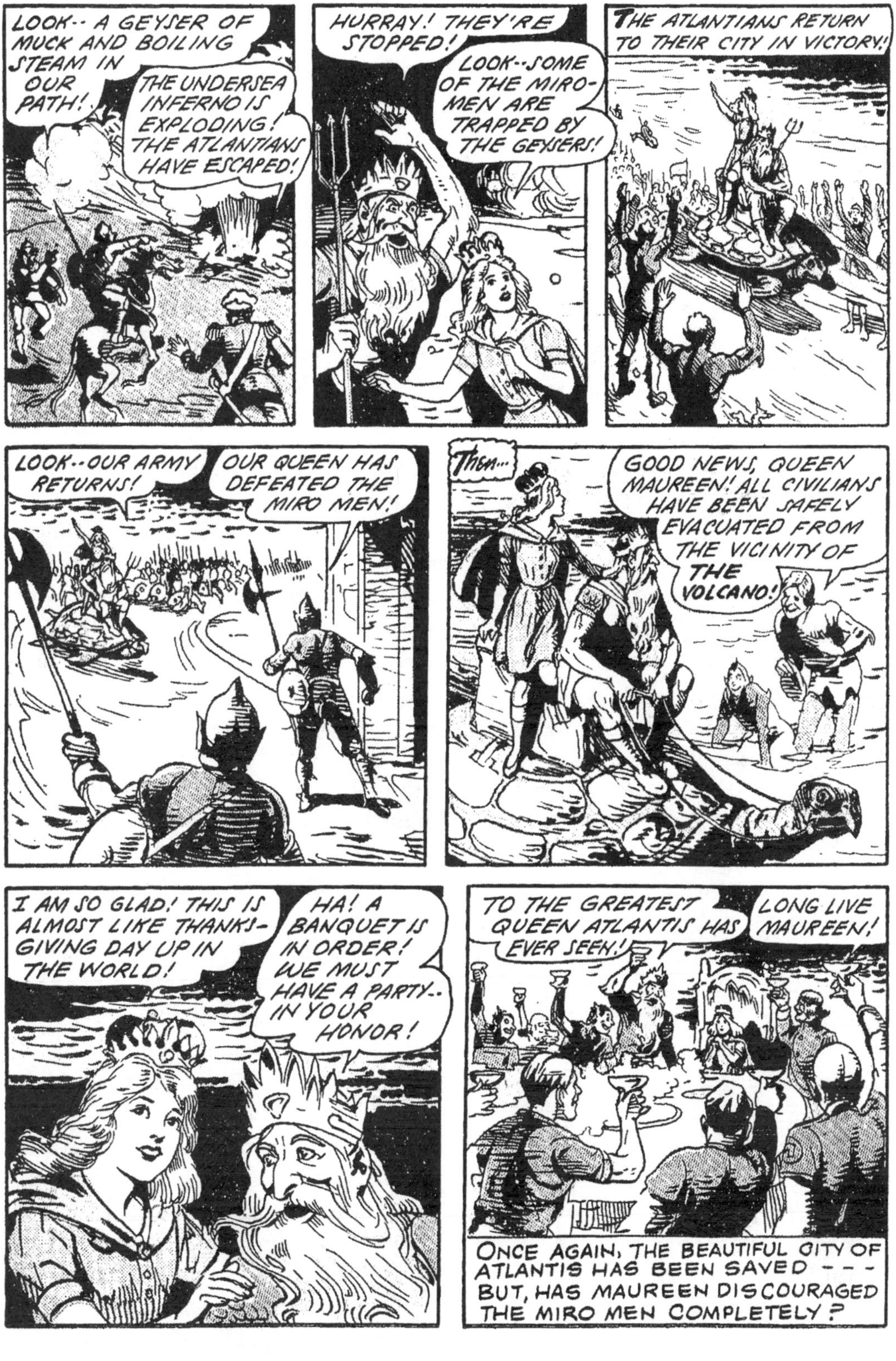
LOOK-- A GEYSER OF MUCK AND BOILING STEAM IN OUR PATH!
THE UNDERSEA INFERNO IS EXPLODING! THE ATLANTIANS HAVE ESCAPED!
HURRAY! THEY'RE STOPPED!
LOOK--SOME OF THE MIRO-MEN ARE TRAPPED BY THE GEYSERS!
THE ATLANTIANS RETURN TO THEIR CITY IN VICTORY!
LOOK--OUR ARMY RETURNS!
OUR QUEEN HAS DEFEATED THE MIRO MEN!
Then...
GOOD NEWS, QUEEN MAUREEN! ALL CIVILIANS HAVE BEEN SAFELY EVACUATED FROM THE VICINITY OF THE VOLCANO!
I AM SO GLAD! THIS IS ALMOST LIKE THANKSGIVING DAY UP IN THE WORLD!
HA! A BANQUET IS IN ORDER! WE MUST HAVE A PARTY-- IN YOUR HONOR!
TO THE GREATEST QUEEN ATLANTIS HAS EVER SEEN!
LONG LIVE MAUREEN!
ONCE AGAIN, THE BEAUTIFUL CITY OF ATLANTIS HAS BEEN SAVED --- BUT, HAS MAUREEN DISCOURAGED THE MIRO MEN COMPLETELY?

WARRIORS & QUEENS

In the seven decades since their debut, comic books have been praised as an American art form, and denounced as a cause of juvenile delinquency. They have been used as both propaganda and educational tools. One has even received the Pulitzer Prize. Comics have become the modern mythology of our culture, so we sometimes forget that they began as escapist entertainment. And while we usually associate comic book stories with the superheroes and crime fighters of the modern world, the early days of the medium offered more than just that. Comic books also took readers on grand adventures to strange and fantastic worlds, where equally fantastic women resided.

Prior to the arrival of the comic book, newspaper comic strips were the primary source of illustrated escapist entertainment in America. During the grim days of the Great Depression in the 1930s, newspaper readers faithfully followed the medieval tales of Prince Valiant, or the sweeping science fiction adventures of Buck Rogers and Flash Gordon. When comic books hit the newsstands in the late '30s, they often looked to the newspaper strips for inspiration. *Inspiration* may be putting it mildly. *Hit Comics'* Blaze Barton was merely a thinly disguised version of newspaper mainstay Flash Gordon, with the art often crudely copied from the original source. But the fantasy series of the comic books did take it a step further than their newspaper inspirations. Prince Valiant, Buck Rogers, and Flash Gordon were all men. The heroes of comic book fantasy tales were often women.

Camilla, Queen of the Lost Empire is one of the earliest heroines of comic books, debuting in *Jungle Comics #1* (January 1940). When Camilla first appeared, she was a femme fatale reminiscent of Ayesha from H. Rider Haggard's novel *She*. The story tells how a young scientist finds a lost city in the heart of the African jungle, populated by Norsemen who came to Africa during the Crusades. Camilla is the wondrous city's 500 year-old monarch, who stays eternally young and beautiful by bathing in a miraculous spring. She rules her people with an iron hand, and will stop at nothing to maintain power, including human sacrifice. At this point, Camilla was not what you'd call a *heroic* character.

But after two subsequent stories, Camilla has a change of heart. She decides to abandon her evil ways and vows to become a good and just ruler. Camilla moves from a traditional female role into a male role, as she is transformed from a slinky silent movie style seductress to a sword wielding warrior queen protecting her kingdom against human and supernatural foes. Like a comic book Boadicea, a zebra-riding Camilla leads her men into battle against any threats to the Lost Empire. "Like a woman possessed, the beautiful queen cuts through the enemy ranks!" reads the text that describes Camilla's victory over her enemies. Brave Camilla even took on Satan himself to protect her people. These stories took place in an exotic and fanciful world, filled with magic and steeped in ancient mystery. At the center of these tales was the proud and fierce Camilla, a female warrior whose likes would not be seen in modern comics until sword wielding heroines like Red Sonja appeared in the 1970s.

The Magician From Mars was perhaps the most unique of the science fiction heroines of early comics. Like Camilla, The Magician's motivations were initially selfish. In a future where interplanetary contact had been established, Jane Q-X 3 was born the daughter of a Martian father and a mother from Earth. As a baby, Jane was accidentally exposed to a cathode ray, giving her fantastic powers. Fearing her daughter would be ostracized, Jane's mother made the young girl hide her powers. After the death of her parents, Jane fell under the control of her elderly aunt, who locked the free-spirited young women away from the world. Using her powers, Jane broke free and stowed away on the first spaceship for Earth. She also used her powers to steal the $3 million in gold in the ship's cargo, which at first doesn't seem like a heroic act. But once on Earth, Jane donated half the gold to a doctor who was trying to cure infantile paralysis, and kept the rest of the money to create a new life for herself. Smart cookie, this girl. Now able to enjoy the freedom she had so desperately craved. Jane became The Magician from Mars, and used her amazing abilities to help her new world.

Aside from being financially independent, The Magician From Mars was also able to live a life of complete freedom because she could access 100% of her brain capacity. This impressive ability enabled her to fly, reshape reality, "destroy time and space," and keep herself young and beautiful forever. Devoting herself to helping the citizens of Earth, she travels the world righting wrongs and performing amazing feats. In one story, the super-intelligent Magician must stop the killing spree of a giant rampaging monster, destroying it by singing a beautiful song. These stories present The Magician every bit as devoted to a heroic role as a man would be, and offered readers epic adventures. "...I'll catch him even if I have to search all the planets in the galaxies of eternal space!!" The Magician vows, after the murderous villain known The Hood has escaped her grasp.

There was a flowering of these strong fantasy heroines in the very early 1940s. But when WWII broke out, comic books needed to switch their focus. Not only was there the Axis to defeat, there were also brave men fighting overseas that needed to be entertained. In a letter to *Wings Comics* #35 (1943), a servicemen made a simple request about the depiction of the much discussed Jane Martin, "We would like her with even less clothes!" The costumes worn by space heroines like Gale Allen got skimpier, and her Girl Squadron started looking more like a chorus line. Camilla fared the worst during this time, as she was transformed from a powerful empress into yet another scantily clad clone of Sheena, Queen of the Jungle.

By the end of the 1940s there was little left in the way of fantasy heroines other than jungle queens like Princess Pantha, Tiger Girl, and Rulah, Jungle Goddess. These simple daughters of nature in animal print bikinis ushered in the 1950s, and an era where comic book heroines had to be little more than pretty.

Now, let's meet the fantastic females who ruled empires and traveled across the cosmos—

★ ★ ★

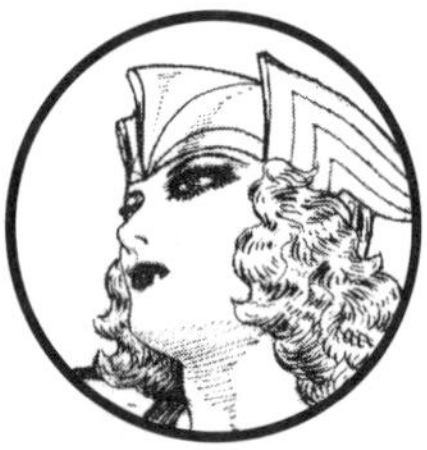

CAMILLA, QUEEN OF THE LOST EMPIRE— Camilla appeared in *Jungle Comics* from 1940-52, one of the longest careers for a woman during the Golden Age of Comics. The story here is from *Jungle Comics* #8, during the period when Camilla was presented as a courageous warrior queen. In it, she must defend her kingdom from an invading army, even enlisting the aid of gorillas to do so. After the handsome Sir Champion was introduced, Camilla eventually became less fearless fighter and more damsel-in-distress. Camilla's character changed dramatically in 1942, when she became lost in the jungle. She traded her queenly armor for a leopard skin bikini, and promptly forgot all about her kingdom. The series was renamed "Queen of the *Jungle* Empire," and Camilla became just another generic shapely nymph swinging from a vine, like Sheena or any of the countless others like her. And that's how she stayed for the next ten years, a sad fate for a once mighty comic book monarch.

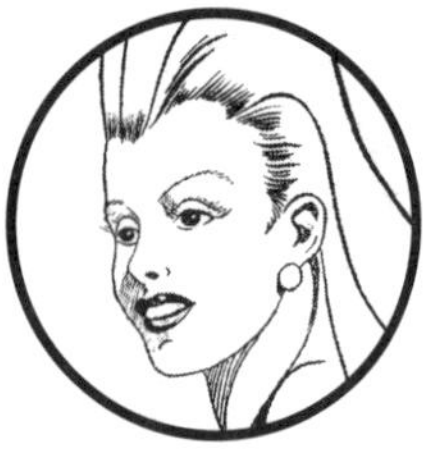

THE SORCERESS OF ZOOM— The Sorceress of Zoom was obsessed with ruling the world. To that end, the haughty and ruthless sorceress swooped about the skies in her magical flying city, searching for the next unfortunate victims to add to her monstrous army of slaves. Most of the Sorceress' stories involved her quest for some mystical object of power. This would usually result in a duel between the Sorceress and some other practitioner of magic. And these battles were wild, since the Sorceress' powers seemed to be as limitless as her capacity to inflict cruelty and pain. This story takes the reader on a rollercoaster ride, complete with young lovers, an invisible cloak, sea monsters, a treacherous foe, deception, and even a Nazi agent. At the story's climax, it appears that the Sorceress is actually working on the side of justice, but it's merely an accident on her part. There were *only* mean bones in her body. Unlike Camilla, the Sorceress did not reform and become an honorable character; she stuck with her malevolent ways for most of her adventures. This was the kind of series that could only have been produced during the dawn of the comic book industry, when there were very few rules. The Sorceress of Zoom appeared in every issue of the aptly named *Weird Comics* between 1940-41.

GALE ALLEN AND THE GIRL SQUADRON— Comic books of the 1940s had plenty of male science fiction heroes like Spurt Hammond, Flint Barton, and Spacehawk bringing justice to the outer reaches of the cosmos. But Gale Allen was one of the few women in comics to explore the spaceways. Gale and her 40th Women's Space Battalion (AKA The Girl Squadron) protected the planet Venus from all manner of evil alien races and one slimy, carnivorous monster after another. Still, Gale found some men were skeptical about the abilities of an all-female crew. "I asked for men to help fight pirates. I didn't send out bids to a knitting circle!" proclaims a male Space Patrol agent when the Girl Squadron arrives to fight Plutonian marauders. But time and again Gale and her leggy "Amazon legion" proved they were just as capable as any platoon of men as they faced "inhuman hordes and sudden death." With WWII at an end in 1945, publishers may have felt that readers were tired of reading about the military. So, that year the Girl Squadron disappeared, leaving Gale to fly solo as a space pilot. Although she may be overlooked in the annals of comic book history, Gale Allen enjoyed a lengthy publication run in *Planet Comics* from 1940-46.

THE MAGICIAN FROM MARS— The Magician from Mars was a heroine with great potential. Sadly, she only made five appearances in *Amazing Man Comics* in 1940. The story presented here is her final appearance, and features the heroine's return to Mars and her rematch with her archenemy The Hood. It feels reminiscent of the original *Star Wars* movies, complete with a desperate plea for help from an embattled planet, epic space battles, the dramatic unmasking of the villain, and The Magician herself leading an army into battle. It's interesting that even in the story's romantic subplot, The Magician plays what would be considered a traditional male role, and puts duty before thoughts of love.

MYSTA OF THE MOON— Mysta made her debut in 1945, as WWII was drawing to a close. Perhaps as a reaction to the horrors the world had experienced for the past several years, Mysta was a new kind of heroine. She was born in a future where the war god Mars had eradicated all knowledge, science, and culture, bringing about a new Dark Age. An aged scientist raised young Mysta and instilled all of mankind's knowledge into her. She was described as "the living temple of man's essential goodness…into whose head is packed all science, all knowledge, all wisdom…" Mysta's mission was to rekindle the fires of knowledge throughout a blighted universe. Alone in her lunar science citadel, Mysta kept watch over the cosmos, waiting for "the next assaults spawned by the lurking terrors of outer space." Mysta could project her mind through space, and was aided by a powerful robot that answered her mental commands. As the '40s drew to a close and more conservative times beckoned, Mysta had to hide her amazing talents behind a secret identity. Her lofty mission now downplayed, she became more of a space detective. By 1949, her series in *Planet Comics* was gone. This story was drawn by the prolific woman artist Fran Hopper.

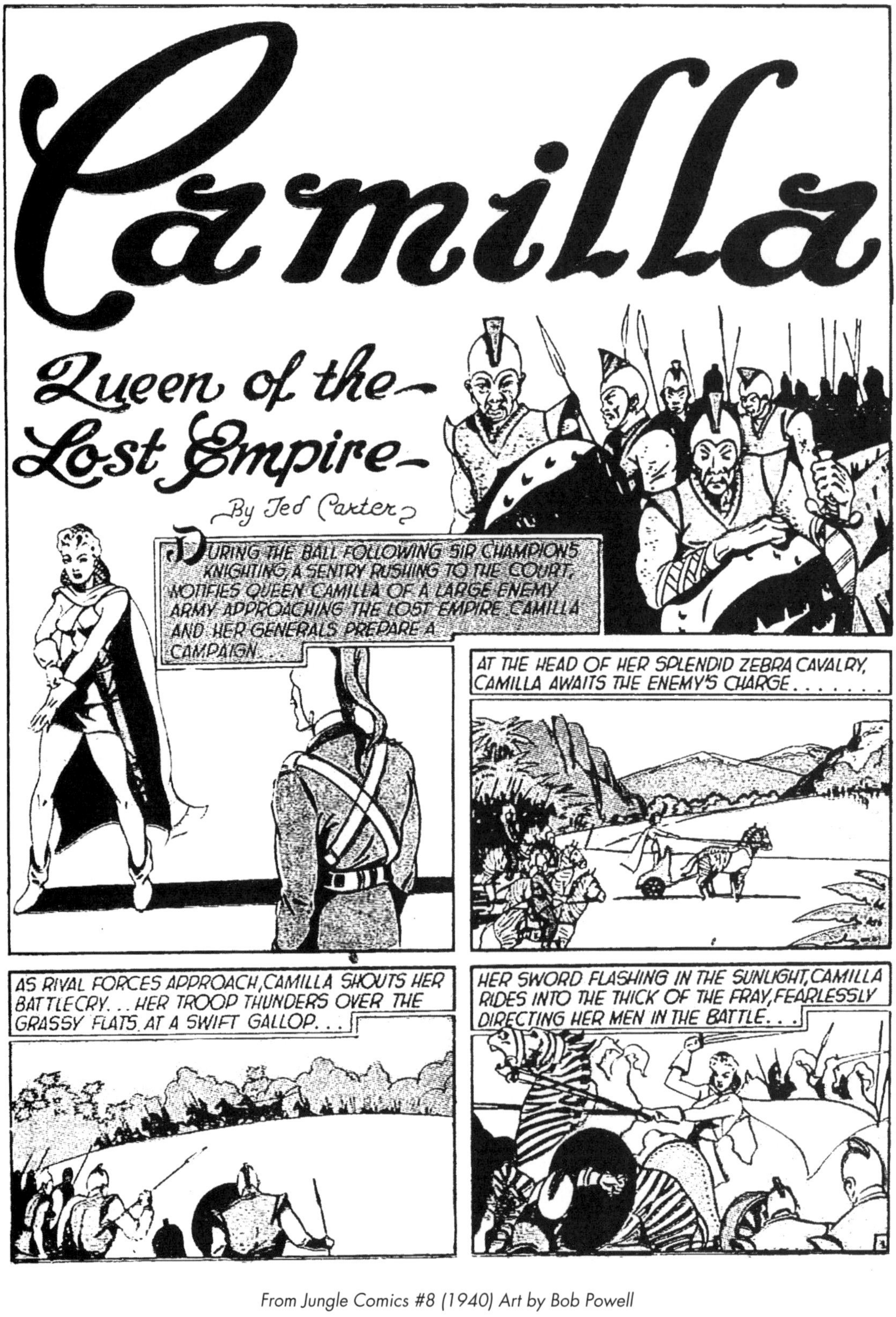
Camilla
Queen of the Lost Empire
By Ted Carter
DURING THE BALL FOLLOWING SIR CHAMPIONS KNIGHTING, A SENTRY RUSHING TO THE COURT, NOTIFIES QUEEN CAMILLA OF A LARGE ENEMY ARMY APPROACHING THE LOST EMPIRE. CAMILLA AND HER GENERALS PREPARE A CAMPAIGN.
AT THE HEAD OF HER SPLENDID ZEBRA CAVALRY, CAMILLA AWAITS THE ENEMY'S CHARGE . . . . . .
AS RIVAL FORCES APPROACH, CAMILLA SHOUTS HER BATTLECRY. . . HER TROOP THUNDERS OVER THE GRASSY FLATS AT A SWIFT GALLOP. . .
HER SWORD FLASHING IN THE SUNLIGHT, CAMILLA RIDES INTO THE THICK OF THE FRAY, FEARLESSLY DIRECTING HER MEN IN THE BATTLE. . .

From Jungle Comics #8 (1940) Art by Bob Powell

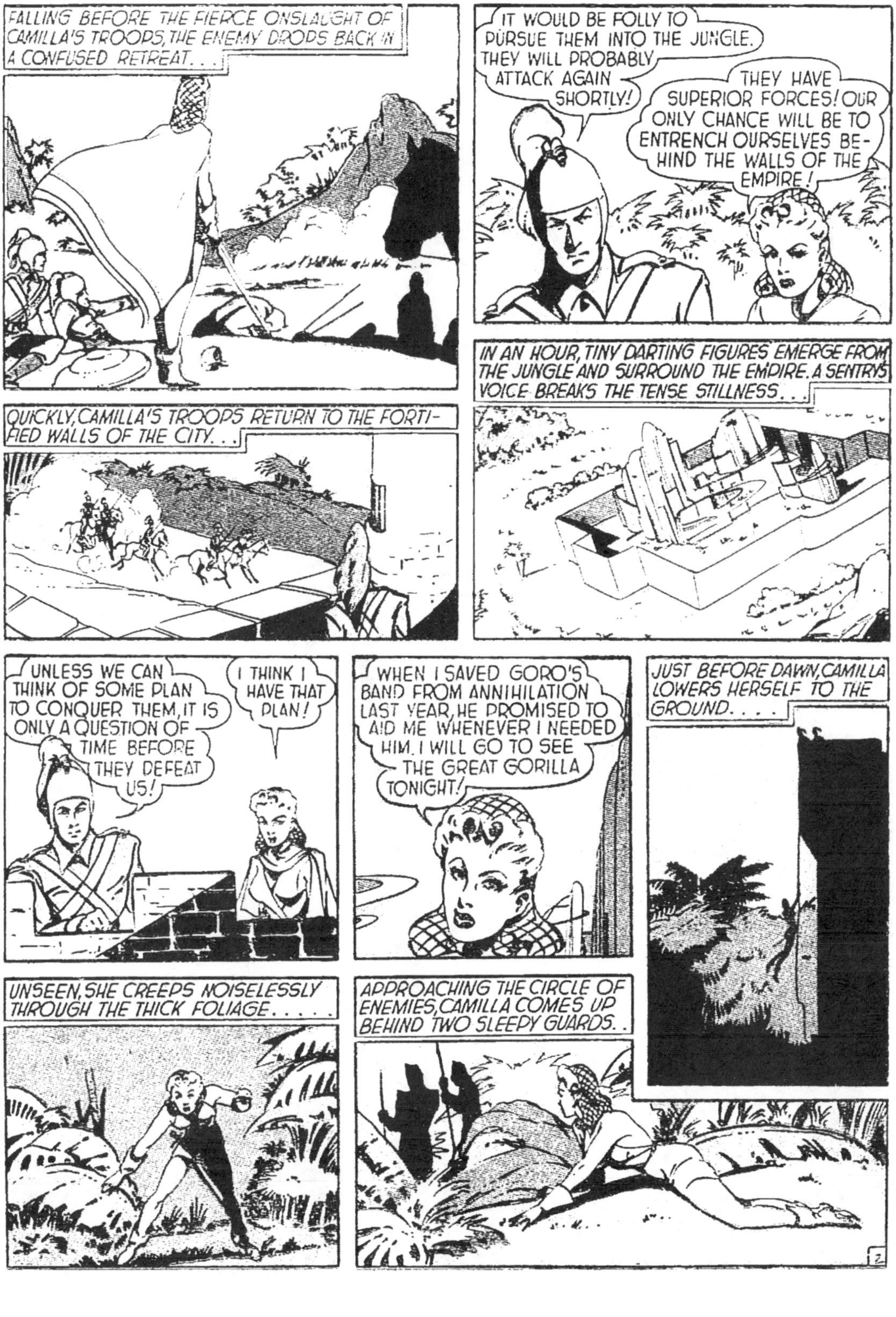

FALLING BEFORE THE FIERCE ONSLAUGHT OF CAMILLA'S TROOPS, THE ENEMY DROPS BACK IN A CONFUSED RETREAT. . .
IT WOULD BE FOLLY TO PURSUE THEM INTO THE JUNGLE. THEY WILL PROBABLY ATTACK AGAIN SHORTLY!
THEY HAVE SUPERIOR FORCES! OUR ONLY CHANCE WILL BE TO ENTRENCH OURSELVES BE-HIND THE WALLS OF THE EMPIRE!
QUICKLY, CAMILLA'S TROOPS RETURN TO THE FORTI-FIED WALLS OF THE CITY. . .
IN AN HOUR, TINY DARTING FIGURES EMERGE FROM THE JUNGLE AND SURROUND THE EMPIRE. A SENTRY'S VOICE BREAKS THE TENSE STILLNESS. . .
UNLESS WE CAN THINK OF SOME PLAN TO CONQUER THEM, IT IS ONLY A QUESTION OF TIME BEFORE THEY DEFEAT US!
I THINK I HAVE THAT PLAN!
WHEN I SAVED GORO'S BAND FROM ANNIHILATION LAST YEAR, HE PROMISED TO AID ME WHENEVER I NEEDED HIM. I WILL GO TO SEE THE GREAT GORILLA TONIGHT!
JUST BEFORE DAWN, CAMILLA LOWERS HERSELF TO THE GROUND. . . .
UNSEEN, SHE CREEPS NOISELESSLY THROUGH THE THICK FOLIAGE. . . . .
APPROACHING THE CIRCLE OF ENEMIES, CAMILLA COMES UP BEHIND TWO SLEEPY GUARDS. .
2

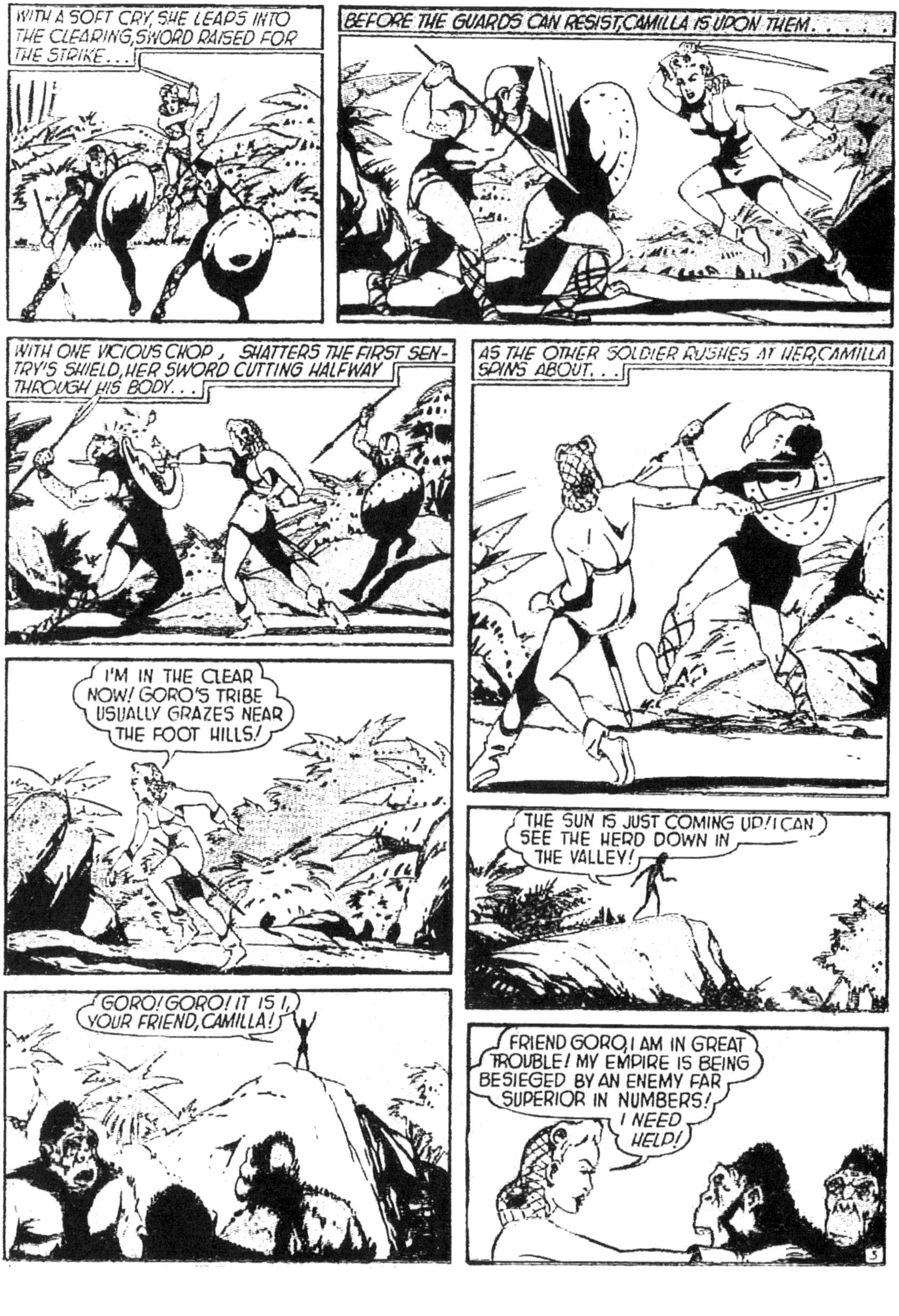
WITH A SOFT CRY, SHE LEAPS INTO THE CLEARING, SWORD RAISED FOR THE STRIKE...
BEFORE THE GUARDS CAN RESIST, CAMILLA IS UPON THEM.....
WITH ONE VICIOUS CHOP , SHATTERS THE FIRST SEN-TRY'S SHIELD, HER SWORD CUTTING HALFWAY THROUGH HIS BODY...
AS THE OTHER SOLDIER RUSHES AT HER, CAMILLA SPINS ABOUT...
I'M IN THE CLEAR NOW! GORO'S TRIBE USUALLY GRAZES NEAR THE FOOT HILLS!
THE SUN IS JUST COMING UP! I CAN SEE THE HERD DOWN IN THE VALLEY!
GORO! GORO! IT IS I, YOUR FRIEND, CAMILLA!
FRIEND GORO, I AM IN GREAT TROUBLE! MY EMPIRE IS BEING BESIEGED BY AN ENEMY FAR SUPERIOR IN NUMBERS! I NEED HELP!
5

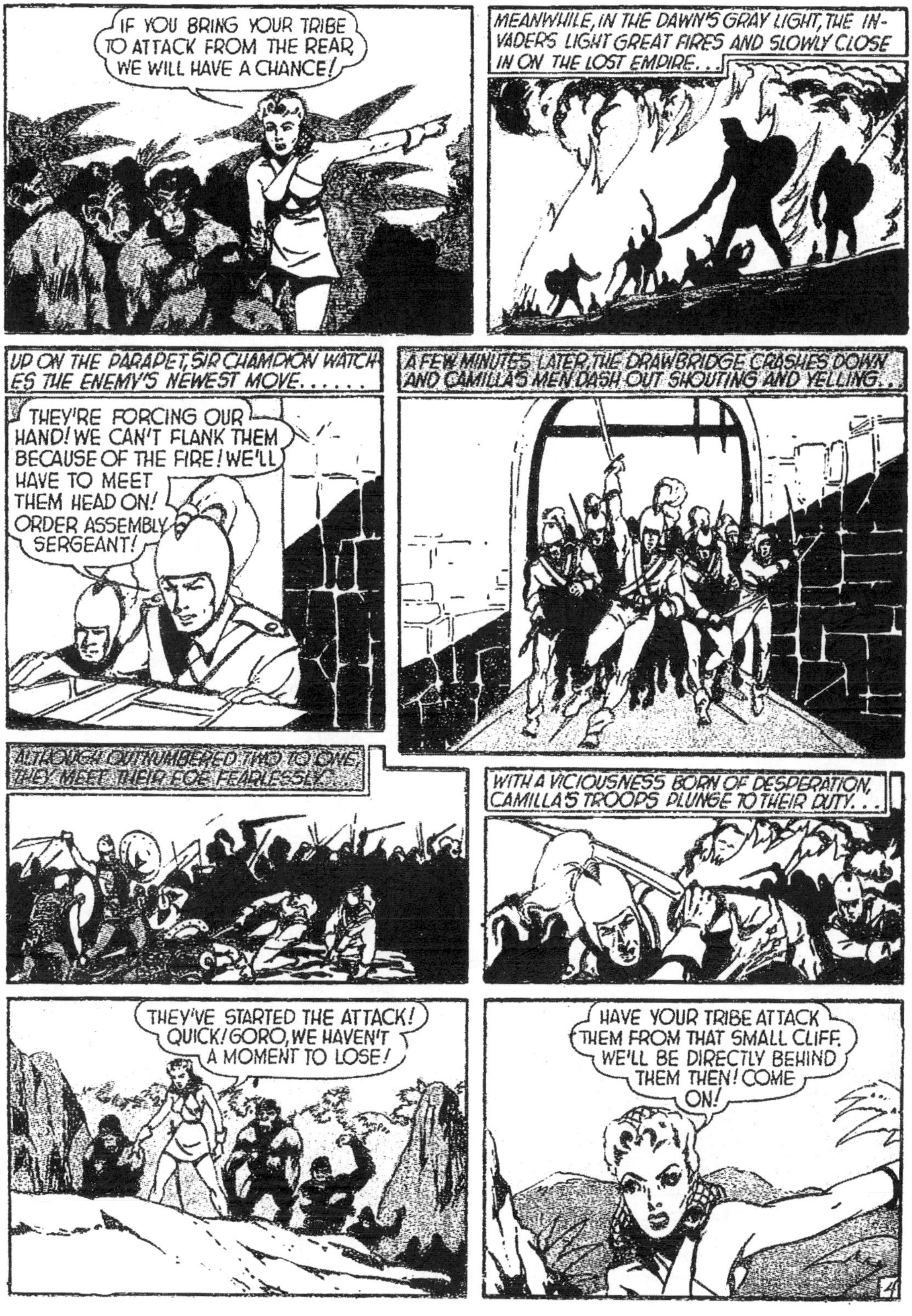
IF YOU BRING YOUR TRIBE TO ATTACK FROM THE REAR WE WILL HAVE A CHANCE!
MEANWHILE, IN THE DAWN'S GRAY LIGHT, THE INVADERS LIGHT GREAT FIRES AND SLOWLY CLOSE IN ON THE LOST EMPIRE...
UP ON THE PARAPET, SIR CHAMPION WATCHES THE ENEMY'S NEWEST MOVE......
THEY'RE FORCING OUR HAND! WE CAN'T FLANK THEM BECAUSE OF THE FIRE! WE'LL HAVE TO MEET THEM HEAD ON! ORDER ASSEMBLY, SERGEANT!
A FEW MINUTES LATER THE DRAWBRIDGE CRASHES DOWN AND CAMILLA'S MEN DASH OUT SHOUTING AND YELLING..
ALTHOUGH OUTNUMBERED TWO TO ONE, THEY MEET THEIR FOE FEARLESSLY...
WITH A VICIOUSNESS BORN OF DESPERATION, CAMILLA'S TROOPS PLUNGE TO THEIR DUTY...
THEY'VE STARTED THE ATTACK! QUICK! GORO, WE HAVEN'T A MOMENT TO LOSE!
HAVE YOUR TRIBE ATTACK THEM FROM THAT SMALL CLIFF. WE'LL BE DIRECTLY BEHIND THEM THEN! COME ON!
4

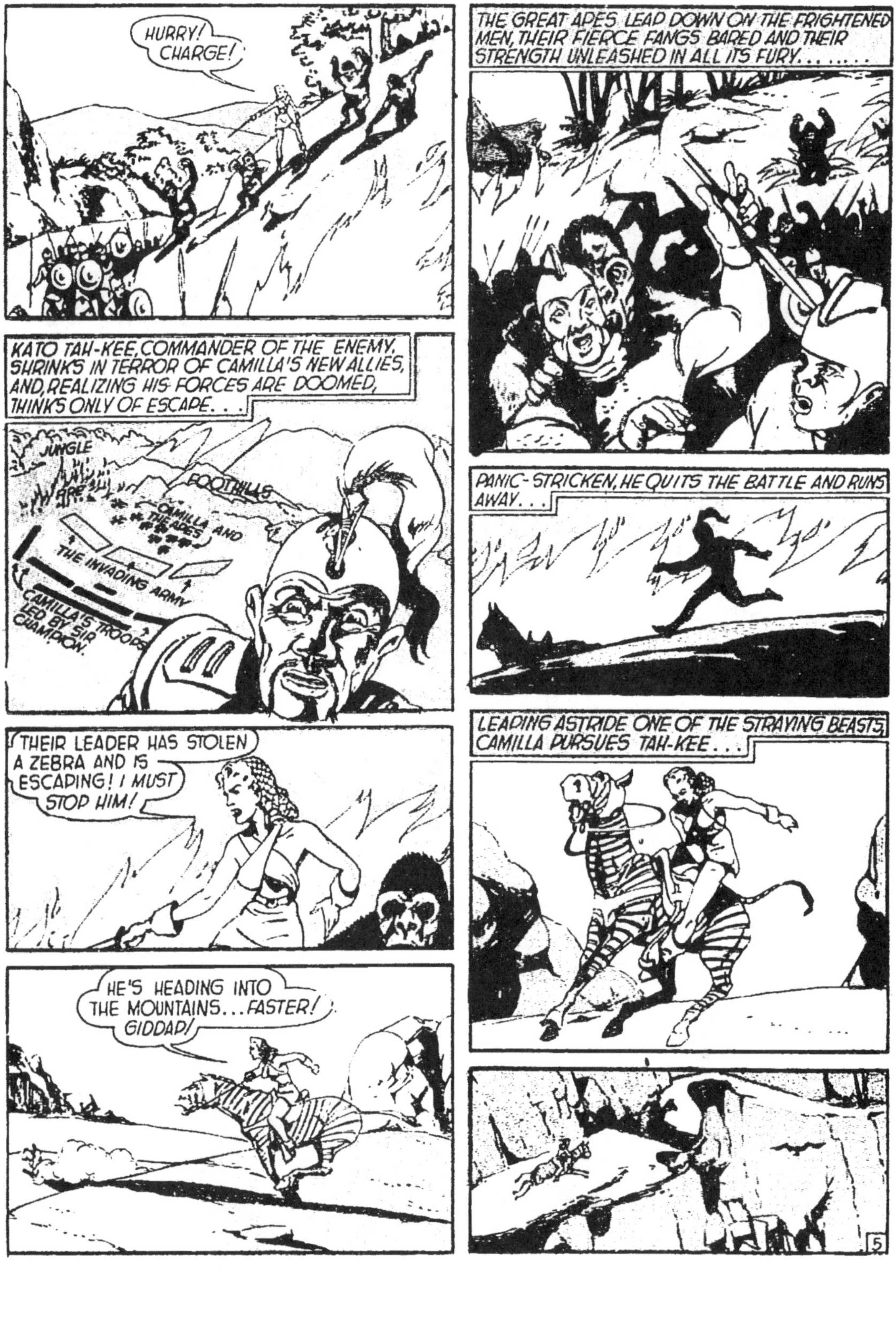
HURRY! CHARGE!
THE GREAT APES LEAP DOWN ON THE FRIGHTENED MEN, THEIR FIERCE FANGS BARED AND THEIR STRENGTH UNLEASHED IN ALL ITS FURY . . . . . .
KATO TAH-KEE, COMMANDER OF THE ENEMY, SHRINKS IN TERROR OF CAMILLA'S NEW ALLIES, AND, REALIZING HIS FORCES ARE DOOMED, THINKS ONLY OF ESCAPE . . .
JUNGLE
FOOTHILLS
CAMILLA AND THE APES
THE INVADING ARMY
CAMILLA'S TROOPS LED BY SIR CHAMPION.
PANIC-STRICKEN, HE QUITS THE BATTLE AND RUNS AWAY . . .
THEIR LEADER HAS STOLEN A ZEBRA AND IS ESCAPING! I MUST STOP HIM!
LEAPING ASTRIDE ONE OF THE STRAYING BEASTS, CAMILLA PURSUES TAH-KEE . . .
HE'S HEADING INTO THE MOUNTAINS . . . FASTER! GIDDAP!
5

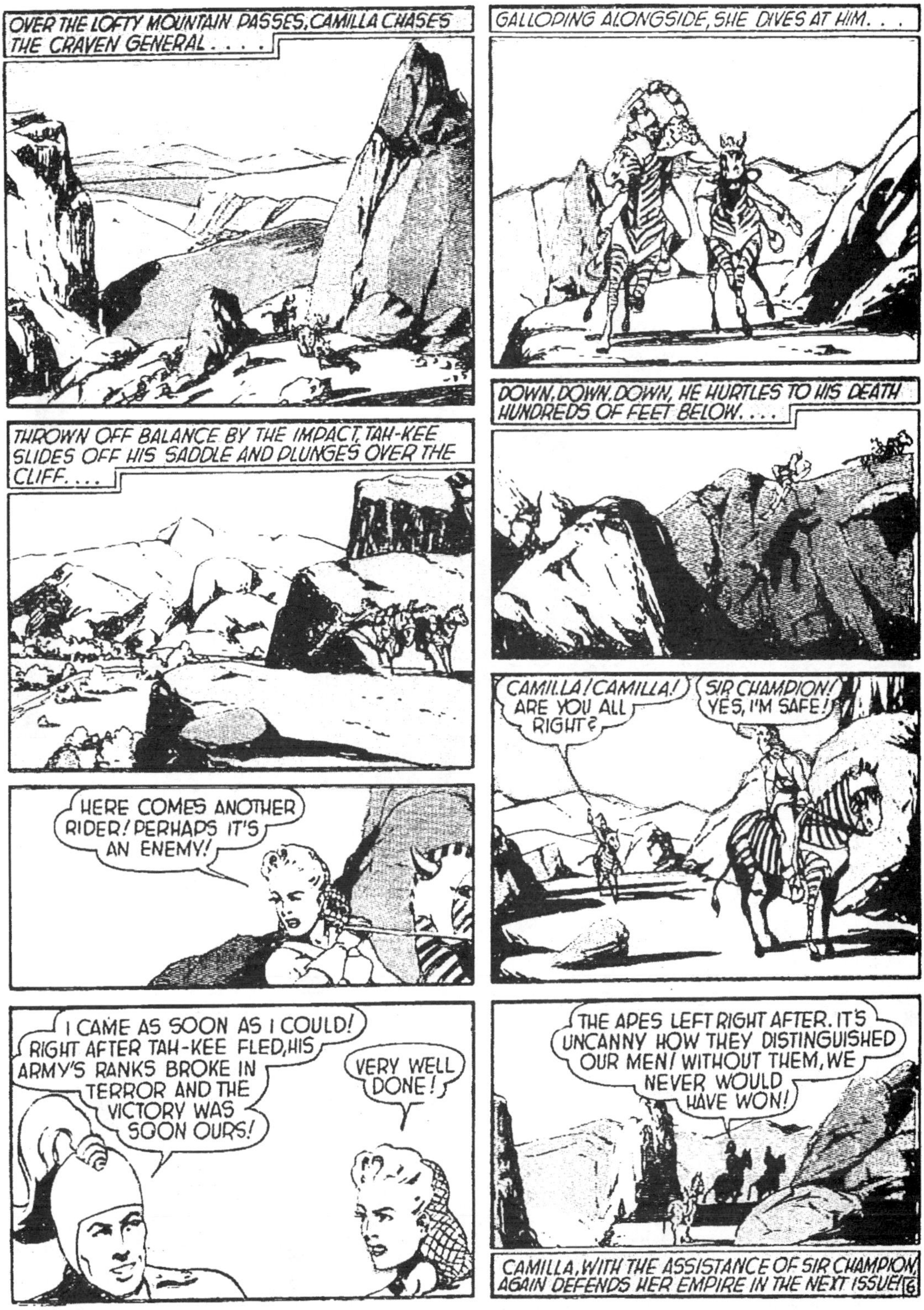
OVER THE LOFTY MOUNTAIN PASSES, CAMILLA CHASES THE CRAVEN GENERAL . . . .
GALLOPING ALONGSIDE, SHE DIVES AT HIM . . .
THROWN OFF BALANCE BY THE IMPACT, TAH-KEE SLIDES OFF HIS SADDLE AND PLUNGES OVER THE CLIFF. . . .
DOWN, DOWN, DOWN, HE HURTLES TO HIS DEATH HUNDREDS OF FEET BELOW. . . .
HERE COMES ANOTHER RIDER! PERHAPS IT'S AN ENEMY!
CAMILLA! CAMILLA! ARE YOU ALL RIGHT?
SIR CHAMPION! YES, I'M SAFE!
I CAME AS SOON AS I COULD! RIGHT AFTER TAH-KEE FLED, HIS ARMY'S RANKS BROKE IN TERROR AND THE VICTORY WAS SOON OURS!
VERY WELL DONE!
THE APES LEFT RIGHT AFTER. IT'S UNCANNY HOW THEY DISTINGUISHED OUR MEN! WITHOUT THEM, WE NEVER WOULD HAVE WON!
CAMILLA, WITH THE ASSISTANCE OF SIR CHAMPION, AGAIN DEFENDS HER EMPIRE IN THE NEXT ISSUE!
6

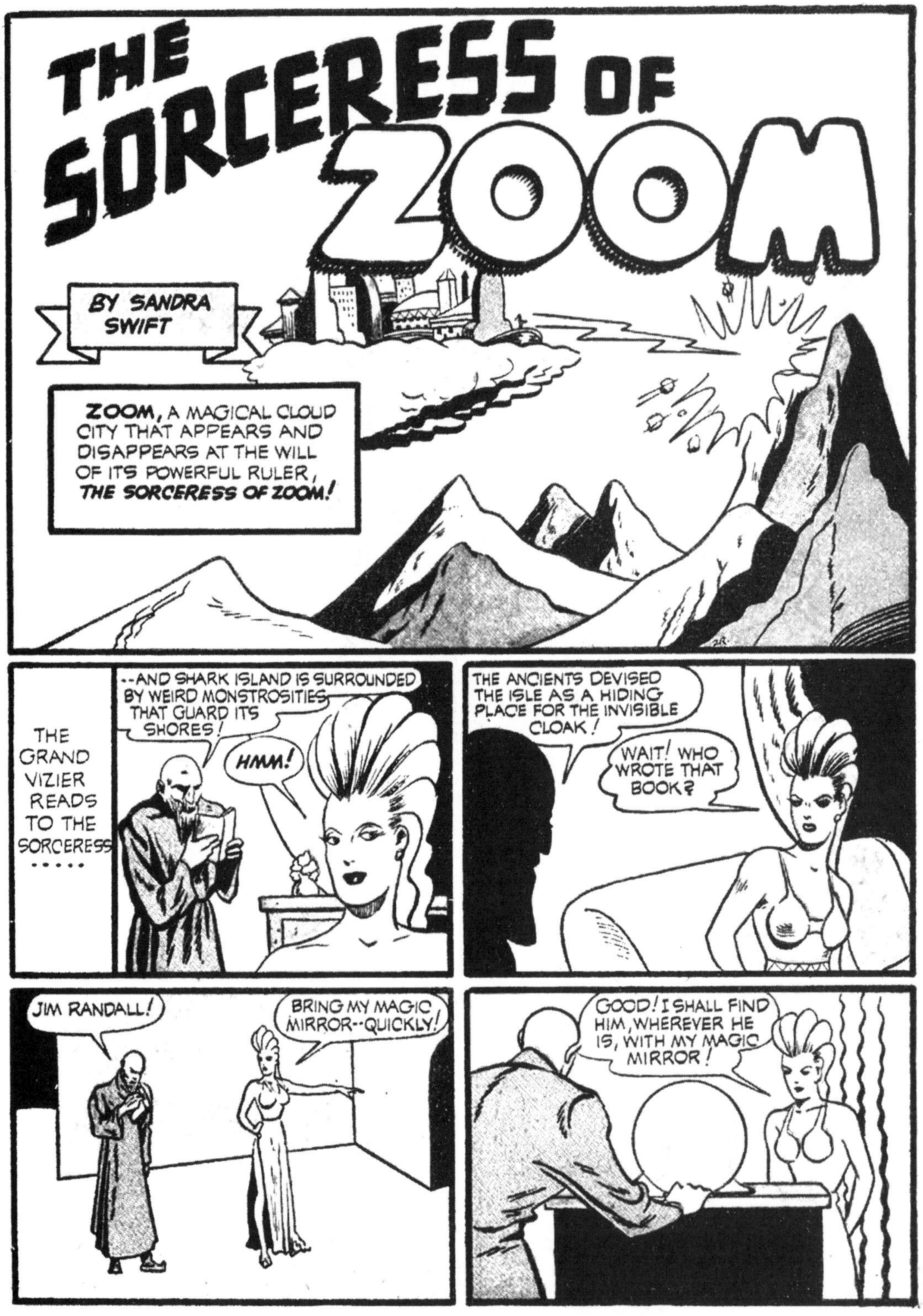
THE SORCERESS OF ZOOM
BY SANDRA SWIFT
ZOOM, A MAGICAL CLOUD CITY THAT APPEARS AND DISAPPEARS AT THE WILL OF ITS POWERFUL RULER, THE SORCERESS OF ZOOM!
THE GRAND VIZIER READS TO THE SORCERESS .....
--AND SHARK ISLAND IS SURROUNDED BY WEIRD MONSTROSITIES THAT GUARD ITS SHORES!
HMM!
THE ANCIENTS DEVISED THE ISLE AS A HIDING PLACE FOR THE INVISIBLE CLOAK!
WAIT! WHO WROTE THAT BOOK?
JIM RANDALL!
BRING MY MAGIC MIRROR--QUICKLY!
GOOD! I SHALL FIND HIM, WHEREVER HE IS, WITH MY MAGIC MIRROR!

From Weird Comics #16 (1941) Art by Don Rico

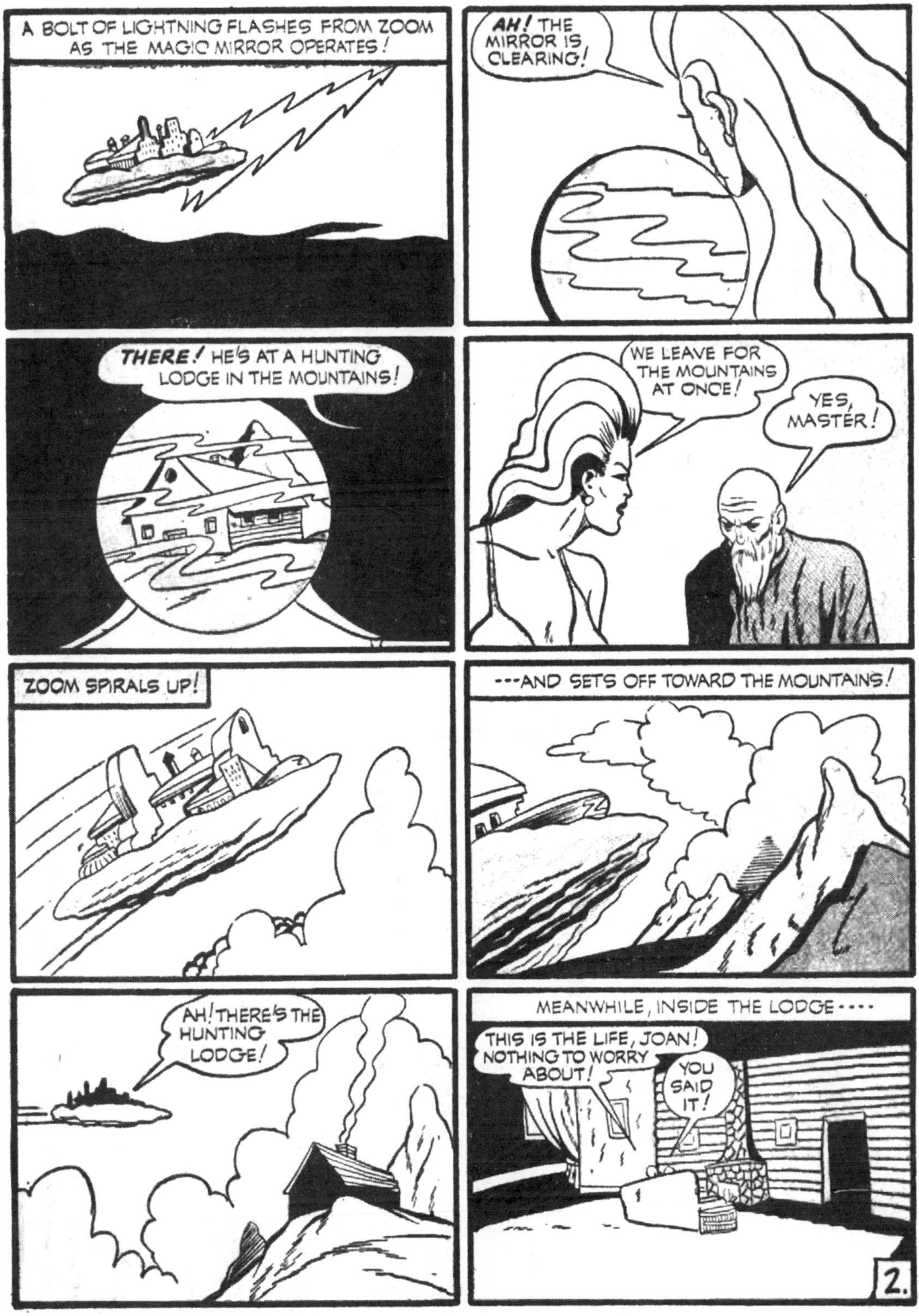
A BOLT OF LIGHTNING FLASHES FROM ZOOM AS THE MAGIC MIRROR OPERATES!
AH! THE MIRROR IS CLEARING!
THERE! HE'S AT A HUNTING LODGE IN THE MOUNTAINS!
WE LEAVE FOR THE MOUNTAINS AT ONCE!
YES, MASTER!
ZOOM SPIRALS UP!
---AND SETS OFF TOWARD THE MOUNTAINS!
AH! THERE'S THE HUNTING LODGE!
MEANWHILE, INSIDE THE LODGE----
THIS IS THE LIFE, JOAN! NOTHING TO WORRY ABOUT!
YOU SAID IT!
2.

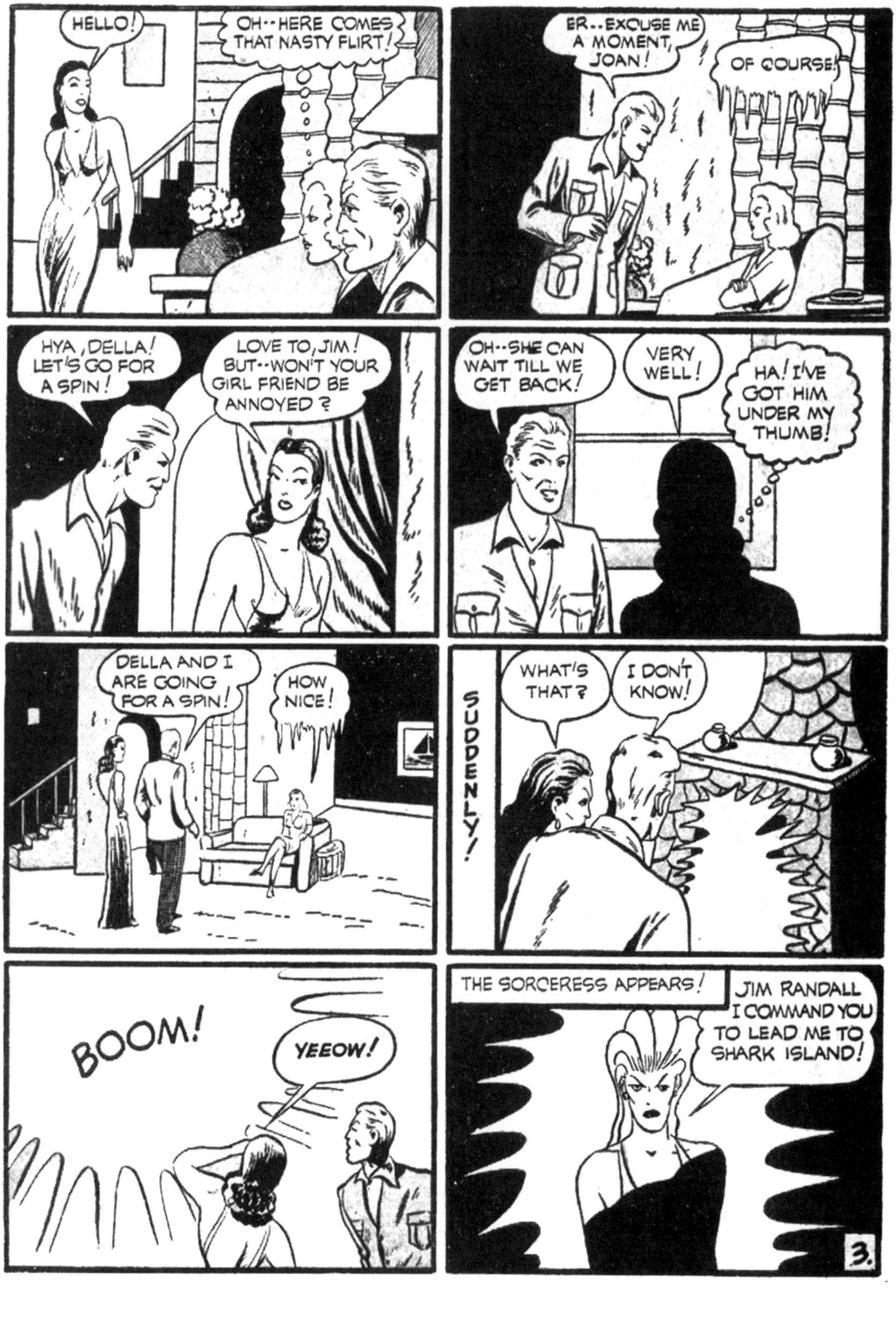
HELLO!
OH--HERE COMES THAT NASTY FLIRT!
ER..EXCUSE ME A MOMENT, JOAN!
OF COURSE!
HYA, DELLA! LET'S GO FOR A SPIN!
LOVE TO, JIM! BUT--WON'T YOUR GIRL FRIEND BE ANNOYED ?
OH--SHE CAN WAIT TILL WE GET BACK!
VERY WELL!
HA! I'VE GOT HIM UNDER MY THUMB!
DELLA AND I ARE GOING FOR A SPIN!
HOW NICE!
SUDDENLY!
WHAT'S THAT ?
I DON'T KNOW!
BOOM!
YEEOW!
THE SORCERESS APPEARS!
JIM RANDALL I COMMAND YOU TO LEAD ME TO SHARK ISLAND!
3.

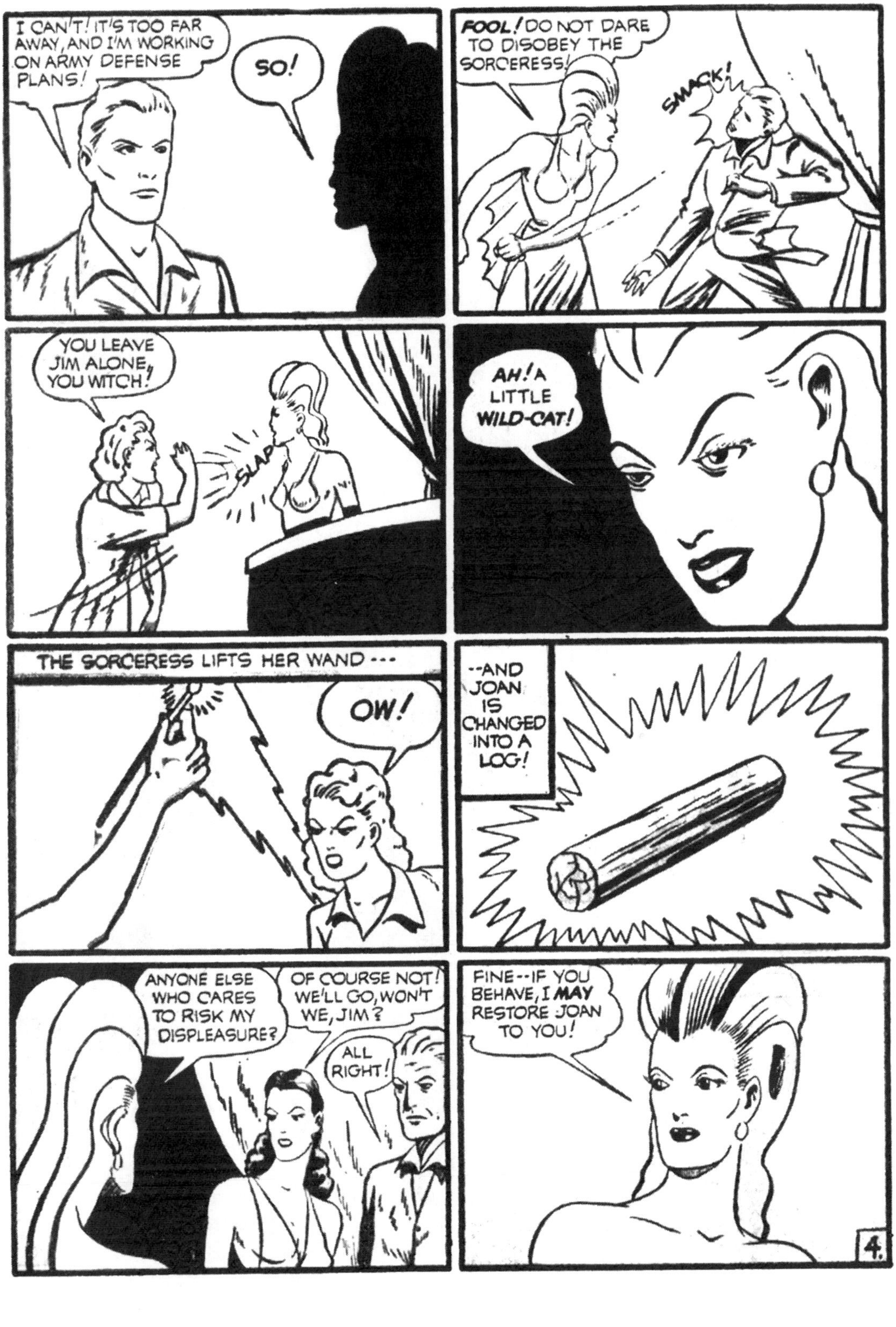
I CAN'T! IT'S TOO FAR AWAY, AND I'M WORKING ON ARMY DEFENSE PLANS!
SO!
FOOL! DO NOT DARE TO DISOBEY THE SORCERESS!
SMACK!
YOU LEAVE JIM ALONE, YOU WITCH!
SLAP
AH! A LITTLE WILD-CAT!
THE SORCERESS LIFTS HER WAND---
OW!
--AND JOAN IS CHANGED INTO A LOG!
ANYONE ELSE WHO CARES TO RISK MY DISPLEASURE?
OF COURSE NOT! WE'LL GO, WON'T WE, JIM?
ALL RIGHT!
FINE--IF YOU BEHAVE, I MAY RESTORE JOAN TO YOU!
4.

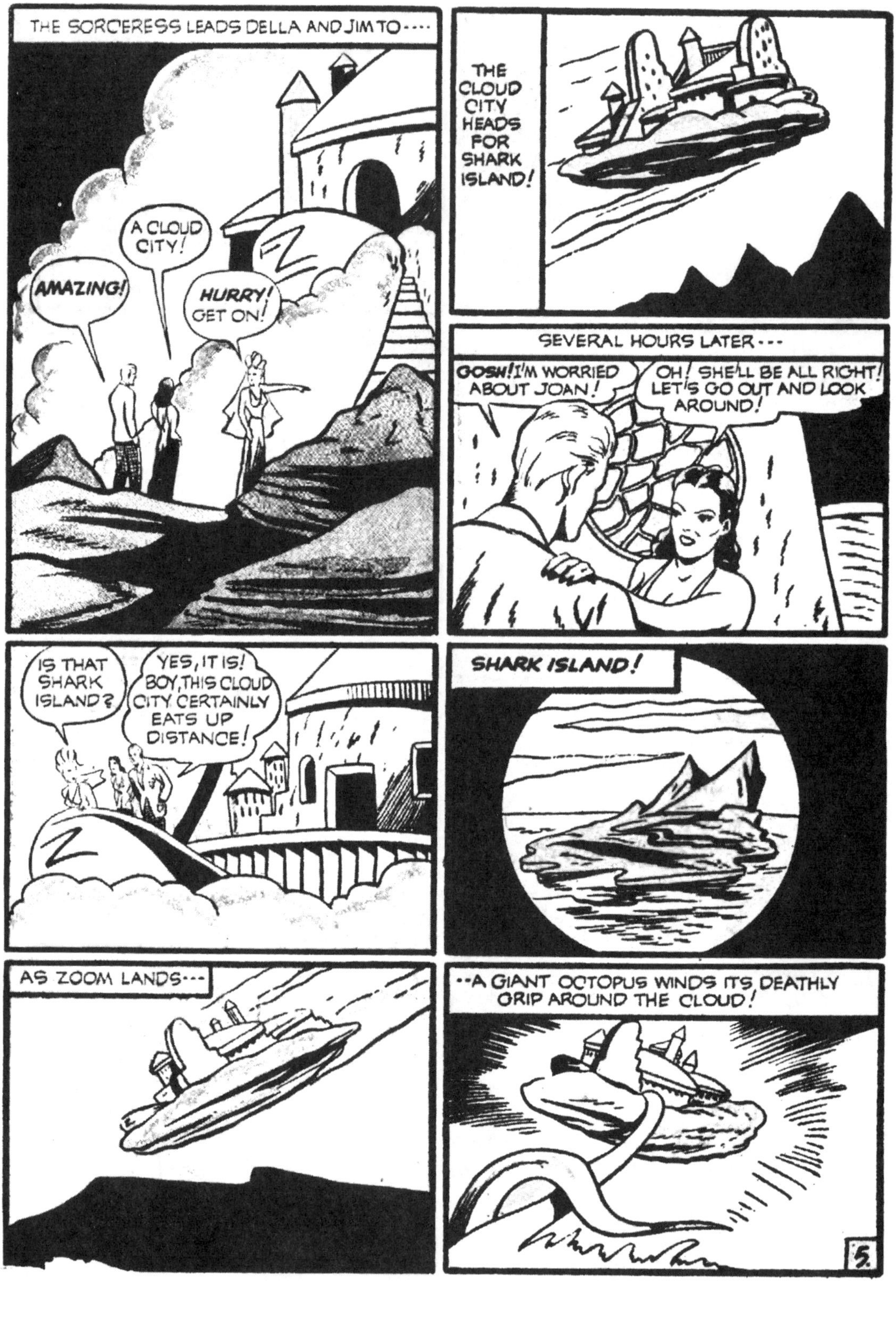
THE SORCERESS LEADS DELLA AND JIM TO----
AMAZING!
A CLOUD CITY!
HURRY! GET ON!
THE CLOUD CITY HEADS FOR SHARK ISLAND!
SEVERAL HOURS LATER---
GOSH! I'M WORRIED ABOUT JOAN!
OH! SHE'LL BE ALL RIGHT! LET'S GO OUT AND LOOK AROUND!
IS THAT SHARK ISLAND?
YES, IT IS! BOY, THIS CLOUD CITY CERTAINLY EATS UP DISTANCE!
SHARK ISLAND!
AS ZOOM LANDS---
--A GIANT OCTOPUS WINDS ITS DEATHLY GRIP AROUND THE CLOUD!
5.

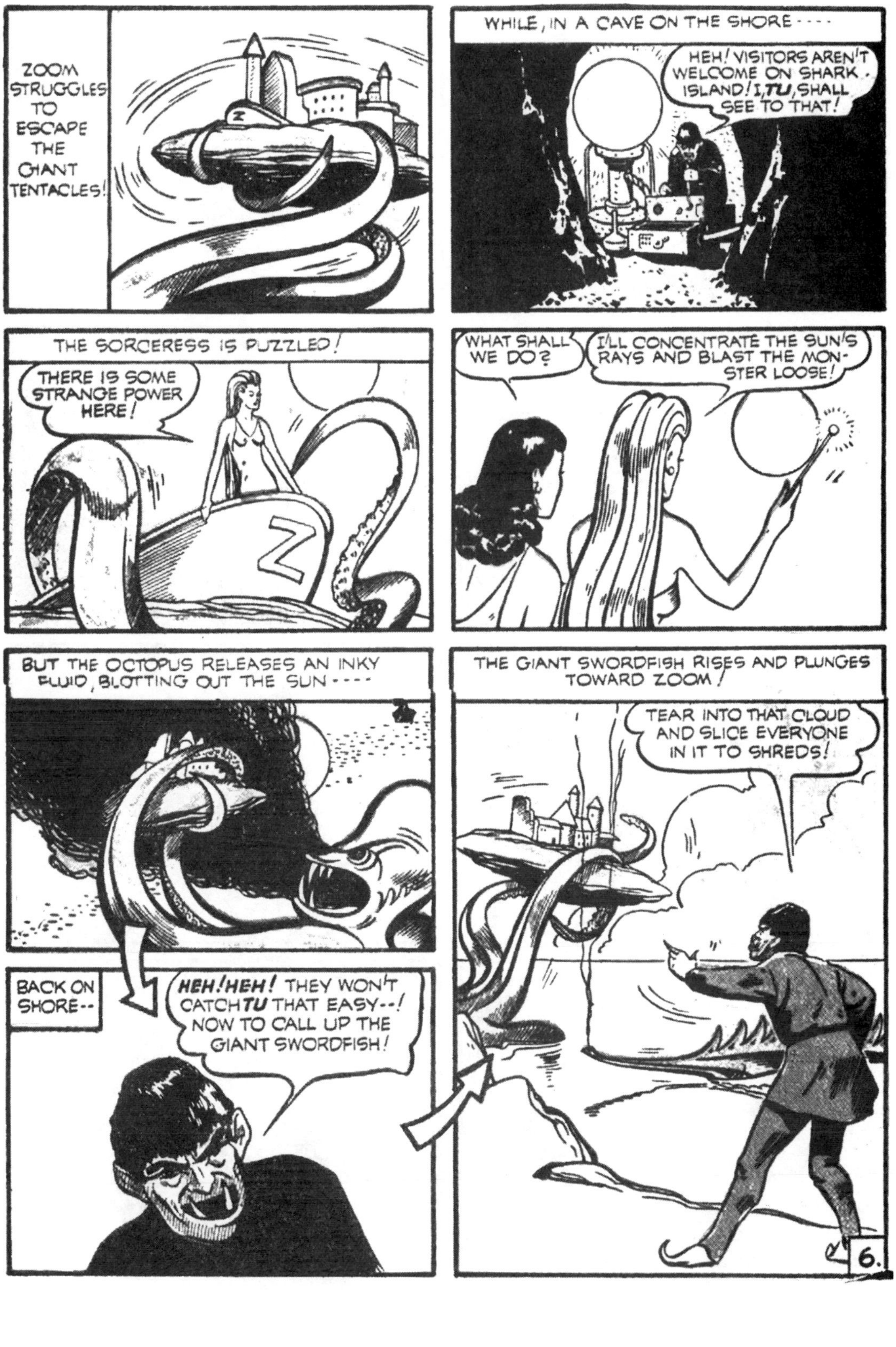
ZOOM STRUGGLES TO ESCAPE THE GIANT TENTACLES!
WHILE, IN A CAVE ON THE SHORE - - - -
HEH! VISITORS AREN'T WELCOME ON SHARK ISLAND! I, TU, SHALL SEE TO THAT!
THE SORCERESS IS PUZZLED!
THERE IS SOME STRANGE POWER HERE!
WHAT SHALL WE DO?
I'LL CONCENTRATE THE SUN'S RAYS AND BLAST THE MONSTER LOOSE!
BUT THE OCTOPUS RELEASES AN INKY FLUID, BLOTTING OUT THE SUN - - - -
THE GIANT SWORDFISH RISES AND PLUNGES TOWARD ZOOM!
TEAR INTO THAT CLOUD AND SLICE EVERYONE IN IT TO SHREDS!
BACK ON SHORE - -
HEH! HEH! THEY WON'T CATCH TU THAT EASY - -! NOW TO CALL UP THE GIANT SWORDFISH!
6.

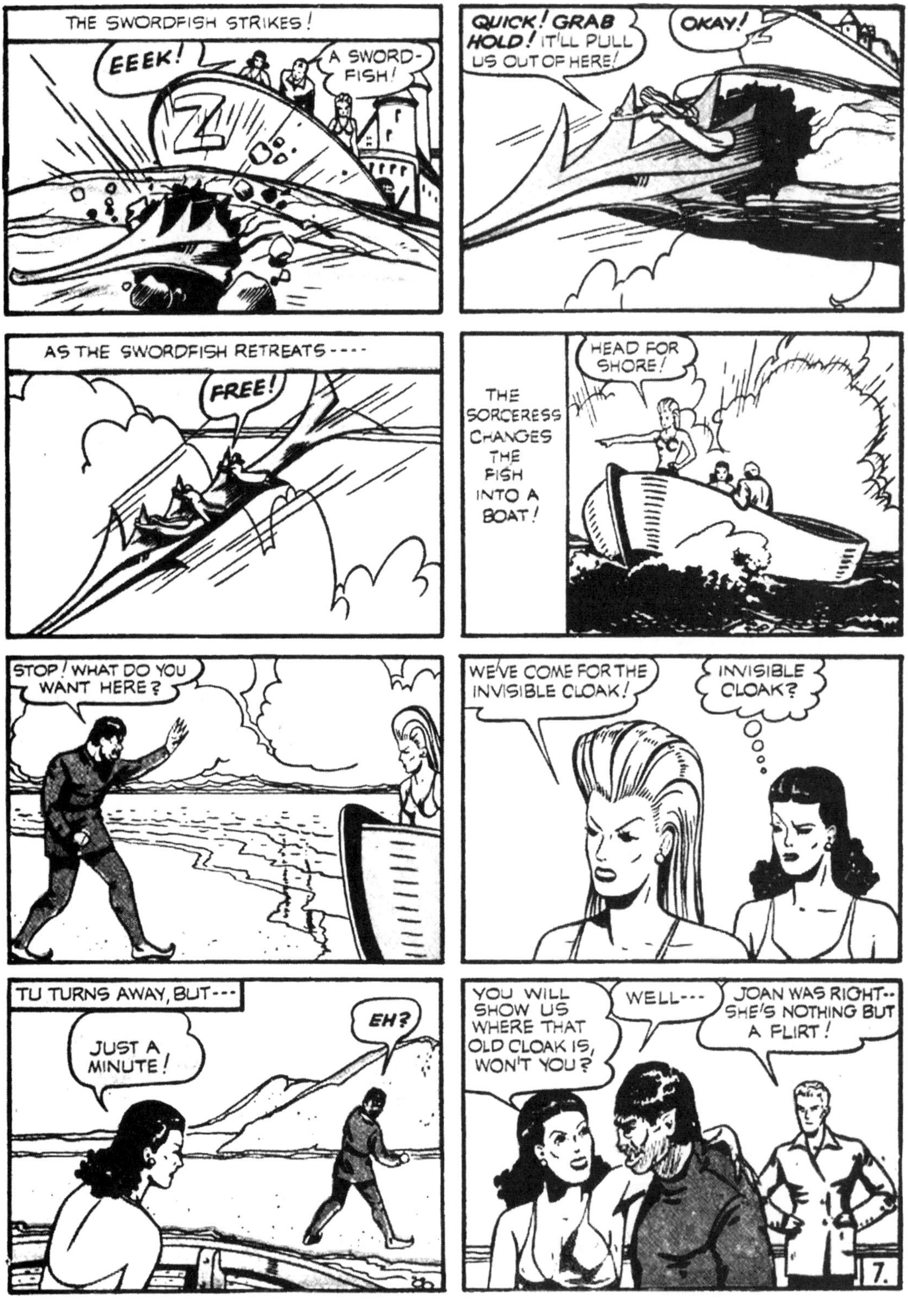
THE SWORDFISH STRIKES!
EEEK!
A SWORD-FISH!
QUICK! GRAB HOLD! IT'LL PULL US OUT OF HERE!
OKAY!
AS THE SWORDFISH RETREATS----
FREE!
THE SORCERESS CHANGES THE FISH INTO A BOAT!
HEAD FOR SHORE!
STOP! WHAT DO YOU WANT HERE?
WE'VE COME FOR THE INVISIBLE CLOAK!
INVISIBLE CLOAK?
TU TURNS AWAY, BUT---
JUST A MINUTE!
EH?
YOU WILL SHOW US WHERE THAT OLD CLOAK IS, WON'T YOU?
WELL---
JOAN WAS RIGHT-- SHE'S NOTHING BUT A FLIRT!
7.

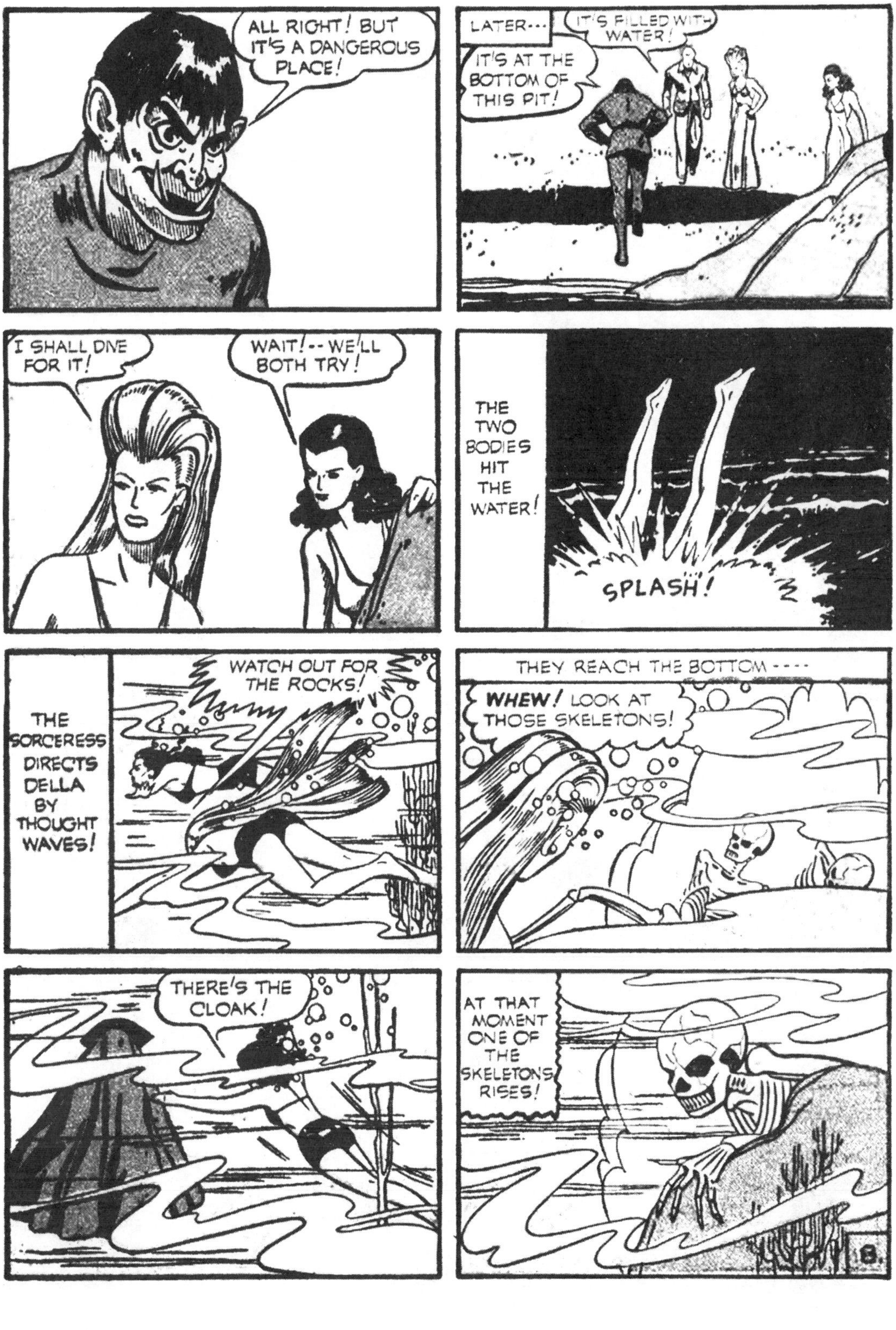
ALL RIGHT! BUT IT'S A DANGEROUS PLACE!
LATER---
IT'S AT THE BOTTOM OF THIS PIT!
IT'S FILLED WITH WATER!
I SHALL DIVE FOR IT!
WAIT!--WE'LL BOTH TRY!
THE TWO BODIES HIT THE WATER!
SPLASH!
THE SORCERESS DIRECTS DELLA BY THOUGHT WAVES!
WATCH OUT FOR THE ROCKS!
THEY REACH THE BOTTOM----
WHEW! LOOK AT THOSE SKELETONS!
THERE'S THE CLOAK!
AT THAT MOMENT ONE OF THE SKELETONS RISES!
8.

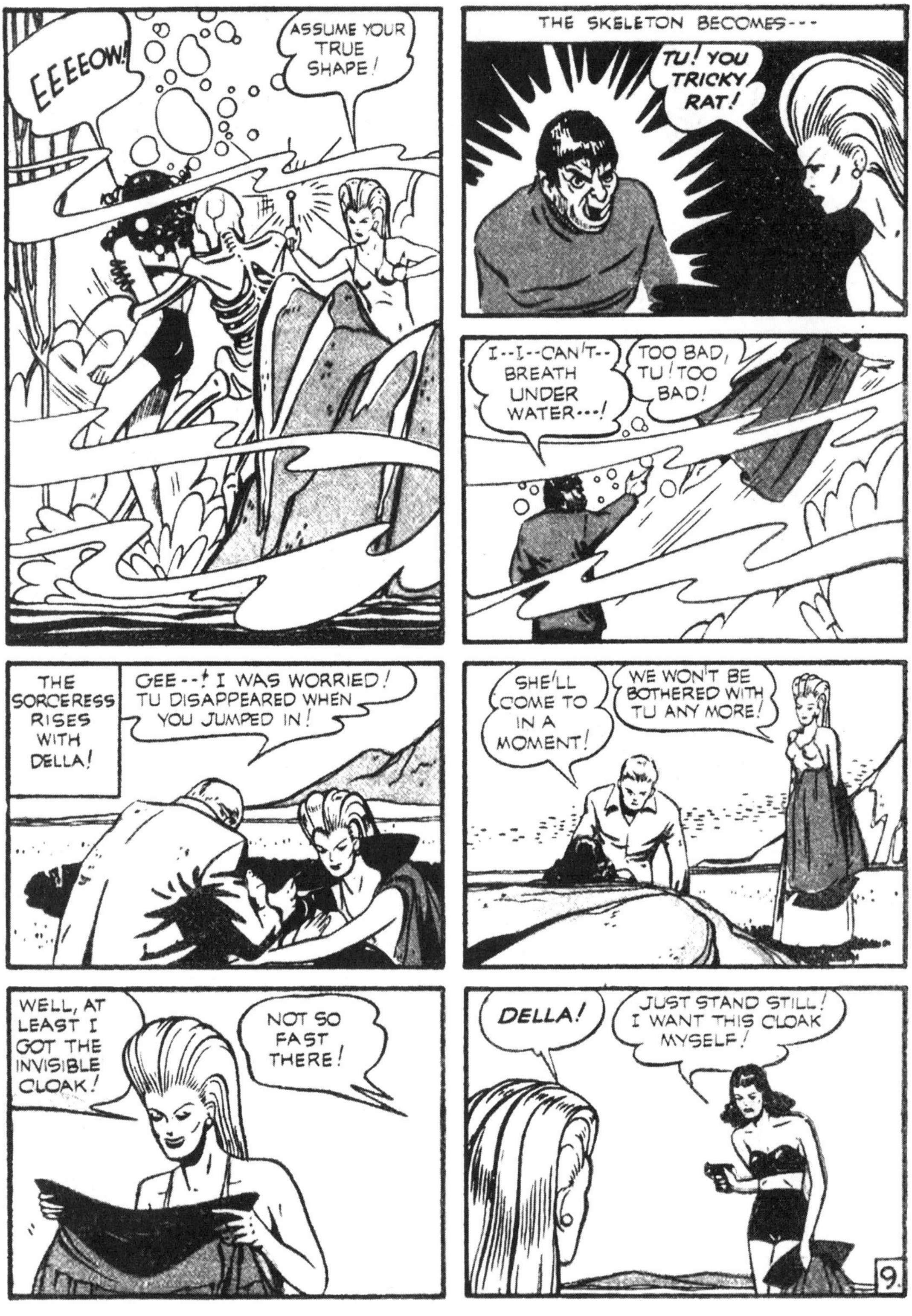
EEEEOW!
ASSUME YOUR TRUE SHAPE!
THE SKELETON BECOMES---
TU! YOU TRICKY RAT!
I--I--CAN'T--BREATH UNDER WATER---!
TOO BAD, TU! TOO BAD!
THE SORCERESS RISES WITH DELLA!
GEE--! I WAS WORRIED! TU DISAPPEARED WHEN YOU JUMPED IN!
SHE'LL COME TO IN A MOMENT!
WE WON'T BE BOTHERED WITH TU ANY MORE!
WELL, AT LEAST I GOT THE INVISIBLE CLOAK!
NOT SO FAST THERE!
DELLA!
JUST STAND STILL! I WANT THIS CLOAK MYSELF!
9.

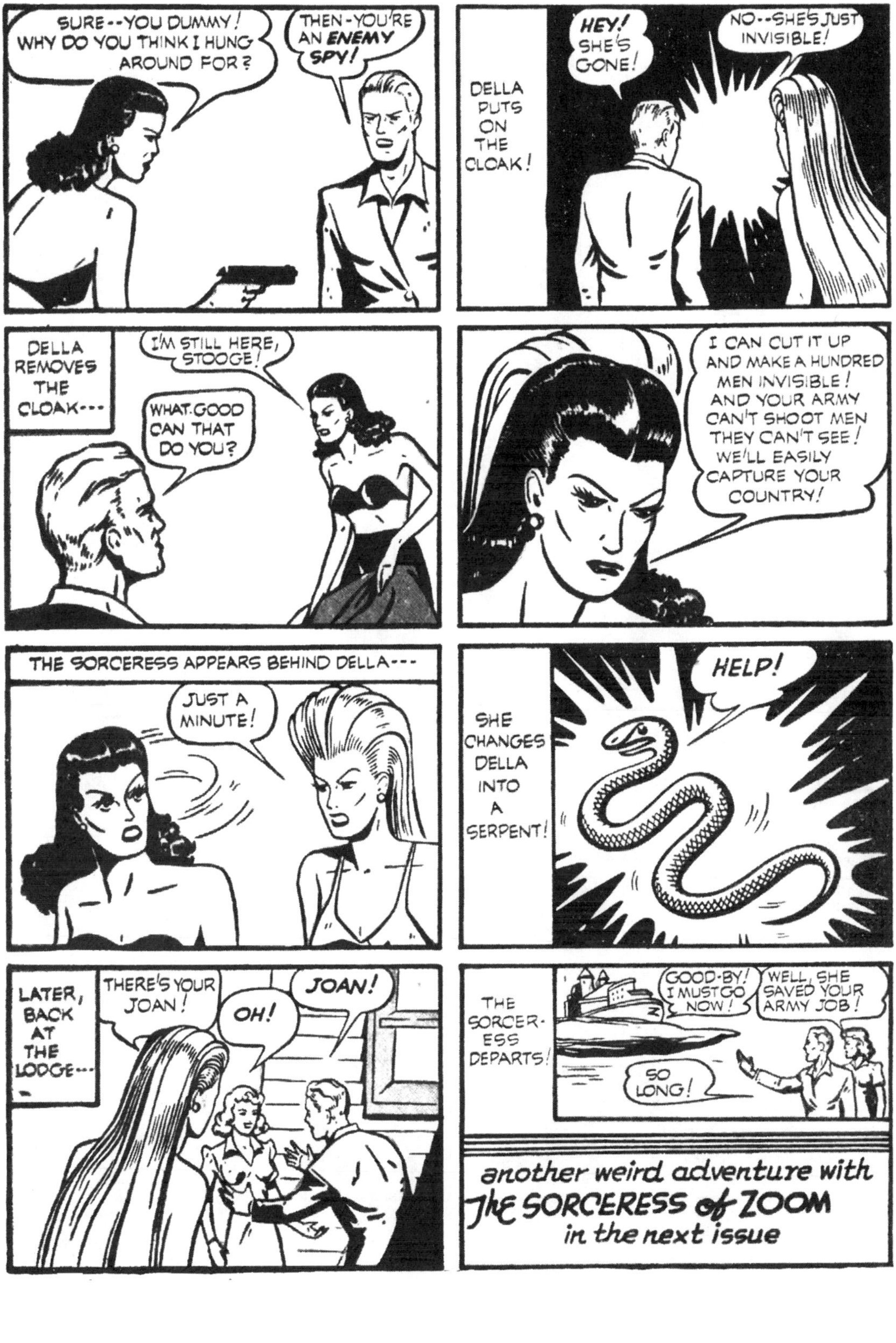
SURE--YOU DUMMY! WHY DO YOU THINK I HUNG AROUND FOR?
THEN-YOU'RE AN ENEMY SPY!
DELLA PUTS ON THE CLOAK!
HEY! SHE'S GONE!
NO--SHE'S JUST INVISIBLE!
DELLA REMOVES THE CLOAK---
I'M STILL HERE, STOOGE!
WHAT GOOD CAN THAT DO YOU?
I CAN CUT IT UP AND MAKE A HUNDRED MEN INVISIBLE! AND YOUR ARMY CAN'T SHOOT MEN THEY CAN'T SEE! WE'LL EASILY CAPTURE YOUR COUNTRY!
THE SORCERESS APPEARS BEHIND DELLA---
JUST A MINUTE!
SHE CHANGES DELLA INTO A SERPENT!
HELP!
LATER, BACK AT THE LODGE---
THERE'S YOUR JOAN!
JOAN!
OH!
THE SORCERESS DEPARTS!
GOOD-BY! I MUST GO NOW!
WELL, SHE SAVED YOUR ARMY JOB!
SO LONG!
another weird adventure with
THE SORCERESS of ZOOM
in the next issue

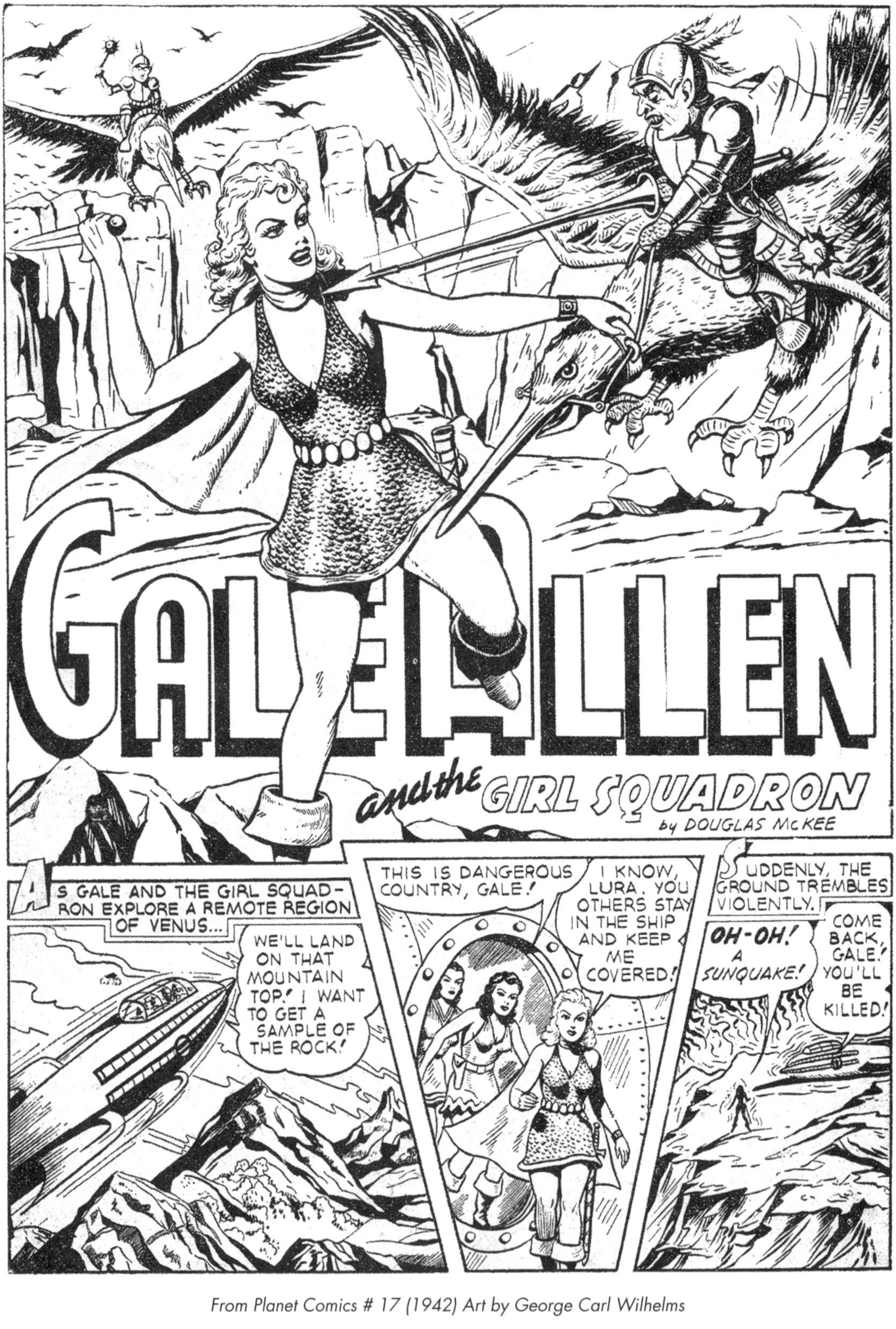
GALE ALLEN
and the GIRL SQUADRON
by DOUGLAS McKEE
AS GALE AND THE GIRL SQUADRON EXPLORE A REMOTE REGION OF VENUS...
WE'LL LAND ON THAT MOUNTAIN TOP! I WANT TO GET A SAMPLE OF THE ROCK!
THIS IS DANGEROUS COUNTRY, GALE!
I KNOW, LURA. YOU OTHERS STAY IN THE SHIP AND KEEP ME COVERED!
SUDDENLY, THE GROUND TREMBLES VIOLENTLY.
OH-OH! A SUNQUAKE!
COME BACK, GALE! YOU'LL BE KILLED!

From Planet Comics # 17 (1942) Art by George Carl Wilhelms

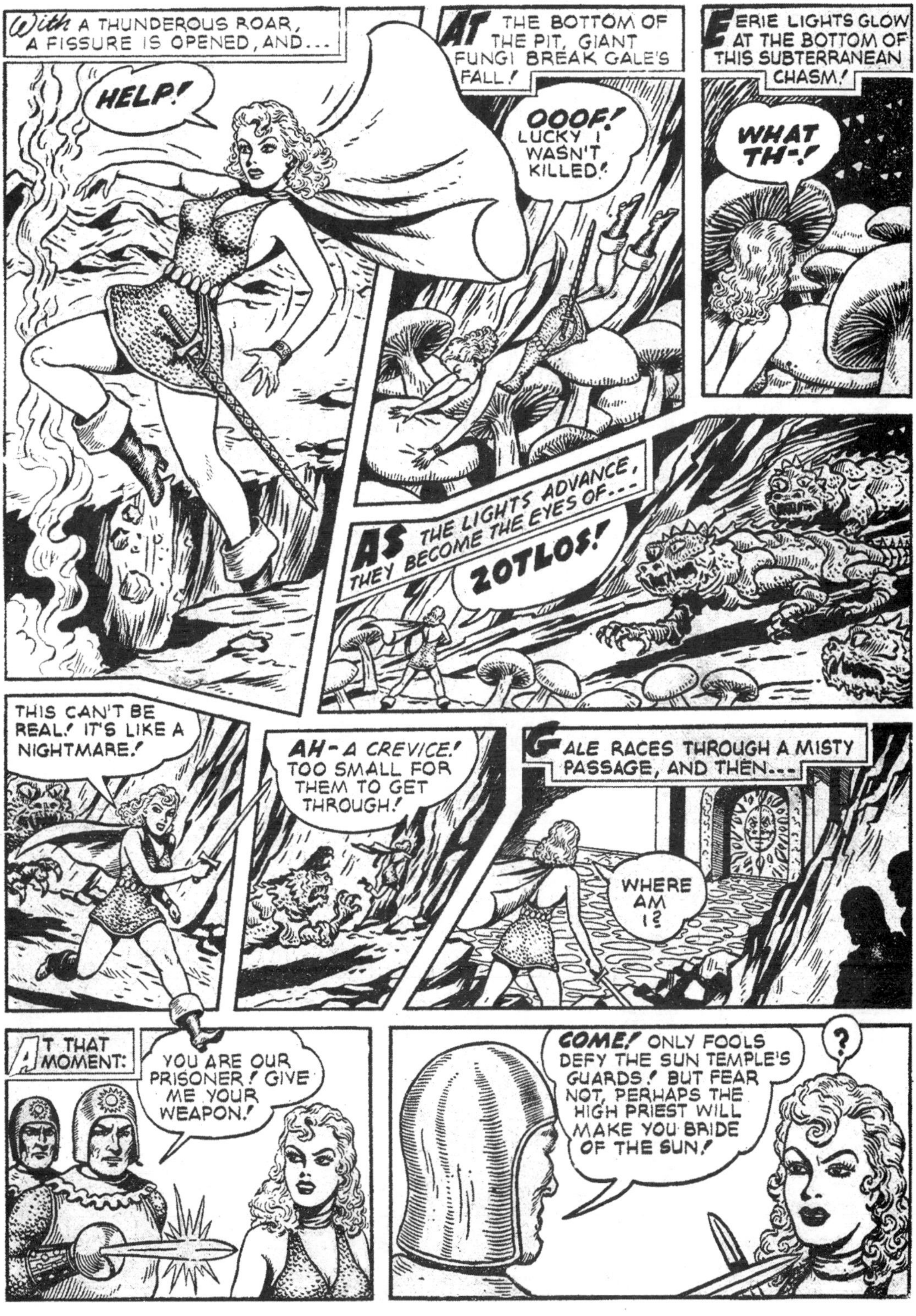

WITH A THUNDEROUS ROAR, A FISSURE IS OPENED, AND...
HELP!
AT THE BOTTOM OF THE PIT, GIANT FUNGI BREAK GALE'S FALL!
OOOF! LUCKY I WASN'T KILLED!
EERIE LIGHTS GLOW AT THE BOTTOM OF THIS SUBTERRANEAN CHASM!
WHAT TH-!
AS THE LIGHTS ADVANCE, THEY BECOME THE EYES OF...
ZOTLOS!
THIS CAN'T BE REAL! IT'S LIKE A NIGHTMARE!
AH- A CREVICE! TOO SMALL FOR THEM TO GET THROUGH!
GALE RACES THROUGH A MISTY PASSAGE, AND THEN...
WHERE AM I?
AT THAT MOMENT:
YOU ARE OUR PRISONER! GIVE ME YOUR WEAPON!
COME! ONLY FOOLS DEFY THE SUN TEMPLE'S GUARDS! BUT FEAR NOT, PERHAPS THE HIGH PRIEST WILL MAKE YOU BRIDE OF THE SUN!
?

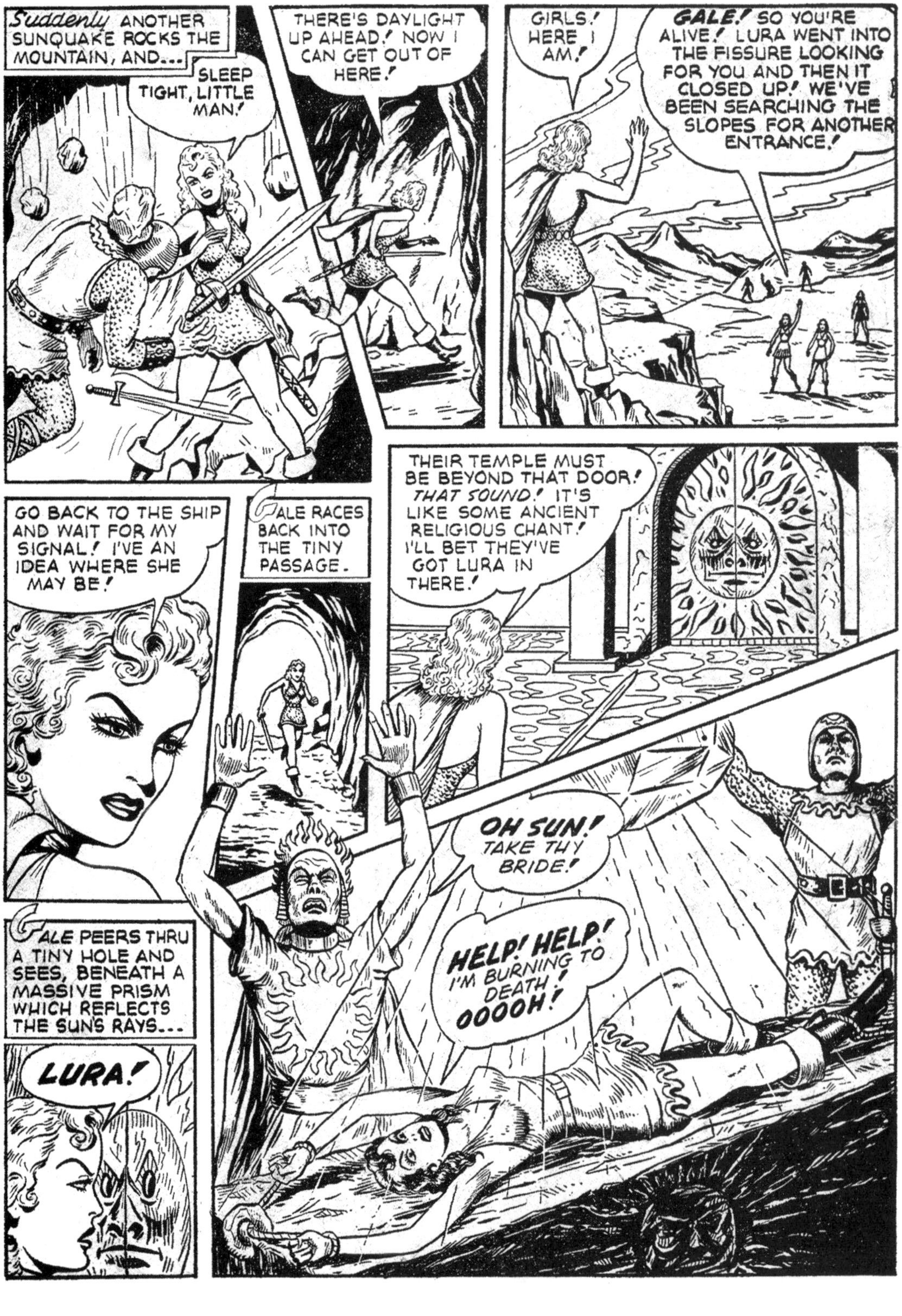
Suddenly ANOTHER SUNQUAKE ROCKS THE MOUNTAIN, AND...
SLEEP TIGHT, LITTLE MAN!
THERE'S DAYLIGHT UP AHEAD! NOW I CAN GET OUT OF HERE!
GIRLS! HERE I AM!
GALE! SO YOU'RE ALIVE! LURA WENT INTO THE FISSURE LOOKING FOR YOU AND THEN IT CLOSED UP! WE'VE BEEN SEARCHING THE SLOPES FOR ANOTHER ENTRANCE!
GO BACK TO THE SHIP AND WAIT FOR MY SIGNAL! I'VE AN IDEA WHERE SHE MAY BE!
GALE RACES BACK INTO THE TINY PASSAGE.
THEIR TEMPLE MUST BE BEYOND THAT DOOR! THAT SOUND! IT'S LIKE SOME ANCIENT RELIGIOUS CHANT! I'LL BET THEY'VE GOT LURA IN THERE!
GALE PEERS THRU A TINY HOLE AND SEES, BENEATH A MASSIVE PRISM WHICH REFLECTS THE SUN'S RAYS...
LURA!
OH SUN! TAKE THY BRIDE!
HELP! HELP! I'M BURNING TO DEATH! OOOOH!

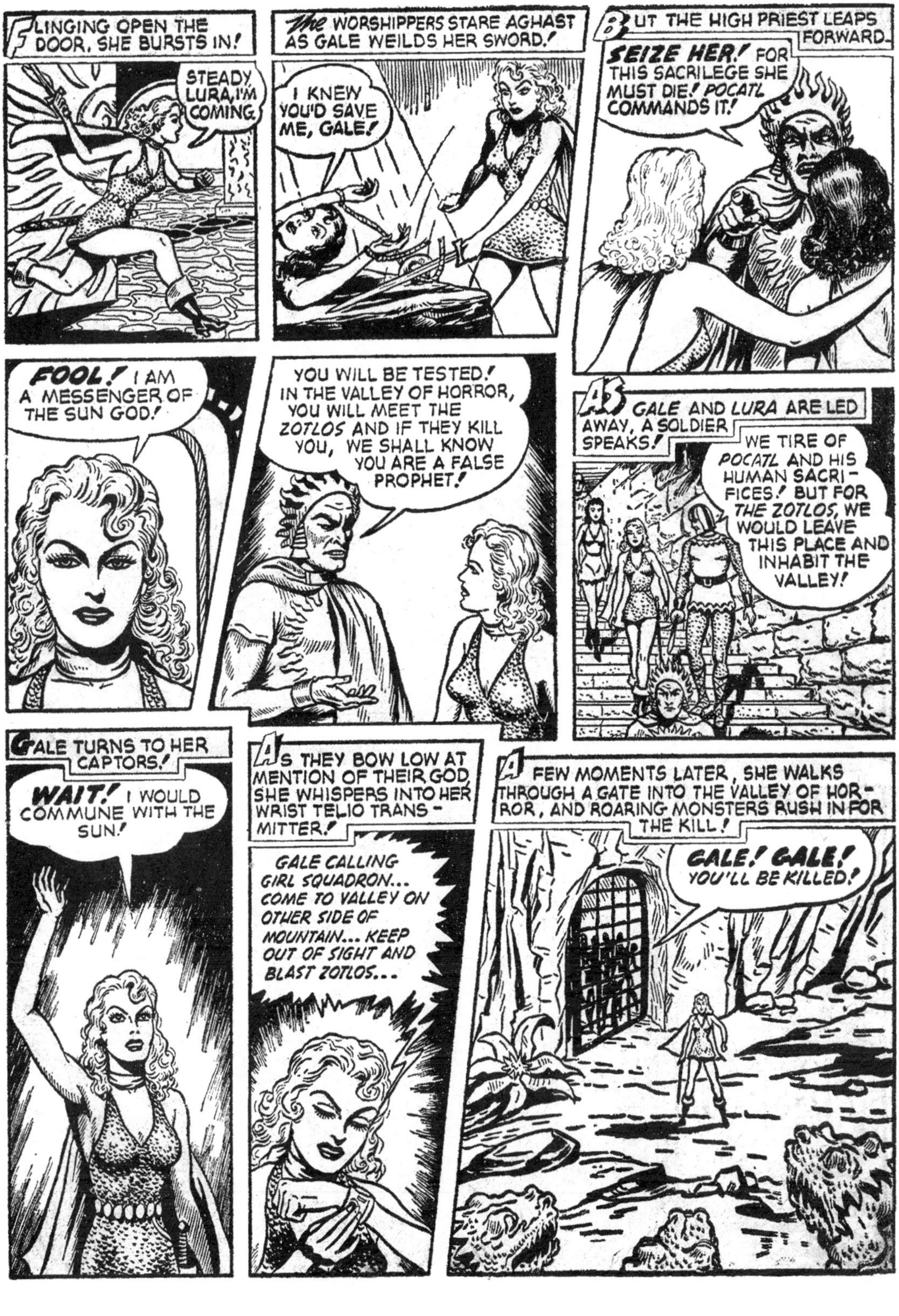
FLINGING OPEN THE DOOR, SHE BURSTS IN!
STEADY, LURA, I'M COMING.
THE WORSHIPPERS STARE AGHAST AS GALE WEILDS HER SWORD!
I KNEW YOU'D SAVE ME, GALE!
BUT THE HIGH PRIEST LEAPS FORWARD.
SEIZE HER! FOR THIS SACRILEGE SHE MUST DIE! POCATL COMMANDS IT!
FOOL! I AM A MESSENGER OF THE SUN GOD!
YOU WILL BE TESTED! IN THE VALLEY OF HORROR, YOU WILL MEET THE ZOTLOS AND IF THEY KILL YOU, WE SHALL KNOW YOU ARE A FALSE PROPHET!
AS GALE AND LURA ARE LED AWAY, A SOLDIER SPEAKS!
WE TIRE OF POCATL AND HIS HUMAN SACRI-FICES! BUT FOR THE ZOTLOS, WE WOULD LEAVE THIS PLACE AND INHABIT THE VALLEY!
GALE TURNS TO HER CAPTORS!
WAIT! I WOULD COMMUNE WITH THE SUN!
AS THEY BOW LOW AT MENTION OF THEIR GOD SHE WHISPERS INTO HER WRIST TELIO TRANS-MITTER!
GALE CALLING GIRL SQUADRON... COME TO VALLEY ON OTHER SIDE OF MOUNTAIN... KEEP OUT OF SIGHT AND BLAST ZOTLOS...
A FEW MOMENTS LATER, SHE WALKS THROUGH A GATE INTO THE VALLEY OF HOR-ROR, AND ROARING MONSTERS RUSH IN FOR THE KILL!
GALE! GALE! YOU'LL BE KILLED!

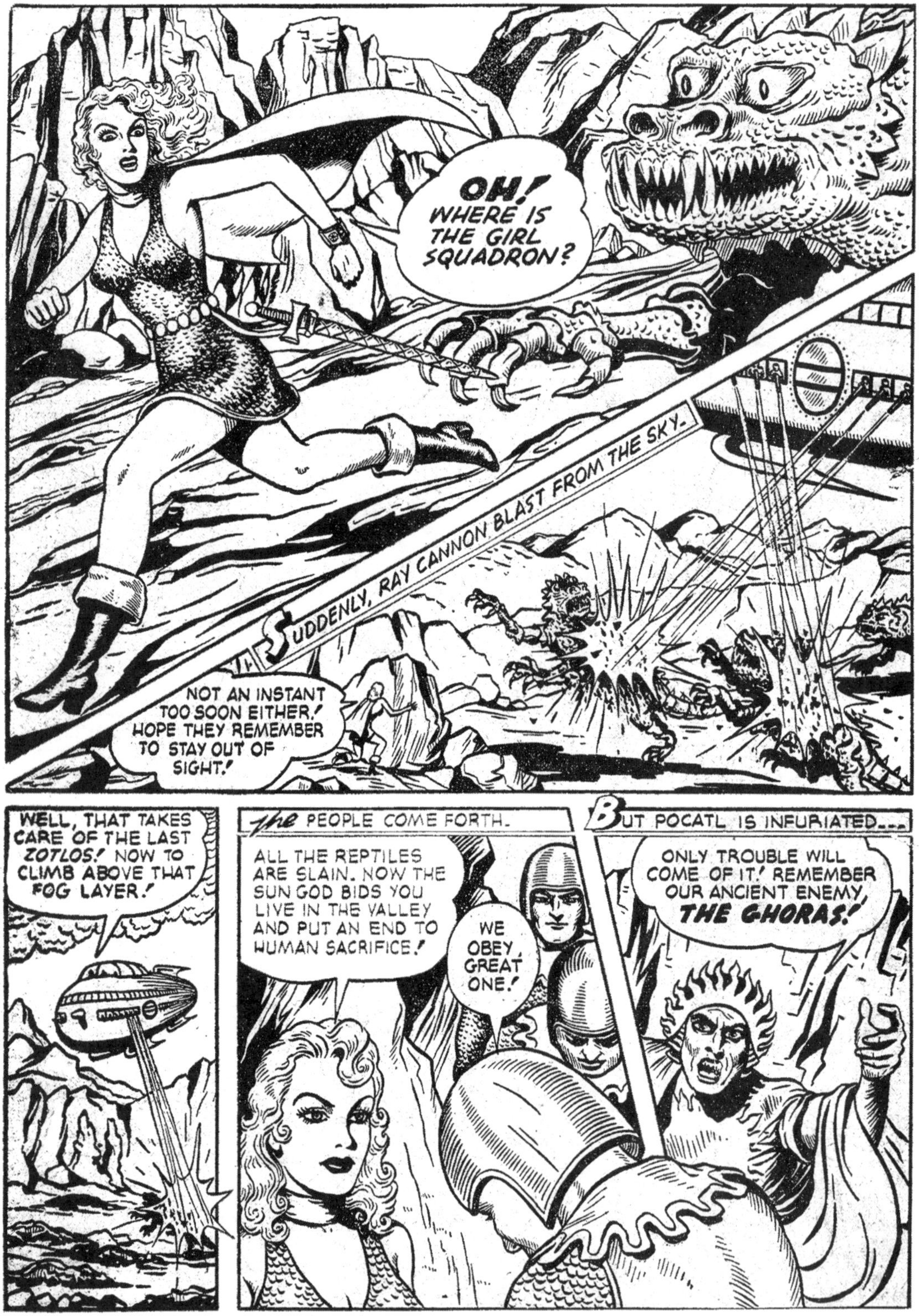
OH! WHERE IS THE GIRL SQUADRON?
SUDDENLY, RAY CANNON BLAST FROM THE SKY.
NOT AN INSTANT TOO SOON EITHER! HOPE THEY REMEMBER TO STAY OUT OF SIGHT!
WELL, THAT TAKES CARE OF THE LAST ZOTLOS! NOW TO CLIMB ABOVE THAT FOG LAYER!
THE PEOPLE COME FORTH.
ALL THE REPTILES ARE SLAIN. NOW THE SUN GOD BIDS YOU LIVE IN THE VALLEY AND PUT AN END TO HUMAN SACRIFICE!
WE OBEY, GREAT ONE!
BUT POCATL IS INFURIATED...
ONLY TROUBLE WILL COME OF IT! REMEMBER OUR ANCIENT ENEMY, THE GHORAS!

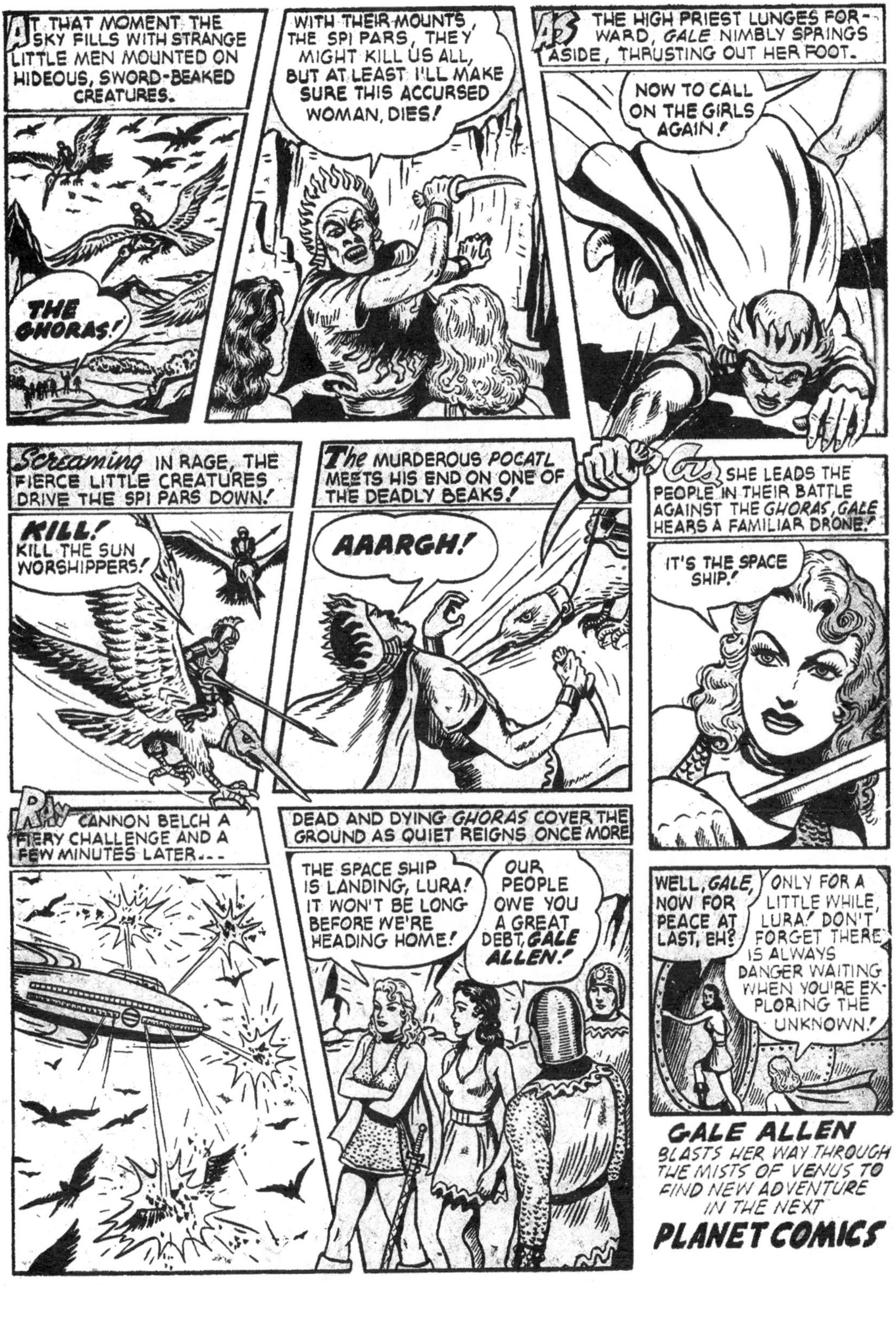
AT THAT MOMENT THE SKY FILLS WITH STRANGE LITTLE MEN MOUNTED ON HIDEOUS, SWORD-BEAKED CREATURES.
THE GHORAS!
WITH THEIR MOUNTS, THE SPI PARS, THEY MIGHT KILL US ALL, BUT AT LEAST I'LL MAKE SURE THIS ACCURSED WOMAN, DIES!
AS THE HIGH PRIEST LUNGES FORWARD, GALE NIMBLY SPRINGS ASIDE, THRUSTING OUT HER FOOT.
NOW TO CALL ON THE GIRLS AGAIN!
Screaming IN RAGE, THE FIERCE LITTLE CREATURES DRIVE THE SPI PARS DOWN!
KILL! KILL THE SUN WORSHIPPERS!
The MURDEROUS POCATL MEETS HIS END ON ONE OF THE DEADLY BEAKS!
AAARGH!
AS SHE LEADS THE PEOPLE IN THEIR BATTLE AGAINST THE GHORAS, GALE HEARS A FAMILIAR DRONE.
IT'S THE SPACE SHIP!
RAY CANNON BELCH A FIERY CHALLENGE AND A FEW MINUTES LATER---
DEAD AND DYING GHORAS COVER THE GROUND AS QUIET REIGNS ONCE MORE
THE SPACE SHIP IS LANDING, LURA! IT WON'T BE LONG BEFORE WE'RE HEADING HOME!
OUR PEOPLE OWE YOU A GREAT DEBT, GALE ALLEN!
WELL, GALE, NOW FOR PEACE AT LAST, EH?
ONLY FOR A LITTLE WHILE, LURA! DON'T FORGET THERE IS ALWAYS DANGER WAITING WHEN YOU'RE EXPLORING THE UNKNOWN!
GALE ALLEN
BLASTS HER WAY THROUGH THE MISTS OF VENUS TO FIND NEW ADVENTURE IN THE NEXT
PLANET COMICS

The
MAGICIAN
from
MARS
by GIUNTA MIRANDO
WAR! UNKNOWN TO EARTH CHAOS REIGNS ON MARS. THAT HORRIBLE— RAVAGING— DISEASE OF MANKIND--- WAR!! BRINGING
CHAOS
DEATH
HORROR
MEANWHILE WE FIND THE LOVED KING OF MARS CONFERRING WITH HIS TRUSTED AMBASSADOR & FRIEND.
—AND REACH OUR MAGICIAN OF MARS AT ANY COST-KAR-LO!- SHE IS THE ONLY ONE WHO CAN AID OUR FIGHT AGAINST THE HOOD & HIS REVOLUTIONISTS
YES SIRE!
—AND SOON KAR-LO IS OFF!

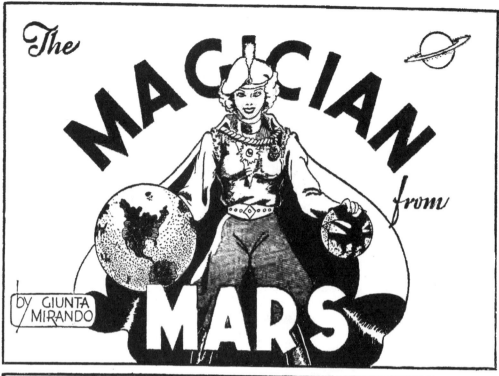

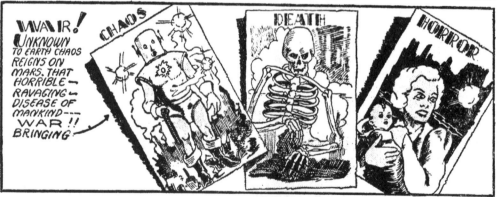

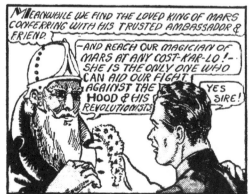

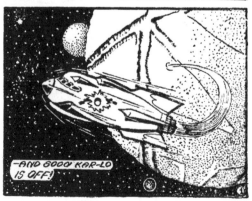

From Amazing Man #11 (1940) Art by John Giunta and Michael Mirando

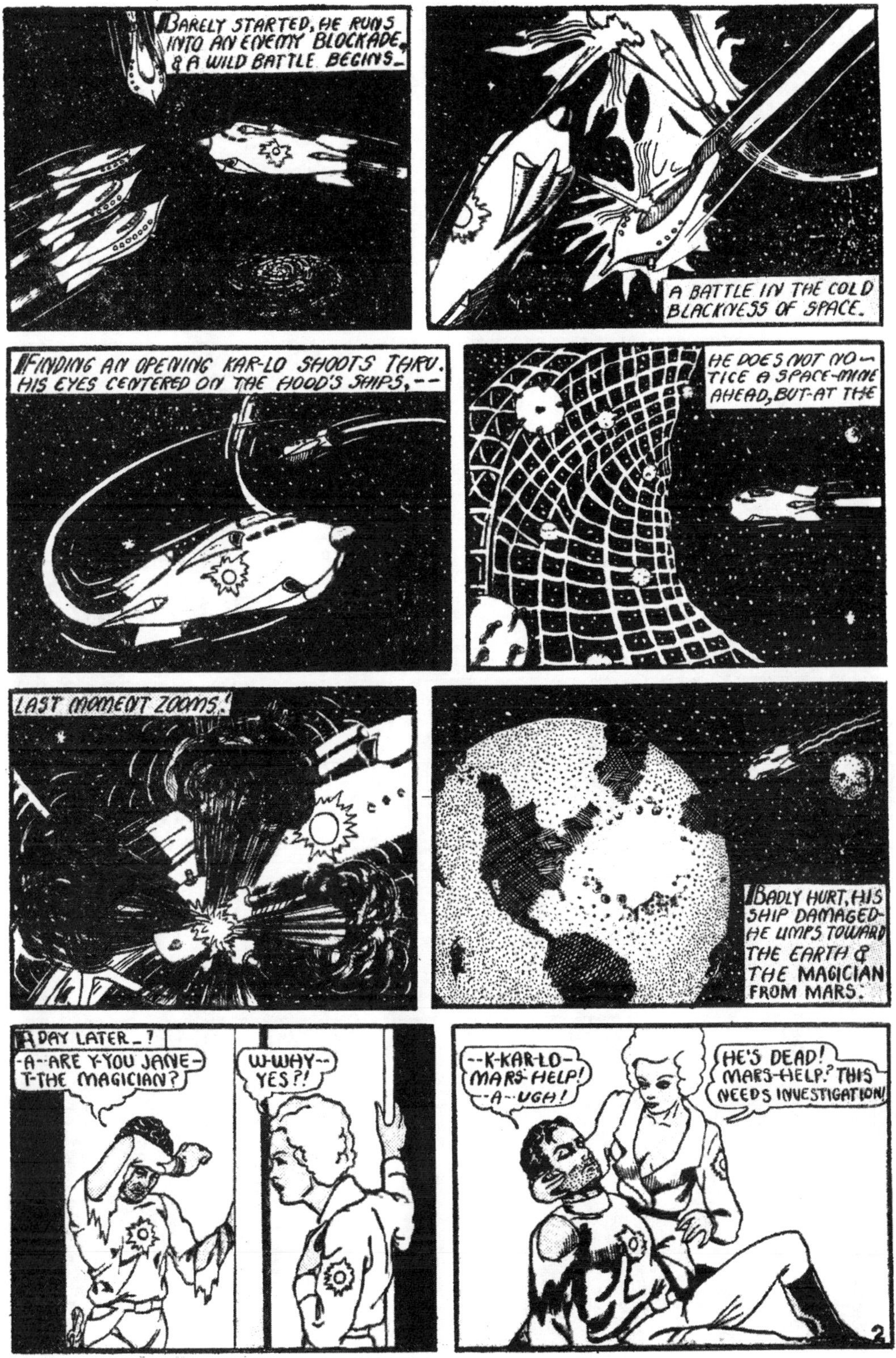
BARELY STARTED, HE RUNS INTO AN ENEMY BLOCKADE, & A WILD BATTLE BEGINS_
A BATTLE IN THE COLD BLACKNESS OF SPACE.
FINDING AN OPENING KAR-LO SHOOTS THRU. HIS EYES CENTERED ON THE HOOD'S SHIPS,--
HE DOES NOT NO-TICE A SPACE-MINE AHEAD, BUT-AT THE
LAST MOMENT ZOOMS!
BADLY HURT, HIS SHIP DAMAGED- HE LIMPS TOWARD THE EARTH & THE MAGICIAN FROM MARS.
A DAY LATER_?
-A--ARE Y-YOU JANE T-THE MAGICIAN?
W-WHY-- YES?!
--K-KAR-LO- MARS-HELP! --A--UGH!
HE'S DEAD! MARS-HELP? THIS NEEDS INVESTIGATION!
2

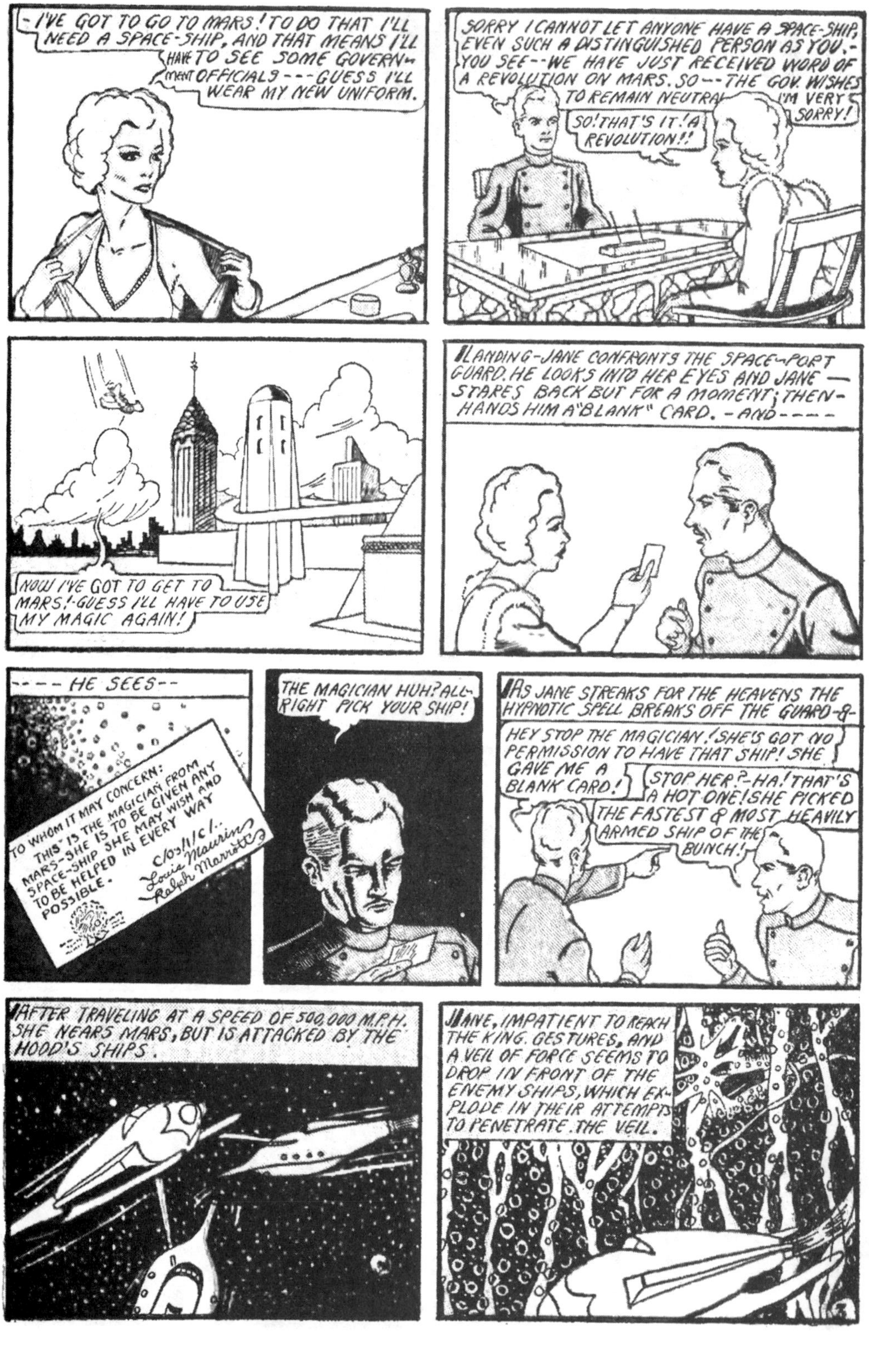
-I'VE GOT TO GO TO MARS! TO DO THAT I'LL NEED A SPACE-SHIP, AND THAT MEANS I'LL HAVE TO SEE SOME GOVERNMENT OFFICIALS---GUESS I'LL WEAR MY NEW UNIFORM.
SORRY I CANNOT LET ANYONE HAVE A SPACE-SHIP, EVEN SUCH A DISTINGUISHED PERSON AS YOU.-YOU SEE--WE HAVE JUST RECEIVED WORD OF A REVOLUTION ON MARS. SO--THE GOV. WISHES TO REMAIN NEUTRA
I'M VERY SORRY!
SO! THAT'S IT! A REVOLUTION!!
NOW I'VE GOT TO GET TO MARS!-GUESS I'LL HAVE TO USE MY MAGIC AGAIN!
LANDING-JANE CONFRONTS THE SPACE-PORT GUARD. HE LOOKS INTO HER EYES AND JANE—STARES BACK BUT FOR A MOMENT; THEN-HANDS HIM A "BLANK" CARD. -AND----
----HE SEES--
TO WHOM IT MAY CONCERN:
THIS IS THE MAGICIAN FROM MARS-SHE IS TO BE GIVEN ANY SPACE-SHIP SHE MAY WISH AND TO BE HELPED IN EVERY WAY POSSIBLE.
C/O's/1/c/.
Louis Maurin
Ralph Marrotte
THE MAGICIAN HUH? ALL RIGHT PICK YOUR SHIP!
AS JANE STREAKS FOR THE HEAVENS THE HYPNOTIC SPELL BREAKS OFF THE GUARD-&-
HEY STOP THE MAGICIAN! SHE'S GOT NO PERMISSION TO HAVE THAT SHIP! SHE GAVE ME A BLANK CARD!
STOP HER?-HA! THAT'S A HOT ONE! SHE PICKED THE FASTEST & MOST HEAVILY ARMED SHIP OF THE BUNCH!
AFTER TRAVELING AT A SPEED OF 500,000 M.P.H. SHE NEARS MARS, BUT IS ATTACKED BY THE HOOD'S SHIPS.
JANE, IMPATIENT TO REACH THE KING. GESTURES, AND A VEIL OF FORCE SEEMS TO DROP IN FRONT OF THE ENEMY SHIPS, WHICH EXPLODE IN THEIR ATTEMPTS TO PENETRATE THE VEIL.
3

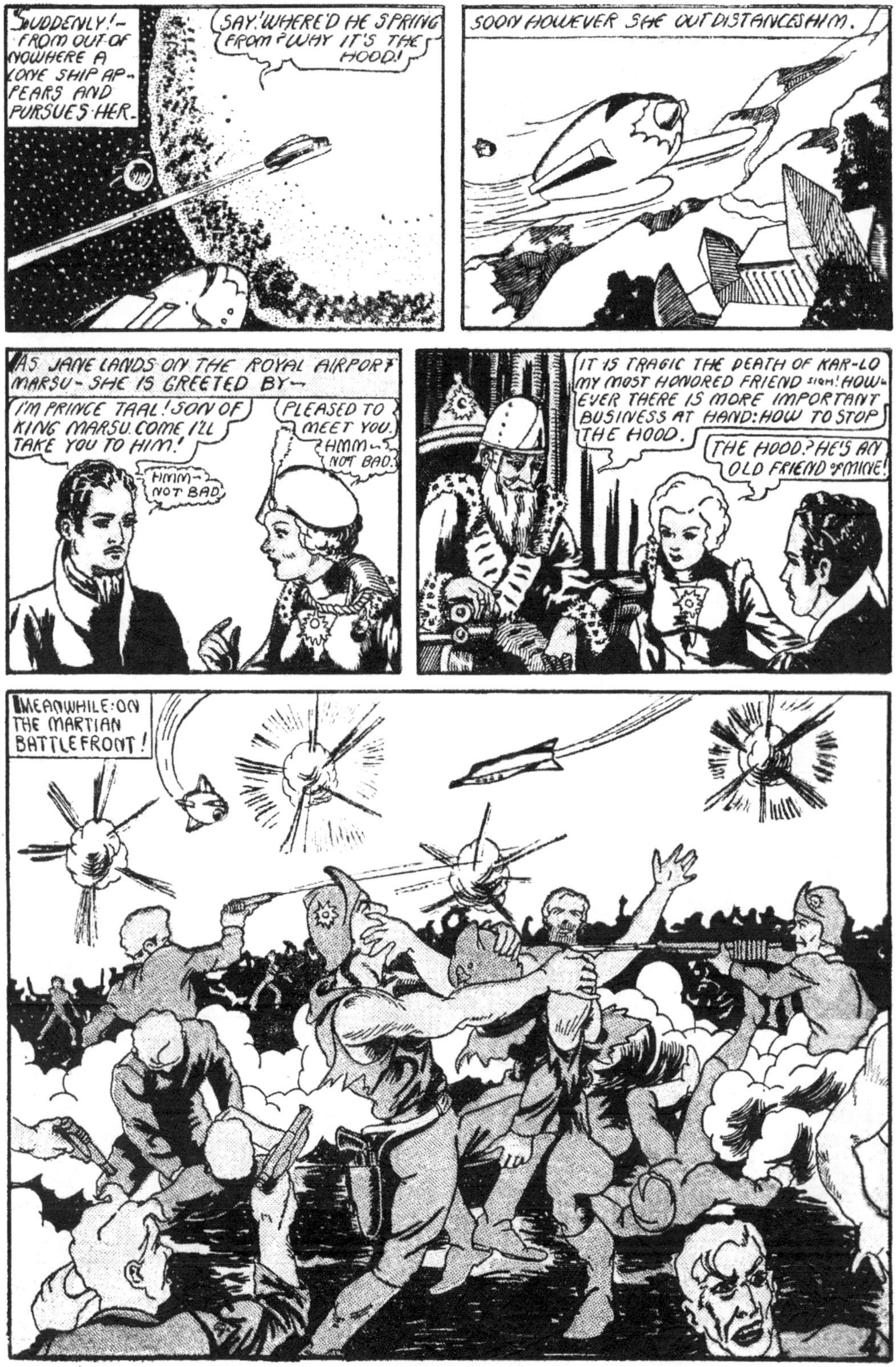
SUDDENLY!— FROM OUT-OF NOWHERE A LONE SHIP AP- PEARS AND PURSUES HER—
SAY! WHERE'D HE SPRING FROM? WHY IT'S THE HOOD!
SOON HOWEVER SHE OUT DISTANCES HIM.
AS JANE LANDS ON THE ROYAL AIRPORT MARSU— SHE IS GREETED BY—
I'M PRINCE TAAL! SON OF KING MARSU. COME I'LL TAKE YOU TO HIM!
PLEASED TO MEET YOU. HMM— NOT BAD.
HMM— NOT BAD.
IT IS TRAGIC THE DEATH OF KAR-LO MY MOST HONORED FRIEND sigh! HOW- EVER THERE IS MORE IMPORTANT BUSINESS AT HAND: HOW TO STOP THE HOOD.
THE HOOD? HE'S AN OLD FRIEND of MINE!
MEANWHILE: ON THE MARTIAN BATTLEFRONT!

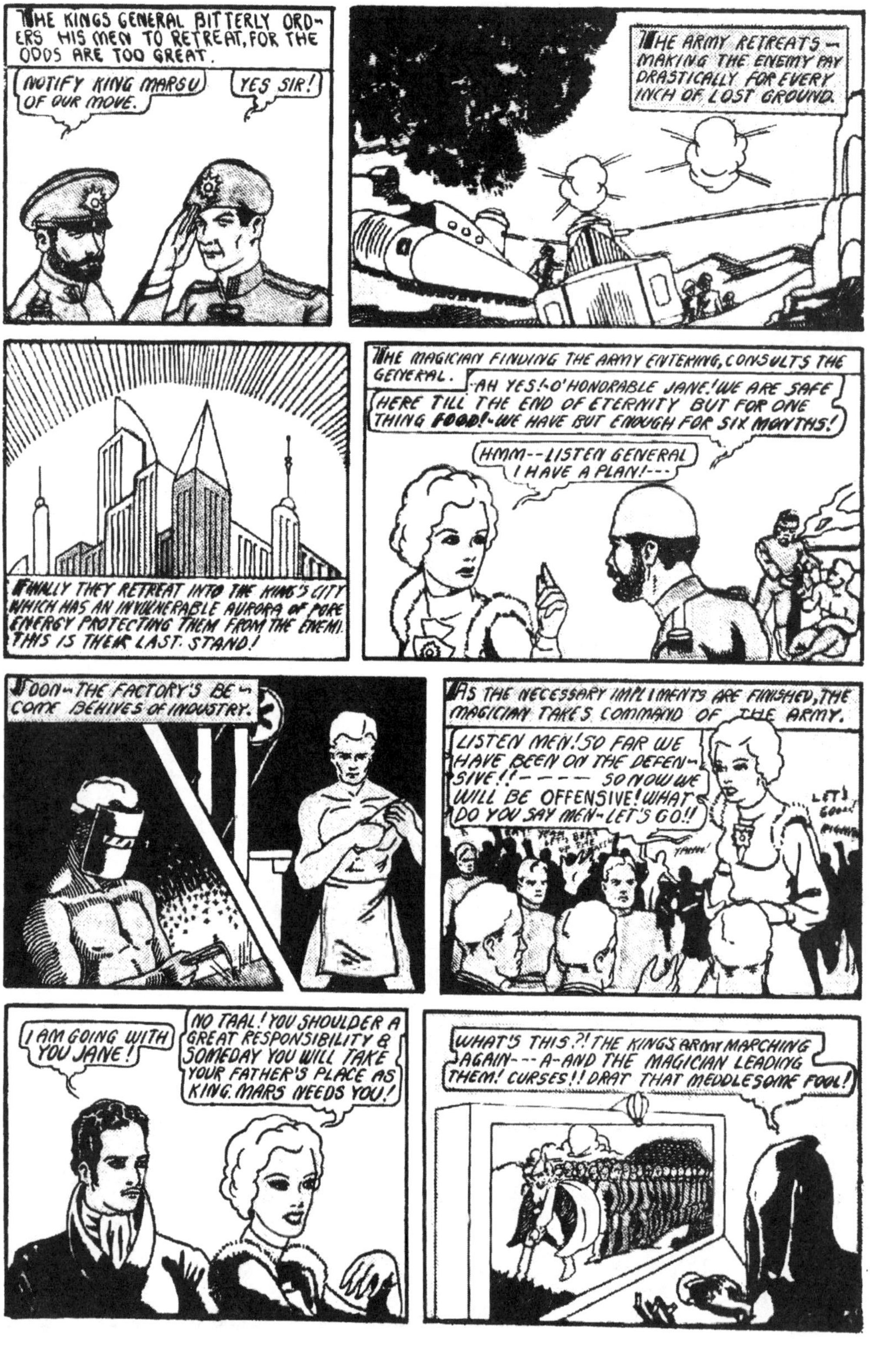
THE KINGS GENERAL BITTERLY ORDERS HIS MEN TO RETREAT, FOR THE ODDS ARE TOO GREAT.
NOTIFY KING MARSU OF OUR MOVE.
YES SIR!
THE ARMY RETREATS — MAKING THE ENEMY PAY DRASTICALLY FOR EVERY INCH OF LOST GROUND.
FINALLY THEY RETREAT INTO THE KING'S CITY WHICH HAS AN INVULNERABLE AURORA OF PURE ENERGY PROTECTING THEM FROM THE ENEMI. THIS IS THEIR LAST. STAND!
THE MAGICIAN FINDING THE ARMY ENTERING, CONSULTS THE GENERAL.
AH YES!-O'HONORABLE JANE! WE ARE SAFE HERE TILL THE END OF ETERNITY BUT FOR ONE THING FOOD!-WE HAVE BUT ENOUGH FOR SIX MONTHS!
HMM--LISTEN GENERAL I HAVE A PLAN!---
SOON-THE FACTORY'S BECOME BEHIVES OF INDUSTRY.
AS THE NECESSARY IMPLIMENTS ARE FINISHED, THE MAGICIAN TAKES COMMAND OF THE ARMY.
LISTEN MEN! SO FAR WE HAVE BEEN ON THE DEFENSIVE!!---- SO NOW WE WILL BE OFFENSIVE! WHAT DO YOU SAY MEN-LET'S GO!!
I AM GOING WITH YOU JANE!
NO TAAL! YOU SHOULDER A GREAT RESPONSIBILITY & SOMEDAY YOU WILL TAKE YOUR FATHER'S PLACE AS KING. MARS NEEDS YOU!
WHAT'S THIS?! THE KING'S ARMY MARCHING AGAIN---A-AND THE MAGICIAN LEADING THEM! CURSES!! DRAT THAT MEDDLESOME FOOL!

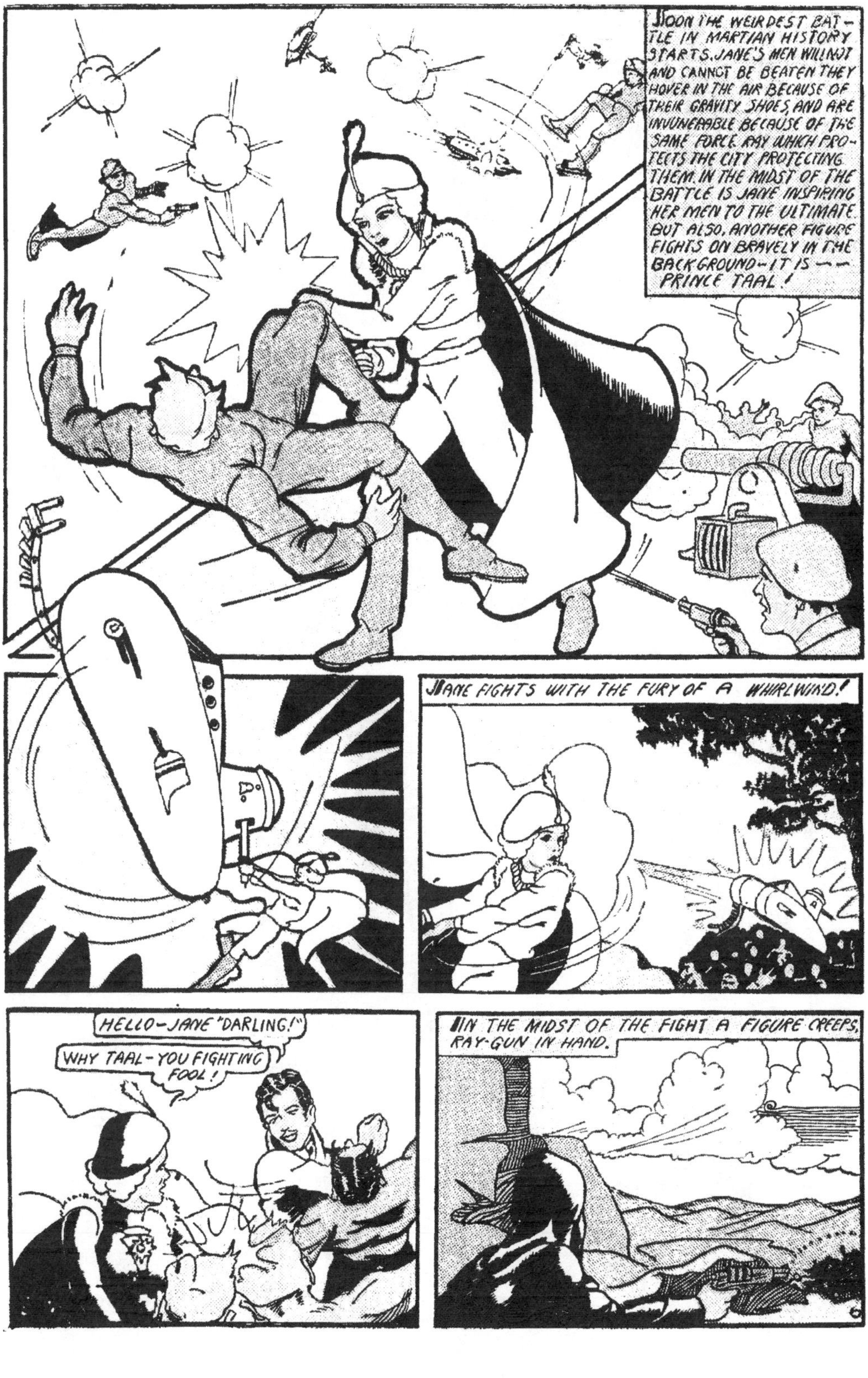
SOON THE WEIRDEST BATTLE IN MARTIAN HISTORY STARTS. JANE'S MEN WILL NOT AND CANNOT BE BEATEN THEY HOVER IN THE AIR BECAUSE OF THEIR GRAVITY SHOES, AND ARE INVULNERABLE BECAUSE OF THE SAME FORCE RAY WHICH PROTECTS THE CITY PROTECTING THEM. IN THE MIDST OF THE BATTLE IS JANE INSPIRING HER MEN TO THE ULTIMATE. BUT ALSO, ANOTHER FIGURE FIGHTS ON BRAVELY IN THE BACKGROUND - IT IS -- PRINCE TAAL!
JANE FIGHTS WITH THE FURY OF A WHIRLWIND!
HELLO-JANE "DARLING!"
WHY TAAL-YOU FIGHTING FOOL!
IN THE MIDST OF THE FIGHT A FIGURE CREEPS, RAY-GUN IN HAND.

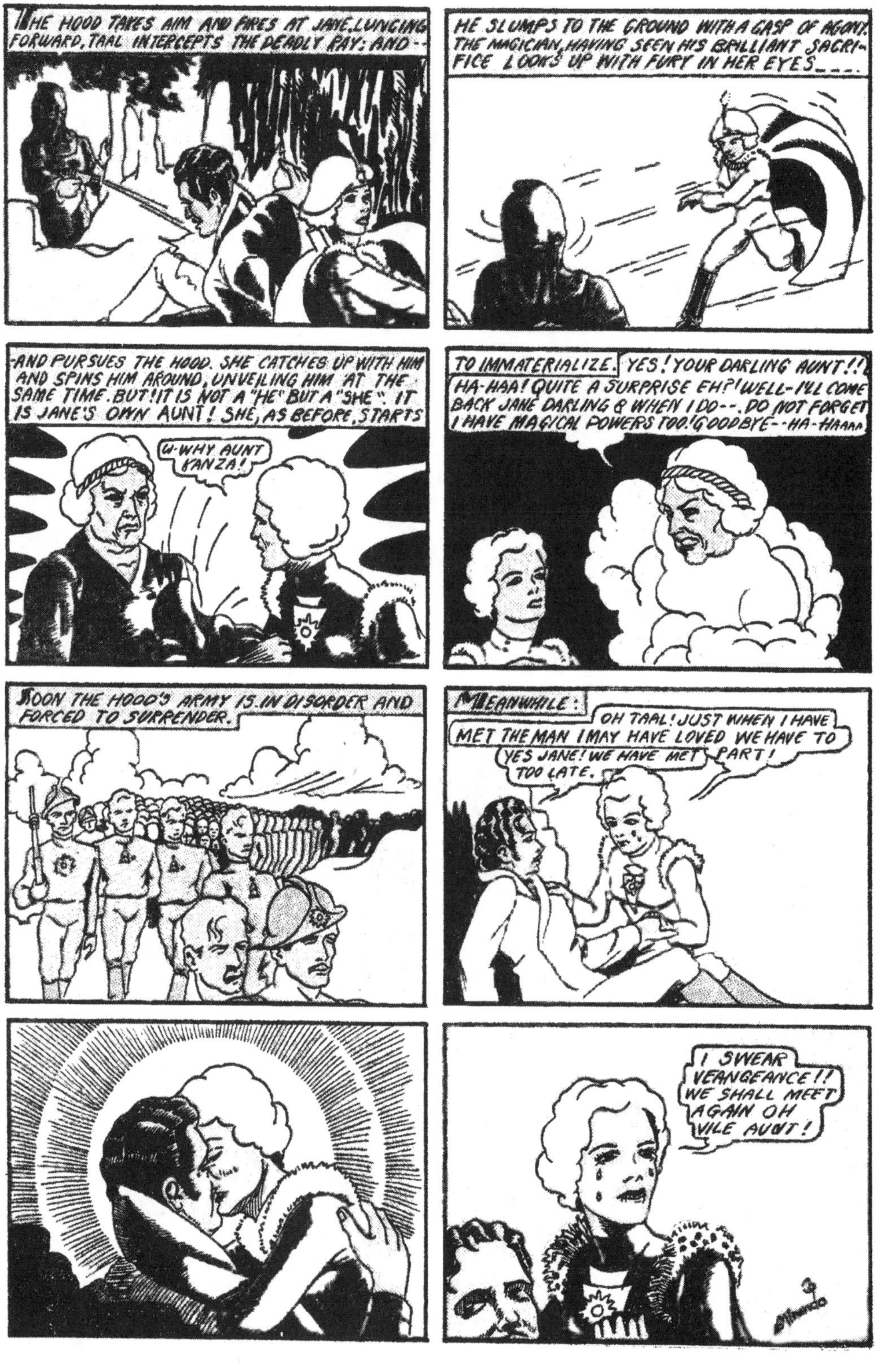
THE HOOD TAKES AIM AND FIRES AT JANE. LUNGING FORWARD, TAAL INTERCEPTS THE DEADLY RAY: AND--
HE SLUMPS TO THE GROUND WITH A GASP OF AGONY. THE MAGICIAN, HAVING SEEN HIS BRILLIANT SACRIFICE LOOKS UP WITH FURY IN HER EYES___.
-AND PURSUES THE HOOD. SHE CATCHES UP WITH HIM AND SPINS HIM AROUND, UNVEILING HIM AT THE SAME TIME. BUT! IT IS NOT A "HE" BUT A "SHE". IT IS JANE'S OWN AUNT! SHE, AS BEFORE, STARTS
W-WHY AUNT KANZA!
TO IMMATERIALIZE.
YES! YOUR DARLING AUNT!! HA-HAA! QUITE A SURPRISE EH?! WELL-I'LL COME BACK JANE DARLING & WHEN I DO--. DO NOT FORGET I HAVE MAGICAL POWERS TOO! GOODBYE--HA-HAAAA
SOON THE HOOD'S ARMY IS IN DISORDER AND FORCED TO SURRENDER.
MEANWHILE:
OH TAAL! JUST WHEN I HAVE MET THE MAN I MAY HAVE LOVED WE HAVE TO PART!
YES JANE! WE HAVE MET TOO LATE.
I SWEAR VEANGEANCE!! WE SHALL MEET AGAIN OH VILE AUNT!

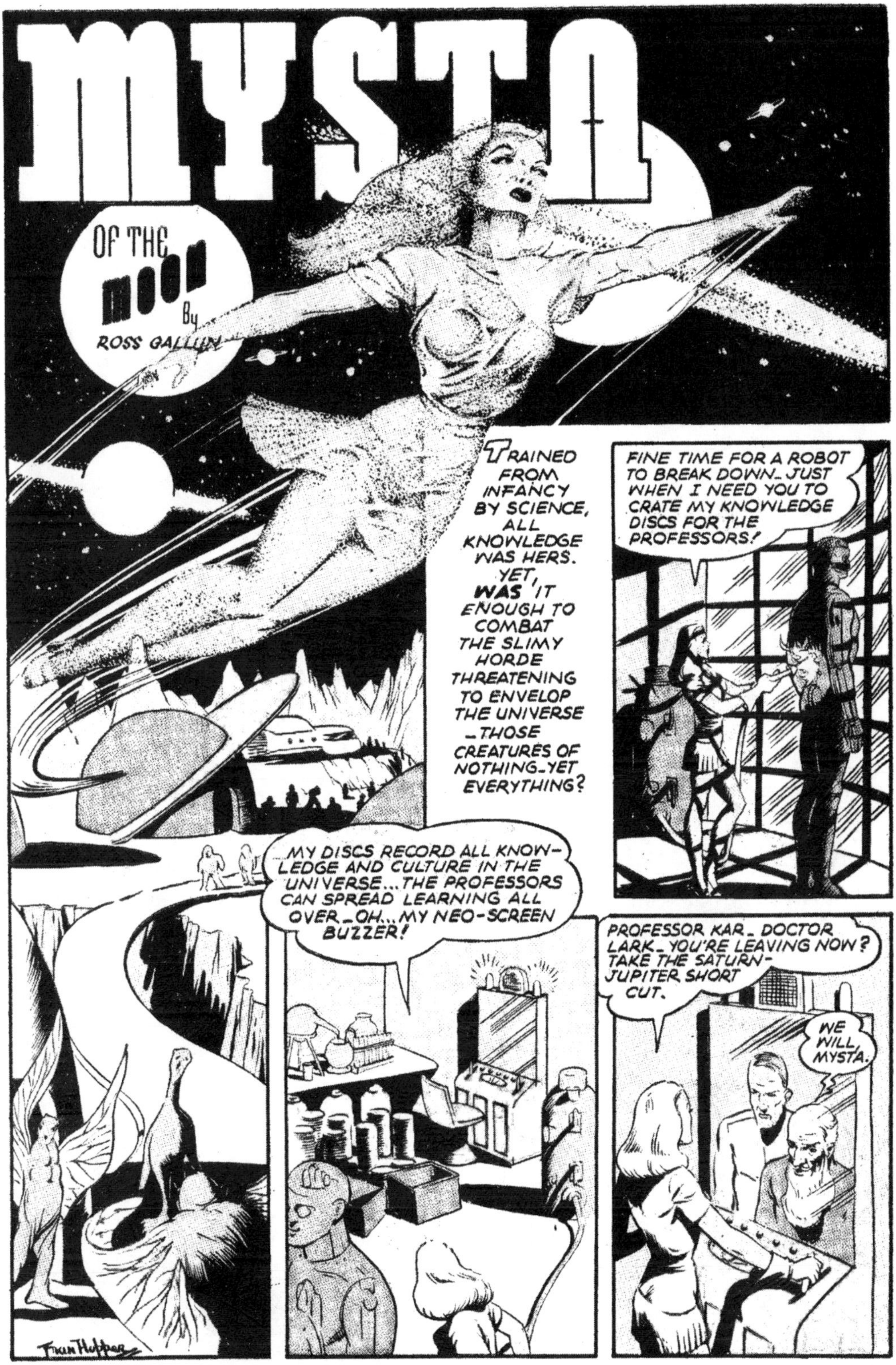
MYSTA
OF THE MOON
By ROSS GALLUN
TRAINED FROM INFANCY BY SCIENCE, ALL KNOWLEDGE WAS HERS. YET, WAS IT ENOUGH TO COMBAT THE SLIMY HORDE THREATENING TO ENVELOP THE UNIVERSE _THOSE CREATURES OF NOTHING_YET EVERYTHING?
FINE TIME FOR A ROBOT TO BREAK DOWN_ JUST WHEN I NEED YOU TO CRATE MY KNOWLEDGE DISCS FOR THE PROFESSORS!
...MY DISCS RECORD ALL KNOW-LEDGE AND CULTURE IN THE UNIVERSE... THE PROFESSORS CAN SPREAD LEARNING ALL OVER_OH... MY NEO-SCREEN BUZZER!
PROFESSOR KAR_ DOCTOR LARK_ YOU'RE LEAVING NOW? TAKE THE SATURN-JUPITER SHORT CUT.
WE WILL, MYSTA.
Fran Hopper

From Planet Comics #38 (1945) Art by Fran Hopper

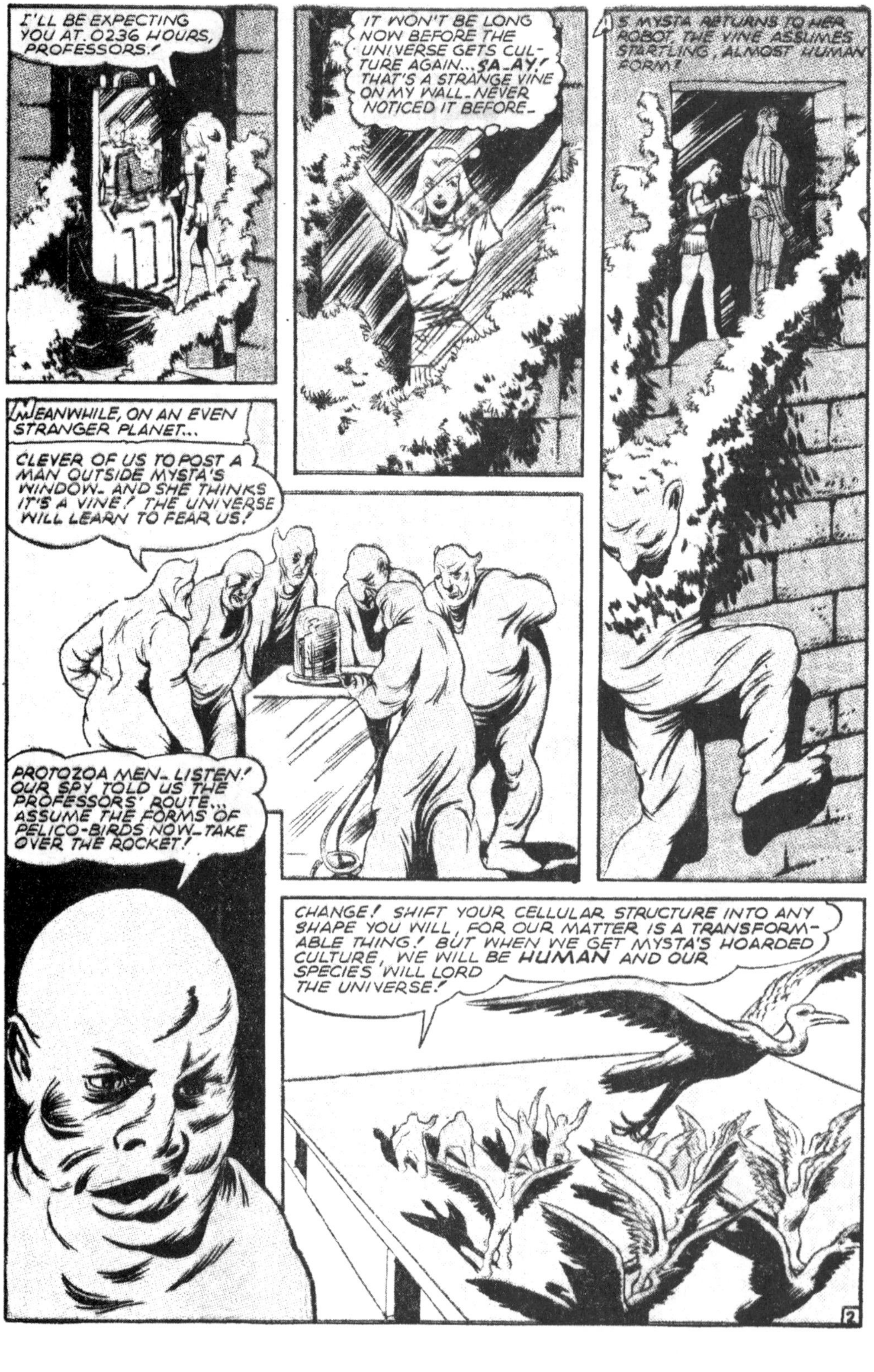
I'LL BE EXPECTING YOU AT 0236 HOURS, PROFESSORS!
IT WON'T BE LONG NOW BEFORE THE UNIVERSE GETS CULTURE AGAIN... SA-AY! THAT'S A STRANGE VINE ON MY WALL- NEVER NOTICED IT BEFORE-
AS MYSTA RETURNS TO HER ROBOT, THE VINE ASSUMES STARTLING, ALMOST HUMAN FORM!
MEANWHILE, ON AN EVEN STRANGER PLANET...
CLEVER OF US TO POST A MAN OUTSIDE MYSTA'S WINDOW- AND SHE THINKS IT'S A VINE! THE UNIVERSE WILL LEARN TO FEAR US!
PROTOZOA MEN- LISTEN! OUR SPY TOLD US THE PROFESSORS' ROUTE... ASSUME THE FORMS OF PELICO-BIRDS NOW- TAKE OVER THE ROCKET!
CHANGE! SHIFT YOUR CELLULAR STRUCTURE INTO ANY SHAPE YOU WILL, FOR OUR MATTER IS A TRANSFORMABLE THING! BUT WHEN WE GET MYSTA'S HOARDED CULTURE, WE WILL BE HUMAN AND OUR SPECIES WILL LORD THE UNIVERSE!
2

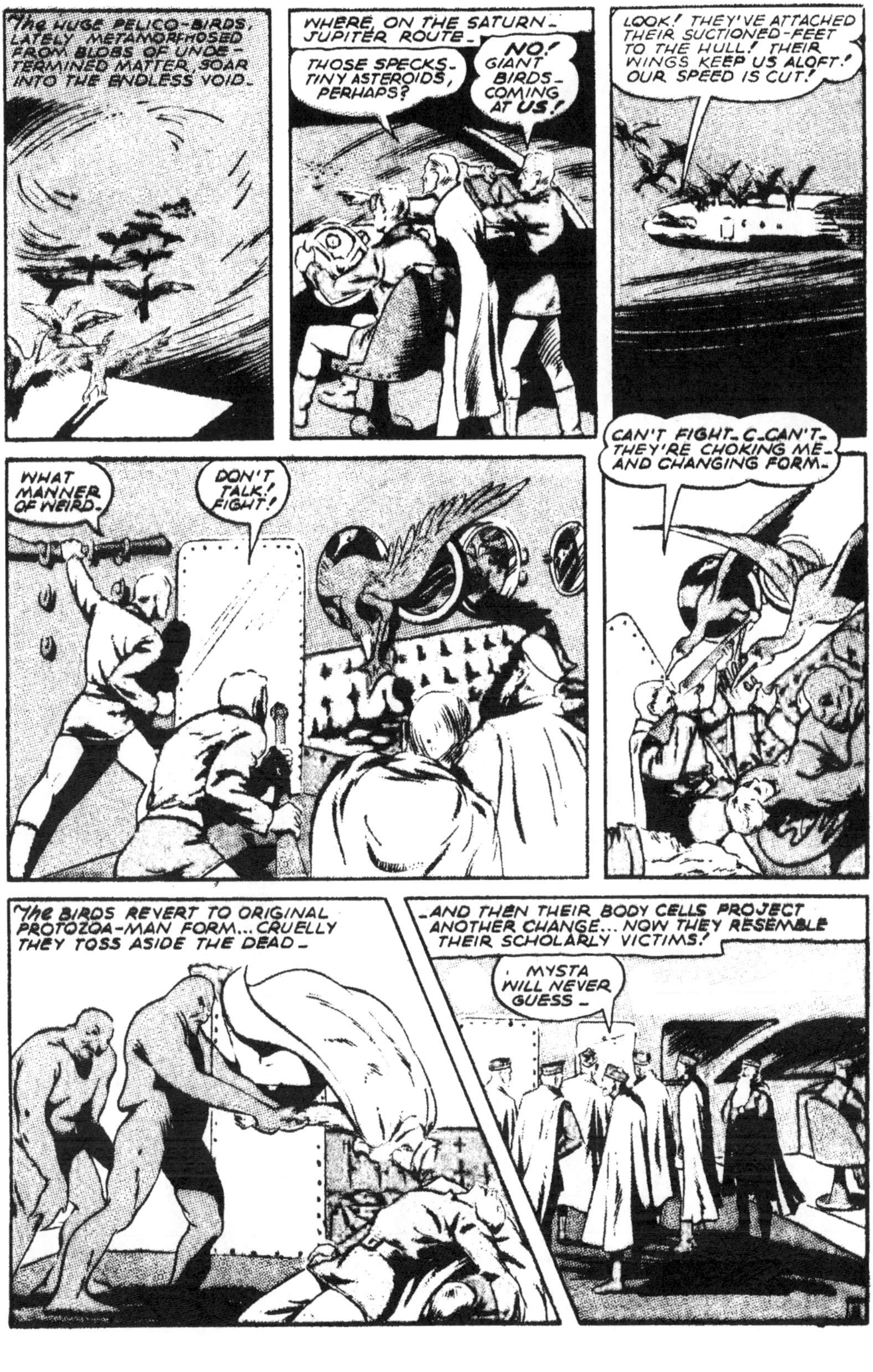
The huge pelico-birds, lately metamorphosed from blobs of undetermined matter, soar into the endless void-
Where, on the Saturn-Jupiter route-
Those specks-tiny asteroids, perhaps?
No! Giant birds-coming at us!
Look! They've attached their suctioned-feet to the hull! Their wings keep us aloft! Our speed is cut!
What manner of weird-
Don't talk! Fight!
Can't fight-c-can't-they're choking me-and changing form-
The birds revert to original protozoa-man form... cruelly they toss aside the dead-
-And then their body cells project another change... now they resemble their scholarly victims!
Mysta will never guess-

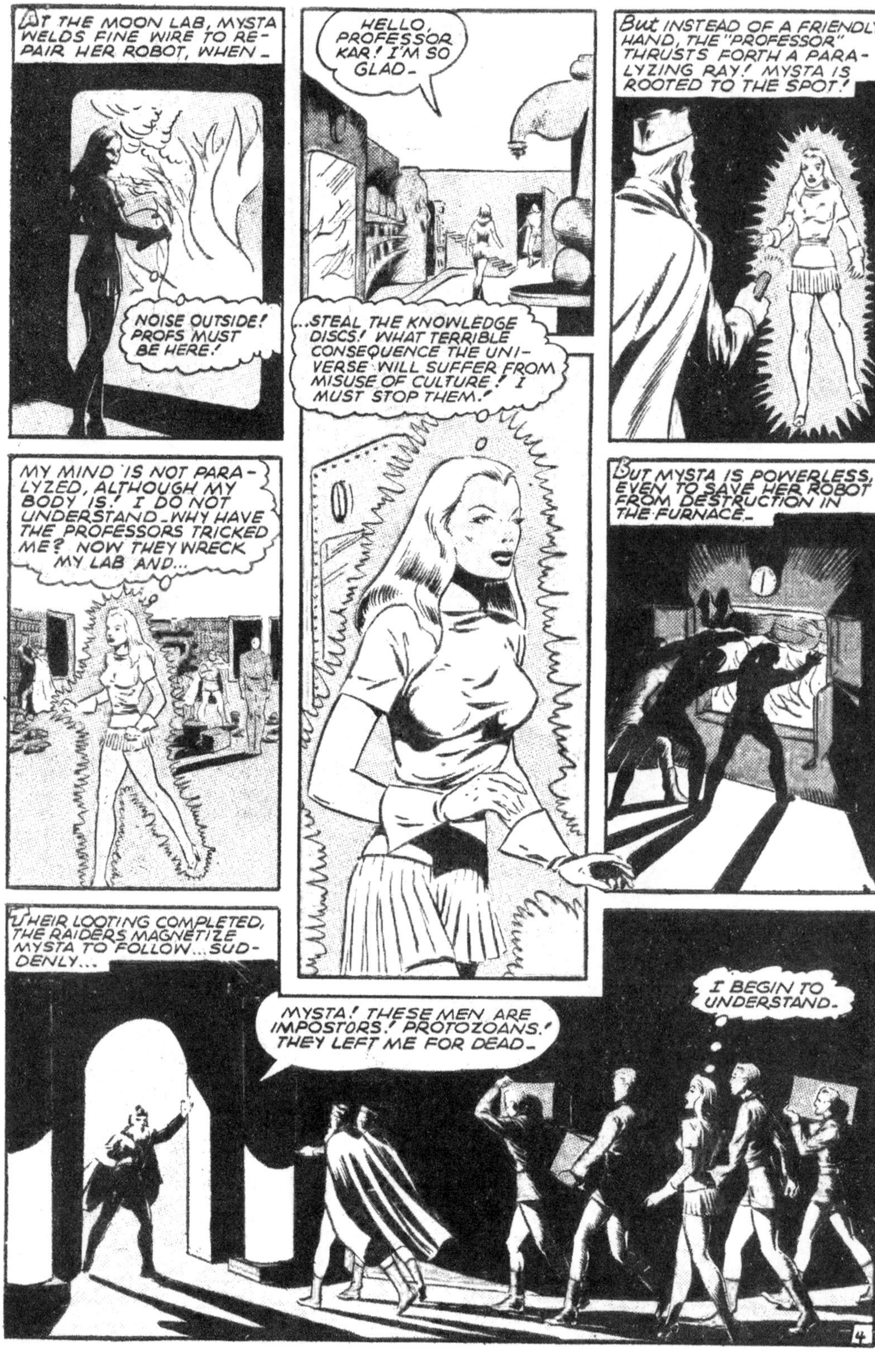
AT THE MOON LAB, MYSTA WELDS FINE WIRE TO REPAIR HER ROBOT, WHEN–
NOISE OUTSIDE! PROFS MUST BE HERE!
HELLO, PROFESSOR KAR! I'M SO GLAD–
BUT INSTEAD OF A FRIENDLY HAND, THE "PROFESSOR" THRUSTS FORTH A PARALYZING RAY! MYSTA IS ROOTED TO THE SPOT!
MY MIND IS NOT PARALYZED, ALTHOUGH MY BODY IS! I DO NOT UNDERSTAND–WHY HAVE THE PROFESSORS TRICKED ME? NOW THEY WRECK MY LAB AND...
...STEAL THE KNOWLEDGE DISCS! WHAT TERRIBLE CONSEQUENCE THE UNIVERSE WILL SUFFER FROM MISUSE OF CULTURE! I MUST STOP THEM!
BUT MYSTA IS POWERLESS, EVEN TO SAVE HER ROBOT FROM DESTRUCTION IN THE FURNACE–
THEIR LOOTING COMPLETED, THE RAIDERS MAGNETIZE MYSTA TO FOLLOW... SUDDENLY...
MYSTA! THESE MEN ARE IMPOSTORS! PROTOZOANS! THEY LEFT ME FOR DEAD–
I BEGIN TO UNDERSTAND–
4

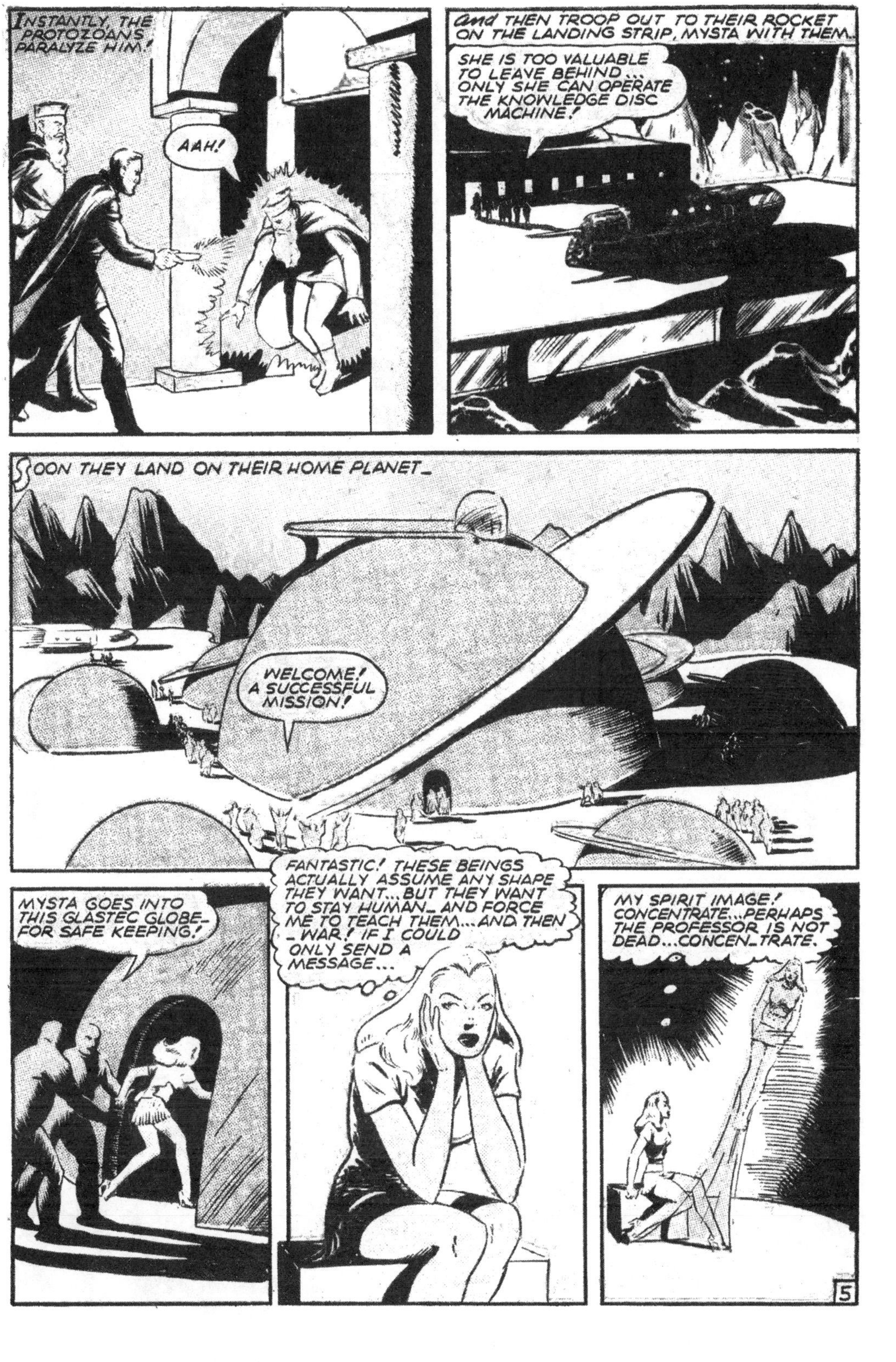
INSTANTLY, THE PROTOZOANS PARALYZE HIM!
AAH!
And THEN TROOP OUT TO THEIR ROCKET ON THE LANDING STRIP, MYSTA WITH THEM.
SHE IS TOO VALUABLE TO LEAVE BEHIND... ONLY SHE CAN OPERATE THE KNOWLEDGE DISC MACHINE!
SOON THEY LAND ON THEIR HOME PLANET_
WELCOME! A SUCCESSFUL MISSION!
MYSTA GOES INTO THIS GLASTEC GLOBE_ FOR SAFE KEEPING!
FANTASTIC! THESE BEINGS ACTUALLY ASSUME ANY SHAPE THEY WANT... BUT THEY WANT TO STAY HUMAN_ AND FORCE ME TO TEACH THEM... AND THEN _WAR! IF I COULD ONLY SEND A MESSAGE...
MY SPIRIT IMAGE! CONCENTRATE... PERHAPS THE PROFESSOR IS NOT DEAD... CONCEN_TRATE.
5

HER ETHEREAL SPIRIT IMAGE BREACHES VAST SPACE... HOVERS OVER THE MOON LAB...

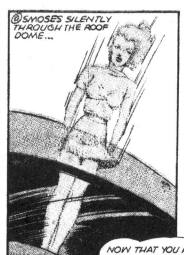

...OSMOSES SILENTLY THROUGH THE ROOF DOME...

AND... THE PROFESSOR IS *NOT* DEAD!

MYSTA...M— MYSTA...IS IT REALLY? YOUR TELEPATHIC IMAGE IS VERY CLEAR—

YES...I RECEIVE THE MESSAGE...THE ROBOT IS UNDAMAGED IN THE FURNACE BECAUSE IT IS HEAT RESISTANT...REPAIR THE WIRING...THEN SEEK YOU! 78 LEAGOMETERS PAST SATURN, 3 ALTIGRADES OVER JUPITER...WE WILL COME! HAVE FAITH, MYSTA!

NOW THAT YOU HAVE WISELY DECIDED TO WORK WITH US, PLAY YOUR KNOWLEDGE DISCS...WE PROTOZOANS WILL LEARN ANYTHING TO HELP US MASTER THE UNIVERSE!

MEANWHILE

A VERY WORTHY PLAN! NOW I SET THE DISC...

I SWITCHED DISCS! THEY'LL GO CRAZY FROM THIS ONE!

WEIRD HIGH-PITCHED MUSIC BREAKS THE EXPECTANT SILENCE...WITH PRIMEVAL SAVAGERY, THE BLOBBY CREATURES RESPOND TO THE SHRILLING VIOLENCE OF THE SOUNDS!

I MUST FLEE!

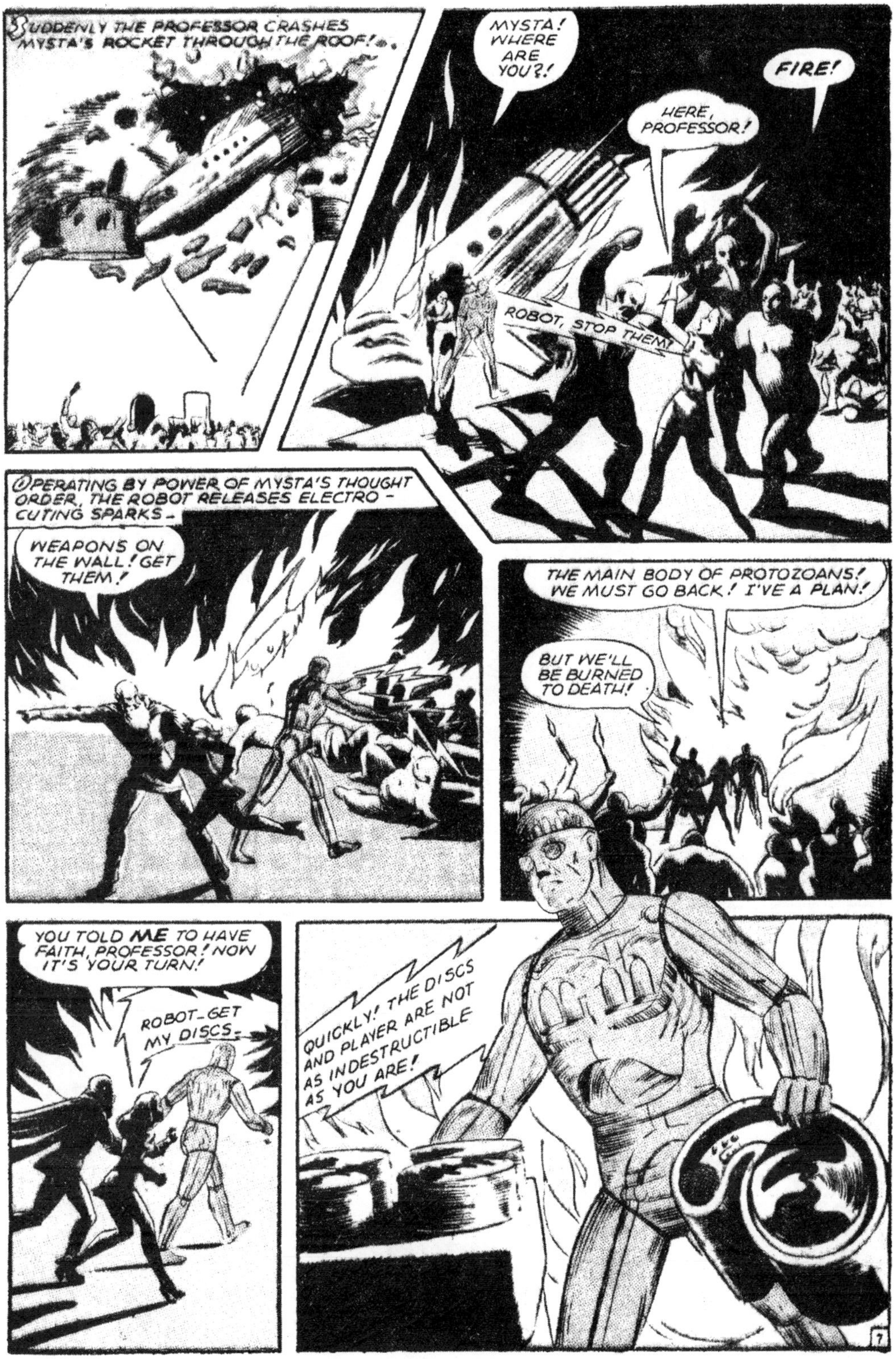
SUDDENLY THE PROFESSOR CRASHES MYSTA'S ROCKET THROUGH THE ROOF!
MYSTA! WHERE ARE YOU?!
FIRE!
HERE, PROFESSOR!
ROBOT, STOP THEM!
OPERATING BY POWER OF MYSTA'S THOUGHT ORDER, THE ROBOT RELEASES ELECTRO-CUTING SPARKS-
WEAPONS ON THE WALL! GET THEM!
THE MAIN BODY OF PROTOZOANS! WE MUST GO BACK! I'VE A PLAN!
BUT WE'LL BE BURNED TO DEATH!
YOU TOLD ME TO HAVE FAITH, PROFESSOR! NOW IT'S YOUR TURN!
ROBOT-GET MY DISCS-
QUICKLY! THE DISCS AND PLAYER ARE NOT AS INDESTRUCTIBLE AS YOU ARE!
7

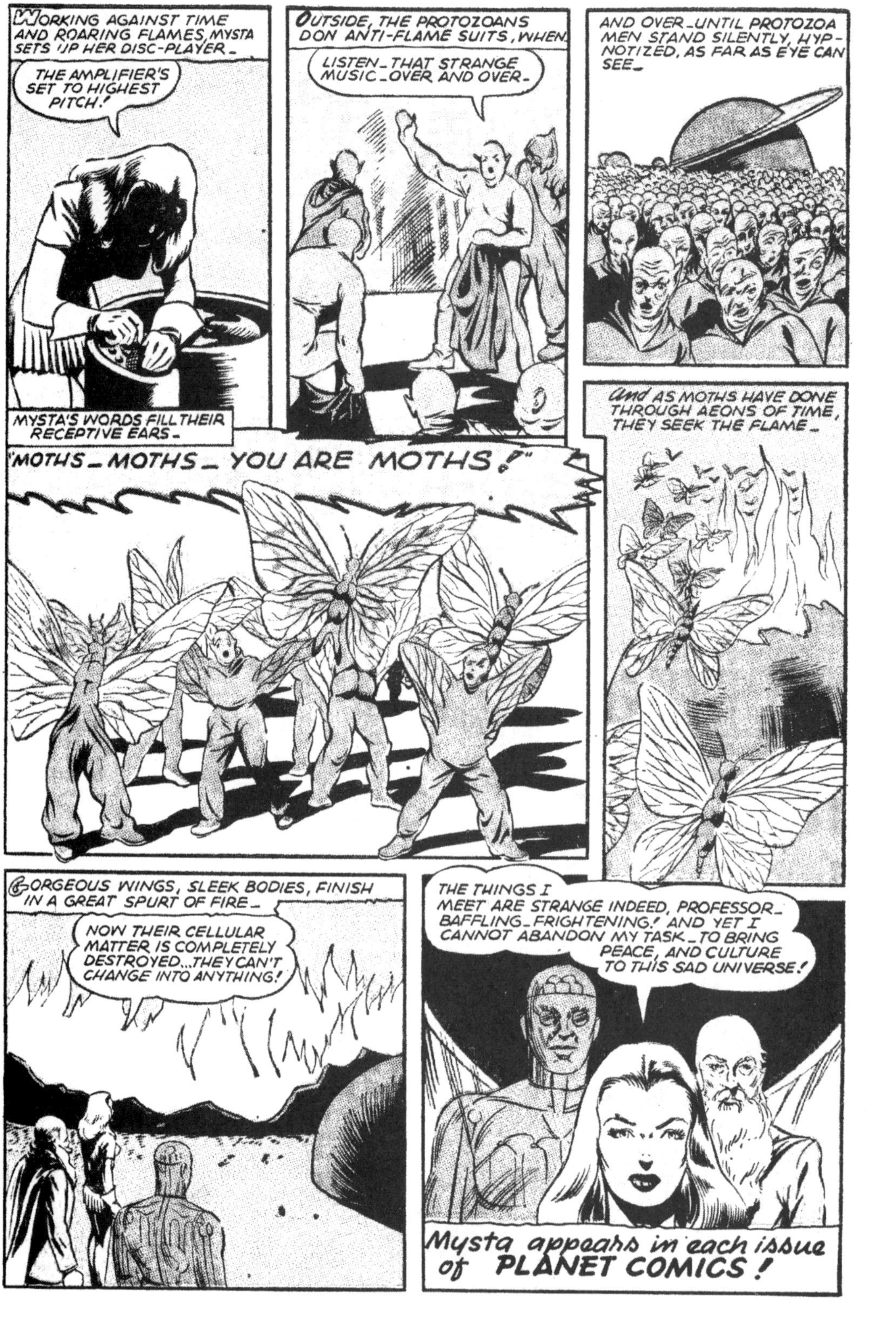
WORKING AGAINST TIME AND ROARING FLAMES, MYSTA SETS UP HER DISC-PLAYER –
THE AMPLIFIER'S SET TO HIGHEST PITCH!
MYSTA'S WORDS FILL THEIR RECEPTIVE EARS –
OUTSIDE, THE PROTOZOANS DON ANTI-FLAME SUITS, WHEN
LISTEN – THAT STRANGE MUSIC – OVER AND OVER –
AND OVER – UNTIL PROTOZOA MEN STAND SILENTLY, HYPNOTIZED, AS FAR AS EYE CAN SEE –
"MOTHS – MOTHS – YOU ARE MOTHS!"
And AS MOTHS HAVE DONE THROUGH AEONS OF TIME, THEY SEEK THE FLAME –
GORGEOUS WINGS, SLEEK BODIES, FINISH IN A GREAT SPURT OF FIRE –
NOW THEIR CELLULAR MATTER IS COMPLETELY DESTROYED... THEY CAN'T CHANGE INTO ANYTHING!
THE THINGS I MEET ARE STRANGE INDEED, PROFESSOR – BAFFLING – FRIGHTENING! AND YET I CANNOT ABANDON MY TASK – TO BRING PEACE, AND CULTURE TO THIS SAD UNIVERSE!
Mysta appears in each issue of PLANET COMICS!

A MOMENT  IN TIME

The end of WWII promised a new era of peace for the world. But it presented a challenge for comic books. The scores of red, white, and blue, star-spangled heroes and heroines who had fought so bravely during the war years were now obsolete. Peace had eliminated the perfect evil foe for freedom-loving heroes. Who needed a Mr. America, Liberty Belle, or Yankee Doodle Jones if there was no longer a great menace threatening democracy? Patriotic heroes disappeared quickly, as the anthology comics of the Golden Age began to change to reflect the postwar world. *Military Comics* became *Modern Comics* in 1945. By the early 1950s, Captain America was billed as a "Commie Smasher," as comic books looked for the next big menace for superheroes to take on. But the Communists just didn't possess the same dramatic evil the Nazis had. Superheroes were becoming passé, and readers wanted new kinds of thrills. Colorfully clad heroes vanished from the covers, replaced by cowboys and horrific monsters. *All-Star Comics* became *All-Star Western*, *Sensation Comics* became *Sensation Mystery*, and superheroes became an endangered species.

It makes sense that comic books would evolve to adapt to changing times. That is the nature of business—change or die. But the demise of the anthology superhero comics had larger implications for women. Heroic women now had nowhere to go. Popular heroines like The Black Cat, Mary Marvel and Sheena were gone by the early '50s, and a significantly less powerful Wonder Woman hobbled her way into the next decade. The final nail in the coffin was *Seduction of the Innocent*, Dr. Frederic Wertham's 1954 book that charged that comic books corrupted the young minds of readers. Following a Senate investigation of comic books, publishers developed the Comics Code Authority. Comic books would no longer be violent and prurient. Just as Eve had tempted Adam, the sexy and daring women of comics were accused of leading children astray with their antics. From now on females would have to be content to remain in the background, while men took center stage

With the anthology comics gone, there was now a more definite line drawn between what were considered "girl comics" and "boy comics." Girls read romance comics; boys read action and adventure comics. So girls read stories where women went on dates and got married, while boys read stories where women were rescued by men. When heroines began to reemerge beginning in the late '50s, they were shadows of the adventurous women of the previous decade. Batwoman was continually berated for her incompetence by Batman, while the Invisible Girl worried more about her hairstyles than she did about fighting evil. The new heroines were depicted as frivolous females who mainly wanted to get married. As a result, a generation of new comic book readers in the '60s grew up thinking that women were useless, and had no place in superhero comics.

Comic books by their very nature present a fantastic world where all is possible. In that world, people can achieve great things, and be elevated to supreme heights. And for a few years, that privilege was granted to women as well as men. And then the fantastic world became more like the world that we live in, where things aren't always that egalitarian. The stories collected in this book represent a moment in time when women could be as heroic as men. It may not have lasted long, and these heroines may have become *lost* over the course of several decades. But they are worth revisiting to see where comic books began, and to remind us how far comics of today still need to go.

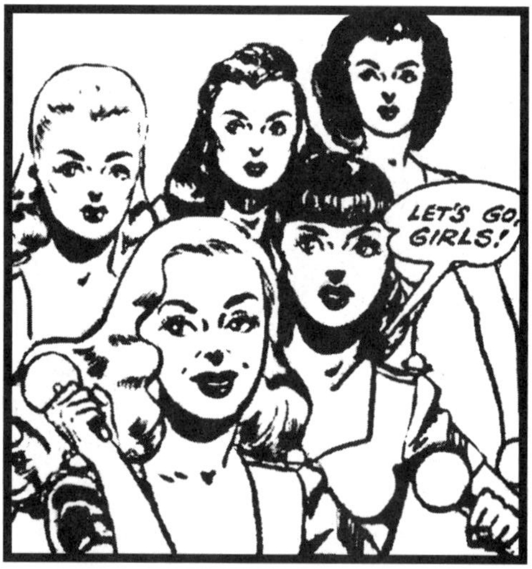
LET'S GO, GIRLS!

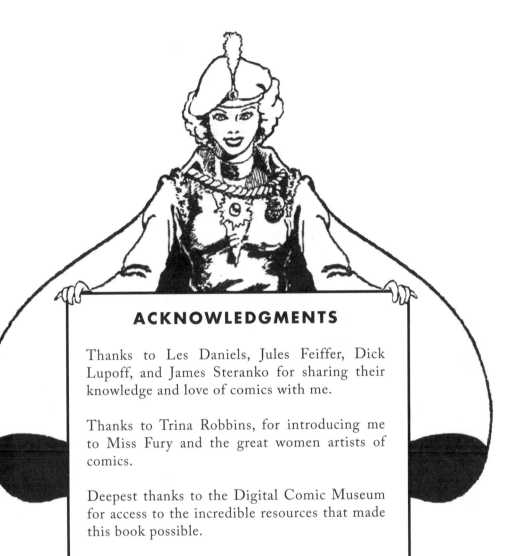

ACKNOWLEDGMENTS

Thanks to Les Daniels, Jules Feiffer, Dick Lupoff, and James Steranko for sharing their knowledge and love of comics with me.

Thanks to Trina Robbins, for introducing me to Miss Fury and the great women artists of comics.

Deepest thanks to the Digital Comic Museum for access to the incredible resources that made this book possible.

Thanks to Don Markstein's Toonepedia, Grand Comics Database, and Public Domain Super Heroes for information used in researching this book.

Thanks to Bob Irwin for moral support, and for making me laugh.

And a special thanks to D.V., for inspiration...

Also by **MIKE MADRID**
THE SUPERGIRLS

Comic book superheroines bend steel, travel across time and space, and wield the mighty forces of nature. These powerful females do everything that male heroes do. But they have to work their wonders in skirts and high heels.

The Supergirls, a cultural history of comic book heroines, asks whether their world of fantasy is that different from our own. Are the stories of Wonder Woman's search for an identity, Batwoman and Power Girl's battle for equality, and Manhunter's juggling of her crime fighting career and motherhood also an alternative saga of modern American women?

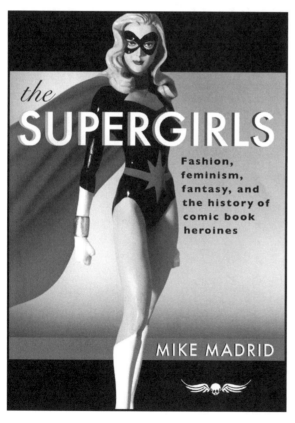

the
SUPERGIRLS

Fashion,
feminism,
fantasy, and
the history of
comic book
heroines

MIKE MADRID

Praise for
THE SUPERGIRLS
Fashion, Feminism, Fantasy, and the History of Comic Book Heroines

"*The Supergirls* is a long overdue tribute to the fabulous fighting females whose beauty and bravery brighten the pages of your favorite comics."—Stan Lee

"Sharp and lively—and just obsessive enough about women who wear capes and boots to be cool but not creepy. [Madrid] clearly loves this stuff. And he's enough of a historian to be able to trace the ways in which the portrayal of sirens and supergirls has echoed society's ever-changing feelings about women and sex. A-"— *Entertainment Weekly*

"From the super heroines of today to 'Goddesses of Tomorrow,' Madrid questions the position of women in the world of superhero fantasy, showing the parallels between society's expectations and the depiction of American women in comic fiction." —ALA Amelia Bloomer Project

"A thoughtful, comprehensive history of women in comics ... *The Supergirls* gleefully celebrates the medium itself, in all its goofy, glorious excess." —*NPR*

"Hopefully [*Supergirls*] will start some new discussions not just about female superheroes, but their cultural significance in American pop culture." —*BITCH* magazine

"There comes a time in every comic book geek slash fashionista's life when she must ask herself 'What do costumes and couture have in common?' *The Supergirls* sets out to answer that question. .... A quick read that skims over the history of publishing powerhouses Marvel and DC, making it informative enough and providing sufficient cultural context for those who may have no prior comic book knowledge." —*WORN Fashion Journal*

"Any comics or graphic novel library needs *The Supergirls*. It provides a cultural history of comic book heroines and asks whether their fantasy world has any connection to our own, offering a fine survey of different super-women in comic history." —*Midwest Book Review*

"Weird and wonderful all the way through." —*Portland Mercury*

"*The Supergirls* is fascinating and informative. Combine that with Madrid's enjoyable writing style, and you have a book that any fan of comics should read. A book like this has been a long time coming, and it's been worth the wait." —*Sequential Tart*

"Entertaining and informative, *Supergirls* is a breezy and thoroughly accessible history of the comic book heroine. A great resource!" —Marc Andreyko, writer, *Manhunter* and *Torso*

"Mike Madrid's fast-moving, encyclopedic, and often funny *Supergirls* shows the author's lifelong affection for these heroines on every page. He has a great feel for the genre and its history, with evident sensitivity to issues of female power and powerlessness. The section on the She-Hulk is not to be missed!" —Larry Gonick, author, *Cartoon History of the Universe*

National Public Radio *"Best Book To Share With Your Friends"*
American Library Association Amelia Bloomer Project Notable Book

---

Available in print, electronic and audiobook editions
wherever books are sold

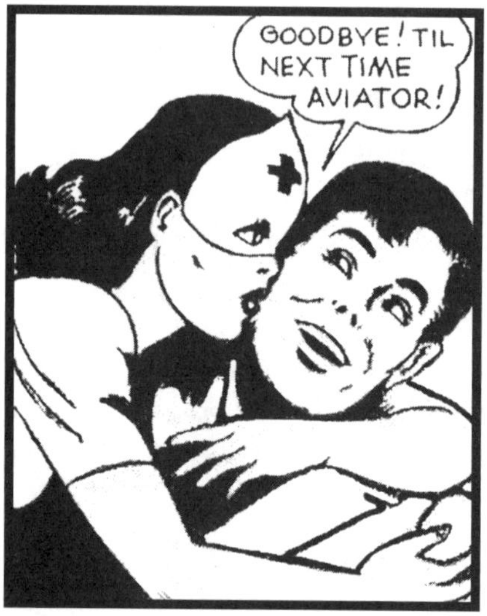
GOODBYE! TIL NEXT TIME AVIATOR!

MIKE MADRID is the author of *The Supergirls: Fashion, Feminism, Fantasy, and the History of Comic Book Heroines* (also from Exterminating Angel Press). A San Francisco native and lifelong fan of comic books and popular culture, he also appears in the documentary *Wonder Women! The Untold Story of American Superheroines*.

For more information visit **heaven4heroes.com**

★ ★ ★